# AGRICULTURAL PRICE DISTORTIONS, INEQUALITY, AND POVERTY

# AGRICULTURAL PRICE DISTORTIONS, INEQUALITY, AND POVERTY

*Kym Anderson,*
*John Cockburn, and*
*Will Martin, Editors*

**THE WORLD BANK**
Washington, D.C.

ISBN: 978-0-8213-8184-7
eISBN: 978-0-8213-8185-4
DOI: 10.1596/978-0-8213-8184-7

**Library of Congress Cataloging-in-Publication Data**

Agricultural price distortions, inequality, and poverty / Kym Anderson, John Cockburn and Will Martin, editors.
   p. cm.
  ISBN 978-0-8213-8184-7 — ISBN 978-0-8213-8185-4 (electronic)
  1. Agricultural prices—Government policy. 2. Farm income—Developing countries. 3. Agricultural wages—Developing countries. 4. Poverty.　I. Anderson, Kym. II. Cockburn, John. III. Martin, Will, 1953 -
  HD1447.A37 2010
  339.4'6—dc22

2009041807

# OTHER TITLES IN THE SERIES

*Distortions to Agricultural Incentives: A Global Perspective, 1955–2007*
edited by Kym Anderson, 2009

*Distortions to Agricultural Incentives in Africa*
edited by Kym Anderson and William A. Masters, 2009

*Distortions to Agricultural Incentives in Asia*
edited by Kym Anderson and Will Martin, 2009

*Distortions to Agricultural Incentives in Europe's Transition Economies*
edited by Kym Anderson and Johan Swinnen, 2008

*Distortions to Agricultural Incentives in Latin America*
edited by Kym Anderson and Alberto Valdés, 2008

# CONTENTS

Foreword     xvii

Acknowledgments     xix

Contributors     xxi

Abbreviations     xxv

**PART I**     **INTRODUCTION**     1

**1**     **Introduction and Summary**     3
*Kym Anderson, John Cockburn, and Will Martin*

**PART II**     **GLOBAL CGE APPROACHES**     47

**2**     **Global Welfare and Poverty Effects:**
**Linkage Model Results**     49
*Kym Anderson, Ernesto Valenzuela, and*
*Dominique van der Mensbrugghe*

**3**     **Global Poverty and Distributional Impacts:**
**The GIDD Model**     87
*Maurizio Bussolo, Rafael De Hoyos, and Denis Medvedev*

**4**     **Poverty Impacts in 15 Countries: The GTAP Model**     119
*Thomas W. Hertel and Roman Keeney*

**PART III**     **NATIONAL CGE APPROACHES: ASIA**     145

**5**     **China**     147
*Fan Zhai and Thomas W. Hertel*

**6**     **Indonesia**     179
*Peter Warr*

**7**     **Pakistan**     209
*Caesar B. Cororaton and David Orden*

8       The Philippines                                           247
        *Caesar B. Cororaton, Erwin Corong, and John Cockburn*

9       Thailand                                                  283
        *Peter Warr*

PART IV  NATIONAL CGE APPROACHES: AFRICA                          301

10      Mozambique                                                303
        *Channing Arndt and James Thurlow*

11      South Africa                                              331
        *Nicolas Hérault and James Thurlow*

PART V   NATIONAL CGE APPROACHES: LATIN AMERICA                   357

12      Argentina                                                 359
        *Martín Cicowiez, Carolina Díaz-Bonilla,*
        *and Eugenio Díaz-Bonilla*

13      Brazil                                                    391
        *Joaquim Bento de Souza Ferreira Filho and Mark Horridge*

14      Nicaragua                                                 423
        *Marco V. Sánchez and Rob Vos*

        Appendix: Border Price and Export Demand
        Shocks in Developing Countries from
        Rest-of-the-World Trade Liberalization:
        The Linkage Model                                         457
        *Dominique van der Mensbrugghe,*
        *Ernesto Valenzuela, and Kym Anderson*

        Index                                                     489

# Figures

3.1     Income Distributions among Agricultural and Nonagricultural
        Populations of the World, 2000                                      90
3.2     Relationship between Income Levels and Share of Employment
        in Agriculture, by Country, 2000                                    92
3.3     Share of the Population in Agriculture and of Agriculture
        in Total Income, Developing Countries, 2000                         93
3.4     Inequality Variation in Agricultural, Nonagricultural,
        and All Households, Developing Countries, 2000                      95
3.5     The GIDD Methodological Framework                                   97
3.6     The Effects on Real National Consumption of the Global
        Removal of Agricultural and All Merchandise Trade Distortions      100
3.7     The Effects on National Real Factor Rewards of the Global
        Removal of Only Agricultural Price and Trade Policies              102
3.8     National GICs: The Effects on the Per Capita Household Income
        Distribution of a Hypothetical 1 Percent Increase in Agricultural
        Versus Nonagricultural Incomes, Developing Countries               104
3.9     Regional and National GICs: The Effects on the Per Capita
        Household Income Distribution of Full Global Agricultural
        Policy Reform                                                      108
3.10    Changes in Poverty as a Share of the Total Change among the
        Greatest Winners and Losers in Full Global Agricultural
        Policy Reform, Developing Countries                                110
3.11    The Theil Index of Overall and Between-Group Income
        Distributional Changes after Full Global Agricultural
        Policy Reform                                                      114
5.1     The Impacts of Prospective Liberalizations on Welfare of
        Five Types of Households, China                                   167
6.1     Initial and Simulated Levels of Poverty Incidence, Indonesia      201
7.1     Poverty Incidence, Pakistan, 1986–87 to 2004–05                   224
8.1     Trends in Poverty Indexes, the Philippines, 1985–2000             253
12.1    Export Taxes, Argentina, 2001–07                                  362
12.2    Tax Revenue, Argentina, 1991–2007                                 363
12.3    Agricultural Producer Price Indexes, Argentina, 1992–2006         364
12.4    Indexes of International Agricultural Prices, Relative Domestic
        Agricultural Prices, and the Real Effective Exchange Rate,
        Argentina, 1996–2008                                              365
13.1    The Share of the Poor, by State, Brazil, 2001                     399
14.1    Tariff Rates on Agricultural and Total Imports from the United
        States under DR-CAFTA, Nicaragua, 2003–20                         428
14.2    The NRAs for Exportable, Importable, and All Covered Farm
        Products, Nicaragua, 1991–2004                                    429
14.3    The NRAs for Agricultural and Nonagricultural Tradable Sectors
        and the RRAs for Farmers, Nicaragua, 1991–2004                    430
14.4    The Fiscal Cost of Trade Liberalization, Nicaragua                446

## Tables

1.1     Global Poverty and Inequality, by Region, 1981–2005                    4
1.2     The NRAs for Tradable Agricultural and Nonagricultural
        Products and the RRA, Focus Regions, 1980–2004                        7
1.3     The Linkage Model's Effects of Full Global Liberalization of
        Agricultural and All Merchandise Trade on Economic
        Welfare and Real GDP, by Country and Region                          15
1.4     The Linkage Model's Effects of Full Global Merchandise
        Trade Liberalization on Real Factor Prices, by Country and Region    17
1.5     The Linkage Model's Effects of Full Global Merchandise
        Trade Liberalization on the Number of Extreme Poor, by Region        18
1.6     The GIDD Model's Effects of the Removal of Agricultural and
        All Merchandise Trade Distortions on the Number of Extreme
        Poor, by Region                                                      20
1.7     The GIDD Model's Effects of the Removal of Agricultural
        and All Merchandise Trade Distortions on Global Poverty and
        Inequality, Farm and Nonfarm Households                              21
1.8     The GIDD Model's Effects of the Removal of Agricultural and
        All Merchandise Trade Distortions on Global Poverty and
        Inequality, Farm and Nonfarm Households, by Region                   22
1.9     The GTAP Model's Effects of Full Global Liberalization of
        Agricultural and All Merchandise Trade on the Number of
        Extreme Poor, by Country                                             24
1.10    Characteristics of the Models in the Global and National
        Country Studies                                                      26
1.11    The Impact of Reform on the Incidence of Extreme Poverty,
        by Country                                                           28
1.12    The Impact of Reform on the Incidence of Income
        Inequality, by Country                                               32
1.13    The Direction of the Effects of Global Reform on Extreme
        Poverty, by Country                                                  36
2.1     Structure of Producer Price Distortions in Global Goods
        Markets, 2004                                                        53
2.2     The Impact on Real Income of the Full Liberalization of Global
        Merchandise Trade, by Country and Region, 2004                       58
2.3     Regional and Sectoral Sources of the Welfare Gains from the
        Full Liberalization of Global Merchandise Trade, 2004                61
2.4     The Impact of Full Global Liberalization on the Shares of
        Global Output Exported, by Product, 2004                             62
2.5     The Impact of Full Global Trade Liberalization on Agricultural
        and Food Output and Trade, by Country and Region, 2004               63
2.6     The Impact of Global Liberalization on the Share of Agricultural
        and Food Production Exports, by Country and Region, 2004             65

2.7    The Impact of Global Liberalization on Self-sufficiency in
       Agricultural and Other Products, by Region, 2004                    66
2.8    Shares of Production Exported and of Consumption Imported
       before and after Full Global Liberalization of all Merchandise
       Trade, by Product, 2004                                             67
2.9    The Impact of Full Global Liberalization on Real International
       Product Prices, 2004                                               68
2.10   The Impacts of Full Global Merchandise Trade Liberalization
       on Real Pretax Factor Prices, by Country and Region, 2004          70
2.11   The Effects of the Full Global Liberalization of Agricultural
       and Merchandise Trade on Sectoral Value Added, by Country
       and Region, 2004                                                   73
2.12   The Poverty Effects of Full Global Liberalization of Merchandise
       Trade Reform, by Region, 2004                                      77
3.1    Characteristics of the Poor in Agricultural and Nonagricultural
       Households, Developing Countries, 2000                             91
3.2    The Household Effects of the Removal of Agricultural and All
       Merchandise Trade Distortions on Global Poverty and Inequality     105
3.3    The GIDD Model: The Effects of the Removal of Agricultural
       and All Merchandise Trade Distortions on the Incidence of
       Poverty, by Region                                                 107
3.4    The Effects of the Full Global Liberalization of Agricultural
       and All Merchandise Trade on the Incidence of Inequality and
       Poverty, Developing Countries                                      111
4.1    Estimates of Elasticities of the US$1-a-Day Poverty
       Headcount with Respect to Total Income, 15 Countries               122
4.2    Stratum Contributions to the US$1-a-Day Poverty
       Population, 15 Countries                                           124
4.3    Stratum- and Earnings-Specific Poverty Elasticities, Bangladesh    126
4.4    The Contributions of Earnings to the Total US$1-a-Day Poverty
       Response, 15 Countries                                             127
4.5    Summary of the Poverty Impacts of Global Reforms, 15 Countries     131
4.6    Earnings Differences after Agricultural and Nonagricultural
       Reforms, 15 Countries                                              136
4.7    Earnings-Specific Differences between Agricultural and
       Nonagricultural Reforms in the Changes in Poverty, 15 Countries    137
4.8    Stratum-Specific Differences in the Changes in Poverty after
       Agricultural and Nonagricultural Reforms, 15 Countries            138
4.9    Change in Poverty after Commodity-Specific Reforms,
       15 Countries                                                       140
4.10   Change in Poverty Caused by Foodgrain and Feedgrain
       Reforms, 15 Countries                                              141
5.1    The Sectoral Structure of GDP, Trade, Import Tariffs, and
       Export Subsidies, China, Around 2004                               154

5.2    Modeled Liberalization Scenarios, China    157
5.3    Exogenous Demand and Price Shocks Caused by Liberalization in the Rest of the World, China    158
5.4    Aggregate Simulation Results of Prospective Liberalizations, China    161
5.5    The Effects of Prospective Liberalizations on Income Inequality and Poverty, China    164
5.6    The Effects of Prospective Liberalizations on Sectoral Outputs and Trade, China    171
5.7    Sensitivity Analysis of the Simulation Results, China    174
6.1    The Cost Shares of Major Factors of Production, Paddy and Other Industries, Indonesia, 2000    184
6.2    Sources of the Factor Incomes of 10 Broad Household Groups, Indonesia, 2000    187
6.3    Expenditure and Poverty Incidence by Household Category, Indonesia, 2000    187
6.4    Industry Assistance Rates Used in Modeling, Indonesia, 2004    191
6.5    Exogenous Border Price Shocks That Would Result from Rest-of-the-World Liberalization, Indonesia    193
6.6    Aggregate Simulation Results of the Prospective Liberalization of All Commodities, Indonesia    195
6.7    Poverty Effects of the Prospective Liberalization of All Commodities, Indonesia    198
6.8    Income Inequality Effects of the Prospective Liberalization of All Commodities, Indonesia    202
6.9    Aggregate Simulation Results of the Prospective Liberalization Only of Agricultural Commodities, Indonesia    203
6.10   Poverty Effects of the Prospective Liberalization of Only Agricultural Commodities, Indonesia    204
6.11   Income Inequality Effects of the Prospective Liberalization of Only Agricultural Commodities, Indonesia    206
7.1    Elasticity Parameters and Production Structure, Pakistan, 2001–02    215
7.2    Model Household Categories, Pakistan    218
7.3    Parameters and Exogenous Demand and Price Shocks Caused by Rest-of-the-World Liberalization, Pakistan    220
7.4    Household Income Sources and Income Taxes, Pakistan, 2001–02    222
7.5    Poverty Estimates, Pakistan, 1998–99, 2001–02, and 2004–05    224
7.6    The Poverty Effects of Prospective Liberalizations, Pakistan    227
7.7    Aggregate Simulation Results of Prospective Agricultural and Nonagricultural Liberalization, Pakistan    228
7.8    Household Welfare and Price Effects of the Liberalization in All Goods Trade by the Rest of the World, Pakistan    232

7.9     The Sectoral Effects of the Unilateral Liberalization of All
        Goods Trade, Pakistan                                            236
7.10    Sensitivity Analysis of Household Welfare Effects, Two
        Tax Replacement Schemes, Pakistan                                242
7.11    Sensitivity Analysis of Poverty Effects, Two Tax Replacement
        Schemes, Pakistan ·                                              243
8.1     The NRAs to Major Agricultural Commodities, the Philippines,
        1960–2004                                                        251
8.2     Poverty Incidence and Food Expenditure Shares,
        the Philippines, 1997 and 2000                                   252
8.3     Production Structure, the Philippines, 2000                      255
8.4     Trade Structure and Elasticity Parameters,
        the Philippines, 2000                                            258
8.5     Structure of Household Expenditure, by Decile,
        the Philippines, 2000                                            261
8.6     Exogenous Demand and Price Shocks Caused by
        Rest-of-the-World Liberalization                                 263
8.7     Aggregate Simulation Results of Prospective Liberalizations
        in Agriculture and Nonagriculture, the Philippines               268
8.8     Effects of Prospective Liberalizations on Real Household
        Consumption, by Income Group, the Philippines                    273
8.9     Income Inequality and the Poverty Effects of Prospective
        Liberalizations, by Location, Gender, and Skills, the Philippines  277
9.1     Cost Shares of the Major Factors of Production, Paddy and
        Other Industries, Thailand, 2000                                 286
9.2     Sources of the Factor Incomes of Broad Household Groups,
        Thailand, 2000                                                   286
9.3     Characteristics of the Major Household Categories,
        Thailand, 2000                                                   287
9.4     Industry Assistance Rates Used in Modeling, Thailand, 2004       289
9.5     Exogenous Border Price Shocks Caused by Rest-of-the-World
        Liberalization, Thailand                                         290
9.6     Aggregate Simulation Results of the Prospective Liberalization
        of All Commodities, Thailand                                     291
9.7     The Poverty and Inequality Effects of the Prospective
        Liberalization of All Commodities, Thailand                      293
9.8     Aggregate Simulation Results of the Prospective Liberalization
        of Only Agricultural Commodities, Thailand                       295
9.9     The Poverty and Inequality Effects of the Prospective
        Liberalization of Only Agricultural Commodities, Thailand        296
10.1    The Economic Structure in 2002 and Price Distortions
        in 2004, Mozambique                                              306
10.2    Factor Intensities of Production, Mozambique, 2002               309

| | | |
|---|---|---|
| 10.3 | Household Income and Expenditure Shares, Mozambique, 2002 | 312 |
| 10.4 | The Exogenous Demand and Price Shocks Caused by Rest-of-the-World Liberalization, Mozambique | 316 |
| 10.5 | The Macroeconomic Simulation Results of Prospective Liberalization Abroad and Nationally, Mozambique | 318 |
| 10.6 | The Effects of Prospective Liberalization Abroad and Nationally on GDP, by Sector, Mozambique | 319 |
| 10.7 | The Effects of Prospective Liberalization Abroad and Nationally on the Real Value of Exports, Mozambique | 321 |
| 10.8 | The Effects of Prospective Liberalization Abroad and Nationally on the Real Value of Imports, Mozambique | 323 |
| 10.9 | The Effects of Prospective Liberalization Abroad and Nationally on Employment, Welfare, and Poverty, Mozambique | 325 |
| 11.1 | Economic Structure and Price Distortions, South Africa, 2002 | 333 |
| 11.2 | Direct Tax Rates on Households, South Africa, 2000 | 337 |
| 11.3 | Household Income Shares, South Africa, 2000 | 338 |
| 11.4 | Household Expenditure Shares, South Africa, 2000 | 339 |
| 11.5 | Exogenous Demand and Border Price Shocks of Rest-of-the-World Liberalization, South Africa | 341 |
| 11.6 | Macroeconomic Simulation Results of Prospective Liberalization Abroad and Nationally, South Africa | 342 |
| 11.7 | The Effects of Prospective Liberalization Abroad and Nationally on GDP, by Sector at Factor Cost, South Africa | 343 |
| 11.8 | Factor Intensity Structure, South Africa, 2002 | 345 |
| 11.9 | The Effects of Prospective Liberalization Abroad and Nationally on Factor Rewards, Employment, and Welfare, South Africa | 346 |
| 11.10 | The Effects of Prospective Liberalization Abroad and Nationally on Sectoral Employment, Income Inequality, and Poverty, South Africa | 347 |
| 12.1 | Components of the Social Accounting Matrix, Argentina, 2005 | 367 |
| 12.2 | External Trade Structure, Argentina, 2005 | 369 |
| 12.3 | Export Taxes and Import Tariffs, Argentina, 2005 | 370 |
| 12.4 | Aggregate Simulation Results of Prospective Liberalization, Argentina | 375 |
| 12.5 | Sectoral Simulation Results of Prospective Liberalization, Argentina | 377 |
| 12.6 | Poverty Effects of Prospective Liberalization, Argentina | 380 |
| 12.7 | Income Inequality Effects of Prospective Liberalization, Argentina | 381 |
| 12.8 | Fiscal and Real Investment Effects of Prospective Liberalization, Argentina | 384 |
| 13.1 | Poverty Indicators, by Poverty Group, Brazil, 2001 | 398 |
| 13.2 | Poverty and Income Inequality by State, Brazil, 2001 | 400 |

| | | |
|---|---|---|
| 13.3 | Share of Occupations in the Activity Labor Bill, by Wage Group, Brazil, 2001 | 402 |
| 13.4 | The Structure of External Trade, Brazil, 2001 | 405 |
| 13.5 | Exogenous Demand and Border Price Shocks Caused by Prospective Global Trade Liberalization, Brazil | 407 |
| 13.6 | The Macroeconomic Impacts of Prospective Trade Liberalizations, Brazil | 410 |
| 13.7 | The Effects of Prospective Global Trade Liberalization on Sectoral Outputs, Exports, and Imports, Brazil | 411 |
| 13.8 | The Effects of Prospective Global Trade Liberalization on Output, by State, Brazil | 413 |
| 13.9 | The Effects of Prospective Global Trade Liberalization on Poverty and Income Inequality, by Household Income Group, Brazil | 414 |
| 13.10 | Decomposition of the Effects of Liberalization on Real Incomes, by Household Income Group, Brazil | 416 |
| 13.11 | The Effects of Prospective Global Trade Liberalization on Poverty, by State, Brazil | 417 |
| 14.1 | Macroeconomic Indicators, Nicaragua, 1990–2005 | 425 |
| 14.2 | Structure of Value Added by Sector at Factor Cost, Nicaragua, 1995, 2000, and 2004 | 426 |
| 14.3 | The Poverty Headcount Ratio and the Gini Coefficient of Income Inequality, Nicaragua, 1993–2005 | 431 |
| 14.4 | Trade Structure and World Price Shocks Imposed in the Global Trade Liberalization Simulations, Nicaragua, 2004 | 440 |
| 14.5 | The Impact of Prospective Trade Liberalization on the Macroeconomy, Nicaragua, 2004 | 441 |
| 14.6 | The Impact of Prospective Trade Liberalization on Real Sectoral GDP, Nicaragua | 443 |
| 14.7 | The Impact of Prospective Trade Liberalization on Employment and Real Wages, Nicaragua | 447 |
| 14.8 | The Impact of Prospective Trade Liberalization on Employment, by Sector, Nicaragua | 448 |
| 14.9 | Microsimulation Results for Poverty and Inequality, Nicaragua | 451 |
| A.1 | Sectoral Concordance of the Linkage Model and the GTAP Version 7 Database | 459 |
| A.2 | Regional Concordance of the Linkage Model and the GTAP Version 7 Database | 460 |
| A.3 | Key Elasticities in the Linkage Model | 464 |
| A.4 | Price Distortion Structure in GTAP Version 7p5 and the Distortion Rates Drawn from the World Bank Project, 2004 | 468 |
| A.5 | Export Price, Import Price, and Export Demand Shocks to National Models from Rest-of-the-World Agricultural and Trade Policy Reform, Selected Developing Countries | 471 |

# FOREWORD

The vast majority of the world's poorest households depend to a considerable extent on farming for their incomes, while food represents a large component of the consumption of all poor households. The prices of farm products are thus crucial determinants of the extent of poverty and inequality in the world. Yet, for generations, these prices have been heavily distorted by government policies in high-income countries and in developing countries. True, many countries began to reform their agricultural price and trade policies in the 1980s, but *Distortions to Agricultural Incentives: A Global Perspective, 1955–2007* (edited by Kym Anderson), a 2009 World Bank publication, shows that the extent of government policy intervention is still considerable and still favors farmers in high-income countries at the expense of farmers in developing countries.

What would be the poverty and inequality consequences of the removal of the remaining distortions to agricultural incentives? This question is of great relevance to governments in evaluating ways to engage in multilateral and regional trade negotiations or to improve their own policies unilaterally. The answer is often not clear in any one country and is certainly an empirical matter for groups of countries because the positive and negative effects in different settings may be offsetting. Some analysts have sought answers in past events using ex post econometric analysis of historical data, but it is not easy to find natural experiments that are suitable for analysis and from which it is possible to generalize. An alternative approach—the one adopted in the present study—is to undertake ex ante analysis using economy-wide models, including global models, so as to be able to simulate the prospective effects of the multilateral removal of all price-distorting policies.

This volume represents a first attempt to exploit new methodologies, models, and databases (developed partly as a consequence of recent World Bank–sponsored research) to assess the relative impacts on national, regional, and global poverty and inequality of agricultural and nonagricultural trade policies at home and abroad. While clear, definitive answers are not easy to determine, the volume extends our understanding of the contributions of various policies to inequality and poverty in selected developing countries and regions. Its broad finding is that the removal of all current price-distorting policies is likely to reduce global poverty and inequality, but there may be a few countries in which such a policy change on its own might worsen poverty nationally. In particular, it highlights the fact that the results are sensitive to assumptions about the changes in taxation needed to compensate the national treasury for losses in trade tax revenue, the degree of flexibility in each country's labor markets, the complementary measures taken to increase the opportunities for farm families and mitigate any adverse poverty impacts, and so on. As always, agricultural and trade policy reforms have better prospects of becoming politically and socially sustainable, the more governments also provide optimal domestic safety net policies.

Justin Yifu Lin
Senior Vice President and Chief Economist
The World Bank

# ACKNOWLEDGMENTS

This book analyzes the effects of agricultural policies and farm and nonfarm trade policies around the world on national and regional economic welfare, on income inequality among and within countries, and, most importantly, on the level and incidence of poverty in developing countries. The studies in this volume include economy-wide analyses of the inequality and poverty effects of own-country policies compared with rest-of-the-world policies for 10 individual developing countries in three continents. In addition, the book includes three chapters that each use a separate global economic model to examine the effects of policies on aggregate poverty and the distribution of poverty across many identified developing countries.

The book is motivated by two policy issues: first, the World Trade Organization's struggle to conclude the Doha Round of multilateral trade negotiations, in which agricultural policy reform is, once again, one of the most contentious topics in the talks, and, second, the struggle of the developing countries to achieve their Millennium Development Goals by 2015, notably the alleviation of hunger and poverty, which depends crucially on policies that affect agricultural incentives. The study's timing is facilitated by recent methodological developments involving microsimulation modeling based on household survey data, in conjunction with economy-wide computable general equilibrium modeling. Recent surveys are now available at the World Bank on more than 100 countries. Moreover, the World Bank has recently compiled a comprehensive new global database that updates and expands substantially our understanding of the distortions to agricultural incentives, particularly in developing countries. The authors of the chapters in this book are therefore indebted to the many contributors to these recent developments in methodology and data. In turn, we are grateful to the authors for taking part in our project, which is an extension of the project that generated the new distortions database (details of which are available at http://go.worldbank.org/5XY7A7LH40).

We extend our thanks to the senior advisory board of the overall project. The board's members have provided advice and encouragement throughout the planning and implementation stages of the project. The board consists of Yujiro Hayami, Bernard Hoekman, Anne Krueger, John Nash, Johan Swinnen, Stefan Tangermann, Alberto Valdés, Alan Winters, and, until his untimely death in March 2008, Bruce Gardner.

The editors, the other authors, and the advisory board are all grateful for the untiring administrative support provided throughout the entire project by Michelle Chester in the trade unit of the Development Research Group of the World Bank. They also appreciate the feedback and helpful comments of colleagues at the 2008 and 2009 annual Global Economic Analysis Conference, in Helsinki and Santiago, respectively, where earlier versions of many of the chapters herein were presented.

For financial assistance, grateful thanks go to the Development Research Group of the World Bank and the trust funds of the governments of the Netherlands and the United Kingdom. This combined support has made it possible for the study to include a wide range of developing countries.

Kym Anderson, John Cockburn, and Will Martin
August 2009

# CONTRIBUTORS

*Kym Anderson* is George Gollin Professor of Economics at the University of Adelaide, Australia and a fellow of the Centre for Economic Policy Research, London. During 2004–07, he was on an extended sabbatical as lead economist (trade policy) in the Development Research Group of the World Bank in Washington, DC.

*Channing Arndt*, following a five-year period based in Maputo, Mozambique, is a professor at the Department of Economics at the University of Copenhagen. His publications cover poverty measurement, trade policy, the macroeconomic implications of HIV/AIDS, agricultural productivity growth, and demand systems estimation.

*Maurizio Bussolo* is a senior economist at the World Bank in Washington, DC. At the time of his contribution to this volume, he was with the Development Prospects Group; he is now in the economic policy unit of the Latin America and the Caribbean Region of the World Bank.

*Martin Cicowiez* is a research economist and lecturer at the Center for Distributional, Labor, and Social Studies at the Universidad Nacional de La Plata, in Buenos Aires, Argentina.

*John Cockburn* is a professor of economics at the Université Laval in Quebec and co-director of the Poverty and Economic Policy Research Network. He conducts research on child welfare, poverty, growth, and trade policy.

*Erwin Corong* is a PhD student at the Centre of Policy Studies at Monash University, Melbourne. At the time of his contribution to this volume, he was with the Poverty and Economic Policy Research Network at the Université Laval in Quebec. He was subsequently with the International Food Policy Research Institute in Washington, DC.

*Caesar B. Cororaton* is a research fellow at the Global Issues Initiative at the Institute for Society, Culture, and Environment of Virginia Polytechnic and State University in Alexandria, Virginia. At the time of his contribution to this volume, he was with the International Food Policy Research Institute in Washington, DC.

*Carolina Díaz-Bonilla* is an economist in the Poverty Reduction and Economic Management Network of the Latin America and the Caribbean Region at the World Bank in Washington, DC. At the time of her contribution to this volume, she was in the Development Prospects Group of the World Bank.

*Eugenio Díaz-Bonilla* is executive director for Argentina and Haiti at the Inter-American Development Bank, in Washington, DC. He was formerly a senior fellow in the Macro and Trade Division of the International Food Policy Research Institute in Washington, DC.

*Joaquim Bento de Souza Ferreira Filho* is a professor in the Department of Economics in the Escola Superior de Agricultura "Luiz de Queiroz," Universidade de São Paulo at Piracicaba, São Paulo, Brazil. He has served as president of the Brazilian Society of Rural Economics, Management, and Sociology.

*Nicolas Hérault* is a research fellow with the Melbourne Institute of Applied Economic and Social Research at the University of Melbourne, which he joined in March 2007 following doctoral studies at the University of Bordeaux IV in France, where he began his microsimulation analyses of South Africa.

*Thomas W. Hertel* is a distinguished professor, Department of Agricultural Economics, and founding executive director, Center for Global Trade Analysis at Purdue University, West Lafayette, Indiana, where he teaches and conducts research on the economy-wide impacts of trade and environmental policies.

*Mark Horridge* is a professor of economics at the Centre of Policy Studies at Monash University in Melbourne. He specializes in computable general equilibrium modeling, including the ongoing development of widely used economic modeling software such as Gempack.

*Rafael De Hoyos*, at the time of his contribution to this volume, was a senior economist in the Development Prospects Group of the World Bank in Washington, DC. He is now chief of advisers to the Mexican Under-Secretary of Education, Mexico City.

*Roman Keeney* is an assistant professor in the Department of Agricultural Economics, Purdue University, West Lafayette, Indiana, where he specializes in teaching and research on the global economy-wide modeling of economic policies.

*Will Martin* is the research manager of the Rural Development Unit in the Development Research Group at the World Bank in Washington, DC. He specializes in trade and agricultural policy issues globally, especially in Asia, and has written extensively on trade policies affecting developing countries.

*Denis Medvedev* is a young professional in the World Bank in Washington, DC. At the time of his contribution to this volume, he was with the Development Prospects Group at the World Bank. He specializes in the global economy-wide modeling of economic policies, especially as these policies affect inequality and poverty.

*David Orden* is a senior research fellow at the International Food Policy Research Institute in Washington, DC and director of the Global Issues Initiative at the Institute for Society, Culture, and Environment at Virginia Polytechnic Institute and State University in Alexandria, Virginia. His research focuses on the economics and political economy of agricultural policies.

*Marco V. Sánchez* is economic affairs officer at the Department of Economic and Social Affairs of the United Nations, New York. He was previously associated with the Sub-Regional Office in Mexico City of the United Nations Economic Commission for Latin America and the Caribbean.

*James Thurlow* is a research fellow at the University of Copenhagen and at the International Food Policy Research Institute in Washington, DC. His research focuses on the role of agricultural transformation in the development process, particularly strategies for growth and poverty reduction in Sub-Saharan Africa.

*Ernesto Valenzuela* is a lecturer and research fellow at the School of Economics and the Centre for International Economic Studies at the University of Adelaide, Australia. During 2005–07, he was a consultant at the Development Research Group of the World Bank in Washington, DC.

*Dominique van der Mensbrugghe* is lead economist in the Development Prospects Group of the Development Economics Vice-Presidency of the World Bank in Washington, DC, where he specializes in global economy-wide modeling. He is the architect of the global Linkage model.

*Rob Vos* is the director of the Development Policy and Analysis Division at the Department of Economic and Social Affairs of the United Nations, New York, and affiliated professor of finance and development at the Institute of Social Studies in The Hague.

*Peter Warr* is the John Crawford Professor of Agricultural Economics and founding director of the Poverty Research Centre in the Arndt-Corden Division of Economics, Research School of Pacific and Asian Studies, at the Australian National University, Canberra.

*Fan Zhai* was, at the time of his contribution to this volume, an economist in the Asian Development Bank in Manila on secondment to the Asian Development Bank Institute in Tokyo as a research fellow. He is now with the China Investment Bank in Beijing. His research has focused on modeling Asian economies.

# ABBREVIATIONS

| | |
|---|---|
| CGE | computable general equilibrium (model) |
| DR CAFTA | Dominican Republic–Central America Free Trade Agreement |
| EU15 | The 15 members of the European Union prior to 2004 |
| GDP | gross domestic product |
| GIC | growth incidence curve |
| GIDD | Global Income Distribution Dynamics (data set) |
| GTAP | Global Trade Analysis Project |
| MS | microsimulation |
| NRA | nominal rate of assistance |
| OECD | Organisation for Economic Co-operation and Development |
| PPP | purchasing power parity |
| RRA | relative rate of assistance |
| SAM | social accounting matrix |
| WTO | World Trade Organization |

*Note:* All dollar amounts are U.S. dollars (US$) unless otherwise indicated.

# PART I

# INTRODUCTION

# INTRODUCTION
# AND SUMMARY

*Kym Anderson, John Cockburn, and Will Martin*

For decades, the earnings from farming in many developing countries have been depressed because of a pro-urban, antiagricultural bias in own-country policies and because governments in more well off countries are favoring their farmers by imposing import barriers and providing subsidies. These policies have reduced national and global economic welfare, inhibited economic growth, and added to inequality and poverty because no less than three-quarters of the billion poorest people in the world have been dependent directly or indirectly on farming for their livelihoods (World Bank 2007). Over the past two or three decades, however, numerous developing-country governments have reduced sectoral and trade policy distortions, while governments in some high-income countries have also begun reforming protectionist farm policies. Partly as a consequence of these and associated domestic policy reforms and the consequent growth in incomes in many developing countries, the number of people living on less than US$1 a day fell by nearly half between 1981 and 2005, while the share of these people fell from 42 to 16 percent of the global population (table 1.1).

Notwithstanding the dramatic achievement in poverty reduction, there were still almost 900 million extremely poor people in 2005, and the number may have risen following the eruption of the global financial crisis in 2008. Moreover, most of the improvement has been in Asia (especially China), while, in Sub-Saharan Africa, the incidence of poverty was not much different in 2005 than in 1981, at around 40 percent (amounting to 300 million people in 2005). Despite the success of China, more than 100 million people were still living on less than US$1 a day there in 2005, 90 percent of whom lived in rural areas. In India, the number of

**Table 1.1. Global Poverty and Inequality, by Region, 1981–2005**
*(number and percent of people living on less than 2005 PPP US$1 a day)*

| Region | 1981 | 1987 | 1993 | 1999 | 2005 | Share of poor who are rural, 2002, % | Index of income inequality, 2004[a] |
|---|---|---|---|---|---|---|---|
| *Number of people, millions* | | | | | | | |
| World | 1,528 | 1,228 | 1,237 | 1,146 | 879 | 74 | — |
| Sub-Saharan Africa | 157 | 202 | 247 | 299 | 299 | 69 | — |
| East Asia and Pacific | 948 | 598 | 600 | 425 | 180 | 85 | 0.37 |
| China | 730 | 412 | 444 | 302 | 106 | 90 | 0.36 |
| South Asia | 387 | 384 | 341 | 359 | 350 | 75 | 0.35 |
| India | 296 | 285 | 280 | 270 | 267 | 74 | 0.33 |
| Latin America and the Caribbean | 27 | 35 | 34 | 40 | 28 | 34 | 0.52 |
| Rest of world | 9 | 9 | 15 | 23 | 22 | 50 | — |
| East and South Asia share in world, % | 87 | 80 | 76 | 68 | 60 | — | — |
| *Share of population, %* | | | | | | | |
| World | 42 | 30 | 27 | 23 | 16 | — | — |
| Sub-Saharan Africa | 40 | 42 | 44 | 46 | 39 | — | — |
| East Asia and Pacific | 69 | 39 | 36 | 24 | 10 | — | — |
| China | 74 | 38 | 38 | 24 | 8 | — | — |
| South Asia | 42 | 37 | 29 | 27 | 24 | — | — |
| India | 42 | 36 | 31 | 27 | 24 | — | — |
| Latin America and the Caribbean | 7 | 8 | 7 | 8 | 5 | — | — |

*Sources:* Chen and Ravallion (2008); for the rural share, Ravallion, Chen, and Sangraula (2007); for the Gini coefficient, PovcalNet (2008). — = no data are available.

*Note:* The calculations are based on 2005 PPP (purchasing power parity) dollars. — = no data are available.

a. The index is the Gini coefficient calculated as the population-weighted cross-country average of national Gini coefficients in the region for the available year nearest to 2004.

extreme poor remains stubbornly close to 300 million (74 percent in rural areas) despite large farm subsidies.

Less pressing than the problem of extreme poverty, though nonetheless still important to the welfare of individuals, is the extent of income inequality.[1] In the past, only inequality at the local level affected the utility of individuals, but the information and communication technology revolution has increased awareness of income differences nationally and even internationally. At national levels, there are concerns about rural-urban inequality, as well as inequality within other classifications. Within rural areas, for example, differences in incomes may be vast among landless unskilled farm workers, subsistence farmers, the owners of larger commercial farms, and nonfarm workers in rural towns.[2]

At the global level, Milanovic (2005) points to three possible means of assessing the changes in income distribution in recent decades. One revolves around *intercountry* inequality, the comparison of average incomes across countries wherein each country has an equal weight in the world distribution regardless of population size; measured in this way, income distribution appears to have become more unequal. The second focuses on *international* inequality, the comparison of average incomes across countries wherein each country is weighted by population; measured in this way, income inequality appears to have decreased, although the decrease has occurred mostly because of rapid population growth in China and India (see Bourguignon, Levin, and Rosenblatt 2004; Atkinson and Brandolini 2004). The third method of assessment focuses on *global* inequality, the comparison of individual incomes regardless of the country of citizenship. This method thus takes into account within-country inequality, which is ignored in the intercountry and international inequality approaches wherein individuals are all assumed to earn the average income in their countries. The rapid growth in the large emerging economies has tended to offset the increase in inequality within countries, and, so, by this last methodology, global inequality appears to have remained roughly constant since the late 1980s.[3]

Given the evidence currently available, our book focuses on one main question: how much scope is there to reduce poverty and inequality in the world and in specific developing countries by unilaterally or globally eliminating the distortions in the incentives affecting the producers and consumers of tradable goods? This question is of great interest to the agricultural, trade, and development policy communities in many developing countries and in nongovernmental organizations and international agencies. The answer is by no means obvious. While it is true that recent studies indicate that agricultural policies are responsible for the majority of the global welfare costs of the remaining distortions to goods markets, removing these policies could affect national poverty levels either negatively or positively. The answer in each country to our question depends on current food and agricultural policies at home and abroad, as well as on earning and spending patterns and the taxes on the poor, among other factors. Account also needs to be taken of three other facts. First, the dependence of the extreme poor on agriculture for their livelihoods has been declining in numerous countries as alternative opportunities have emerged outside agriculture, especially in off-farm, part-time employment. Second, the lowering of trade barriers has improved the opportunities for farmers to specialize in cash crops for export, increasing their potential benefits from any improvements in market access abroad for these crops or related products. Third, practical realities too important to ignore in some countries are high levels of unemployment (as in South Africa) or policies that inhibit intersectoral labor mobility (as in China).

Empirical studies undertaken as background for the World Trade Organization's ongoing Doha Round of multilateral trade negotiations suggest that, in 2001, when the Doha Round was launched, policy-driven distortions to agricultural incentives contributed around two-thirds of the global welfare cost of merchandise trade barriers and subsidies (for example, see Anderson, Martin, and van der Mensbrugghe 2006). While these studies did not have access to comprehensive estimates of the distortions to farmer and food consumer incentives in developing countries other than the applied tariffs on imports, a more recent study that draws on a new database of distortions to agricultural incentives has confirmed the earlier result. Valenzuela, van der Mensbrugghe, and Anderson (2009) find that agricultural price and trade policies as of 2004 accounted for 60 percent of the global welfare cost of these and other merchandise trade policies. This is a striking outcome given that the shares of agriculture and food in global gross domestic product (GDP) and trade are less than 6 percent. The contribution of farm and food policies to the welfare cost of global trade-distorting policies in developing countries alone is estimated by these authors to be even greater, at 83 percent, of which a little more than one-third is generated by the policies of the developing countries themselves. Nonetheless, the price distortion estimates used in the modeling study (see Anderson and Valenzuela 2008) show that many developing countries protect their less-competitive farmers from import competition; so, some of this subset of farmers might be hurt if all markets were opened.

Thus, despite much reform over the past quarter century in policies leading to distortions in world trade, many of the relevant intervention measures, especially the agricultural ones, are still in place. Table 1.2 summarizes the average extent of these measures in developing and high-income countries. It shows that the rate of assistance to farmers relative to producers of nonfarm tradables has fallen by one-third in high-income countries since the late 1980s (from 51 to 32 percent), while, in developing countries, this relative rate of assistance has risen from −41 percent in the early 1980s to 1 percent in 2000–04. The latter trend in developing countries is caused partly by the phasing out of agricultural export taxes and partly by the

## Table 1.2. The NRAs for Tradable Agricultural and Nonagricultural Products and the RRA, Focus Regions, 1980–2004

*(percent)*

| Region, indicator | 1980–84 | 1985–89 | 1990–94 | 1995–99 | 2000–04 |
|---|---|---|---|---|---|
| *Africa* | | | | | |
| NRA agricultural exportables | −35 | −37 | −36 | −26 | −25 |
| NRA agricultural import-competing | 13 | 58 | 5 | 10 | 2 |
| NRA agricultural tradables | −14 | 0 | −15 | −9 | −12 |
| NRA nonagricultural tradables | 2 | 9 | 3 | 2 | 7 |
| RRA | −13 | −8 | −17 | −10 | −18 |
| *South Asia* | | | | | |
| NRA agricultural exportables | −28 | −21 | −16 | −12 | −6 |
| NRA agricultural import-competing | 38 | 63 | 25 | 15 | 27 |
| NRA agricultural tradables | 2 | 47 | 0 | −2 | 13 |
| NRA nonagricultural tradables | 55 | 40 | 19 | 15 | 10 |
| RRA | −33 | 5 | −16 | −15 | 3 |
| *China and Southeast Asia* | | | | | |
| NRA agricultural exportables | −50 | −41 | −21 | −2 | 0 |
| NRA agricultural import-competing | 1 | 15 | 3 | 13 | 12 |
| NRA agricultural tradables | −35 | −28 | −12 | 5 | 7 |
| NRA nonagricultural tradables | 21 | 23 | 20 | 10 | 6 |
| RRA | −43 | −42 | −26 | −4 | 2 |
| *Latin America* | | | | | |
| NRA agricultural exportables | −27 | 25 | −11 | −4 | −5 |
| NRA agricultural import-competing | 14 | 5 | 19 | 13 | 21 |
| NRA agricultural tradables | −13 | −11 | 4 | 6 | 5 |
| NRA nonagricultural tradables | 19 | 17 | 7 | 7 | 5 |
| RRA | −27 | −24 | −3 | −1 | −1 |
| *All developing countries* | | | | | |
| NRA agricultural exportables | −41 | −36 | −19 | −6 | −3 |
| NRA agricultural import-competing | 17 | 38 | 23 | 22 | 23 |
| NRA agricultural tradables | −21 | −16 | −4 | 4 | 7 |
| NRA nonagricultural tradables | 35 | 27 | 17 | 10 | 6 |
| RRA | −41 | −34 | −18 | −5 | 1 |
| *High-income countries* | | | | | |
| NRA agricultural exportables | 12 | 22 | 16 | 8 | 7 |
| NRA agricultural import-competing | 58 | 71 | 62 | 54 | 51 |
| NRA agricultural tradables | 43 | 56 | 48 | 37 | 34 |
| NRA nonagricultural tradables | 3 | 3 | 3 | 2 | 1 |
| RRA | 38 | 51 | 45 | 34 | 32 |

*Source:* Anderson and Valenzuela (2008), based on estimates reported in the project country studies.

*Note:* The relative rate of assistance (RRA) is defined as $100 * [(100 + NRAag^t)/(100 + NRAnonag^t) − 1]$, where $NRAag^t$ and $NRAnonag^t$ are the percentage nominal rates of assistance (NRAs) for the tradables parts of the agricultural and nonagricultural sectors, respectively, and $NRAag^t$ is the weighted average of the nominal rates of assistance for the exporting and import-competing subsectors of agriculture.

rise in assistance via food import restrictions over the period. Thus, both in high-income countries and in developing countries, there is now a large gap between the nominal rates of assistance for import-competing and export agriculture, as well as a continuing gap (albeit smaller than the corresponding gap in the 1980s) between the relative rates of assistance in the two groups of countries. In light of this evidence, our question above may be expressed more specifically for any developing country of interest as two additional questions: How important are a developing country's own agricultural and other trade policies compared with those of the rest of the world in determining the welfare of the poor in the country? And what is the contribution of agricultural policies to these outcomes? Clear answers to these questions are crucial in guiding countries in national policy making and in negotiating bilateral and multilateral trade agreements.

Now is an appropriate time to address these multifaceted questions for at least two policy reasons. One is that the World Trade Organization is struggling to conclude the Doha Round of multilateral trade negotiations, and agricultural policy reform is once again one of the most contentious issues in these talks. The other is that poorer countries are striving to achieve their United Nations–encouraged Millennium Development Goals by 2015, and the prime goals are the reduction of hunger and poverty. Farm-subsidizing rich countries are not alone in resisting reform; some developing countries likewise do not wish to remove food import barriers and farmer subsidies.

There are also several analytical reasons for focusing more thoroughly on this issue now. First, methodologies to address the issue have been improving rapidly, most notably through the combination of economy-wide computable general equilibrium (CGE) modeling and microsimulation modeling based on household survey data. Prominent examples include the studies in Hertel and Winters (2006) and in Bourguignon, Bussolo, and Pereira da Silva (2008). Household income information is increasingly important for poverty and inequality analysis because farm households and rural areas in developing countries are rapidly diversifying their sources of income beyond the income generated by agricultural land and farm labor, including part-time off-farm work and remittances (Otsuka and Yamano 2006; Otsuka, Estudillo, and Sawada 2009). Hence, the once close correspondence between net farm income or agricultural GDP and farm household welfare is fading even in low-income countries (Davis, Winters, and Carletto 2009).

Second, the compilation of national household surveys that are comparable for the purpose of cross-country analysis has progressed rapidly. Recent surveys are now available at the World Bank for more than 100 countries. The Global Income Distribution Dynamics (GIDD) data set has already begun to be used in conjunction with the World Bank's Linkage model of the global economy to assess global income distribution issues (for example, see Bussolo, De Hoyos, and Medvedev 2008; see also the GIDD Database).

Third, the World Bank has recently compiled a comprehensive global database that substantially updates and expands our information on the distortions to agricultural incentives in developing countries.[4] The estimates in this database have since been expressed so as to make them usable in national and global economy-wide models (Valenzuela and Anderson 2008). They differ from the usual estimates relied on by trade modelers of developing-country policies in that they are based on direct domestic-to-border price comparisons rather than on applied rates of import tariffs and other key border measures (see Narayanan and Walmsley 2008 for the latest compilation of the Global Trade Analysis Project [GTAP] data set).

The present volume is a first attempt to exploit these new methodologies and databases to assess the relative impacts on national, regional, and global poverty and inequality of agricultural and nonagricultural trade policies at home and abroad. Poverty is defined in purchasing power parity terms at a threshold of US$1 a day per capita (the extreme poverty line) and also sometimes at a threshold of US$2 a day (the moderate poverty line). If these indicators are not available, then the national poverty line is used. The incidence of poverty (the share of the population below the poverty line) and the headcount (the absolute number of poor people) are also used. The Gini coefficient of income distribution is the key measure of inequality adopted here. Where possible, the national indicators for both poverty and inequality are calculated for farm and nonfarm households separately, in addition to the national averages.

In undertaking this set of studies, we are acutely aware that agricultural and trade or domestic price subsidies are by no means the first-best policy instruments for achieving national poverty or income distribution objectives; this is largely the prerogative of public finance policies such as the supply of public goods or tax and transfer measures, including the provision of social safety nets funded through general tax revenues. However, should studies reveal that national trade-related policies are worsening poverty or inequality in particular countries, they provide a reason, in addition to the usual national gains-from-trade reason, for unilateral policy reform in these countries. Should the inequality- and poverty-reducing effects of national trade-related policy reforms be contingent on the rest of the world also reforming, this would provide another reason for a country to participate actively in promoting multilateral trade negotiations at the World Trade Organization. Furthermore, if global modeling studies reveal that multilateral trade reform would reduce global inequality and poverty, this would underline the importance of bringing the Doha Development Agenda of the World Trade Organization expeditiously to a successful conclusion through commitments to ambitious agricultural reform.

A negative finding—for example, that trade liberalization or farm subsidy cuts would increase poverty in a particular developing country—need not be a reason to shun welfare-enhancing reform, but would be a reason to use the results to provide guidance to determine where tax or social programs might become more well targeted so that all groups in society share in the economic benefits of reform (see Ravallion 2008). The results of global reform also provide bargaining power to developing countries that are seeking aid-for-trade side payments to reduce any increase in poverty projected to be generated by trade reform that has been multilaterally agreed upon.

The purpose of the rest of this chapter is to outline the analytical framework and the common empirical methodology adopted in the global and national case studies reported in subsequent chapters, to summarize and compare the modeling results from the global and national models, and to draw some general policy implications. The findings are based on three chapters (part II) that each use a global model to examine the effects of farm and nonfarm price and trade policies on global poverty and the distribution of poverty within and across many of the countries identified, plus 10 individual developing-country studies (parts III–V) spanning the three key regions: Asia (where nearly two-thirds of the world's poor live), Sub-Saharan Africa, and Latin America.

## Analytical Framework

To capture the poverty and inequality effects of price-distorting policies adequately, one must give careful consideration to the impacts of the policies on household incomes and expenditures. Many farm households in developing countries rely on the farm enterprise for virtually all of their incomes, and, in the world's poorest countries, the share of national poverty concentrated in such households is large. That the poorest households in the poorest countries are concentrated in agriculture means these households are likely to benefit from farm producer price increases generated by global trade policy reform, all else being equal. However, this outcome is not certain for several reasons. First, if a country provides protection from import competition for the farm commodities produced by the poor, the domestic prices of the commodities may decline after liberalization. Second, poor farm households also spend the majority of their incomes on staple foods (Cranfield et al. 2003); so, if food prices rise as a consequence of reform, then this adverse effect on household expenditure may more than offset any beneficial effect of higher earnings. Third, the rural nonfarm and urban poor, too, would be adversely affected by a rise in the consumer prices of staple foods. However, it is possible that a trade reform that induced a rise in food prices may also raise the demand for unskilled labor (according to the relative factor intensity of production in the economy's expanding sectors), which—depending on the intersectoral mobility of labor—might raise the incomes of poor households more than it raises the price of the consumption bundle of these households. The outcome is therefore not always going to be clear for any particular country and is certainly an empirical matter for groups of countries because the positive and negative effects in different settings will be more or less offsetting.

Some analysts have sought answers in past events by using ex post econometric or micro household data analysis (as in the set of studies in Harrison 2007), but it is not easy to find natural experiments of specific policy reforms that are appropriate for analysis and from which it is possible to generalize. An alternative approach—the one adopted in the present study—is to undertake ex ante analysis using economy-wide models. While such models have well-recognized limitations, they are the only option available if one is seeking to simulate the prospective effects of the removal of all remaining price-distorting policies (see, for example, Francois and Martin 2007). This is particularly the case if global reform is one of the scenarios of interest and, even more so, if insights into the effects on overall world poverty and inequality are being sought.

The approach adopted in our study is a variant on the pathbreaking approach pioneered by Hertel and Winters (2006) in their study of the poverty consequences of a prospective Doha Round agreement under the World Trade Organization. Like Hertel and Winters (2006), our study uses global models to assess the implications of global reform for poverty, plus a series of national models to focus more attention on specific aspects of importance to particular countries. However, the present study contrasts with the earlier one compiled by Hertel and Winters in three key respects. First, our study focuses on the impacts of agricultural policies and distinguishes these from the impacts of other merchandise trade policies; moreover, it relies on the new database on distortions to agricultural incentives in developing countries that has only recently become available in a format that is readily usable by CGE modelers (Valenzuela and Anderson 2008). These distortion estimates (for 2004) are used to represent agricultural and food policies in each of the 10 national CGE models employed in our country case studies in parts III–V, as well as in the three global models described in part II. A second distinction is that our study examines inequality, in addition to poverty. The third difference is that the present study is able to draw on the massive data collection and modeling effort undertaken for the GIDD Database, which includes data on more than a million surveyed households in a set of countries representing more than 90 percent of the world's population.

The national CGE models are able, on their own, to provide estimates of the effects of the unilateral reform of agricultural policies or of all merchandise trade-distorting policies in each relevant country. To estimate the effects of the policies of other countries, however, a national modeler requires input from a global model. We have decided to use the World Bank Linkage model for this purpose. It is based on version 7 of the GTAP Database on global protection that is calibrated to 2004 except that we have replaced the applied agricultural tariffs for developing countries in the GTAP Database with the more comprehensive set of estimates of distortion rates derived during the World Bank's research project, Distortions to Agricultural Incentives, as collated by Valenzuela and Anderson (2008), which are also calibrated to 2004.[5] The latter distortion estimates suggest that, despite reforms over the past 25 years, there was still a considerable range of price distortions across commodities and countries in 2004, including a strong antitrade bias in national agricultural policies in many developing countries, plus considerable nonagricultural protection in some developing countries (see table 1.2 above).

There are various ways to transmit the results derived from a global CGE model such as Linkage to a single-country CGE model. Like Hertel and Winters (2006), we adopt the approach developed by Horridge and Zhai (2006). For imports, Horridge and Zhai propose the use of border price changes from the global model's simulation of rest-of-the-world liberalization (that is, without the developing country that is the focus). For the exports of the developing country of interest, the shift in the export demand curve following liberalization in the rest of the world is given as percentage changes, as follows:

$$x = (1/\sigma) \cdot q, \tag{1.1}$$

where $x$ is the percentage vertical shift in the export demand curve; $\sigma$ is the elasticity of substitution between the exports of country $i$ and the exports of other countries; and $q$ is the percentage change in the quantity of exports under the scenario of liberalization in the rest of the world, excluding the country of focus.

All the CGE models used in the present study are applied in the comparative static mode, and they assume constant returns to scale and perfectly competitive product markets and homogeneous firms. In all cases other than the exceptional case of South Africa and, to a much smaller extent, the cases of Argentina and Nicaragua, unemployment is assumed to be unaffected by changes in the trade policy regime. These assumptions are imposed simply because of insufficient empirical evidence for the use of alternative assumptions across all the countries modeled in our study. This application of a standard set of assumptions reduces the risk that differences in the results across countries are driven by differing assumptions about investment behavior, productivity growth, the degree of monopolistic competition or firm heterogeneity, economies of scale, or the aggregate employment response to changes in trade policy (see Helpman, Itskhoki, and Redding 2009). Our workhorse specifications almost certainly lead to underestimations of the welfare gains that would accrue from trade reform, however. In particular, without dynamics, the models will not generate a growth dividend from the freeing up of markets or from the eventual productivity gains from trade. This dividend may be substantial.[6] Moreover, because economic growth is the predominant way poverty is reduced in developing countries (see the literature review in Ravallion 2006), the absence of dynamics implies that the results of this study will grossly underestimate the potential poverty-reducing consequences of liberalization and might, in some situations, indicate poverty increases when, in fact, they would be decreases had the growth consequences been incorporated.

All the country case studies and two of the global modeling studies presented in this volume make use of household survey data, in addition to a social accounting matrix. The matrix is the basis for the data in the CGE model, while the household survey data are used in microsimulation modeling.

Typically, the experiments are performed in two stages. The first stage involves the imposition on the national CGE model of the policy shock (either unilateral liberalization, or an exogenous shock to border prices and export demand provided by the Linkage model). This generates changes in domestic product and factor markets. The consequent changes in consumer and factor prices are then transmitted to the microsimulation model to determine how they alter the earnings of various household types (according to the shares of household income generated by the various factors) and the cost of living of these households (according to the shares of their expenditure on the various consumer products). In turn, this provides information on changes in the distribution of real household incomes and, hence, in inequality, as well as in the number of people living below any poverty line, such as the US$1-a-day extreme poverty line.

In all the country case studies, a common set of simulations has been run to compare the inequality and poverty effects of the own-country versus rest-of-the-world policies affecting the markets for agricultural goods (including lightly processed food) relative to the markets for other merchandise. The precise nature of the rest-of-the-world simulation, which employs the global Linkage model, is made clear in the next chapter and in the appendix. The other two global studies in part II use the same 2004 global protection data set, but rely on a different global model that includes national household survey data for microsimulations. In most cases, additional simulations have also been run, often to illustrate the sensitivity of the results to key assumptions pertinent to the particular case study. One assumption that the contributors to Hertel and Winters (2006) find important and that is confirmed in our study as well revolves around the nature of the change in raising tax revenue required to make up for the loss in tariff revenue associated with trade policy reform.

Although the models used in this study are all standard, perfectly competitive, constant-returns-to-scale, comparative static, economy-wide CGE models, they nonetheless differ somewhat so as to capture important realities, such as labor market characteristics or data limitations, in the particular national settings. However, to ensure the comparability of the models within this volume, we have aimed at conforming the models to a common set of factor market assumptions and closure rules, in addition to our use of 2004 as the base year for the data and undertaking a common set of simulations with the same global distortions data set.

We know from trade theory that factor market assumptions are crucial determinants of the income distributional effects of trade policies; so, all modelers have assumed the following: (1) a fixed aggregate stock of factors (including no international mobility in labor or capital or in international technology transfers), with the exception of labor in the studies on Argentina, Nicaragua, and South Africa, in which some aggregate employment responsiveness to trade policy is allowed because of the high level of unemployment in the baseline; (2) possibly some sector-specific capital and labor, but most capital and labor types are assumed to be intersectorally mobile and have a common, flexible rate of return or wage, except in the case of Argentina, in which the labor market is modeled with a switching regime between employment or wage adjustments; and (3) land is assumed to be specific to the agricultural sector, but mobile across crop and livestock activities within the sector.

The key agreed macroeconomic closure rules that the authors have aimed to adopt in each case study are a fixed current account in foreign currency (so as to avoid foreign debt considerations) and fixed real government spending and fiscal balance (so as not to affect household utility other than through traceable changes in factor and product prices and taxes). Fiscal balance is achieved by using a uniform (generally direct income) tax to replace the net losses in revenue caused by the elimination of sectoral trade taxes and subsidies. Technologies are also assumed to be unchanged by reform; so, no account is taken of any dynamic gains arising from the opening of trade and the prospective impacts on poverty and inequality generated by more rapid productivity growth.

## Synopsis of Empirical Findings: Global Model Results

This section summarizes the results of the three global models (denoted Linkage, GIDD, and GTAP). The subsequent section then brings together the results from the 10 more-detailed national case studies. Finally, we draw together the lessons learned from both sets of analyses. It would be surprising if all the studies came to the same conclusions, but the strength of this blend of somewhat different global and national models is the fact that it is more likely to expose the various determinants of the measured effects in different settings than would be the case if only a single type of model were employed.

*Linkage model results*

Chapter 2, by Anderson, Valenzuela, and van der Mensbrugghe, sets the scene for the rest of the book in that it uses the World Bank's global Linkage model (see van der Mensbrugghe 2005) to assess the market effects of the world's agricultural and trade policies as of 2004. It serves two purposes. One is to provide the basis for estimating, in each of the 10 country case studies in parts III–V, the effects of rest-of-the-world policies on the import and export prices and the demand for the various exports of any one developing country. The details of these results are reported in the appendix. The other purpose of chapter 2 is to provide estimates of various economic effects on individual countries and country groups so as to be able to say something about international inequality (in the Milanovic [2005] sense, that is, taking into account the economic size of countries) and poverty (using a simple elasticities approach).

The Linkage model results reported in chapter 2 suggest that developing countries would gain nearly two times more than high-income countries in welfare terms if 2004 agricultural and trade policies were removed globally (an average welfare increase of 0.9 percent in developing countries compared with 0.5 percent in high-income countries; see table 1.3, column 1). Thus, in this broad sense of a world of only two large country groups, completing the global trade reform

**Table 1.3. The Linkage Model's Effects of Full Global Liberalization of Agricultural and All Merchandise Trade on Economic Welfare and Real GDP, by Country and Region**

*(percent change relative to benchmark data)*

| Region | Policies in all sectors Economic welfare (EV) | Agricultural policies Agric GDP | Agricultural policies Nonag GDP | Policies in all sectors Agric GDP | Policies in all sectors Nonag GDP |
|---|---|---|---|---|---|
| East and South Asia | 0.9 | −0.3 | 0.7 | 0.5 | 2.9 |
| China | 0.2 | 2.8 | 0.2 | 5.7 | 3.0 |
| India | −0.2 | −6.1 | 1.4 | −8.3 | −0.3 |
| Africa | 0.2 | 0.1 | 0.8 | −0.9 | 0.0 |
| Latin America | 1.0 | 36.3 | 2.8 | 37.0 | 2.3 |
| All developing countries | 0.9 | 5.4 | 1.0 | 5.6 | 1.9 |
| Eastern Europe and Central Asia | 1.2 | −4.4 | 0.3 | −5.2 | 0.3 |
| All high-income countries | 0.5 | −13.8 | 0.2 | −14.7 | 0.1 |
| World total | 0.6 | −1.0 | 0.4 | −1.2 | 0.5 |

*Source:* Linkage model simulations of Anderson, Valenzuela, and van der Mensbrugghe (chapter 2).

*Note:* EV = equivalent variation in income. Agric = agricultural. Nonag = nonagricultural.

process would reduce international inequality.[7] The results vary widely across developing countries, however, ranging from slight losses in the case of some South Asian and Sub-Saharan African countries that would suffer exceptionally large adverse changes in the terms of trade to an 8 percent increase in the case of Ecuador (of which the main export item, bananas, is currently facing heavy discrimination in the markets of the European Union, where former colonies and least developed countries enjoy preferential duty-free access).[8]

Because three-quarters of the world's poorest people depend directly or indirectly on agriculture for their main incomes and because farm sizes are far larger in high-income countries than in developing countries, chapter 2 also looks at the extent to which agricultural and trade policies in place as of 2004 reduced the rewards of farming in developing countries and thereby added to international inequality in farm incomes.[9] It finds that net farm incomes in developing countries would rise by 5.6 percent, compared with 1.9 percent in nonagricultural value added, if these policies were eliminated (see table 1.3, the final two columns). This suggests that the inequality between farm and nonfarm households in developing countries would fall. In contrast, in high-income countries, net farm incomes would fall by 15 percent on average, compared with a slight rise in real nonfarm value added, that is, inequality between farm and nonfarm households in high-income countries would probably increase.[10] However, inequality between farm households in developing countries and those in high-income countries would decline substantially. These inequality results would not be so different if only agricultural policies were to be removed (see table 1.3, columns 2 and 3), underscoring the large magnitude of the distortions caused by agricultural trade policies relative to the effects of nonagricultural trade policies.

Chapter 2 also reports that unskilled workers in developing countries—the majority of whom work on farms—would benefit most from reform (followed by skilled workers and then capital owners): the average change in the real unskilled wage over all developing countries would be a rise of 3.5 percent. However, the most relevant consumer prices for the poor, including those many poor farm households and other rural households that earn most of their income from their labor and are net buyers of food, are the prices relating to food and clothing. Hence, if we deflate by a food and clothing price index rather than the aggregate consumer price index, we obtain a better indication of the welfare change among the poor. As shown in the final column of table 1.4, the real unskilled wage over all developing countries would show a rise of 5.9 percent if we use the food and clothing deflator, that is, the inequality in real incomes between unskilled wage earners and the much wealthier owners of (human or physical) capital within developing countries would likely be reduced if there were full trade reform.

## Table 1.4. The Linkage Model's Effects of Full Global Merchandise Trade Liberalization on Real Factor Prices, by Country and Region

*(percent change relative to benchmark data)*

| Region | Nominal change deflated by the aggregate CPI | | | Real change in unskilled wages, deflated | | |
| --- | --- | --- | --- | --- | --- | --- |
| | Skilled wages | Capital user cost[a] | Land user cost[a] | By aggregate CPI | By food CPI | By food and clothing CPI |
| East and South Asia | 3.4 | 3.0 | −1.8 | 3.2 | 4.6 | 4.8 |
| Africa | 4.7 | 4.3 | 0.1 | 4.4 | 5.8 | 6.9 |
| Latin America | 1.4 | 1.9 | 21.1 | 4.5 | 2.4 | 4.1 |
| All developing countries | 3.0 | 2.9 | 1.6 | 3.5 | 5.5 | 5.9 |
| Eastern Europe and Central Asia | 3.2 | 2.6 | −4.5 | 1.7 | 4.2 | 4.5 |
| High-income countries | 1.0 | 0.5 | 17.9 | 0.2 | 3.3 | 3.3 |
| World total | 1.3 | 1.2 | −3.1 | 0.9 | 3.6 | 3.8 |

*Source:* Anderson, Valenzuela, and van der Mensbrugghe (chapter 2).

*Note:* CPI = consumer price index.

a. The user cost of capital and land represents the subsidy-inclusive rental cost.

The results on real factor rewards and net farm incomes suggest that poverty, as well as international and intra-developing-country inequality, might be reduced globally by agricultural and trade policy liberalization. The authors of chapter 2 take a further step to assess the impacts of reform on poverty explicitly even though the Linkage model has only a single representative household per country. They do so using the elasticities approach, which involves taking the estimated impact on real household income and applying an estimated income to poverty elasticity to estimate the impacts on the poverty headcount index for each country. They focus on the change in the average wage of unskilled workers, deflated by the food and clothing consumer price index and assume that these workers are exempt from the direct income tax imposed to replace the lost customs revenue following trade reform (a realistic assumption for many developing countries).

Table 1.5 reports that, under the full merchandise trade reform scenario, extreme poverty—the number of people surviving on less than US$1 a day—would drop by 26 million people in developing countries relative to the baseline level of slightly less than 1 billion, a reduction of 2.7 percent. The proportional reduction is much higher in China and Sub-Saharan Africa, falling in each by around 4 percent. It is even higher in Latin America (7 percent) and in South Asia outside India (10 percent). In contrast, the number of extreme poor in India is

# Table 1.5. The Linkage Model's Effects of Full Global Merchandise Trade Liberalization on the Number of Extreme Poor, by Region

| Region | Real change in average unskilled wage,[a] % | Baseline headcount, % | | New levels, US$1 a day | | New levels, US$2 a day | | Change in number of poor relative to baseline levels, millions | | Change in number of poor relative to baseline levels, % | |
|---|---|---|---|---|---|---|---|---|---|---|---|
| | | US$1 a day | US$2 a day | Headcount, % | Total poor, millions | Headcount, % | Total poor, millions | US$1 a day | US$2 a day | US$1 a day | US$2 a day |
| East Asia | 4.4 | 9 | 37 | 8 | 151 | 34 | 632 | −17 | −52 | −10.3 | −7.6 |
| China | 2.1 | 10 | 35 | 9 | 123 | 34 | 440 | −5 | −12 | −4.0 | −2.7 |
| Other East Asia | 8.1 | 9 | 50 | 6 | 29 | 42 | 192 | −12 | −40 | −30.1 | −17.1 |
| South Asia | −1.9 | 31 | 77 | 32 | 454 | 78 | 1,124 | 8 | 8 | 1.8 | 0.7 |
| India | −3.8 | 34 | 80 | 36 | 386 | 82 | 883 | 15 | 15 | 4.2 | 1.7 |
| Other South Asia | 4.0 | 29 | 94 | 26 | 68 | 92 | 241 | −8 | −7 | −9.9 | −2.7 |
| Sub-Saharan Africa | 5.3 | 41 | 72 | 39 | 287 | 70 | 508 | −11 | −14 | −3.8 | −2.7 |
| Latin America | 4.1 | 9 | 22 | 8 | 44 | 21 | 115 | −3 | −6 | −6.8 | −4.7 |
| Middle East and North Africa | 14.3 | 1 | 20 | 1 | 3 | 13 | 40 | −2 | −19 | −36.4 | −32.7 |
| Developing-country total | 5.9 | 18 | 48 | 18 | 944 | 46 | 2,462 | −26 | −87 | −2.7 | −3.4 |
| Excluding China | 6.5 | 21 | 52 | 20 | 820 | 50 | 2,022 | −21 | −74 | −2.5 | −4.7 |
| Eastern Europe and Central Asia | 4.5 | 1 | 10 | 1 | 4 | 9 | 43 | −0 | −4 | −6.8 | −8.0 |

*Source:* Anderson, Valenzuela, and van der Mensbrugghe (chapter 2).

a. Nominal unskilled wage deflated by the food and clothing consumer price index.

estimated to rise, by 4 percent.[11] This follows from the estimated decline in overall income in India following trade liberalization that is noted in table 1.3. Under the more moderate definition of poverty (people living on no more than US$2 per day), the number of poor in developing countries would fall by nearly 90 million compared to an aggregate baseline level of slightly less than 2.5 billion in 2004, or by 3.4 percent (although the number of people in India living on less than US$2 a day would still increase, but by only 1.7 percent).

### The GIDD model results

Bussolo, De Hoyos, and Medvedev, in chapter 3, make direct use of the global CGE Linkage model, but combine it with the newly developed GIDD tool (Bussolo, De Hoyos, and Medvedev 2008). The GIDD is a framework for ex ante analysis of the effects on income distribution and poverty of changes in macroeconomic, trade, and sectoral policies or trends in global markets. It thus offers an alternative to the elasticity approach adopted in chapter 2. It complements a global CGE analysis by providing global microsimulations based on standardized household surveys. The tool pools information from most of the currently available household surveys covering 1.2 million households in 73 developing countries. Information on households in developed countries and Eastern European transition economies completes the data set. Overall, the GIDD sample countries cover more than 90 percent of the world's population.[12] In contrast to the modeling approach used in chapter 2, the GIDD approach is able to distinguish between farm and nonfarm households by examining the employment of heads of household. However, because of differences across surveys in the coverage of sources of household income, the database does not provide precise information on the sources of income for each household, and behind the data is the assumption that the proportional change in household incomes is driven only by changes in wages.

The key inputs in the microsimulation model are the results on changes in incomes from labor that have been obtained through the use of a variation on the Linkage model that assumes full labor mobility.[13] Two liberalization scenarios are examined: first, the full liberalization of the markets for agricultural products and lightly processed food without the liberalization of nonfarm goods markets and, second, the full liberalization of the markets for all goods. Neither scenario is accompanied by large effects on global poverty according to the GIDD. The results summarized in table 1.6 show the incidence of extreme poverty (US$1 a day) rising by 1.0 percent (0.5 percent each from full global trade reform in the farm sector and the nonfarm sector). This increase in poverty is largely caused by the increase in poverty in South Asia, where the number of poor people rises by 3.9 percent after complete global trade reform, a result

**Table 1.6. The GIDD Model's Effects of the Removal of Agricultural and All Merchandise Trade Distortions on the Number of Extreme Poor, by Region**
*(millions and percent)*

| | | Change in number of poor after global trade reform | | | |
| | | Agricultural reform only | | All merchandise trade reform | |
| Region | Share of global poverty, % | millions | % | millions | % |
|---|---|---|---|---|---|
| *Extreme poverty, US$1 a day* | | | | | |
| East Asia | 24 | −6.4 | −2.8 | −6.3 | −2.8 |
| South Asia | 50 | 15.4 | 3.3 | 18.2 | 3.9 |
| Sub-Saharan Africa | 21 | −1.0 | −0.5 | 0.5 | 0.3 |
| Latin America | 4 | −2.8 | −6.9 | −3.5 | −8.7 |
| Global[a] | 100 | 5.0 | 0.5 | 8.9 | 1.0 |
| *Moderate and extreme poverty, US$2 a day* | | | | | |
| East Asia | 33 | −12.8 | −1.6 | −13.2 | −1.7 |
| South Asia | 46 | −3.6 | −0.3 | −2.0 | −0.2 |
| Sub-Saharan Africa | 14 | 0.1 | 0.0 | 1.1 | 0.3 |
| Latin America | 4 | −4.8 | −4.6 | −5.7 | −5.4 |
| Global[a] | 100 | −22.1 | −0.9 | −19.8 | −0.8 |

*Source:* Bussolo, De Hoyos, and Medvedev (chapter 3).

a. Includes Middle East and North Africa, Eastern Europe and Central Asia, and high-income countries, which, together, account for no more than 2 percent of the world's poor.

similar to the result reported in chapter 2. Moderate poverty (US$2 a day), on the other hand, is projected to *fall* by a similar amount (0.9 percent because of agricultural reform alone and 0.8 percent if nonfarm reform is included).

These small aggregate global changes are produced by a combination of offsetting trends among farm and nonfarm households (table 1.7). At the US$1-a-day extreme poverty level, global liberalization would raise the share of agricultural households among the world's total poor households by one percentage point (from 76 to 77 percent). It would also increase the incidence of poverty among the world's agricultural households (from 32 to 33 percent), while the incidence of poverty among the world's nonfarm households would drop slightly, to 8 percent. However, at the moderate poverty line of US$2 a day, both agricultural and all merchandise trade liberalization would globally *lower* the incidence of poverty by nearly 1 percent, and it would reduce poverty among farm and nonfarm households (compare table 1.7, last two columns).

There are several possible explanations for the differences between the signs of the effects of reforms on extreme poverty in chapters 2 and 3. First is that the

**Table 1.7.  The GIDD Model's Effects of the Removal of Agricultural and All Merchandise Trade Distortions on Global Poverty and Inequality, Farm and Nonfarm Households**

| Indicator | Gini coefficient | Real average monthly income, 2000 US$ PPP | US$1-a-day poverty incidence | US$1-a-day poverty share | US$2-a-day poverty incidence | US$2-a-day poverty share |
|---|---|---|---|---|---|---|
| *Initial levels* | | | | | | |
| Agricultural | 0.45 | 65 | 31.5[a] | 76[a] | 73.8[a] | 70[a] |
| Nonagricultural | 0.63 | 320 | 8.3[a] | 24[a] | 26.7[a] | 30[a] |
| All households | 0.67 | 204 | 18.9[a] | 100[a] | 48.2[a] | 100[a] |
| *Agricultural liberalization, change from baseline, percentage points* | | | | | | |
| Agricultural | 0.7 | 1.1[a] | 0.86 | 1.1 | −0.86 | 0.5 |
| Nonagricultural | −0.1 | 0.2[a] | −0.29 | −1.1 | −0.90 | −0.5 |
| All households | −0.1 | 0.3[a] | 0.23 | 0.0 | −0.88 | 0.0 |
| *All merchandise trade liberalization, change from baseline, percentage points* | | | | | | |
| Agricultural | 0.8 | 0.0[a] | 1.09 | 1.0 | −0.66 | 0.6 |
| Nonagricultural | −0.2 | 0.4[a] | −0.19 | −1.0 | −0.95 | −0.6 |
| All households | −0.0 | 0.4[a] | 0.39 | 0.0 | −0.82 | 0.0 |

*Source:* Bussolo, De Hoyos, and Medvedev (chapter 3).

*Note:* PPP = purchasing power parity.

a. Expressed in percentages.

GIDD poverty data refer to 2000, whereas the Linkage poverty numbers relate to 2004. A large share of the developing-country population was bunched around the extreme poverty line in 2000 (see chapter 3, figure 3.1), but, by 2004, poverty had shrunk quite a bit, at least in East Asia. Second, the GIDD results are based on changes in labor incomes only rather than on changes in incomes from all factors of production. In particular, by not including the effect on nonlabor (especially land) incomes, the study presented in chapter 3 understates the poverty-reducing impacts of trade reform on farm households, thereby contributing to its finding that extreme poverty among farm households would increase. Third, the assumption of full labor mobility implies that unskilled farm workers share in the gains from increased agricultural prices, along with their nonfarm counterparts, because less labor is required to migrate to nonfarm jobs.

The GIDD results suggest that there might also be a considerable change in inequality following global trade reform. Indeed, table 1.7 shows that agricultural incomes would increase by twice as much as nonfarm household incomes in the all-goods reform scenario (0.8 compared with 0.4 percent) and by five times as much in the reform in agriculture only scenario (1.1 compared with 0.2 percent). While this reduction in the nonagricultural income premium on its own would reduce inequality, income dispersion within the agricultural sector would also increase

**Table 1.8. The GIDD Model's Effects of the Removal of Agricultural and All Merchandise Trade Distortions on Global Poverty and Inequality, Farm and Nonfarm Households, by Region**

*(percentage point change)*

| | Agricultural reform only | | | All merchandise trade reform | | |
|---|---|---|---|---|---|---|
| Region | Gini coefficient | US$1 a day, headcount | US$2 a day, headcount | Gini coefficient | US$1 a day, headcount | US$2 a day, headcount |
| East Asia | −0.72 | −0.38 | −0.76 | −0.62 | −0.37 | −0.78 |
| South Asia | 0.82 | 1.16 | −0.27 | 0.81 | 1.37 | −0.15 |
| India | 1.01 | 1.49 | −0.33 | 1.04 | 1.71 | −0.26 |
| Other South Asia | 0.22 | 0.06 | −0.09 | 0.02 | 0.21 | 0.17 |
| Africa | −0.04 | −0.23 | 0.02 | 0.06 | 0.11 | 0.25 |
| Latin America | −0.51 | −0.61 | −1.06 | −0.65 | −0.77 | −1.26 |
| World | −0.10 | 0.23 | −0.88 | −0.00 | 0.39 | −0.82 |

*Source:* Bussolo, De Hoyos, and Medvedev (chapter 3).

a. Weighted averages across the selected countries in each region.

given the differences in the impacts of reform on income distribution across developing-country regions, such that the final change in global inequality would be close to zero (table 1.7, column 1).

Chapter 3 also provides results on poverty and inequality at the national and regional levels; these are summarized in table 1.8. Improvements (that is, reductions) in these indicators are pervasive among the 19 countries of Latin America and the Caribbean and the 5 East Asian countries. There are far fewer African examples of improvements, regardless of whether the reform scenario is only in agriculture or also includes nonfarm goods, but most of the changes in the indicators on these countries are close to zero. It is mainly in India where extreme poverty—but not moderate poverty—would worsen according to the GIDD results; this was also the finding derived in the study in chapter 2 through the application of poverty elasticities directly to the Linkage model results.

The impact of agricultural reform on poverty in India is important, but the existing evidence is quite mixed. In an econometric analysis of historical data, Topalova (2007) concludes that the reductions in agricultural protection associated with India's tariff reforms of the 1990s increased national poverty. In contrast, using detailed information on household incomes and expenditures, Cai, de Janvry, and Sadoulet (2008) conclude that 70 percent of the farmers in India (86 percent of those with less than 0.2 hectares, 73 percent of those with between 0.2 and 1 hectare, and 49 percent of those with more than 1 hectare) would have lost from increases in the prices of staple foods during 2007–08. According to their data, this is because even the smallest farmers receive only about half their incomes from farming. Unfortunately, we have been unable to locate an appropriate model or commission a study for India to include in part III.

One needs to bear in mind that the GIDD microsimulation model assumes that changes in total household incomes are proportional to the changes in the wage rates for the agricultural or nonagricultural labor of the households. While labor income is the most important source of income for households at or near the poverty line, it is not the only one. Thus, accounting for changes in other factor returns may yield somewhat different results, especially in terms of inequality. In the remaining studies under review, all sources of income are taken into account so that we may provide more reliable national results, albeit for a smaller sample of developing countries.

### *GTAP model results*

Hertel and Keeney, in chapter 4, draw on the widely used global economy wide GTAP model. The model adopts the same price distortions as the other studies in this volume and runs the same scenarios, but generates its own world price changes from the GTAP model for scenarios of multilateral trade reform scenarios. These price changes alter the border prices in the various countries in the GTAP model, a subset of which has associated detailed household survey data. This allows the authors to make statements about poverty impacts across a range of diverse economies using an internally consistent framework that represents an alternative to the framework used by Bussolo, De Hoyos, and Medvedev in chapter 3. While the number of countries on which household survey data are available to Hertel and Keeney is much smaller, the income data are richer, allowing the authors to capture the distributive effects of all changes in factor incomes rather than restricting their examination only to labor income shocks, as in chapter 3.

The multicountry study described in chapter 4 focuses on 15 developing countries: four African (Malawi, Mozambique, Uganda, and Zambia), five Asian (Bangladesh, Indonesia, the Philippines, Thailand, and Vietnam), and six Latin American countries (Brazil, Chile, Colombia, Mexico, Peru, and República Bolivariana de Venezuela). Overall, it concludes that the removal of current agricultural and trade policies globally would tend to reduce poverty, primarily via the agricultural reforms (table 1.9). The unweighted average for all 15 developing countries is a decline in the headcount for extreme poverty (US$1 a day) of 1.7 percent. The average fall for the Asian subsample is two times higher, however, and nearly two-thirds of the world's extremely poor people live in Asia (although the sample does not include China and India). The results of Hertel and Keeney on specific countries indicate that, in the sample, the greatest reduction in poverty would occur among the exporters of agricultural products, namely, Chile, Thailand, and Vietnam (table 1.9, column 3). The majority of the

**Table 1.9. The GTAP Model's Effects of Full Global Liberalization of Agricultural and All Merchandise Trade on the Number of Extreme Poor, by Country**

*(percentage point change in US$1-a-day poverty)*

| Country | Default tax replacement | | | Alternative tax replacement[a] |
|---|---|---|---|---|
| | Agricultural reform only | Nonagricultural reform only | All merchandise trade reform | All merchandise trade reform |
| *Asia* | | | | |
| Bangladesh | −0.3 | 0.5 | 0.3 | −5.3 |
| Indonesia | −1.1 | 0.5 | −0.6 | −5.2 |
| Philippines | −1.4 | 0.4 | −1.0 | −6.4 |
| Thailand | −11.2 | 0.9 | −10.3 | −28.1 |
| Vietnam | −0.5 | −5.3 | −5.7 | −23.6 |
| *Africa* | | | | |
| Malawi | −1.6 | −0.3 | −1.9 | −5.6 |
| Mozambique | −1.2 | 0.2 | −1.0 | −4.3 |
| Uganda | −0.0 | 0.1 | 0.1 | −6.0 |
| Zambia | −0.0 | 0.1 | 0.1 | −2.0 |
| *Latin America* | | | | |
| Brazil | −2.5 | 0.4 | −2.2 | −10.0 |
| Chile | −4.8 | 0.1 | −4.6 | −12.3 |
| Colombia | −0.7 | 0.6 | −0.1 | −4.1 |
| Mexico | 0.8 | 0.4 | 1.1 | −0.5 |
| Peru | −0.6 | −0.2 | −0.8 | −5.2 |
| Venezuela, R.B. de | 0.2 | 0.7 | 0.9 | −2.1 |
| *Unweighted average* | | | | |
| Asia | −2.9 | −0.6 | −3.5 | −13.7 |
| Africa | −0.7 | 0.1 | −0.7 | −4.5 |
| Latin America | −1.3 | 0.3 | −1.0 | −5.7 |
| All 15 developing countries | −1.7 | −0.1 | −1.7 | −8.0 |

*Source:* Hertel and Keeney (chapter 4), table 4.5.

a. The poor are exempt under the alternative tax replacement.

15 countries would experience small increases in poverty after nonagricultural reforms, although the unweighted average across the 15 countries suggests that there would be a slight decrease, primarily because of a significant decline in Vietnam (table 1.9, column 2).

The magnitude of the estimated reduction in extreme poverty in Asia and Latin America is somewhat larger according to Hertel and Keeney (chapter 4) than the average reductions estimated for the same countries by Bussolo, De Hoyos, and Medvedev (chapter 3, table 3.4) using the GIDD model. Hertel and Keeney also estimate a small reduction in poverty in Africa.[14] These GTAP results are thus closer to the results of the Linkage model described in chapter 2.

Hertel and Keeney explore the relative poverty-friendliness of agricultural trade reforms in detail by examining the differential impacts on real after-tax factor returns of agricultural versus nonagricultural trade policy reforms. They extend their analysis to the distribution of households by looking at changes in stratum-specific poverty. They find that the more favorable impacts of agricultural reforms are driven by increased returns to the labor of farm households, as well as higher returns to unskilled work off-farm. They also find that the liberalization of foodgrain markets accounts for the largest contribution to poverty reduction and that the removal of import tariffs in these commodity markets dominates among the poverty-increasing impacts of the removal of subsidies by high-income countries.

The final column of table 1.9 reports the percentage change in the national poverty headcount if the poor are not subject to the rise in the income tax required to replace trade tax revenue following trade reform. This assumption represents a significant implicit income transfer from nonpoor to poor households and thus generates a marked difference in the predicted reduction in poverty. Trade reforms are no longer marginally poverty reducing in most of the 15 cases, but, instead, are poverty reducing in all cases and by a considerable magnitude. This lowers the poverty rate by roughly one-quarter in Thailand and Vietnam, for example. Overall, the regional and total average extent of poverty reduction is around four times larger under this scenario relative to the scenario whereby the poor are also assumed to be subject to the income taxes levied to replace lost trade tax revenue.

The reduction in the unweighted average poverty headcount in the three regions shown in the final column of table 1.9 is remarkably similar to the reduction in the population-weighted averages found by Anderson, Valenzuela, and van der Mensbrugghe (chapter 2) and reported in table 1.5, above, under a similar tax-replacement assumption: the 17 percent for Asia, excluding China and India, and the 6.4 percent for Latin America found by the latter authors are only slightly above the 14 and 5.7 percent, respectively, of Hertel and Keeney, while the 3.7 percent for Sub-Saharan Africa in chapter 2 is only slightly below the 4.5 percent obtained by Hertel and Keeney.

## Synopsis of the Empirical Findings: National Model Results

We turn now to a comparison of the results of the 10 detailed individual country case studies with the results obtained from the global models described above. The features of the national models are summarized in table 1.10.[15] Like the three global models, they focus on price-distorting policies as of 2004, even though the database for the CGE models and the household survey data on

**Table 1.10. Characteristics of the Models in the Global and National Country Studies**

| Study | Chapter | Protection data, year | SAM,[a] year | Household survey, year | Sectors, number | Products, number | Types of labor, number | Intersectoral labor mobility |
|---|---|---|---|---|---|---|---|---|
| *Global* | | | | | | | | |
| Linkage | 2 | 2004 | 2004 | None | 23 | 23 | 2 | Yes |
| GIDD | 3 | 2004 | 2004 | circa 2000 | 23 | 23 | 4 | Partial |
| GTAP | 4 | 2004 | 2001 | circa 2000 | 31 | 6 | 6 | Partial |
| *National* | | | | | | | | |
| China | 5 | 2004 | 2002 | 2000 | 48 | 48 | 8 | Partial |
| Indonesia | 6 | 2004 | 2000 | 1999 | 65 | 20 | 2 | Yes |
| Pakistan | 7 | 2004 | 2000–01 | 2001–02 | 34 | 28 | 3 | Farm, no |
| Philippines | 8 | 2004 | 2000 | 2000 | 41 | 34 | 2 | Yes |
| Thailand | 9 | 2004 | 2000 | 2000 | 65 | 65 | 2 | Yes |
| Mozambique | 10 | 2004 | 2003 | 2002 | 56 | 56 | 8 | No |
| South Africa | 11 | 2004 | 2002 | 2000 | 110 | 110 | 3 | Unemployment |
| Argentina | 12 | 2004 | 2005 | 2005 | 24 | 26 | 6 | Unemployment |
| Brazil | 13 | 2004 | 2001 | 2001 | 42 | 52 | 10 | Yes |
| Nicaragua | 14 | 2004 | 2000 | 2001 | 40 | 40 | 4 | Unemployment |

*Sources:* Global and country case studies in parts II–V.

a. Social accounting matrix of production and trade data.

which these models are based typically date back a little earlier in the decade. They all include more sectoral and product disaggregation than the global models and cover multiple types of households and labor. All the national studies include microsimulations that draw on the CGE model results, as in the GIDD and GTAP global models.

The results of the national studies on real GDP and household consumption suggest that GDP would increase after full global trade reform, but only by 1 or 2 percent, in all 10 countries (except in Argentina if export taxes are removed during full liberalization).[16] Given falling consumer prices, real household consumption would increase by considerably more in most cases. (Argentina would again be the notable exception for the reasons discussed elsewhere below.) Generally, these numbers are a little larger than the numbers generated by the global Linkage model, but they are still usually much lower than would be the case had the authors used dynamic models. Like the global models, the studies therefore underestimate the poverty-reducing benefits of trade reform given the broad consensus in the literature that trade liberalization increases growth, which is, in turn, a major contributor to poverty reduction.

Comparative tables 1.11 and 1.12 summarize the national results on the incidence of extreme poverty and income inequality, respectively, resulting from own-country and rest-of-the-world full global liberalization of either agricultural trade or the trade in all goods.[17] Some authors ran only six of the nine simulations shown in these tables, but the authors who ran all nine found that the simulations sum almost exactly (to within one decimal place). We have therefore inferred the three missing results in the other country studies by assuming that the results in the agriculture only and nonagriculture only simulations sum to the results of the reform in the trade for all goods. The inferred numbers are shown in italics in tables 1.11 and 1.12. In each case, the total effects on poverty and inequality are subdivided into rural and urban effects.

One should not necessarily expect the unweighted averages of the poverty results for each region to be similar to those generated by Hertel and Keeney (chapter 4) because only half of the 10 countries on which we have case studies are included among the 15 countries sampled by Hertel and Keeney. Nonetheless, the unweighted averages of the national poverty effects for each of the key developing country regions computed by Hertel and Keeney are reported in parentheses in the last 4 rows of table 1.11, panel c so that these may be easily compared with the unweighted regional averages derived from our national case studies. In all but 3 of the 12 comparisons on global liberalization (agriculture, nonagriculture, and all merchandise), the projected regional average reductions in poverty after global liberalization are larger in our sample of national case studies than in the sample of 15 countries examined by Hertel and Keeney. This may mean that the poverty

**Table 1.11. The Impact of Reform on the Incidence of Extreme Poverty, by Country**
(percentage point change in the national or US$1-a-day poverty line)

**a. Rural poverty**

| Country study | Base % | Agricultural reform only | | | Nonagricultural reform only | | | All merchandise trade reform | | |
|---|---|---|---|---|---|---|---|---|---|---|
| | | Unilateral | R of W | Global | Unilateral | R of W | Global | Unilateral | R of W | Global |
| China (US$2/day) | 58 | 0.3 | -1.4 | -1.1 | 0.2 | -0.5 | -0.3 | 0.5 | -1.9 | -1.4 |
| Indonesia | 29 | 0.1 | -1.1 | -1.1 | -0.2 | -3.2 | -3.3 | -0.1 | -4.3 | -4.4 |
| Pakistan | 38 | -1.4 | -0.1 | -1.5 | -6.2 | -1.1 | -7.1 | -7.6 | -1.2 | -8.6 |
| Philippines | 49 | 0.0 | -0.6 | -0.3 | 0.6 | -0.3 | 0.2 | 0.6 | -0.9 | -0.1 |
| Thailand | 30 | 0.3 | -1.6 | -1.3 | -3.8 | 0.7 | -3.1 | -3.5 | -0.9 | -4.4 |
| Mozambique | 36 | -1.6 | 0.0 | -1.6 | -0.5 | -1.5 | -2.0 | -2.1 | -1.5 | -3.6 |
| South Africa | 17 | -0.3 | -0.3 | -0.7 | -0.8 | 0.0 | -0.8 | -1.1 | -0.4 | -1.4 |
| Argentina | — | — | — | — | — | — | — | — | — | — |
| Brazil | — | — | — | — | — | — | — | — | — | — |
| Nicaragua | 63 | -0.7 | 0.3 | -0.4 | -0.6 | -0.3 | -0.9 | -1.3 | 0.0 | -1.3 |

## b. Urban poverty

| Country study | Base % | Agricultural reform only | | | Nonagricultural reform only | | | All merchandise trade reform | | |
|---|---|---|---|---|---|---|---|---|---|---|
| | | Unilateral | R of W | Global | Unilateral | R of W | Global | Unilateral | R of W | Global |
| China (US$2/day) | 3 | 0.0 | 0.0 | 0.0 | 0.0 | −0.1 | −0.1 | 0.0 | −0.1 | −0.1 |
| Indonesia | 12 | −0.1 | −0.3 | −0.4 | −0.1 | −1.7 | −1.8 | −0.2 | −2.0 | −2.2 |
| Pakistan | 20 | −2.4 | −0.1 | −2.7 | 4.7 | −1.4 | 3.1 | 2.3 | −1.5 | 0.4 |
| Philippines | 19 | 0.8 | −0.9 | −0.2 | 1.2 | −0.7 | 0.3 | 2.0 | −1.6 | 0.1 |
| Thailand | 6 | 0.0 | −0.8 | −0.7 | −3.3 | 0.2 | −3.2 | −3.3 | −0.6 | −3.9 |
| Mozambique | 37 | −0.5 | 0.0 | −0.5 | −0.4 | −1.3 | −1.7 | −0.9 | −1.3 | −2.2 |
| South Africa | 4 | −0.1 | −0.2 | −0.3 | −0.4 | 0.0 | −0.4 | −0.5 | −0.2 | −0.7 |
| Argentina | 13 | 1.3 | 0.1 | 1.5 | −0.4 | −0.1 | −0.5 | 0.9 | 0.0 | 1.0 |
| Brazil | — | — | — | — | — | — | — | — | — | — |
| Nicaragua | 27 | 0.3 | −0.5 | −0.2 | −1.0 | 1.4 | 0.4 | −0.7 | 0.9 | 0.2 |

(Table continues on the following page.)

**Table 1.11. The Impact of Reform on the Incidence of Extreme Poverty, by Country (continued)**
*(percentage point change in the national or US$1-a-day poverty line)*

**c. Total poverty**

| Country study | Base % | Agricultural reform only | | | Nonagricultural reform only | | | All merchandise trade reform | | |
|---|---|---|---|---|---|---|---|---|---|---|
| | | Unilateral | R of W | Global | Unilateral | R of W | Global | Unilateral | R of W | Global |
| China (US$2/day) | 36 | 0.2 | −0.8 | −0.6 | 0.1 | −0.4 | −0.3 | 0.3 | −1.2 | −0.9 |
| Indonesia | 23 | −0.0 | −0.8 | −0.8 | −0.1 | −2.7 | −2.8 | −0.1 | −3.5 | −3.6 |
| Pakistan | 31 | −1.6 | −0.1 | −1.8 | −3.6 | −1.2 | −4.6 | −5.2 | −1.3 | −6.4 |
| Philippines | 34 | 0.4 | −0.6 | −0.1 | 0.7 | −0.3 | 0.2 | 1.1 | −0.9 | 0.1 |
| Thailand | 14 | 0.1 | −1.1 | −0.8 | −3.5 | 0.4 | −3.3 | −3.4 | −0.7 | −4.1 |
| Mozambique | 36 | −1.3 | 0.0 | −1.3 | −0.4 | −1.4 | −1.8 | −1.7 | −1.4 | −3.1 |
| South Africa | 10 | −0.2 | −0.3 | −0.5 | −0.6 | −0.1 | −0.6 | −0.8 | −0.3 | −1.1 |
| Argentina | — | — | — | — | — | — | — | — | — | — |
| Brazil | 31 | −0.5 | −2.3 | −2.8 | −0.4 | −0.1 | −0.5 | −0.9 | −2.4 | −3.5 |
| Nicaragua | 41 | −0.1 | −0.2 | −0.3 | −0.9 | 0.3 | −0.6 | −1.0 | 0.1 | −0.9 |
| *Unweighted averages* | | | | | | | | | | |
| Asia | 28 | −0.2 | −0.7 | (−2.9) −0.8 | −1.2 | −0.8 | (−0.6) −2.2 | −1.5 | −1.6 | (−3.5) −3.0 |
| Africa | 32 | −0.8 | −0.2 | (−0.7) −0.9 | −0.5 | −0.7 | (0.1) −1.2 | −1.3 | −0.9 | (−0.7) −2.1 |
| Latin America | 36 | −0.3 | −1.3 | (−1.3) −1.6 | −0.7 | 0.1 | (0.3) −0.6 | −1.0 | −1.2 | (−1.0) −2.2 |
| All 9 developing countries[a] | 43 | −0.4 | −0.6 | (−1.7) −1.0 | −0.9 | −0.7 | (−0.1) −1.6 | −1.3 | −1.3 | (−2.6) −2.6 |

*Sources:* Studies in parts II–V. Hertel and Keeney (chapter 4), table 4.5, for the numbers in parentheses.

*Note:* R of W = rest of the world. The numbers in italics for individual countries have been inferred on the assumption that linearity holds (see the text). The numbers in parentheses are from the GTAP model results and are provided for comparison (see table 1.9). Numbers may not sum because of rounding or interaction effects.
— = no estimates are available.

a. Excludes Argentina.

elasticities used in the latter study (and also in the Linkage model, which generated similar results) are too small given the greater possibilities for adaptation reflected in most of the national models.[18]

The individual country results show that poverty would be reduced in all countries by both global agricultural and, with the exception of the Philippines, nonagricultural liberalization (table 1.11, panel c). If all merchandise trade were liberalized, the extent of the reduction in poverty ranges from close to zero to about 3.5 percentage points, except in Pakistan, where it is more than 6.0 percentage points.[19] If we examine the unweighted averages, we find that a greater share of the reduction in poverty is generated by nonfarm trade reform, with the important exception of Brazil, where agricultural reform is the major contributor to the significant pro-poor outcome. However, if the average is weighted according to the number of people involved, agricultural reform would dominate, as it does in the results of the global modeling. The extreme Brazil result occurs despite the existence of tariff protection for the country's poor import-competing farmers; it is a consequence of the increase in the demand for unskilled labor following liberalization, which evidently outweighs the poverty impact of the removal of farm tariffs. The contribution of own-country reforms to the decline in poverty appears to be as important as the rest-of-the-world reforms, on average, although there is considerable cross-country divergence in the extent of this parity in the farm reforms and in the nonfarm reforms.

The reduction in poverty is divided into rural and urban sources of reduction in table 1.11, panels a and b. A glance at the final column in these panels reveals that rural poverty declines much more than urban poverty in every case. This is true after farm or nonfarm trade reform, as well as after own-country or rest-of-the-world reform. Since the rural poor are much poorer, on average, than the urban poor, this would lead one to expect trade reform to reduce inequality also (see Bussolo, De Hoyos, and Medvedev, chapter 3, figure 3.1).

Indeed, the results shown at the bottom of table 1.12, panel c on this sample of countries indicate that inequality would decline in all three developing-country regions after full trade liberalization of all goods or of only agricultural products in the case of both own-country reform and rest-of-the-world reform. The effect of nonfarm trade reform alone is more mixed, providing another reason trade negotiators should not neglect agricultural reform in their discussions. Rest-of-the-world and global agricultural reform both lead to a reduction in inequality in every country in the sample except Thailand (plus Argentina and the Philippines slightly in the case of global reform). Meanwhile, unilateral agricultural reform reduces (or leaves constant) inequality in a small majority of countries; the exceptions are Argentina, China, the Philippines, and Thailand (although the effects are small). Nonfarm global reform increases inequality slightly in only three countries.

**Table 1.12. The Impact of Reform on the Incidence of Income Inequality, by Country**
*(percentage point change in the Gini coefficient)*

**a. Rural**

| Country study | Base % | Agricultural reform only | | | Nonagricultural reform only | | | All merchandise trade reform | | |
|---|---|---|---|---|---|---|---|---|---|---|
| | | Unilateral | R of W | Global | Unilateral | R of W | Global | Unilateral | R of W | Global |
| China | 0.32 | 0.0 | −0.2 | −0.2 | 0.0 | 0.0 | 0.0 | 0.0 | −0.2 | −0.2 |
| Indonesia | 0.29 | 0.0 | 0.0 | 0.0 | 0.1 | 0.0 | 0.1 | 0.1 | 0.0 | 0.1 |
| Pakistan | 0.26 | −0.1 | −0.0 | −0.1 | 0.3 | 0.0 | 0.3 | 0.2 | −0.0 | 0.2 |
| Philippines | 0.43 | 0.2 | −0.1 | 0.1 | 0.3 | 0.0 | 0.1 | 0.5 | −0.1 | 0.2 |
| Thailand | 0.33 | 0.0 | 0.5 | 0.5 | 0.4 | 0.0 | 0.4 | 0.4 | 0.5 | 0.9 |
| Mozambique | — | — | — | — | — | — | — | — | — | — |
| South Africa | 0.63 | −0.1 | −0.1 | −0.2 | −0.3 | 0.0 | −0.3 | −0.4 | −0.1 | −0.5 |
| Argentina | — | — | — | — | — | — | — | — | — | — |
| Brazil | — | — | — | — | — | — | — | — | — | — |
| Nicaragua | — | — | — | — | — | — | — | — | — | — |

## b. Urban

| Country study | Base % | Agricultural reform only | | | Nonagricultural reform only | | | All merchandise trade reform | | |
|---|---|---|---|---|---|---|---|---|---|---|
| | | Unilateral | R of W | Global | Unilateral | R of W | Global | Unilateral | R of W | Global |
| China | 0.26 | 0.0 | 0.1 | 0.1 | 0.0 | −0.1 | −0.1 | 0.0 | 0.0 | 0.0 |
| Indonesia | 0.36 | 0.0 | −0.1 | −0.1 | 0.3 | 0.3 | 0.6 | 0.3 | 0.2 | 0.5 |
| Pakistan | 0.40 | −0.1 | −0.0 | −0.1 | −1.9 | 0.0 | −1.9 | −2.0 | −0.0 | −2.0 |
| Philippines | 0.48 | 0.3 | −0.2 | 0.1 | 0.1 | 0.0 | 0.1 | 0.4 | −0.2 | 0.2 |
| Thailand | 0.15 | 0.1 | 0.6 | 0.7 | 0.5 | 0.0 | 0.5 | 0.6 | 0.6 | 1.2 |
| Mozambique | — | — | — | — | — | — | — | — | — | — |
| South Africa | 0.62 | −0.1 | −0.1 | −0.2 | −0.5 | 0.0 | −0.5 | −0.6 | −0.1 | −0.7 |
| Argentina | 0.50 | 0.3 | −0.1 | 0.2 | −0.2 | −0.1 | −0.3 | 0.1 | −0.2 | 0.0 |
| Brazil | — | — | — | — | — | — | — | — | — | — |
| Nicaragua | — | — | — | — | — | — | — | — | — | — |

*(Table continues on the following page.)*

**Table 1.12. The Impact of Reform on the Incidence of Income Inequality, by Country (*continued*)**
*(percentage point change in the Gini coefficient)*

**c. Total**

| Country study | Base % | Agricultural reform only | | | Nonagricultural reform only | | | All merchandise trade reform | | |
|---|---|---|---|---|---|---|---|---|---|---|
| | | Unilateral | R of W | Global | Unilateral | R of W | Global | Unilateral | R of W | Global |
| China | 0.44 | 0.1 | −0.4 | −0.3 | 0.0 | −0.1 | −0.1 | 0.1 | −0.5 | −0.4 |
| Indonesia | 0.34 | 0.0 | −0.1 | −0.1 | 0.2 | 0.2 | 0.4 | 0.2 | 0.1 | 0.3 |
| Pakistan | 0.34 | −0.1 | −0.0 | −0.2 | −3.2 | −0.1 | −3.1 | −3.3 | −0.1 | −3.3 |
| Philippines | 0.51 | 0.3 | −0.2 | 0.1 | 0.1 | 0.0 | 0.1 | 0.4 | −0.2 | 0.2 |
| Thailand | 0.34 | 0.1 | 0.7 | 0.8 | 0.4 | 0.0 | 0.4 | 0.5 | 0.7 | 1.2 |
| Mozambique | 0.48 | −1.2 | −0.1 | −1.3 | −0.3 | 0.2 | −0.1 | −1.5 | 0.1 | −1.4 |
| South Africa | 0.67 | −0.1 | −0.1 | −0.2 | −0.4 | 0.0 | −0.4 | −0.5 | −0.1 | −0.6 |
| Argentina | — | — | — | — | — | — | — | — | — | — |
| Brazil | 0.58 | −0.2 | −1.4 | −1.6 | 0.1 | −0.1 | 0.0 | −0.1 | −1.5 | −1.7 |
| Nicaragua | 0.53 | −0.1 | 0.1 | 0.0 | −0.1 | −0.2 | −0.3 | −0.2 | −0.1 | −0.3 |
| *Unweighted averages* | | | | | | | | | | |
| Asia | 0.39 | 0.1 | −0.0 | 0.1 | −0.5 | 0.0 | −0.5 | −0.4 | −0.0 | −0.4 |
| Africa | 0.58 | −0.7 | −0.1 | −0.8 | −0.4 | 0.1 | −0.3 | −1.0 | −0.0 | −1.0 |
| Latin America | 0.56 | −0.2 | −0.7 | −0.8 | 0.0 | −0.2 | −0.1 | −0.2 | −0.8 | −1.0 |
| All 9 developing countries[a] | 0.59 | −0.2 | −0.2 | −0.4 | −0.3 | −0.0 | −0.3 | −0.5 | −0.2 | −0.7 |

*Sources:* Country case studies in parts III–V.

*Note:* R of W = rest of the world. The numbers in italics for individual countries have been inferred on the assumption that linearity holds (see the text). Numbers may not sum because of rounding or interaction effects. — = no data are available.

a. Excludes Argentina.

In Indonesia and Thailand, the inequality-increasing impact of nonfarm reform more than offsets the egalitarian effect of farm trade reform, whereas both types of reform increase inequality in the Philippines and Thailand.

Inequality within the rural or urban household groups is not altered much by trade reform relative to overall national inequality (compare table 1.12, panels a and b with panel c). This underlines the point that trade reform would tend to reduce urban-rural inequality predominantly rather than inequality separately within either group.

Several of the national studies investigate the impact of reforms that might complement trade reform, notably various approaches to address the elimination of trade tax revenue. If the revenues can be recouped through taxes that do not bear on the poor, then the impact of reform on poverty reduction is more favorable. The China study focuses on lowering the barriers to migration out of agriculture by improving the operation of land markets and diminishing the barriers to mobility created by the *hukou* system, the household registration system in China. Each of these two initiatives, along with international trade liberalization (which increases access to foreign markets), would reduce poverty, and a combination of such measures would benefit all major household groups.

Argentina is a special case in several respects. First, Cicowiez, Díaz-Bonilla, and Díaz-Bonilla, the authors of the country study (chapter 12), had access only to an urban household survey; they were thus unable to make any determinations about the effect of policy reform on rural poverty or urban-rural income inequality. Second, Argentina imposed export taxes on farm products in 2002 and has increased the taxes a number of times since then. Removing these taxes as part of a shift toward free trade would clearly benefit farmers and rural areas, but would also raise the price of food in urban areas, which, all else being equal, would tend to increase urban poverty (see the results in table 1.11, panel b). Third, by their assumptions, the authors allow reform to alter aggregate employment, unlike most of the other studies, making their results less comparable. Together, these features mean that the authors have found that global trade reform would reduce urban poverty and inequality in Argentina, but only if export taxes are not included in the reform. If export taxes are eliminated as well, the results in table 1.11, panel b and table 1.12, panel b show that urban inequality would change little, but urban poverty would rise. Although, on its own, nonfarm reform would reduce urban poverty in Argentina, urban poverty would rise because of the strong negative impact on the urban poor of the higher food prices resulting from the removal of export taxes. In a global reform scenario in which export taxes are left unchanged, the authors find that both poverty and inequality would fall in Argentina because there would be less unemployment with respect to the scenario involving the removal of export taxes.

## What Have We Learned?

As in previous studies, whether based on ex post econometrics (as in Harrison 2007) or on ex ante economy-wide simulation (as in Hertel and Winters 2006), this study also finds that the results are mixed and not easy to summarize, particularly with regard to the poverty effects. There is nonetheless a high degree of similarity in the most important sign: the direction of the estimated national effect on extreme poverty that would result from freeing all merchandise trade globally. The greatest amount of overlap across the studies occurs in relation to this effect; the signs, summarized in table 1.13, agree in all but one-seventh of our available cases. Moreover, apart from India, there is no case in which the majority of the signs indicate that reform would increase poverty.

This beneficial impact of the full liberalization of global merchandise trade on the world's poor would be more readily generated by agricultural reform than by

**Table 1.13. The Direction of the Effects of Global Reform on Extreme Poverty, by Country**

*(sign of the change in the share of the population living on less than US$1 a day or the national poverty line)*

| Country | Agricultural reform only | | | All merchandise trade reform | | | |
|---|---|---|---|---|---|---|---|
| | GIDD model | GTAP model | National model | Linkage model | GIDD model | GTAP model | National model |
| Brazil | − | − | − | | − | − | − |
| Chile | + | − | | | − | − | |
| China | | | − | − | | | − |
| Colombia | − | − | | | − | − | |
| India | + | | | + | + | | |
| Indonesia | − | − | − | | − | − | − |
| Mexico | − | + | | | − | + | |
| Mozambique | − | − | | | | − | − |
| Nicaragua | − | | − | | − | | − |
| Pakistan | + | − | | | + | | − |
| Peru | − | − | | | − | − | |
| Philippines | − | − | − | | − | − | + |
| South Africa | + | − | | | + | | − |
| Thailand | − | − | − | | − | − | − |
| Uganda | − | − | | | + | + | |
| Venezuela, R.B. de | − | + | | | − | + | |
| Vietnam | − | − | | | − | − | |

*Sources:* Country case studies in parts III–V.

*Note:* The table shows the only countries in our study on which results are available from at least two of the models reported in the subsequent chapters. Blank cells indicate that there are no estimates.

nonagricultural reform and, within agricultural reform, by the removal of the substantial supports provided to farmers in developed countries rather than by policy reform in developing countries. According to the economy-wide models used in our study, such reform would raise the real earnings of unskilled laborers in developing countries, most of whom are working in agriculture. The earnings of these laborers would rise relative to the earnings of unskilled workers in developed countries and relative to the earnings of other income earners in developing countries. In addition to reducing poverty, such reform would thus lower the inequality within developing countries and between developing countries and developed countries.

According to the estimates of the Linkage model, the number of extremely poor people in developing countries—people living on less than US$1 a day—would fall by 2.7 percent after the global opening of all goods markets; the number would decline by 4.0 percent in China and Sub-Saharan Africa, but rise by 4.0 percent in India (or by 1.7 percent if the more moderate US$2-a-day poverty line is used). The GIDD model suggests that the decline in moderate poverty would be less than the decline estimated in the Linkage model and that extreme poverty would actually rise by 1.0 percent globally after full global trade reform (almost all because of a rise in India). However, we should recall that the GIDD model only takes labor income effects into account. The results for the 15 countries in the GTAP model are more in line with the Linkage results. They suggest that, in Asia and Latin America, the poverty-reducing effect of global reform would be twice as large as the estimates in the GIDD model and that, in Africa, there would be a small decline (rather than a small rise) in poverty. The 10 national case studies all find that global trade liberalization is poverty reducing (if the removal of export taxes is not part of the full liberalization in Argentina), regardless of whether the reform involves only agricultural goods or all goods; the benefit would arise roughly equally from reform at home and from reform abroad. The case studies also find that rural poverty would be cut much more than urban poverty in all cases, whether by reform at home or abroad and whether or not the reform includes nonfarm goods.

Again according to the Linkage model, global trade liberalization would reduce international inequality between developing countries and high-income countries both in total and among only farm households. However, it cannot be guaranteed that every developing country would be made more well off unless there is a strong economic growth dividend associated with reform (which is not captured in the comparative static modeling used in our study). The message emerging from the GIDD analysis is less optimistic: the model finds that inequality would change little after full global reform (inequality would fall in Latin America, but rise in South Asia). This is mainly because of increased income dispersion within the agricultural sector, despite a reduction in the gap in farm-nonfarm household incomes. The analysis based on the GTAP model, which reinforces the findings in the Linkage model with respect to poverty, does not cover the inequality effects.

The full trade liberalization of all goods or only of agricultural products would also cause inequality to decline after both own-country reform and rest-of-the-world reform within each of the three developing country regions covered by our sample. Inequality within the rural or urban household groups would not alter much following full trade reform, suggesting that the predominant impact of trade reform would be a reduction in urban-rural inequality.

The mechanism used by governments to adapt to the fall in tariff revenue is shown to be crucial. If one assumes that, rather than distributing it proportionately, governments do not require the poor to bear any of the tax burden in the effort to replace lost trade tax revenue, the estimated degree of poverty reduction is about four times greater in the 15 countries studied in the GTAP model.

The results of the three global analyses all indicate that the removal of the remaining agricultural policies would have a much stronger impact on poverty and inequality than would nonagricultural trade reforms. A weighted average across the 10 country case studies would probably show similar results. This contrasts with the outcomes of reforms over the past three decades according to Valenzuela, van der Mensbrugghe, and Anderson (2009): they estimate that global reforms in nonfarm trade policy between the early 1980s and 2004 boosted the value added in developing-country agriculture by more than twice as much as the global reforms in agricultural policy lowered it, and the former might therefore be expected to have had a dominant impact in any reduction in poverty and inequality over the period.

The 10 national case studies also shine some light on the relative importance of domestic versus rest-of-the-world reform in these countries. The contribution of own-country reforms to the fall in poverty appears to be equally as important as the contribution of rest-of-the-world reform, on average, although there is considerable cross-country divergence in the extent of the effects of both farm reform and nonfarm reform.

## Caveats

The impacts of agricultural and other trade reforms are complex. Such reforms simultaneously affect product and factor markets, government budgets, and external trade. The studies in this volume provide a broad range of ex ante modeling perspectives, including global and national models. They devote considerable attention to capturing poverty effects through microsimulation and poverty elasticity approaches and to using the same price distortion estimates, the same global model for measuring rest-of-the-world border shocks in the 10 national models, and similar behavioral assumptions, tax replacement assumptions, and model closures. Nonetheless, there is ample scope for further exploration of this issue through additional comparisons, including by drilling down to examine the origins of each modeling result. Our space limitations mean that such exploratory work needs to be left to future research efforts.

The reforms considered here cover only the liberalization of the trade in goods. Freeing up the global trade in services would also likely produce gains in most national economies, including among farmers. Freeing up capital would add to the gains, as would freeing the international movement of low-skilled labor from developing countries to higher-income countries (Prasad et al. 2007, World Bank 2005). How those reforms would interact with farm and other goods trade reforms in terms of the impacts on global poverty and inequality awaits the development of more sophisticated global simulation models.

Another key challenge that remains is to capture the growth effects of liberalization and, in particular, the general equilibrium distributive (poverty and inequality) consequences. This area of research has only recently been addressed in the empirical literature by building on the advances in the theoretical literature in the 1990s on endogenous growth (beginning with Grossman and Helpman 1991). Existing partial equilibrium analyses strongly suggest that the trade-growth-poverty nexus is extremely important, possibly much more important than the static reallocative impacts captured in the current set of studies. There is every reason to believe that, once dynamics are included, they will reinforce the basic finding of our study that agricultural and other merchandise trade policy reforms are poverty and inequality reducing.

A further modeling change involves introducing a stochastic dimension so as to capture changes in the *probability* of falling into poverty. This is important if greater openness alters the risk of food price spikes given, for example, that an upward spike might cause a food-deficit household to starve. Such general equilibrium empirical modeling that contains sufficient sectoral and household detail to be useful for poverty analysis, even without a dynamic component, is still in infancy. However, this field may develop rapidly in response to the demand for climate change studies; an early prototype is Ahmed, Diffenbaugh, and Hertel (2009).

There is significant scope also for exploring empirically the possible effects of complementary domestic reforms that might accompany agricultural price and trade policy reforms. This is well illustrated in the China case study, which shows that, if labor market reform were to accompany trade reform, the reduction in poverty would be several times greater. Even in the extreme case of India, trade reform would probably not increase poverty if more efficient transfer mechanisms were in place and high-payoff infrastructure investments were undertaken. The politics behind implementing first-best domestic policies is not necessarily any less complex than the politics associated with trade policies, however; this underscores the need for comprehensive political economy analysis that is not limited only to border policy measures.[20]

## Policy Implications

The empirical findings described above have a number of policy implications. First, the generally attractive results in terms of the poverty- and inequality-reducing effects of trade policy reforms, whether unilateral or multilateral, provide yet another reason why it is in the interest of countries to seek the further liberalization of national and world markets.

Second, a recurring theme in the national case studies is that the gains in terms of poverty and inequality reduction, in addition to the standard aggregate real income gains associated with trade liberalization, are generally much greater after global reform than after only own-country reform. In the Indonesia study, for example, unilateral trade liberalization is expected to reduce poverty only slightly, but liberalization by the rest of the world is expected to lower poverty substantially. In the Philippines, domestic reform of the current levels of protection alone may marginally increase poverty rates, whereas rest-of-the-world liberalization would almost fully offset this increase (and more than offset it in the case of only agricultural reform).

Third, the results of this set of studies show that the winners in trade reform would overwhelmingly be found among the poorer countries and the poorest individuals within countries. However, it is also clear that, even among the extreme poor, some will lose out. Hence, there is merit in compensatory policies, ideally ones that focus not on private goods, but on public goods that reduce underinvestment in pro-growth factors such as rural human capital. At the national level, India appears to be an important example of a potential loser from global trade reform in terms of welfare, poverty, and inequality. The government of India might therefore consider replacing its current extensive agricultural input subsidies and import tariffs by targeted assistance aimed only at the poorest farmers and rural areas (which may also help the urban poor, save government spending on fair price shops to offset the effects of tariffs on food, and reduce the adverse environmental effects of subsidies for irrigation and farm chemicals).[21]

Fourth, the most substantial benefits would be generated by agricultural reform. This underscores the economic and social importance of securing reforms in the agricultural sector, in addition to manufacturing, notwithstanding the political sensitivities involved. Other domestic policy instruments would more directly address the Millennium Development Goals of governments in poverty and hunger reduction and, hence, be more efficient than trade policies in this effort. However, the former generally represent a greater net drain on the treasury, which may be a challenge in low-income countries that still rely heavily on trade tax revenue. One solution to this dilemma involves expanding aid-for-trade funding as part of official development assistance programs.

Finally, most of the national case studies find that unilateral policy reform alone may represent a way to reduce poverty and inequality. This suggests that developing countries should not hold back on national reforms while they are negotiating in the World Trade Organization Doha Round or other international forums. It also suggests that, from a poverty-reducing perspective, developing countries have little to gain and, potentially, much to lose by negotiating exemptions or delays in national reforms within the framework of World Trade Organization multilateral agreements.

## Notes

1. For a review of the theoretical literature and the empirical evidence on individual and societal preferences for redistribution, see Alesina and Giuliano (2009). Prasad et al. (2007) make the point that, as the number of the extreme poor declines, concerns about poverty will diminish and be gradually replaced by concerns about income inequality.

2. Political economists are also interested in the ways policies affect the incomes and asset values of various vested interests, but this is not a focus of our analysis.

3. A study by Sala-i-Martin (2006) finds that economies have converged in the sense that disparities in GDP per capita across countries have shrunk in recent decades. Analyses based on household survey data rather than GDP per capita include the studies by Milanovic (2002, 2005, 2006). A recent review of the evidence on global poverty and inequality is available in Ferreira and Ravallion (2008).

4. The distortions database is documented fully in Anderson and Valenzuela (2008). It is based on the methodology summarized in Anderson et al. (2008) and detailed in appendix A of Anderson (2009).

5. We were fortunate to have early access to the P5 preliminary version of the GTAP Database ahead of the final release. Details on the GTAP Database are available in Narayanan and Walmsley (2008).

6. See Wacziarg and Welch (2008) and Krueger (2010), as well as the collection of seminal papers in Winters (2007). Rutherford and Tarr (2002) bring together these ideas using a numerical open-economy growth model. This model allows for product variety, imperfect competition, economies of scale, and international capital flows. It is also dynamic so that the model may be used to trace out an adjustment path to trade reform. It is stochastic in that it draws randomly from uniform probability distributions for eight key parameters of the model. The authors simulate a halving of the only policy intervention (a 20 percent tariff on imports) and thereby fully replace the government's lost tariff revenue by a lump-sum tax. This modest trade reform produces a welfare increase (in terms of a Hicksian equivalent variation) of 11 percent of the present value of consumption in the central model. Systematic sensitivity analysis with 34,000 simulations shows that there is virtually no chance of a welfare gain of less than 3 percent and a 7 percent chance of a welfare gain larger than 18 percent of consumption. See also the empirical study of four developing countries in Cockburn et al. (2008).

7. This would continue a process that was initiated in the 1980s when many countries began to reform trade and exchange rate regimes. Using the same Linkage model and database as the present study, Valenzuela, van der Mensbrugghe, and Anderson (2009) find that the global reforms between 1980–84 and 2004 also boosted economic welfare proportionately more in developing countries than in high-income economies (by 1.0 percent compared with 0.7 percent, respectively).

8. Even so, if one were to treat each of the 60 countries or the groups of countries in the global study described in chapter 2 in terms of a single household (that is, ignoring intracountry inequality), then intercountry income inequality (not taking account of the differing economic size of countries) would be reduced at least slightly, as measured by the Gini coefficient, from 0.8513 to 0.8506.

9. According to data in the FAOSTAT Database, less than 15 million relatively wealthy farmers in developed countries, with an average of almost 80 hectares per worker, are currently being helped, at the expense of not only consumers and taxpayers in these rich countries, but also the majority of the 1.3 billion relatively impoverished farmers and their large families in developing countries, who, on average, must earn a living from only 2.5 hectares per worker.

10. In some high-income economies, however, farm households now have higher incomes than nonfarm households (Gardner and Sumner 2007, OECD 2009).

11. The rise in India is caused partly by the removal of the large subsidies and import tariffs that assist Indian farmers and partly by the greater imports of farm products that raise the border prices of these imports.

12. Information on the GIDD data set, methodology, and applications are available at http://go.worldbank.org/YADEAFEJ30.

13. While changes in incomes from labor are the most important income change among households at or near the poverty line, accounting for the changes in other sources of income may yield somewhat different results, particularly as they relate to inequality. The results for the Linkage model used in chapter 3 are not identical to those in chapter 2 because, to make their results compatible with the GIDD, the authors of chapter 3 had to assume that labor is less than fully mobile across sectors.

14. An African comparison is not possible because there was only one African country common to the two sets of sample countries.

15. The 10 national studies cover Argentina (Cicowiez, Díaz-Bonilla, and Díaz-Bonilla; chapter 12), Brazil (Ferreira Filho and Horridge; chapter 13), China (Zhai and Hertel; chapter 5), Indonesia (Warr; chapter 6), Mozambique (Arndt and Thurlow; chapter 10), Nicaragua (Sanchez and Vos; chapter 14), Pakistan (Cororaton and Orden; chapter 7), the Philippines (Cororaton, Corong, and Cockburn; chapter 8), South Africa (Hérault and Thurlow; chapter 11), and Thailand (Warr; chapter 9).

16. The results on Argentina are included only in the urban parts of tables 11 and 12 because the relevant household survey does not include rural areas. However, it should be kept in mind that Argentina is the most urbanized developing country in the sample; only 8 percent of the population was living in rural areas in 2007. Hence, even if the poverty effects in rural areas had the opposite sign, they might not offset substantially the results in the urban sector.

17. The data are based on national or US$1-a-day poverty lines, except in the case of China; the results on China are available only at the US$2-a-day poverty line.

18. Hertel and Keeney (chapter 4) use stratum-specific poverty elasticities to map the impacts on poverty of the changes in average incomes from all sources.

19. The Pakistan results have been generated on the assumption that the loss in trade taxes would be offset by a rise in direct income taxes. Only nonpoor urban households pay direct taxes in Pakistan; so, the removal of tariffs would raise the direct taxes paid by the urban nonpoor such that the benefits of trade reform would go mainly to the poor.

20. A beginning has been made in such political econometric analysis in a set of studies reported in Anderson (2010) that use the World Bank agricultural distortions database compiled by Anderson and Valenzuela (2008).

21. Caution is needed, as always, in proposing such interventions in countries in which it is difficult to implement even the most well intentioned policy. As Pritchett (2009) vividly points out, India especially suffers from this problem of underdevelopment.

# References

Ahmed, S. A., N. S. Diffenbaugh, and T. W. Hertel. 2009. "Climate Volatility Deepens Poverty Vulnerability in Developing Countries." Purdue Climate Change Research Center Paper 0921, Purdue University, West Lafayette, IN. Also published in *Environmental Research Letters* 4 (3): 034004 (1–8).

Alesina, A. F., and P. Giuliano. 2009. "Preferences for Redistribution." NBER Working Paper 14825, National Bureau of Economic Research, Cambridge, MA.

Anderson, K., ed. 2009. *Distortions to Agricultural Incentives: A Global Perspective, 1955–2007*. London: Palgrave Macmillan; Washington, DC: World Bank.

———, ed. 2010. *The Political Economy of Agricultural Price Distortions*. New York: Cambridge University Press.

Anderson, K., M. Kurzweil, W. Martin, D. Sandri, and E. Valenzuela. 2008. "Measuring Distortions to Agricultural Incentives, Revisited." *World Trade Review* 7 (4): 1–30.

Anderson, K., W. Martin, and D. van der Mensbrugghe. 2006. "Distortions to World Trade: Impacts on Agricultural Markets and Incomes." *Review of Agricultural Economics* 28 (2): 168–94.

Anderson, K., and E. Valenzuela. 2008. "Estimates of Global Distortions to Agricultural Incentives, 1955–2007." Data spreadsheet, October, World Bank, Washington, DC. http://go.worldbank.org/YAO39F35E0.

Atkinson, A. B., and A. Brandolini. 2004. "Global World Inequality: Absolute, Relative or Intermediate." Paper prepared for the 28th Conference of the International Association for Research in Income and Wealth, Cork, Ireland, August 22–28.

Bourguignon, F., M. Bussolo, and L. A. Pereira da Silva, eds. 2008. *The Impact of Macroeconomic Policies on Poverty and Income Distribution: Macro-Micro Evaluation Techniques and Tools*. London: Palgrave Macmillan; Washington, DC: World Bank.

Bourguignon, F., V. Levin, and D. Rosenblatt. 2004. "Declining International Inequality and Economic Divergence: Reviewing the Evidence through Different Lenses." *Economie Internationale* (4Q): 13–26.

Bourguignon, F., and C. Morrison. 2002. "Inequality among World Citizens: 1820–1992." *American Economic Review* 92 (4): 727–44.

Bussolo, M., R. De Hoyos, and D. Medvedev. 2008. "Is the Developing World Catching Up? Global Convergence and National Rising Dispersion." Policy Research Working Paper 4733, World Bank, Washington, DC.

Cai, J., A. de Janvry, and E. Sadoulet. 2008. "Rural Households in India: Sources of Income and Incidence of Burden of Rising Prices." Unpublished report, July, University of California Berkeley, Berkeley, CA.

Chen, S., and M. Ravallion. 2008. "The Developing World Is Poorer Than We Thought, but No Less Successful in the Fight against Poverty." Policy Research Working Paper 4703, World Bank, Washington, DC.

Cockburn, J., B. Decaluwé, I. Fofana, and V. Robichaud. 2008. "Trade, Growth, and Gender in Developing Countries: Comparison of Ghana, Honduras, Senegal, and Uganda." In *Gender Aspects of the Trade and Poverty Nexus: A Macro-Micro Approach*, ed. M. Bussolo and R. De Hoyos, 111–63. London: Palgrave Macmillan; Washington, DC: World Bank.

Cranfield, J. A. L., P. V. Preckel, J. S. Eales, and T. W. Hertel. 2003. "Estimating Consumer Demands across the Development Spectrum: Maximum Likelihood Estimates of an Implicit Direct Additivity Model." *Journal of Development Economics* 68 (2): 289–307.

Davis, B., P. Winters, and G. Carletto. 2009. "A Cross-Country Comparison of Rural Income-Generating Activities." Unpublished report, January, Agricultural Development Economics Division, Food and Agriculture Organization of the United Nations, Rome.

FAOSTAT Database. Food and Agriculture Organization of the United Nations. http://faostat.fao.org/default.aspx (accessed June 2008).

Ferreira, F. H.G., and M. Ravallion. 2008. "Global Poverty and Inequality: A Review of the Evidence," Policy Research Working Paper 4623, Poverty Team, Development Research Group, World Bank, Washington, DC.

Francois, J. F., and W. Martin. 2007. "Great Expectations: Ex Ante Assessments of the Welfare Impacts of Trade Reforms." Unpublished report, January, Erasmus University, Rotterdam.

Gardner, B. L., and D. A. Sumner. 2007. "U.S. Agricultural Policy Reform in 2007 and Beyond." Short publication, American Enterprise Institute, Washington, DC.

GIDD Database (Global Income Distribution Dynamics Database). World Bank. http://go.worldbank.org/YADEAFEJ30.

Grossman, G. M., and E. Helpman. 1991. *Innovation and Growth in the Global Economy*. Cambridge, MA: MIT Press.

Harrison, A. E., ed. 2007. *Globalization and Poverty*. National Bureau of Economic Research Conference Report Series. Chicago: University of Chicago Press; Cambridge, MA: National Bureau of Economic Research.

Helpman, E., O. Itskhoki, and S. J. Redding. 2009. "Inequality and Unemployment in a Global Economy." CEPR Discussion Paper 7375, Centre for Economic Policy Research, London.

Hertel, T. W., M. Ivanic, P. V. Preckel, and J. A. L. Cranfield. 2004. "The Earnings Effects of Multilateral Trade Liberalization: Implications for Poverty." *World Bank Economic Review* 18 (2): 205–36.

Hertel, T. W., and L. A. Winters, eds. 2006. *Poverty and the WTO: Impacts of the Doha Development Agenda*. London: Palgrave Macmillan; Washington, DC: World Bank.

Horridge, M., and F. Zhai. 2006. "Shocking a Single-Country CGE Model with Export Prices and Quantities from a Global Model." In *Poverty and the WTO: Impacts of the Doha Development Agenda*, ed. T. W. Hertel and L. A. Winters, 94–104. London: Palgrave Macmillan; Washington, DC: World Bank.

Ivanic, M., and W. Martin. 2008. "Implications of Higher Global Food Prices for Poverty in Low-Income Countries." Policy Research Working Paper 4594, World Bank, Washington, DC.

Krueger, A. O. 2010. "Trade Liberalization and Growth in Developing Countries." In *Better Living through Economics*, ed. J. J. Siegfried. Cambridge, MA: Harvard University Press.

Milanovic, B. 2002. "True World Income Distribution, 1988 and 1993: First Calculation Based on Household Surveys Alone." *Economic Journal* 112 (476): 51–92.

———. 2005. *Worlds Apart: Measuring International and Global Inequality*. Princeton, NJ: Princeton University Press.

———. 2006. "Global Income Inequality: What It Is and Why It Matters." Policy Research Working Paper 3865, World Bank, Washington, DC.

Narayanan, B. G., and T. L. Walmsley, eds. 2008. *Global Trade, Assistance, and Production: The GTAP 7 Data Base*. West Lafayette, IN: Center for Global Trade Analysis, Department of Agricultural Economics, Purdue University. https://www.gtap.agecon.purdue.edu/databases/v7/v7_doco.asp.

OECD (Organisation for Economic Co-operation and Development). 2009. *The Role of Agriculture and Farm Household Diversification in the Rural Economy: Evidence and Initial Policy Implications*. Report TAD/CA/APM/WP(2009)1/Final (April 21). Paris: OECD.

Otsuka, K., J. P. Estudillo, and Y. Sawada, eds. 2009. *Rural Poverty and Income Dynamics in Asia and Africa*. New York: Routledge.

Otsuka, K., and T. Yamano. 2006. "Introduction to the Special Issue on the Role of Nonfarm Income in Poverty Reduction: Evidence from Asia and East Africa." *Agricultural Economics* 35 (supplement): 373–97.

PovcalNet. World Bank, Washington, DC. http://go.worldbank.org/NT2A1XUWP0 (accessed May 2008).

Prasad, E. S., K. Rogoff, S.-J. Wei, and M. A. Kose. 2007. "Financial Globalization, Growth, and Volatility in Developing Countries." In *Globalization and Poverty*, ed. A. E. Harrison, 457–516. National

Bureau of Economic Research Conference Report Series. Chicago: University of Chicago Press; Cambridge, MA: National Bureau of Economic Research.

Pritchett, L. 2009. "A Review of Edward Luce's *In Spite of the Gods: The Strange Rise of Modern India*." *Journal of Economic Literature* 97 (3): 771–80.

Ravallion, M. 2006. "Looking Beyond Averages in the Trade and Poverty Debate." *World Development* 34 (8): 1374–92.

———. 2008. "Bailing Out the World's Poorest." Policy Research Working Paper 4763, World Bank, Washington, DC.

Ravallion, M., S. Chen, and P. Sangraula. 2007. "New Evidence on the Urbanization of Poverty." Policy Research Working Paper 4199, World Bank, Washington, DC.

Rutherford, T. F., and D. G. Tarr. 2002. "Trade Liberalization, Product Variety, and Growth in a Small Open Economy: A Quantitative Assessment." *Journal of International Economics* 56 (2): 247–72.

Sala-i-Martin, X. 2006. "The World Distribution of Income: Falling Poverty and . . . Convergence, Period." *Quarterly Journal of Economics* 121 (2): 351–97.

Topalova, P. 2007. "Trade Liberalization, Poverty, and Inequality: Evidence from Indian Districts." In *Globalization and Poverty*, ed. A. E. Harrison, 291–336. National Bureau of Economic Research Conference Report Series. Chicago: University of Chicago Press; Cambridge, MA: National Bureau of Economic Research.

Valenzuela, E., and K. Anderson. 2008. "Alternative Agricultural Price Distortions for CGE Analysis of Developing Countries, 2004 and 1980–84." Research Memorandum 13 (December), Center for Global Trade Analysis, Department of Agricultural Economics, Purdue University, West Lafayette, IN. https://www.gtap.agecon.purdue.edu/resources/res_display.asp?RecordID=2925.

Valenzuela, E., D. van der Mensbrugghe, and K. Anderson. 2009. "General Equilibrium Effects of Price Distortions on Global Markets, Farm Incomes, and Welfare." In *Distortions to Agricultural Incentives: A Global Perspective, 1955–2007*, ed. K. Anderson, chap. 13. London: Palgrave Macmillan; Washington, DC: World Bank.

van der Mensbrugghe, D. 2005. "Linkage Technical Reference Document: Version 6.0." December, World Bank, Washington, DC. http://go.worldbank.org/7NP2KK1OH0.

Wacziarg, R., and K. H. Welch. 2008. "Trade Liberalization and Growth: New Evidence." *World Bank Economic Review* 22 (2): 187–231.

Winters, L. A., ed. 2007. *The WTO and Poverty and Inequality*. 2 vols. Critical Perspectives on the Global Trading System and the WTO 13. London: Edward Elgar.

World Bank. 2005. *Global Economic Prospects 2006: Economic Implications of Remittances and Migration*. Washington, DC: World Bank.

———. 2007. *World Development Report 2008: Agriculture for Development*. Washington, DC: World Bank.

PART II

# GLOBAL CGE APPROACHES

# GLOBAL WELFARE AND POVERTY EFFECTS: LINKAGE MODEL RESULTS

*Kym Anderson, Ernesto Valenzuela,
and Dominique van der Mensbrugghe**

Despite much reform over the past quarter century in the policy distortions to agricultural incentives, many relevant intervention measures remain active (Anderson 2009). How these policies affect economic welfare, inequality, and poverty levels is an issue of great interest to the agricultural, trade, and development policy communities in international agencies and in many developing countries. More specifically, for any developing country of interest, how important are its own policies compared with those of the rest of the world in affecting the welfare of the poor in that country? And, given that three-quarters of the world's poor depend on agriculture directly or indirectly for their livelihoods and that, according to an earlier finding, farm policies in 2001 were responsible for more than three-fifths of the global welfare cost of trade distortions, what contributions do agricultural policies contribute to these outcomes (World Bank 2007; Anderson, Martin, and van der Mensbrugghe 2006a, 2006b)?

Now is an appropriate time to address this set of questions for at least three reasons. One is that the World Trade Organization is struggling to conclude the Doha Round of multilateral trade negotiations; agricultural policy reform is once again one of the most contentious issues in these talks. Another reason is that

*The authors are grateful for the distortion estimates provided by authors of the focus country case studies; for the assistance with spreadsheets by Johanna Croser, Marianne Kurzweil, and Signe Nelgen; and for the helpful comments of workshop participants.

poorer countries and their development partners are striving to achieve the United Nations–encouraged Millennium Development Goals by 2015, of which the prime goals are the reduction of hunger and poverty. The third reason is that a new set of estimates of distortions to agricultural incentives in many countries has been brought together recently by the World Bank (Anderson and Valenzuela 2008), and these estimates have since been provided as alternative measures of price distortions for use in computable general equilibrium models (Valenzuela and Anderson 2008). The estimates differ from the usual ones used by trade modelers in that they are based on direct domestic-to-border price comparisons rather than on merely applied import tariff rates (as with the Global Trade Analysis Project [GTAP] data set; see Narayanan and Walmsley 2008).

This chapter serves two purposes. The first is to offer an analysis of the economic effects of agricultural price and merchandise trade policies around the world as of 2004 on global markets, net farm incomes, and national and regional economic welfare and poverty, that is, it assesses the effort still necessary to remove the disarray in world agriculture—to use the title of the seminal study by Johnson (1991)—and to provide at least a crude indication of the poverty that might be reduced by such a reform. In doing so, the chapter also serves a second purpose: to explain the origin of the exogenous shocks used in the global modeling described in the following chapter and in the national modeling studies described in parts III–V that show the market effects on particular developing countries of rest-of-the-world agricultural and trade policies.

To quantify the impacts of current policies, we first amend the distortions in version 7 of the GTAP global protection database (Narayanan and Walmsley 2008) by replacing the applied tariffs there with distortion rates that reproduce the distortions estimated by contributors to the World Bank's research project, Distortions to Agricultural Incentives, as collated by Valenzuela and Anderson (2008).[1] These distortion estimates suggest that, despite the reforms of the past 25 years, there was still a considerable range of rates across commodities and countries in 2004, including a strong antitrade bias in national agricultural and trade policies in many developing countries. Furthermore, nonagricultural protectionism is still rife in some developing countries, and agricultural price supports in some high-income countries remain high.

The present analysis addresses the following questions: To what extent were policies as of 2004 still reducing the rewards of farming in developing countries and thereby adding to inequality in farm household incomes *across* countries? Are policies depressing value added more in primary agriculture than in the rest of the economies of developing countries? And are they depressing the earnings of unskilled workers more than the earnings of the owners of other factors of production, thereby potentially contributing to inequality and poverty *within* these developing countries (given that farm incomes are well below nonfarm incomes in most developing countries and that agriculture in these countries is intensive in the use of unskilled labor)?

To provide answers to these and related questions, we use our amended GTAP distortion database in a global computable general equilibrium model (the Linkage model; see van der Mensbrugghe 2005). We use the model to assess how agricultural markets, factor prices, and the value added in agriculture versus in nonfarm sectors would differ if all price and trade policies that distort the markets for farm and nonfarm goods (as of 2004) were removed. It is important to include nonagricultural trade policies in the reform experiment because, as shown in the new study reported in Anderson (2009), these policies may have been more harmful than agricultural policies in depressing farmer incentives in many developing countries.

We present the results for the key countries and regions of the world and for the world as a whole. While no one anticipates a complete freeing of global markets in the near future, this prospective analysis serves as a benchmark to appreciate the stakes in terms of further reforms through rounds of multilateral World Trade Organization negotiations. At the same time, by showing how different the trade patterns of various countries would be without distortions, we also provide indications of agricultural comparative advantages in different parts of the world that are more accurate than the perspective offered through an examination of actual trade and self-sufficiency indicators derived in the current distortion-ridden situation.

The chapter begins with an examination of the extent of price distortions in 2004 provided by various policy instruments as calibrated in Valenzuela and Anderson (2008). The emphasis is mainly on import tariffs in the case of nonfarm products, but, in the case of agriculture, it is on the full range of production, consumption, and trade taxes and subsidies and their equivalent in the case of quantitative restrictions on markets. This is followed by a description of the Linkage model of the global economy that we use to analyze the consequences of the removal of the distortions. The key results of the two simulations are then presented: the full global liberalization of markets for all merchandise and—to understand the relative contribution of farm policies to these outcomes—the full global reform only of agricultural policies.[2] The chapter concludes by highlighting the main messages that emerge from the results. They are as follows: in a shift to free markets, income inequality across countries would be reduced at least slightly; all but one-sixth of the gains to developing countries would be generated by agricultural policy reform; unskilled workers in developing countries—the majority of whom work on farms—would benefit most from reform; net farm incomes in developing countries would rise by 6 percent compared with 2 percent in nonagricultural value added; and the number of people surviving on less than US$1 a day would drop by 3 percent globally.

## Key Distortions in Global Markets

Border measures have traditionally been the main means by which governments distort prices in their domestic markets for tradable products, given that the relative prices of the various goods are affected by trade taxes or subsidies. Product-specific domestic output subsidies and farm input subsidies have played a more limited role in part because of their much greater overt cost to the treasury.[3]

To quantify the impacts of current policies, we use the Altertax procedure (Malcolm 1998) to amend the distortions in the prerelease of version 7 of the GTAP global protection database. The amendments relate mainly to developing countries, but, following Anderson and Valenzuela (2007b), we also alter cotton distortions in the United States to reflect the policies there more accurately. To simplify the discussion below, we treat European transition economies (among which we include Turkey) as one of the world's developing-country regions, alongside Africa, Asia, and Latin America.[4]

Version 7 of the GTAP database includes estimates of bilateral tariffs and export subsidies and of domestic supports as of 2004 for more than 100 countries and country groups spanning the world. As with version 6 of the GTAP data set (which relates to 2001; see Dimaranan 2006), the protection data come from MAcMaps, a joint project of the Centre d'Etudes Prospectives et d'Informations Internationale (Paris) and the International Trade Centre (Geneva). MAcMaps is a detailed database on bilateral import protection at the Harmonized System 6-digit tariff line classification level that integrates trade preferences, specific and compound tariffs, and a partial evaluation of nontariff barriers such as tariff rate quotas.[5] The new 2004 version 7 of the GTAP database has lower tariffs than the previous, 2001 version 6 database because of major reforms such as the completion of the implementation of the Uruguay Round agreements and unilateral reforms, including those resulting from the World Trade Organization accession negotiations of China and other recent acceding countries.

As noted above, the agricultural price distortion rates in the GTAP version 7 database have been replaced here by an alternative data set for numerous developing countries based on the estimates of the nominal rates of assistance for 2004 contained in Valenzuela and Anderson (2008). The sectoral averages of these amended values are shown in table 2.1. In the case of the amendments to the import tariffs on individual farm products for any particular developing country, the bilateral tariff structure in the GTAP version 7 database is preserved by simply lowering or raising the bilateral tariffs by the same proportion we use to amend the country's average import tariff on each product for 2004.

According to this amended data set, the weighted average applied tariff for agriculture and lightly processed food in 2004 was 21.8 percent for developing countries and 22.3 percent for high-income countries, while, for nonfarm goods, it was

**Table 2.1. Structure of Producer Price Distortions in Global Goods Markets, 2004**

*(percent)*

| Region, country | Primary agriculture — Domestic support | Agriculture and lightly processed food — Export subsidy | Agriculture and lightly processed food — Tariff | Other goods — Tariff |
|---|---|---|---|---|
| Africa | −0.8 | 0.1 | 20.4 | 11.2 |
| Egypt, Arab Rep. | 0.0 | 0.0 | 5.0 | 13.5 |
| Madagascar | 0.0 | −4.4 | 3.4 | 2.7 |
| Mozambique | 0.2 | 0.0 | 14.5 | 10.9 |
| Nigeria | 0.1 | 0.0 | 76.1 | 17.2 |
| Senegal | 0.0 | −1.1 | 6.2 | 8.9 |
| South Africa | 0.0 | 0.0 | 10.2 | 6.5 |
| Tanzania | 0.3 | 0.0 | 11.8 | 13.7 |
| Uganda | 0.0 | −2.6 | 9.2 | 5.5 |
| Zambia | −0.8 | 0.0 | 7.0 | 9.0 |
| Zimbabwe | −3.2 | 0.0 | 8.9 | 15.4 |
| Rest of Africa | −1.2 | 0.3 | 19.0 | 13.4 |
| East and South Asia | 2.4 | 0.6 | 29.6 | 8.1 |
| China | 0.0 | 0.2 | 6.5 | 7.1 |
| Indonesia | 0.0 | −1.6 | 7.3 | 4.9 |
| Korea, Rep. | 0.0 | 0.0 | 319.4 | 5.9 |
| Malaysia | 0.0 | −0.2 | 5.0 | 5.9 |
| Philippines | −4.7 | 0.0 | 7.1 | 3.4 |
| Taiwan, China | −0.4 | 0.0 | 84.2 | 3.9 |
| Thailand | −0.2 | 0.0 | 26.2 | 12.9 |
| Vietnam | −3.6 | −0.5 | 21.5 | 18.5 |
| Bangladesh | −1.0 | 0.0 | 9.9 | 22.5 |
| India | 10.1 | 2.5 | 2.9 | 20.8 |
| Pakistan | 0.0 | −0.2 | 19.4 | 18.5 |
| Sri Lanka | 0.6 | −0.3 | 23.8 | 5.8 |
| Rest of East and South Asia | −0.7 | 0.0 | 4.3 | 2.7 |
| Latin America | −0.2 | −1.4 | 7.2 | 6.7 |
| Argentina | 0.0 | −14.8 | 0.0 | 5.8 |
| Brazil | 0.0 | 0.0 | 4.8 | 8.9 |
| Chile | 0.0 | 0.0 | 2.4 | 1.8 |
| Colombia | 0.0 | 0.0 | 21.6 | 9.8 |
| Ecuador | 0.0 | 0.0 | 13.4 | 10.4 |
| Mexico | 1.2 | 0.0 | 6.2 | 3.4 |
| Nicaragua | 0.0 | −2.8 | 9.6 | 3.9 |
| Rest of Latin America | −1.7 | 0.3 | 9.9 | 9.9 |

*(Table continues on the following page.)*

**Table 2.1. Structure of Producer Price Distortions in Global Goods Markets, 2004 (*continued*)**

*(percent)*

| Region, country | Primary agriculture | Agriculture and lightly processed food | | Other goods |
|---|---|---|---|---|
| | Domestic support | Export subsidy | Tariff | Tariff |
| Eastern Europe and Central Asia | 0.8 | −0.3 | 15.9 | 4.8 |
| Baltic States | 3.4 | 0.0 | 8.2 | 0.9 |
| Bulgaria | 0.6 | 0.0 | 14.8 | 11.5 |
| Czech Republic | 0.6 | 0.0 | 3.0 | 0.5 |
| Hungary | 3.1 | 0.0 | 6.2 | 0.5 |
| Poland | 0.4 | 0.0 | 6.2 | 0.8 |
| Romania | 1.3 | 0.0 | 18.0 | 9.8 |
| Russian Federation | 1.7 | −0.9 | 18.9 | 7.4 |
| Slovak Republic | 0.0 | 0.0 | 5.2 | 0.4 |
| Slovenia | 0.0 | 0.0 | 7.8 | 0.4 |
| Kazakhstan | −0.9 | 0.0 | 3.4 | 2.7 |
| Turkey | 0.8 | 0.0 | 33.3 | 3.1 |
| Rest of Eastern Europe and Central Asia | −1.1 | −0.9 | 9.7 | 5.7 |
| High-income countries | 2.6 | 7.2 | 22.3 | 1.2 |
| Australia | 0.0 | 0.0 | 0.5 | 3.3 |
| Canada | 1.6 | 3.6 | 18.9 | 1.4 |
| EU15 | 1.2 | 12.8 | 6.9 | 0.7 |
| Japan | 2.0 | 0.0 | 151.7 | 1.7 |
| New Zealand | 0.0 | −0.2 | 0.7 | 3.3 |
| Rest of Western Europe | 2.6 | 13.4 | 53.9 | 2.2 |
| United States | 5.2 | 0.6 | 6.1 | 1.3 |
| Developing countries | 1.4 | 0.0 | 21.8 | 7.5 |
| Africa | −0.8 | 0.1 | 20.4 | 11.2 |
| East Asia | −0.3 | 0.0 | 41.6 | 6.7 |
| South Asia | 7.2 | 1.7 | 6.9 | 20.2 |
| Latin America | −0.2 | −1.4 | 7.2 | 6.7 |
| Middle East | −12.4 | 0.0 | 7.5 | 5.7 |
| Eastern Europe and Central Asia | 0.8 | −0.3 | 15.9 | 4.8 |
| World total | 1.9 | 3.5 | 22.1 | 3.3 |

*Sources:* Valenzuela and Anderson (2008) based on calculations compiled by Anderson and Valenzuela (2008).

*Note:* Data are weighted by the value of production at undistorted prices. EU15 = the 15 members of the European Union prior to 2004.

7.5 percent for developing countries and only 1.2 percent for high-income countries. Export subsidies for farm products in a few high-income regions and export taxes in a few developing countries were still in place in 2004, but they are generally small in impact compared with tariffs, as are production subsidies and taxes.[6]

The averages alone are not necessarily good indicators of the overall distortions to farmer incentives. Also of importance is the composition of each country's trade. Two examples serve to illustrate the point. First, if the tariffs of high-income countries are at a near-prohibitive level for temperate farm products, but are zero on tropical products such as coffee beans, the import-weighted average agricultural tariff of these countries may be quite low even if the agricultural value added has been enhanced substantially in these rich countries. Second, the nonagricultural primary sector and the farm sector may receive a similar level of import protection (but less than the manufacturing sector), although the former is much more export-focused than agriculture. In this case, trade reform may cause the nonagricultural primary sector to expand at the expense not only of manufacturing, but also of farming.

Although we have used production rather than trade weights to obtain sectoral average rates of distortion in table 2.1 and although the ratio of agricultural tariffs to the tariffs on other goods in 2004 shown in the table is well above unity in many of the regions, it is not possible to say from those distortion rates alone whether developing-country policies have an antiagricultural bias. Likewise, it is not possible to know how the benefits of the removal of agricultural tariffs in the protective countries would be distributed among the various agricultural exporting countries. To address such issues, a global general equilibrium model is needed to estimate the net effects of the distortions in all sectors in all countries in terms of the agricultural markets and net farm incomes of the various nations. We now turn to such a model.

## The Linkage Model of the Global Economy

The model used for this analysis is the World Bank's global computable general equilibrium model known as Linkage (van der Mensbrugghe 2005). For most of this decade, this model has formed the basis for the standard World Bank long-term projections of the world economy, for much of world trade policy analysis, and, more recently, for migration policy analysis (see World Bank 2001, 2003, 2004, 2005, 2006). It is a relatively straightforward computable general equilibrium model, but has some characteristics that distinguish it from other comparative static models such as the GTAP model (described in Hertel 1997). Factor stocks are fixed, which means, in the case of labor, that the extent of unemployment (if any) in the baseline remains unchanged. Producers minimize costs, subject to constant returns to scale in production; consumers maximize utility; and all markets, including for labor, are cleared with flexible prices. There are three types of production structures. The crop sectors reflect the substitution possibilities between extensive and intensive farming; the livestock sectors reflect the substitution possibilities between pasture and intensive feeding; and all other sectors reflect standard capital-labor substitution. There are two types of labor, skilled and unskilled, and the total employment of each is assumed to be fixed (so there is no change in unemployment levels), although both are assumed to be intersectorally mobile. There is a single representative household per modeled region, and this household allocates income to consumption using the extended linear expenditure system. Trade is modeled using a nested Armington structure whereby aggregate import demand is the outcome of the allocation of domestic absorption between domestic goods and aggregate imports, and then aggregate import demand is allocated across source countries to determine the bilateral trade flows.[7]

Government fiscal balances are fixed in U.S. dollar terms, and the fiscal objective is met by changing the level of lump sum taxes on households. This implies that the losses in tariff revenues are replaced by higher direct taxes on households. The current account balance is also fixed. Given that other external financial flows are fixed, this implies that ex ante changes to the trade balance are reflected in ex post changes to the real exchange rate. For example, if import tariffs are reduced, the propensity to import increases, and additional imports are financed by boosting export revenues. This last step is typically achieved through depreciation of the real exchange rate. Finally, investment is driven by savings. With fixed public and foreign savings, investment occurs through changes in the savings behavior of households and changes in the unit cost of investment. The model only solves for relative prices; the numéraire, or price anchor, is the export price index of manufactured exports from high-income countries. This price is fixed at unity in the base year.

A virtue of beginning with the latest GTAP database is that the database includes bilateral tariffs that capture not only reciprocal, but also nonreciprocal preferential trade agreements; the latter provide low-income exporters duty-free access to protected markets in high-income countries. This allows us to take into account the fact that future reform may cause a decline in the international terms of trade in those developing countries that are enjoying preferential access to the agricultural markets and other markets in high-income countries (in addition to those that are net food importers because their comparative advantage lies in other sectors, such as labor-intensive manufacturing).

The version of the Linkage model used in our study is based on an aggregation involving 23 sectors and 49 individual countries, plus 11 country groups spanning the world (see the appendix). There is an emphasis on agriculture and food, which account for 16 of the 23 sectors. Note that, consistent with the World Trade Organization, we include the Republic of Korea and Taiwan, China in the developing-country category.[8]

The results below are comparative static results; so, they do not include the (often much larger) dynamic gains that result from an acceleration in investment arising from the reduction in tariffs on industrial goods that lowers the cost of investment. Also missing are therefore any costs of adjustment to reform. Moreover, because this version of the Linkage model assumes perfect competition and constant returns to scale, it captures none of the benefits of freeing markets that might be generated by accelerated productivity growth, scale economies, and the creation of new markets (extensification versus intensification). There is also a dampening effect on the estimates of welfare gains because of product and regional aggregation, which hides many of the differences across products in rates of distortions. The results should thus be treated as much lower-bound estimates of the net economic welfare benefits of policy reform.[9]

## The Prospective Effects of the Global Removal of Price-Distorting Policies

In this section, to explore the possible outcome of the removal of the policies in force as of 2004, we examine the results of two modeling simulations. The main one involves the full global liberalization of agricultural policies and of trade policies in nonagricultural goods. We also discuss an additional simulation, which involves the global liberalization of agricultural policies only, to give a sense of the relative contribution of farm policies to various outcomes.

### Global and national economic welfare

Beginning with the baseline projection of the world economy in 2004, we remove globally all agricultural subsidies and taxes, plus import tariffs on other merchandise (as summarized in table 2.1).[10] Our Linkage model suggests that this would lead to a global gain of US$168 billion per year (table 2.2). As a share of national income, developing countries would gain nearly twice as much as high-income countries by completing the reform process (an average increase of 0.9 compared with 0.5 percent, respectively). Thus, in this broad sense of a world of only two large country groups, completing the global reform process would reduce international inequality, to use the Milanovic (2005) term, taking in to account the economic size of each country.[11] The results vary widely across developing countries, however, ranging from slight losses in the case of some South Asian and Sub-Saharan African countries that would suffer exceptionally large adverse terms of trade changes to 8 percent increases in the case of Ecuador (of which the main export item, bananas, is currently facing heavy discrimination in the markets of the European Union, where former colonies and least developed countries enjoy preferential duty-free access).

**Table 2.2. The Impact on Real Income of the Full Liberalization of Global Merchandise Trade, by Country and Region, 2004**

*(2004 U.S. dollars and percent)*

| Country and region | Change in annual real income, US$, billions | | Change in real income, % of benchmark | |
|---|---|---|---|---|
| | Total income gain | Change deriving from change in terms of trade | Total income gain | Change deriving from terms of trade effects |
| North Africa and Sub-Saharan Africa | 0.9 | −6.0 | 0.2 | −1.1 |
| Egypt, Arab Rep. | −0.2 | −0.6 | −0.3 | −0.9 |
| Madagascar | 0.0 | 0.0 | −0.9 | −1.2 |
| Mozambique | 0.1 | −0.1 | 2.4 | −2.0 |
| Nigeria | 0.3 | −0.6 | 0.7 | −1.3 |
| Senegal | 0.0 | −0.1 | −2.3 | −4.0 |
| South Africa | 0.2 | −0.7 | 0.1 | −0.5 |
| Tanzania | 0.0 | 0.0 | −0.5 | −0.4 |
| Uganda | 0.0 | 0.0 | −0.6 | −0.1 |
| Zambia | 0.0 | 0.0 | 0.1 | −0.3 |
| Zimbabwe | 0.1 | 0.0 | 3.4 | 0.5 |
| Rest of Africa | 0.5 | −3.8 | 0.2 | −1.5 |
| East and South Asia | 29.7 | −4.9 | 0.9 | −0.1 |
| China | 3.3 | 0.5 | 0.2 | 0.0 |
| Indonesia | 0.5 | 0.0 | 0.2 | 0.0 |
| Korea, Rep. | 14.0 | 0.2 | 2.8 | 0.0 |
| Malaysia | 4.2 | −1.0 | 4.7 | −1.1 |
| Philippines | 0.0 | −0.5 | 0.1 | −0.7 |
| Taiwan, China | 1.0 | 0.0 | 0.4 | 0.0 |
| Thailand | 3.3 | −0.1 | 1.4 | −0.1 |
| Vietnam | 1.9 | −0.9 | 5.3 | −2.5 |
| Bangladesh | −0.2 | −0.8 | −0.4 | −1.7 |
| India | −0.8 | −2.9 | −0.2 | −0.6 |
| Pakistan | −0.1 | −0.6 | −0.2 | −0.8 |
| Sri Lanka | 0.8 | 0.5 | 5.1 | 3.1 |
| Rest of East and South Asia | 1.9 | 0.8 | 1.4 | 0.5 |
| Latin America | 15.8 | 2.5 | 1.0 | 0.2 |
| Argentina | 3.2 | −0.7 | 2.6 | −0.6 |
| Brazil | 6.8 | 5.6 | 1.6 | 1.3 |
| Chile | 0.3 | 0.2 | 0.4 | 0.3 |
| Colombia | 2.2 | 0.7 | 3.1 | 1.0 |
| Ecuador | 2.0 | 1.1 | 8.2 | 4.4 |
| Mexico | −0.7 | −3.4 | −0.1 | −0.6 |
| Nicaragua | 0.0 | 0.0 | 1.3 | 0.4 |
| Rest of Latin America | 2.0 | −1.0 | 0.5 | −0.3 |

**Table 2.2.  The Impact on Real Income of the Full Liberalization of Global Merchandise Trade, by Country and Region, 2004 (*continued*)**

*(2004 U.S. dollars and percent)*

| Country and region | Change in annual real income, US$, billions | | Change in real income, % of benchmark | |
|---|---|---|---|---|
| | Total income gain | Change deriving from change in terms of trade | Total income gain | Change deriving from terms of trade effects |
| Eastern Europe and Central Asia | 14.2 | −3.6 | 1.2 | −0.3 |
| Baltic States | 0.5 | 0.1 | 1.8 | 0.3 |
| Bulgaria | 0.2 | −0.2 | 1.4 | −1.4 |
| Czech Republic | 1.0 | −0.1 | 1.4 | −0.2 |
| Hungary | 0.4 | −0.1 | 0.6 | −0.1 |
| Poland | 2.0 | 0.1 | 1.2 | 0.1 |
| Romania | −0.1 | −0.7 | −0.3 | −1.9 |
| Russian Federation | 5.4 | 3.1 | 1.2 | −0.7 |
| Slovak Republic | 0.7 | 0.1 | 2.3 | 0.4 |
| Slovenia | 0.3 | 0.1 | 1.5 | 0.3 |
| Kazakhstan | 0.4 | 0.2 | 1.1 | 0.6 |
| Turkey | 1.3 | −0.5 | 0.6 | −0.2 |
| Rest of Eastern Europe and Central Asia | 2.2 | 0.5 | 2.1 | 0.4 |
| High-income countries | 102.8 | 11.3 | 0.5 | 0.1 |
| Australia | 2.4 | 1.9 | 0.5 | 0.4 |
| Canada | 0.6 | −1.2 | 0.1 | −0.2 |
| EU15 | 56.8 | −3.8 | 0.7 | 0.0 |
| Japan | 23.1 | 10.4 | 0.7 | 0.3 |
| New Zealand | 2.2 | 1.8 | 3.2 | 2.6 |
| Rest of Western Europe | 13.1 | −0.1 | 2.7 | 0.0 |
| United States | 2.8 | 0.9 | 0.0 | 0.0 |
| Hong Kong, China; Singapore | 1.7 | 1.4 | 1.4 | 1.1 |
| Developing countries | 64.9 | −12.2 | 0.9 | −0.2 |
| North Africa | 0.9 | −2.8 | 0.5 | −1.5 |
| Sub-Saharan Africa | 0.0 | −3.2 | 0.0 | −0.9 |
| East Asia | 30.1 | −1.0 | 1.1 | 0.0 |
| South Asia | −0.4 | −3.9 | −0.1 | −0.6 |
| Latin America | 15.8 | 2.5 | 1.0 | 0.2 |
| Middle East | 4.2 | −0.2 | 0.8 | 0.0 |
| Eastern Europe and Central Asia | 14.2 | −3.6 | 1.2 | −0.3 |
| World total | 167.7 | −1.0 | 0.6 | 0.0 |

*Source:* World Bank Linkage model simulations by the authors.

*Note:* The table shows results relative to the 2004 benchmark data. EU15 = the 15 members of the European Union prior to 2004.

If one were to represent each of the 60 countries and regions in table 2.2 by a single household (that is, ignoring intraregional inequality), the income inequality across countries as measured by the Gini coefficient would be reduced at least slightly, from 0.8513 to 0.8506.[12]

The second and fourth columns in table 2.2 show the amount of the welfare gain deriving from changes in the international terms of trade for each country. For developing countries as a group, this terms of trade effect is slightly negative; the converse is true for high-income countries.

### The regional and sectoral distribution of welfare effects

One way to decompose the real income gains from the full removal of price distortions globally so that we may understand more clearly the sources of the gains for each region is to assess the impacts in various economic sectors of liberalization in developing countries versus liberalization in high-income countries. These results are provided in table 2.3. They suggest that the global liberalization of agriculture and food markets would contribute 70 percent of the total global gains from merchandise reform. This is slightly greater than the 63 percent found for 2015 by Anderson, Martin, and van der Mensbrugghe (2006b) using the earlier version 6 of the GTAP database anchored on 2001 estimates of distortions. This result is remarkable given the low shares of agriculture and food in global GDP and global merchandise trade (3 and 6 percent, respectively). For developing countries, the importance of agricultural policies is even slightly greater, at 72 percent (see row 7 in table 2.3).

Slightly more than two-thirds of the global gains that may arise because of the removal of agricultural policies are accounted for by the farm policies of high-income countries (column 3 in table 2.3; US$82 billion of the US$117 billion per year). These policies also account for nearly one-quarter of the overall gains to developing countries from all global agricultural and trade policy reforms (column 1 in table 2.3; US$15 billion of the US$65 billion per year).

### The quantities produced and traded

The results of full global liberalization suggest that there would be little change in the aggregate shares of developing countries in the global output and exports of nonfarm products other than textiles and apparel. The shares of these countries in agricultural and processed food markets change noticeably, however. The export share rises from 54 to 64 percent, and the output share rises from 46 to 50 percent. More significantly, the rises occur in nearly all agricultural and food industries. The share of the global production of farm products that is exported thus rises dramatically in many industries and, for the sector as a whole, increases from 8 to 13 percent, excluding intra–European Union trade (table 2.4). This thickening of international food markets would reduce substantially the fluctuations in food prices and in the quantities of food traded in these markets.

**Table 2.3. Regional and Sectoral Sources of the Welfare Gains from the Full Liberalization of Global Merchandise Trade, 2004**

*(2004 U.S. dollars and percent)*

| Sector | Gains by region,[a] US$, billions | | | Share of regional gain, % | | |
|---|---|---|---|---|---|---|
| | Developing | High-income | World | Developing | High-income | World |
| *Developing countries liberalize* | | | | | | |
| Agriculture and light processing | 31.8 | 3.9 | 35.6 | 48.6 | 3.8 | 21.2 |
| Manufacturing and services | 5.6 | 36.7 | 42.3 | 3.6 | 35.9 | 25.2 |
| Total | 37.4 | 40.6 | 77.9 | 57.2 | 39.6 | 46.5 |
| *High-income countries liberalize* | | | | | | |
| Agriculture and light processing | 15.1 | 66.4 | 81.6 | 23.2 | 64.9 | 48.6 |
| Manufacturing and services | 12.8 | –4.6 | 8.2 | 19.6 | –4.5 | 4.9 |
| Total | 28.0 | 61.8 | 89.8 | 42.8 | 60.4 | 53.5 |
| *All countries liberalize* | | | | | | |
| Agriculture and light processing | 46.9 | 70.3 | 117.2 | 71.8 | 68.7 | 69.9 |
| Manufacturing and services | 18.4 | 32.1 | 50.5 | 28.2 | 31.3 | 30.1 |
| Total | 65.3 | 102.3 | 167.7 | 100.0 | 100.0 | 100.0 |

*Source:* World Bank Linkage model simulations by the authors.

*Note:* The table shows results relative to the 2004 benchmark data.

a. Small interaction effects are distributed proportionately, and the numbers are rounded to sum to 100 percent.

**Table 2.4. The Impact of Full Global Liberalization on the Shares of Global Output Exported, by Product, 2004**
(percent)

| | Share in global output exported | | Developing countries in global output | | Developing countries in global exports | |
|---|---|---|---|---|---|---|
| | Benchmark | Full global liberalization | Benchmark | Full global liberalization | Benchmark | Full global liberalization |
| Paddy rice | 1 | 2 | 81 | 82 | 56 | 42 |
| Wheat | 16 | 22 | 67 | 71 | 25 | 39 |
| Other grains | 11 | 15 | 55 | 57 | 35 | 56 |
| Oilseeds | 21 | 28 | 69 | 74 | 54 | 68 |
| Plant-based fibers | 25 | 25 | 74 | 83 | 50 | 79 |
| Vegetables and fruits | 9 | 15 | 72 | 77 | 69 | 80 |
| Other crops | 14 | 17 | 49 | 49 | 75 | 62 |
| Cattle, sheep, and so on | 2 | 2 | 43 | 48 | 56 | 59 |
| Other livestock | 4 | 4 | 65 | 67 | 43 | 46 |
| Wool | 13 | 14 | 82 | 81 | 16 | 18 |
| Beef and sheep meat | 7 | 21 | 27 | 41 | 31 | 68 |
| Other meat products | 7 | 12 | 32 | 34 | 42 | 45 |
| Vegetable oils and fats | 20 | 30 | 52 | 58 | 80 | 84 |
| Dairy products | 5 | 11 | 29 | 33 | 28 | 41 |
| Processed rice | 5 | 7 | 76 | 79 | 85 | 87 |
| Refined sugar | 8 | 42 | 52 | 85 | 78 | 90 |
| Other food, beverages, tobacco | 9 | 12 | 35 | 36 | 50 | 59 |
| Other primary products | 31 | 33 | 64 | 63 | 76 | 76 |
| Textiles and wearing apparel | 28 | 35 | 53 | 57 | 74 | 77 |
| Other manufacturing | 24 | 26 | 32 | 31 | 43 | 43 |
| Services | 3 | 3 | 20 | 20 | 31 | 30 |
| Agriculture and food | 8 | 13 | 46 | 50 | 54 | 64 |
| Agriculture | 8 | 11 | 62 | 65 | 55 | 64 |
| Processed foods | 8 | 14 | 37 | 40 | 52 | 63 |

*Source:* World Bank Linkage model simulations by the authors.

*Note:* The developing-country shares of global output and exports exclude intra–European Union trade.

The impact of full trade reform on agricultural and food output and trade for each country and region is shown in table 2.5. It is clear that global farm trade is enhanced by more than one-third (39 percent), whereas the global value of output is virtually unchanged (dropping only 2.6 percent). This suggests that, in aggregate, the pro-agricultural policies of high-income countries are not quite fully offset by the

**Table 2.5. The Impact of Full Global Trade Liberalization on Agricultural and Food Output and Trade, by Country and Region, 2004**

*(2004 U.S. dollars and percent)*

| Country, region | US$, billions | | | Change relative to baseline, % | | |
|---|---|---|---|---|---|---|
| | Output | Exports | Imports | Output | Exports | Imports |
| North Africa and sub Saharan Africa | 13.8 | 20.5 | 10.0 | 7.2 | 99.1 | 16.0 |
| Egypt, Arab Rep. | 0.4 | 0.5 | −0.1 | 2.2 | 39.2 | −4.2 |
| Madagascar | 0.0 | 0.0 | 0.0 | −0.4 | 2.7 | −4.3 |
| Mozambique | 0.9 | 1.0 | 0.1 | 52.3 | 597.1 | 33.3 |
| Nigeria | −0.5 | 0.4 | 0.7 | −2.9 | 92.8 | 43.1 |
| Senegal | 0.0 | 0.0 | 0.0 | −1.9 | 35.0 | 0.3 |
| South Africa | 0.7 | 0.9 | 0.8 | 2.4 | 26.7 | 42.9 |
| Tanzania | 0.0 | 0.2 | 0.1 | −0.7 | 28.5 | 31.2 |
| Uganda | 0.0 | 0.0 | 0.0 | −0.6 | 1.3 | 1.5 |
| Zambia | 0.1 | 0.1 | 0.0 | 5.2 | 22.3 | 35.9 |
| Zimbabwe | 0.4 | 0.3 | 0.1 | 25.7 | 38.0 | 39.2 |
| Rest of Africa | 12.0 | 17.0 | 8.3 | 10.5 | 133.1 | 64.3 |
| East and South Asia | 25.0 | 39.5 | 24.7 | 2.7 | 83.4 | 36.7 |
| China | 6.2 | 7.7 | 6.7 | 1.7 | 76.5 | 27.5 |
| Indonesia | 1.1 | 1.6 | 1.0 | 1.8 | 21.6 | 21.5 |
| Korea, Rep. | −1.0 | 1.0 | 6.2 | −1.7 | 194.1 | 75.0 |
| Malaysia | 1.6 | 1.3 | 0.7 | 8.9 | 17.0 | 17.8 |
| Philippines | 1.1 | 1.9 | 0.8 | 3.5 | 120.5 | 35.0 |
| Taiwan, China | −1.9 | 0.3 | 1.5 | −9.1 | 62.8 | 35.5 |
| Thailand | 9.5 | 8.3 | 1.9 | 17.4 | 133.0 | 78.1 |
| Vietnam | 0.5 | 1.1 | 0.6 | 3.3 | 54.0 | 55.6 |
| Bangladesh | −0.6 | 0.4 | 0.8 | −2.4 | 261.2 | 38.3 |
| India | 1.1 | 9.0 | 1.4 | 0.5 | 131.2 | 24.2 |
| Pakistan | −0.6 | 0.5 | 1.0 | −1.3 | 45.0 | 43.0 |
| Sri Lanka | −0.1 | −0.1 | 0.6 | −1.2 | −18.2 | 69.3 |
| Rest of East and South Asia | 8.0 | 6.4 | 1.4 | 41.5 | 266.1 | 29.5 |

*(Table continues on the following page.)*

**Table 2.5. The Impact of Full Global Trade Liberalization on Agricultural and Food Output and Trade, by Country and Region, 2004 (continued)**

*(2004 U.S. dollars and percent)*

| Country, region | US$, billions | | | Change relative to baseline, % | | |
|---|---|---|---|---|---|---|
| | Output | Exports | Imports | Output | Exports | Imports |
| Latin America | 87.2 | 71.5 | 7.2 | 26.8 | 106.4 | 29.8 |
| Argentina | 12.2 | 15.1 | 0.3 | 37.8 | 95.6 | 81.8 |
| Brazil | 45.8 | 25.7 | 2.1 | 45.3 | 100.7 | 94.8 |
| Chile | 0.5 | 0.4 | 0.2 | 4.7 | 11.3 | 15.8 |
| Colombia | 3.1 | 4.9 | 1.1 | 14.6 | 161.4 | 81.7 |
| Ecuador | 4.2 | 4.6 | 0.3 | 46.1 | 198.7 | 71.8 |
| Mexico | −0.3 | 0.3 | 0.4 | −0.4 | 5.8 | 4.3 |
| Nicaragua | 0.0 | 0.1 | 0.0 | 2.9 | 21.6 | 19.4 |
| Rest of Latin America | 21.6 | 20.4 | 2.8 | 25.7 | 175.9 | 30.4 |
| Eastern Europe and Central Asia | −10.4 | 17.4 | 20.3 | −2.6 | 79.7 | 77.6 |
| Baltic States | −1.2 | −0.1 | 0.4 | −16.9 | −15.5 | 30.9 |
| Bulgaria | 4.2 | 2.6 | 0.6 | 6.6 | 366.5 | 118.1 |
| Czech Republic | −2.2 | −0.1 | 0.7 | −12.0 | −10.9 | 40.5 |
| Hungary | −0.9 | 0.4 | 0.8 | −6.0 | 17.1 | 66.6 |
| Poland | 1.7 | 2.5 | 2.5 | 3.9 | 80.7 | 88.8 |
| Romania | −0.2 | 1.3 | 1.1 | −1.0 | 190.5 | 78.3 |
| Russian Federation | −12.9 | 3.2 | 8.8 | −13.1 | 179.4 | 98.9 |
| Slovak Republic | −0.9 | −0.1 | 0.4 | −11.3 | −12.0 | 64.1 |
| Slovenia | −0.6 | −0.1 | 0.2 | −17.1 | −54.1 | 26.2 |
| Kazakhstan | 1.5 | 1.4 | 0.0 | 11.8 | 142.9 | 11.6 |
| Turkey | −2.0 | 2.3 | 2.9 | −3.1 | 61.5 | 92.1 |
| Rest of Eastern Europe and Central Asia | 3.0 | 4.1 | 2.0 | 7.7 | 71.3 | 53.4 |
| High-income countries | −233.2 | −9.2 | 89.8 | −13.1 | −4.0 | 38.3 |
| Australia | 12.0 | 7.0 | 0.2 | 19.8 | 41.2 | 11.1 |
| Canada | −1.6 | 3.6 | 2.7 | −2.4 | 24.1 | 32.8 |
| EU15 | −190.9 | −38.8 | 50.9 | −21.2 | −29.2 | 31.9 |
| Japan | −39.1 | 0.4 | 16.8 | −22.9 | 87.7 | 69.1 |
| New Zealand | 10.6 | 6.4 | 0.2 | 46.6 | 74.3 | 27.1 |
| Rest of Western Europe | −11.6 | 11.7 | 9.8 | −19.4 | 312.0 | 132.7 |
| United States | −12.8 | 0.6 | 9.3 | −2.6 | 1.1 | 32.4 |
| Hong Kong, China; Singapore | 0.1 | 0.0 | 0.1 | 2.1 | 6.3 | 1.6 |
| Developing countries | 137.6 | 163.6 | 64.6 | 7.1 | 100.0 | 40.4 |
| North Africa | 11.4 | 13.3 | 6.1 | 17.3 | 377.2 | 62.5 |
| Sub-Saharan Africa | 2.5 | 7.2 | 3.8 | 1.9 | 41.9 | 32.3 |
| East Asia | 25.1 | 29.5 | 20.8 | 4.0 | 77.4 | 37.4 |
| South Asia | −0.1 | 10.0 | 3.9 | 0.0 | 108.3 | 33.2 |
| Latin America | 87.2 | 71.5 | 7.2 | 26.8 | 106.4 | 29.8 |
| Middle East | 22.0 | 14.8 | 2.5 | 21.5 | 222.7 | 12.1 |
| Eastern Europe and Central Asia | −10.4 | 17.4 | 20.3 | −2.6 | 79.7 | 77.6 |
| World total | −95.7 | 154.4 | 154.4 | −2.6 | 39.1 | 39.1 |

*Source:* World Bank Linkage model simulations by the authors.

*Note:* The table shows results relative to the 2004 benchmark data. EU15 = the 15 members of the European Union prior to 2004.

**Table 2.6. The Impact of Global Liberalization on the Share of Agricultural and Food Production Exports, by Country and Region, 2004**

(percent)

| Country, region | 2004 benchmark data | Full global liberalization |
|---|---|---|
| Developing countries | 9.5 | 16.9 |
| North Africa | 6.3 | 20.6 |
| Sub-Saharan Africa | 13.8 | 19.3 |
| East Asia | 8.4 | 15.1 |
| South Asia | 3.7 | 7.5 |
| Latin America | 18.1 | 28.2 |
| Middle East | 7.4 | 17.2 |
| Eastern Europe and Central Asia | 6.8 | 11.1 |
| High-income countries | 13.0 | 14.1 |
| World total | 11.4 | 13.1 |

Source: World Bank Linkage model simulations by the authors.

antiagricultural policies of developing countries, whereas the antitrade bias in the policies of both groups of countries reinforce each other. The increase in the exports of these goods from developing countries would be a huge US$163 billion per year. Latin America accounts for nearly half this increase, but the exports of all developing regions expand. This means that the share of these countries in production for export would be much higher. It would increase in the case of almost all developing countries, rising in aggregate for the group from 10 to 17 percent (table 2.6).

Also of interest is the course of agricultural imports. Developing countries as a group would see them growing less than farm exports (table 2.5). This means that the food and agricultural self-sufficiency of these countries would rise, although, in aggregate, only slightly. For high-income countries, it would fall five percentage points (slightly less if Eastern Europe is included); for East Asia and Africa, it would rise two or three points; for South Asia, it would be unchanged; and, for Latin America, it would jump from 112 to 126 percent (table 2.7).

Such reform also raises substantially the share of agricultural and food production that is exported globally, thereby thickening international markets. This would restrict international food price fluctuations and thereby reduce the concerns about vulnerability to import dependence. The extent of this global public good aspect of agricultural and trade reform may be sensed for various products from the results reported in table 2.8. The case of highly protected sugar and milk, as well as grains and oilseeds, is especially noteworthy. Also noteworthy is the extent to which the developing-country shares of output exported rise for certain products. The share of grain production that is exported by these countries would double, and

**Table 2.7. The Impact of Global Liberalization on Self-sufficiency in Agricultural and Other Products, by Region, 2004**
(percent)

| Product | High-income countries | | Developing countries | | North Africa and Sub-Saharan Africa | | Latin America | | East Asia | | South Asia | | Eastern Europe and Central Asia | |
|---|---|---|---|---|---|---|---|---|---|---|---|---|---|---|
| | BK | GL | BK | GL | BK | GL | BK | GL | BK | GL | BK | GL | BK | GL |
| Paddy rice | 101 | 105 | 100 | 99 | 97 | 96 | 93 | 72 | 100 | 101 | 101 | 101 | 95 | 92 |
| Wheat | 141 | 140 | 88 | 89 | 67 | 46 | 80 | 98 | 68 | 65 | 100 | 98 | 102 | 117 |
| Other grains | 108 | 102 | 94 | 98 | 94 | 91 | 98 | 119 | 88 | 81 | 103 | 105 | 103 | 113 |
| Oilseeds | 104 | 92 | 97 | 103 | 104 | 130 | 140 | 167 | 66 | 51 | 100 | 101 | 106 | 115 |
| Plant-based fibers | 161 | 112 | 88 | 97 | 177 | 265 | 94 | 107 | 54 | 58 | 93 | 95 | 104 | 118 |
| Vegetables and fruits | 90 | 78 | 105 | 109 | 108 | 103 | 153 | 221 | 102 | 104 | 99 | 98 | 99 | 92 |
| Other crops | 90 | 91 | 113 | 110 | 138 | 138 | 143 | 133 | 110 | 104 | 104 | 104 | 90 | 88 |
| Cattle, sheep, and so on | 100 | 100 | 100 | 100 | 101 | 99 | 102 | 102 | 98 | 97 | 100 | 100 | 102 | 102 |
| Other livestock | 101 | 101 | 100 | 100 | 101 | 100 | 101 | 100 | 99 | 99 | 100 | 100 | 99 | 98 |
| Wool | 161 | 180 | 92 | 91 | 103 | 104 | 103 | 102 | 78 | 75 | 96 | 93 | 96 | 99 |
| Beef and sheep meat | 101 | 85 | 97 | 134 | 96 | 102 | 108 | 183 | 83 | 77 | 126 | 652 | 95 | 85 |
| Other meat products | 100 | 99 | 100 | 103 | 92 | 85 | 121 | 143 | 101 | 103 | 96 | 95 | 96 | 93 |
| Vegetable oils and fats | 95 | 85 | 103 | 114 | 69 | 191 | 141 | 143 | 115 | 116 | 78 | 66 | 93 | 96 |
| Dairy products | 103 | 100 | 94 | 101 | 76 | 79 | 97 | 102 | 78 | 78 | 99 | 99 | 102 | 104 |
| Processed rice | 99 | 95 | 100 | 101 | 69 | 63 | 94 | 85 | 104 | 108 | 104 | 104 | 92 | 87 |
| Refined sugar | 98 | 41 | 102 | 133 | 95 | 100 | 131 | 227 | 98 | 196 | 96 | 91 | 98 | 70 |
| Other food, beverages, tobacco | 99 | 97 | 103 | 105 | 101 | 100 | 108 | 112 | 105 | 113 | 106 | 94 | 100 | 98 |
| Other primary products | 76 | 76 | 122 | 122 | 180 | 189 | 148 | 155 | 84 | 82 | 75 | 69 | 115 | 116 |
| Textiles and wearing apparel | 81 | 76 | 123 | 128 | 98 | 91 | 104 | 91 | 144 | 155 | 144 | 153 | 101 | 95 |
| Other manufacturing | 101 | 102 | 98 | 96 | 77 | 74 | 96 | 91 | 106 | 105 | 90 | 89 | 95 | 95 |
| Services | 101 | 101 | 101 | 101 | 101 | 102 | 100 | 100 | 101 | 100 | 100 | 101 | 101 | 101 |
| Agriculture and food | 100 | 95 | 101 | 105 | 100 | 103 | 112 | 126 | 100 | 102 | 100 | 100 | 99 | 98 |
| Agriculture | 99 | 96 | 100 | 102 | 104 | 103 | 115 | 126 | 96 | 95 | 100 | 100 | 100 | 101 |
| Processed foods | 100 | 95 | 101 | 108 | 94 | 103 | 110 | 126 | 104 | 111 | 100 | 101 | 99 | 96 |

Source: World Bank Linkage model simulations by the authors.

Note: Self-sufficiency = domestic production as a percentage of domestic consumption measured in value terms at free-on-board prices. BK = benchmark. GL = global liberalization.

**Table 2.8. Shares of Production Exported and of Consumption Imported before and after Full Global Liberalization of all Merchandise Trade, by Product, 2004**

*(percent)*

| Product | Share of production exported | | | | Share of consumption imported | | | |
|---|---|---|---|---|---|---|---|---|
| | High-income countries | | Developing countries | | High-income countries | | Developing countries | |
| | 2004 benchmark | Global liberalization | 2004 benchmark | Global liberalization | 2004 benchmark | Global liberalization | 2004 benchmark | Global liberalization |
| Paddy rice | 3 | 7 | 1 | 1 | 2 | 3 | 1 | 2 |
| Wheat | 37 | 47 | 6 | 12 | 11 | 25 | 17 | 21 |
| Other grains | 15 | 16 | 7 | 15 | 9 | 14 | 11 | 15 |
| Oilseeds | 31 | 34 | 16 | 25 | 26 | 36 | 16 | 22 |
| Plant-based fibers | 50 | 31 | 17 | 24 | 18 | 22 | 26 | 25 |
| Vegetables and fruits | 10 | 13 | 9 | 15 | 18 | 30 | 4 | 7 |
| Other crops | 7 | 13 | 21 | 22 | 16 | 20 | 11 | 14 |
| Cattle, sheep, and so on | 1 | 2 | 2 | 2 | 2 | 2 | 2 | 2 |
| Other livestock | 6 | 7 | 3 | 3 | 6 | 6 | 3 | 3 |
| Wool | 60 | 62 | 2 | 3 | 35 | 31 | 10 | 12 |
| Beef and sheep meat | 6 | 11 | 7 | 35 | 5 | 24 | 10 | 13 |
| Other meat products | 6 | 10 | 9 | 16 | 6 | 12 | 8 | 14 |
| Vegetable oils and fats | 8 | 11 | 31 | 43 | 12 | 24 | 26 | 34 |
| Dairy products | 5 | 10 | 4 | 14 | 2 | 10 | 10 | 14 |
| Processed rice | 3 | 4 | 5 | 8 | 4 | 9 | 5 | 7 |
| Refined sugar | 4 | 30 | 12 | 44 | 5 | 66 | 10 | 25 |
| Other food, beverages, tobacco | 7 | 8 | 12 | 20 | 8 | 10 | 9 | 16 |
| Other primary products | 20 | 21 | 37 | 39 | 38 | 39 | 22 | 24 |
| Textiles and wearing apparel | 15 | 19 | 39 | 48 | 30 | 37 | 23 | 31 |
| Other manufacturing | 20 | 21 | 32 | 36 | 19 | 20 | 32 | 38 |
| Services | 3 | 3 | 5 | 4 | 2 | 2 | 5 | 5 |
| Agriculture and food | 7 | 9 | 9 | 17 | 8 | 13 | 8 | 12 |
| Agriculture | 9 | 11 | 7 | 11 | 10 | 15 | 7 | 9 |
| Processed foods | 6 | 9 | 12 | 23 | 7 | 13 | 10 | 16 |

*Source:* World Bank Linkage model simulations by the authors.

*Note:* The data on the high-income countries exclude intra–European Union trade.

the corresponding share of meat would more than double, while the share of sugar would rise nearly fourfold. Global exports of cotton (plant-based fibers) would become more dominated by developing countries, while the share of cotton production exported by high-income countries would fall from 50 to 31 percent.

### The effects on product and factor prices

The average real international prices of agricultural and lightly processed food products would be only 1.3 percent higher in the absence of all merchandise trade distortions, or 2.0 percent if only agricultural policies were liberalized (see table 2.9). The

**Table 2.9. The Impact of Full Global Liberalization on Real International Product Prices, 2004**
(percent relative to 2004 baseline)

| Product | Agricultural policies | Policies in all goods sectors |
|---|:---:|:---:|
| Paddy rice | 6.9 | 6.6 |
| Wheat | 1.8 | 1.4 |
| Other grains | 2.6 | 2.7 |
| Oilseeds | −2.2 | −2.4 |
| Sugarcane and beets | −1.1 | −2.0 |
| Plant-based fibers | 4.7 | 2.9 |
| Vegetables and fruits | 2.4 | 1.8 |
| Other crops | 1.7 | 1.0 |
| Cattle, sheep, and so on | −0.2 | −1.1 |
| Other livestock | −1.2 | −2.1 |
| Raw milk | 0.7 | −0.2 |
| Wool | 3.5 | 3.3 |
| Beef and sheep meat | 5.6 | 4.6 |
| Other meat products | 1.3 | 0.6 |
| Vegetable oils and fats | −1.4 | −1.9 |
| Dairy products | 4.6 | 3.8 |
| Processed rice | 2.8 | 2.9 |
| Refined sugar | 2.5 | 1.3 |
| Other food, beverages, tobacco | −1.7 | −1.3 |
| Textiles and wearing apparel | 0.3 | −1.2 |
| Other manufacturing | 0.2 | −0.2 |
| Merchandise trade | 0.3 | −0.2 |
| Agriculture and food | 0.8 | 0.3 |
|   Agriculture | 1.5 | 0.9 |
|   Agriculture and light processing | 2.0 | 1.3 |

Source: World Bank Linkage model simulations by the authors.

Note: The model numéraire is the export price index of the manufactured exports of high-income countries.

net effects of distortions (as of 2004) are especially dampening on the international prices of beef, milk, rice, and cotton. However, they prop up the international prices of some other products because export taxes are still in place in some developing countries, most notably Argentina.

The size of the redistribution of welfare among groups within each country following trade reform may be much larger than the aggregate change partly because of the impacts on real pretax rewards to labor, capital, and land. These effects are reported in table 2.10, in which the data on factor rewards are deflated by the overall consumer price index and also, in the case of unskilled wages, by the food and the food plus clothing consumer price indexes (since these items are so prominent in the spending of unskilled workers). Consistent with trade theory, these results suggest that unskilled workers in developing countries—the majority of whom work on farms—would benefit most from reform, followed by skilled workers, then capital owners. The returns to immobile agricultural land would also rise in developing countries, but by less than the rise in more mobile factors. Land returns fall substantially in highly protected Japan and Western Europe, change little in the United States, rise considerably in Australia and Canada, and rise dramatically in dairy-intensive New Zealand.

### The effects on sectoral value added

Also of crucial interest in terms of the impact of these policies on inequality and poverty is the effect the policies have on value added in agriculture, that is, on net farm incomes. The results of this issue in full global reform are reported in the first four columns of table 2.11. They show that, for developing countries as a group, the value added in agriculture rises by 5.6 percent following full global reform of all merchandise trade. This compares with only 1.9 percent for nonagriculture. Net farm income expands the most in Latin America, where the average rise is 37 percent, but exceeds 100 percent in Argentina and Ecuador and 40–50 percent in Brazil and Colombia. In East Asia, it also expands considerably, more than the expansion in nonagricultural value added, including in China. However, among the countries listed in Africa, net farm incomes would increase substantially only in Mozambique, Zambia, and Zimbabwe, and, in the continent as a whole, including North Africa, they would fall only slightly (by less than 1 percent). Partly this is because the nonagricultural primary sector—in which numerous African countries have a strong comparative advantage—would expand (raising Africa's self-sufficiency in that sector from 180 to 189 percent; see table 2.7), and this would, in turn, boost the production and employment in nontradable goods and services. It is estimated that net farm incomes would also fall in South Asia (by 7 percent), although, there, textiles and clothing would expand (raising the self-sufficiency in

**Table 2.10. The Impacts of Full Global Merchandise Trade Liberalization on Real Pretax Factor Prices, by Country and Region, 2004**

*(percent)*

| Country, region | Nominal change deflated by the aggregate CPI | | | Real change in unskilled wages, deflated | | |
|---|---|---|---|---|---|---|
| | Skilled wages | Capital[a] user cost | Land[a] user cost | By aggregate CPI | By food CPI | By food and clothing CPI |
| North Africa and Sub-Saharan Africa | 4.7 | 4.3 | 0.1 | 4.4 | 5.8 | 6.9 |
| Egypt, Arab Rep. | 3.2 | 1.7 | 3.4 | 2.3 | 2.2 | 2.9 |
| Madagascar | 2.0 | −0.2 | −0.3 | −0.8 | −0.8 | −0.7 |
| Mozambique | −0.2 | 4.3 | −5.8 | 10.7 | 12.0 | 13.0 |
| Nigeria | 10.1 | 10.5 | −1.3 | 3.2 | 7.7 | 8.6 |
| Senegal | 2.4 | 3.2 | 0.7 | 3.1 | 2.6 | 3.6 |
| South Africa | 1.8 | 2.4 | −0.1 | 1.6 | 1.7 | 3.6 |
| Tanzania | 2.1 | 2.4 | 1.6 | 2.8 | 2.6 | 3.0 |
| Uganda | 2.2 | 0.7 | −0.8 | 0.2 | 0.2 | 0.5 |
| Zambia | 2.6 | 3.2 | 0.7 | 3.0 | 3.1 | 3.5 |
| Zimbabwe | 6.7 | 11.8 | 23.1 | 13.6 | 15.9 | 16.8 |
| Rest of Africa | 6.2 | 5.5 | 1.1 | 6.4 | 7.2 | 8.5 |
| East and South Asia | 3.4 | 3.0 | −1.8 | 3.2 | 4.6 | 4.8 |
| China | 1.9 | 2.0 | 3.6 | 2.6 | 1.6 | 2.1 |
| Indonesia | 0.7 | 0.7 | 0.1 | 1.4 | 1.5 | 1.8 |
| Korea, Rep. | 7.1 | 6.5 | −14.5 | 5.8 | 26.6 | 22.7 |
| Malaysia | 10.7 | 10.2 | 3.6 | 11.1 | 32.3 | 29.2 |
| Philippines | −1.0 | 1.4 | 7.2 | 8.5 | 9.2 | 9.4 |
| Taiwan, China | 2.4 | 2.8 | −11.8 | 3.3 | 10.9 | 10.3 |
| Thailand | 2.6 | 3.5 | 7.5 | 5.6 | 8.5 | 7.8 |

| | | | | | |
|---|---|---|---|---|---|
| Vietnam | 17.7 | 16.0 | 9.1 | 19.6 | 23.9 | 26.7 |
| Bangladesh | 2.1 | 2.8 | 2.8 | 3.3 | 4.5 | 5.3 |
| India | 2.1 | 0.2 | -8.5 | -1.9 | -4.4 | -3.8 |
| Pakistan | 3.9 | 3.5 | 1.5 | 3.8 | 3.3 | 3.5 |
| Sri Lanka | 0.1 | 14.1 | 0.9 | 3.0 | 4.8 | 4.8 |
| Rest of East and South Asia | 2.0 | 2.9 | 6.5 | 5.1 | 8.3 | 9.1 |
| Latin America | 1.4 | 1.9 | 21.1 | 4.5 | 2.4 | 4.1 |
| Argentina | -3.1 | 4.1 | 43.6 | 8.8 | 4.9 | 7.2 |
| Brazil | 1.3 | 2.7 | 26.5 | 1.4 | 0.2 | 1.1 |
| Chile | 1.3 | 0.5 | 3.0 | 1.3 | 1.1 | 1.9 |
| Colombia | -0.8 | 0.3 | 30.2 | 5.0 | 4.4 | 5.6 |
| Ecuador | 2.1 | -1.2 | 61.7 | 15.1 | 12.1 | 13.9 |
| Mexico | 0.5 | 0.5 | 2.3 | 0.8 | -2.3 | 0.9 |
| Nicaragua | 1.9 | 2.5 | 2.1 | 3.8 | 3.9 | 4.7 |
| Rest of Latin America | 0.8 | 1.5 | 18.0 | 5.4 | 4.9 | 6.1 |
| Eastern Europe and Central Asia | 3.2 | 2.6 | -4.5 | 1.7 | 4.2 | 4.5 |
| Baltic States | 3.9 | 2.0 | -9.8 | 1.3 | 5.6 | 5.0 |
| Bulgaria | 0.3 | 1.6 | 5.9 | 2.5 | 1.8 | 2.3 |
| Czech Republic | 2.4 | 1.5 | -26.1 | 0.7 | 3.9 | 3.3 |
| Hungary | 2.2 | 1.1 | -19.9 | -1.0 | 1.6 | 1.4 |
| Poland | 3.9 | 2.6 | -24.6 | 0.5 | 5.2 | 4.6 |
| Romania | 4.5 | 3.5 | -3.4 | 3.4 | 4.5 | 5.7 |
| Slovak Republic | 2.9 | 2.2 | -15.9 | 1.0 | 4.9 | 4.0 |
| Slovenia | 2.3 | 1.8 | -17.2 | 1.3 | 4.9 | 4.2 |
| Russian Federation | 3.9 | 3.8 | -1.9 | 2.5 | 4.3 | 5.1 |
| Kazakhstan | 1.0 | 1.4 | 14.0 | 3.0 | 2.4 | 3.3 |
| Turkey | 2.1 | 1.4 | -3.4 | 0.4 | 1.8 | 1.8 |
| Rest of Eastern Europe and Central Asia | 3.7 | 4.2 | 12.7 | 6.3 | 9.7 | 10.3 |

(Table continues on the following page.)

**Table 2.10. The Impacts of Full Global Merchandise Trade Liberalization on Real Pretax Factor Prices, by Country and Region, 2004 (continued)**

(percent)

| Country, region | Nominal change deflated by the aggregate CPI | | | Real change in unskilled wages, deflated | | |
|---|---|---|---|---|---|---|
| | Skilled wages | Capital[a] user cost | Land[a] user cost | By aggregate CPI | By food CPI | By food and clothing CPI |
| High-income countries | 1.0 | 0.5 | −17.9 | 0.2 | 3.3 | 3.3 |
| Australia | 0.4 | 0.8 | 9.4 | 1.3 | 0.0 | 1.6 |
| Canada | 0.5 | 0.4 | 6.3 | 0.4 | 1.7 | 2.7 |
| EU15 | 1.7 | 0.6 | −39.5 | −0.1 | 4.2 | 3.6 |
| Japan | 1.7 | 1.2 | −29.3 | 0.9 | 6.5 | 6.0 |
| New Zealand | −1.2 | 1.5 | 34.8 | 5.9 | 6.2 | 7.3 |
| Rest of Western Europe | 3.1 | 3.1 | −50.6 | 0.8 | 19.3 | 14.0 |
| United States | 0.2 | 0.1 | −2.9 | −0.1 | −2.0 | 0.0 |
| Hong Kong, China; Singapore | 0.3 | 0.8 | 0.4 | 2.2 | 1.8 | 2.4 |
| Developing countries | 3.0 | 2.9 | 1.6 | 3.5 | 5.5 | 5.9 |
| North Africa | 7.7 | 5.3 | −0.5 | 7.0 | 9.3 | 10.4 |
| Sub-Saharan Africa | 3.2 | 3.8 | 0.2 | 3.2 | 4.4 | 5.3 |
| East Asia and Pacific | 3.4 | 3.3 | 1.9 | 4.0 | 6.9 | 6.9 |
| South Asia | 2.3 | 1.2 | −6.2 | −0.6 | −2.5 | −1.9 |
| Latin America | 1.4 | 1.9 | 21.1 | 4.5 | 2.4 | 4.1 |
| Middle East | 2.9 | 4.7 | 43.8 | 8.3 | 17.0 | 16.5 |
| Eastern Europe and Central Asia | 3.2 | 2.6 | −4.5 | 1.7 | 4.2 | 4.5 |
| World total | 1.3 | 1.2 | −3.1 | 0.9 | 3.6 | 3.8 |

*Source:* World Bank Linkage model simulations by the authors.

*Note:* The table shows results relative to the 2004 benchmark data. CPI = consumer price index. EU15 = the 15 members of the European Union prior to 2004.

a. The user cost of capital and land represents the subsidy-inclusive rental cost.

**Table 2.11. The Effects of the Full Global Liberalization of Agricultural and Merchandise Trade on Sectoral Value Added, by Country and Region, 2004**

*(2004 U.S. dollars and percent)*

| | US$, billions | | | | Percent | | | |
| | Agricultural policies | | Policies in all sectors | | Agricultural policies | | Policies in all sectors | |
| Country, region | Ag | Nonag | Ag | Nonag | Ag | Nonag | Ag | Nonag |
|---|---|---|---|---|---|---|---|---|
| North and Sub Saharan Africa | 0.1 | 5.1 | −0.9 | −0.2 | 0.1 | 0.8 | −0.9 | 0.0 |
| Egypt, Arab Rep. | 0.1 | 0.2 | 0.0 | −0.7 | 1.3 | 0.4 | −0.1 | −1.1 |
| Madagascar | 0.0 | 0.0 | 0.0 | −0.1 | −3.2 | 0.1 | −3.4 | −3.1 |
| Mozambique | 0.3 | 0.0 | 0.3 | 0.0 | 23.6 | 0.6 | 22.7 | 0.1 |
| Nigeria | −0.6 | 0.2 | −1.2 | −0.3 | −4.8 | 0.5 | −9.3 | −1.7 |
| Senegal | 0.0 | 0.0 | 0.0 | 0.0 | −.5 | −0.8 | −1.1 | −0.8 |
| South Africa | −0.2 | 0.7 | −0.1 | 0.1 | −2.7 | 0.4 | −0.7 | 0.1 |
| Tanzania | 0.0 | 0.0 | 0.0 | −0.1 | 0.6 | −0.3 | −0.3 | −1.3 |
| Uganda | −0.1 | 0.0 | −0.1 | −0.1 | −1.6 | −0.4 | −2.9 | −1.6 |
| Zambia | 0.0 | 0.0 | 0.0 | 0.0 | 0.7 | 0.5 | 0.6 | 0.6 |
| Zimbabwe | 0.1 | 0.0 | 0.2 | 0.2 | 24.2 | 0.8 | 38.9 | 4.9 |
| Rest of Africa | 0.5 | 3.9 | 0.0 | 1.4 | 0.7 | 1.4 | 0.1 | 0.5 |
| East and South Asia | −1.4 | 24.4 | 2.0 | 100.7 | −0.3 | 0.7 | 0.5 | 2.9 |
| China | 4.6 | 2.5 | 9.4 | 37.5 | 2.8 | 0.2 | 5.7 | 3.0 |
| Indonesia | 0.3 | 1.1 | 0.2 | 2.7 | 1.1 | 0.5 | 0.8 | 1.2 |
| Korea, Rep. | −4.0 | 7.2 | −3.2 | 31.3 | −18.7 | 1.2 | −15.1 | 5.4 |
| Malaysia | −0.2 | 0.9 | −0.1 | 4.0 | −6.3 | 0.8 | −2.0 | 3.8 |
| Philippines | 1.7 | 0.3 | 1.9 | 1.0 | 13.8 | 0.5 | 15.6 | 1.7 |
| Taiwan, China | −0.5 | 0.8 | −0.5 | 10.7 | −11.3 | 0.3 | −9.9 | 3.7 |

*(Table continues on the following pages.)*

**Table 2.11. The Effects of the Full Global Liberalization of Agricultural and Merchandise Trade on Sectoral Value Added, by Country and Region, 2004 (continued)**

*(2004 U.S. dollars and percent)*

| Country, region | US$, billions | | | | Percent | | | |
|---|---|---|---|---|---|---|---|---|
| | Agricultural policies | | Policies in all sectors | | Agricultural policies | | Policies in all sectors | |
| | Ag | Nonag | Ag | Nonag | Ag | Nonag | Ag | Nonag |
| Thailand | 2.9 | 2.7 | 3.0 | 7.3 | 14.0 | 1.0 | 14.3 | 2.8 |
| Vietnam | 1.4 | 0.0 | 1.2 | 4.5 | 22.8 | 0.0 | 18.8 | 15.6 |
| Bangladesh | −0.2 | 0.4 | −0.3 | −2.1 | −2.6 | 0.9 | −3.8 | −4.4 |
| India | −7.8 | 6.3 | −10.6 | −1.3 | −6.1 | 1.4 | −8.3 | −0.3 |
| Pakistan | −0.2 | −0.1 | −0.1 | 0.2 | −1.0 | −0.1 | −0.5 | 0.2 |
| Sri Lanka | 0.0 | 0.0 | 0.3 | 1.3 | 0.0 | 0.1 | 7.1 | 9.6 |
| Rest of East and South Asia | 0.6 | 2.3 | 0.7 | 4.3 | 9.6 | 1.4 | 11.2 | 2.7 |
| Latin America | 40.0 | 42.2 | 40.7 | 34.6 | 36.3 | 2.8 | 37.0 | 2.3 |
| Argentina | 12.4 | 8.1 | 10.9 | 15.1 | 116.8 | 7.4 | 103.5 | 13.8 |
| Brazil | 12.2 | 22.7 | 13.0 | 21.3 | 40.1 | 4.4 | 42.6 | 4.2 |
| Chile | 0.2 | 0.3 | 0.2 | 0.7 | 5.0 | 0.3 | 5.5 | 0.9 |
| Colombia | 5.0 | 2.1 | 5.0 | 1.2 | 53.5 | 2.7 | 53.5 | 1.5 |
| Ecuador | 2.6 | 2.9 | 2.9 | 1.7 | 113.1 | 11.4 | 126.0 | 6.7 |
| Mexico | −0.2 | 0.6 | 0.1 | −3.4 | −1.0 | 0.2 | 0.3 | −1.0 |
| Nicaragua | 0.0 | 0.0 | 0.0 | 0.1 | 3.0 | 1.4 | 2.4 | 2.3 |
| Rest of Latin America | 7.9 | 5.5 | 8.6 | −2.1 | 26.3 | 1.5 | 28.7 | −0.6 |
| Eastern Europe and Central Asia | −5.2 | 4.4 | −6.2 | 4.4 | −4.4 | 0.3 | −5.2 | 0.3 |
| Baltic States | −0.1 | 0.1 | −0.1 | 0.2 | −7.5 | 0.3 | −8.9 | 0.5 |
| Bulgaria | 0.3 | −0.1 | 0.4 | 0.1 | 5.1 | −0.4 | 5.6 | 0.3 |
| Czech Republic | −0.7 | 0.4 | −0.7 | −0.3 | −19.2 | 0.4 | −20.9 | −0.3 |

| | | | | | | | | |
|---|---|---|---|---|---|---|---|---|
| Hungary | −0.7 | 0.3 | −0.7 | −0.1 | −16.8 | 0.4 | −17.9 | −0.1 |
| Poland | −2.4 | 2.1 | −2.5 | 1.7 | −21.8 | 1.1 | −22.6 | 0.9 |
| Romania | −0.3 | 0.2 | −0.5 | 0.3 | −3.7 | 0.4 | −5.8 | 0.5 |
| Russian Federation | −2.2 | −0.7 | −2.3 | −1.3 | −6.3 | −0.2 | −6.6 | −0.3 |
| Slovak Republic | −0.1 | 0.1 | −0.1 | 0.1 | −11.8 | 0.2 | −13.5 | 0.4 |
| Slovenia | 0.0 | 0.1 | 0.0 | 0.1 | −9.2 | 0.4 | −11.1 | 0.4 |
| Kazakhstan | 0.5 | 0.4 | 0.5 | 0.5 | 23.1 | 1.1 | 23.0 | 1.2 |
| Turkey | −1.0 | 0.9 | −1.5 | 0.9 | −3.2 | 0.4 | −4.7 | 0.4 |
| Rest of Eastern Europe and Central Asia | 1.5 | 0.5 | 1.5 | 2.0 | 11.1 | 0.4 | 11.1 | 1.8 |
| High-income countries | −55.1 | 61.9 | −58.5 | 28.6 | −13.8 | 0.2 | −14.7 | 0.1 |
| Australia | 2.2 | 8.4 | 2.7 | 11.7 | 10.9 | 1.5 | 13.7 | 2.1 |
| Canada | 0.4 | 2.5 | 0.7 | −4.6 | 3.4 | 0.3 | 5.3 | −0.5 |
| EU15 | −42.9 | 16.7 | −47.4 | −45.9 | −23.0 | 0.2 | −25.4 | −0.4 |
| Japan | −7.6 | 4.5 | −7.6 | 93.2 | −16.7 | 0.1 | −16.8 | 2.3 |
| New Zealand | 2.7 | 4.1 | 2.7 | 4.4 | 57.7 | 5.0 | 57.2 | 5.4 |
| Rest of Western Europe | −3.6 | 6.5 | −3.6 | −8.4 | −25.8 | 1.0 | −25.8 | −1.3 |
| United States | −6.4 | 18.6 | −6.0 | −25.4 | −5.7 | 0.2 | −5.3 | −0.2 |
| Hong Kong, China; Singapore | 0.0 | 0.6 | 0.0 | 3.4 | 3.7 | 0.4 | 2.2 | 2.1 |
| Developing countries | 42.7 | 79.5 | 44.4 | 145.4 | 5.4 | 1.0 | 5.6 | 1.9 |
| North Africa | −0.1 | 3.9 | −0.3 | 1.4 | −0.4 | 1.8 | −1.1 | 0.8 |
| Sub-Saharan Africa | 0.2 | 1.2 | −0.6 | −2.2 | 0.3 | 0.3 | −0.8 | −0.5 |
| East Asia | 6.8 | 17.7 | 12.6 | 102.4 | 2.6 | 0.6 | 4.7 | 3.5 |
| South Asia | −8.2 | 6.7 | −10.7 | −2.1 | −5.1 | 1.1 | −6.7 | −0.3 |
| Latin America | 40.0 | 42.2 | 40.7 | 34.5 | 36.3 | 2.8 | 37.0 | 2.3 |
| Eastern Europe and Central Asia | −5.2 | 4.4 | −6.2 | 4.4 | −4.4 | 0.3 | −5.2 | 0.3 |
| World total | −12.4 | 141.4 | −14.2 | 174.2 | −1.0 | 0.4 | −1.2 | 0.5 |

*Source:* World Bank Linkage model simulations by the authors.

*Note:* The table shows results relative to the 2004 benchmark data. Ag = agriculture. Nonag = nonagriculture. EU15 = the 15 members of the European Union prior to 2004.

the sector from 144 to 153 percent). For India, the skilled-unskilled wage differential rises, as does skill-intensive goods and services production.

### The effects on poverty measured using the elasticities approach

The results for real factor rewards and net farm income suggest that inequality and poverty might be reduced globally through agricultural and trade policy liberalization. It is possible for us to take a step or two further in assessing the impacts of reform on poverty through a global model, even with only a single representative household per country. This involves using the elasticities approach, which is employed here in two ways. The first way focuses on the impact on real household income by applying an estimated income-to-poverty elasticity and then assessing the impacts on the poverty headcount index for each country. This simple approach assumes that there is distributional neutrality: the poor receive the same proportional increase in real income as the average household in the economy, and all are subject to the same higher rate of direct income taxation to replace the customs revenue forgone because of trade liberalization.

A slightly more complex, but more reasonable approach involves linking key model variables to the possible change in the average per capita consumption of the poor, that is, to capture from the model's results some of the distributional aspects of the changes in real income, rather than simply the average gain. We have accomplished this by calculating the change in the average (pretax) wage of unskilled workers, deflated by the food and clothing consumer price index. (Food and clothing prices are presumably the most relevant consumer items among the poor, including people in the many poor farm households and other rural households who earn most of their income from wages and are net buyers of food.) These workers are assumed to be exempt from the direct income tax imposed to replace the lost customs revenue following trade reform, a realistic assumption for many developing countries.[13]

Table 2.12 summarizes the key poverty results that emerge from the global reform scenario using these two approaches. As is clear from the comparison, the more naive first approach yields little change in poverty numbers. We therefore concentrate our attention here on the results generated using the more realistic second approach.

Under the full merchandise trade reform scenario, extreme poverty—the number of people surviving on less than US$1 a day—would drop in developing countries by 26 million relative to the baseline level of slightly under 1 billion, a reduction of 2.7 percent. The proportional reduction is much higher in China than in other developing countries, however: 3.7 compared with 2.6 percent. This would continue the trend of the recent past whereby China has been the region in which

**Table 2.12. The Poverty Effects of Full Global Liberalization of Merchandise Trade Reform, by Region, 2004**
*(number and percent)*

**a. The benchmark**

| Region | Benchmark US$1 a day | | Benchmark US$2 a day | | Poverty elasticities | |
|---|---|---|---|---|---|---|
| | Headcount, % | Number of poor, millions | Headcount, % | Number of poor, millions | US$1 a day | US$2 a day |
| East Asia | 9 | 169 | 37 | 684 | n.a. | n.a. |
| China | 10 | 128 | 35 | 452 | −1.9 | −1.3 |
| Other East Asia | 9 | 41 | 50 | 232 | −3.7 | −2.1 |
| South Asia | 31 | 446 | 77 | 1,116 | n.a. | n.a. |
| India | 34 | 371 | 80 | 868 | −1.1 | −0.5 |
| Other South Asia | 29 | 76 | 94 | 248 | −2.5 | −0.7 |
| Eastern Europe and Central Asia | 1 | 4 | 10 | 46 | −1.7 | −1.7 |
| Middle East and North Africa | 1 | 4 | 20 | 59 | −2.5 | −2.3 |
| Sub-Saharan Africa | 41 | 298 | 72 | 522 | −0.7 | −0.5 |
| Latin America | 9 | 47 | 22 | 121 | −1.7 | −1.1 |
| Developing-country total | 18 | 969 | 43 | 2,548 | n.a. | n.a. |
| Excluding China | 21 | 841 | 52 | 2,096 | n.a. | n.a. |

*(Table continues on the following page.)*

**Table 2.12. The Poverty Effects of Full Global Liberalization of Merchandise Trade Reform, by Region, 2004** (*continued*)

*(number and percent)*

b. All are assumed to obtain the average income gain

| Region | Average income change, real, % | US$1 a day | | US$2 a day | | Change in number of poor | |
|---|---|---|---|---|---|---|---|
| | | Headcount, % | Number of poor, millions | Headcount, % | Number of poor, millions | US$1 a day, millions | US$2 a day, millions |
| East Asia | 1.1 | 9 | 166 | 36 | 675 | −2.9 | −8.9 |
| China | 0.2 | 10 | 128 | 35 | 451 | −0.6 | −1.4 |
| Other East Asia | 1.9 | 8 | 38 | 49 | 224 | −2.3 | −7.5 |
| South Asia | −0.1 | 31 | 446 | 77 | 1,116 | 0.1 | 0.3 |
| India | −0.2 | 34 | 371 | 80 | 868 | 0.6 | 0.7 |
| Other South Asia | 0.3 | 29 | 75 | 94 | 248 | −0.5 | −0.4 |
| Eastern Europe and Central Asia | 1.2 | 1 | 4 | 10 | 45 | −0.1 | −1.0 |
| Middle East and North Africa | 0.7 | 1 | 4 | 19 | 58 | −0.1 | −1.0 |
| Sub-Saharan Africa | 0.0 | 41 | 298 | 72 | 522 | 0.0 | 0.0 |
| Latin America | 1.0 | 9 | 46 | 22 | 119 | −0.8 | −1.3 |
| Developing-country total | 0.9 | 18 | 966 | 47 | 2,536 | −3.7 | −12.0 |
| Excluding China | 1.1 | 21 | 838 | 51 | 2,085 | −3.1 | −10.6 |

**c. The gain in the real earnings of unskilled workers**

| Region | Average income change, real,[a] % | US$1 a day | | US$2 a day | | Change in number of poor | |
|---|---|---|---|---|---|---|---|
| | | Headcount, % | Number of poor, millions | Headcount, % | Number of poor, millions | US$1 a day, millions | US$2 a day, millions |
| East Asia | 4.4 | 8 | 151 | 34 | 632 | −17 | −52 |
| China | 2.1 | 9 | 123 | 34 | 440 | −5 | −12 |
| Other East Asia | 8.1 | 6 | 29 | 42 | 192 | −12 | −40 |
| South Asia | −1.9 | 32 | 454 | 78 | 1,124 | 8 | 8 |
| India | −3.8 | 36 | 386 | 82 | 883 | 15 | 15 |
| Other South Asia | 4.0 | 26 | 68 | 92 | 241 | −8 | −7 |
| Eastern Europe and Central Asia | 4.5 | 1 | 4 | 9 | 43 | −0 | −4 |
| Middle East and North Africa | 14.3 | 1 | 3 | 13 | 40 | −2 | −19 |
| Sub-Saharan Africa | 5.3 | 39 | 287 | 70 | 508 | −11 | −14 |
| Latin America | 4.1 | 8 | 44 | 21 | 115 | −3 | −6 |
| Developing-country total | 5.9 | 18 | 944 | 46 | 2,462 | −26 | −87 |
| Excluding China | 6.5 | 20 | 820 | 50 | 2,022 | −21 | −74 |

*Source:* World Bank Linkage model simulations by the authors.

*Note:* n.a. = not applicable.

a. Nominal unskilled wage deflated by the food and clothing consumer price index.

poverty reduction has been most numerous (see Chen and Ravallion 2007, 2008). Nonetheless, in this scenario, the number of the extreme poor in Sub-Saharan Africa would fall by 3.7 percent. In India (though not in the rest of South Asia), by contrast, we estimate that the number of the extreme poor would climb by 4.0 percent.

Recall that this set of poverty calculations is based on the change in the real wage of unskilled workers, deflated by the food and clothing consumer price index. The average change in real unskilled wages across all developing countries is 5.9 percent, which is six times greater than the average net income increase in developing countries, after accounting for a rise in direct taxes to offset the loss in tariff revenues and assuming that the change in unskilled wages is fully passed through to households. This suggests that such a reform would deliver a marked average reduction in income inequality within developing countries.

Under the broader definition of poverty (a subsistence threshold of no more than US$2 a day), the number of poor in developing countries would fall by 87 million under the full reform scenario relative to the aggregate baseline level of nearly 2.5 billion poor. This represents a somewhat larger proportionate reduction in the number of poor in developing countries, by 3.4 percent, or 3.7 percent if China is excluded. The proportionate decline in Sub-Saharan Africa is 2.7 percent, while, in India, there is an increase by 1.7 percent.

## Caveats

As with all modeling, our results depend on our assumptions in structuring the model. Several assumptions place a downward bias on our estimates of the welfare gains arising from trade. They include the assumptions that returns to scale are constant (rather than increasing), that there are no productivity effects of reform (for example, of the sort stressed by Melitz 2003), and that there is no possibility for the creation of new markets following reform. There is also always the issue of product and regional aggregation: the less disaggregated the specification of the world economy, the smaller the estimated benefits of reform. This is because there is no accounting for welfare gains from adjustments within aggregated sectors or regions.

As for the effects on poverty, the crude methodology used at the end of the previous subsection is meant simply as a beginning in our examination of the poverty consequences of global trade reform. The results of global reform that we have identified based on the Linkage model and presented above are used in the next chapter, in association with microsimulation survey data on individual countries, to assess the effects on the distribution of income across and within 101 countries. Bussolo, De Hoyos, and Medvedev, the authors of the next chapter, are thus able to identify much more precisely the inequality and poverty effects worldwide of the policies as of 2004. In parts III–V, in individual developing-country case studies, authors examine—also with the help of national microsimulation survey data—the effects of own-country policies, but also the effects of policies in the rest of the world. The border price and export demand shocks associated with rest-of-the-world liberalization are almost the same as those outlined above. The only difference is that, for each of the countries in the case studies, a separate global simulation has been run that excludes the reforms undertaken by the countries under examination. The border shocks in all the case studies are reported in the appendix.

## Conclusions

The findings presented above are aimed at indicating the global economic effects of the agricultural and trade policies in place as of 2004. They may be summarized as follows:

- As a share of national income, developing countries would gain nearly twice as much as high-income countries by removing the policies (an average increase of 0.9 percent compared with 0.5 percent, respectively), thereby reducing income inequality across countries.
- Even intercountry inequality (not taking into account differences in the economic size of nations) as measured by the Gini coefficient would improve slightly, although some developing countries (notably in South Asia) would lose, and a few (for example, Ecuador) would gain many times more than the average.
- Of the prospective welfare gains from global liberalization, 60 percent would be generated by agricultural and food policy reform, which is a striking result given that the shares of agriculture and food in global GDP and global merchandise trade are less than 9 percent.
- The contribution of agricultural policy reform to the prospective welfare gain in developing countries is even greater, at 83 percent.
- Through the full liberalization of the trade in goods, the share of exports in the global production of farm products would rise from 8 to 13 percent (excluding intra–European Union trade), thereby thickening international food markets and reducing the price fluctuations and the instability in the quantities traded on these markets.
- Unskilled workers in developing countries—the majority of whom work on farms—would benefit most from reform, followed by skilled workers and then capital owners. The average change in the real unskilled wage across all

developing countries would rise 3.8 percent or nearly five times more than the average increase in net incomes in developing countries.

- Net farm incomes in developing countries would rise by 5.6 percent, compared with 1.9 percent for nonagricultural value added, suggesting that inequality between farm and nonfarm households in developing countries would fall.
- In contrast, in high-income countries, net farm incomes would fall by 15 percent on average (compared with a slight rise in real nonfarm value added). So, inequality between farm households in these countries and farm households in developing countries would decline substantially.
- The number of people in extreme poverty—the number surviving on less than US$1 a day—in developing countries would drop by 26 million relative to the baseline level of slightly under 1 billion, a reduction of 3 percent (4 percent if the more moderate US$2-a-day poverty level is used).

To obtain a more precise sense of the inequality and poverty effects within countries and to explore the extent to which own-country policies rather than rest-of world policies are causing the harm, we need country case studies using national economy-wide models that are enhanced through the inclusion of detailed earning and expenditure information on numerous types of urban and rural households. This is the purpose of parts III–V.

## Notes

1. This distortions database is documented fully in Anderson and Valenzuela (2008). It is based on the methodology summarized in Anderson et al. (2008a, 2008b).

2. Some of the questions raised here have been addressed by Anderson, Martin, and van der Mensbrugghe (2006a, 2006b), who use the same Linkage model we use in the present analysis, and by Anderson and Valenzuela (2007a), who use the GTAP-AGR model. However, in each case, these authors have relied on the GTAP version 6 protection database for 2001, which includes only the applied import tariffs in developing countries.

3. In principle, service trade and foreign investment distortions may also affect incentives in the agricultural and industrial sectors, but they are ignored here because much controversy still surrounds the measurement of these distortions and the way they should be modeled. This is reflected in the widely differing results emerging from attempts to include service distortions in trade reform modeling. Compare, for example, Brown, Deardorff, and Stern (2003); Francois, van Meijl, and van Tongeren (2005); and Hertel and Keeney (2006).

4. We have no new distortion estimates for countries in the Middle East; so, in what follows, we give little attention to this small and relatively affluent part of the global agricultural economy.

5. More information on the MAcMaps database is available in Bouët et al. (2008) and at http://www.cepii.fr/anglaisgraph/bdd/macmap.htm. For details on the incorporation of the database into the GTAP version 7 data set, see Narayanan and Walmsley (2008).

6. Using the GTAP version 6 protection database for 2001, Anderson, Martin, and Valenzuela (2006) find that agricultural production and export subsidies together contributed only 7 percent of the global welfare cost of agricultural protection.

7. The size of the Armington elasticities is important; see Valenzuela, Anderson, and Hertel (2008) and Zhang and Osborne (2009). The Linkage model assumes larger values relative to some other

models because it is seeking to estimate the long-run consequences of liberalization. An example of the differences this may generate in the results is detailed in Anderson and Martin (2006, table 12A.2).

8. The more affluent economies of Hong Kong, China and of Singapore are in our high-income category, but, since they have trade policies that approximate free trade policies and almost no farm production anyway, their influence on the results is not noticeable.

9. The model also does not include any divergences between the private and social marginal costs and the benefits that might arise from externalities, market failures, and other behind-the-border policies not represented in our amended GTAP protection database. These omissions may affect the welfare estimates in either direction.

10. The only other policy change is the removal of the export taxes on nonfarm products in Argentina. We do this because these taxes were introduced at the same time (at the end of 2001) and for the same reason (so the government might gain the support of the urban poor) as the country's export taxes on farm products.

11. This would continue a process that began in the 1980s when many countries began to reform their trade and exchange rate regimes. Using the same Linkage model and database as the present study, Valenzuela, van der Mensbrugghe, and Anderson (2009) find that the global reforms between 1980–84 and 2004 also boosted economic welfare proportionately more in developing countries than in high-income economies (by 1.0 percent compared with 0.7 percent, respectively).

12. The Gini coefficient is a measure of intercountry inequality in the Milanovic (2005) sense, whereby each country is treated as a single observation without regard to the economic size of the country. The measure is calculated using the 60 regions and Deaton's Gini coefficient calculation:

$$ G = \frac{N+1}{N-1} - \frac{2}{N(N-1)u} (\Sigma_{i=1}^{n} P_i X_i) $$

where $N$ is the number of regions, $u$ is the sample average GDP, $P_i$ is the GDP sample rank (setting the highest at 1 and the lowest at $N$), and $X_i$ is the GDP of country $i$.

13. Even if the fiscal closure affects a domestic sales or value added tax instead of direct taxes on households, food is exempt from taxation in many countries, or the tax is difficult to collect in practice because of the informal nature of many food markets.

# References

Anderson, K., ed. 2009. *Distortions to Agricultural Incentives: A Global Perspective, 1955–2007*. London: Palgrave Macmillan; Washington, DC: World Bank.

Anderson, K., and Y. Hayami, eds. 1986. *The Political Economy of Agricultural Protection: East Asia in International Perspective*. Sydney: Allen and Unwin.

Anderson, K., M. Kurzweil, W. Martin, D. Sandri, and E. Valenzuela. 2008a. "Methodology for Measuring Distortions to Agricultural Incentives." In *Distortions to Agricultural Incentives: A Global Perspective, 1955–2007*, ed. K. Anderson, Appendix A. London: Palgrave Macmillan; Washington, DC: World Bank.

———. 2008b. "Measuring Distortions to Agricultural Incentives, Revisited." *World Trade Review* 7 (4): 1–30.

Anderson, K., and W. Martin, eds. 2006. *Agricultural Trade Reform and the Doha Development Agenda*. London: Palgrave Macmillan; Washington, DC: World Bank.

Anderson, K., W. Martin, and D. van der Mensbrugghe. 2006a. "Distortions to World Trade: Impacts on Agricultural Markets and Incomes." *Review of Agricultural Economics* 28 (2): 168–94.

———. 2006b. "Market and Welfare Implications of the Doha Reform Scenarios." In *Agricultural Trade Reform and the Doha Development Agenda*, ed. K. Anderson and W. Martin, chap. 12. London: Palgrave Macmillan; Washington, DC: World Bank.

Anderson, K., W. Martin, and E. Valenzuela. 2006. "The Relative Importance of Global Agricultural Subsidies and Market Access." *World Trade Review* 5 (3): 357–76.

Anderson, K., and E. Valenzuela. 2007a. "Do Global Trade Distortions Still Harm Developing Country Farmers?" *Review of World Economics* 143 (1): 108–39.

———. 2007b. "The World Trade Organization's Doha Cotton Initiative: A Tale of Two Issues." *World Economy* 30 (8): 1281–1304.

———. 2008. "Estimates of Global Distortions to Agricultural Incentives, 1955–2007." Data spreadsheet, October, World Bank, Washington, DC. http://go.worldbank.org/YAO39F35E0.

Bautista, R. M., S. Robinson, P. Wobst, and F. Tarp. 2001. "Policy Bias and Agriculture: Partial and General Equilibrium Measures." *Review of Development Economics* 5 (1): 89–104.

Bouët, A., Y. Decreux, L. Fontagné, S. Jean, and D. Laborde. 2008. "Assessing Applied Protection across the World." *Review of International Economics* 16 (5): 850–63.

Brown, D. K., A. V. Deardorff, and R. M. Stern. 2003. "Multilateral, Regional, and Bilateral Trade-Policy Options for the United States and Japan." *World Economy* 26 (6): 803–28.

Chen, S., and M. Ravallion. 2007. "Absolute Poverty Measures for the Developing World, 1981–2004." Policy Research Working Paper 4211, World Bank, Washington, DC.

———. 2008. "The Developing World Is Poorer Than We Thought, but No Less Successful in the Fight against Poverty." Policy Research Working Paper 4703, World Bank, Washington, DC.

Dimaranan, B. D., ed. 2006. *Global Trade, Assistance, and Protection: The GTAP 6 Data Base*. West Lafayette, IN: Center for Global Trade Analysis, Department of Agricultural Economics, Purdue University. https://www.gtap.agecon.purdue.edu/databases/v6/v6_doco.asp.

Francois, J. F., H. van Meijl, and F. van Tongeren. 2005. "Trade Liberalization in the Doha Development Round." *Economic Policy* 20 (42): 349–91.

Hertel, T. W., ed. 1997. *Global Trade Analysis: Modeling and Applications*. New York: Cambridge University Press.

Hertel, T. W., and R. Keeney. 2006. "What's at Stake: The Relative Importance of Import Barriers, Export Subsidies, and Domestic Support." In *Agricultural Trade Reform and the Doha Development Agenda*, ed. K. Anderson and W. Martin, chap. 2. London: Palgrave Macmillan; Washington, DC: World Bank.

Jensen, H. T., S. Robinson, and F. Tarp. 2002. "General Equilibrium Measures of Agricultural Policy Bias in Fifteen Developing Countries." TMD Discussion Paper 105, Trade and Macroeconomics Division, International Food Policy Research Institute, Washington, DC.

Johnson, D. G. 1991. *World Agriculture in Disarray*, rev. ed. London: St. Martin's Press.

Krueger, A. O., M. Schiff, and A. Valdés. 1988. "Agricultural Incentives in Developing Countries: Measuring the Effect of Sectoral and Economy-wide Policies." *World Bank Economic Review* 2 (3): 255–72.

Malcolm, G. 1998. "Adjusting Tax Rates in the GTAP Data Base." GTAP Technical Paper 12 (September), Center for Global Trade Analysis, Department of Agricultural Economics, Purdue University, West Lafayette, IN. https://www.gtap.agecon.purdue.edu/resources/download/580.pdf.

Melitz, M. 2003. "The Impact of Trade on Intra-industry Reallocations and Aggregate Industry Productivity." *Econometrica* 71 (6): 1692–1725.

Milanovic, B. 2005. *Worlds Apart: Measuring International and Global Inequality*. Princeton, NJ: Princeton University Press.

Narayanan, B. G., and T. L. Walmsley, eds. 2008. *Global Trade, Assistance, and Production: The GTAP 7 Data Base*. West Lafayette, IN: Center for Global Trade Analysis, Department of Agricultural Economics, Purdue University. https://www.gtap.agecon.purdue.edu/databases/v7/v7_doco.asp.

Valenzuela, E., and K. Anderson. 2008. "Alternative Agricultural Price Distortions for CGE Analysis of Developing Countries, 2004 and 1980–84." Research Memorandum 13 (December), Center for Global Trade Analysis, Department of Agricultural Economics, Purdue University, West Lafayette, IN. https://www.gtap.agecon.purdue.edu/resources/res_display.asp?RecordID=2925.

Valenzuela, E., K. Anderson, and T. W. Hertel. 2008. "Impacts of Trade Reform: Sensitivity of Model Results to Key Assumptions." *International Economics and Economic Policy* 4 (4): 395–420.

Valenzuela, E., D. van der Mensbrugghe, and K. Anderson. 2009. "General Equilibrium Effects of Price Distortions on Global Markets, Farm Incomes, and Welfare." In *Distortions to Agricultural Incentives: A Global Perspective, 1955–2007*, ed. K. Anderson, chap. 13. London: Palgrave Macmillan; Washington, DC: World Bank.

van der Mensbrugghe, D. 2005. "Linkage Technical Reference Document: Version 6.0." December, World Bank, Washington, DC. http://go.worldbank.org/7NP2KK1OH0.

———. 2006. "Estimating the Benefits: Why Numbers Change." In *Trade, Doha, and Development: A Window into the Issues*, ed. R. Newfarmer, 59–75. Washington, DC: World Bank.

World Bank. 2001. *Global Economic Prospects 2002: Making Trade Work for the World's Poor.* Washington, DC: World Bank.

———. 2003. *Global Economic Prospects 2004: Realizing the Development Promise of the Doha Agenda.* Washington, DC: World Bank.

———. 2004. *Global Economic Prospects 2005: Trade, Regionalism, and Development.* Washington, DC: World Bank.

———. 2005. *Global Economic Prospects 2006: Economic Implications of Remittances and Migration.* Washington, DC: World Bank.

———. 2006. *Global Economic Prospects 2007: Managing the Next Wave of Globalization.* Washington, DC: World Bank.

———. 2007. *World Development Report 2008: Agriculture for Development*, Washington, DC: World Bank.

Zhang, X. G., and M. Osborne. 2009. "Developing an Armington-Heckscher-Ohlin Database: Splitting Global Trade (GTAP) Data into Homogeneous and Differentiated Products." Internal Research Memorandum 09-02 (January), Productivity Commission, Melbourne.

# 3

# GLOBAL POVERTY AND DISTRIBUTIONAL IMPACTS: THE GIDD MODEL

*Maurizio Bussolo, Rafael De Hoyos,*
*and Denis Medvedev*[*]

Trade liberalization is almost always welfare increasing nationally and globally, but it also brings about large redistributions of income. Simulation models calibrated on real world data show that the aggregate gains for a country that eliminates tariffs are, at best, within only a few percentage points of the initial GDP. Similarly, the gains from multilateral trade policy reforms for the whole world tend to be small. In contrast, the losses suffered by specific, initially protected sectors or factors may be much larger. As Rodrik (1998) puts it, the static efficiency consequences of trade reform pale in comparison with the redistributive effects.

These effects often create complicated policy challenges at domestic and international levels because, in most cases, losers tend to be a smaller and more vocal group than winners.[1] Perhaps the most recent and glaring example of this trade-related distributional tension is the impasse in the Doha Round of the World Trade Organization. Disputes over the reduction of agricultural market distortions have stalled the entire multilateral trade negotiation process. The controversy is centered on the demands of developing and agricultural exporting countries to phase out export subsidies and domestic farm supports that are mainly applied in developed countries, in addition to the reduction of import barriers.

This example illustrates that a distributional tension among countries may have important implications for international relations and global welfare. An

*The authors are grateful to Rebecca Lessem for research assistance and to Will Martin, Hans Timmer, and Dominique van der Mensbrugghe for discussions on the issues.

**87**

additional question is this: would resolving trade disputes improve the distribution of income not only between countries, but also within national economies? The answer depends, in part, on own-country distortions to agricultural and other producer incentives in individual developing countries. Frequently, the related policies privilege urban dwellers by protecting urban industries and maintaining low prices for food items, which works to the disadvantage of (often) poorer local farmers, although this is much less so now than it was in the 1960s and 1970s (Krueger, Schiff, and Valdés 1988; Anderson 2009). Given that poverty is greatest among farmers, the poverty reduction potential of agricultural trade liberalization is promising (Chen and Ravallion 2007).

Using an ex ante simulation analysis, this chapter answers the following questions: How much would global inequality and poverty be reduced if all distortions to trade in agricultural and other goods were removed? How much of this change would be generated by agricultural policy reform only? What share of the change in inequality would arise from changes across countries versus changes within countries (one should bear in mind that a lowering of the inequality between agricultural and nonagricultural groups might be offset by, for example, increased inequality within the agricultural sector)? What would happen to global poverty and to the incidence of poverty in specific countries and regions? Does it matter whether we use the US$1-a-day or US$2-a-day international poverty line (because, for example, more nonagricultural households than farm households may be clustered between these two poverty lines)?

The empirical results of the study represented in this chapter have been produced using the World Bank's Linkage global general equilibrium model and the newly developed Global Income Distribution Dynamics tool (GIDD) (van der Mensbrugghe 2005; Bussolo, De Hoyos, and Medvedev 2008; see also the GIDD Database). The GIDD is a framework for ex ante analysis of the income distributional and poverty effects of changes in macroeconomic, trade, and sectoral policies and trends in global markets. It complements a global computable general equilibrium (CGE) analysis by providing global microsimulations based on standardized household surveys. The tool pools most of the currently available household surveys covering 1.2 million households in 73 developing countries. Information on households in developed countries completes the data set. Overall, the GIDD sample countries cover more than 90 percent of the world's population.[2]

The chapter is organized as follows. The next section presents the GIDD data set and the main features of global income distribution as a way of establishing the initial conditions or baseline. This descriptive analysis sets the stage for the subsequent sections, which illustrate the modeling methodology, lay out the reform scenarios, and summarize the main results. The two core simulations involve the case of the liberalization of all merchandise trade and agricultural domestic distortions and—to examine the contribution of farm and food policies—the case of the liberalization of only agricultural trade and domestic price-distorting measures. Final remarks are provided in the concluding section.

## What Is at Stake? The Initial Conditions

Almost 45 percent of the world's people, most of them in developing countries, live in households in which agricultural activities represent the main occupation of the heads of household. A large share of this agriculture-dependent group, close to 32 percent, is poor. Agricultural households thus contribute disproportionably to global poverty: three of every four poor people belong to this group. Improving the economic opportunities available in agriculture may therefore significantly affect global poverty and inequality. The specific opportunity considered in this study is the removal of agricultural subsidies and taxes and all merchandise trade distortions. The direct effects of this global liberalization would include changes in the international prices of food and other agricultural products and changes in the returns to the factors used intensively in agriculture. These changes would determine the winners and losers of reform through the impacts on household earnings and spending.

Before examining these effects in detail, this section describes the stakes involved in the reforms by considering the socioeconomic characteristics of the world's population, especially the people engaged in agriculture. This initial descriptive analysis is based on the GIDD data set that has been recently developed at the World Bank. The data set consists of 73 detailed household surveys on low- and middle-income countries, complemented by more highly aggregated information on income distribution among 25 high-income countries and 22 other developing countries.[3] Together, the 120 countries in the data set cover more than 90 percent of the global population. The country coverage varies by region: while the countries in the GIDD data set represent more than 97 percent of the population in East Asia, South Asia, Latin America, and Eastern Europe and Central Asia, the coverage in Sub-Saharan Africa and in the Middle East and North Africa is limited to 76 and 58 percent of the population, respectively. Among the detailed surveys, the majority (54) rely on per capita consumption as the main indicator of welfare, while the remaining surveys—all but one are on countries in Latin America—rely on per capita income alone as a measure of household welfare. The income and consumption data are monthly; the data are standardized to the year 2000 and are expressed in 1993 purchasing power parity (PPP) prices for consistency with the US$1-a-day and US$2-a-day poverty lines, which are calculated at 1993 PPP exchange rates.[4]

**Figure 3.1. Income Distributions among Agricultural and Nonagricultural Populations of the World, 2000**

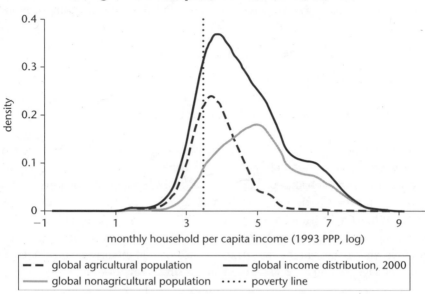

*Source:* Author compilation based on the GIDD Database.

*Note:* See the text for an explanation of the figure.

Three facts about the agricultural sector help identify the welfare effects of a global-scale removal of trade distortions: the proportion of the world's people whose real incomes depend on the agricultural sector, the initial position of the agricultural population in the global income distribution, and the dispersion of incomes among the agricultural population.

Based on the GIDD data set, figure 3.1 shows a kernel density of the global income distribution of household per capita income and consumption and kernel densities of the income and consumption of the population inside and outside the agricultural sector.[5] The area below the kernel density for the agricultural sector is equal to 0.45, indicating that 45 percent of the world population relies on agriculture for their livelihoods. The distribution of the agricultural population is located to the left of the nonagricultural distribution, implying that households in the agricultural sector earn, on average, lower incomes than their counterparts in other sectors. In U.S. PPP dollars, the average agricultural household's per capita monthly income is US$65, only 20 percent of the US$320 per capita income earned by the average household in the nonagricultural group. The differences in the shapes of the two distributions corroborate the hypothesis of Kuznets more than 50 years ago that incomes in the traditional sector are less well dispersed than incomes in the modern sectors. A more egalitarian traditional sector is indicated by the taller and thinner distribution for the agricultural population in figure 3.1.

Income inequality is estimated based on the global income distribution data depicted in figure 3.1. The Gini coefficient for the world is equal to 0.67, which denotes a high level of inequality. In fact, this global Gini is about 0.28 points higher (worse) than the Gini of the United Sates and even higher than the level observed in extremely unequal countries such as Mexico. As Bourguignon, Levin, and Rosenblatt (2004: 15) note, "if the world [were] a country, it would be one of the most unequal countries in the world." How much of this inequality may be explained by the disparity in average incomes between the agricultural group and the rest? Inequality decomposition analysis shows that one-quarter of the global income disparities may be explained by the difference in average incomes between the two groups of households; the remaining three-quarters are generated by within-group income variation.

Based on the preestablished poverty line of US$1 a day in PPP dollars, the GIDD global income data also provide information about the differences in poverty incidence among the two population subgroups. Despite the fact that incomes are more evenly distributed among the agricultural population (the Gini coefficient is 0.10 points lower in agriculture than in nonagriculture), lower average incomes in this sector result in a much higher poverty incidence: 32 percent of agricultural households are poor compared with 8 percent of nonagricultural households.

In terms of the personal characteristics of the poor inside and outside the agricultural sector, no noticeable differences are observed in the average age of the heads of household or in the household size. However, poor people in agriculture tend to have lower educational attainment: only 32 percent have completed primary education compared with 46 percent among nonfarm households. In agriculture, poor woman-headed households are a small minority, less than 9 percent, which is significantly below the 14 percent observed among nonagricultural households (table 3.1).

Up to this point, our welfare information on agricultural and nonagricultural populations has been derived by agglomerating all households within these two groups irrespective of nationality. In fact, the kernel densities in figure 3.1 exploit

**Table 3.1. Characteristics of the Poor in Agricultural and Nonagricultural Households, Developing Countries, 2000**

| Household type | Population share, % | Head of household completed primary school, % | Age of household head, average years | Household members, average number | Woman-headed households, % |
|---|---|---|---|---|---|
| Agricultural | 44.8 | 32.3 | 44.8 | 7.11 | 8.7 |
| Nonagricultural | 55.2 | 46.0 | 44.4 | 7.06 | 14.0 |

*Source:* Author compilation based on the GIDD Database.

**Figure 3.2. Relationship between Income Levels and Share of Employment in Agriculture, by Country, 2000**

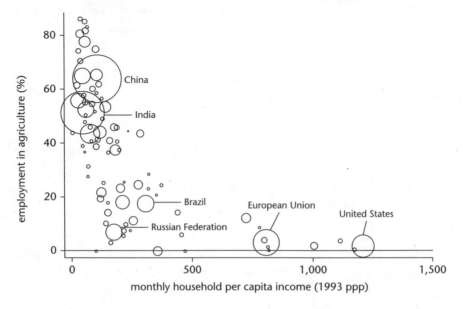

*Source:* Author compilation based on the GIDD Database.

*Note:* Area of symbol proportional to the country's population.

full income heterogeneity across households, including variations across and within countries. Countries display large differences in terms of population size, level of development, and the importance of the agricultural sector in the economy. These three country-specific characteristics are important determinants in any prospective change in global poverty and global inequality. As we may see in figure 3.2, global poverty would be strongly reduced if China and India were to achieve higher income levels. Given the initial large share of these countries in the global population and their position in the global income distribution, the economic expansion of these two giants is a key factor shaping the evolution of the world economy.[6] Figure 3.2 also depicts a negative relationship between income levels and the share of workers in agriculture, and, although it is imperfectly inferred from a cross-section of countries at a particular point in time, this relationship suggests that structural shifts would likely affect income distribution within countries. Figure 3.3 shows this heterogeneity by displaying, for each county in our sample, the shares of agriculture in total population and in national income. Given the large variation in the proportion of the population for which the incomes depend on the agricultural sector, the income effects following a

## Figure 3.3. Share of the Population in Agriculture and of Agriculture in Total Income, Developing Countries, 2000

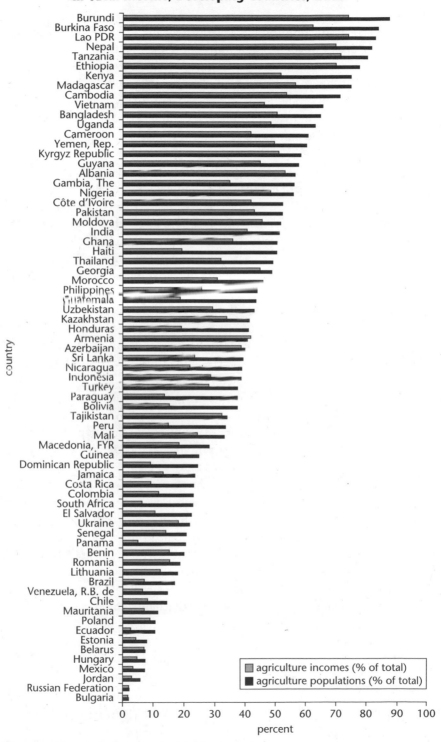

*Source:* Author compilation based on the GIDD Database.

*Note:* The figure is based on the data set for developing countries and transition economies.

removal of agricultural distortions would differ greatly between countries and be especially important in countries in which more than half the population is in agriculture. The majority of these agriculture-based countries are located in the poorest region of the world, namely, Sub-Saharan Africa. Of the 25 countries in the agriculture-based group, 12 are in Sub-Saharan Africa, 4 are in South Asia, 3 are in East Asia, 3 are in Eastern Europe and Central Asia, 2 are in Latin America (Guyana and Haiti), and only 1 (the Republic of Yemen) is in the Middle East and North Africa.

The pattern observed at the global level, namely, that agriculture-dependent households, on average, earn less than other households, is replicated in all developing countries in the GIDD Database (figure 3.3); the share of the total population employed in agricultural activities is always larger than the share of this population in total income. The average income of nonagricultural households is 2.25 times greater than the average agricultural household income. This difference is unconditional in the sense it does not take into account the fact that, in agriculture, low-earning unskilled workers tend to be more abundant than skilled workers or that other factors may explain the observed income gap. However, we have undertaken a simple multivariate regression analysis on the GIDD data set, and it shows that, even controlling for education, age, gender, household size, geographic region, and country fixed-effects, agriculture-related incomes are still 23 percent lower than incomes derived from other sectors.

An important element hidden in figure 3.1 and only partially shown in figure 3.3 is the degree of cross-country variation in income inequality. Figure 3.4 shows that the differences in the Gini coefficient across countries are enormous. Former centrally planned economies such as Hungary, Romania, and Ukraine show a coefficient below 0.3, whereas, in South Africa and much of Latin America, the coefficient reaches values well above 0.5. Once again, the tendency toward higher inequality within the agricultural group observed at the global level is corroborated by analysis of country-specific inequality. For more than three-quarters of the countries included in our data (56 of 73), Gini indicators of inequality within the agricultural group are higher than those within the nonagricultural group (figure 3.4).

A global trade reform would be expected to reallocate resources intersectorally within national states and between them. Given the global variations in the importance of the agricultural sector, the ratio of nonagricultural to agricultural incomes, and the within-sector income inequality, the resource reallocation following the trade reform would have significant distributional effects across and within countries. Is economic theory able to provide guidance on the expected global welfare effects after the removal of agricultural distortions and other trade distortions?

As shown by Winters (2002) and McCulloch, Winters, and Cirera (2001), trade liberalization and household welfare are linked via prices, factor markets, and

# Figure 3.4. Inequality Variation in Agricultural, Nonagricultural, and All Households, Developing Countries, 2000

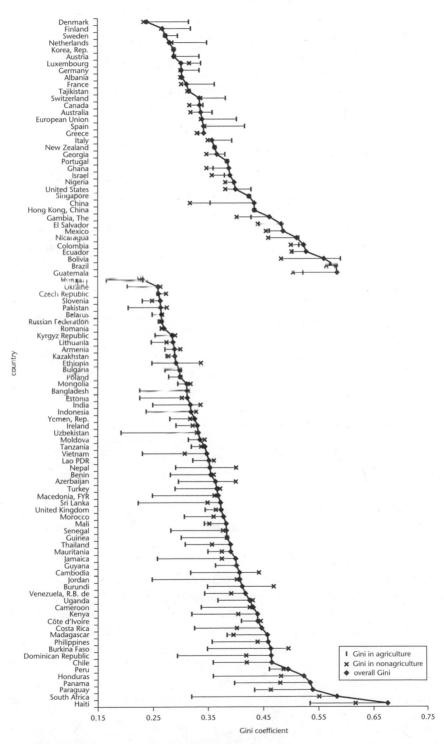

Source: Author compilation based on the GIDD Database.

consumer preferences. The international prices of many agricultural products would increase after the removal of trade barriers (see chapter 2, by Anderson, Valenzuela, and van der Mensbrugghe; see also Anderson and Martin 2005). If we assume some degree of pass-through, the increase in international prices would be followed by a rise in domestic agricultural prices, which would encourage a redistribution of resources from nonagricultural activities to the agricultural sector of the economy. Based on figure 3.1, this redistribution might help reduce global poverty and inequality. However, household consumption patterns would also change as a result of the shift in prices, making the link between trade liberalization and global household welfare more complex. As a consequence of the agricultural price changes, a redistribution of real income would take place between *net* sellers and *net* buyers of agricultural products; the welfare of the former would improve at the expense of the welfare of the latter.[7] Finally, factor prices would also change after trade liberalization, thus changing the real incomes of households that are not directly involved in agricultural production.

The transition from trade theory to real world analysis presents serious challenges. A sound empirical strategy must estimate the effects of the reform on prices, monetary incomes (via profits in the case of farm households and returns to factors of production in the case of nonfarm households), consumption, and transfers.[8] The framework used in this chapter and described in more detail below accounts for the impact of trade liberalization through at least some of these channels.

## Methodology

The empirical analysis in this chapter relies on the GIDD Database, a newly developed tool for analyzing the dynamics of global income distribution.[9] Compiled by the Development Prospects Group of the World Bank, the GIDD combines a consistent set of price and volume changes from a global CGE model with microdata at the household level to create a hypothetical or counterfactual income distribution capturing the welfare effects of policies under evaluation.[10] The GIDD therefore has the ability to map CGE-consistent macroeconomic outcomes to disaggregated household survey data.

The GIDD framework is based on microsimulation methodologies developed in the recent literature, including Bourguignon and Pereira da Silva (2003), Ferreira and Leite (2003, 2004), Chen and Ravallion (2003), and Bussolo, Lay, and van der Mensbrugghe (2006). The starting point is the global income distribution in 2000, which has been assembled using data from household surveys (see above).[11] The hypothetical distribution is then obtained by applying three main exogenous changes to the initial distribution: changes in relative wages across skills and sectors for each country, changes in household purchasing power

**Figure 3.5. The GIDD Methodological Framework**

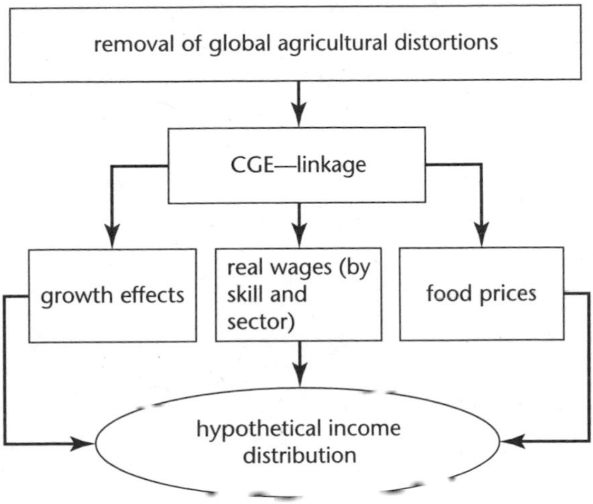

Source: Construction by the authors.

caused by shifts in food prices and other prices, and changes in the average level of welfare (real income) for each country.

The methodological framework used here is depicted in figure 3.5. The starting point is the price and quantity effects after the removal of trade distortions; one computes these by using the global CGE Linkage model (top part of figure 3.5). The CGE model will compute the values of the three variables linking the macro- and microlevels of the model (middle part of figure 3.5): overall economic growth, real wage premiums among agricultural and nonagricultural and skilled and unskilled groups, and the consumption (or real income) effects brought about by the change in the relative prices of food. These CGE results are passed on to the household survey data, creating a new, hypothetical household income distribution (bottom part of figure 3.5). This is accomplished by differentiating four types of households: those in which the household head is an: (1) unskilled agricultural worker, (2) skilled agricultural worker, (3) unskilled nonagricultural worker, or (4) skilled nonagricultural worker. The initial income premium earned by groups (2)–(4) relative to group (1) is changed in accordance with changes in the wage premiums in the CGE model, which uses the GIDD information on a number of workers in each of the segments (1)–(4). For example, if, initially, a household headed by an unskilled worker in nonagriculture earns 50 percent more than a household headed by an unskilled worker in agriculture and if the CGE results show that this premium would decline by a tenth, the microsimulation part of the GIDD changes the incomes of all households headed by unskilled workers in nonagriculture such that the new wage premium is 45 percent. In addition to these wage shocks, the GIDD also accounts for changes in relative prices and changes in per capita incomes, thereby indirectly picking up the impact on the returns to factors other than labor.

In the real world, the changes depicted in figure 3.5 take place simultaneously, but, in the GIDD simplified framework, they are accommodated in a sequential fashion. In the first step, changes in labor remuneration by skill level and sectoral location are applied to each household in the sample, depending on educational attainment and sector of employment. In the second step, consistent with an overall growth rate of real income per capita, real household incomes are affected by the change in the prices of food items versus the prices of nonfood; households with a higher share of household income allocated to food consumption bear a larger proportional impact after a change in the prices of food.

Comparisons between the initial and the counterfactual income distributions capture the welfare and inequality effects of the removal of global trade distortions. By taking into account labor market effects (returns to skills in the agricultural sector and in the rest of the economy) and consumption effects, the GIDD framework closely maps the theoretical links outlined in the previous section.[12] However, the framework reshapes national income distributions under a set of strong assumptions. In particular, income inequality within population subgroups formed by skills and by sector of employment is assumed to remain constant after the trade reform. Moreover, data limitations affect the estimates of the initial inequality and of the evolution of inequality. Although consumption expenditure is a more reliable welfare measure than income and although its distribution is normally more equal than the distribution of income, consumption data are not available in all country surveys. To obtain a global picture, we have been obliged to include countries for which only income data are available, along with countries for which consumption information is available. Finally, measurement errors implicit in the PPP exchange rates that have been used to convert local currency units also affect the comparability across countries. The resulting hypothetical income distribution should thus not be considered a forecast of the future distribution; rather, it should be interpreted as the result of an exercise that captures the distributional effect of trade liberalization, all else being equal.

## What Happens to Poverty and Income Distribution If Trade Is Liberalized Globally?

In this section, we link the macro-outcomes of global agricultural reform and other trade policy reforms to the changes in the distribution of income among and within countries. Our analysis is carried out in three stages. First, we briefly examine the macroeconomic results from the Linkage model simulations of global trade reform (which are similar, but not identical to those presented in chapter 2, by Anderson, Valenzuela, and van der Mensbrugghe) and focus on the variables that are passed on to the household survey data.[13] Second, we consider the income distributional results from a global perspective by quantifying the likely changes in global poverty and inequality and identifying groups of countries and individuals that are likely to benefit the most (least) from global trade reform. Third, we assess the potential trends in the distribution of income within countries by identifying countries in which inequality and poverty pressures may heighten and thus erode the support for additional reforms.

### Macroeconomic general equilibrium results

We have carried out the Linkage simulation analysis using version 7 of the Global Trade Analysis Project Database, which has been amended by Valenzuela and Anderson (2000) to take account of new estimates of the distortions to agricultural incentives in developing countries compiled by these same authors. The Linkage model disaggregates global trade into bilateral flows between more than 100 countries and regions in 57 commodity groups. The base year for the simulations is 2004, and the baseline data have taken into account changes in the global trade and tariff structure generated by the implementation of the Uruguay Round commitments, European Union enlargement, China's accession to the World Trade Organization, and most major preferential trade agreements in place at the time. The model is solved in a comparative static mode, which means that simulations are implemented as one-time shocks and do not take into account potential growth effects through changes in capital accumulation rates or variations in productivity.

Our two simulations envision the full removal globally of trade taxes and subsidies on all agricultural goods and lightly processed food without and then with the trade reform of nonagricultural goods. With these two scenarios, we are able to see the relative contribution to changes in the global economy after the removal of agricultural distortions alone.

The removal of distortions to the trade in agricultural products causes global consumption to rise by 0.29 percent, or two-thirds of the improvement expected under a trade liberalization scenario involving all goods. Developing countries gain more than the average; their consumption rises by 0.47 percent compared with 0.24 percent for high-income countries. No less than 50 of 60 Linkage countries and regions—representing nearly 95 percent of the world's people—would experience positive changes in consumption following the removal of agricultural distortions compared with 47 countries and regions that would enjoy consumption gains from the liberalization of all goods trade (figure 3.6).

**Figure 3.6. The Effects on Real National Consumption of the Global Removal of Agricultural and All Merchandise Trade Distortions**

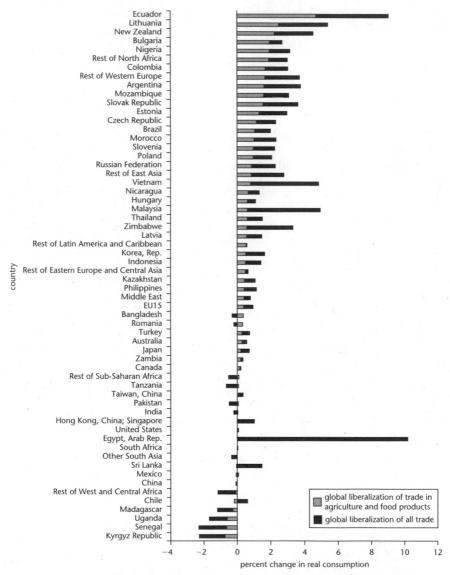

*Source:* Author compilation using Linkage model results similar to those in chapter 2, by Anderson, Valenzuela, and van der Mensbrugghe, except that factor mobility is more limited.

*Note:* The darker bars show the percent increase in consumption (at prereform prices) generated by the removal of price and trade distortions in agriculture and food products (excluding beverages and tobacco). The lighter bars show the additional gains in consumption generated by the removal of all remaining barriers to merchandise trade. The combined length of the two bars shows the consumption gains from the global trade reform of all merchandise. EU15 = the 15 members of the European Union prior to 2004.

There are three main channels that transmit the trade reform shocks to household consumption in the Linkage model and help explain the heterogeneity of the results in figure 3.6. The first channel is changes in the terms of trade, that is, the ratio of export prices to import prices, without taking into account domestic price distortions caused by own-country policies. Net exporters of agriculture and food, such as Brazil, Ecuador, and New Zealand, reap significant welfare gains if the export prices of their farm commodities rise by an average of 8, 19, and 11 percent, respectively.[14] On the other hand, net importers of food, such as China, Mexico, and Senegal, experience real consumption losses due to higher import prices.

The second channel is tightly linked to the first and involves the impact of own-country policies. Thus, countries with high prereform tariffs or export taxes, such as Lithuania, Nigeria, and the group in North Africa, tend to experience larger consumption gains relative to countries in which the initial distortions are low. If initial agricultural import barriers are sufficiently high, consumers may face lower postreform prices for food even if import prices are rising. This is the case in North Africa, which experiences an increase in real consumption although it is a net food importer.

The third channel is the impact of trade reform on government budgets. Since the model does not include an explicit transversality condition, we maintain a fixed budget deficit closure, which means that any losses in public revenue (such as a reduction in tariff income) must be offset by a compensatory increase in the direct tax rate on households.[15] Therefore, welfare gains are more limited in countries, such as Tanzania and Zimbabwe, that rely heavily on international trade taxes as an important provider of public revenue.[16]

In addition to changes in the levels of per capita consumption *across* countries, the Linkage results hint at important distributional consequences of trade reform *within* countries, which come about through changes in returns to labor in different sectors and at varying skill levels. Figure 3.7 shows the contributions of the payments for different factors to the total change in real GDP at factor cost (in percentage points) after the removal of agricultural distortions alone. With the exception of China, all the countries experiencing an increase in the payments for unskilled labor in agriculture also register consumption gains after agricultural policy reform. However, the converse does not hold: real consumption rises in 32 of the 41 countries that show a decline in unskilled agricultural wages. Since unskilled workers in agriculture tend to be in the poorest part of the population, these results suggest that pressures toward increased inequality may intensify.[17] Furthermore, losses and gains in agricultural wages exhibit strong regional patterns: the real wages of unskilled farmers rise in Latin America, the Middle East, and East Asia, but decline in other developing regions and decline much more in high-income countries.

### Figure 3.7. The Effects on National Real Factor Rewards of the Global Removal of Only Agricultural Price and Trade Policies

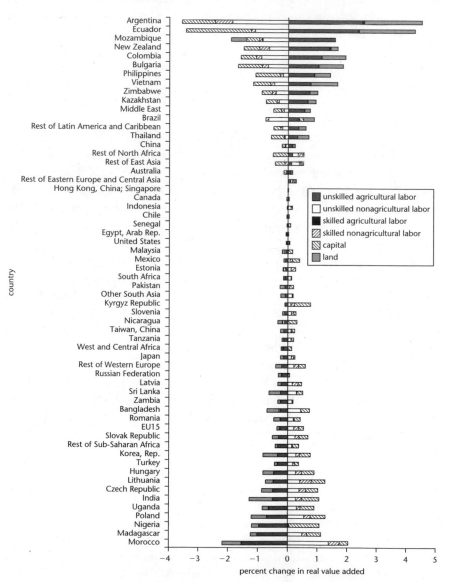

*Source:* Author compilation using Linkage model results similar to those in chapter 2, by Anderson, Valenzuela, and van der Mensbrugghe, except that factor mobility is more limited.

*Note:* Each bar shows a contribution of the changes in the value added by a specific factor to the total change in value added, deflated by the price of GDP at factor cost. Countries are sorted (in descending order) by the increase in the payments to unskilled farm labor.

The initial level of protection in agriculture, combined with the terms of trade shock, represents the main determinant of the trends in farm factor prices. Consider the example of India, where unskilled farm wages decline by 6.1 percent following trade reform.[18] Indian farmers must contend with the falling international prices of imported farm products (a decline of 1.7 percent), as well as a loss in tariff protection (2.0 percent), export subsidies (3.3 percent), and output subsidies (6.9 percent) if all farm policies are scrapped. The first two channels decrease the competitiveness of the farmers on the domestic market and lead to higher import penetration; the third channel erodes their competitiveness on international markets; and the fourth channel increases production costs and makes Indian farmers less competitive overall. Together, these effects result in a strong negative shock to farm labor earnings.

In Mexico, the income losses among unskilled farmers are lower than they are in India. This is partially attributable to the close trading relationship between Mexico and the United States. Mexico purchases 75 percent of its agricultural imports from the United States, the export prices of which rise by 5.7 percent because of the elimination of export and production subsidies. Thus, the removal of agricultural price supports in the United States exerts upward pressure on the import prices of farm products in Mexico, which hurts consumers, but increases the competitiveness of Mexican farmers on the domestic market. The trend is counteracted by the removal of Mexico's tariff protection on agriculture (1.2 percent) and farm output subsidies (0.8 percent), which leads to a decrease in the competitiveness of farmers in Mexico and market share losses among them in the domestic market and in export markets.

In contrast, Brazil is an example of a country in which a number of positive developments combine to produce a nearly 34 percent gain in the wages of unskilled agricultural workers.[19] The import prices of farm products in Brazil rise by 1.8 percent, bolstering the domestic competitiveness of Brazilian farmers, while export prices increase by more than 10 percent. Because the farmers do not receive export or production subsidies, they are well positioned to take advantage of these opportunities and gain market share both domestically and abroad. Although some of the gains among agricultural producers are offset by the loss in domestic protection (import tariffs of 2.4 percent), Brazilian agriculture is still able to increase production volumes by 18 percent after farm trade reform.

### Microsimulation results:
### A first look at global poverty and inequality effects

In this subsection, we use the GIDD model and data to simulate the likely changes in global poverty and inequality arising from the elimination of trade distortions.

Given the richness of the data and the numerous factors affecting global poverty and inequality within the GIDD, this subsection starts with two simulations that illustrate, in a simple way, the expected effects of global trade policy reform. Focusing only on the developing countries in our data set, both simulations raise the average income in the developing world by 1 percent. In the first simulation, national income increases because of an increase in the incomes of agricultural households only, while, in the second simulation, the increase originates entirely in an expansion in nonagricultural incomes. The results of these examples are shown in two growth incidence curves (GICs) in figure 3.8.[20] The broken GIC line captures the effects of assigning income gains only to agricultural households, while the solid GIC line raises incomes only among those households in which the heads work in nonagricultural activities.

As expected, the increase in agricultural incomes is more pro-poor than the same income change taking place in other sectors in which households are relatively richer. This pro-poor bias in the growth in agricultural incomes is reflected in the downward slope of the broken GIC line, indicating that the poorest households

**Figure 3.8. National GICs: The Effects on the Per Capita Household Income Distribution of a Hypothetical 1 Percent Increase in Agricultural Versus Nonagricultural Incomes, Developing Countries**

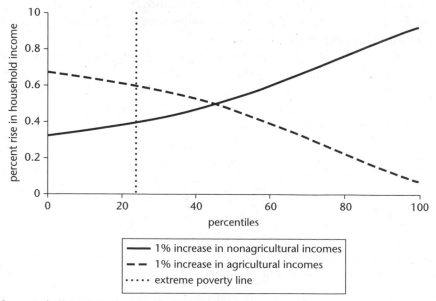

*Source:* Author compilation based on the GIDD Database.

*Note:* The figure is based on the data set for developing countries only.

reap the largest income gains. A different way of interpreting the results shown in figure 3.8 is to observe that, if the agricultural sectors in all developing countries receive income gains above the gains in the nonagricultural sectors as an outcome of the elimination of distortions, global poverty and inequality would fall. As shown in the discussion below, the reality tends to be much more complex than these simple simulations, but the central message of figure 3.8 nonetheless captures the essence of the GIDD simulations.

## Impacts on global poverty and inequality

Using the GIDD to translate the shocks from the Linkage model into poverty and inequality outcomes, we find that the effects of the full removal of agricultural price and trade distortions on extreme poverty globally are close to zero (table 3.2, column 3). This limited impact is explained by several factors. First, the estimated impacts arise from a comparative static model rather than a dynamic model, and, so, they do not capture the growth effects of the reform. Thus, the changes in per capita consumption are small and arise only because of the income boost from more-efficient resource allocation. According to the GIDD, the world's average monthly household

**Table 3.2. The Household Effects of the Removal of Agricultural and All Merchandise Trade Distortions on Global Poverty and Inequality**
*(percentage point change and U.S. dollars)*

| Household type | Gini coefficient | Real average monthly income, 2000 US$ PPP | US$1-a-day poverty, % Incidence | US$1-a-day poverty, % Share | US$2-a-day poverty, % Incidence | US$2-a-day poverty, % Share |
|---|---|---|---|---|---|---|
| *Baseline* | | | | | | |
| Agricultural | 0.45 | 65 | 31.5 | 76 | 73.8 | 70 |
| Nonagricultural | 0.63 | 320 | 8.3 | 24 | 26.7 | 30 |
| All households | 0.67 | 204 | 18.9 | 100 | 48.2 | 100 |
| *Agricultural liberalization, percentage point change* | | | | | | |
| Agricultural | 0.7 | 1.1[a] | 0.86 | 1.13 | −0.86 | 0.47 |
| Nonagricultural | −0.1 | 0.2[a] | −0.29 | −1.13 | −0.90 | −0.47 |
| All households | −0.1 | 0.3[a] | 0.23 | 0.00 | −0.88 | 0.00 |
| *All merchandise trade liberalization, percentage point change* | | | | | | |
| Agricultural | 0.8 | 0.8[a] | 1.09 | 1.02 | −0.66 | 0.57 |
| Nonagricultural | −0.2 | 0.4[a] | −0.19 | −1.02 | −0.95 | −0.57 |
| All households | −0.0 | 0.4[a] | 0.39 | 0.00 | −0.82 | 0.00 |

*Source:* Author compilation based on the GIDD Database and using Linkage model results similar to those in chapter 2, by Anderson, Valenzuela, and van der Mensbrugghe, except that factor mobility is more limited.

a. Changes in average income are expressed in percentages.

income increases 0.3 percent after the removal of only agricultural distortions, passing from an initial level of US$204 to a final value of US$210 at 1993 PPP. If nonagricultural trade is also liberalized, global income rises slightly more, but the total number of households living on less than US$1 a day remains the same.

Second, there is an income redistribution from farm households to nonfarm households, so that the incidence of extreme poverty among farm households rises by around 1 percent in both scenarios, while the incidence among nonfarm households falls by 0.2 or 0.3 percent. As a result, the share of extremely poor households that are farm households rises from 76 to 77 percent (table 3.2, column 4).

Third, the definition of poverty is important. The extreme level, at less than US$1 a day, suggests that only 8 percent of nonfarm households are poor and that they account for only one in four poor households, whereas, at the moderate poverty definition, at less than US$2 a day, the corresponding share is 27 percent, accounting for nearly one in three poor households. If we use the moderate definition of poverty, we find that both agricultural trade liberalization and all merchandise trade liberalization globally lower the total poverty incidence by nearly 1 percent by reducing it among farm and nonfarm households (compare table 3.2, columns 3 and 5).

The policy reforms also have only a slight impact in reducing income inequality at the global level. Incomes rise in both the agricultural and nonagricultural sectors, and agricultural incomes increase by twice as much in the all-goods reform scenario and by five times as much in the reform of agriculture only (1.1 percent compared with only 0.2 percent; see table 3.2, column 2). Yet, while the reduction in the nonagricultural income premium, on its own, reduces inequality, income dispersion *within* the agricultural sector also increases such that the final change in global income distribution is close to zero, judged according to the changes in the Gini coefficient shown in table 3.2, column 1.

Because of these distributional changes taking place within the agricultural sector, the incidence of extreme poverty (under US$1 a day at PPP) rises in the agricultural sector. It increases by 0.9 percentage points as a consequence of the elimination of agricultural price and trade distortions and by 1.1 points if nonfarm trade policies are also reformed. Meanwhile, poverty among nonagricultural households experiences a reduction equal to 0.3 or 0.2 percentage points, respectively. The combination of poverty changes occurring inside and outside the agricultural sector increases extreme poverty by 0.2 percentage points with respect to agricultural reform alone and by 0.4 points if all goods markets are freed, the latter pushing 9 million additional individuals below the extreme poverty line of US$1 a day. We must bear in mind, though, that the poverty effect of these reforms depends on where the poverty line is set. While the global number of people in poverty measured by the US$1-a-day poverty line shows

**Table 3.3. The GIDD Model: The Effects of the Removal of Agricultural and All Merchandise Trade Distortions on the Incidence of Poverty, by Region**
*(number and percent)*

| Region | Share of global poverty, % | Change in number of poor, global trade reform | | | |
| | | Agriculture only | | All merchandise | |
| | | Millions | % | Millions | % |
|---|---|---|---|---|---|
| *Extremely poor, under US$1 a day* | | | | | |
| East Asia | 24 | −6.4 | −2.8 | −6.3 | −2.8 |
| South Asia | 50 | 15.4 | 3.3 | 18.2 | 3.9 |
| Sub-Saharan Africa | 21 | −1.0 | −0.5 | 0.5 | 0.3 |
| Latin America | 4 | −2.8 | −6.9 | −3.5 | −8.7 |
| Global[a] | 100 | 5.0 | 0.5 | 8.9 | 1.0 |
| *Moderately and extremely poor, under US$2 a day* | | | | | |
| East Asia | 33 | −12.8 | −1.6 | −13.2 | −1.7 |
| South Asia | 46 | −3.6 | −0.3 | −2.0 | −0.2 |
| Sub-Saharan Africa | 14 | 0.1 | 0.0 | 1.1 | 0.3 |
| Latin America | 4 | −4.8 | −4.6 | −5.7 | −5.4 |
| Global[a] | 100 | −22.1 | −0.9 | −19.8 | −0.8 |

*Source:* Author compilation based on the GIDD Database and using Linkage model results similar to those in chapter 2, by Anderson, Valenzuela, and van der Mensbrugghe, except that factor mobility is more limited.

a. Includes Middle East and North Africa, Eastern Europe and Central Asia, and high-income countries. Together, these account for no more than 2 percent of the world's poor.

an increase of 1.0 percent as a consequence of the reform in all goods, the number measured using the US$2-a-day criterion actually falls by about 20 million or 0.8 percent (table 3.3, columns 4 and 5).

These results treat the world as a single entity, making no distinction among regions or countries. Indeed, the lack of major changes at the global level may be the outcome of offsetting impacts across regions. Farmers in Latin America are big winners from agricultural price and trade reform, with an impressive increase of 16 percent in household incomes. In contrast, the incomes of farmers in South Asia would shrink more than 3 percent if agricultural distortions were dismantled globally. To show the incidence of these changes among the population across regions, figure 3.9 plots the GICs for Latin America, South Asia, and the rest of the world (see chart a). The GIC for Latin America indicates that agriculture-based growth in the region is quite pro-poor. In contrast, agriculture-based growth in South Asia is highly regressive: the poorest households are the losers in such reform. East Asia and, to a lesser extent, Sub-Saharan Africa would benefit from

**Figure 3.9. Regional and National GICs: The Effects on the Per Capita Household Income Distribution of Full Global Agricultural Policy Reform**

**a. Regional**

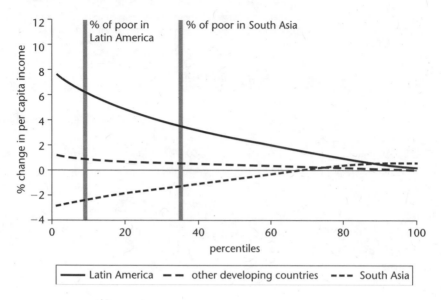

**b. National: Brazil and India**

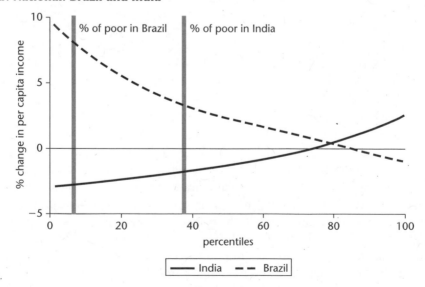

*Source:* Author compilation based on the GIDD Database.

*Note:* The figure is based on the data set for developing countries only.

global agricultural reform, and the effects of such reform would be progressive, albeit small, in the rest of the world.

The differences in reform outcomes across regions help explain the lack of significant change in global poverty. With nearly a half billion of its people in extreme poverty and another 625 million moderately poor, South Asia alone accounts for about half of global poverty, while Latin America accounts for less than 5 percent (table 3.3, column 1). Hence, although removing agricultural distortions reduces extreme poverty in most regions of the world, the increase in the headcount ratio in South Asia slightly more than offsets these gains.

The results based on the US$2-a-day poverty line show a more positive picture. Poverty gauged by this standard is reduced in all key regions except (marginally) Sub-Saharan Africa (table 3.3, final column). The results at the moderate poverty line are particularly interesting in the case of South Asia, where agricultural reform becomes pro-poor, instead of antipoor as it was according to the US$1-a-day extreme poverty line. This result is explained by the large number of nonagricultural households between the two poverty lines in South Asia; these would experience an increase in purchasing power if global agricultural markets were liberalized. The reduction in moderate poverty is somewhat less if the trade in nonfarm goods is also liberalized, but is still 0.8 percent, or 20 million people globally.

### Poverty and inequality effects within regions and countries

Global agricultural liberalization has distributional and poverty effects that vary not only across regions, but also between neighboring countries and within countries. This subsection summarizes the poverty effects and distributional changes in each of the countries included in our sample. Table 3.3 shows that the 5 million individuals who would be pushed into poverty as a consequence of agricultural reform may be broken down into an increase of 15 million people living in poverty in South Asia and a decrease of 10 million people living in poverty in all other regions. Figure 3.10 shows the specific countries that contribute, respectively, the most to the reduction and the most to the increase in global poverty. On the one hand, among the new poor, 92 percent—about 15 million—are in India, while 2.2 percent are in Mexico, and 1.8 percent are in South Africa; both Mexico and South Africa currently protect their farmers and would face higher prices for imported farm products. On the other hand, the gross reduction in global poverty is distributed more evenly among many winners among countries; the great majority are located in East Asia and Latin America. In fact, no country in East Asia and only Chile and Mexico in Latin America experience an increase in the number of extreme poor as a result of global agricultural reform, and even the latter two would experience poverty reduction if the reform were broadened to include nonfarm goods as well (table 3.4).

**Figure 3.10. Changes in Poverty as a Share of the Total Change among the Greatest Winners and Losers in Full Global Agricultural Policy Reform, Developing Countries**

**a. Share of the global increase in poverty**

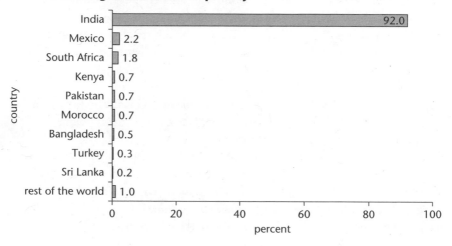

**b. Share of the global reduction in poverty**

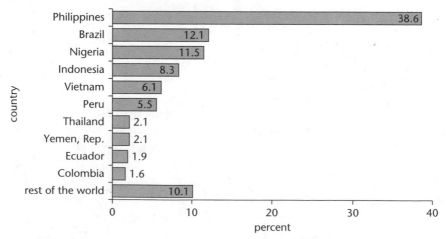

*Source:* Author compilation based on the GIDD Database.

*Note:* The figure is based on the data set for developing countries only.

**Table 3.4. The Effects of the Full Global Liberalization of Agricultural and All Merchandise Trade on the Incidence of Inequality and Poverty, Developing Countries**

*(percentage point change)*

| Region, country | Agricultural reform only | | | All merchandise trade reform | | |
|---|---|---|---|---|---|---|
| | Gini coefficient | US$1 a day, headcount | US$2 a day, headcount | Gini coefficient | US$1 a day, headcount | US$2 a day, headcount |
| East Asia | −0.72 | −0.38 | −0.76 | −0.62 | −0.37 | −0.78 |
| Cambodia | −0.75 | −0.40 | 0.17 | −0.69 | −0.90 | −0.05 |
| China | −0.37 | 0.00 | 0.00 | −0.35 | 0.00 | 0.00 |
| Indonesia | 0.05 | −0.49 | −0.83 | 0.04 | −0.57 | −1.26 |
| Philippines | −6.88 | −6.31 | −9.91 | −6.65 | −6.15 | 9.80 |
| Thailand | −1.25 | −0.40 | −2.29 | −1.10 | −0.38 | −2.29 |
| Vietnam | −1.85 | −0.89 | −3.57 | 0.08 | −0.66 | −2.97 |
| South Asia | 0.82 | 1.16 | −0.27 | 0.81 | 1.37 | 0.15 |
| Bangladesh | 0.06 | 0.06 | 0.19 | −0.09 | 0.07 | 0.05 |
| India | 1.01 | 1.49 | −0.33 | 1.04 | 1.71 | −0.26 |
| Nepal | 0.05 | −0.12 | 0.04 | 0.05 | 0.11 | 0.18 |
| Pakistan | 0.04 | 0.09 | 0.03 | 0.10 | 0.49 | 0.44 |
| Sri Lanka | 0.03 | 0.14 | −0.01 | 0.17 | −0.20 | −0.69 |
| Sub-Saharan Africa | 0.04 | −0.23 | 0.02 | 0.06 | 0.11 | 0.25 |
| Benin | 0.00 | −0.05 | 0.09 | 0.02 | 0.79 | 0.74 |
| Burkina Faso | −0.02 | 0.00 | 0.05 | 0.02 | 0.78 | 0.43 |
| Burundi | 0.27 | −0.35 | 0.17 | 0.26 | 0.12 | 0.37 |
| Cameroon | −0.01 | 0.24 | 0.06 | 0.05 | 0.72 | 0.70 |
| Côte d'Ivoire | 0.02 | 0.14 | 0.61 | 0.06 | 0.43 | 0.89 |
| Ethiopia | −0.13 | −0.27 | −0.20 | −0.07 | 0.24 | 0.22 |
| Gambia, The | −0.12 | 0.05 | 0.00 | −0.11 | 0.61 | 0.40 |
| Ghana | 0.08 | 0.10 | 0.09 | 0.08 | 0.62 | 0.62 |
| Guinea | −0.04 | −0.10 | 0.04 | 0.03 | 0.62 | 0.42 |
| Kenya | 0.30 | 0.41 | 0.54 | 0.38 | 0.52 | 0.94 |
| Madagascar | 0.95 | 0.24 | 0.06 | 0.98 | 0.56 | 0.36 |
| Mali | 0.01 | −0.01 | −0.03 | 0.03 | 0.93 | 0.45 |
| Mauritania | 0.03 | 0.09 | 0.18 | 0.07 | 0.60 | 0.60 |
| Nigeria | 0.10 | −1.04 | −0.30 | 0.27 | −0.75 | −0.21 |
| Senegal | −0.28 | −0.12 | −0.24 | 0.01 | 0.75 | 0.31 |
| South Africa | 0.32 | 0.68 | 0.68 | 0.21 | 0.39 | 0.50 |
| Tanzania | −0.03 | 0.01 | 0.03 | 0.02 | 0.54 | 0.26 |
| Uganda | 0.30 | −0.05 | 0.01 | 0.45 | 0.12 | −0.03 |
| Latin America | −0.51 | −0.61 | −1.06 | −0.65 | −0.77 | −1.26 |
| Bolivia | −0.55 | −0.64 | −0.65 | −0.71 | −0.74 | −0.61 |
| Brazil | −0.58 | −0.82 | −1.16 | −0.70 | −0.92 | −1.31 |
| Chile | 0.03 | 0.02 | 0.02 | 0.09 | −0.02 | −0.10 |
| Colombia | −0.71 | −0.45 | −1.30 | −0.85 | −0.49 | −1.40 |
| Costa Rica | −0.56 | −0.13 | −0.50 | −0.72 | −0.22 | −0.62 |

*(Table continues on the following page.)*

**Table 3.4. The Effects of the Full Global Liberalization of Agricultural and All Merchandise Trade on the Incidence of Inequality and Poverty, Developing Countries (*continued*)**

*(percentage point change)*

| Region, country | Agricultural reform only | | | All merchandise trade reform | | |
|---|---|---|---|---|---|---|
| | Gini coefficient | US$1 a day, headcount | US$2 a day, headcount | Gini coefficient | US$1 a day, headcount | US$2 a day, headcount |
| Dominican Republic | −0.76 | −0.24 | −0.75 | −0.95 | −0.24 | −0.89 |
| Ecuador | −0.90 | −1.75 | −2.78 | −1.29 | −1.98 | −3.09 |
| El Salvador | −1.09 | −1.25 | −0.79 | −1.29 | −1.34 | −0.88 |
| Guatemala | −0.87 | −1.26 | −1.54 | −1.11 | −1.59 | −1.44 |
| Guyana | −1.49 | −0.27 | −0.39 | −1.66 | −0.46 | −0.54 |
| Honduras | −1.06 | −0.57 | −1.58 | −1.30 | −0.72 | −1.63 |
| Haiti | −0.80 | −0.61 | −0.55 | −1.04 | −0.65 | −0.53 |
| Jamaica | −0.75 | −0.10 | −1.44 | −0.91 | −0.05 | −1.49 |
| Mexico | 0.20 | 0.36 | 0.35 | −0.05 | 0.01 | −0.07 |
| Nicaragua | −2.42 | −3.03 | −1.42 | −2.38 | −3.07 | −1.42 |
| Panama | −0.40 | −0.44 | −0.74 | −0.53 | −0.51 | −0.85 |
| Paraguay | −0.77 | −1.30 | −1.41 | −0.99 | −1.38 | −1.92 |
| Peru | −1.21 | −2.92 | −6.41 | −1.51 | −3.10 | −6.77 |
| Venezuela, R.B. de | −0.29 | −0.44 | −0.71 | −0.42 | −0.55 | −0.82 |
| Europe and Central Asia | 0.07 | −0.02 | −0.26 | 0.22 | 0.00 | −0.12 |
| Armenia | 0.42 | 0.34 | 0.14 | 0.45 | 0.23 | 0.13 |
| Azerbaijan | −0.23 | 0.10 | −1.36 | −0.12 | 0.14 | −1.21 |
| Georgia | −0.48 | −0.49 | −0.57 | −0.37 | −0.45 | −0.61 |
| Kazakhstan | −0.97 | −0.39 | −2.07 | −1.00 | −0.43 | −2.22 |
| Kyrgyz Republic | −0.50 | 0.08 | 0.57 | −0.27 | 0.19 | 1.09 |
| Moldova | −0.20 | −0.22 | −0.75 | −0.06 | −0.09 | −0.24 |
| Russian Federation | −0.16 | 0.00 | −0.32 | −0.06 | 0.00 | −0.31 |
| Tajikistan | −0.12 | −0.77 | −0.75 | −0.32 | −0.67 | −0.74 |
| Ukraine | −0.11 | −0.03 | −0.33 | −0.02 | 0.00 | −0.04 |
| Uzbekistan | −0.07 | 0.00 | −0.06 | 0.29 | 0.00 | 0.03 |
| World | −0.10 | 0.23 | −0.88 | −0.00 | 0.39 | −0.82 |

*Source:* Author compilation based on the GIDD Database and using Linkage model results similar to those in chapter 2, by Anderson, Valenzuela, and van der Mensbrugghe, except that factor mobility is more limited.

The contributions to the global entries into and exits out of poverty depicted in figure 3.10 are, to a certain extent, the outcomes of differences in population size. For instance, a populous country such as India may have a substantial contribution to global poverty without necessarily implying a large increase in the headcount ratio of the country. Another way of ranking countries in terms of poverty outcomes is to consider the postreform change in the headcount ratio following all merchandise trade liberalization globally. Undertaking this exercise, we show that, among countries in which poverty falls, Ecuador and Peru would enjoy the largest declines in Latin America, while, in Asia, the Philippines, Thailand, and Vietnam (and Kazakhstan) would be in this category. India is still the country showing the largest increase in the incidence of extreme poverty, but the incidence of moderate poverty (US$2 a day) falls by 0.3 percentage points (table 3.4). Note that these changes in India occur although average household income remains virtually constant; the changes are therefore entirely a result of a deterioration in income distribution. This is reflected in the increase by 1.0 percentage points in the Gini coefficient of India. Three-quarters of this increase in inequality is attributable to a rise in the agricultural-nonagricultural income gap in India. In contrast, the poverty reduction in Brazil is the outcome of a combination of a 1 percent increase in average incomes and a reduction in the Gini coefficient of inequality of around 0.6–0.7 percentage points (table 3.4).

The changes in overall growth and distribution that would take place in Brazil and India after global agricultural reform are summarized through the GICs for these two countries plotted in figure 3.9, chart b. Given the importance of Brazil and India in their respective regions, it is not surprising that the shapes of the GICs for these countries are similar to the GICs of their respective regions plotted in figure 3.9, chart a.

Chart b in Figure 3.9 shows that the only beneficiaries of global agricultural liberalization in India are people in households in the top 22 percent of the distribution; given that 83 percent of the Indian population is living below the US$2-a-day poverty line, part of the top 22 percent is accounted for by households living in moderate poverty.

Agricultural reforms may have important real income distributional effects in terms of the gap between agricultural and nonagricultural households (see elsewhere above). Our results show that, for many countries in our sample, the removal of distortions would have considerable distributional effects. In one-third of the countries listed in table 3.4, the Gini coefficient shows a decline of more than one-half of a percentage point. This pattern is also observed in the changes in the country-specific Theil index plotted in figure 3.11. There are distinguishable regional differences in the distributional effects of the reform; countries in East Asia and Latin America experience a significant reduction in income inequality, while the inequality in countries outside these regions remains constant or rises marginally. The advantage of using the Theil index as the inequality measure is that we are able to decompose the changes in the index into an effect attributable to shifts in the agricultural-to-nonagricultural wage gap (the between effect) and the effects arising from income changes

**Figure 3.11. The Theil Index of Overall and Between-Group Income Distributional Changes after Full Global Agricultural Policy Reform**

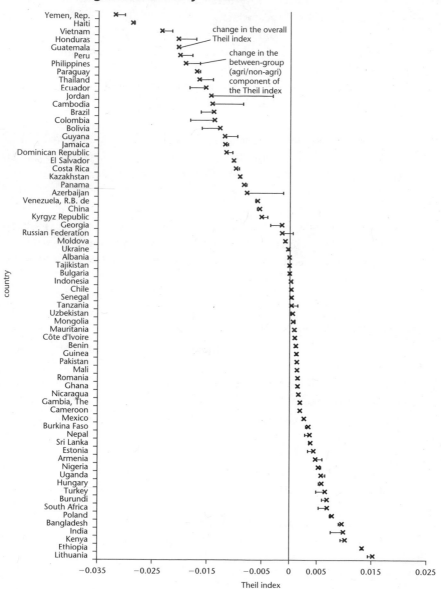

Source: Author compilation based on the GIDD Database.

Note: The Theil index is an inequality measure of the family of general entropy that has the property of yielding perfectly additive inequality decompositions by population subgroups. The figure is based on the data set for developing countries only.

within these two groups. Figure 3.11 shows the total changes in the Theil index (depicted by an x) and the changes attributable to movements in the nonagricultural income premium (the small horizontal bar). Since the between effect is close to the total distributional effect for the majority of countries, we may conclude that the total change in income distribution in these economies is mainly the outcome of changes in the mean incomes in the agricultural and nonagricultural sectors.

## Conclusions

Trade distortions in agriculture and food represent the last major bastion of merchandise protection and continue to be the main point of contention in multilateral and preferential trade negotiations. Using a newly developed data set and methodological approach for evaluating the poverty and inequality effects of policy reforms, the GIDD, this chapter evaluates the potential effects on global income distribution and poverty exerted by the removal of agricultural distortions and other trade distortions.

There are three main messages emerging from our analysis. First, the liberalization of agricultural and food markets is unlikely to have large effects on global poverty. Our results show that the incidence of extreme poverty (US$1 a day, PPP) might rise by 0.5 percent each from farm and nonfarm full global trade reform, while moderate poverty (US$2 a day, PPP) is likely to fall by 0.9 percent from agricultural reform alone. The second message is that these small aggregate changes are produced by a combination of offsetting trends at the regional and national levels. Farmers in Latin America, the region that accounts for less than 5 percent of global poverty, experience significant income gains, while 15 million more people in South Asia, where half of the world's poor reside, would fall below the extreme poverty line after the liberalization of world agricultural markets, and another 2.8 million would fall below this line if the barriers to the trade in nonfarm goods were also removed. Some countries or regions would experience considerable distributional changes following global trade reform. Inequality is projected to fall in regions, such as Latin America, that are characterized by high initial inequality, but is projected to rise in South Asia, which is characterized by low initial inequality. As a result, the projected changes for developing countries as a group are small overall.

There are several important caveats to our analysis. First, it should be emphasized that, although poverty reduction is a most worthy goal, it should not be the only or even the first metric with which to measure trade policy. Trade reform should not be expected to benefit all constituents and may do so only if it is accompanied by other, complementary domestic policies. Second, our analysis is confined to an examination of the effects of static efficiency gains and does not consider the potential growth effects of trade liberalization. Although our results show that the static gains from agricultural reform and other trade reform may not contribute to a reduction in extreme poverty and may do little to combat moderate poverty, they do not imply that this pattern of trade liberalization is not an effective tool for poverty reduction. Finally, our microsimulation model considers only changes in labor income; while this is the most important income source for households at or near the poverty line, accounting for changes in other factor returns may yield somewhat different inequality results.

## Notes

1. According to Anderson and Martin (2005), self-interested vocal groups lobbying aggressively in favor of excluding agricultural liberalization from multilateral negotiations encompass not only farmers in the highly protected countries and net food-importing developing countries, but also food exporters receiving preferential access to these markets, including holders of tariff rate quotas, members of regional trading agreements, and parties to nonreciprocal preference agreements, such as all least developed countries.

2. The GIDD data set, methodology, and applications are available at http://go.worldbank.org/YADEAFEJ30.

3. This more highly aggregated information usually consists of 20 data points for each country, each data point representing the average per capita income (or consumption) of 5 percent of the country's population. In the absence of full survey data, the use of these vingtile data provides a close approximation to most economy-wide measures of inequality.

4. The adjustment procedure for expressing welfare indicators in 1993 international dollars (PPP) is as follows. First, for countries for which the survey year is not 2000, the welfare indicator (household per capita income or consumption) is scaled to the year 2000 using the cumulative growth in real income per capita between the survey year and 2000. Then, the welfare indicator is converted to 1993 national prices by multiplying the welfare indicator by the ratio of the consumer price index in 1993 to the consumer price index in the survey year. Finally, the welfare indicator is converted to 1993 international prices by multiplying the outcome of the above calculations by the 1993 PPP exchange rate.

5. The distributions for the agricultural and nonagricultural populations are not, strictly speaking, density functions because the area below the curve does not add to 1. The densities of the agricultural and nonagricultural populations were rescaled so that the area under the curve represents the share of the world's population in these two groups.

6. For a specific analysis of the importance of China and India to global growth and income distribution, see Bussolo et al. (2007).

7. A household is defined as a net producer (consumer) of agricultural products if the monetary income it derives from merchandising these products is greater (smaller) than the amount spent on them.

8. For empirical applications of the effect of trade on household welfare that take into account these effects, see, for example, the case studies on Mexico by Nicita (2004) and De Hoyos (2007).

9. A detailed methodological description of the GIDD may be found in Bussolo, De Hoyos, and Medvedev (2008).

10. The GIDD uses the Linkage model as a global CGE framework. See van der Mensbrugghe (2005) for a detailed description of the Linkage model.

11. Throughout this chapter, global distribution means the GIDD sample of countries, which include 92 percent of the world's population.

12. The GIDD does not take into account the welfare impacts via any changes in remittances or transfers between households that result from trade reform.

13. The Linkage results used here are not identical to those in chapter 2 because labor mobility in our chapter has been restricted to match the available microdata more closely. In the version of the Linkage model used in chapter 2, the assumption of full factor mobility leads to an equalization of factor prices across sectors. However, the household survey data show large and persistent differences between the labor earnings in agriculture and the labor earnings in nonagriculture after we have controlled for other relevant characteristics. Imposing an equalization of wages in the GIDD would lead to large and implausible changes in the distribution of income; to maintain consistency between macro- and micromodels, we have therefore limited labor mobility in the macromodel.

14. The price increases are calculated using the Paasche price index, that is, using postreform exports as weights to aggregate the prices of individual commodities. Unless explicitly noted, all price indexes in this section are calculated using the Paasche formula. Price indexes differ by country because of differences in the composition of exports (that is, aggregation weights).

15. This closure choice thus gives rise to a consistent measurement of household utility because the utility function does not include the consumption of public goods.

16. In this situation, whether households gain or lose from trade reform, in addition to the impacts of the first two channels, depends on their ability to substitute out of more expensive goods into now-cheaper alternatives.

17. Note that trends in consumption per capita are unlikely to be representative of the welfare of agricultural households given that, because of limited incomes and high poverty incidence, the weight of these households in total consumption is low.

18. The 6.1 percent figure refers to the decline in nominal wages. The change in real wages depends on the choice of deflator: while the consumer price index increases by 2 percent relative to the base year, the GDP deflator falls by 1 percent.

19. This is a nominal increase, not a real increase. Consumer prices in Brazil rise by 4 percent after trade reform.

20. A GIC shows the changes in welfare along the entire income distribution. It therefore captures, in a single graph, the growth and distributional components of overall welfare changes. For a detailed description of the properties of GICs, see Ravallion and Chen (2003).

# References

Anderson, K., ed. 2009. *Distortions to Agricultural Incentives: A Global Perspective, 1955–2007*. London: Palgrave Macmillan; Washington, DC: World Bank.

Anderson, K., and W. Martin. 2005. "Agricultural Trade Reform and the Doha Development Agenda." *World Economy* 28 (9): 1301–27.

Anderson, K., and E. Valenzuela. 2008. "Estimates of Global Distortions to Agricultural Incentives, 1955–2007." Data spreadsheet, October, World Bank, Washington, DC. http://go.worldbank.org/YAO39F35E0.

Bourguignon, F., V. Levin, and D. Rosenblatt. 2004. "Declining International Inequality and Economic Divergence: Reviewing the Evidence through Different Lenses." *Economie Internationale* 2004 (4Q): 13–26.

Bourguignon, F., and L. A. Pereira da Silva, eds. 2003. *The Impact of Economic Policies on Poverty and Income Distribution: Evaluation Techniques and Tools*. London: Oxford University Press; Washington, DC: World Bank.

Bussolo, M., R. De Hoyos, and D. Medvedev. 2008. "Economic Growth and Income Distribution: Linking Macroeconomic Models with Household Survey Data at the Global Level." Paper presented at the International Association for Research in Income and Wealth 30th general conference, Portoroz, Slovenia, August 24–30.

Bussolo, M., R. De Hoyos, D. Medvedev, and D. van der Mensbrugghe. 2007. "Global Growth and Distribution: Are China and India Reshaping the World?" Policy Research Working Paper 4392, World Bank, Washington, DC.

Bussolo, M., J. Lay, and D. van der Mensbrugghe. 2006. "Structural Change and Poverty Reduction in Brazil: The Impact of the Doha Round." In *Poverty and the WTO: Impacts of the Doha Development Agenda*, ed. T. W. Hertel and L. A. Winters, 249–84. London: Palgrave Macmillan; Washington, DC: World Bank.

Chen, S., and M. Ravallion. 2003. "Household Welfare Impacts of China's Accession to the World Trade Organization." *World Bank Economic Review* 18 (1): 29–57.

————. 2007. "Absolute Poverty Measures for the Developing World, 1981–2004." Policy Research Working Paper 4211, World Bank, Washington, DC.

De Hoyos, R. E. 2007. "North-South Trade Agreements and Household Welfare: Mexico under NAFTA." mimeo, World Bank, Washington, DC.

Ferreira, F. H. G., and P. G. Leite. 2003. "Meeting the Millennium Development Goals in Brazil: Can Microsimulations Help?" *Economía* 3 (2): 235–79.

————. 2004. "Educational Expansion and Income Distribution: A Microsimulation for Ceará." In *Growth, Inequality, and Poverty: Prospects for Pro-Poor Economic Development*, ed. A. Shorrocks and R. van der Hoeven, 222–50. London: Oxford University Press.

GIDD Database (Global Income Distribution Dynamics Database). World Bank. http://go.worldbank.org/YADEAFEJ30.

Krueger, A. O., M. Schiff, and A. Valdés. 1988. "Agricultural Incentives in Developing Countries: Measuring the Effect of Sectoral and Economy-wide Policies." *World Bank Economic Review* 2 (3): 255–72.

McCulloch, N., L. A. Winters, and X. Cirera. 2001. *Trade Liberalization and Poverty: A Handbook*. London: Centre for Economic Policy Research.

Nicita, A. 2004. "Who Benefited from Trade Liberalization in Mexico? Measuring the Effects on Household Welfare." Policy Research Working Paper 3265, World Bank, Washington, DC.

Ravallion, M., and S. Chen. 2003. "Measuring Pro-poor Growth." *Economics Letters* 78 (1): 93–99.

Rodrik, D. 1998. "Why Is Trade Reform So Difficult in Africa?" *Journal of African Economies* 7 (0): 43–69.

Valenzuela, E., and K. Anderson. 2008. "Alternative Agricultural Price Distortions for CGE Analysis of Developing Countries, 2004 and 1980–84." Research Memorandum 13 (December), Center for Global Trade Analysis, Department of Agricultural Economics, Purdue University, West Lafayette, IN. https://www.gtap.agecon.purdue.edu/resources/res_display.asp?RecordID=2925.

van der Mensbrugghe, D. 2005. "Linkage Technical Reference Document: Version 6.0." December, World Bank, Washington, DC. http://go.worldbank.org/7NP2KK1OH0.

Winters, L. A. 2002. "Trade Liberalization and Poverty: What Are the Links?" *World Economy* 25 (9): 1339–67.

# 4

# POVERTY IMPACTS IN 15 COUNTRIES: THE GTAP MODEL

## Thomas W. Hertel and Roman Keeney

Despite slow progress toward a multilateral trade reform agreement, the Doha Development Agenda negotiations of the World Trade Organization continue to generate interest because of their poverty reduction potential. A distinguishing feature of the Doha agenda has been the lack of commitment to trade policy reform by developing countries, particularly the poorest countries, which would not be required to commit to reduce tariffs following a Doha agreement (Anderson and Martin 2006).

Recent research suggests that developing-country tariff cuts, particularly in agriculture, are among the most poverty-friendly elements of a broader multilateral trade policy agenda (Hertel et al. 2009). Such analyses hinge critically on the measured protection for agriculture in developing countries. Unlike the countries of the Organisation for Economic Co-operation and Development (OECD), in which the measurement of agricultural protection has received considerable attention over the past two decades through the regular publication of producer support estimates, there was considerable uncertainty about the current support and recent trends in agricultural protection in developing countries, particularly the smaller low-income economies, until the new World Bank agricultural distortions database was compiled (Anderson and Valenzuela 2008).

In this chapter, we incorporate the new information on price distortions in an assessment of the impact of agricultural and other trade reforms on poverty. The new data on developing-country protection in agriculture afford us the opportunity to consider the relative importance of agricultural versus nonagricultural protection at home and abroad more accurately than has been previously possible.[1]

Tracing the impacts of developments in multilateral trade policy from international markets to the household level is a long and complex process (Winters, McCulloch, and McKay 2004). A natural method for accomplishing this is to divide the task into parts. This approach is taken in Hertel and Winters (2006), who use a global model to generate the changes in world prices following various multilateral trade reform scenarios and then national models rich in household-level detail to assess the ensuing national poverty impacts. This method allows the authors to benefit from the comparative advantage of separate modeling tools. It has become widely accepted as the standard method for reaching definitive answers to ex ante questions on the impacts of trade reforms on poverty in individual countries.

An inherent limitation of the country-specific studies underlying the final estimates on the changes in poverty derived through this approach is the shortage of general conclusions on the broad pattern of impacts on poverty. Are rich-country reforms pro-poor on average? How do they compare with poor-country reforms?

For this purpose, it is important to assemble a framework that is based on household surveys. The framework should allow us to make comparisons across countries and develop conclusions about poverty impacts in a wide range of diverse economies that are representative of the developing world. This approach has been adopted by Ivanic (2006) and Hertel et al. (2007) in their analyses of the Doha Development Agenda. These authors find that the set of measures envisioned under the Doha Development Agenda are less poverty-friendly than alternative policy measures not being considered.[2] Hertel et al. (2009) explore this question in detail and determine that an overemphasis on export and domestic production subsidies relative to the attention paid to market access in the rich countries, together with the absence of commitments to deep agricultural tariff cuts in developing countries, is the primary culprit in diminishing the prospects for poverty reduction through the Doha Development Agenda. The international cross-section approach—the framework approach mentioned above—has proven especially fruitful in providing insights that are complementary to those provided by more-detailed country-specific studies, despite the former's relatively undifferentiated treatment of developing-country household behavior.

In addition to making use of the new developing-country protection estimates, we also examine the poverty impacts of trade reform through a different lens, namely, the lens of commodity-specific support. Given that many political economy and distributional causes of agricultural protection are inherently commodity specific, viewing the trade-poverty link through the commodity lens in a comparative fashion represents an area of relative inattention and one that a global model with a diverse developing-country sample is well suited to address. For our present purposes, we focus on 15 developing countries: four in Africa (Malawi, Mozambique, Uganda, and Zambia), five in Asia (Bangladesh, Indonesia, the Philippines, Thailand, and Vietnam), and six in Latin America (Brazil, Chile, Colombia, Mexico, Peru, and República Bolivariana de Venezuela).

## Our Analytical Approach to Poverty Modeling

Our poverty analysis begins with the specification of a utility function and an associated consumer demand system for determining household consumption and the maximum utility attainable at a given level of prices and incomes. The utility of the household at the poverty line is defined as the poverty level of utility. Households with utility at or below this level are deemed to be in poverty. In this study, we follow Hertel et al. (2004, 2007) in using the AIDADS demand system of Rimmer and Powell (1992) to represent consumer preferences. AIDADS (an implicitly directly additive demand system) is particularly effective in poverty analysis because it lends itself to international cross-section estimation and devotes two-thirds of its parameters to consumption behavior in the neighborhood of the poverty line (Cranfield et al. 2003).

The estimation of this demand system is undertaken using the 80-country per capita consumption data set offered in version 6.1 of the Global Trade Analysis Project (GTAP) data set; the resulting parameters are reported in Hertel et al. (2009). The demand system estimates are then calibrated to reproduce base year per capita demands in each country following the approach of Golub and Hertel (2008).

A key finding in the work of Hertel et al. (2004) is the importance of stratifying households by primary source of income. Farm households in developing countries often rely on the farm enterprise for virtually all income, and the share of national poverty concentrated in agriculture-specialized households is large in the poorest countries in our sample: between one-quarter and one-half of the US$1-a-day poverty line headcount in Chile, Colombia, Indonesia, Malawi, Mozambique, and Zambia.

Not only are farm households in the poorest countries more likely to be specialized in farm earnings, these specialized farm households also tend to be poorer than the rest of the population (Hertel et al. 2004). The implication is that the poorest households in the poorest countries are more concentrated in agriculture and therefore more likely to benefit from producer price increases engendered by multilateral trade reforms. We follow Hertel et al. (2004) in identifying five household groups that rely almost exclusively (greater than 95 percent) on one source of income: agricultural self-employment, nonagricultural self-employment, rural wage labor, urban wage labor, or transfer payments. The remaining households are grouped into rural or urban diversified strata, leading to seven total strata.[3]

Hertel et al. (2004) have simulated the impact of trade reform on the full distribution of households within each of the seven strata using a global computable general equilibrium (CGE) model and a household microsimulation framework. Given our emphasis on poverty in this chapter, we follow Hertel et al. (2009) by focusing on the households in the neighborhood of the poverty line and making use of a highly disaggregated poverty elasticity approach. Specifically, we compute the stratum-specific elasticity of the poverty headcount with respect to a change in average income in the stratum. We denote this elasticity by $\varepsilon_{rs}$ and report the computed values for the 15 countries in our sample in table 4.1. The values range from a low of 0.0006 in the self-employed agriculture stratum in Zambia, where nearly

**Table 4.1. Estimates of Elasticities of the US$1-a-Day Poverty Headcount with Respect to Total Income, 15 Countries**

| Country | Ag | Nonag | Urban labor | Rural labor | Transfer | Urban diverse | Rural diverse | National elasticity |
|---------|-----|-------|-------------|-------------|----------|---------------|---------------|---------------------|
| Bangladesh | 1.64 | 2.02 | 1.58 | 0.63 | 0.56 | 1.74 | 1.09 | 1.24 |
| Brazil | 0.75 | 1.28 | 1.94 | 2.19 | 0.34 | 3.63 | 2.69 | 1.35 |
| Chile | 1.90 | 2.24 | 2.06 | 1.55 | 2.45 | 2.29 | 2.60 | 2.18 |
| Colombia | 0.79 | 0.60 | 1.73 | 1.72 | 0.93 | 1.14 | 1.00 | 0.82 |
| Indonesia | 2.35 | 2.14 | 2.38 | 2.89 | 1.17 | 2.58 | 2.87 | 2.47 |
| Malawi | 0.49 | 0.30 | 2.26 | 1.97 | 0.43 | 1.04 | 0.76 | 0.58 |
| Mexico | 1.73 | 1.90 | 3.33 | 2.08 | 2.28 | 1.63 | 1.80 | 2.02 |
| Mozambique | 0.28 | 0.94 | 0.97 | 0.76 | 0.48 | 1.58 | 0.99 | 0.64 |
| Peru | 1.50 | 1.32 | 2.37 | 1.73 | 0.44 | 1.09 | 1.05 | 1.07 |
| Philippines | 2.25 | 1.96 | 2.98 | 2.44 | 1.69 | 2.42 | 1.98 | 2.15 |
| Thailand | 2.30 | 2.42 | 2.98 | 2.45 | 2.78 | 2.42 | 2.59 | 2.57 |
| Uganda | 0.28 | 0.40 | 1.71 | 0.34 | 0.01 | 0.36 | 0.21 | 0.24 |
| Venezuela, R.B. de | 0.69 | 1.16 | 2.57 | 2.17 | 0.01 | 1.72 | 1.53 | 1.20 |
| Vietnam | 0.48 | 1.12 | 2.81 | 8.98 | 0.84 | 0.86 | 1.01 | 0.98 |
| Zambia | 0.00 | 0.64 | 2.28 | 0.91 | 0.45 | 1.29 | 0.37 | 0.61 |

*Source:* Author compilation.

*Note:* The values in the strata columns are the elasticities of the poverty headcount with respect to changes in earnings. National elasticity in the final column is the aggregate elasticity for each country weighted by the poverty share (see table 4.2). The authors have estimated the elasticities using country-specific household survey data. For the first five strata, more than 95 percent of household income is derived from only one income source. Ag = agriculture. Nonag = nonagriculture.

all of the population is living well below the poverty line, to a high of 3.63 in the urban diversified stratum of Brazil, where the population density at the poverty line is quite high.

The proportional change in the real incomes of households at the poverty line in stratum $s$ of region $r$ may be written as the sum of the real after-tax factor earnings of these households weighted by the income share, as follows:

$$\hat{y}_{rs}^{P} = \sum_{j} \alpha_{rsj}^{P}(\hat{W}_{rj} - \hat{C}_{r}^{P}), \tag{4.1}$$

where $\alpha_{rsj}^{P}$ is the share of income obtained from factor $j$ by households at the poverty line in stratum $s$ of region $r$; $\hat{W}_{rj}$ is the proportional change in after-tax earnings of factor $j$ in region $r$; and $\hat{C}_{r}^{P}$ is the proportional change in the cost of living at the poverty line in region $r$, that is, the expenditure required to remain at the poverty level of utility. This last is obtained by solving the AIDADS demand system for the expenditure required to remain at the poverty level of utility given the new prices (that is, the post-trade reform prices).

We may now express the proportional change in the poverty headcount in stratum $s$ of region $r$ as follows:

$$\hat{H}_{rs} = \varepsilon_{rs} \cdot \hat{y}_{rs}^{P} - \varepsilon_{rs} \cdot \sum_{j} \cdot \alpha_{rsj}^{P}(\hat{W}_{rj} - \hat{C}_{r}^{P}) \tag{4.2}$$

The earnings shares at the poverty line, $\alpha_{rsj}^{P}$, will play a critical role in our analysis. Regardless of the household type (with the exception of transfer-dependent households), the income from unskilled labor tends to dominate the stratum-specific earnings shares (Hertel et al. 2009). For example, in the case of agriculture-dependent households, most earnings show up in unskilled agricultural labor. In the case of rural diversified households, earnings usually show a mix of sources, including agricultural self-employed unskilled labor, unskilled wage labor, and unskilled nonfarm (self-employed) labor. The fact that these households are so poor means that they have little income from land or capital.

Having established the determinants of the stratum poverty headcount, we may now progress to the national poverty headcount, $H_r$, which may be expressed as a function of the stratum headcounts and stratum populations ($POP_{rs}$):

$$H_r = \left[ \sum_{s} POP_{rs} * H_{rs} \right] / POP_r, \tag{4.3}$$

where $POP_r = \sum_{s} POP_{rs}$. So, the proportional change in the national poverty headcount is $\hat{H}_r = \sum_{s} \beta_{rs} * H_{rs}$ .

Here,

$$\beta_{rs} = \left[(POP_{rs} * H_{rs})/POP_r\right]/H_r = (POP_{rs} * H_{rs})/\sum_s (POP_{rs} * H_{rs}) \qquad (4.4)$$

is the share of stratum $s$ poverty in nationwide poverty within region $r$. These shares are reported in table 4.2 for our 15 focus countries. Agriculture-specialized households and rural diversified households tend to dominate in the poverty headcount although exceptions are evident in Colombia, Peru, and República Bolivariana de Venezuela, where self-employed nonagricultural households represent a large share of the poor.

Combining equations (4.2) and (4.4), we obtain a useful expression for evaluating the change in the national poverty headcount in response to a small change in factor and commodity prices:

$$\hat{H}_r = \sum_s \beta_{rs} \cdot \varepsilon_{rs} \cdot \sum_j \alpha_{rsj}^p (\hat{W}_{rj} - C_r^p) \qquad (4.5)$$

**Table 4.2. Stratum Contributions to the US$1-a-Day Poverty Population, 15 Countries**

*(percentage shares)*

| Country | Ag | Nonag | Urban labor | Rural labor | Transfer | Urban diverse | Rural diverse | Total |
|---|---|---|---|---|---|---|---|---|
| Bangladesh | 0.15 | 0.13 | 0.04 | 0.22 | 0.03 | 0.07 | 0.37 | 1.00 |
| Brazil | 0.14 | 0.09 | 0.24 | 0.15 | 0.32 | 0.04 | 0.03 | 1.00 |
| Chile | 0.26 | 0.01 | 0.09 | 0.09 | 0.28 | 0.15 | 0.12 | 1.00 |
| Colombia | 0.28 | 0.43 | 0.03 | 0.04 | 0.12 | 0.05 | 0.04 | 1.00 |
| Indonesia | 0.42 | 0.12 | 0.02 | 0.07 | 0.04 | 0.06 | 0.28 | 1.00 |
| Malawi | 0.54 | 0.11 | 0.00 | 0.03 | 0.07 | 0.01 | 0.25 | 1.00 |
| Mexico | 0.05 | 0.06 | 0.05 | 0.12 | 0.28 | 0.14 | 0.29 | 1.00 |
| Mozambique | 0.41 | 0.13 | 0.01 | 0.05 | 0.14 | 0.06 | 0.19 | 1.00 |
| Peru | 0.07 | 0.35 | 0.01 | 0.02 | 0.22 | 0.11 | 0.23 | 1.00 |
| Philippines | 0.12 | 0.06 | 0.03 | 0.05 | 0.03 | 0.23 | 0.49 | 1.00 |
| Thailand | 0.06 | 0.02 | 0.00 | 0.06 | 0.11 | 0.07 | 0.68 | 1.00 |
| Uganda | 0.10 | 0.04 | 0.00 | 0.03 | 0.02 | 0.07 | 0.75 | 1.00 |
| Venezuela, R.B. de | 0.08 | 0.24 | 0.17 | 0.10 | 0.28 | 0.08 | 0.05 | 1.00 |
| Vietnam | 0.04 | 0.11 | 0.00 | 0.00 | 0.05 | 0.10 | 0.70 | 1.00 |
| Zambia | 0.34 | 0.23 | 0.10 | 0.07 | 0.07 | 0.09 | 0.11 | 1.00 |

*Source:* Author compilation.

*Note:* The values are the shares of the impoverished population that are specialized in a particular stratum of earnings. The shares are derived from country-specific household surveys. The total column reflects the assumption that the entire population in poverty is allocated among the seven strata. Ag = agriculture. Nonag = nonagriculture.

Because the expression in parentheses in equation (4.5) denotes the proportional change in the real after-tax income associated with each of the factors of production ($\hat{W}_{rj}^R$), we may rewrite this as follows:

$$\hat{H}_r = \sum_s \sum_j \beta_{rs} \cdot \varepsilon_{rs} \cdot \alpha_{rsj}^p \cdot \hat{W}_{rj}^R \qquad (4.6)$$

From equation (4.6), it is clear that, to obtain the change in national poverty, each real after-tax factor return must be premultiplied by a region-, stratum-, and factor-specific poverty elasticity.

For example, table 4.3 reports the product $\beta_{rs} \cdot \varepsilon_{rs} \cdot \alpha_{rsj}^p$ for Bangladesh. The rows in the table correspond to strata, and the columns to earnings types. Because $\sum_j \alpha_{rsj} = 1$, the sums in the rows of the table simply give the elasticity of national poverty with respect to a 1 percent rise in stratum income, that is, $\beta_{rs} \cdot \varepsilon_{rs}$. The sums are obviously heavily influenced by the national poverty shares reported in the Bangladesh row of table 4.2. The rural diversified stratum comprises nearly 37 percent of the poor, so it is not surprising that this row total is the largest in table 4.3. This stratum is followed in importance by the self-employed agricultural and nonagricultural strata, which show relatively high stratum-specific poverty elasticities (recall the first row of table 4.1), and then by the rural labor stratum and the urban diversified stratum.

The column sums in table 4.3 allow us to identify the factors that are most important to poverty reduction in Bangladesh. In this case, it is clear that unskilled labor is the primary endowment of the poor in Bangladesh. The key issues are the strata of these workers and the effect of trade reform on their relative wages. From the bottom row in table 4.3, we learn that unskilled wage labor is the most important stratum from the perspective of national poverty reduction, followed closely by self-employed nonagricultural labor and unskilled agricultural labor. Transfer payments, skilled wage labor, capital, and land play a much smaller role in poverty reduction at the margin, according to the final row in the table. The grand total in table 4.3 gives the national US$1-a-day poverty elasticity (bottom right corner, 1.24) with respect to a uniform 1 percent rise in real after-tax income from all sources.

The first row of table 4.4 takes the final row of table 4.3 for Bangladesh and divides all the entries by 1.24 so that we may see the share of each earnings source in national poverty reduction in the context of an across-the-board rise in real after-tax incomes. Thus, unskilled wage labor (the fifth column entry in row 1) contributes 33 percent of the total and so on. The remaining rows in table 4.4 provide the same calculation for the other 14 developing countries in our sample.

If we treat each country as an observation, we find that unskilled wage labor shows the highest average share (table 4.4, bottom row), followed by agricultural unskilled labor and then nonagricultural unskilled labor and transfers. Transfer

**Table 4.3. Stratum- and Earnings-Specific Poverty Elasticities, Bangladesh**

| Strata | Land | Ag unskilled labor | Ag skilled labor | Ag capital | Unskilled wage labor | Skilled wage labor | Nonag unskilled labor | Nonag skilled labor | Nonag capital | Transfers | Total |
|---|---|---|---|---|---|---|---|---|---|---|---|
| Ag | 0.01 | 0.23 | 0.00 | 0.01 | 0.00 | 0.00 | 0.00 | 0.00 | 0.00 | 0.00 | 0.24 |
| Nonag | 0.00 | 0.00 | 0.00 | 0.00 | 0.00 | 0.00 | 0.25 | 0.00 | 0.01 | 0.00 | 0.26 |
| Urban labor | 0.00 | 0.00 | 0.00 | 0.00 | 0.06 | 0.00 | 0.00 | 0.00 | 0.00 | 0.00 | 0.06 |
| Rural labor | 0.00 | 0.00 | 0.00 | 0.00 | 0.12 | 0.01 | 0.00 | 0.00 | 0.00 | 0.00 | 0.14 |
| Transfer | 0.00 | 0.00 | 0.00 | 0.00 | 0.00 | 0.00 | 0.00 | 0.00 | 0.00 | 0.01 | 0.02 |
| Urban diverse | 0.00 | 0.02 | 0.00 | 0.00 | 0.05 | 0.01 | 0.02 | 0.00 | 0.00 | 0.01 | 0.12 |
| Rural diverse | 0.00 | 0.07 | 0.00 | 0.00 | 0.17 | 0.02 | 0.08 | 0.00 | 0.01 | 0.04 | 0.40 |
| Total | 0.01 | 0.33 | 0.00 | 0.01 | 0.41 | 0.03 | 0.36 | 0.00 | 0.02 | 0.07 | 1.24 |

*Source:* Author compilation.

*Note:* The table refers to households living on less than US$1 a day. The elasticities are calculated by multiplying earnings shares by stratum-specific elasticities for Bangladesh. The total column shows the change in stratum poverty resulting from a 1 percent increase in income for each household type. The total row shows the national change in poverty resulting from a 1 percent increase in the factor income of each column type. Ag = agriculture. Nonag = nonagriculture.

**Table 4.4. The Contributions of Earnings to the Total US$1-a-Day Poverty Response, 15 Countries**
*(percent share of total)*

| Country | Land | Ag unskilled labor | Ag skilled labor | Ag capital | Unskilled wage labor | Skilled wage labor | Nonag unskilled labor | Nonag skilled labor | Nonag capital | Transfers | Total |
|---|---|---|---|---|---|---|---|---|---|---|---|
| Bangladesh | 0.01 | 0.27 | 0.00 | 0.01 | 0.33 | 0.02 | 0.29 | 0.00 | 0.02 | 0.06 | 1.00 (1.24) |
| Brazil | 0.00 | 0.07 | 0.03 | 0.01 | 0.60 | 0.04 | 0.10 | 0.01 | 0.00 | 0.15 | 1.00 (1.35) |
| Chile | 0.07 | 0.15 | 0.00 | 0.10 | 0.26 | 0.00 | 0.02 | 0.00 | 0.00 | 0.40 | 1.00 (2.18) |
| Colombia | 0.00 | 0.29 | 0.00 | 0.00 | 0.18 | 0.00 | 0.34 | 0.00 | 0.01 | 0.16 | 1.00 (0.82) |
| Indonesia | 0.03 | 0.50 | 0.00 | 0.02 | 0.19 | 0.01 | 0.15 | 0.00 | 0.04 | 0.03 | 1.00 (2.47) |
| Malawi | 0.03 | 0.52 | 0.00 | 0.07 | 0.12 | 0.02 | 0.15 | 0.00 | 0.05 | 0.14 | 1.00 (0.58) |
| Mexico | 0.00 | 0.09 | 0.00 | 0.00 | 0.38 | 0.00 | 0.05 | 0.00 | 0.00 | 0.43 | 1.00 (2.02) |
| Mozambique | 0.00 | 0.35 | 0.00 | 0.02 | 0.11 | 0.00 | 0.14 | 0.00 | 0.15 | 0.20 | 1.00 (0.64) |
| Peru | 0.01 | 0.16 | 0.00 | 0.01 | 0.09 | 0.00 | 0.15 | 0.07 | 0.06 | 0.14 | 1.00 (1.07) |
| Philippines | 0.23 | 0.00 | 0.01 | 0.12 | 0.31 | 0.01 | 0.14 | 0.00 | 0.07 | 0.10 | 1.00 (2.15) |
| Thailand | 0.03 | 0.20 | 0.02 | 0.02 | 0.24 | 0.05 | 0.04 | 0.01 | 0.01 | 0.38 | 1.00 (2.57) |
| Uganda | 0.13 | 0.13 | 0.00 | 0.25 | 0.08 | 0.08 | 0.12 | 0.00 | 0.13 | 0.08 | 1.00 (0.24) |
| Venezuela, R.B. de | 0.00 | 0.06 | 0.00 | 0.00 | 0.58 | 0.03 | 0.28 | 0.01 | 0.00 | 0.05 | 1.00 (1.20) |
| Vietnam | 0.01 | 0.12 | 0.00 | 0.00 | 0.00 | 0.00 | 0.18 | 0.00 | 0.47 | 0.20 | 1.00 (0.98) |
| Zambia | 0.00 | 0.02 | 0.00 | 0.02 | 0.43 | 0.16 | 0.20 | 0.00 | 0.13 | 0.08 | 1.00 (0.61) |
| Average | 0.04 | 0.19 | 0.00 | 0.04 | 0.26 | 0.03 | 0.15 | 0.01 | 0.08 | 0.17 | n.a. |

*Source:* Author compilation.

*Note:* The values are earnings-specific elasticities, divided by national poverty elasticities (in parentheses in the total column). The average row is the simple average across countries of the contribution of a specific earnings source to total poverty responsiveness. The total column reflects the fact that contributions to total responsiveness add to 1. Ag = agriculture. Nonag = nonagriculture. n.a. = not applicable.

payments are important in some of the richer developing countries (Brazil, Chile, Colombia, Mexico, Thailand), as well as in lower-income countries with a large share of migrant labor (for example, Mozambique). The entries in table 4.4 give a clear idea of the factor price increases that are most likely to lower the national poverty headcount in each country.

## The Global CGE Model

Because the household-level poverty impacts hinge critically on factor rewards that depend not only on the type of endowment, but also on where it is employed, we need a global modeling framework with sufficient detail to separate out these differential returns. We have adopted the GTAP model (Hertel 1997) and the version 6.1 GTAP Database calibrated to 2001 (Dimaranan 2006). We have modified both to be consistent with our needs for differentiated factor returns, as well as the changes in price distortions identified in Anderson and Valenzuela (2008) and prepared for CGE modeling by Valenzuela and Anderson (2008). We must also make some updates to account for changes in market conditions and policy reforms since 2001, the year of the version 6.1 database. The model is implemented in Gempack software (Harrison and Pearson 1996).

We now turn to a discussion of the modeling assumptions and data changes incorporated into our CGE modeling framework.

### Database adjustments

Our starting point for the global CGE analysis of the impacts of trade policy is the GTAP version 6.1 database (Dimaranan 2006). For our present purposes, we have aggregated the database to 31 productive sectors and six groups of household consumption items, following Ivanic (2006). We have updated this database by solving an experiment that accounts for key policy reforms in border protection that were undertaken between 2001 and 2005, most notably the accession of China to the World Trade Organization, the enlargement of the European Union, and the completion of the Uruguay Round commitments by some members of the World Trade Organization. We have also altered the database, now with a base year of 2005, to reflect the recent estimates of agricultural price distortions in developing countries by Anderson and Valenzuela (2008). We have likewise altered our database to reflect the most recent OECD commodity support data on agricultural output subsidies as of 2004. The aggregate changes in commodity support as measured by the producer support estimate are relatively small over this time frame (OECD 2007). However, in some instances, the support for particular commodities changed dramatically. Because of our desired emphasis on viewing poverty impacts through a commodity lens, our use of the most recent available information on initial protection is warranted. In total, this has meant that we have adjusted the output subsidy levels among 25 OECD members in the initial database.[4]

### Modifications to the GTAP model

Our modifications to the standard GTAP model focus on features that enhance the analysis of agricultural reforms and the simulation of impacts on poverty. We retain the simplistic, yet empirically robust assumptions of constant returns to scale and perfect competition typically featured in agricultural trade studies.[5] The remaining modifications are aimed at permitting us to shed new light on the distributional consequences of trade reforms. They focus particularly on unraveling the puzzle involved in the question, why is such reform not more poverty-friendly?

On the demand side of the model, we ensure consistency with the poverty analysis by modifying the GTAP model to incorporate the AIDADS demand system as discussed in Hertel et al. (2007). Thus, the aggregate preferences are consistent with the preferences used to evaluate the impact of price changes on households at the poverty line although expenditure patterns differ across income levels because of the nonhomotheticity of demands.

The other modifications relate to the factor markets and follow from the model changes made by Keeney and Hertel (2005). Frictions in agricultural factor markets have featured prominently in the development economics literature, particularly as an explanation for low agricultural supply response (de Janvry, Fafchamps, and Sadoulet 1991). Modeling the complex processes leading to limited farm-nonfarm and rural-urban mobility for the full range of countries in our model is beyond the scope of this chapter and is better suited to the individual country case study approach (see elsewhere above).

To maintain a general framework that reflects the imperfect factor mobility between rural and urban employment, we specify a constant elasticity of transformation function that transforms farm-employed factors into nonfarm employment and vice-versa.[6] This allows factor rewards to diverge between the farm and nonfarm sectors and supplies us with the factor market segmentation we require for our distributional analysis. We use the factor supply parameters that have been adopted by Keeney and Hertel (2005) and that are drawn from the OECD (2001).

We assume that aggregate endowment levels are fixed in our static analysis. This reflects a belief that the aggregate supply of factors is unaffected by trade policy. This is not the full employment assumption sometimes ridiculed by advocates of structural models of development. Rather, it holds that aggregate employment is primarily determined by factors, such as labor market norms and regulation, that are largely independent of trade policy in the long run.

Recalling equation (4.6), we must tie our results to the factor earnings shares for all household types in each region. We map the factor returns from the general equilibrium model to the various earnings types according to the following method. Agricultural labor and capital receive the corresponding farm factor returns from the general equilibrium model, as do nonagricultural labor and capital. Wage labor in the household surveys is not distinguished by place of employment; so, we use the economy-wide average change. Transfer payments represent an important source of earnings for many households and have no obvious corollary in the CGE model. We choose to index these to the growth rate in net national incomes, which allows us to maintain consistency with the representative household approach of the global model (see Hertel et al. 2007).

Finally, a few words about our macroclosure are in order. In this chapter, we fix the ratio of key macroeconomic aggregates relative to net national income. These include government spending, total tax revenues (net of subsidies), net national savings, and the trade balance. In this way, we also ensure that public transfer payments (not explicitly modeled in our study) are implicitly fixed relative to net national income. This provides a convenient method for indexing the transfer payments accruing to households. Because tariff liberalization typically results in a reduction in tax revenues, a replacement tax is needed. In this chapter, we assume that income taxes on all earnings rise by an equal proportion so to ensure that tax revenues remain fixed relative to net national income. Of course, in those rich countries in which tariffs are low and agricultural subsidies are high, this tax rate may fall in the wake of trade liberalization. While we do not believe that the income tax will be the replacement tax of choice in many economies, particularly the poorest economies, it is a convenient tool, and we do not possess sufficient detail on the tax structure in many of these economies to improve greatly on this simple assumption. As we show below, the omission of the tax replacement effect has a dramatic impact on our poverty results. This impact is thereby highlighted as a key issue for consideration in the country-specific case studies in this volume and elsewhere.

## Model Results and Discussion

In this chapter, we report the results of only one core simulation: the removal globally of all agricultural production and export subsidies and all agricultural and nonagricultural merchandise trade taxes.[7] Table 4.5 reports our estimates of the percent change in the national poverty headcount for each of our focus countries based on this global liberalization simulation. We use the decomposition method of Harrison, Horridge, and Pearson (2000) to identify the impacts of agricultural and nonagricultural policy reform separately from the total in

*(percent change in the headcount)*

| Country | Core results of this study | | | | Different data, GTAP 6 | Different tax replacement | |
| --- | --- | --- | --- | --- | --- | --- | --- |
| | Ag reform | Nonag reform | Total | Level change, 1,000s | | Poor are exempt | VAT |
| Bangladesh | -0.25 | 0.51 | 0.26 | 116 | 0.28 | -5.30 | -0.01 |
| Brazil | -2.53 | 0.38 | -2.15 | -50 | -1.41 | -10.00 | -1.42 |
| Chile | -4.76 | 0.12 | -4.64 | -14 | -4.99 | -12.25 | -4.79 |
| Colombia | -0.72 | 0.63 | -0.09 | -3 | 0.10 | -4.05 | 0.03 |
| Indonesia | -1.05 | 0.49 | -0.56 | -84 | -1.45 | -5.23 | -0.53 |
| Malawi | -1.64 | -0.26 | -1.91 | -87 | -1.84 | -5.62 | -1.31 |
| Mexico | 0.78 | 0.35 | 1.13 | 105 | 1.35 | -0.48 | 1.15 |
| Mozambique | -1.15 | 0.15 | -1.00 | -61 | -0.69 | -4.34 | 0.29 |
| Peru | -0.64 | -0.16 | -0.80 | -35 | -0.79 | -5.24 | -0.67 |
| Philippines | -1.37 | 0.42 | -0.95 | -108 | -0.75 | -6.39 | -1.92 |
| Thailand | -11.19 | 0.93 | -10.26 | -121 | -8.87 | -28.05 | -5.83 |
| Uganda | -0.01 | 0.09 | 0.09 | 15 | 0.06 | -5.96 | 0.09 |
| Venezuela, R.B. de | 0.15 | 0.71 | 0.86 | 28 | 0.86 | -2.12 | 1.14 |
| Vietnam | -0.48 | -5.26 | -5.74 | -88 | -5.85 | -23.58 | -6.96 |
| Zambia | -0.02 | 0.13 | 0.11 | 7 | 0.09 | -2.00 | 1.25 |
| Average | -1.66 | -0.05 | -1.71 | n.a. | -1.59 | -8.04 | -1.30 |
| Absolute average | 1.78 | 0.71 | 2.04 | n.a. | 1.96 | 8.04 | 1.83 |
| Sign consistency | -0.93 | -0.07 | -0.84 | n.a. | -0.81 | -1.00 | -0.71 |

*Source:* Model simulations by the authors.

*Note:* The table shows the results of simulations by the authors using Gempack software (Harrison and Pearson 1996) and the GTAP Database (Dimaranan 2006). The impacts of agricultural (Ag) and nonagricultural (Nonag) reform add to the total percent change in poverty. We use the subtotal routine in Gempack that has been developed by Harrison, Horridge, and Pearson (2000) to isolate these portions of the total impact. Level change is the calculated number of persons moving out of poverty given the initial headcount and the predicted percent change. The different data simulation uses the GTAP version 6 (base year 2001) protection data with the modifications of Hertel et al. (2007, 2009). The different tax replacement, poor are exempt scenario assumes that the poor are not subject to the higher income tax needed to replace lost tariff revenue. The different tax replacement, value added tax (VAT) scenario replaces lost tariff revenue through a consumption tax that may be viewed as a value added tax equivalent under which imports are taxed, while exports are exempted. Sign consistency measures the consistency between the direction of effects and the level of impact and is calculated as the ratio of the average to the absolute value of individual percent changes. Absolute average is the simple average of the absolute value of the percent changes, while average is the simple average of the percent changes, while AV/AEV (Ivanic 2006). n.a. = not applicable.

percentage terms. We also provide level changes (in thousands) in the national poverty headcount (table 4.5, column 4).

### Impacts of the new data on price distortions

Table 4.5 offers a comparison of the total poverty reduction based on previous work (Hertel et al. 2009) that did not feature the distortion estimates compiled by Anderson and Valenzuela (2008) or the updated OECD estimates of protection in OECD member countries. Comparing table 4.5, columns 3 and 5, we find mostly small differences in the percent changes in the poverty headcount of our study (column 3) compared with the changes calculated in the GTAP Database (column 5). However, some differences are worth noting. For Colombia, the previous results indicated that global liberalization would lead to a slight increase in poverty (a 0.1 percent rise in the national headcount), whereas our results anticipate that global trade reform will lead to a slight reduction in poverty. Colombia is one of the countries in which the information on agricultural protection changed significantly because of the incorporation of the estimates of Anderson and Valenzuela (2008). More significantly, our predicted poverty reduction in Indonesia is somewhat lower and, in Brazil, somewhat higher than the poverty reduction estimates reported previously.

### The crucial role of tax replacement

The last two columns of table 4.5 present differing estimates of the predicted poverty changes that follow if we alter our assumption about tax adjustments. One variant is to assume that the poor are not subjected to the income tax replacement mechanism. Another is to use an alternative tax replacement instrument, namely, a value added tax equivalent. This allows us to compare our results with the results of studies that rely on different assumptions, and it highlights the importance of the tax replacement assumption on the predicted changes in poverty.

Table 4.5, column 6 reports the percent changes in the national poverty headcounts if the poor are not subject to the replacement income tax. This is the assumption of Anderson, Martin, and van der Mensbrugghe (2006) in their analysis of the poverty impacts of the Doha Development Agenda. As one may see, this accounts for a marked difference in the predicted poverty reduction. Trade reforms that, without this assumption, were marginally poverty reducing in most cases are now universally poverty reducing by a considerable magnitude. The assumption reduces the poverty rate by roughly one-quarter in Thailand and Vietnam, for example. In this scenario, the poor are being given access to commodities or are able to sell them at undistorted prices without having to bear any of the direct tax burden involved in replacing the lost tariff revenue. Indeed, this reform represents a significant implicit income transfer from nonpoor households to poor households. We do not argue that such a fiscal transfer is not to be desired, of course, because the transfer would have tremendous poverty reduction benefits. However, we do not believe this is the measure that would most likely be used, given that most developing countries seek to make up for lost tariff revenue by resorting to a value added tax.

The final column in table 4.5 reports the poverty results if we replace the lost tariff revenue by adjusting the value added tax. However, care must be taken in adjusting this tax because some sectors are exempt from the tax (public consumption, for example, and, often, basic foods). In this alternative scenario, we adjust the tax through an equiproportional adjustment in the power of the consumption tax (that is, one, plus the consumption tax rate) on taxable items in each focus country. This might be viewed as equivalent, in effect, to a value added tax replacement experiment if the value added tax applies to all imports and exempts all exports. However, if the existing consumption tax structure is already distorted (as in the case in our model, for example, because some sectors are exempt), this replacement consumption tax exacerbates the distortions. In particular, because it does not apply to public consumption, the tax distorts the allocation of resources between public consumption and private consumption. Therefore, in our framework, this value added tax scenario is expected to produce less beneficial outcomes in terms of poverty reduction relative to the core scenario. Indeed, this is confirmed by a comparison of table 4.5, columns 3 and 7: if lost tariff revenue is replaced by a consumption tax instead of an income tax, the poverty gains are more modest, and the mix of countries that reduce poverty is altered slightly.

### Summary of the poverty impacts

In the final three rows of table 4.5, columns 1–3, we report on the summary measures introduced by Ivanic (2006). Specifically, we compute, first, the average value across countries (treating each country as an observation with equal weight); then, we report the average absolute value, which indicates the importance of a given change regardless of sign; and, finally, we report the ratio of these two: $AV/AAV = SC$ (average/absolute average = sign consistency). Note that this ratio—which may be viewed as the tendency for trade reforms to reduce (or increase) poverty—is constructed such that $-1 \leq SC \leq +1$. If $SC = -1$, then a given trade reform (or set of reforms) is poverty reducing for all countries in the sample because the average change and the absolute value of the changes are of the same magnitude, but opposite in sign.

From the average across countries, we see that our current results, based on updated protection data, predict larger poverty-reducing impacts in developing countries relative to the previous analysis ($AV = -1.71$ versus $AV = -1.59$) and a slightly greater prevalence of poverty-reducing impacts across the countries in our sample ($AAV = -0.84$ versus $AAV = -0.81$). In summary, the results predict that full global trade liberalization would reduce poverty in 10 of our 15 focus countries. Even if we ignore the growth-enhancing effects of trade reform (which are not included in our comparative static framework), this would mean that no less than 816,000 people would be lifted out of poverty.

The decomposition of total impacts between agricultural and nonagricultural reforms (table 4.5, first two columns) shows that the impact of the global agricultural reforms on the poor is more than twice the impact of the nonagricultural reforms ($AAVag = 1.78$ versus $AAVnonag = 0.71$). Furthermore, the agricultural reforms are nearly always poverty reducing ($SC = -0.93$), whereas the nonagricultural reforms tend to be only marginally poverty reducing among this sample of countries ($SC = -0.07$). Of the five countries experiencing increases in poverty in the wake of combined agricultural and nonagricultural trade reforms, Bangladesh and Mexico are the most important in terms of absolute numbers (more than 100,000 in each case). These countries currently enjoy preferential market access in their most important markets (the European Union for Bangladesh and the United States for Mexico). Global trade liberalization would lead to substantial preference erosion for both countries in these preferred markets.

### Why are agricultural reforms more poverty-friendly than nonfarm trade reform?

We begin our quest to understand the differential impact of trade reforms across products by focusing on the difference between the poverty impacts of agricultural and nonagricultural reforms; we then turn to an individual commodity decomposition of agricultural reforms.

A natural method of investigating the difference between farm and nonfarm reforms is via the decomposition proposed in equation (4.6). Because the elasticities in this expression are the same (initially) in both experiments, the entire difference in the change in the poverty headcount is accounted for by real after-tax wage changes. Specifically, we have the following decomposition of the difference in poverty headcount by region:

$$\hat{H}_{r,diff} = \sum_{s} \sum_{j} \beta_{rs} \cdot \varepsilon_{rs} \cdot \alpha_{rsj}^{P} (\hat{W}_{rj,agr}^{R} - \hat{W}_{rj,nagr}^{R}), \tag{4.7}$$

where $\hat{W}_{rj,agr}^{R}$ is the real after-tax change in earnings for endowment $j$ in region $r$ owing to agricultural reforms, and $\hat{W}_{rj,nagr}^{R}$ is the nonagricultural counterpart.

Our first task is to explain why the earnings are differentially affected; then, we must consider the interaction of these changes with region, stratum, and factor elasticities to determine the differential impact on national poverty.

Table 4.6 reports the values of ($\hat{W}^R_{rj,agr} - \hat{W}^R_{rj,nagr}$) for all sources of earnings and all focus regions in our analysis. Relative to nonagricultural trade reforms, agricultural trade reforms raise the returns to farming in all our focus developing countries. Relative to nonagricultural reforms, they also raise the returns to unskilled wage labor in most countries as the unskilled labor-intensive agricultural sector expands and boosts wages among unskilled labor. (Indonesia, Mexico, and Vietnam are the exceptions because the nonagricultural reforms exert a stronger influence on unskilled wages there.) Agricultural reforms are less favorable for skilled labor, but the reward of this factor is relatively unimportant for the poor (see table 4.4).

Continuing across the columns in table 4.6, we see that agricultural reforms often, but not always lead to relatively lower real after-tax earnings relative to nonagricultural reforms for self-employed nonagricultural endowments. This is evident in the many negative entries in columns 7–9. Relative to nonagricultural reforms, agricultural reforms that increase food prices tend to hurt transfer-dependent households because transfers (by assumption) are indexed to net national income and not to the cost of living at the poverty line (column 10). This effect is attributable to the relatively large share of food expenditures in the consumption baskets of the poorest households.

If we take into account the aggregate poverty elasticities with respect to factor earnings reported in table 4.4, it is not immediately clear from the pattern of earnings differences shown in table 4.6 why agricultural trade reforms dominate nonagricultural reforms as a poverty reduction tool. However, this result depends on the responsiveness of the national poverty headcounts to each of the sources of earnings. We gain more insight into this issue by examining table 4.7, which reports the poverty-weighted elasticity counterparts to the earnings differences reported in table 4.6, that is, $\sum_s \beta_{rs} \cdot \varepsilon_{rs} \cdot \alpha^P_{rsj}(\hat{W}^R_{rj,farm} - \hat{W}^R_{rj,nfarm})$.

If we sum across a row in table 4.7 (that is, if we sum across all endowments in a given country), we obtain the percent difference in the poverty headcount stemming from agricultural and nonagricultural reforms (subject to any rounding error arising from the differencing of percentages; this is the reason these entries differ from the simple difference between the first two columns of table 4.5). The final column in table 4.7 indicates that, in all countries except Mexico and Vietnam, agricultural reforms are more poverty friendly relative to nonagricultural reforms.

What is special about Mexico and Vietnam? We note that these are two of the three countries in which real after-tax unskilled wages rise more under nonagricultural trade reforms (the other country is Indonesia; see table 4.6). Unlike Indonesia, where the share of the poor in agriculture-specialized households is

**136**

**Table 4.6. Earnings Differences after Agricultural and Nonagricultural Reforms, 15 Countries**
(percent change)

| Country | Land | Ag unskilled labor | Ag skilled labor | Ag capital | Unskilled wage labor | Skilled wage labor | Nonag unskilled labor | Nonag skilled labor | Nonag capital | Transfers |
|---|---|---|---|---|---|---|---|---|---|---|
| Bangladesh | 0.33 | 0.38 | 0.95 | 0.86 | 0.56 | 1.68 | 0.62 | 1.69 | 1.52 | 1.17 |
| Brazil | 40.01 | 16.35 | 15.10 | 14.81 | 1.34 | −0.75 | −0.72 | −0.91 | −1.58 | −0.13 |
| Chile | 15.35 | 7.57 | 6.93 | 6.74 | 0.29 | −0.86 | −1.03 | −0.88 | −1.33 | −0.85 |
| Colombia | 8.22 | 4.40 | 3.97 | 3.49 | 1.10 | 0.30 | 0.36 | 0.30 | −0.81 | 0.35 |
| Indonesia | 3.87 | 1.76 | 1.59 | 1.49 | −0.50 | −0.83 | −1.53 | −0.86 | −1.09 | −0.59 |
| Malawi | 4.76 | 3.20 | 2.68 | 2.82 | 1.75 | 0.77 | 0.75 | 0.77 | 0.68 | 1.21 |
| Mexico | −0.18 | −0.10 | −0.06 | −0.06 | −0.19 | −0.10 | −0.21 | −0.10 | −0.20 | −0.26 |
| Mozambique | 8.58 | 4.93 | 3.52 | 4.16 | 1.42 | −1.41 | −0.18 | −1.43 | −0.50 | 0.60 |
| Peru | 12.95 | 6.94 | 5.69 | 5.92 | 1.07 | −1.25 | −1.44 | −1.49 | −0.92 | −0.11 |
| Philippines | 3.07 | 1.68 | 1.53 | 1.21 | 0.35 | 0.07 | −0.56 | 0.03 | −0.67 | −0.36 |
| Thailand | 34.07 | 17.46 | 14.29 | 12.92 | 4.19 | −1.59 | −2.01 | −1.99 | −4.38 | −2.11 |
| Uganda | 0.62 | 0.50 | 0.47 | 0.44 | 0.40 | 0.34 | 0.25 | 0.34 | 0.20 | 0.37 |
| Venezuela, R.B. de | 0.87 | 0.68 | 0.70 | 0.44 | 0.49 | 0.55 | 0.46 | 0.55 | 0.01 | −0.11 |
| Vietnam | 15.75 | 3.87 | 3.89 | 5.83 | −9.07 | −8.93 | −12.81 | −8.93 | −4.87 | −6.40 |
| Zambia | 4.00 | 1.87 | 1.60 | 1.47 | 0.56 | 0.03 | 0.17 | 0.02 | −0.49 | −0.15 |
| Average | 10.15 | 4.76 | 4.19 | 4.17 | 0.25 | −0.80 | −1.19 | −0.86 | −0.96 | −0.49 |
| Absolute average | 10.17 | 4.78 | 4.20 | 4.18 | 1.55 | 1.30 | 1.54 | 1.35 | 1.28 | 0.98 |
| Sign consistency | 1.00 | 1.00 | 1.00 | 1.00 | 0.16 | −0.62 | −0.77 | −0.64 | −0.75 | −0.50 |

Source: Model simulations by the authors.

Note: The table shows the differences in impacts on real after-tax earnings according to endowment following agricultural and nonagricultural reforms. See the note to table 4.5 for simulation information.

## Table 4.7. Earnings-Specific Differences between Agricultural and Nonagricultural Reforms in the Changes in Poverty, 15 Countries

(percent change in the headcount)

| Country | Land | Ag unskilled labor | Ag skilled labor | Ag capital | Unskilled wage labor | Skilled wage labor | Nonag unskilled labor | Nonag skilled labor | Nonag capital | Transfers | Total |
|---|---|---|---|---|---|---|---|---|---|---|---|
| Bangladesh | 0.00 | −0.12 | 0.00 | −0.01 | −0.23 | −0.05 | −0.22 | 0.00 | −0.04 | −0.08 | −0.76 |
| Brazil | −0.10 | −1.43 | −0.60 | −0.15 | −1.09 | 0.04 | 0.10 | 0.00 | 0.00 | 0.03 | −3.21 |
| Chile | −2.30 | −2.45 | 0.00 | −1.48 | −0.16 | 0.00 | 0.04 | 0.00 | 0.00 | 0.75 | −5.60 |
| Colombia | 0.00 | −1.07 | 0.00 | 0.00 | −0.17 | 0.00 | −0.10 | 0.00 | 0.01 | −0.04 | −1.38 |
| Indonesia | −0.30 | −2.16 | −0.02 | −0.08 | 0.23 | 0.02 | 0.66 | 0.01 | 0.10 | 0.05 | −1.49 |
| Malawi | −0.10 | −0.95 | 0.00 | −0.11 | −0.12 | 0.00 | −0.03 | 0.00 | −0.02 | −0.10 | −1.43 |
| Mexico | 0.00 | 0.02 | 0.00 | 0.00 | 0.15 | 0.00 | 0.03 | 0.00 | 0.00 | 0.23 | 0.43 |
| Mozambique | −0.04 | −1.12 | 0.00 | −0.04 | −0.11 | 0.00 | 0.02 | 0.00 | 0.05 | −0.08 | −1.31 |
| Peru | −0.12 | −1.17 | 0.00 | −0.07 | −0.11 | 0.01 | 0.70 | 0.11 | 0.06 | 0.02 | −0.59 |
| Philippines | −1.54 | −0.01 | −0.04 | −0.32 | −0.23 | 0.00 | 0.17 | 0.00 | 0.09 | 0.08 | −1.79 |
| Thailand | −2.95 | −9.08 | −0.89 | −0.54 | −2.55 | 0.21 | 0.21 | 0.03 | 0.13 | 2.06 | −13.38 |
| Uganda | −0.02 | −0.02 | 0.00 | −0.03 | −0.01 | −0.01 | 0.00 | 0.00 | −0.01 | −0.01 | −0.10 |
| Venezuela, R.B. de | 0.00 | −0.05 | 0.00 | 0.00 | −0.34 | −0.02 | −0.16 | 0.00 | 0.00 | 0.01 | −0.56 |
| Vietnam | −0.17 | −0.45 | 0.00 | −0.03 | 0.01 | 0.00 | 2.27 | 0.01 | 2.24 | 1.31 | 5.20 |
| Zambia | −0.01 | −0.01 | 0.00 | −0.01 | −0.14 | 0.00 | −0.02 | 0.00 | 0.04 | 0.01 | −0.15 |
| Average | −0.51 | −1.34 | −0.10 | −0.19 | −0.32 | 0.01 | 0.24 | 0.01 | 0.18 | 0.28 | −1.74 |
| Absolute average | 0.51 | 1.34 | 0.10 | 0.19 | 0.38 | 0.02 | 0.32 | 0.01 | 0.19 | 0.32 | 2.49 |
| Sign consistency | −1.00 | −1.00 | −1.00 | −1.00 | −0.86 | 0.53 | 0.77 | 0.93 | 0.95 | 0.87 | −0.70 |

*Source:* Model simulations by the authors.

*Note:* The results correspond with equation (4.7) and represent the differences in the impacts of agricultural and nonagricultural reforms on poverty according to endowment. See the note to table 4.5 for simulation information.

about 40 percent (see table 4.2), Mexico and Vietnam show relatively low shares of agricultural households in total poverty. Both these countries have relatively high shares of rural diversified households in poverty that rely heavily on unskilled wage labor, which is more favorably affected by nonagricultural trade reforms.

While higher returns to unskilled family labor in agriculture represent the dominant driver of agricultural poverty reduction relative to nonagricultural poverty reduction in most countries, there are important exceptions. In Bangladesh and Zambia, agricultural reforms have a more favorable impact on poverty than do nonagricultural reforms largely because of the wage labor channel. In the Philippines, farm households benefit relatively more from higher returns to agricultural land.

We also examine the relative impact of agricultural and nonagricultural trade reforms on poverty by stratum. This is shown in table 4.8, which reports the

**Table 4.8. Stratum-Specific Differences in the Changes in Poverty after Agricultural and Nonagricultural Reforms, 15 Countries**
*(contribution to percent change in the headcount)*

| Country | Ag | Nonag | Urban labor | Rural labor | Transfer | Urban diverse | Rural diverse | Total |
|---|---|---|---|---|---|---|---|---|
| Bangladesh | −0.10 | −0.17 | −0.03 | −0.09 | −0.02 | −0.08 | −0.27 | −0.76 |
| Brazil | −1.67 | 0.08 | −0.55 | −0.40 | 0.01 | −0.46 | −0.23 | −3.21 |
| Chile | −4.47 | 0.02 | −0.05 | −0.04 | 0.58 | −0.97 | −0.67 | −5.60 |
| Colombia | −0.98 | −0.09 | −0.06 | −0.07 | −0.04 | −0.08 | −0.06 | −1.38 |
| Indonesia | −1.76 | 0.39 | 0.02 | 0.10 | 0.03 | −0.03 | −0.23 | −1.49 |
| Malawi | −0.86 | −0.02 | 0.00 | −0.09 | −0.03 | −0.02 | −0.40 | −1.43 |
| Mexico | 0.01 | 0.02 | 0.03 | 0.05 | 0.17 | 0.05 | 0.10 | 0.43 |
| Mozambique | −0.58 | 0.04 | −0.02 | −0.05 | −0.04 | −0.21 | −0.45 | −1.31 |
| Peru | −0.68 | 0.64 | −0.01 | −0.03 | 0.01 | −0.18 | −0.33 | −0.59 |
| Philippines | −0.62 | 0.06 | −0.03 | −0.04 | 0.02 | −0.41 | −0.77 | −1.79 |
| Thailand | −2.62 | 0.09 | −0.05 | −0.57 | 0.63 | −0.94 | −9.94 | −13.38 |
| Uganda | −0.01 | 0.00 | 0.00 | 0.00 | 0.00 | −0.01 | −0.06 | −0.10 |
| Venezuela, R.B. de | −0.04 | −0.13 | −0.21 | −0.11 | 0.00 | −0.04 | −0.03 | −0.56 |
| Vietnam | −0.08 | 1.16 | 0.00 | 0.00 | 0.27 | 0.11 | 3.74 | 5.20 |
| Zambia | 0.00 | 0.01 | −0.08 | −0.03 | 0.00 | −0.04 | −0.01 | −0.15 |
| Average | −0.96 | 0.14 | −0.07 | −0.09 | 0.11 | −0.22 | −0.64 | −1.74 |
| Absolute average | 0.97 | 0.20 | 0.08 | 0.11 | 0.12 | 0.24 | 1.15 | 2.49 |
| Sign consistency | −1.00 | 0.72 | −0.91 | −0.82 | 0.86 | −0.91 | −0.56 | −0.70 |

*Source:* Model simulations by the authors.

*Note:* The results correspond with equation (4.7) and represent the differences in the impacts of agricultural and nonagricultural reforms on poverty according to household type. See the note to table 4.5 for simulation information.

elements of $\Sigma_j \beta_{rs} \cdot \varepsilon_{rs} \cdot \alpha_{rsj}^P (\hat{W}_{rj,farm}^R - \hat{W}_{rj,nfarm}^R)$ for all 15 countries and all seven strata. The columns now refer to strata, and each element represents the combined impact of all changes in earnings (adjusted for changes in taxes and the cost of living) on national poverty through the changes in poverty in the individual household strata. Once again, the final column records the differences between agricultural and nonagricultural reforms in terms of the percent change in the national poverty headcount. Here, we see that agricultural trade reforms reduce poverty among agriculture-specialized households in nearly all countries (note that $SC$, the ratio of the average and absolute average headcounts, is $-1.00$ under this stratum).

The contribution of the agricultural stratum to poverty reduction is negligible only in Mexico and Vietnam, and these are the only two countries in which poverty among diversified rural households would fall more after nonagricultural trade reforms than after agricultural reforms (leading to positive entries in the rural diversified column in table 4.8). In both Mexico and Vietnam, the contribution of all nonagricultural household strata to reductions in poverty are more significant after multilateral nonagricultural reforms than after agricultural reforms.

### Understanding the impacts on poverty of particular farm commodity policies

Because of the importance of agricultural reform, we now turn to the task of decomposing poverty impacts according to agricultural commodity. In table 4.9, we decompose the reduction in poverty after agricultural reform (see table 4.5) into component parts; in this case, our breakdown is according to the global commodity market in which the reform has occurred. Thus, the first set of columns reports the percent change in national poverty headcounts caused by global reforms in the foodgrains sector. As a result, we see that, with the exception of Vietnam (and Mexico and República Bolivariana de Venezuela, in which there is no effect), the liberalization in foodgrain markets is generally poverty reducing. The disaggregation of the foodgrains reforms according to instrument reveals that tariff cuts in foodgrains—as well as feedgrains, which are also shown in table 4.10—are universally poverty reducing (the sign consistency index is $-1$). If poverty increases in a country because of reforms in food or feedgrains, this effect is caused by adverse price impacts that arise from the elimination of export subsidies and domestic support (see the export subsidies and domestic subsidies columns in table 4.10). Apart from foodgrains, the reforms in other crops are the most poverty friendly. These

**Table 4.9. Change in Poverty after Commodity-Specific Reforms, 15 Countries**

*(percent change in the headcount)*

| Country | Foodgrains | Feedgrains | Sugar | Cotton | Other crops | Dairy | Meat |
|---|---|---|---|---|---|---|---|
| Bangladesh | −0.07 | −0.16 | −0.02 | −0.18 | 0.11 | 0.04 | 0.02 |
| Brazil | −0.29 | −0.20 | −0.20 | −0.01 | −0.27 | 0.01 | −1.56 |
| Chile | −0.18 | −0.04 | −0.03 | 0.03 | −3.11 | −0.40 | −1.03 |
| Colombia | −0.11 | 0.06 | −0.08 | 0.01 | −0.55 | −0.09 | 0.04 |
| Indonesia | −0.09 | 0.00 | 0.29 | 0.00 | −0.36 | −0.03 | −0.86 |
| Malawi | −0.14 | 0.02 | 0.05 | −0.04 | −1.51 | −0.02 | 0.00 |
| Mexico | 0.00 | 0.48 | 0.03 | 0.06 | 0.23 | −0.03 | 0.02 |
| Mozambique | −0.10 | −0.17 | −0.53 | −0.08 | −0.36 | −0.01 | 0.09 |
| Peru | −0.07 | 0.01 | −0.01 | 0.02 | −0.01 | 0.02 | −0.60 |
| Philippines | −0.20 | −0.23 | −0.01 | −0.07 | −0.79 | 0.11 | −0.19 |
| Thailand | −5.63 | −0.91 | −0.88 | 0.06 | −2.89 | 0.01 | −0.93 |
| Uganda | −0.01 | −0.02 | 0.00 | −0.02 | 0.03 | 0.01 | 0.00 |
| Venezuela, R.B. de | 0.00 | 0.02 | 0.00 | 0.00 | 0.04 | 0.03 | 0.04 |
| Vietnam | 0.03 | −0.40 | −0.07 | 0.00 | −0.18 | 0.13 | 0.01 |
| Zambia | −0.01 | −0.04 | 0.01 | 0.01 | −0.04 | 0.01 | 0.03 |
| Average | −0.46 | −0.11 | −0.10 | −0.01 | −0.64 | −0.01 | −0.33 |
| Absolute average | 0.46 | 0.18 | 0.15 | 0.04 | 0.70 | 0.06 | 0.36 |
| Sign consistency | −0.99 | −0.57 | −0.65 | −0.31 | −0.92 | −0.23 | −0.90 |

*Source:* Model simulations by the authors.

*Note:* The results correspond with equation (4.7) and represent the impacts of reforms on poverty according to commodity sector. See the note to table 4.5 for simulation information.

crops include many of the tropical products of which developing countries are net exporters. We report only foodgrains and feedgrains here, but an all-commodity ranking on poverty friendliness, as we have used the term, would appear as follows: foodgrains, other food and beverages, other crops, meats, sugar, feedgrains, cotton, and dairy. In terms of the absolute size of the impacts on poverty, the liberalization of other crops is the most significant, followed by liberalization in foodgrains and then meats.

## Summary and Conclusions

This chapter offers a complementary perspective to the detailed country case studies of trade reform and poverty provided by others in this volume. By looking at a wide range of developing countries in Africa, Asia, and Latin America, we

**Table 4.10. Change in Poverty Caused by Foodgrain and
Feedgrain Reforms, 15 Countries**
(percent change in the headcount)

| Country | Foodgrains | | | | Feedgrains | | | |
|---|---|---|---|---|---|---|---|---|
| | Tariffs | Export subsidies | Domestic subsidies | Total | Tariffs | Export subsidies | Domestic subsidies | Total |
| Bangladesh | −0.02 | −0.02 | −0.03 | −0.07 | −0.17 | 0.00 | 0.01 | −0.16 |
| Brazil | −0.31 | 0.01 | 0.01 | −0.29 | −0.07 | −0.01 | −0.13 | −0.20 |
| Chile | −0.22 | −0.01 | 0.05 | −0.18 | 0.00 | −0.02 | −0.02 | −0.04 |
| Colombia | −0.14 | 0.00 | 0.02 | −0.11 | −0.12 | 0.03 | 0.14 | 0.06 |
| Indonesia | −0.18 | 0.01 | 0.08 | −0.09 | −0.05 | 0.01 | 0.04 | 0.00 |
| Malawi | −0.18 | 0.00 | 0.03 | −0.14 | −0.02 | 0.00 | 0.04 | 0.02 |
| Mexico | −0.16 | 0.00 | 0.15 | 0.00 | −0.44 | 0.01 | 0.92 | 0.48 |
| Mozambique | −0.13 | 0.01 | 0.02 | −0.10 | −0.17 | 0.00 | −0.01 | −0.17 |
| Peru | −0.11 | 0.01 | 0.04 | −0.07 | −0.05 | 0.02 | 0.04 | 0.01 |
| Philippines | −0.54 | 0.02 | 0.02 | −0.49 | −0.21 | 0.01 | 0.00 | 0.23 |
| Thailand | −5.45 | −0.03 | −0.15 | −5.63 | −1.09 | 0.00 | 0.18 | −0.91 |
| Uganda | −0.02 | 0.00 | 0.01 | −0.01 | −0.02 | 0.00 | 0.00 | −0.02 |
| Venezuela, R.B. de | −0.02 | 0.00 | 0.02 | 0.00 | −0.03 | 0.00 | 0.05 | 0.02 |
| Vietnam | −0.02 | 0.01 | 0.04 | 0.03 | −0.44 | 0.02 | 0.01 | 0.40 |
| Zambia | 0.01 | 0.00 | 0.00 | −0.01 | 0.05 | 0.00 | 0.01 | 0.04 |
| Average | −0.19 | 0.00 | 0.03 | −0.46 | −0.20 | 0.01 | 0.09 | −0.11 |
| Absolute average | 0.49 | 0.01 | 0.05 | 0.46 | 0.20 | 0.01 | 0.11 | 0.18 |
| Sign consistency | −1.00 | 0.17 | 0.54 | −0.99 | −1.00 | 0.60 | 0.82 | −0.57 |

Source: Model simulations by the authors.

Note: The results correspond with equation (4.7) and represent the impacts of reforms on poverty
according to type of reform in two commodity sectors. The totals are the sums across instruments and
reflect the total contribution of sector-specific reforms to the percent change in poverty headcounts
nationwide. See the note to table 4.5 for simulation information.

provide more general conclusions about the poverty impacts of commodity trade
reform. We find that, overall, trade reform tends to reduce poverty, and it does so
because of the agricultural trade reform components in the total package of
reforms. Indeed, nonagricultural trade reforms tend to increase poverty in most
of our focus developing countries.

We explore the relative poverty friendliness of agricultural trade reforms in
more detail by examining the differential impacts (relative to nonagricultural
reforms) on real after-tax factor returns and on poverty by stratum. Overall, the
more favorable impacts of agricultural reforms are driven by the increased factor
rewards for farm households, as well as the higher returns to unskilled wage labor,
which we have evaluated relative to the real cost of living at the poverty line.

Finally, we have examined the poverty impacts of trade reform according to agricultural commodity groups across our sample of countries. Not surprisingly, foodgrain reforms are the most poverty-friendly group.

## Notes

1. Note that, throughout this chapter, as with the rest of the book, nonagriculture includes highly processed foods and beverages, while farm goods that require light processing before they may be traded easily, such as rice, sugar, dairy products, and meat, are included in agriculture.

2. Specifically, the set of measures envisioned under the Doha Development Agenda focus on the implementation of the July 2004 framework agreement of the Doha Development Agenda.

3. A clear limitation of this approach stems from the rigidity of the households' classification by earnings specialization. Obviously, households may be induced to change their specialization or diversify in response to changing relative factor returns. We believe that the relatively broad definition of the seven strata circumvents this problem for the majority of households in the face of modest earnings changes. However, this important qualification is considered in more detail in the subsequent results section.

4. We make adjustments to the output subsidy ad valorem rate in instances in which the difference between the reported output subsidy rate in 2001 and the corresponding rate in 2004 is at least 1 percent. Most of the changes occur in the case of the United States, where the ad valorem output subsidy for rice falls by 77 points and the subsidy for oilseeds falls by 24 points. The world prices for oilseeds and rice were low in 2001 relative to 2004, and these commodities factor heavily in our updates of protection in the OECD countries.

5. Francois, van Meijl, and van Tongeren (2005) introduce monopolistic competition in the manufacturing sector into their analysis of World Trade Organization reforms. The resulting variety and scale effects generally boost the gains to rich countries and dampen the gains to poor countries generated by rich-country reforms. However, this makes their model less stable, and, given our focus on agricultural reforms, this feature seems less critical.

6. Land in the GTAP Database is specific to agriculture. Therefore, we model imperfect mobility across agricultural uses to represent the cost of converting land from one use to another.

7. More specifically, our global liberalization includes the removal of all border measures (export subsidies and trade taxes) in all regions of the model and the removal of all input and output subsidies in agriculture in the OECD and in those developing countries on which Anderson and Valenzuela (2008) provide new information (see the text for explanations).

## References

Anderson, K., and W. Martin, eds. 2006. *Agricultural Trade Reform and the Doha Development Agenda.* London: Palgrave Macmillan; Washington, DC: World Bank.

Anderson, K., W. Martin, and D. van der Mensbrugghe. 2006. "Global Impacts of the Doha Scenarios on Poverty." In *Poverty and the WTO: Impacts of the Doha Development Agenda,* ed. T. W. Hertel and L. A. Winters, 497–528. London: Palgrave Macmillan; Washington, DC: World Bank.

Anderson, K., and E. Valenzuela. 2008. "Estimates of Global Distortions to Agricultural Incentives, 1955–2007." Data spreadsheet, October, World Bank, Washington, DC. http://go.worldbank.org/YAO39F35E0.

Cranfield, J. A. L., P. V. Preckel, J. S. Eales, and T. W. Hertel. 2003. "Estimating Consumer Demands across the Development Spectrum: Maximum Likelihood Estimates of an Implicit Direct Additivity Model." *Journal of Development Economics* 68 (2): 289–307.

de Janvry, A., M. Fafchamps, and E. Sadoulet. 1991. "Peasant Household Behavior with Missing Markets: Some Paradoxes Explained." *Economic Journal* 101 (409): 1400–17.

Dimaranan, B. D., ed. 2006. *Global Trade, Assistance, and Protection: The GTAP 6 Data Base.* West Lafayette, IN: Center for Global Trade Analysis, Department of Agricultural Economics, Purdue University. https://www.gtap.agecon.purdue.edu/databases/v6/v6_doco.asp.

Francois, J. F., H. van Meijl, and F. van Tongeren. 2005. "Trade Liberalization in the Doha Development Round." *Economic Policy* 20 (42): 349–91.

Golub, A., and T. W. Hertel. 2008. "Global Economic Integration and Land Use Change." *Journal of Economic Integration* 23 (3): 463–88.

Harrison, W. J., M. Horridge, and K. R. Pearson. 2000. "Decomposing Simulation Results with Respect to Exogenous Shocks." *Computational Economics* 15 (3): 227–49.

Harrison, W. J., and K. R. Pearson. 1996. "Computing Solutions for Large General Equilibrium Models using Gempack." *Computational Economics* 9 (2): 83 127.

Hertel, T. W., ed. 1997. *Global Trade Analysis: Modeling and Applications.* New York: Cambridge University Press.

Hertel, T. W., M. Ivanic, P. V. Preckel, and J. A. L. Cranfield. 2004. "The Earnings Effects of Multilateral Trade Liberalization: Implications for Poverty." *World Bank Economic Review* 18 (2): 205–36.

Hertel, T. W., R. Keeney, M. Ivanic, and L. A. Winters. 2007. "Distributional Effects of WTO Agricultural Reforms in Rich and Poor Countries." *Economic Policy* 22 (50): 289–337,

———. 2009. "Why Isn't the Doha Development Agenda More Poverty Friendly?" *Review of Development Economics.* Wiley InterScience. http://www3.interscience.wiley.com/journal/122211891/abstract (published online February 23).

Hertel, T. W., and L. A. Winters, eds. 2006. *Poverty and the WTO: Impacts of the Doha Development Agenda.* London: Palgrave Macmillan; Washington, DC: World Bank.

Ivanic, M. 2006. "The Effects of a Prospective Multilateral Trade Reform on Poverty in Developing Countries." In *Poverty and the WTO: Impacts of the Doha Development Agenda,* ed. T. W. Hertel and L. A. Winters, 405–26. London: Palgrave Macmillan; Washington, DC: World Bank.

Keeney, R., and T. W. Hertel. 2005. "GTAP-AGR: A Framework for Assessing the Implications of Multilateral Changes in Agricultural Policies." GTAP Technical Paper 24 (August), Center for Global Trade Analysis, Department of Agricultural Economics, Purdue University, West Lafayette, IN. https://www.gtap.agecon.purdue.edu/resources/res_display.asp?RecordID=1869.

OECD (Organisation for Economic Co-operation and Development). 2001. *Market Effects of Crop Support Measures.* Paris: OECD.

———. 2007. *Agricultural Policies in OECD Countries: Monitoring and Evaluation 2007.* Paris: OECD.

Rimmer, M., and A. Powell. 1992. "An Implicitly Additive Demand System." *Applied Economics* 28 (12): 1613–22.

Valenzuela, E., and K. Anderson. 2008. "Alternative Agricultural Price Distortions for CGE Analysis of Developing Countries, 2004 and 1980–84." Research Memorandum 13 (December), Center for Global Trade Analysis, Department of Agricultural Economics, Purdue University, West Lafayette, IN. https://www.gtap.agecon.purdue.edu/resources/res_display.asp?RecordID=2925.

Winters, L. A., N. McCulloch, and A. McKay. 2004. "Trade Liberalization and Poverty: The Evidence So Far." *Journal of Economic Literature* 42 (1): 72–115.

# PART III

# NATIONAL CGE APPROACHES: ASIA

# 5

# CHINA

### Fan Zhai and Thomas W. Hertel

As the most populous nation in the world, China plays a critical role in the determination of the global poverty headcount. Indeed, a considerable portion of the reduction in the headcount may be attributable to the remarkable reduction in the incidence of poverty in China over the past two decades. Chen and Ravallion (2004) find that, in 1981, 65 percent of the population in China was in extreme poverty (US$1 a day), whereas by 2001, this share had fallen to around 12 percent. They show that much of this poverty reduction was driven by reforms in the agricultural sector. These advances notwithstanding, rural poverty continues to dominate the national poverty headcount in China, and the headcount is highest among households that are specialized in farming. Furthermore, there is evidence that, despite rapid economic growth, the rural-urban wage gap is widening (Sicular et al. 2007). Within the rural sector, rapid nonagricultural income growth and slow agricultural income growth since the 1990s is contributing to increased rural inequality (Benjamin et al. 2007). The agricultural sector therefore continues to play an important role in the determination of national poverty and inequality in China. In this chapter, we focus on the impact on poverty and inequality in China of agricultural, trade, and rural policy reforms both at home and abroad.

The impact of trade reforms on poverty and inequality in China has been a topic of intense research over the past decade, culminating in a number of studies focusing on the impact on poverty of China's accession to the World Trade Organization (WTO) (for example, see Bhattasali, Li, and Martin 2004). Chen and Ravallion (2004) examine these impacts at a highly disaggregate level using earnings and price estimates from another study; they estimate that WTO accession will benefit urban households, particularly poor urban households. However, they predict that, as a result of the WTO accession, falling rural wages and increases in the consumer prices faced by rural households are likely to hurt the rural poor. In a companion study, Hertel, Zhai, and Wang (2004) aggregate households to a greater degree, but incorporate them directly into their computable general equilibrium (CGE) model of China. They, too, conclude that WTO accession will be relatively more favorable for urban households, but they argue that whether or not rural households will lose from these reforms depends critically on the degree of off-farm labor mobility. At low (or zero) mobility, as assumed by Chen and Ravallion, the poorest rural households lose from reform, but, as the off-farm labor supply elasticity rises, the potential for farm households to gain increases.

In closely related work, Hertel and Zhai (2006) contrast the impacts of commodity market reforms, such as those initiated through China's WTO accession, with factor market reforms aimed at facilitating an improved flow of labor out of agriculture and between the rural and urban markets. They find that the latter may result in significant gains for rural households. Specifically, these authors explore the implications of (1) reforming agricultural land markets to permit arm's-length land rental in all rural areas, thereby facilitating the permanent movement of labor out of farming; (2) enhancing off-farm labor mobility; and (3) abolishing the *hukou* system, the household registration system in China, thereby reducing the transaction costs imposed on rural-urban migrants. If combined, these reforms reduce the estimated 2007 urban-rural income ratio from 2.58 (in the absence of WTO accession) to 2.09. If WTO accession is added to this mix of policy reforms, the 2007 urban-rural income ratio is still reduced, though not quite as much, to 2.12. Given the importance of labor market distortions to poverty and inequality in China, we pay special attention in our study to their presence as well.

In this chapter, we update the model used in earlier studies (to reflect the most recent social accounting matrix for China) and capitalize on the most recent estimates of agricultural price distortions, which have changed significantly since China's accession to the WTO. We also bring to bear new farm price distortion estimates for other developing countries to assess the impact of global trade reform on poverty and inequality in China.[1] Unlike our earlier work (see below), which focused solely on China's own reforms associated with WTO accession, we explore here the impacts of reforms in the rest of the world, as well as in China. Additionally, we decompose these impacts in two ways: first, by region (China versus the rest of the world) and, second, by sector (agriculture versus nonagriculture). We also examine the interplay between these commodity market reforms and the factor market reforms aimed at improving the allocation of labor within the Chinese economy.

This chapter is organized as follows. The next section describes the specification of the CGE model used in this study. We then assess the effects on the macroeconomy, agricultural production, and poverty in China that are generated by the elimination of agricultural price distortions in the rest of the world, as well as by the reduction of China's own distortions in commodity and factor markets. The final section offers conclusions.

## The Model and the Data

The Chinese model we use is an updated version of the household-disaggregated CGE model that we have relied on previously to study the economic and poverty effects in China of WTO accession and Doha Round trade liberalization (see Hertel, Zhai, and Wang 2004; Hertel and Zhai 2006; Zhai and Hertel 2006). The model has intellectual roots in the group of single-country applied general equilibrium models used over the past two decades to analyze the impact of trade policy reform. The updated version in this chapter has a more recent benchmark data set based on the 2002 input-output table (NBS 2006) and a detailed sectoral disaggregation for agriculture and food. In this section, we describe the main features of the model.

### Household behavior

Following our previous work, we disaggregate rural and urban households into 40 rural and 60 urban representative households according to primary source of income and relative income level. In light of the fact that our focus here is on agricultural incentives, we seek to highlight those households that depend exclusively on farming for their incomes. Accordingly, we stratify the rural households by agriculture-specialized households (more than 95 percent of household income is obtained through farming) and diversified (all other sources of income). We are also interested in the impacts of restrictions on rural-urban labor mobility; so, we separately identify urban households and group them into three strata: transfer-specialized, labor-specialized, and diversified households. Within each stratum, we order households from poorest to richest based on per capita income and then group them into 20 vingtiles, each containing 5 percent of the stratum population.

Household income is derived from labor income, the profits from family-owned agricultural and nonagricultural enterprises, property income, and transfers. Households consume goods and services according to a preference structure determined by the extended linear expenditure system. Through the specification of a subsistence quantity of each good or service, this expenditure function generates nonhomothetic demands, whereby the greater the relative importance of subsistence consumption to a household (for example, it would be high for rice, but low for automobiles), the more income inelastic the demand of the household for that good.

The other important dimension of household behavior is the supply of labor for off-farm activities. In China, the off-farm labor supply decision is complicated by institutional factors that have been built into the system to keep the agricultural population in place; among these, the rural land tenure system is one of the most widely discussed (Zhao 1999a). The absence of well-defined land tenure has served to raise the opportunity cost of leaving the farm (Yang 1997). Households that cease to farm the land may lose the rights to the land; so, they have a strong incentive to continue some level of agricultural activity even if profitability is quite low (Zhao 1999b). Because of only modest growth in rural nonfarm activities, this seriously limits the ability of households to obtain off-farm work (Zhao 1999a).[2] Although an active land rental market has emerged in some regions in recent years, the overall level of land rental transactions is still low; only around 10–15 percent of rural households rent land out or are land renters (Deininger and Jin 2005, 2007; Wang, Herzfeld, and Glauben 2007). Empirical studies have found that the transaction costs associated with land rental are significant, and the absence of an efficient land rental market remains a substantial barrier to the facilitation of off-farm labor participation by rural labor (Deininger and Jin 2005; Wang, Herzfeld, and Glauben 2007).

In this chapter, we model rural households as if they maximize the total return to their labor supply, which is offered on both the on-farm and the off-farm labor markets. However, the ability of households to shift labor between these two labor markets is constrained by a number of factors, including education, experience, and simple geography, which may isolate farm households from the nonfarm labor market. We proxy the combined impact of these factors through a single, finite, constant elasticity of transformation. The labor allocation between farm and off-farm jobs is determined by the ratio of the shadow value of labor in agriculture relative to the off-farm wage rate and this elasticity of transformation.[3] The constant elasticity of transformation parameter governs the off-farm labor supply elasticity, for which we adopt the estimate of 2.67 of Sicular and Zhao (2004) as the overall farm–off-farm transformation elasticity for the total rural labor force. The empirical study by Zhang, Huang, and Rozelle (2002) suggests that this elasticity increases by 0.58 for an additional year of schooling. This is translated into the farm–off-farm transformation elasticity of 0.68 for unskilled labor and 4.01 for semiskilled labor.[4]

Owing to the absence of an effective land market, the shadow value of labor in agriculture in this function takes into account the potential impact that reducing agricultural employment would have on the household's claim to farmland. This incremental factor is calculated as the marginal value product of land, multiplied by the probability that the household will lose its land as a result of off-farm migration. To make this amenable to use in a model of a representative farm household with continuously variable labor and land use, we translate the probability into a simple elasticity of land income with respect to on-farm labor. The higher this elasticity, the greater the probability that the farm household will lose its land if the farmer shifts to an off-farm job. The benchmark elasticity in our model is 0.5, that is, a 10 percent reduction in on-farm work results in a 5 percent loss of land income. However, for purposes of sensitivity analysis, we also report results from two extreme simulations. In the first, the elasticity of land income with respect to off-farm work is zero. This is the case of a perfectly functioning land rental market with no chance of land loss. In the second sensitivity analysis, the elasticity is set equal to 1, such that the farmer leaving the farm to work in the city is virtually guaranteed to lose his land. By comparing these two extremes, we gain an appreciation of the importance of land market reform in addressing inequality.

### Rural-urban migration

Migration is a key part of the rural economy in China. According to rural household survey data collected in 2003 and compiled by Liu, Park, and Zhao (2006), 19.4 percent of all rural workers participated in migratory work in 2003, and more than 40 percent of all households had at least one member who was a labor migrant in that year. More than half the migrants had left their provinces, and most of these had migrated to the coastal provinces, where manufacturing activity and exports have been booming. The 2000 census estimated that the total number of migrants in China was 131 million, of which nearly two-thirds were non-hukou migrants. (Households lacking the hukou urban registration face limited access to many urban amenities, including housing and education.) Rural-urban migration was the largest form of migration and accounted for more than 50 million people in the 2000 census (Cai, Park, and Zhao 2007). This massive migration is a rational response to the enormous rural-urban wage gap that exists in China, which Sicular et al. (2007) recently placed at 2.27 (the ratio of urban to rural per capita disposable income in 2002) after adjusting for housing subsidies and spatial price differences. Sicular et al. find no evidence of this gap declining. Indeed, the ratio of urban to rural incomes appears to have risen slightly between 1997 and 2002. This is hardly the outcome that a standard general equilibrium model with perfect labor mobility would predict. Clearly, there are important barriers to labor movement in China that need to be considered if one hopes to assess accurately the impact of commodity market reforms on rural and urban employment, wages, and household incomes.

While the rural-urban per capita income gap is an indication of a potential labor market distortion, we are more interested in discovering the hourly wage differential among workers of comparable skill and ability. If there were no barriers to the movement of labor between rural and urban areas, we would expect real wages to be equalized for an individual worker with given characteristics. In an exploration of the issue of rural-urban inequality in greater detail in nine provinces using the China Health and Nutrition Survey, Shi, Sicular, and Zhao (2002) conclude that the apparent labor market distortion is about 42 percent of the rural-urban labor income differential and 48 percent of the hourly earnings differential.[5] Applied to their estimated average wage differential, this amounts to an ad valorem apparent transactions tax rate on rural wages of 81 percent.[6]

We model these transaction costs as real costs that are assumed by the temporary rural migrants who move to urban areas without possessing hukou urban registrations. Of course, these migrants are heterogeneous, and the extent of the burden varies widely. Individuals who are single and live close to the urban area in which they are working are likely to experience minor inconvenience as a result of the temporary migration. We expect them to be the first to migrate (all else being equal) in response to higher urban wages. Other migrants have large families and must travel a great distance. Their urban living conditions are often poor, and, among these migrants, it is not uncommon to be robbed on their return home by train after their jobs. For such individuals, the decision to migrate temporarily is likely to be difficult, and they may or may not choose to repeat the experience. With this heterogeneous population in mind, we postulate a transaction cost function in which the cost increases in proportion to the increase in the rural population engaged in temporary work. This transaction cost function has a simple constant elasticity functional form, which begins at the origin, reflecting those migrants for whom there is essentially no cost because of their proximity to urban areas, and reaches the observed wage gap (adjusted for transportation and living costs) at the current level of temporary migration (about 70 million workers). We assume that additional increases in temporary migration have only a modest impact on these transaction costs.[7] Finally, only a portion of these observed transaction costs may be attributed to the government's formal policy of migration restriction, the hukou system. Indeed, Shi (2002) finds that only 28 percent of the rural-urban wage difference may be explained directly by the coefficient on the hukou registration variable. We take this into account elsewhere below in our investigation of prospective labor market reforms by the Chinese government.

### Production and trade

Production in each sector of the economy is modeled using nested constant elasticity of substitution functions, and constant returns to scale are assumed. In the top level of the nest, value added and a composite of intermediate inputs produce outputs. Then, another constant elasticity of substitution function disaggregates the value added into a capital-labor composite and agricultural land. The capital-labor composite is split into the capital–skilled labor composite and aggregated less-skilled labor. The capital–skilled labor composite consists of capital and skilled labor, while aggregated less-skilled labor is composed of semiskilled labor and unskilled labor. A low substitution elasticity of 0.3 between capital and skilled labor is assumed to introduce the capital-skill complementarity. The elasticity of substitution between semiskilled labor and unskilled labor is set at 1.5 based on estimates for the United States by Katz and Murphy (1992) and Heckman, Lochner, and Taber (1998).

Each sector employs a labor composite comprising both rural and urban labor that substitute imperfectly. This is an indirect means of building a geographic flavor into the model because some sectors will be located largely in urban areas, while others will be predominantly in rural areas. By limiting the substitutability of rural and urban labor in each sector, we are able to proxy the economic effect of geographically distributed activity. Ideally, we would model the geographic distribution of industrial activity, but the data do not exist to support this split.

All commodity and factor markets are assumed to clear through prices. In the case of rural labor markets, there is a segmentation between agricultural and nonagricultural labor: these two markets are linked imperfectly through the constant elasticity of transformation parameter (see elsewhere above). Once the transaction costs associated with temporary migration are accounted for, rural wages are equated with urban wages. Capital is assumed to be fully mobile across sectors. Import demand is modeled using the Armington assumption, that is, domestic products are assumed to be differentiated from foreign products. On the export side, it is assumed that firms treat the domestic and export markets equally. Thus, the law of one price holds, that is, the export price is identical to the price of domestic supply. The small country assumption is assumed for imports; so, world import prices are exogenous in terms of foreign currency. Exports are demanded according to constant elasticity demand curves. The terms of trade for China are therefore endogenous in the simulations. The value of export demand and the Armington elasticities are based on the elasticities used in the global CGE Linkage model (van der Mensbrugghe 2005).

### The benchmark data

A social accounting matrix is estimated for China for the year 2002 to serve as the benchmark data set for model calibration. The matrix contains 48 sectors of production and 100 representative households based on 2000 household survey data for three provinces (Guangdong, Liaoning, and Sichuan) and the 2002 input-output table (NBS 2006). Because the 2002 input-output table has only one crop sector and one livestock sector, we disaggregate these two sectors into eight crop sectors and four livestock sectors according to the corresponding Global Trade Analysis Project sector classification (Hertel 1997). The information on the structure of production, demand, inputs, and trade in the Global Trade Analysis Project Database, version 7 are used for the sectoral disaggregation, and we employ the cross-entropy method to balance the social accounting matrix (see Robinson, Cattaneo, and El-Said 2001).

The base year tariffs and export subsidies and taxes are reported in table 5.1. Protection rates for lightly processed food and agricultural products have been obtained from Huang et al. (2009) and from the Global Trade Analysis Project Database, version 7. For other primary goods and manufacturing products, tariffs are estimated based on the collected revenue from import tariffs and base year imports by commodity. As shown in table 5.1, China's tariff structure provides more protection for food and agricultural products than for nonfood manufacturing

**Table 5.1. The Sectoral Structure of GDP, Trade, Import Tariffs, and Export Subsidies, China, Around 2004**

(percent)

| Product | Tariff rate | Export subsidy rate[a] | GDP share | Export share | Import share |
|---|---|---|---|---|---|
| Agriculture | 6.5 | 0.8 | 13.4 | 1.6 | 2.5 |
| Paddy rice | 0.0 | −1.0 | 0.8 | 0.0 | 0.0 |
| Wheat | 4.0 | 0.0 | 0.3 | 0.0 | 0.1 |
| Other grains | 3.4 | 13.0 | 0.3 | 0.1 | 0.0 |
| Vegetables and fruits | 14.8 | 0.0 | 5.5 | 0.7 | 0.1 |
| Oilseeds | 15.9 | 0.0 | 0.4 | 0.1 | 0.7 |
| Sugarcane and beets | 15.3 | 0.0 | 0.0 | 0.0 | 0.0 |
| Plant-based fibers | −5.3 | 0.0 | 0.2 | 0.0 | 0.3 |
| Other crops | 9.4 | 0.0 | 0.1 | 0.3 | 0.0 |
| Cattle, sheep, and so on | 3.9 | 0.0 | 0.3 | 0.0 | 0.0 |
| Other livestock | 0.0 | 0.0 | 2.7 | 0.1 | 0.2 |
| Raw milk | 0.0 | 0.0 | 0.1 | 0.0 | 0.0 |
| Wool | 7.0 | 0.0 | 0.1 | 0.0 | 0.1 |
| Forestry | 2.8 | 0.0 | 1.3 | 0.0 | 0.9 |
| Fishing | 5.2 | 0.0 | 1.3 | 0.1 | 0.0 |
| Mining | 0.7 | 0.0 | 4.9 | 1.5 | 6.2 |
| Coal mining | 3.1 | 0.0 | 1.9 | 0.5 | 0.1 |
| Crude oil and natural gas | 0.9 | 0.0 | 1.9 | 0.4 | 4.1 |
| Ore mining | 0.0 | 0.0 | 0.5 | 0.1 | 1.4 |
| Other mining | 0.5 | 0.0 | 0.6 | 0.5 | 0.7 |

(Table continues on the following page.)

**Table 5.1. The Sectoral Structure of GDP, Trade, Import Tariffs, and Export Subsidies, China, Around 2004 (*continued*)**

*(percent)*

| Product | Tariff rate | Export subsidy rate[a] | GDP share | Export share | Import share |
|---|---|---|---|---|---|
| Food manufacturing | 5.0 | −0.0 | 3.8 | 3.0 | 2.0 |
| Meat products | 10.5 | 0.0 | 0.2 | 0.5 | 0.3 |
| Vegetable oils | 12.5 | 0.0 | 0.3 | 0.1 | 0.5 |
| Grain, milled | 0.0 | −1.0 | 0.2 | 0.0 | 0.0 |
| Sugar, refined | 17.3 | 0.0 | 0.1 | 0.0 | 0.1 |
| Forage | 11.5 | 0.0 | 0.2 | 0.0 | 0.0 |
| Prepared fish products | 0.9 | 0.0 | 0.2 | 1.0 | 0.7 |
| Other processed food | 9.4 | 0.0 | 0.8 | 1.1 | 0.3 |
| Beverages | 12.7 | 0.0 | 0.6 | 0.2 | 0.1 |
| Tobacco products | 8.9 | 0.0 | 1.1 | 0.1 | 0.1 |
| Nonfood manufacturing | 2.9 | 0.0 | 20.6 | 74.9 | 80.3 |
| Textiles | 0.2 | 0.0 | 2.0 | 9.1 | 4.5 |
| Apparel and leather | 0.2 | 0.0 | 1.5 | 9.3 | 1.6 |
| Sawmills and furniture | 1.9 | 0.0 | 0.9 | 2.2 | 0.7 |
| Paper, printing, and so on | 3.0 | 0.0 | 2.0 | 3.3 | 2.0 |
| Petroleum refining | 3.6 | 0.0 | 0.9 | 0.9 | 1.5 |
| Chemicals | 3.3 | 0.0 | 4.9 | 7.3 | 13.0 |
| Building materials | 2.7 | 0.0 | 1.6 | 1.4 | 0.7 |
| Metals | 1.7 | 0.0 | 3.1 | 1.5 | 5.9 |
| Metal products | 2.1 | 0.0 | 1.2 | 3.6 | 2.0 |
| Machinery | 3.3 | 0.0 | 3.1 | 4.4 | 11.6 |
| Transport equipment | 16.4 | 0.0 | 2.1 | 2.2 | 3.7 |
| Electrical machinery | 2.9 | 0.0 | 1.5 | 6.8 | 6.2 |
| Electronics | 1.4 | 0.0 | 2.3 | 16.6 | 20.7 |
| Instruments | 2.1 | 0.0 | 0.4 | 5.0 | 6.0 |
| Other manufacturing goods | 0.7 | 0.0 | 1.2 | 1.4 | 0.4 |
| Utilities, construction, services | 0.0 | 0.0 | 49.3 | 19.0 | 8.8 |

*Sources:* Huang et al. (2009), drawing on version 7 of the Global Trade Analysis Database and the social accounting matrix for China for 2002.

a. Negative numbers indicate the existence of an export tax.

goods. Moreover, the import tariff rates show considerable cross-sectoral variation within agriculture: vegetables and fruits, oilseeds, and sugarcane and beets have high tariff rates of around 15 percent, while imports of plant-based fibers appear to be effectively subsidized.

Table 5.1, columns 3–5 present China's sectoral shares of GDP, exports, and imports. Despite the diminishing importance of the agricultural sector in the Chinese economy over the last two decades, agriculture still accounts for 13.4 percent of GDP. Vegetables, fruits, and livestock are key sources of agricultural value added. Manufacturing value added represents 32 percent of the economy-wide total. Chemicals, metals, and machinery lead the way, followed by sectors related to electronics, textiles, and apparel. Nonfood manufacturing is export intensive, accounting for 75 percent of Chinese exports. Electronics, textiles, apparel, chemicals, and machinery are the major exporting sectors. These sectors also represent a relatively large share of imports, reflecting the significant presence of the processing trade in China. Meanwhile, China's agricultural and food manufacturing sectors have limited trade exposure. Agriculture accounts for only 1.6 percent of exports and 2.5 percent of imports. Vegetables and fruits are major agricultural exports, while agricultural imports are concentrated in oilseeds, cotton, and forestry products.

## Simulation Design

To explore the implications for the Chinese economy of agricultural distortions at home and abroad, we consider six policy reform scenarios that eliminate various distortions in global trade and in China's domestic commodity and factor markets. These scenarios are summarized in table 5.2. The first two scenarios examine the effects of trade liberalization in the rest of the world. *ROW-Ag* considers the impact of agricultural liberalization in the form of the elimination of import tariffs and export subsidies, as well as subsidies for domestic production, in the agricultural and lightly processed food sectors in the rest of the world. The second scenario involving the rest of the world policies across all merchandise commodities (*ROW*) looks at more broadly based trade liberalization. It combines the removal of policy distortions in the agricultural and lightly processed food sectors in scenario 1 and the elimination of tariffs on nonagricultural goods in the rest of the world.

We incorporate the impacts of trade reforms in the rest of the world in the Chinese CGE model through exogenous changes in import prices and export demands. The sizes of these exogenous trade shocks are obtained from the global CGE Linkage model, omitting China's reforms in the process. Table 5.3 lists the external shocks imposed in the *ROW* and *ROW-Ag* scenarios.[8] It shows that enormous percent increases in China's agricultural and food export volumes (export demand) are generated by the elimination of high rates of protection elsewhere in Asia. Rice, other grains, vegetables and fruits, and refined sugar all show large proportionate increases. Of course, the associated changes in output volume are often quite modest because China is not a large exporter of most of these products (see table 5.1). China's export volume declines in most livestock subsectors, reflecting the relatively smaller *ROW* barriers faced by China's exporters in these subsectors.

**Table 5.2. Modeled Liberalization Scenarios, China**

| Scenario | Description |
|---|---|
| | *Agricultural liberalization in the rest of the world* |
| ROW-Ag | – Elimination of production taxes and subsidies in the agricultural and lightly processed food sectors |
| | – Elimination of export taxes and subsidies in the agricultural and lightly processed food sectors |
| | – Elimination of import tariffs in the agricultural and lightly processed food sectors |
| | *All merchandise trade liberalization in the rest of the world* |
| ROW | – Elimination of production taxes and subsidies in the agricultural and lightly processed food sectors |
| | – Elimination of export taxes and subsidies in the agricultural and lightly processed food sectors |
| | – Elimination of import tariffs in all sectors |
| | *Agricultural liberalization in China* |
| DOM-Ag | – Elimination of export taxes and subsidies in the agricultural and lightly processed food sectors |
| | – Elimination of import tariffs in the agricultural and lightly processed food sectors |
| | *All merchandise trade liberalization in China* |
| DOM | – Elimination of export taxes and subsidies in the agricultural and lightly processed food sectors |
| | – Elimination of import tariffs in all sectors |
| | *Relaxation of the hukou system* |
| LABOR | – Cut the indirect transaction costs from 81 to 34 percent of the nonfarm rural wage |
| | *Introduction of land reform* |
| LAND | – Farm households do not include the returns to land in decisions to migrate temporarily |

*Source*: Specifications of the authors.

In the case of broadbased trade reform, the average export price in China increases by 2.4 percent, while the average import price increases by only 0.6 percent (both relative to the price of the manufacturing exports of members of the Organisation for Economic Co-operation and Development), indicating a gain in the country's terms of trade if other countries liberalize and China does not. However, given the relatively greater importance to China of manufacturing exports, if liberalization is confined to the agricultural sector, the improvement in the terms of trade diminishes; the average increase in the export price is only 0.6 percent, and the average increase in the import price is only 0.4 percent.

**Table 5.3. Exogenous Demand and Price Shocks Caused by Liberalization in the Rest of the World, China**

*(percent change)*

| Sector, products | Elimination of all trade distortions in ROW | | | Elimination of agricultural distortions in ROW | | |
|---|---|---|---|---|---|---|
| | Export demand | Export prices | Import prices | Export demand | Export prices | Import prices |
| *Agriculture* | | | | | | |
| Paddy rice | 94.9 | 4.2 | n.a. | 123.6 | 0.0 | 1.8 |
| Wheat | 15.5 | 3.5 | 2.8 | 45.8 | 1.4 | 3.6 |
| Other grains | 105.1 | 3.9 | 6.5 | 157.7 | 1.6 | 6.5 |
| Vegetables and fruits | 185.5 | 4.2 | 1.9 | 232.9 | 1.8 | 1.6 |
| Oilseeds | 10.3 | 4.0 | −2.8 | 42.9 | 1.7 | −2.3 |
| Sugarcane and beets | n.a. | n.a. | n.a. | n.a. | n.a. | n.a. |
| Plant-based fibers | 30.0 | 3.3 | 10.0 | 51.4 | 1.3 | 11.5 |
| Other crops | −12.7 | 4.5 | 1.3 | 8.4 | 2.0 | 1.5 |
| Cattle, sheep, and so on | −18.6 | 4.4 | 6.5 | −3.1 | 1.9 | 6.6 |
| Other livestock | −20.8 | 3.8 | 0.7 | −0.2 | 1.6 | 1.6 |
| Raw milk | −48.3 | 4.1 | −1.8 | −31.7 | 1.7 | −0.7 |
| Wool | −13.1 | 3.8 | 4.9 | 10.1 | 1.6 | 4.9 |
| Other primary products | −7.8 | 2.7 | 0.5 | 2.0 | 0.6 | 1.1 |
| *Lightly processed food* | | | | | | |
| Meat products | 29.2 | 3.5 | 4.9 | 56.3 | 1.3 | 5.6 |
| Vegetable oils | −6.4 | 1.8 | −0.2 | 5.7 | 0.3 | −0.9 |
| Grain, milled | 148.8 | 3.0 | 4.2 | 192.1 | 0.9 | 3.4 |
| Sugar, refined | 410.2 | 3.0 | 1.4 | 560.4 | 0.8 | 2.0 |
| Highly processed food | 67.3 | 2.9 | 0.8 | −14.1 | 0.8 | −0.2 |
| *Nonfood manufacturing* | | | | | | |
| Textiles; apparel and leather | 13.7 | 2.6 | −0.2 | −2.1 | 0.8 | 0.4 |
| Other manufacturing sectors | −3.3 | 2.2 | 0.7 | −1.6 | 0.5 | 0.3 |
| Services | −10.5 | 2.5 | 0.1 | −0.9 | 0.5 | 0.2 |
| Total | 2.2 | 2.4 | 0.6 | −0.3 | 0.6 | 0.4 |

*Source*: Linkage model simulations by van der Mensbrugghe, Valenzuela, and Anderson (see the appendix).

*Note*: n.a. = not applicable.

The increase in sectoral export prices range from 1.8 to 4.5 percent in the case of broadbased trade liberalization and from 0.3 to 2.0 percent in the case of agricultural liberalization only; food and agricultural prices rise relative to nonfood prices in both cases.

The changes in China's import prices show much greater sectoral variation. The import prices of most food and agricultural products rise more than the import prices of nonfood products, reflecting the elimination of agricultural subsidies in the countries of the Organisation for Economic Co-operation and Development. However, the world price of China's oilseed imports declines by 2.8 and 2.3 percent, respectively, in these two scenarios, largely because of the elimination of the high export taxes on soybean exports from Argentina; in the wake of the elimination of these export taxes, the soybean exports become a dominant source of oilseed imports into China.

The next two scenarios focus on the impacts of China's own trade liberalization. Scenario 3 (*DOM-Ag*) eliminates the import tariffs and export taxes and subsidies on China's agricultural goods and lightly processed foods. In scenario 4, *DOM*, the tariff elimination is extended to nonagricultural sectors. These two scenarios are intended to show the effects of distortions in China's factor markets. Scenario 5 (*LABOR*) examines the impact of a relaxation of the hukou system such that the ad valorem tax equivalent of the indirect transaction costs are reduced from 81 to 34 percent (if evaluated at current levels of migration). This is the portion of the observed differential in wages that has been directly attributed to possession of a hukou certificate (see elsewhere above). In scenario 6 (*LAND*), we consider the impact of the relaxation of one of the important barriers to off-farm labor mobility, namely, the absence of well-defined property rights for agricultural land. The existence of this barrier leads to the retention of additional labor in the farm sector. The reason for this is that farm households presently tend to include the returns to communal land in their decision to work on- or off-farm because leaving the farm means potentially forgoing the rights to the farmland. Scenario 6 introduces a land reform whereby farm households migrating to cities may keep full land returns by renting their land out; they thereby only need to consider the ratio of the marginal value of the products of their labor in agriculture to their nonfarm rural wages in deciding where to work.

In all six scenarios, government real spending and real savings (deflated by the GDP deflator) are fixed at the levels of the base year. Thus, the policy reforms are assumed to be revenue neutral and associated with a unified, endogenous factor income tax designed to replace lost government tariff revenue. The goal of this tax replacement closure is to avoid unrealistic macroeconomic effects of tariff removal, while exerting a relatively neutral impact on inequality. Foreign savings are also fixed in foreign currency terms, and the real exchange rate adjusts endogenously to maintain the current account balance. Total investment is endogenously adjusted according to changes in the savings levels of households and enterprises.

## The Impacts of the Reforms on China's Economy

In this section, we examine the impacts of the six scenarios on the macroeconomy, on poverty and inequality, and on households and sectors.

### Macroeconomic effects

The macroeconomic outcomes of these simulations are reported in table 5.4. We begin by focusing on the two scenarios of broadbased commodity trade liberalization (*ROW* and *DOM*, reported in the first two columns). The elimination of trade distortions in all commodity sectors gives a substantial boost to trade in China; exports and imports rise by more than 5 percent in the unilateral liberalization scenario and by 2–4 percent in the scenario of trade liberalization in the rest of the world.

Aggregate welfare effects, which we proxy using the sum of the equivalent variation of individual households and a representative firm, are generally quite small, as one would expect in a model with fixed endowments, perfect competition, and constant returns to scale.[9] The composite equivalent variation is projected to increase by 0.5 percent of GDP in the case of trade liberalization in the rest of the world because of improved terms of trade. In contrast, there is a small deterioration in welfare under unilateral liberalization because of a deterioration in China's terms of trade. This reflects China's relatively limited import protection following the WTO accession, as well as the country's growing influence in world export markets, in which trade expansion tends to depress export prices.

At fixed labor endowments and capital stocks and on the assumption of fixed unemployment and no productivity changes, real GDP changes little under both trade liberalization scenarios. The small decrease under *ROW* is driven by the ensuing labor reallocation from nonagriculture to agriculture. The stronger demand for China's agricultural exports following the elimination of trade barriers in the rest of the world diverts the labor force from high-productivity manufacturing sectors to lower-productivity agricultural subsectors.[10] As a consequence, real GDP declines slightly. This contrasts with the case of China's unilateral trade liberalization, whereby the elimination of the relatively higher import protection in the agricultural sector encourages the movement of the labor force from the rural agricultural sector to urban nonagricultural activities, leading to an increase in GDP.

As the bottom section of table 5.4 indicates, temporary migration from the rural to urban sectors slows down as a result of the trade liberalization in the rest of the world; this boosts the economic prospects in agriculture. Under *ROW*, there are about 5.9 million fewer rural-urban migrants in the new equilibrium relative to the base year. The larger rural labor force is mainly generated by the retention

**Table 5.4. Aggregate Simulation Results of Prospective Liberalizations, China**

| Indicator | ROW | DOM | ROW-Ag | DOM-Ag | LABOR | LAND |
|---|---|---|---|---|---|---|
| *Macroeconomy, % change* | | | | | | |
| Welfare, equivalent variation | 0.5 | −0.1 | 0.04 | 0.01 | 1.0 | 0.1 |
| Real GDP | −0.1 | 0.2 | −0.2 | 0.1 | 0.8 | 0.3 |
| Exports | 1.9 | 5.8 | −0.3 | 0.7 | 1.6 | 0.6 |
| Imports | 4.3 | 5.5 | 0.1 | 0.7 | 1.4 | 0.6 |
| Terms of trade | 1.8 | −0.8 | 0.3 | −0.1 | −0.3 | −0.1 |
| Consumer price index | 2.9 | −0.9 | 1.0 | −0.3 | 1.4 | 0.7 |
| *Factor prices, %* | | | | | | |
| Return to agricultural land | 16.3 | −3.5 | 13.5 | −3.1 | −7.3 | 2.5 |
| Return to capital | 2.2 | −0.8 | 0.0 | 0.0 | 1.5 | 0.6 |
| *Unskilled wages* | | | | | | |
| Urban | 3.7 | 1.1 | 1.2 | −0.3 | −17.7 | 3.1 |
| Rural nonagricultural | 3.9 | −1.3 | 1.3 | −0.4 | 6.9 | −3.9 |
| Agricultural | 4.4 | −1.8 | 1.3 | −0.4 | 23.7 | 8.8 |
| *Semiskilled wages* | | | | | | |
| Urban | 3.9 | −1.2 | 1.3 | −0.3 | −5.4 | −3.1 |
| Rural nonagricultural | 4.9 | −1.1 | 2.2 | −0.4 | 25.5 | −4.5 |
| Agricultural | 2.7 | 1.1 | 0.0 | 0.0 | 20.1 | 11.7 |
| *Skilled wages* | | | | | | |
| Urban | 1.9 | −0.9 | 0.0 | 0.0 | 0.9 | 0.3 |
| Rural nonagricultural | 1.9 | −1.0 | −0.1 | 0.0 | 0.9 | 0.2 |
| *Labor force, millions* | | | | | | |
| Farm labor | 6.4 | −1.6 | 5.7 | −1.5 | −27.9 | −13.2 |
| Unskilled | 0.7 | −0.2 | 0.6 | −0.2 | −15.6 | −1.8 |
| Semiskilled | 5.7 | −1.4 | 5.1 | −1.3 | −12.3 | −11.3 |
| Rural-urban temporary migration | −5.9 | 1.5 | −5.3 | 1.4 | 35.7 | 12.1 |
| Unskilled | −0.6 | 0.1 | −0.5 | 0.1 | 18.2 | 1.5 |
| Semiskilled | −5.3 | 1.3 | −4.8 | 1.3 | 17.6 | 10.6 |
| Skilled | 0.0 | 0.0 | 0.0 | 0.0 | 0.0 | 0.0 |
| *Labor force, %* | | | | | | |
| Farm labor | 1.7 | −0.4 | 1.6 | −0.4 | −7.6 | −3.6 |
| Unskilled | 0.4 | −0.1 | 0.4 | −0.1 | −9.8 | −1.2 |
| Semiskilled | 2.7 | −0.7 | 2.4 | −0.6 | −5.9 | −5.4 |
| Rural-urban temporary migration | −6.0 | 1.5 | −5.4 | 1.4 | 36.5 | 12.3 |
| Unskilled | −1.5 | 0.4 | −1.4 | 0.4 | 46.7 | 3.9 |
| Semiskilled | −10.4 | 2.6 | −9.3 | 2.5 | 34.3 | 20.6 |
| Skilled | 0.0 | 0.0 | 0.0 | 0.0 | 0.0 | 0.0 |

*Source*: CGE model simulations of the authors.

of additional on-farm labor (increased by 6.4 million) in the *ROW* scenario. In contrast, China's unilateral trade liberalization accelerates off-farm migration; about 1.5 million to 1.6 million workers would leave agriculture and migrate to urban areas (relative to the baseline).

Table 5.4 also reports changes in factor prices. It is clear from these that trade liberalization in the rest of the world favors unskilled and semiskilled labor over skilled labor and rural labor over urban labor. This is caused by the relative increase in the demand for agricultural exports and the rise in the prices of competing agricultural imports. Agricultural profitability in China is also boosted by the trade reforms in the rest of the world; this is reflected in the rise in the returns to agricultural land under *ROW*. The returns to capital and skilled wages increase less than the consumer price index, which rises by 2.9 percent under *ROW*. This pattern of changes in factor prices contrasts sharply with the pattern emerging after China's unilateral liberalization, whereby the returns to capital and skilled wages increase the most relative to the consumer price index, while the returns to agricultural land decrease the most.

In the macroeconomic results reported in table 5.4, columns 3 and 4, namely, the results stemming from the liberalization of the agricultural and lightly processed food sectors only, we see that agricultural liberalization has only modest impacts on aggregate exports and imports, reflecting the minor role of the agricultural and food sectors in China's total trade (see table 5.1). Consequently, China's welfare gains from agricultural liberalization are trivial, ranging from 0.01 to 0.04 percent of GDP. In contrast to unilateral trade liberalization in all sectors, China's unilateral agricultural liberalization leads to an aggregate gain in equivalent variation of 0.01 percent of GDP, mainly because of much smaller losses in the terms of trade. The changes in factor prices induced by agricultural liberalization show patterns that are similar to the patterns resulting from broadbased commodity trade liberalization, that is, agricultural liberalization in the rest of the world would favor unskilled and semiskilled labor, as well as agricultural land, in China, while China's unilateral agricultural reforms would favor the capital and skilled labor that are intensively employed in the relatively lightly protected manufacturing sectors. The changes in off-farm employment and rural-urban migration under the two agricultural liberalization scenarios are comparable to the corresponding changes in the broadbased trade liberalization scenarios, indicating the dominant role played by distortions in the agricultural subsectors in determining the mobility of the rural labor force in China.

Relative to the reduction in China's trade distortions, the labor market reforms investigated in scenarios *LABOR* and *LAND* generally have larger impacts on welfare, GDP, and other macroeconomic aggregates. This reflects the large and persistent rural-urban distortions in China's labor markets. It is evident from the last two columns of table 5.4 that both the factor market reforms serve to increase migration out of the relatively low-productivity agricultural sector into the higher-productivity nonagricultural sectors and from the rural to the urban economy. In the case of land reform, 13.2 million additional workers leave agriculture after they have been assured that they will retain ownership of their land even if they migrate (see the farm labor row in table 5.4, final column). These individuals initially migrate to the off-farm rural labor market, which releases an additional 12.1 million temporary rural migrants to the urban sector to restore equality in rural and urban wages, net of transaction costs. The release of workers from agriculture tends to depress wages in the rural nonfarm economy, where wages fall by 3.9 percent in the case of land reform. This wage drop plays a role in dampening the out-migration from agriculture.

While the *LAND* reform scenario focuses on the barriers to the off-farm mobility of labor, the *LABOR* scenario focuses on rural-urban migration. If the transaction costs associated with temporary migration are reduced because of the elimination of the hukou system, rural-urban migration expands by 35.7 million workers. Because the transaction costs associated with temporary rural-urban migration operate, in effect, as a tax on rural labor, the first impact of their reduction is to increase the supply of rural labor to the urban economy, thereby boosting rural wages and depressing urban wages. This represents a redistribution of the rents associated with the hukou system from urban to rural households. In addition, by raising rural wages, this hukou reform scenario also draws 27.9 million additional workers out of agriculture.

### Poverty and inequality impacts

Because poverty and income distribution are central to our study, we provide several related measures of inequality and poverty in table 5.5. The first column in the table reports the initial level of each indicator in our database, while subsequent columns report changes or percentage changes in the indicators. The initial urban-rural income ratio, at 3.5, is higher than the ratios in some of the studies cited elsewhere above that are based on household surveys. This is largely because of our inability to adjust for spatial price variations which, if taken fully into account, would reduce the ratio considerably. The initial Gini coefficient in our model, 0.442, is heavily influenced by rural-urban income disparity. This estimate is also consistent with the recent work of Benjamin et al. (2007), who identify limitations with many of the existing estimates of inequality and place the Gini in the 0.4–0.5 range.

Using the US$2-a-day poverty line and the 1993 purchasing power parity exchange rate, the World Bank estimates that 58.1 percent of the rural population

**Table 5.5. The Effects of Prospective Liberalizations on Income Inequality and Poverty, China**

| Indicator | Base | ROW | DOM | ROW-Ag | DOM-Ag | LABOR | LAND |
|---|---|---|---|---|---|---|---|
| *Inequality* | | | | | | | |
| Urban/rural income ratio | 3.538 | −0.052 | 0.009 | −0.042 | 0.010 | −0.303 | −0.167 |
| Gini coefficient | 0.442 | −0.005 | 0.001 | −0.004 | 0.001 | −0.021 | −0.008 |
| Urban | 0.259 | 0.000 | 0.000 | 0.001 | 0.000 | 0.006 | 0.003 |
| Rural | 0.315 | −0.002 | 0.000 | −0.002 | 0.000 | −0.008 | −0.003 |
| *Poverty headcount, US$2 a day* | *Ratio, %* | *Changes, percentage points* | | | | | |
| Total | 36.4 | −1.2 | 0.3 | −0.8 | 0.2 | −4.1 | −1.0 |
| Urban | 2.5 | −0.1 | 0.0 | 0.0 | 0.0 | 0.7 | 0.3 |
| Transfer specialized | 0.5 | 0.0 | 0.0 | 0.0 | 0.0 | 0.0 | 0.0 |
| Labor specialized | 4.0 | −0.1 | 0.0 | 0.0 | 0.0 | 0.9 | 0.4 |
| Diversified | 1.6 | 0.0 | 0.0 | 0.0 | 0.0 | 0.6 | 0.3 |
| Rural | 58.1 | −1.9 | 0.5 | −1.4 | 0.3 | −7.1 | −1.9 |
| Agriculture specialized | 63.6 | −1.8 | 0.4 | −1.4 | 0.3 | −6.8 | −3.5 |
| Diversified | 57.5 | −1.9 | 0.5 | −1.4 | 0.3 | −7.1 | −1.7 |
| *Poverty headcount, US$2 a day* | *Millions* | *Changes, millions* | | | | | |
| Total | 467.3 | −14.9 | 3.6 | −10.8 | 2.3 | −52.1 | −13.4 |
| Urban | 12.6 | −0.3 | 0.1 | 0.0 | 0.0 | 3.3 | 1.6 |
| Transfer specialized | 0.1 | 0.0 | 0.0 | 0.0 | 0.0 | 0.0 | 0.0 |
| Labor specialized | 8.1 | −0.2 | 0.1 | 0.0 | 0.0 | 1.7 | 0.9 |
| Diversified | 4.4 | −0.1 | 0.0 | 0.0 | 0.0 | 1.6 | 0.8 |
| Rural | 454.7 | −14.6 | 3.5 | −10.8 | 2.4 | −55.5 | −15.0 |
| Agriculture specialized | 52.2 | −1.5 | 0.4 | −1.1 | 0.3 | −5.6 | −2.9 |
| Diversified | 402.5 | −13.1 | 3.2 | −9.7 | 2.1 | −49.9 | −12.1 |

*Source:* CGE model simulations of the authors.

and 2.5 percent of the urban population were living in poverty in China in 2004.[11] We start with these target rates of poverty and compute the poverty line in our data set that reproduces this same poverty headcount. This yields a poverty line of Y 3,520 per person for urban areas and Y 2,591 per person for rural areas. By assuming a uniform distribution of the population within each of the income vingtiles in our source data from the National Bureau of Statistics of China (NBS 2006), we are able to estimate the poverty headcounts in each stratum. This information is also reported in table 5.5. As one may see there, the national poverty situation in China is largely driven by rural poverty; 455 million poor reside in rural areas. The poverty headcount rate is highest in the agriculture-dependent household stratum, in which nearly two-thirds (63.7 percent) of the population is poor.

The two reform scenarios that do not reduce the rural-urban income disparity are *DOM* and *DOM-Ag* (China's unilateral liberalization) because rural households generally lose if agricultural factor returns decline. Although the magnitude of the change in the rural urban income ratio is small in the cases of trade liberalization, it is substantial in the factor market reform scenarios. In the case where the hukou registration system is abolished (*LABOR*), for example, the ratio declines from 3.54 to 3.23. The decline in the land reform scenario (*LAND*) is likewise large, at 0.17 points.

Table 5.5 also reports the absolute changes in Gini coefficients. Because income inequality in China is dominated by urban rural inequality, the narrower urban-rural income gaps in the scenarios of trade liberalization in the rest of the world and of reforms in factor markets are reflected in an improvement in overall inequality, as measured in the national Gini coefficient. There are no discernible changes in inequality within urban and rural areas in the unilateral liberalization scenarios. However, in the two factor market reform scenarios, the Gini coefficients show a slight increase in inequality within urban areas and a slight decline within rural areas. This is because low-income urban households dependent on the earnings from unskilled labor are hurt most by the increase in the rural-urban migration of unskilled workers after labor market reforms, whereas low-income, diversified rural households gain more from the resulting increase in rural unskilled wages than do households at high-income levels.

In the scenario of broadbased trade liberalization in the rest of the world (*ROW*), the monetary poverty line increases by 2.9 percent after the change in the consumer price index (table 5.4). Nonetheless, higher factor earnings mean that the poverty headcount ratio declines among all household groups living in significant poverty. Urban poverty decreases by 0.3 million people (the bottom panel reports changes in poverty in millions), while rural households enjoy a 1.9 percentage point reduction in the poverty headcount (the middle panel reports percentage point changes in poverty). Because of the large population base in rural China, this translates into a rural poverty reduction of 14.6 million people. In the case of agricultural liberalization in the rest of the world, the poverty reduction is smaller, but still significant; the rural poverty headcount declines by 10.8 million.

Given the adverse impacts on agricultural subsectors after China's unilateral liberalization, rural poverty increases slightly, by 3.5 million people, in the *DOM* scenario and by 2.4 million in the *DOM-Ag* scenario. Because of the predominance of rural poverty in China, these increases in rural poverty translate into comparable changes in total poverty. However, labor market reforms would significantly reduce rural poverty, but slightly increase urban poverty. The rural poverty headcount ratio declines from 58.1 percent in the base year to 51.0 percent in the *LABOR* scenario and 56.2 percent in the *LAND* scenario, while the urban headcount ratio rises slightly, from 2.5 to 2.8–3.2 percent. Overall, the share of the national population that is impoverished falls quite sharply in the case of hukou reforms, from 36.4 percent of the total population to 32.3 percent in the *LABOR* scenario (hukou reforms) and to 35.4 percent in the *LAND* scenario. If combined, these two scenarios, together, generate a poverty reduction of 65.5 million. It is thus clear that, if poverty reduction and greater income equality are the objectives of the next round of reforms in China, then factor market reforms should be part of the package.

### Household impacts

It is important to dig below the aggregate indicators of poverty and inequality and consider the disaggregated household incidence curves reported in figure 5.1, charts a-f. These show the percentage changes in welfare (the equivalent variation as a percentage of initial income) by stratum across the income vingtile spectrum. The largest increases in welfare after both trade and agricultural liberalization in *ROW* (on the order of 2 percent) accrue to agriculture-specialized households (figure 5.1, charts a and b). These households benefit from the fact that the returns to agricultural land increase relative to other factor prices. Real incomes rise less among rural diversified households because of the dominance of nonfarm wage earnings in the income portfolios of these households. Among urban households, the largest welfare increases in chart a of figure 5.1 are associated with labor-specialized households, followed by urban diversified households. This is consistent with the larger increases in wage rates relative to the returns to capital. Because the transfers are constant in real terms and because transfers make up most of the incomes of these households, the real incomes of the transfer group are little affected by the agricultural reform. However, because the share of food consumption in the total expenditure of households at low income levels tend to be larger, the relative increase in food prices leads to a higher household-specific consumer price index for these low-income households relative to the national average consumer price index, causing the modest welfare losses among the lowest income transfer groups.

## Figure 5.1. The Impacts of Prospective Liberalizations on Welfare of Five Types of Households, China

### a. All goods liberalization in the rest of the world (*ROW*)

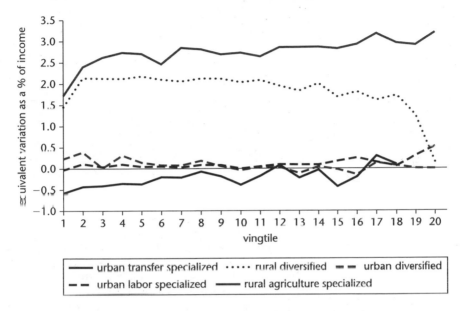

### b. Agricultural liberalization in the rest of the world (*ROW-ag*)

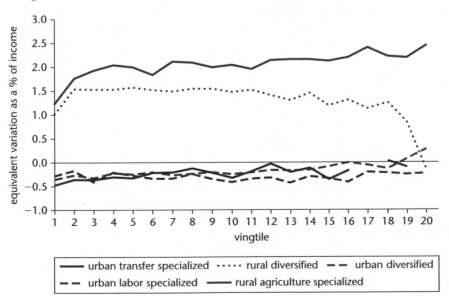

(*Figure continues on the following page.*)

**Figure 5.1.** (*continued*)

**c. Unilateral liberalization of all goods trade (*TRA*)**

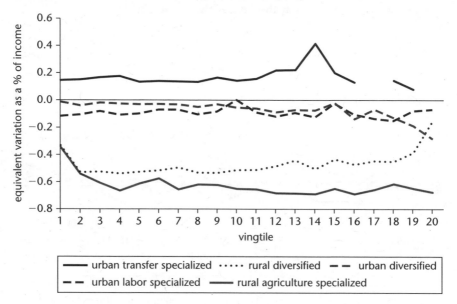

**d. Unilateral liberalization of agricultural trade (*TRA-ag*)**

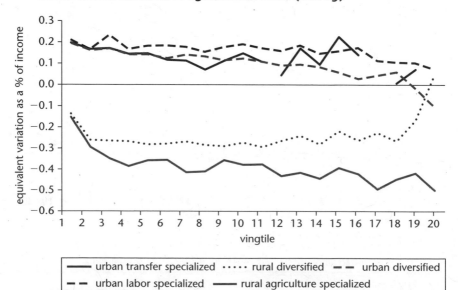

**Figure 5.1.** (*continued*)

**e. Hukou reform (*LABOR*)**

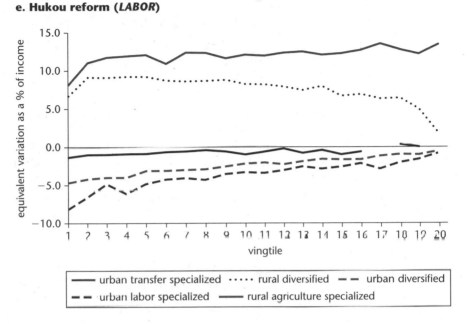

**f. Land reform (*LAND*)**

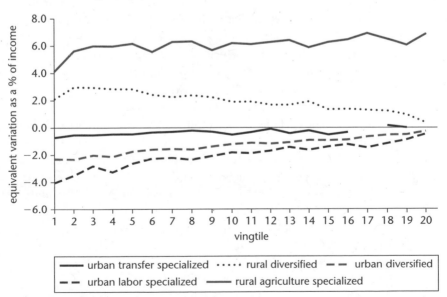

*Source:* Author simulations.

China's unilateral trade liberalization hurts all households except urban transfer-specialized households (figure 5.1, chart c), although the magnitude of the welfare losses is small. Rural agriculture-specialized households experience the largest welfare losses, followed by rural diversified households, which suffer from the depressed returns to agricultural activity. The welfare losses of urban households are small, amounting to only around 0.1–0.2 percent of household income among diversified households and labor-specialized households. The increased income tax rate required to replace the loss in tariff revenue is the major factor contributing to the welfare losses among urban households. In the case of China's unilateral agricultural liberalization, rural households are still the major losers, but all urban households gain slightly because of the smaller tax replacement effects associated with the less serious loss in tariff revenue (figure 5.1, chart d).

Recall from the preceding discussion that the largest poverty and inequality impacts stem from the hukou reform. Chart e, figure 5.1 shows why this is true. The population stratum showing the highest poverty headcount, the agriculture-specialized households, is also the one reaping the largest proportionate gains in this labor market reform scenario. The stratum benefits from the significant increase in agricultural wages. Diversified rural households also benefit from the rise in rural wages, although their welfare gains are somewhat less. These households supply less of the temporary migrant labor to urban areas. These migrants bear the direct burden of the heightened transaction costs associated with the hukou system; so, if this burden is eliminated, the migrants benefit the most. While the benefits from hukou reform are spread relatively evenly across income levels within each of the rural strata, the higher-income households within the diversified strata, which have more capital earnings in their incomes, tend to experience smaller proportionate gains; this contributes to the decline in the Gini coefficient within the rural sector.

Most urban households suffer from the influx of unskilled and semiskilled rural migrants, whose presence drags down the wage rates in urban areas. Almost all urban households experience welfare losses, with the minor exception of the richest transfer-specialized households. Overall, the urban index of income inequality worsens slightly. However, this is overwhelmed by the reduction in between-sector, rural-urban inequality; if coupled with the decline in rural inequality, this leads to a decline in the national Gini coefficient of inequality of 0.021 (from 0.442 to 0.421). This is a substantial movement in a coefficient that is generally quite robust in the face of policy reforms.

Similar to the case of the hukou reform, the largest gains from land reform accrue to agriculture-specialized rural households (figure 5.1, chart f). These households are currently constrained to remain active on the farm if they wish to retain the rights to their land. By permitting some of these households to rent the land and migrate to the city if they wish, land market reform raises the shadow value of the labor remaining in agriculture substantially across all income levels. Diversified rural households also gain; some of the highest gains come at the lowest income levels, where households are more heavily reliant on incomes from agriculture. Urban household welfare falls across the board in this experiment, and it falls most among the poorest households. This is because of the large boost in rural-urban migration among unskilled and semiskilled labor, as well as the increase in food prices following the reduction in the agricultural labor force. As a consequence, the urban Gini coefficient rises. However, from the point of view of overall inequality in China, the main consequence of this experiment is to redistribute income from urban to rural households, which lowers the Gini coefficient by 0.008.

### Sectoral impacts

In table 5.6, we report the effects of the policy reforms in the six aggregated scenarios we have investigated on output, exports, and imports. The first row of the table shows that highly processed food products are the major winners from the

### Table 5.6. The Effects of Prospective Liberalizations on Sectoral Outputs and Trade, China

(percent)

| Subsector | ROW | DOM | ROW-Ag | DOM-Ag | LABOR | LAND |
|---|---|---|---|---|---|---|
| *Output* | | | | | | |
| Agriculture | 1.7 | −0.3 | 1.6 | −0.4 | −2.9 | −1.3 |
| Other primary goods | −0.8 | −0.1 | −0.2 | 0.1 | −0.8 | −0.5 |
| Lightly processed food | 1.7 | −2.0 | 1.7 | −2.2 | −2.6 | −1.1 |
| Highly processed food | 5.4 | 0.03 | −1.6 | 0.44 | −2.3 | −1.1 |
| Nonfood manufacturing | −0.5 | 0.4 | −0.9 | 0.3 | 2.0 | 0.9 |
| Services | −0.4 | 0.2 | −0.2 | 0.1 | 1.3 | 0.5 |
| *Exports* | | | | | | |
| Agriculture | 71.5 | 5.7 | 100.2 | 3.0 | −39.2 | −23.6 |
| Other primary goods | −6.0 | 5.6 | 1.7 | 0.6 | 3.7 | 1.3 |
| Lightly processed food | 31.2 | 11.0 | 58.3 | 7.7 | −25.0 | −14.4 |
| Highly processed food | 64.8 | 7.0 | −14.8 | 2.8 | −17.4 | −9.6 |
| Nonfood manufacturing | 1.6 | 6.4 | −2.1 | 0.7 | 3.0 | 1.4 |
| Services | −10.2 | 2.7 | −1.2 | 0.3 | 2.1 | 1.1 |
| *Imports* | | | | | | |
| Agriculture | 11.6 | 21.0 | 1.2 | 22.1 | 18.6 | 9.8 |
| Other primary goods | 5.5 | 1.2 | −2.4 | −0.1 | 6.9 | 3.0 |
| Lightly processed food | 8.8 | 46.4 | −0.1 | 48.6 | 10.3 | 5.8 |
| Highly processed food | 8.8 | 16.3 | 3.5 | −0.9 | 8.0 | 4.3 |
| Nonfood manufacturing | 3.9 | 5.7 | 0.2 | 0.0 | 0.5 | 0.1 |
| Services | 4.8 | −1.2 | 0.3 | −0.1 | 0.4 | 0.1 |

*Source*: CGE model simulations of the authors.

elimination of market distortions in the rest of the world, with an average output expansion of 5.4 percent. Production in the agriculture and lightly processed food sectors expands by 1.7 percent. Substantial increases in exports are the key drivers of the expansion in China's food and agricultural sectors; this flows from the significant increase in international demand. Exports of agricultural products, lightly processed food, and highly processed food increase by 72, 31, and 65 percent, respectively, in the *ROW* scenario. Despite the absence of any decline in protection for agriculture in the *ROW* scenario, China's agricultural and food imports increase by around 10 percent following agricultural liberalization in the rest of the world because of the decline in the world prices of some of China's major agricultural imports such as oilseeds and vegetable oils. In addition, there is a real appreciation in China's currency that tends to boost the demand for imports across the board.

If *ROW* liberalization is confined to the agricultural and lightly processed food sectors, they become the only two aggregate sectors with expanding exports and output. All the other aggregate sectors experience declining output and exports. The impact of agricultural liberalization in the rest of the world on China's imports is modest in comparison with the impact of broadbased trade liberalization because the decline in total exports and a depreciation in the real exchange rate both serve to dampen the expansion of imports in the *ROW-Ag* scenario.

The sectoral impacts of China's own reforms suggest that the current distortions arising from China's tariff protection and labor market barriers generally support the size of agriculture relative to the size of other industries. Under all four scenarios involving China's own reforms, agriculture experiences output losses, while the nonfood manufacturing sectors and services expand. The impact of reducing China's distortions in commodity and factor markets on highly processed food is mixed: this sector benefits from the elimination of import tariffs, but loses from the reforms in factor markets.

In the two scenarios involving liberalization in the rest of the world, the disaggregated changes in sectoral output (not shown) generally follow the changes in export demand reported in table 5.3: the sectors with larger increases (decreases) in export demand and higher export dependence, such as prepared fish products, sugar, textiles, and apparel and leather, experience relatively large increases (decreases) in output. However, imports also play a role in determining changes in sectoral output in oilseeds, in which output shrinks by 7.4 percent in the *ROW* scenario as a result of the 2.8 percent decline in import prices, which spurs the growth of oilseed imports.

Under China's unilateral trade liberalization (*DOM*), instruments, electronics, textiles, apparel and leather are major manufacturing sectors with rapid output expansion. As the most highly export-oriented sectors, they benefit from the real depreciation in the Chinese currency in the wake of the country's unilateral trade liberalization. At the other end of the spectrum, the most heavily protected sectors, with sizable trade exposure, experience declining output, including oilseeds, sugar, transportation equipment, other grains, and vegetable oil. In the case of China's unilateral agricultural liberalization, the agricultural subsectors with high levels of protection experience significant contractions in output.

In the scenarios of hukou reform (reduced transaction costs) and land reform, agricultural output falls sharply because the farm labor force is diverted to off-farm rural activities, as well as urban-based manufacturing. Within manufacturing, the consumption goods subsectors experience declining output, but most capital goods sectors expand because the changes in final demand favor investment over consumption in these two scenarios.

### The sensitivity of the results to the land rental market assumption

China's rural land markets have been undergoing reform, and a nascent market for land is emerging in many areas (see elsewhere above). In principle, this should facilitate off-farm migration because migrants may no longer risk losing control of their land if they leave their farms. However, to date, these reforms have been restricted to certain regions, and it is not clear how efficiently this market is functioning even in those special cases. Therefore, in our base case results, we have assumed that the transfer of rural labor from farm activities to off-farm activities would diminish the earnings from land rents by 50 percent, on average (that is, there is a 50 percent probability that migrants will lose control of their land). Since this parameter choice is somewhat arbitrary, we contrast the base case results with the results arising from the two extreme assumptions about the functioning of the rural land rental market: one in which there is a zero loss in land returns following the onset of off-farm employment and the other in which there is no land rental market (representing a 100 percent loss in land returns if farmers switch to off-farm jobs). We then repeat the two trade liberalization scenarios, *ROW* and *DOM*. The key simulation results are presented in table 5.7. Since the macro aggregate results are essentially unchanged from our base line results, only revised results on factor prices and labor migration are reported.

The first pair of columns in table 5.7 report the results if the land market is entirely absent so that migration produces the loss of all land farmed by the migrants. The second pair of columns reports the results under the opposite assumption, namely, the existence of a fully functioning land market. Consider, first, the case of trade reforms in the rest of the world (*ROW*). In this case, the returns to land and the wage rates in agriculture rise. Furthermore, the rise in

**Table 5.7. Sensitivity Analysis of the Simulation Results, China**

| | No land rental market | | Fully functioning land market | |
|---|---|---|---|---|
| Indicator | ROW | DOM | ROW | DOM |
| *Factor prices, %* | | | | |
| Return to agricultural land | 16.8 | −3.6 | 15.8 | −3.4 |
| Return to capital | 2.1 | −0.7 | 2.2 | −0.8 |
| *Unskilled wages* | | | | |
| Urban | 4.0 | −1.1 | 3.4 | −1.0 |
| Rural nonagricultural | 4.3 | −1.3 | 3.5 | −1.3 |
| Agricultural | 3.5 | −1.3 | 5.3 | −1.8 |
| *Semiskilled wages* | | | | |
| Urban | 4.4 | −1.3 | 3.5 | −1.1 |
| Rural nonagricultural | 5.6 | −1.1 | 4.1 | −1.1 |
| Agricultural | 1.5 | −0.8 | 4.2 | −1.5 |
| *Skilled wages* | | | | |
| Urban | 1.8 | −0.9 | 1.9 | −0.9 |
| Rural nonagricultural | 1.7 | −1.0 | 1.9 | −1.0 |
| *Labor force, millions* | | | | |
| Farm labor | 8.0 | −1.9 | 4.7 | −1.3 |
| Unskilled | 0.8 | −0.2 | 0.5 | −0.1 |
| Semiskilled | 7.2 | −1.7 | 4.2 | −1.1 |
| Rural-urban temporary migration | −7.4 | 1.7 | −4.4 | 1.2 |
| Unskilled | −0.7 | 0.2 | −0.4 | 0.1 |
| Semiskilled | −6.7 | 1.6 | −4.0 | 1.1 |
| Skilled | 0.0 | 0.0 | 0.0 | 0.0 |

*Source*: CGE model simulations of the authors.

the returns to land is greater than the rise in wages. Therefore, households that had hitherto been considering leaving agriculture because of depressed factor returns have an even stronger incentive to continue to devote their labor to agriculture than do those households that, at the margin, had been indifferent to the wage differential between the farm and nonfarm sectors (the fully functioning land market). Thus, the movement of labor into agriculture in the *ROW* scenario is greater if the land market is not functioning rather than functioning, provided there is no change in the underlying structure of the land market.

The same situation applies, but in reverse, in the case of unilateral trade reforms if labor is leaving agriculture. Here, by including the returns to land in the off-farm migration decision (because these fall more than the fall in wages), the incentive to work off-farm is accentuated in the absence of a land market. As we see above, the shift from the lack of a land market to a fully functioning land market (the *LAND* experiment) generates a much larger flow of workers from agriculture to the rest of the economy (more than 13 million), as well as a significant reduction in poverty. So, we are not concluding that a poorly functioning land market is good for poverty reduction. Because the impact of land reforms dominates the impacts of trade reform on labor markets, the former rules the day if both are undertaken together. However, this sensitivity analysis does show that our predictions about the impact of trade reforms on intersectoral labor mobility depend importantly on the extent to which farmers are able to lease their land if they are migrating to the city for work.

## Conclusions and Policy Implications

Absolute poverty in China is now largely a rural problem, and, within the rural sector, the intensity of poverty is greatest on the farm. Thus, policy reforms that either boost the returns to farming or enhance the off-farm opportunities for those individuals presently working in agriculture offer the best prospects for reducing poverty and inequality in China. Of the reforms considered, trade reforms in the rest of the world, land reform, and hukou reform all reduce poverty in China, while unilateral trade reforms result in a small increase in poverty. Domestic agricultural distortions are important factors in determining the distributional and poverty effects of trade reform packages, although the impacts of the reforms on aggregate trade and welfare are small. Furthermore, the *ROW* trade reforms, as well as the land and hukou reforms tend to favor rural households over urban households, while the opposite is true of the unilateral tariff reforms. So, it would seem desirable to bundle these reforms together in such a way that all these broad household groups stand to benefit from the reform package. For example, by combining the *ROW* and domestic trade reforms, a policy package would reduce poverty and inequality, while benefitting all the household groups in our study.

The land reform and the hukou reform scenarios benefit rural areas much more significantly than urban ones. In the case of land reform, the changes may hurt the lower-income urban households that currently benefit from the artificial restriction of rural-urban labor mobility. This outcome may be avoided, however, if the reforms are phased in over time; in the context of continued rapid economic growth in the urban and coastal regions in China, the urban losses are likely to be more than offset by ongoing income growth. Indeed, this is what appears to be happening in many regions of China in which the restrictions on labor mobility are being eroded, and land markets are emerging. This study suggests that such labor and land market reforms are particularly impressive in their potential for reducing inequality and rural poverty in China, as well as their scope for allowing China to realize more effectively the potential of the vast rural labor force.

## Notes

1. Estimates of agricultural protection and assistance for China based on Huang et al. (2009) are incorporated in the World Bank's Distortions to Agricultural Incentives Project Database (Anderson and Valenzuela 2008). The former cover five decades, but the representative values for developing-country agriculture as of 2004 that are used in the global CGE modeling for this study are summarized in Valenzuela and Anderson (2008).

2. However, as noted by Parish, Zhe, and Li (1995), the rural labor market is looking more and more like an open market.

3. See Hertel and Zhai (2006) for details on the behavior of off-farm labor supply in the model.

4. Given the small number of skilled farm workers in China, we ignore this group in our analysis. See Zhai and Hertel (2006) for details of the derivation of the off-farm labor supply elasticity.

5. There are likely other, unobserved factors inducing this rural-urban wage differential, in which case, the estimation of the labor market distortion via the subtraction of known factors is biased in the direction of overstating the hukou-related distortion. Therefore, it is useful also to estimate the direct impact of household registration status on the observed wage difference among households. Shi (2002) takes this approach to the problem. Using the same China Health and Nutrition Survey data set, he finds that only 28 percent of the rural-urban wage difference may be explained directly via the coefficient on the hukou registration variable. This is quite a bit less than the 48 percent left unexplained by the subtraction approach of Shi, Sicular, and Zhao (2002).

6. See Hertel and Zhai (2006) for a detailed description of the way this ad valorem distortion is obtained.

7. We assume that a doubling in the number of temporary migrants would only increase the marginal cost of migration by 10 percent.

8. Zhai and Hertel (2009), appendix table A.1 provides the mapping between 48 sectors in the Chinese CGE model and 23 sectors in the Linkage model.

9. The equivalent variation of the representative firm is calculated based on the firm's utility derived from the part of investment financed by the firm's retained earnings.

10. In reality, this is likely to show up in slower rates of out-migration from agriculture.

11. The World Bank's poverty estimates are available at http://go.worldbank.org/NT2A1XUWP0.

## References

Anderson, K., and E. Valenzuela. 2008. "Estimates of Global Distortions to Agricultural Incentives, 1955–2007." Data spreadsheet, October, World Bank, Washington, DC. http://go.worldbank.org/YAO39F35E0.

Benjamin, D., L. Brandt, J. Giles, and S. Wang. 2007. "Inequality and Poverty in China during Reform." PEP-PMMA Working Paper 2007-07 (March), Poverty Monitoring, Measurement, and Analysis Program, Poverty and Economic Policy Research Network, Université Laval, Quebec.

Bhattasali, D., S. Li, and W. Martin. 2004. *China and the WTO: Accession, Policy Reform, and Poverty Reduction Strategies*. London: Oxford University Press; Washington, DC: World Bank.

Cai, F., A. Park, and Y. Zhao. 2007. "The Chinese Labor Market in the Reform Era." In *China's Great Economic Transformation*, ed. L. Brandt and T. G. Rawski, 167–214. New York: Cambridge University Press.

Chen, S., and M. Ravallion. 2004. "Welfare Impacts of China's Accession to the WTO." In *China and the WTO: Accession, Policy Reform, and Poverty Reduction Strategies*, ed. D. Bhattasali, S. Li, and W. Martin, 261–82. London: Oxford University Press; Washington, DC: World Bank.

Deininger, K., and S. Jin. 2005. "The Potential of Land Rental Markets in the Process of Economic Development: Evidence from China." *Journal of Development Economics* 78 (1): 241–70.

———. 2007. "Land Rental Markets in the Process of Rural Structural Transformation: Productivity and Equity Impacts in China." Policy Research Working Paper 4454, World Bank, Washington, DC.

Heckman, J. J., L. Lochner, and C. Taber. 1998. "Explaining Rising Wage Inequality: Explanations with a Dynamic General Equilibrium Model of Labor Earnings with Heterogeneous Agents." *Review of Economic Dynamics* 1 (1): 1–58.

Hertel, T. W., ed. 1997. *Global Trade Analysis: Modeling and Applications*. New York: Cambridge University Press.

Hertel, T. W., P. V. Preckel, J. Cranfield, and M. Ivanic. 2004. "Poverty Impacts of Multilateral Trade Liberalization." *World Bank Economic Review* 18 (2): 205–36.

Hertel, T. W., and F. Zhai. 2006. "Labor Market Distortions, Rural-Urban Inequality, and the Opening of China's Economy." *Economic Modeling* 23 (1): 76–109.

Hertel, T. W., F. Zhai, and Z. Wang. 2004. "Implications of WTO Accession for Poverty in China." In *China and the WTO: Accession, Policy Reform, and Poverty Reduction Strategies*, ed. D. Bhattasali, S. Li, and W. Martin, 283–303. London: Oxford University Press; Washington, DC: World Bank.

Huang, J., S. Rozelle, W. Martin, and Y. Liu. 2009. "China." In *Distortions to Agricultural Incentives in Asia*, ed. K. Anderson and W. Martin, 117–61. Washington, DC: World Bank.

Katz, L. F., and K. M. Murphy. 1992. "Changes in Relative Wages, 1963–1987: Supply and Demand Factors." *Quarterly Journal of Economics* 107 (1): 35–78.

Liu, X., A. Park, and Y. Zhao. 2006. "Determinants of Labor Migration: Recent Evidence from Rural China." Unpublished paper, Beijing University, Beijing.

NBS (National Bureau of Statistics of China). 2006. *Input-Output Table of China 2002*. Beijing: China Statistics Press.

Parish, W. L., X. Zhe, and F. Li. 1995. "Nonfarm Work and Marketization of the Chinese Countryside." *China Quarterly* 143 (September): 697–730.

Robinson, S., A. Cattaneo, and M. El-Said. 2001. "Updating and Estimating a Social Accounting Matrix Using Cross Entropy Methods." *Economic Systems Research* 13 (1): 47–64.

Shi, X. 2002. "Empirical Research on Urban-Rural Income Differentials: The Case of China." Unpublished paper, China Center for Economic Research, Beijing University, Beijing.

Shi, X., T. Sicular, and Y. Zhao. 2002. "Analyzing Urban-Rural Income Inequality in China." Paper presented at "International Symposium on Equity and Social Justice in Transitional China," Beijing, July 11–12.

Sicular, T., and Y. Zhao. 2004. "Earnings and Labor Mobility in Rural China: Implications for China's Accession to the WTO." In *China and the WTO: Accession, Policy Reform, and Poverty Reduction Strategies*, ed. D. Bhattasali, S. Li, and W. Martin, 239–60. London: Oxford University Press; Washington, DC: World Bank.

Sicular, T., Y. Ximing, B. Gustafsson, and S. Li. 2007. "The Urban-Rural Income Gap and Inequality in China." *Review of Income and Wealth* 53 (1): 93–126.

Valenzuela, E., and K. Anderson. 2008. "Alternative Agricultural Price Distortions for CGE Analysis of Developing Countries, 2004 and 1980–84." Research Memorandum 13 (December), Center for Global Trade Analysis, Department of Agricultural Economics, Purdue University, West Lafayette, IN. https://www.gtap.agecon.purdue.edu/resources/res_display.asp?RecordID=2925.

van der Mensbrugghe, D. 2005. "Linkage Technical Reference Document: Version 6.0." December, World Bank, Washington, DC. http://go.worldbank.org/7NP2KK1OH0.

Wang, X., T. Herzfeld, and T. Glauben. 2007. "Labor Allocation in Transition: Evidence from Chinese Rural Households." *China Economic Review* 18 (3): 287–308.

Yang, D. T. 1997. "China's Land Arrangements and Rural Labor Mobility." *China Economic Review* 8 (2): 101–16.

Zhai, F., and T. W. Hertel. 2006. "Impacts of the Doha Development Agenda on China: The Role of Labor Markets and Complementary Education Reforms." In *Poverty and the WTO: Impacts of the Doha Development Agenda*, ed. T. W. Hertel and L. A. Winters, 285–318. London: Palgrave Macmillan; Washington, DC: World Bank.

———. 2009. "Economic and Poverty Impacts of Agricultural, Trade, and Factor Market Reforms in China." Agricultural Distortions Working Paper 98, World Bank, Washington, DC.

Zhang, L., J. Huang, and S. Rozelle. 2002. "Employment, Emerging Labor Markets, and the Role of Education in Rural China." *China Economic Review* 13 (2–3): 313–28.

Zhao, Y. 1999a. "Leaving the Countryside: Rural-to-Urban Migration Decisions in China." *American Economic Review* 89 (2): 281–86.

———. 1999b. "Labor Migration and Earnings Differences: The Case of Rural China." *Economic Development and Cultural Change* 47 (4): 767–82.

# 6

# INDONESIA

## Peter Warr[*]

Since the independence of Indonesia, the country's trade policies have taxed agriculture relative to manufacturing. However, since around 2000, the net impact of the trade policies has been roughly neutral between these broad sectors. The reversal occurred immediately following the Asian financial crisis of the late 1990s. It took the form of increases in the protection of the import-competing commodities sugar and rice, declines in the taxation of agricultural exports, especially rubber and copra, and declines in manufacturing protection. The shift toward a more democratic form of government has weakened the influence of Indonesia's technocrats, who have generally favored liberal trade policies. The greater protection of some key agricultural commodities has been a consequence.

The protection of agriculture has primarily involved import restrictions in the import-competing sugar and rice sectors. Other agricultural sectors receive virtually no direct protection. Subsidies for fertilizer and other inputs have been an indirect source of assistance to agriculture, but the rates of these subsidies have declined.

The political explanations for the protection of the sugar and rice industries are quite distinct to each case. The protection of the sugar industry is a consequence of the political power of the highly concentrated sugar refining industry, including the state-owned component of this industry, which is closely linked with large-scale sugar plantations.[1] In contrast, Indonesia's paddy industry—the farm-level production of rice—is dominated by small-scale farm-level producers. The rice milling sector is much more concentrated and well organized, however,

*The author has benefited greatly from the research assistance of Arief Anshory Yusuf in conducting the model simulations, from helpful discussions with Ernesto Valenzuela, and from the comments of John Cockburn.

**179**

and this is relevant because imports compete with milled rice rather than with the raw unmilled product (paddy) produced by farmers. The political power of the rice millers has been an important source of support for the protection of the rice industry. The enhanced political power of the Indonesian parliament since the upheavals induced by the Asian crisis, together with the economic nationalism that dominates the membership of the parliament, has strengthened this support for the protection of the rice industry. Since 2000, imports of rice have officially been banned. In part, this policy has reflected the dubious claim, advanced by supporters of rice industry protection, that restricting rice imports reduces poverty. A general equilibrium analysis presented in Warr (2005) indicates that the policy boosts poverty in rural and urban areas because the poverty-increasing effects of raising the consumer price of rice far exceed the poverty-reducing effects of raising the producer price.

The purpose of our study is to analyze the effects of agricultural and other trade policies both in Indonesia and at a global level. We focus particularly on the effects on the incidence of poverty in Indonesia. We examine the effects of liberalization in the markets for all tradable goods and the effects of liberalization in agricultural markets alone. For this kind of analysis, a general equilibrium approach is essential.

For illustrative purposes, consider the impact of reducing the protection of the rice industry, a highly controversial issue in Indonesia. An adequate analysis of the distributional impact of this policy needs to take account of the policy effects on the expenditures of households, disaggregated by household group, but also the policy effects on household incomes. This requires an examination of the impact on wages, which operate through effects on the labor market, as well as the impact on the returns to the agricultural land and capital owned by poor people. In undertaking this analysis, however, we should not consider the rice industry in isolation. A reduction in rice prices will induce some contraction in rice (paddy) production. The paddy industry is a large employer of unskilled labor in absolute terms. Depending on the labor intensity of this industry relative to the labor intensity of other industries, a contraction of output might induce an increase or a decrease in real unskilled wages. Any change in unskilled wages would affect the profitability in other industries and generate impacts on outputs and prices in those industries as well. These effects would have repercussions on household incomes. The repercussions on incomes would have to be balanced against the effects on consumers of a reduction in the price of rice. Moreover, the consumption of rice may not be considered in isolation either. A reduction in the price of rice will have implications for the demand for other staple foods, such as corn and wheat flour, another significant import. Finally, the reduced protection may lower government revenue if the instrument of protection is a tariff, or it may lower private rents if the instrument is an import quota. The way this revenue is spent by the government or the private quota holders will also influence the net distributional outcome.

The debate over Indonesia's rice protection illustrates the necessity of a general equilibrium approach. The economic issues involved are complex and interrelated. A framework is required that accounts for these interactions and simultaneously satisfies all relevant market clearing conditions and macroeconomic constraints. To address the issues of poverty and inequality, such a framework must include a disaggregated household sector. Moreover, as the above discussion illustrates, the full impact of a reduction in the protection of the rice industry depends on the values of key economic parameters. In the case of the rice example, these include the supply response of domestic producers and the elasticity of supply of rice imports in Indonesia. However, the true values of these parameters are uncertain. A framework is therefore needed in which the values of key parameters may be varied, where appropriate, in determining the sensitivity of the results to the assumed values of the parameters.

The next section describes the Wayang general equilibrium model of the Indonesian economy, the principal analytic tool we use in this study. The subsequent section describes the simulations performed with this model, in combination with the World Bank Linkage model of the world economy (van der Mensbrugghe 2005). The simulations involve unilateral agricultural and trade policy reform in Indonesia and reform in the rest of the world. Our purpose is to assess the relative importance of own-country versus rest-of-the-world policies in terms of the effects on Indonesian households. The results are presented with a focus on the implications for the incidence of poverty in Indonesia. The final section concludes.

## The Wayang General Equilibrium Model of the Indonesian Economy

This section briefly describes the major elements of the Wayang model. The household sector of the model is crucial to the analysis of the incidence of poverty. The most important features of the model are summarized in the overview below. Following the overview, we describe the theoretical structure of the model and the related database. We then discuss important features of the parameter assumptions.

### Overview

The Wayang model identifies 10 household types, which represent 10 socioeconomic groups as defined in the social accounting matrix (SAM) published by

Statistics Indonesia (BPS 2005). For the purposes of our study, each of these 10 SAM household categories is divided into centile groups—100 subcategories, with an equal population segment in each—arranged by per capita consumption expenditure. Working with a general equilibrium model containing a highly disaggregated household sector allows us to conduct controlled experiments that focus on the consequences for household incomes, expenditures, poverty, and inequality that arise from selected economic shocks, taken one at a time.

The Wayang model also has a disaggregated industry and commodity structure. According to the assumptions adopted about microeconomic behavior, all firms seek competitive profit maximization, and all consumers seek competitive utility maximization. In the simulations reported in this chapter, the markets for final outputs, intermediate goods, and factors of production are all assumed to clear at prices that are determined endogenously within the model.[2] The nominal exchange rate between the rupiah and the U.S. dollar may be thought of as exogenously fixed. The role in the model of the exogenous nominal exchange rate is to determine, along with international prices, the nominal domestic price level. Given that prices adjust flexibly to clear markets, a 1 percent increase in the rupiah-dollar exchange rate will result in a 1 percent increase in all nominal domestic prices, leaving all real variables unchanged.

The Wayang model belongs to the class of general equilibrium models that are linear in proportional changes, meaning that relative effects are not altered by the size of a shock. These models are sometimes referred to as Johansen models, after the seminal work of Johansen (1964), who used this approach. The Wayang model shares many structural features with the highly influential ORANI general equilibrium model of the Australian economy (Dixon et al. 1982) and the general equilibrium model of the global economy established through the Global Trade Analysis Project (Hertel 1997). These two models also belong to the Johansen category. The specific structure of the Wayang model draws on an earlier version of the model (Warr et al. 1998) and on a revised version of the ORANI model, called ORANI-G (Horridge 2004). The features of the Wayang model have been adapted to reflect important aspects of the Indonesian economy and to facilitate the analysis of poverty and inequality in Indonesia.[3] The principal components of the model are summarized below.

### Industries

The national model contains 65 producer goods and services offered by 65 corresponding industries, of which 18 are agricultural industries, 6 are resource sectors (wood, other forestry, fishing, minerals mining, crude oil, and other mining), and 41 are other industries. Each industry produces a single output; so, the set of commodities coincides with the set of industries. The various industries in the model are classified as either export oriented or import competing. The level of exports of an export-oriented industry is treated as endogenous, while any exports of an import-competing industry are treated as exogenous.[4] The criterion used to classify these industries is the ratio of an industry's imports to the industry's exports. If this ratio exceeds 1.5, then the industry is said to be producing an importable. If the import-export ratio is less than 0.5, then the industry is deemed export oriented. For ratios between 0.5 and 1.5, additional relevant information is used to classify the industry.

### Commodities

The Wayang model contains two types of commodities: producer goods and consumer goods. Producer goods are either domestically produced or imported. All 65 producer goods are, in principle, capable of being imported, although some show very important levels in the database, in which services and utilities account for most of the examples. The 20 consumer goods identified in the model are each transformed from the producer goods. The proportions of domestically produced and imported producer goods of each kind used in this transformation are sensitive to the (Armington) elasticities of substitution and the relative price changes of the goods.

### Factors of production

The mobility of factors of production is a critical feature of any general equilibrium system. Mobility here means mobility across economic activities (industries) rather than geographical mobility, although the two are clearly connected. The greater the factor mobility built into the model, the greater the economy's simulated capacity to respond to changes in the economic environment. It is essential that assumptions about the mobility of factors of production be consistent with the length of the run that the model is intended to represent.

Two types of labor are identified: unskilled and skilled. They are distinguished by the educational characteristics of the workforce. Skilled labor is defined as those workers with at least a lower secondary education. Both types of labor are assumed to be fully mobile across all sectors. These assumptions imply that skilled wages must be equal in all sectors and move together. The same applies to unskilled wages, although the two need not be the same and need not move together.

An alternative treatment, popular in general equilibrium modeling studies, is to assume labor mobility within the agricultural and nonagricultural sectors, but not between them. This approach is rejected here because it denies a central reality of the Indonesian economy (and of many other developing economies): the mobility of labor between rural and urban areas even in the short run. The approach would rule out all resource mobility between the agricultural and nonagricultural industries, greatly limiting the scope for economic adjustment to changes in patterns of incentives such as the changes that would be produced by trade liberalization. In Indonesia, unskilled and semiskilled workers move readily, often seasonally, between the agricultural and nonagricultural sectors of the economy. Indeed, this mobility is more important than direct mobility among the various agricultural regions of the country, although the latter sort of mobility also occurs.

The mobility of capital is a somewhat different case. It is assumed that there are two kinds of mobile capital: one kind that is mobile among agricultural sectors and another kind that is mobile among nonagricultural industries. Mobile agricultural capital cannot be used outside agriculture, and mobile nonagricultural capital cannot be used in agriculture. Mobile agricultural capital includes machinery such as tractors of various types, which may be used in a range of agricultural activities. It is best to consider land (as we use the term) as an immobile form of agricultural capital, which, in the short run, includes much true land. In nonagriculture, plant and buildings are classified as mobile because they may be used for many purposes. A factory building is a good example. Machinery is considered immobile because most such machinery is more industry specific than are tractors in agriculture.

Table 6.1 summarizes some features of the cost structure of the paddy industry and compares this cost structure with the situation in the rest of the agricultural sector and the rest of the economy. The paddy industry is intensive in its use of unskilled labor, which accounts for 18.5 percent of the total costs and 31 percent of the total variable costs excluding capital and land. Both shares are well above the

**Table 6.1. The Cost Shares of Major Factors of Production, Paddy and Other Industries, Indonesia, 2000**
*(percent of total costs)*

| Cost components | Paddy | Other agriculture | Non-agriculture | All Industries |
|---|---|---|---|---|
| Unskilled labor | 18.5 | 9.0 | 6.3 | 8.1 |
| Skilled labor | 3.1 | 6.6 | 7.1 | 7.0 |
| Mobile agricultural capital | 20.6 | 21.3 | 0.0 | 1.7 |
| Mobile nonagricultural capital | 0.0 | 0.0 | 25.3 | 23.2 |
| Land | 18.1 | 20.2 | 0.0 | 1.6 |
| Nonland fixed capital | 0.0 | 0.0 | 25.3 | 21.2 |
| Intermediate inputs | 39.7 | 42.9 | 36.0 | 37.2 |
| Total | 100.0 | 100.0 | 100.0 | 100.0 |

*Source:* Wayang model database, based on data of Statistics Indonesia (BPS 2001) and unpublished agricultural cost survey data accessed at the Center for Agro-Social and Economic Research, Ministry of Agriculture, Bogor, Indonesia, in March 2008.

shares in other agricultural industries and the rest of the economy, on average. This point is important in our discussion elsewhere below.

It is assumed that, in every sector, the production technology is characterized by constant elasticity of substitution and diminishing returns to scale to variable factors alone. However, we introduce a sector-specific fixed factor in each sector to assure that there are constant returns to scale in production to all factors. We refer to the set of specific factors in the agricultural sectors as land and to the set of specific factors in the nonagricultural sectors as fixed capital. The assumption of constant returns means that all factor demand functions are homogeneous of degree 1 in output. In each sector, there is a zero profit condition that equates the price of output to the minimum unit cost of production. This condition may be thought of as determining the price of the fixed factor in that sector.

## Households

The model contains 10 major household categories—seven rural and three urban—that are differentiated by socioeconomic group. The sources of income of each household type depend on the ownership by the households of factors of production. These differ among the household categories and are estimated from the 2000 SAM compiled by Statistics Indonesia (BPS 2005). The SAM is based primarily on the National Socioeconomic Survey—the Susenas Survey—conducted by Statistics Indonesia. Drawing on the 1999 Susenas data (BPS 2000), we subdivide each of the 10 household categories into 100 subcategories, each of which has the same population size, and arrange them according to per capita real consumption expenditure, thus establishing a total of 1,000 subcategories.[5] The consumer demand equations for the various household types are based on the linear expenditure system. Within each of the 10 major categories, the 100 subcategories differ according to the budget shares in consumption.

Because the focus of our study centers on income distribution, the sources of income of the various households are of particular interest. The source of the factor ownership matrix used in the model is the SAM for Indonesia in 2000. The households are described as follows:

- Rural 1, agricultural employees: agricultural workers who do not own land
- Rural 2, small farmers: agricultural workers with less than 0.5 hectare of land
- Rural 3, medium farmers: agricultural workers with 0.5 to 1 hectare of land
- Rural 4, large farmers: agricultural workers with more than 1 hectare of land
- Rural 5, low-income nonagricultural rural households: small retail store owners, small entrepreneurs, small personal service providers, and clerical and manual workers in rural areas

- Rural 6, nonlabor rural households: nonlabor-force and unclassified households in rural areas
- Rural 7, high-income nonagricultural rural households: managers, technicians, professionals, military officers, teachers, large entrepreneurs, large retail store owners, large personal service providers, and skilled clerical workers in rural areas
- Urban 1, low-income urban households: small retail store owners, small entrepreneurs, small personal service providers, and clerical and manual workers in urban areas
- Urban 2, nonlabor urban households: nonlabor-force and unclassified households in urban areas
- Urban 3, high-income urban households: managers, technicians, professionals, military officers, teachers, large entrepreneurs, large retail store owners, large personal service providers, and skilled clerical workers in urban areas

In the SAM, the income and expenditure items of each household are classified as follows: wages and salaries, rent from capital, incoming transfers, outgoing transfers, income taxes, final consumption, and savings.

The wages and salaries and rent from capital categories are each subdivided into various subcategories. These categories do not correspond exactly to the categories in the model. In agriculture, returns to land and capital are not separated in the SAM, but returns to owner-provided labor are separated. We have used a previous study on the cost structure of paddy production to allocate returns among the land and capital categories, and the various farming households receive the same proportionate breakdown from this total (see Warr 2005).

The factor ownership characteristics of the 10 major household categories are summarized in table 6.2. These household categories vary considerably in the composition of factor incomes, but, for the purposes of our study, the limitations in the available data have obliged us to impose the assumption that the composition of factor incomes is uniform across the 100 subcategories in each of the 10 major categories. These 100 subcategories thus obtain incomes from factors of production in the same proportions. Of course, because the incomes of these 100 subcategories vary greatly, we should think of them as owning different quantities of a uniform bundle of factors. The composition of the factor bundles varies across the 10 major household categories, but is uniform within each category. The composition of expenditures on final commodities does vary among the 100 subcategories, however, and also across the 10 major household categories.

The characteristics of the 10 household categories described above are summarized in table 6.3. The table shows the importance of each category in the overall incidence of poverty in Indonesia using the government's official poverty line. As

**Table 6.2. Sources of the Factor Incomes of 10 Broad Household Groups, Indonesia, 2000**

| Category | Land | Skilled labor | Unskilled labor | Mobile agricultural capital | Mobile nonagricultural capital | Fixed capital and land | Total factor income |
|---|---|---|---|---|---|---|---|
| Rural 1 | 4.1 | 1.4 | 53.6 | 2.1 | 9.3 | 29.5 | 100.0 |
| Rural 2 | 1.6 | 6.1 | 26.7 | 1.4 | 16.3 | 47.9 | 100.0 |
| Rural 3 | 9.8 | 2.7 | 14.1 | 4.8 | 16.1 | 52.6 | 100.0 |
| Rural 4 | 9.7 | 4.0 | 7.8 | 4.9 | 17.4 | 56.3 | 100.0 |
| Rural 5 | 7.6 | 7.0 | 43.3 | 3.6 | 8.7 | 30.0 | 100.0 |
| Rural 6 | 2.8 | 29.2 | 15.2 | 1.7 | 12.7 | 38.4 | 100.0 |
| Rural 7 | 12.6 | 20.7 | 4.5 | 5.9 | 12.4 | 44.0 | 100.0 |
| Urban 1 | 4.1 | 12.8 | 24.4 | 2.4 | 13.8 | 42.5 | 100.0 |
| Urban 2 | 3.2 | 22.0 | 42.3 | 1.7 | 7.4 | 23.4 | 100.0 |
| Urban 3 | 4.1 | 23.8 | 1.3 | 2.5 | 17.0 | 51.4 | 100.0 |

Source: Wayang model database (see Warr et al. 1998), based on data of Statistics Indonesia (BPS 2000).

**Table 6.3. Expenditure and Poverty Incidence by Household Category, Indonesia, 2000**

| Category | Share of total population, % | Mean per capita monthly expenditure, Rp | Share of poor in category, % | Share of category in all poor, % |
|---|---|---|---|---|
| Rural 1 | 8.0 | 6,358 | 39.8 | 13.9 |
| Rural 2 | 14.8 | 3,608 | 34.9 | 22.4 |
| Rural 3 | 7.1 | 7,584 | 32.3 | 9.9 |
| Rural 4 | 9.0 | 6,618 | 27.8 | 10.9 |
| Rural 5 | 16.0 | 3,891 | 23.8 | 16.5 |
| Rural 6 | 4.9 | 12,795 | 28.0 | 5.9 |
| Rural 7 | 5.0 | 16,060 | 10.5 | 2.3 |
| Urban 1 | 20.4 | 4,210 | 15.2 | 13.4 |
| Urban 2 | 6.1 | 17,813 | 11.2 | 2.9 |
| Urban 3 | 8.7 | 14,353 | 5.0 | 1.9 |
| Indonesia | 100.0 | 12,084 | 23.1 | 100.0 |
| *Memorandum items* | | | | |
| Headcount poverty incidence, national,% | | | | 23.10 |
| Headcount poverty incidence, rural, % | | | | 29.09 |
| Headcount poverty incidence, urban, % | | | | 11.97 |
| Gini coefficient, national | | | | 0.335 |
| Gini coefficient, rural | | | | 0.291 |
| Gini coefficient, urban | | | | 0.356 |

Source: Wayang model database (see Warr et al. 1998), based on data of Statistics Indonesia (BPS 2000).

in many developing countries, the incidence of poverty in Indonesia is highest among the rural socioeconomic categories. Rural households account for 82 percent of all poor people in Indonesia, but only 65 percent of the total population.

### Theoretical structure of the model

The analytical structure of the model includes the following major components:

- The household consumption demands of each of the 10 broad household types for 20 categories of consumer goods are derived from the linear expenditure system.
- The household supplies of skilled and unskilled labor are assumed to be exogenous.
- The factor demand system is based on an assumption of constant elasticity of substitution in production technology that relates the demand for each primary factor to industry outputs and to the prices of each of the primary factors. This reflects the assumption that factors of production may be substituted for one another in ways that depend on factor prices and on the elasticities of substitution between the factors.
- The distinction between skilled and unskilled labor, which are nested within the sectoral production functions, is addressed in each nonagricultural sector by allowing skilled and unskilled labor to enter a constant elasticity of substitution production function to produce effective labor. Effective labor, variable capital, and fixed capital then enter the production functions for domestic output.
- Leontief assumptions are used to represent the demand for intermediate goods. The demand for each intermediate good in each sector is assumed to be in fixed proportion to the gross output of the sector.
- The demand for imported and domestically produced versions of each good incorporates Armington elasticities of substitution between the two versions.
- The set of equations that determines the incomes of the 10 household types from the (exogenous) household ownership of factors of production reflects data derived from the official 2000 SAM (BPS 2005), the (endogenous) rates of return to these factors, and any net transfers from elsewhere into the system.
- The import tariff and excise tax rates across commodities; the rates of business taxes, value added taxes, and corporate income taxes across industries; and the rates of personal income taxes across household types reflect the structure of the Indonesian tax system and rely on data of the Ministry of Finance.[6]
- A set of macroeconomic identities ensure that standard macroeconomic accounting conventions are observed.

## The Wayang model database

This subsection provides a description of Indosam 2000, a disaggregated SAM for Indonesia with a base year of 2000. This SAM is intended to serve as the database for Wayang, but it has other, potential uses as well. At the time of our study, 2000 is the most recent year on which it is possible to assemble the information required for the construction of a SAM for Indonesia.

Four data sources, all compiled by Statistics Indonesia, have been used to construct Indosam 2000: the input-output tables for 2000 (BPS 2001), the 2000 SAM (BPS 2005), the 1999 Susenas National Socioeconomic Survey (BPS 2000), and supplementary data sources used in the construction of specific tables. The principal data source is the 2000 SAM, produced by Statistics Indonesia (BPS 2005). It contains 22 production sectors, which is insufficient for the purposes of our study. Moreover, the SAM does not include adequate detail on tax payments and household sources of income that is also required for the study. The 2000 input-output tables specify 66 production sectors.

For the purposes of our study, modifications to the data contained in the input-output tables are needed for three reasons. First, the table specifies only the total transactions for intermediate goods and services for each pair of producing and purchasing industries at producer prices. Unlike the 1990 tables (BPS 1990), these transactions are not divided into goods and services provided through domestic and imported sources. Second, the tables include a sector—number 66, labeled as an unspecified sector—as a balancing item. Sector 66 does not describe a true sector of the economy, and, in any case, the data on this sector indicate negative final demand, an economic impossibility. Third, the tables obtained from Statistics Indonesia are not fully balanced. The major imbalance is that, for most industries defined in the table, the industry-specific elements in row 210 (total input) are not equivalent to the corresponding elements in row 600 (total output), and the elements in row 200 (total imports), plus row 600 (total output) are not equivalent to the elements in row 700 (total supply).

We have overcome these problems as follows. First, we have used the shares of imported intermediate goods and domestically produced intermediate goods for each cell of the table, as implied by the 1990 input-output tables (BPS 1990), to divide the transactions in intermediate goods into domestic and imported components, a distinction that is required by the Armington theoretical structure of the demand for intermediate goods. Second, we have aggregated sector 66 with the much larger sector 65 (other services), which has eliminated the problem of negative final demand. Third, we have balanced the revised table using the RAS adjustment method to ensure that all required accounting identities are observed.

*The model's elasticities*

All export demand elasticities are set equal to 20. The elasticities of supply of imports in Indonesia are assumed to be infinite (import prices are set exogenously) except in the case of rice, for which the assumed elasticity is 10. All production functions are assumed to be constant elasticity of substitution functions in primary factors with elasticities of substitution of 0.5, except for the paddy production industry, for which this elasticity is set at 0.25, reflecting the empirical observation of low elasticities of supply response in this industry. The Armington elasticities of substitution in demand between imports and domestically produced goods are set equal to 2, except for the case of rice, for which the assumed value is 6. The higher value for rice reflects the assumption that imported and domestically produced rice are close substitutes, unlike the situation in most other commodities.

## Simulations

We first describe the policy shocks that are simulated and then summarize the model closure characteristics.

*The shocks*

We simulate the effects of policy reform using the Wayang model of the Indonesian economy, combined with the Linkage model of the world economy (van der Mensbrugghe 2005). The simulations involve unilateral agricultural and trade policy reform in Indonesia and reform in the rest of the world. We do this to assess the relative importance of the impacts of own-country versus rest-of-the-world policies on Indonesian households. We also compare reform in agriculture alone with reform in all goods markets to gauge the relative contribution of agricultural policies to the measured impacts on Indonesian households.

We use the word reform here to mean the complete elimination of all tariffs, the tariff equivalents of any nontariff barriers, export taxes and export subsidies, and domestic agricultural policies in so far as they alter the producer or consumer prices of farm products in various countries. We consider three sets of policy reforms below: unilateral reform in Indonesia (simulation A); global reform, excluding Indonesia (simulation B); and the combination, that is, global reform, including Indonesia (simulation C).

In all three sets of simulations, the Wayang model treats as exogenous: (1) all rates of industry assistance in Indonesia (tariffs, the tariff equivalents of nontariff barriers, and export subsidies), (2) all import prices in Indonesia, and (3) all shifters in the inverse export demand functions in Indonesia

**Table 6.4. Industry Assistance Rates Used in Modeling,
          Indonesia, 2004**

*(percent)*

| Commodity | Tariff | Export subsidy | Output subsidy |
|---|---|---|---|
| Paddy rice | 15.0 | 0.0 | 0.0 |
| Wheat | 0.8 | 0.0 | 0.0 |
| Other grains | 15.0 | 0.0 | 0.0 |
| Vegetables and fruits | 4.8 | 0.0 | 0.0 |
| Oilseeds | 4.7 | −9.0 | 0.0 |
| Sugarcane | 0.0 | 0.0 | 0.0 |
| Plant-based fibers | 3.7 | 0.0 | 0.0 |
| Other crops | 4.5 | −8.0 | 0.0 |
| Cattle, sheep, and so on | 3.1 | 0.0 | 0.0 |
| Other livestock | 3.1 | 0.0 | 0.0 |
| Raw milk | 0.0 | 0.0 | 0.0 |
| Wool | 3.8 | 0.0 | 0.0 |
| Other primary products | 2.9 | −0.6 | 0.3 |
| Beef and sheep meat | 4.8 | 0.0 | 0.0 |
| Other meat products | 4.5 | 0.0 | 0.0 |
| Vegetable oils and fats | 2.9 | 0.0 | 0.0 |
| Dairy products | 3.9 | 0.0 | 0.0 |
| Processed rice | 15.0 | 0.0 | 0.0 |
| Refined sugar | 18.3 | 0.0 | 0.0 |
| Other food, beverages, tobacco | 15.3 | 0.0 | 0.0 |
| Textiles and wearing apparel | 8.0 | −1.4 | 0.0 |
| Other manufacturing | 5.1 | −1.2 | 0.1 |
| Services | 0.0 | 0.0 | 0.2 |

*Source:* Valenzuela and Anderson (2008), based on the estimates compiled by Anderson and Valenzuela (2008).

(equivalent to shifts in the prices at which Indonesia may export a given volume of exports).

*Simulation A* depicts reform in Indonesia alone. This simulation relies only on the Wayang model and does not involve the Linkage model. The assumed rates of industry assistance in Indonesia are set out in table 6.4, and the database of the Wayang model has been amended to match these rates. Exogenous variables (1) are set to zero (changed exogenously by −100 percent) in this scenario, in which all Indonesian tariffs, the tariff equivalents of quantitative restrictions, and all export subsidies are eliminated. Exogenous variables (2) and (3), import prices and export demand shifters, do not change. Export prices are determined endogenously in the Wayang model by export demand equations for Indonesia that relate the export price of each commodity to the quantity of the commodity exported.[7]

The export quantities are endogenously determined within the Wayang model, and export prices are determined simultaneously by movements *along* the export demand equations (recalling that the export demand shifters are zero).

*Simulation B* depicts reforms in the rest of the world (all countries except Indonesia). In this case, exogenous variables (1) do not change, but exogenous variables (2) and (3) do. The simulation uses the changes in import prices in Indonesia and the shifts in the export demand equations for Indonesia that are generated by simulations in the Linkage model. These Linkage model simulations, conducted by van der Mensbrugghe, Valenzuela, and Anderson (see the appendix), estimate the changes to these import prices and export demand shifters that result from liberalization in all countries except Indonesia; these results are then applied as shocks to the Wayang model. The changes to border prices derived from the Linkage model are shown in table 6.5.

*Simulation C* combines simulations A and B to depict global reform, including Indonesia. In this case, exogenous variables (1), (2), and (3) all change. The non-linear approximation techniques used to solve the Wayang model mean that the results of simulation C are not exactly the arithmetic sum of the results of simulations A and B, but they are similar to the arithmetic sum.

Each of the above simulations is conducted twice: once to show the case in which the reductions in the protection in Indonesia and in the rest of the world apply to all traded commodities (labeled simulations A1, B1, and C1) and once to show the case in which the reductions in protection apply only to agricultural and lightly processed food commodities (labeled simulations A2, B2, and C2).

### Model closure

Because we have chosen the real consumption expenditure of each household as the basis for welfare measurement and the calculation of the incidence of poverty, we must make the macroeconomic closure compatible with this measure and with the single-period horizon of the model. We do this by ensuring that the full economic effects of the shocks to be introduced are channeled into current-period household consumption and do not leak in other directions so that we are unable to capture real world intertemporal welfare implications in our welfare measure. The choice of macroeconomic closure may thus be seen partly as a mechanism to minimize inconsistencies between the use of a single-period model to analyze welfare results and the multiperiod reality that the model imperfectly represents.

To prevent intertemporal and other welfare leakages from occurring, we conduct the simulations for the case of balanced trade (the exogenous balance on the current account). This ensures that the potential benefits of the liberalization do not flow to foreigners through a current account surplus or that increases in

## Table 6.5. Exogenous Border Price Shocks That Would Result from Rest-of-the-World Liberalization, Indonesia

*(percent deviation from base)*

| Commodity | Export price shocks[a] | | Import price shocks[b] | |
|---|---|---|---|---|
| | Reform of all goods | Only agricultural reform | Reform of all goods | Only agricultural reform |
| Paddy rice | 0.0 | 0.0 | 4.3 | 2.7 |
| Wheat | 0.0 | 0.0 | 6.8 | 7.1 |
| Other grains | 3.1 | 1.4 | −2.7 | −2.8 |
| Oilseeds | 3.0 | 1.3 | −1.8 | −1.3 |
| Sugarcane and beets | 0.0 | 0.0 | 0.0 | 0.0 |
| Plant-based fibers | 3.1 | 1.4 | 7.6 | 8.7 |
| Vegetables and fruits | 3.1 | 1.4 | 2.6 | 1.9 |
| Other crops | 3.0 | 1.3 | 1.5 | 1.0 |
| Cattle, sheep, and so on | 3.0 | 1.3 | 5.6 | 5.5 |
| Other livestock | 2.7 | 1.1 | −1.9 | −0.6 |
| Raw milk | 0.0 | 0.0 | 0.0 | 0.0 |
| Wool | 0.0 | 0.0 | 9.8 | 10.0 |
| Beef and sheep meat | 3.0 | 1.4 | 5.6 | 5.7 |
| Other meat products | 2.5 | 0.8 | 3.3 | 3.6 |
| Vegetable oils and fats | 2.5 | 0.9 | 0.4 | 1.1 |
| Dairy products | 2.7 | 1.1 | 8.6 | 8.8 |
| Processed rice | 3.0 | 1.3 | 3.7 | 2.8 |
| Refined sugar | 2.6 | 1.0 | 2.9 | 2.5 |
| Other food, beverages, tobacco | 2.4 | 0.9 | −0.8 | −0.7 |
| Other primary products | 2.1 | 0.6 | 1.3 | 0.8 |
| Textiles and wearing apparel | 2.1 | 1.0 | −0.3 | 0.4 |
| Other manufacturing | 1.9 | 0.6 | 0.4 | 0.4 |
| Services | 2.1 | 0.6 | −0.2 | 0.2 |
| Agriculture and food | 2.5 | 1.0 | 3.0 | 3.2 |
| Agriculture | 3.0 | 1.3 | 4.1 | 4.5 |
| Processed foods | 2.5 | 0.9 | 1.7 | 1.8 |
| Other manufacturing | 2.0 | 0.6 | 0.4 | 0.4 |
| Nontradables | 2.1 | 0.6 | −0.2 | 0.2 |
| Total | 2.1 | 0.7 | 0.5 | 0.6 |
| Merchandise trade | 2.1 | 0.7 | 0.7 | 0.8 |

*Source:* Linkage model simulations by van der Mensbrugghe, Valenzuela, and Anderson (see the appendix).

a. Simulated as shocks to the inverse export demand equations for Indonesia.

b. Simulated as shocks to the exogenous import prices for Indonesia.

domestic consumption are not achieved at the expense of borrowing from abroad in the case of a current account deficit. For the same reason, we exogenously fix real government spending and real investment demand for each good. We hold the government budget deficit fixed in nominal terms. We achieve this by endogenous across-the-board adjustments to the sales tax rate so as to restore the base level of the budgetary deficit. As the combined outcome of these features of the closure, the full effects of the changes in policy are channeled into household consumption and not into effects that are, in fact, relevant to economic welfare, but are ignored in the single-period focus of the model.

## The results of the liberalization of the markets for all goods

While the emphasis in our study is on the effects on poverty and income inequality, an understanding of these effects requires that we first look at the macroeconomic impacts.

### Macroeconomic effects

The macroeconomic effects of trade reform in the markets for all commodities are summarized in table 6.6. Real GDP rises in Indonesia under all three reform scenarios. The increases are small in the case of unilateral liberalization (Sim A1) and moderate if other countries liberalize as well (Sim B1 and Sim C1). Under unilateral liberalization, the domestic price levels in Indonesia decline (measured as the GDP deflator and the consumer price index). Aggregate real household consumption rises marginally under unilateral reform (Sim A1) and rises more substantially if the rest of the world reforms (B1) and under global reform, including Indonesia (C1).

As our description of model closure indicates, real investment, real inventories, and real government spending (each deflated by the relevant price deflator), as well as the real trade balance (measured in foreign exchange terms), are all held constant in these simulations. The nominal values of each of these categories thus change as the price levels of the components change. The nominal values of GDP and consumption change in line with the fact that the GDP deflator and the consumer price index both decline as tariffs are removed in Indonesia. The same is true of investment and inventories.

However, nominal government spending increases. The reason is evident from the changes in factor prices. The real value of skilled labor increases by a proportion (5.7 percent) greater than the decline in the consumer price index (2.2 percent). Nominal skilled wages therefore rise (3.5 percent). Because government expenditure is heavily concentrated in the employment of skilled (educated) labor, nominal government spending must rise to maintain the real value of

**Table 6.6. Aggregate Simulation Results of the Prospective Liberalization of All Commodities, Indonesia**

| Indicator | Sim A1, unilateral liberalization | Sim B1, rest-of-the-world liberalization | Sim C1, global liberalization |
|---|---|---|---|
| *Macroeconomic aggregates, % change from base* | | | |
| Real GDP, expenditure side, GDP deflator | 0.54 | 1.12 | 1.37 |
| Real household consumption, CPI deflator | 0.54 | 5.21 | 5.78 |
| Import volume index, duty-paid weights | 11.95 | 12.54 | 27.09 |
| Export volume index | 9.84 | 4.59 | 15.56 |
| GDP price index, expenditure side | −1.75 | 9.06 | 7.59 |
| Consumer price index | −2.19 | 8.79 | 6.50 |
| *Nominal change, Rp, billions* | | | |
| GDP | −17,923 | 150,926 | 133,071 |
| Consumption | −14,854 | 129,693 | 113,574 |
| Investment | −4,561 | 12,890 | 9,135 |
| Inventory | −109 | −1,580 | −1,829 |
| Government expenditure | 1,600 | 9,922 | 12,191 |
| Exports, net of imports | 0 | 0 | 0 |
| *Real return to factors, % change from base, using the CPI deflator* | | | |
| Unskilled labor | 0.2 | 7.1 | 8.5 |
| Skilled labor | 5.7 | 1.8 | 8.1 |
| Agricultural capital | −5.6 | 11.9 | 9.0 |
| Nonagricultural capital | 3.1 | −4.6 | −1.5 |
| Land | −2.9 | 21.0 | 19.1 |
| *Real household expenditure, % change from base, using the CPI deflator* | | | |
| Rural 1 | −0.8 | 3.9 | 3.0 |
| Rural 2 | −1.1 | 5.9 | 4.7 |
| Rural 3 | −0.1 | 6.8 | 6.8 |
| Rural 4 | 0.7 | 4.4 | 5.1 |
| Rural 5 | 1.0 | 5.5 | 6.7 |
| Rural 6 | 0.3 | 5.6 | 6.0 |
| Rural 7 | 1.1 | 5.2 | 6.3 |
| Urban 1 | −0.1 | 4.6 | 4.5 |
| Urban 2 | 1.6 | 5.1 | 7.0 |
| Urban 3 | 1.9 | 5.5 | 7.4 |

*Source:* CGE model simulations for Indonesia by the author.

*Note:* CPI = consumer price index.

government spending. Consumption is the only component of expenditure on GDP the real value of which is not fixed exogenously. The increase in nominal government spending therefore limits the amount by which real household consumption may increase in response to the decline in protection.

The real value of skilled wages rises because, according to the rates of industry assistance in Indonesia used in these simulations (see table 6.4), the country's protective structure acts against the interests of industries that are intensive in the use of skilled labor. The protective structure is virtually neutral with regard to unskilled labor. The existence of this protection reduces the real value of skilled wages, and the removal of the protection accomplishes the reverse.

The bottom panel of table 6.6 summarizes the changes in the real consumption expenditures of each of the 10 household groups. Under unilateral liberalization (Sim A1), the poorer rural household groups (Rural 1, 2, and 3) and the poorest urban household group (Urban 1) lose, and all other household groups gain. The changes in real factor prices and in the sources of household incomes (see table 6.2) provide the main explanation for these outcomes. Real unskilled wages remain virtually unchanged, and the real return to agricultural land and capital decline in this simulation, thus harming poorer rural households. At the same time, the real returns to skilled labor and nonagricultural capital increase, favoring the richer households, especially households in urban areas. In addition, the reduced protection directly lowers the consumer prices of the imported goods subject to the protection.

These results necessarily reflect the structure of protection in Indonesia that is assumed in our study, as represented in the Distortions to Agricultural Incentives Project Database (Anderson and Valenzuela 2008). According to our model results, protection disfavors skilled labor-intensive industries overall, while favoring agricultural industries that are intensive in the use of land and agricultural capital. The removal of the protection harms agricultural land and capital and benefits skilled labor and nonagricultural capital. These factors are owned most intensively by the richest urban households, and these households are, in consequence, the largest beneficiaries of unilateral liberalization in Indonesia.

Liberalization in the rest of the world (Sim B1) produces international price changes that raise real GDP in Indonesia by about twice the increase that would result from unilateral liberalization by Indonesia, but the effects within Indonesia are qualitatively different. Liberalization in the rest of the world raises the real value of both skilled and unskilled wages in Indonesia, especially the former, and also raises the returns to agricultural capital and (especially) agricultural land. This occurs because liberalization in the rest of the world raises agricultural prices relative to nonagricultural prices internationally, favoring the agricultural sectors in Indonesia. These results are important in our discussion of poverty (see below).

The real returns to nonagricultural capital decline, but all other factor returns increase. A key point is that rest-of-the-world liberalization benefits unskilled labor proportionately more than skilled labor in Indonesia. The increase in real consumption in Indonesia in the scenario of rest-of-the-world liberalization is 10 times the corresponding increase in the scenario of unilateral liberalization. Real household expenditures increase in all 10 socioeconomic categories in the rest-of-the-world liberalization scenario.

Global reform (Sim C1) is a combination of the previous two simulations and is dominated by rest-of-the-world liberalization. The results are qualitatively similar to the effects of simulation B1.

### Effects on inequality and the incidence of poverty

The simulated effects on the incidence of poverty according to socioeconomic group broadly mimic the effects on average household consumption among these groups, which is discussed above. The level of the incidence of poverty depends on the poverty line used in the calculations, and this may also be true of the simulated changes in the incidence of poverty that result from particular economic shocks. The shifts in real expenditures generated by particular economic shocks are not uniform across income groups because of differences in expenditure patterns. Different poverty lines act on different sections of the cumulative distribution of real expenditures and may thus produce different patterns of change in the incidence of poverty within the same simulation.

We use three poverty lines to investigate the effects on the incidence of poverty: the government's national poverty line, the international US$1-a-day (extreme) poverty line at purchasing power parity, and the international US$2-a-day (moderate) poverty line at purchasing power parity.

In the case of each of these poverty lines, we apply the following calibration method. First, we use the ex ante distribution of household expenditures revealed in the model database to calculate the particular level of poverty incidence associated with the poverty line.

Second, we use the published level of poverty incidence based on the particular poverty line to calculate the value of the poverty line in the domestic currency in Indonesia. The published levels of poverty incidence are contained in the *Statistical Yearbook of Indonesia* in the case of the national poverty line (BPS 2007) and the World Bank's World Development Indicators in the case of the US$1-a-day and US$2-a-day poverty lines (PovcalNet 2008). These calculations yield the base levels of the poverty lines used in subsequent calculations.

Third, we simulate the ex post levels of real expenditure for each household in the model to reflect the effects of the shocks. These calculations of real expenditure are performed using the individual household consumer price index as the deflator to reflect the particular household's consumption bundle.

Fourth, we compare these ex post real expenditures with the poverty lines described above to obtain ex post levels of poverty incidence.

Fifth, the changes in poverty incidence reported in table 6.7 (see also table 6.10 elsewhere below) are the ex post levels of poverty incidence, minus the ex ante levels corresponding to each of the three poverty lines described above. A positive number thus indicates an increase in the simulated level of poverty incidence as a result of the relevant shocks.

In addition to the effects on the incidence of poverty, we also report simulated effects on inequality in the distribution of household real expenditures using the Gini coefficient as the measure. The Gini coefficient has values between 0 and 1; the higher values reflect greater inequality. These coefficients are estimated by constructing Lorenz curves from the distributions of ex ante and ex post real expenditures and then calculating the Gini coefficients corresponding to these distributions. (These results are presented in tables 6.8 and 6.11; see elsewhere below.)

Panel a in table 6.7 indicates that unilateral liberalization in Indonesia applied to all commodities (simulation A1) raises the incidence of poverty in the poorest

### Table 6.7. Poverty Effects of the Prospective Liberalization of All Commodities, Indonesia

**a. Measured at the national poverty line**

| Household category | Ex ante level of poverty incidence, % of group population | Changes in poverty incidence (%), ex post − ex ante | | |
|---|---|---|---|---|
| | | Sim A1, unilateral liberalization | Sim B1, rest-of-the-world liberalization | Sim C1, global liberalization |
| Rural 1 | 39.81 | 0.81 | −4.82 | −3.52 |
| Rural 2 | 34.89 | 0.76 | −5.71 | −4.95 |
| Rural 3 | 32.29 | 0.09 | −5.53 | −5.49 |
| Rural 4 | 27.82 | −0.44 | −2.64 | −4.17 |
| Rural 5 | 23.78 | −0.82 | −3.91 | −4.60 |
| Rural 6 | 28.01 | −0.13 | −3.45 | −3.85 |
| Rural 7 | 10.50 | −0.77 | −2.07 | −2.35 |
| Urban 1 | 15.22 | 0.02 | −2.31 | −2.27 |
| Urban 2 | 11.16 | −0.52 | −2.35 | −3.09 |
| Urban 3 | 5.00 | −0.39 | −1.03 | −1.36 |
| Urban households | 11.98 | −0.16 | −1.99 | −2.18 |
| Rural households | 29.09 | −0.05 | −4.26 | −4.36 |
| All households | 23.10 | −0.12 | −3.49 | −3.60 |

**b. Measured at the US$1-a-day poverty line**

| Household category | Ex ante level of poverty incidence, % of group population | Changes in poverty incidence (%), ex post − ex ante | | |
| --- | --- | --- | --- | --- |
| | | Sim A1, unilateral liberalization | Sim B1, rest-of-the-world liberalization | Sim C1, global liberalization |
| Rural 1 | 2.40 | 0.11 | −0.47 | −0.39 |
| Rural 2 | 13.09 | 0.43 | −3.46 | −2.72 |
| Rural 3 | 8.74 | 0.06 | −2.07 | −2.06 |
| Rural 4 | 18.55 | −0.67 | −3.13 | −3.48 |
| Rural 5 | 8.67 | −0.54 | −2.20 | −2.73 |
| Rural 6 | 1.80 | 0.03 | −0.47 | −0.51 |
| Rural 7 | 0.00 | 0.00 | 0.00 | 0.00 |
| Urban 1 | 7.08 | 0.00 | −1.43 | −1.40 |
| Urban 2 | 2.66 | 0.10 | 0.51 | 0.60 |
| Urban 3 | 0.00 | 0.00 | 0.00 | 0.00 |
| Urban households | 4.56 | −0.03 | −0.91 | −0.93 |
| Rural households | 9.09 | −0.11 | −2.09 | −2.09 |
| All households | 7.50 | −0.08 | −1.68 | −1.68 |

**c. Measured at the US$2-a-day poverty line**

| Household category | Ex ante level of poverty incidence, % of group population | Changes in poverty incidence (%), ex post − ex ante | | |
| --- | --- | --- | --- | --- |
| | | Sim A1, unilateral liberalization | Sim B1, rest-of-the-world liberalization | Sim C1, global liberalization |
| Rural 1 | 48.79 | 2.03 | −3.29 | −2.87 |
| Rural 2 | 74.36 | 0.62 | −5.05 | −3.28 |
| Rural 3 | 66.73 | 0.28 | −6.32 | −6.30 |
| Rural 4 | 78.64 | −0.26 | −2.79 | −3.49 |
| Rural 5 | 66.93 | −0.63 | −4.56 | −5.84 |
| Rural 6 | 30.59 | −0.72 | −4.66 | −4.81 |
| Rural 7 | 2.38 | −0.19 | −0.53 | −0.59 |
| Urban 1 | 53.11 | 0.05 | −4.04 | −3.95 |
| Urban 2 | 31.43 | −0.96 | −2.96 | −4.48 |
| Urban 3 | 6.79 | −0.62 | −1.39 | −1.78 |
| Urban households | 37.87 | −0.29 | −3.19 | −3.50 |
| Rural households | 60.27 | 0.16 | −4.16 | −4.13 |
| All households | 52.40 | 0.00 | −3.82 | −3.91 |

*Source*: CGE model simulations for Indonesia by the author.

three rural household categories, but lowers it among the richer rural categories and in all but the poorest urban categories. The aggregate urban and rural incidence of poverty both decline, but the decline is larger among urban households. National poverty incidence necessarily declines. All these effects are quite small. Table 6.7, panels b and c show that these effects are not particularly sensitive to the poverty line used except that, at the US$2-a-day poverty line, the incidence of rural poverty rises.

The effects of liberalization in the rest of the world (simulation B1) are quite different. The incidence of poverty in Indonesia declines significantly in this scenario. The decline occurs in all 10 socioeconomic groups, but is largest in rural areas. At the national level, poverty incidence declines by 3.5 percent (national poverty line). This pattern of results is not sensitive to the poverty line used. At the US$1-a-day and national poverty lines, the incidence of poverty declines significantly in both rural and urban areas. The explanation for these outcomes is evident from the changes in real factor returns described above. Rest-of-the-world liberalization raises the international prices of agricultural commodities relative to nonagricultural prices, and this produces an increase in the real value of unskilled wages and of the returns to agricultural capital and land in Indonesia. These effects benefit poor households, especially those in rural areas. The incidence of poverty in both urban and, especially, rural areas declines.

Finally, we may compare the combined effects of unilateral reform in Indonesia and liberalization elsewhere, summarized in the tables as the effects of global reform (simulation C1). As in the case of simulation B1, the real returns to unskilled and skilled labor rise significantly, along with the returns to agricultural land and capital. But the real return to nonagricultural capital declines marginally. Both rural poverty and urban poverty decline significantly, but, especially, rural poverty. The central result is that the effects of the rest-of-the-world reform dominate the effects of unilateral liberalization. The outcomes in this scenario are essentially the same as those of the rest-of-the-world scenario (B1) tempered by the counteracting domestic liberalization (A1) effects.

The method we use to estimate the changes in the incidence of poverty is illustrated in figure 6.1. The figure shows the ex ante (initial) distribution of expenditures for the socioeconomic household group Rural 3 (medium-size farmers with 0.5 to 1 hectare of land), along with the simulated ex post (new) distribution of expenditures that results from simulation C1. The two curves thus indicate the cumulative distribution of expenditures per person at constant (year 2000) prices before and after the shock, that is, the change in nominal expenditures for each household is deflated by a household-specific index of consumer prices, reflecting that household's base-period (initial) expenditure pattern. For any level of expenditure (horizontal axis), each curve shows (on the vertical axis) the share

## Figure 6.1. Initial and Simulated Levels of Poverty Incidence, Indonesia

*(as illustrated by socioeconomic household category Rural 3, simulation C1)*

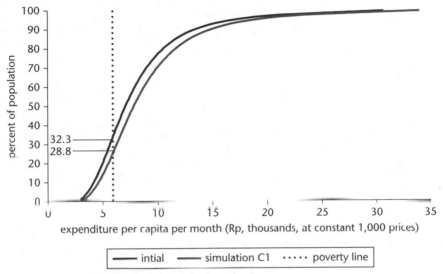

*Source:* CGE model simulations for Indonesia by the author.

*Note:* The cumulative distributions of expenditures corresponding to simulation C1 are calculated in real terms using household-specific consumer price indexes at year 2000 prices as the deflator for each household. It is therefore possible to compare the initial (year 2000) distribution of expenditures and the distribution marked simulation C1 with the poverty line for the year 2000. The initial and simulated (postliberalization) levels of poverty incidence for this household category, using the national poverty line, resulting from simulation C1 are 32.3 percent and 26.8 percent, respectively. See table 6.7, panel a.

of the population with expenditures less than or equal to that level of expenditure. For any poverty line, the incidence of poverty may thus be read as the vertical value of the intersection between the poverty line (horizontal axis) and the cumulative distribution.

Using the national poverty line for 2000, we find that the initial level of poverty incidence among the Rural 3 group was 32.3 percent, the intersection of the poverty line with the cumulative initial distribution in figure 6.1. Simulation C1 (global reform in all commodities) shifts the entire distribution to the right, though not uniformly, producing the simulated cumulative distribution of expenditures at constant prices, which is labeled simulation C1 in the figure. It is important to note that this is a shift in real expenditures measured at 2000 prices. The new level of poverty incidence may therefore be read using the same poverty line that we use elsewhere above. Poverty incidence declines to 26.8 percent, a decrease of 5.5 percent. It is apparent from figure 6.1 that the incidence of poverty declined no matter which

**Table 6.8. Income Inequality Effects of the Prospective Liberalization of All Commodities, Indonesia**

| Household category | Ex ante level of Gini coefficient | Changes in Gini coefficient, ex post − ex ante | | |
|---|---|---|---|---|
| | | Sim A1, unilateral liberalization | Sim B1, rest-of-the-world liberalization | Sim C1, global liberalization |
| Urban households | 0.3559 | 0.0025 | 0.0019 | 0.0045 |
| Rural households | 0.2912 | 0.0011 | 0.0002 | 0.0013 |
| All households | 0.3351 | 0.0023 | 0.0006 | 0.0030 |

*Source:* CGE model simulations for Indonesia by the author.

poverty line might be chosen. In the case of our simulation here, the conclusion that the incidence of poverty declined among socioeconomic group Rural 3 is therefore not dependent on the particular poverty line that we have selected, although the magnitude of the decline is affected by the choice of poverty line.

The effects on inequality in Indonesia are summarized in table 6.8. Both unilateral liberalization and global liberalization in all commodities raise inequality. This effect is largest in the case of unilateral liberalization. The effect operates through the increased returns to skilled labor and nonagricultural capital, which are factors owned primarily by more affluent urban households.

### Results of the liberalization only of agricultural markets

If liberalization is confined to agricultural and lightly processed food products only (simulations A2, B2, and C2), unilateral liberalization in Indonesia (simulation A2) lowers the returns to unskilled labor, agricultural capital, and land and raises the returns to skilled labor and nonagricultural capital (table 6.9). Rice and sugar dominate agricultural protection in Indonesia. These industries are intensive in unskilled labor and land relative to the rest of the economy. Reducing protection in Indonesia reduces the real incomes of the owners of unskilled labor and agricultural land (table 6.10, panels a and c). Real incomes fall in most rural household categories and rise in urban categories, but reduced agricultural protection also lowers food prices. The net effects on real expenditures are small. Most rural household categories are small net losers, and all urban categories are net gainers.

It has been argued elsewhere that the reduced protection of the rice industry alone reduces the incidence of poverty among both urban and rural households in Indonesia (Warr 2005). Rice differs from the rest of agriculture in two important respects. First, it is more intensive in the use of unskilled labor than the rest of agriculture. Second, rice is a staple food for most Indonesians and forms a high share of the total expenditures among the poorest groups. Thus, reductions in the

**Table 6.9. Aggregate Simulation Results of the Prospective Liberalization Only of Agricultural Commodities, Indonesia**

| Indicator | Sim A2, unilateral liberalization | Sim B2, rest-of-the-world liberalization | Sim C2, global liberalization |
|---|---|---|---|
| *Macroeconomic aggregates, % change from base* | | | |
| Real GDP, expenditure side, GDP deflator | 0.01 | 0.25 | 0.26 |
| Real household consumption, CPI deflator | 0.00 | 1.07 | 1.08 |
| Import volume index, duty-paid weights | 0.51 | 0.57 | 1.17 |
| Export volume index | 0.42 | −0.43 | 0.05 |
| GDP price index, expenditure side | −0.17 | 1.16 | 1.15 |
| Consumer price index | 0.20 | 1.55 | 1.20 |
| *Nominal change, Rp, billions* | | | |
| GDP | −2,411 | 25,137 | 22,206 |
| Consumption | −2,556 | 23,709 | 20,658 |
| Investment | −1 | 2,319 | 2,322 |
| Inventory | −81 | −728 | −840 |
| Government expenditure | 228 | −162 | 65 |
| Exports, net of imports | 0 | 0 | 0 |
| *Real return to factors, % change from base, using the CPI deflator* | | | |
| Unskilled labor | −0.5 | 3.2 | 2.7 |
| Skilled labor | 0.7 | −2.5 | −1.8 |
| Agricultural capital | −2.0 | 15.7 | 13.4 |
| Nonagricultural capital | 0.4 | −1.6 | −1.2 |
| Land | −1.1 | 29.7 | 28.8 |
| *Real household expenditure, % change from base, using the CPI deflator* | | | |
| Rural 1 | 0.0 | 1.1 | 1.2 |
| Rural 2 | −0.4 | 2.1 | 1.7 |
| Rural 3 | −0.3 | 2.3 | 2.0 |
| Rural 4 | −0.1 | 1.4 | 1.3 |
| Rural 5 | 0.1 | 0.6 | 0.8 |
| Rural 6 | −0.2 | 1.8 | 1.6 |
| Rural 7 | 0.0 | 1.1 | 1.1 |
| Urban 1 | 0.0 | 1.1 | 1.1 |
| Urban 2 | 0.2 | 0.8 | 1.0 |
| Urban 3 | 0.2 | 0.2 | 0.4 |

*Source:* CGE model simulations for Indonesia by the author.

*Note:* CPI = consumer price index.

### Table 6.10. Poverty Effects of the Prospective Liberalization of Only Agricultural Commodities, Indonesia

#### a. Measured at the national poverty line

| Household category | Ex ante level of poverty incidence, % of group population | Changes in poverty incidence (%), ex post − ex ante | | |
| --- | --- | --- | --- | --- |
| | | Sim A2, unilateral liberalization | Sim B2, rest-of-the-world liberalization | Sim C2, global liberalization |
| Rural 1 | 39.81 | 0.00 | −1.93 | −2.00 |
| Rural 2 | 34.89 | 0.25 | −1.73 | −1.37 |
| Rural 3 | 32.29 | 0.17 | −1.40 | −1.25 |
| Rural 4 | 27.82 | 0.06 | −0.78 | −0.74 |
| Rural 5 | 23.78 | −0.15 | −0.39 | −0.58 |
| Rural 6 | 28.01 | 0.11 | −0.76 | −0.70 |
| Rural 7 | 10.50 | 0.02 | −0.73 | −0.72 |
| Urban 1 | 15.22 | −0.11 | −0.47 | −0.52 |
| Urban 2 | 11.16 | −0.05 | −0.16 | −0.25 |
| Urban 3 | 5.00 | −0.05 | 0.00 | −0.06 |
| Urban households | 11.97 | −0.08 | −0.29 | −0.35 |
| Rural households | 29.09 | 0.05 | −1.11 | −1.06 |
| All households | 23.10 | −0.02 | −0.85 | −0.83 |

#### b. Measured at the US$1-a-day poverty line

| Household category | Ex ante level of poverty incidence, % of group population | Changes in poverty incidence (%), ex post − ex ante | | |
| --- | --- | --- | --- | --- |
| | | Sim A2, unilateral liberalization | Sim B2, rest-of-the-world liberalization | Sim C2, global liberalization |
| Rural 1 | 2.40 | 0.00 | −0.14 | −0.15 |
| Rural 2 | 13.09 | 0.13 | −0.81 | −0.67 |
| Rural 3 | 8.74 | 0.11 | −0.84 | −0.77 |
| Rural 4 | 18.55 | 0.09 | −0.96 | −0.92 |
| Rural 5 | 8.67 | −0.10 | −0.23 | −0.35 |
| Rural 6 | 1.80 | 0.01 | −0.15 | −0.14 |
| Rural 7 | 0.00 | 0.00 | 0.00 | 0.00 |
| Urban 1 | 7.08 | −0.04 | −0.30 | −0.35 |
| Urban 2 | 2.66 | −0.03 | −0.05 | −0.09 |
| Urban 3 | 0.00 | 0.00 | 0.00 | 0.00 |
| Urban households | 4.56 | −0.03 | −0.18 | −0.22 |
| Rural households | 9.09 | 0.03 | −0.50 | −0.48 |
| All households | 7.50 | 0.01 | −0.38 | −0.39 |

## c. Measured at the US$2-a-day poverty line

| Household category | Ex ante level of poverty incidence, % of group population | Changes in poverty incidence (%), ex post − ex ante | | |
|---|---|---|---|---|
| | | Sim A2, unilateral liberalization | Sim B2, rest-of-the-world liberalization | Sim C2, global liberalization |
| Rural 1 | 48.79 | −0.01 | −0.89 | −0.92 |
| Rural 2 | 74.36 | 0.20 | −1.27 | −1.03 |
| Rural 3 | 66.73 | 0.41 | −2.42 | −2.21 |
| Rural 4 | 78.64 | 0.05 | −0.56 | −0.51 |
| Rural 5 | 66.93 | −0.09 | −0.39 | −0.51 |
| Rural 6 | 30.59 | 0.46 | −1.70 | −1.58 |
| Rural 7 | 2.38 | 0.00 | −0.17 | −0.17 |
| Urban 1 | 53.11 | −0.04 | −1.04 | −1.12 |
| Urban 2 | 31.43 | −0.38 | 0.00 | −0.69 |
| Urban 3 | 6.79 | −0.08 | −0.01 | −0.10 |
| Urban households | 37.87 | −0.11 | −0.71 | −0.79 |
| Rural households | 60.27 | 0.11 | −0.98 | −0.92 |
| All households | 52.40 | 0.03 | −0.89 | −0.88 |

*Source:* CGE model simulations for Indonesia by the author.

protection of rice reduce real unskilled wages, but they also reduce the consumer price of rice, the staple food of the poor. The latter effect dominates.

However, if the reduction in protection applies to all agricultural products, including sugar, the effect on the incidence of poverty becomes more ambiguous. Reductions in protection still reduce unskilled wages, but the poverty-reducing effect of lowering consumer prices is less strong in protected agriculture in general than in rice alone. Unilateral agricultural liberalization causes the incidence of poverty to rise in rural areas and to fall in urban areas. The net effect on the national incidence of poverty is a small decline, measured by the national poverty line, but a small increase, measured by the US$1-a-day and US$2-a-day poverty lines.

Agricultural liberalization in the rest of the world (simulation B2) raises the prices of agricultural commodities relative to the prices of nonagricultural commodities on international markets. The effect is to raise the returns to unskilled labor in Indonesia and to lower the returns to skilled labor. The incidence of poverty declines in both rural and urban areas, and this qualitative result holds regardless of the poverty line. If the world liberalizes, including Indonesia (simulation C2), the quantitative effects of this liberalization also dominate the effects of domestic liberalization. The results of global agricultural liberalization are thus qualitatively similar to the results of rest-of-the-world liberalization.

**Table 6.11. Income Inequality Effects of the Prospective Liberalization of Only Agricultural Commodities, Indonesia**

| Household category | Ex ante level of Gini coefficient | Changes in Gini coefficient, ex post − ex ante | | |
|---|---|---|---|---|
| | | Sim A2, unilateral liberalization | Sim B2, rest-of-the-world liberalization | Sim C2, global liberalization |
| Urban households | 0.3559 | 0.0001 | −0.0006 | −0.0006 |
| Rural households | 0.2912 | 0.0000 | 0.0001 | 0.0000 |
| All households | 0.3351 | 0.0002 | −0.0007 | −0.0006 |

Source: CGE model simulations for Indonesia by the author.

Inequality in Indonesia rises slightly under unilateral agricultural liberalization because unskilled wages decline relative to skilled wages. Within rural areas alone, there is no change in inequality because, although real wages decline, this effect is offset by the reduced returns to agricultural capital and land. Rest-of-the-world reform and global agricultural reform reduce inequality in Indonesia because the returns to unskilled labor, agricultural capital, and land (owned by the poor, especially the rural poor) rise relative to other factor returns. These effects are summarized in table 6.11.

Comparing the results of the liberalization in all commodities (simulations A1 to C1) with the liberalization in agricultural products only (simulations A2 to C2), six key points emerge, as follows:

- Trade liberalization reduces the incidence of poverty in Indonesia, but the effects are large only if they apply at a global level and to all commodities.
- The effects of rest-of-the-world liberalization dominate the effects of unilateral liberalization, and rest-of-the-world liberalization is more strongly poverty reducing than liberalization in Indonesia alone.
- Unilateral across-the-board liberalization in Indonesia reduces food prices and raises the real returns to skilled labor, while lowering the returns to agriculture-specific factors of production, which produces small net reductions in the incidence of poverty overall, though the effects on individual rural household categories are mixed.
- Liberalization in all commodities is more strongly poverty reducing in Indonesia than is liberalization in agricultural products alone, whether the liberalization occurs unilaterally in Indonesia, or in the rest of the world, or both.
- Unilateral liberalization confined to agricultural products generates benefits mainly among urban households; these benefits operate through reduced food prices, plus increased returns to skilled labor and nonagricultural capital.

- Liberalization in all commodities raises inequality in Indonesia, whether the liberalization is unilateral or global, but especially the former, whereas liberalization only in agricultural products raises inequality slightly if the liberalization is unilateral and reduces inequality if the liberalization is global.

## Conclusions

The comparative static nature of our analysis in this chapter limits our capacity to capture the full economic gains available through liberalization. Dynamic effects are not captured, and these may be significant sources of additional welfare gains and poverty reduction from trade policy liberalization. Nonetheless, within this comparative static limitation, the analysis indicates that the global reform of trade policies in all commodities would be a significant potential source of poverty reduction in Indonesia. The poor in Indonesia—rural and urban—have a strong interest in global trade policy reform, whether Indonesia is part of the liberalization or not. If Indonesia liberalizes unilaterally, poverty incidence also declines, but the comparative static benefits are much smaller.

If liberalization is confined to agricultural products, the pattern of the effects is similar, but the declines in the incidence of poverty in Indonesia are much more modest. Global reform in agricultural products generates significant reductions in both rural and urban poverty. Indonesia's rural and urban poor have a strong interest in the global reform of agricultural trade policy, but—according to the comparative static analysis of our study—the rural poor do not necessarily have an interest in unilateral agricultural liberalization because some rural socioeconomic groups would lose out from this sort of liberalization.

## Notes

1. For a fuller discussion of agricultural assistance in Indonesia, see Fane and Warr (2008, 2009). The estimates by these authors of agricultural assistance in Indonesia are incorporated in the World Bank database on global agricultural distortions (see Anderson and Valenzuela 2008). These estimates cover over four decades. The representative values for the computable general equilibrium modeling as of 2004 that are used here are available in Valenzuela and Anderson (2008).

2. Variations on this assumption are possible. For example, the possibility of unemployment may be introduced by varying the closure to make either real or nominal wages exogenous, thereby allowing the level of employment to be endogenously determined by demand.

3. For an application of an earlier version of this model to the relationship between economic growth and the incidence of poverty in Indonesia, see Fane and Warr (2003).

4. Given that the exported and domestically sold goods are considered identical, this assumption is required to separate the domestic price of the import-competing good from the price of the exported good. Otherwise, the Armington structure we have described above would be redundant. An alternative treatment is to distinguish between the exported commodity and the commodity sold domestically; between them would be a finite elasticity of transformation in production.

5. The population size of each of the 10 major categories is not the same, but, within each of these 10 categories, the population size of each of the 100 subcategories is the same.

6. Unpublished tax rate data of the Ministry of Finance were accessed in Jakarta in March 2008.

7. The assumption that each export demand elasticity is 20 means that export prices are close to exogenous.

## References

Anderson, K., and E. Valenzuela. 2008. "Estimates of Global Distortions to Agricultural Incentives, 1955–2007." Data spreadsheet, October, World Bank, Washington, DC. http://go.worldbank.org/YAO39F35E0.

BPS (Badan Pusat Statistik, Statistics Indonesia). 1990. *Input-Output Tables of Indonesia.* Jakarta: BPS.

———. 2000. *The National Socioeconomic Survey (Susenas), 1999.* Jakarta: BPS.

———. 2001. *Input-Output Tables of Indonesia, 2000.* Jakarta: BPS.

———. 2005. *Social Accounting Matrix for Indonesia, 2000.* Jakarta: BPS.

———. 2007. *Statistik Indonesia: Statistical Yearbook of Indonesia 2007.* Jakarta: BPS.

Dixon, P. B., B. R. Parmenter, J. Sutton, and D. P. Vincent. 1982. *ORANI: A Multisectoral Model of the Australian Economy.* Amsterdam: North-Holland.

Fane, G., and P. Warr. 2003. "How Economic Growth Reduces Poverty: A General Equilibrium Analysis for Indonesia." In *Perspectives on Growth and Poverty,* ed. R. van der Hoeven and A. Shorrocks, 217–34. New York: United Nations University Press.

———. 2008. "Agricultural Protection in Indonesia." *Bulletin of Indonesian Economic Studies* 44 (1): 133–50.

———. 2009. "Indonesia." In *Distortions to Agricultural Incentives in Asia,* ed. K. Anderson and W. Martin, 165–96. Washington, DC: World Bank.

Hertel, T. W., ed. 1997. *Global Trade Analysis: Modeling and Applications.* New York: Cambridge University Press.

Horridge, M. 2004. "ORANI-G: A Generic Single-Country Computable General Equilibrium Model." Centre of Policy Studies, Monash University, Melbourne.

Johansen, L. 1964. *A Multi-sectoral Study of Economic Growth.* Amsterdam: North-Holland.

PovcalNet. World Bank, Washington, DC. http://go.worldbank.org/NT2A1XUWP0 (accessed May 2008).

Valenzuela, E., and K. Anderson. 2008. "Alternative Agricultural Price Distortions for CGE Analysis of Developing Countries, 2004 and 1980–84." Research Memorandum 13 (December), Center for Global Trade Analysis, Department of Agricultural Economics, Purdue University, West Lafayette, IN. https://www.gtap.agecon.purdue.edu/resources/res_display.asp?RecordID=2925.

van der Mensbrugghe, D. 2005. "Linkage Technical Reference Document: Version 6.0." December, World Bank, Washington, DC. http://go.worldbank.org/7NP2KK1OH0.

Warr, P. 2005. "Food Policy and Poverty in Indonesia: A General Equilibrium Analysis." *Australian Journal of Agricultural and Resource Economics* 49 (4): 429–51.

Warr, P., M. Aziz, H. da Costa, and P. J. Thapa. 1998. "Wayang: An Empirically Based Applied General Equilibrium Model of the Indonesian Economy." Unpublished report, Australian National University, Canberra.

# 7

# PAKISTAN

*Caesar B. Cororaton and David Orden*

This chapter analyzes the macroeconomic, sectoral, and poverty implications of the removal of agricultural and nonagricultural price distortions in the domestic markets of Pakistan and in the rest of the world. Our analysis uses the simulated results of rest-of-the-world trade liberalization in the World Bank's global Linkage model (hereafter referred to as the global model; see van der Mensbrugghe 2005) and derives results for rest-of-the-world and own country liberalization from the Pakistan computable general equilibrium (CGE) model of Cororaton and Orden (2008). The global model incorporates new estimates of assistance to farm industries for various developed and developing countries, including Pakistan, from the World Bank's research project, Distortions to Agricultural Incentives.[1] Using these new estimates, the global model simulates two separate scenarios: one involving full trade liberalization and one involving trade liberalization in agriculture alone. Both scenarios exclude Pakistan. The global model simulations generate changes in the import prices for Pakistan at the border, together with changes in world export prices and shifts in the export demand for Pakistan products. We utilize these results, along with the new estimates of industry assistance in Pakistan generated by Dorosh and Salam (2009), to analyze various liberalization scenarios and measure their impacts on national welfare, income inequality, and poverty using the Pakistan CGE model.

Trade reform entails a fiscal revenue loss to the government because trade taxes are an important source of revenue. We conduct experiments using two alternative tax replacement schemes to retain a fixed fiscal balance: a direct tax on household incomes and an indirect tax on consumption. We are thus able to show how the results differ according to the choice of the tax replacement method.

The simulation analysis is conducted in stages. In the first stage, we run two separate experiments. One experiment involves using the changes in the border prices and the computed shifts in the world export demand for Pakistan products from the global model (see the appendix by van der Mensbrugghe, Valenzuela, and Anderson) as an exogenous shock to the Pakistan model without altering the existing structure of price-distorting policies in Pakistan. The other experiment involves simulating unilateral trade liberalization in Pakistan without incorporating the changes from the global model. In the second stage, we combine these two separate experiments to examine the total effects. We conduct separate experiments in each stage for trade liberalization in all tradable goods sectors and in agriculture only (including lightly processed food). The simulations generate vectors of household income and consumer prices, which we use in conjunction with data from the 2001–02 Pakistan Household Integration Economic Survey (Federal Bureau of Statistics 2003) to calculate the impact on national income inequality and poverty.

The chapter is organized as follows. The next section discusses the structure of agricultural and trade distortions in Pakistan based on the new estimates of industry assistance. The Pakistan CGE model is then outlined. This section covers the model database (which reveals the structure of sectoral production, trade, and consumption), the sources of household income, and the tax structure based on the 2001–02 social accounting matrix (SAM). This is followed by a description of trends in rural and urban poverty in Pakistan. The policy experiments and the results generated by the various modeling scenarios are subsequently discussed in detail. The last section presents a summary of the findings and policy insights. The choice of tax replacement schemes plays an important role in the results we discuss.

## Agricultural Policies and Industry Assistance in Pakistan

The period from the 1960s to the mid-1980s involved heavy government intervention in Pakistan (Dorosh and Salam 2009). The government's hand on agricultural markets, trade policies, and the market for foreign exchange depressed the real prices of tradable agricultural commodities. The fixed exchange rate policy during these years, together with high domestic inflation, eroded significantly the competitiveness of the export sectors. However, during these years, the green revolution took place in agriculture. The revolution involved a package of inputs such as seeds, fertilizer, and irrigation that boosted agricultural production through higher farm productivity. Then, from the mid-1980s to the early 1990s, the government started to liberalize the agricultural sector, though it maintained control over the domestic wheat market and imposed high tariffs on vegetable oils and milk products.

Prior to the 1990s, Pakistan had been pursuing an import-substituting industrialization strategy that involved high tariff rates and quantitative import restrictions to promote the manufacturing sector. Then, major reforms were implemented in 1991 and 1997 that involved a series of tariff rate cuts and the phasing out of the quantitative import restrictions. The maximum tariff rates were reduced from 65 to 45 percent, and the number of tariff categories was cut from 13 to 5. This led to a significant drop in government revenue from trade taxes because tariffs had been the major contributor to government funds.

The key policy changes affecting agricultural prices are summarized in the rest of this section, while the policy changes affecting the manufacturing sector are described elsewhere below.

Wheat is the staple food in Pakistan. The wheat market is still heavily controlled by the government through various instruments, including government procurement (to stabilize supply), support pricing (to assist farmers), and ceiling prices (to ensure affordability among consumers). However, Pakistan's trade and pricing policies on wheat effectively tax wheat producers, while providing substantial fiscal subsidies to wheat millers through the government sale of wheat at below market prices (Dorosh 2005).

Government involvement in the market for cotton, which is the largest cash crop in Pakistan, has changed substantially over time. In 1974, the government prevented the private sector from engaging in the international cotton trade, but this changed in 1989, when the private sector was allowed to buy cotton directly from ginners, export, and sell cotton domestically. Also, exports of cotton were subjected to an export tax. After the abolition of the export duty on cotton in 1994, domestic prices were more in line with international prices (Cororaton and Orden 2008). Since the mid-1990s, exports and imports of cotton have been practically duty free, although seed cotton continues to enjoy indirect protection because of import tariffs on vegetable oils that increase the price of cotton seed oil. Otherwise, government intervention has recently been limited to an annual review of the support prices for seed cotton and some public sector procurement to maintain these prices.

Rice is the third largest crop after wheat and cotton. There were heavy controls on rice in the early 1970s when the government instituted a monopoly procurement scheme to limit domestic consumption and expand exports. The two varieties of rice (basmati and the ordinary coarse rice called IRRI rice) are exported. The intervention system still exists but, since 2003–04, government procurement has been minimal. There were no export taxes on rice in the mid-2000s, but imports were subject to a 10 percent customs duty. The average domestic price of rice is below the export price (often about 20 percent) because of quality differences.

The domestic marketing and processing of sugarcane were highly regulated until the mid-1980s. The zoning of sugar mills required farmers to sell sugarcane to mills inside their zone until 1987. There has been no government procurement of sugarcane, but the government annually announces a support price that greatly assists sugarcane and refined sugar production, and it adjusts import tariffs and the related taxes to stabilize domestic prices. There are export bans on sugarcane and refined sugar, but they do little to reduce the high level of assistance to the industry.

There was a minor tax on vegetable oils in the 1970s and 1980s, but, since the 1990s, vegetable oil imports have been taxed heavily. For example, in 2005–06, the tariff was 32 percent on imported soybean oil and 40 percent on palm oil. Likewise, the domestic prices of sunflower oil are considerably higher than the border price. Nonetheless, two-thirds of the edible oil requirements of Pakistan are supplied by imports.

Maize is mainly used as feed in the livestock and poultry sectors. Maize production has expanded rapidly in recent years because of the strong demand for poultry products. The government has not intervened in the production and marketing of maize. However, there are tariffs on imported maize; these range from 10 to 25 percent. Maize was a nontradable crop between 1990 and 2005; thus, import tariffs had only minor effects on domestic prices.

The import tariffs on milk are high. In the 1970s and 1980s, the average protection was estimated at 74 percent, but the extent of protection has diminished, and, in the first half of the present decade, protection averaged about 35 percent (Dorosh and Salem 2009).

## The Pakistan CGE Model

This section summarizes the structure of the Pakistan CGE model; more details may be found in Cororaton and Orden (2008). It also discusses the method we use to introduce changes in the model to interface with the results generated by the global model. The model database representing the Pakistan economy is also summarized, along with the key parameters of the model.

### Structure of the national model

The Pakistan CGE model of Cororaton and Orden (2008) is calibrated to the 2001–02 SAM constructed by Dorosh, Niazi, and Nazli (2004).[2] The model has 34 production sectors in primary agriculture, lightly processed food, other manufacturing, and services. There are five categories of productive factors: three types of labor (skilled labor, unskilled labor, and farm labor), as well as capital and land. There are also 19 household categories, a government sector, a firm sector, and the rest of the world.

In the model, output ($X$) is a composite of value added ($VA$) and intermediate inputs. Output is sold to the domestic market ($D$) and may also be sold to the export market ($E$). Goods $E$ and goods $D$ are perfect substitutes. The sources of supply in the domestic market are domestic output and imports ($M$); substitution between $D$ and $M$ are dependent on the change in the relative prices of $D$ and $M$ and on the substitution parameter in a constant elasticity of substitution function.

The primary factors of production in agriculture are unskilled labor (a composite of the labor of farmers and hired unskilled labor), land, and capital, while, in nonagriculture, they are skilled labor, unskilled labor, and capital. The on-farm labor of farmers is used only in primary agriculture. Other unskilled labor (including by farmers) is mobile across sectors and is employed in agricultural and nonagricultural sectors, while skilled labor is only mobile among nonagricultural sectors. Capital is fixed in each sector; so, the rates of return may differ across sectors.[3] The use of land may shift among agricultural industries.

The sources of household income are factors of production, transfers, foreign remittances, and dividends. Household savings are a fixed proportion of disposable income. According to the SAM, nonpoor urban households pay direct income taxes to the government, while other households do not. Household demand is specified as a linear expenditure system.

The government obtains revenue from direct taxes on household and firm incomes, tariffs, other receipts, and indirect (consumption) taxes on domestic and imported goods. It spends on the consumption of goods and services, transfers, and other payments. We assume a fixed government fiscal balance in nominal terms. Tariff policy reforms result in changes in government income and expenditure, but the government balance is fixed through a tax replacement. We use a direct income tax replacement, but also compare the results under an adjustment via an indirect sales tax replacement on domestic consumption.[4] In either case, the tax replacement is endogenously determined so as to maintain a fixed level of government balance.

Foreign savings are also fixed. The numéraire is a weighted index of the price of value added in which the weights are the shares of the sectoral value added in the base calibration. The nominal exchange rate is flexible. Furthermore, we introduce a weighted price of investment and derive total investment in real prices. We hold total investment in real prices fixed by introducing an adjustment factor in the household savings function. Equilibrium in the model is achieved if the supply and demand of goods and services are equal and if investment is equal to savings.

### Linking the global model and the Pakistan model

There are various methods for transmitting the results derived from a global CGE model to a single-country CGE model. Horridge and Zhai (2006) propose, for imports, the use of border price changes from the global model simulation of rest-of-the-world liberalization (that is, without Pakistan). For Pakistan's exports, their proposed scheme is as follows.

The export demand in the Pakistan model is

$$E = E0 \left[ \frac{PWE0}{PWE} \right]^{\eta},$$ (7.1)

where $E$ is exports; $PWE0$ is international prices; $PWE$ is the free on board (border) prices of Pakistan's exports; $\eta$ is the export supply elasticity, the value of which is equal to $ESUBM$ (the Armington parameter in the global model); and $E0$ is the scale parameter in the demand function. Because exports and domestic goods are perfect substitutes, the export price in local currency is equal to the local price, which does not include indirect taxes.

The change in the export demand shifter, $E0$, is derived as:

$$E0 = 100 \cdot (a - 1),$$ (7.2)

where $a = (1 + 0.01p)([1 + 0.01q]^{[1/ESUBM]})$, in which $p$ is the change in the border export price, and $q$ is the change in the export volume from the global model of rest-of-the-world liberalization, excluding Pakistan (Horridge and Zhai 2006). The purpose of the introduction of the export demand shift calculated in (7.2) is to allow the Pakistan model—not the simpler representation of Pakistan in the global model—to determine export supply behavior and the equilibrium prices and quantities of Pakistan's exports, taking into account the world demand shift in the global model.

### Economic structure in the SAM and key parameters in the Pakistan model

Table 7.1 shows the sectoral structure of production and trade in the model based on the 2001–02 SAM. Of the 34 sectors, 12 are primary agricultural sectors (sectors 1 to 12), while sectors 14 to 18, which represent lightly processed food, are part of the broadly defined agricultural sector in this analysis. The nonagricultural sectors include the mining industry (sector 13), other food (sector 19), manufacturing industries (sectors 20 to 27), energy (sector 28), construction (sector 29), and five service sectors (sectors 30 to 34). Among these broad sectoral groupings, agriculture produces 27 percent of the sectoral value added and 28 percent of the gross value of sectoral output. In the SAM, it accounts for 13 percent of total employment.[5]

There are 19 household groups in the model. The agriculture-based groups are categorized according to household location (Punjab, Sindh, and other Pakistan) and the size of land holdings (large, medium, and small farms; landless small-farm renters, and agricultural workers without land). In addition, there are four nonfarm national aggregates: rural nonfarm poor, rural nonfarm nonpoor, urban poor, and urban nonpoor. Table 7.2 shows the 19 households in the SAM and the corresponding characteristics of the 19 household groups in the Household Integration Economic Survey.

# Table 7.1. Elasticity Parameters and Production Structure, Pakistan, 2001–02

| Sectors | Value added ratio va/x, % | Value added share, % | Output share, % | Capital-labor ratio[a] | Employment share, % | Share (%) Skilled labor | Unskilled labor | Farmers | value-added-output ratio, % | sig_va[b] | Indirect tax rate, % | eta[c] | sig_m[d] | Exports (%) share | Exports (%) intensity[e] | Imports (%) share | Imports (%) intensity[f] |
|---|---|---|---|---|---|---|---|---|---|---|---|---|---|---|---|---|---|
| *Agriculture* | 26.8 | 23.2 | 27.7 | | 12.6 | | | | | | | | | 8.5 | | 6.6 | |
| *Primary agriculture* | 23.2 | 20.1 | 20.1 | | 10.7 | | | | | | | | | 3.9 | | 3.1 | |
| 1. Wheat, irrigated | 50.8 | 1.8 | 1.8 | 0.3 | 1.58 | | 18.86 | 81.14 | 27.82 | 0.75 | 0.10 | 5.85 | 2.93 | 0.64 | 3.56 | 0.30 | 2.53 |
| 2. Wheat, nonirrigated | 50.9 | 0.1 | 0.1 | 0.3 | 0.07 | | 18.85 | 81.15 | 27.25 | 0.75 | 0.00 | 5.85 | 2.93 | | | | |
| 3. Paddy, IRRI | 60.2 | 0.2 | 0.2 | 0.5 | 0.10 | | 18.84 | 81.16 | 5.35 | 0.75 | 0.30 | 4.45 | 2.23 | | | | |
| 4. Paddy, basmati | 60.2 | 0.5 | 0.4 | 0.5 | 0.12 | | 18.86 | 81.14 | 7.27 | 0.75 | 0.00 | 4.45 | 2.23 | | | | |
| 5. Raw cotton | 61.2 | 1.4 | 1.1 | 0.3 | 1.11 | | 18.87 | 81.13 | 1.97 | 0.75 | 0.04 | 3.94 | 1.97 | | | | |
| 6. Sugarcane | 60.0 | 1.0 | 0.8 | 0.7 | 0.32 | | 18.87 | 81.13 | 46.68 | 0.75 | 0.07 | 5.91 | 2.96 | | | | |
| 7. Other major crops | 71.0 | 2.8 | 2.0 | 0.3 | 2.42 | | 18.87 | 81.13 | 38.88 | 0.75 | 0.05 | 3.94 | 1.97 | 0.52 | 2.65 | 0.60 | 4.53 |
| 8. Fruits and vegetables | 64.2 | 3.6 | 2.8 | 0.6 | 1.75 | | 18.87 | 81.13 | 41.37 | 0.75 | 0.34 | 3.94 | 1.97 | 1.05 | 3.78 | 1.31 | 6.94 |
| 9. Livestock, cattle and dairy | 53.2 | 10.3 | 9.7 | 9.0 | 2.56 | | 100.00 | | | 0.75 | 0.00 | 3.94 | 1.97 | 0.05 | 0.06 | 0.70 | 1.08 |
| 10. Poultry | 51.6 | 0.7 | 0.7 | 9.0 | 0.18 | | 100.00 | | | 0.75 | 0.00 | 3.94 | 1.97 | 0.01 | 0.11 | | |
| 11. Forestry | 82.1 | 0.3 | 0.2 | 0.0 | 0.12 | | 13.88 | 81.12 | 8.58 | 0.75 | 0.00 | 4.31 | 2.15 | 0.48 | 31.36 | 0.23 | 25.16 |
| 12. Fishing industry | 57.1 | 0.6 | 0.5 | 2.3 | 0.41 | | 100.00 | | | 0.75 | 0.00 | 4.31 | 2.15 | 1.14 | 23.79 | 0.00 | 0.08 |
| *Lightly processed food* | | 3.6 | 7.6 | | 1.8 | | | | | | | | | 4.6 | | 3.4 | |
| 14. Vegetable oil | 7.9 | 0.2 | 1.4 | 6.7 | 0.07 | 60.28 | 39.72 | | | 1.50 | 0.02 | 3.94 | 1.97 | 0.00 | 0.02 | 2.33 | 19.99 |
| 15. Wheat, milled | 21.8 | 1.2 | 2.8 | 4.4 | 0.56 | 64.94 | 35.06 | | | 1.50 | 0.02 | 4.45 | 2.22 | 0.51 | 1.82 | 0.82 | 4.31 |
| 16. Rice, milled IRRI | 30.7 | 0.2 | 0.4 | 3.7 | 0.12 | 56.75 | 43.25 | | | 1.50 | 0.00 | 4.45 | 2.22 | 1.72 | 46.60 | | |
| 17. Rice, milled basmati | 29.0 | 0.5 | 0.8 | 3.7 | 0.25 | 56.77 | 43.23 | | | 1.50 | 0.00 | 4.45 | 2.22 | 2.34 | 28.58 | | |
| 18. Sugar | 32.2 | 1.4 | 2.2 | 3.3 | 0.82 | 69.96 | 30.04 | | | 1.50 | 6.75 | 5.91 | 2.96 | 0.03 | 0.11 | 0.28 | 1.89 |

(Table continues on the following pages.)

**Table 7.1. Elasticity Parameters and Production Structure, Pakistan, 2001–02 (continued)**

| Sectors | Value added ratio va/x, % | Value added share, % | Output share, % | Capital-labor ratio[a] | Employment share, % | Skilled labor | Unskilled labor | Farmers | Land-output ratio, % | sig_va[b] | Indirect tax rate, % | eta[c] | sig_m[d] | Exports share (%) | Exports intensity[e] | Imports share (%) | Imports intensity[f] |
|---|---|---|---|---|---|---|---|---|---|---|---|---|---|---|---|---|---|
| *Nonagriculture* | *73.2* | | *72.3* | | *87.4* | | | | | | | | | *91.5* | | *93.4* | |
| *Mining and manufacturing* | | *13.2* | *24.2* | | *7.9* | | | | | | | | | *74.1* | | *88.2* | |
| 13. Mining | 74.6 | 0.6 | 0.4 | 2.3 | 0.47 | 85.00 | 15.00 | | | 1.50 | 14.50 | 4.31 | 2.16 | 0.78 | 18.61 | 9.29 | 80.53 |
| 19. Other food | 36.9 | 1.7 | 2.3 | 4.7 | 0.75 | 61.57 | 38.43 | | | 1.50 | 44.69 | 3.94 | 1.97 | 12.07 | 51.47 | 1.06 | 12.45 |
| 20. Cotton lint and yarn | 21.6 | 1.4 | 3.3 | 3.3 | 0.82 | 85.52 | 14.48 | | | 1.50 | 12.05 | 4.11 | 2.06 | 8.97 | 27.10 | 0.71 | 4.27 |
| 21. Textiles | 22.2 | 3.6 | 8.0 | 2.7 | 2.43 | 78.91 | 21.09 | | | 1.50 | 0.00 | 4.11 | 2.06 | 31.91 | 39.66 | 1.61 | 4.81 |
| 22. Leather | 8.3 | 0.1 | 0.5 | 2.9 | 0.06 | 60.36 | 39.64 | | | 1.50 | 0.00 | 4.11 | 2.06 | 2.27 | 42.79 | 0.11 | 5.21 |
| 23. Wood products | 36.3 | 0.7 | 0.9 | 1.8 | 0.57 | 67.98 | 32.02 | | | 1.50 | 0.18 | 4.09 | 2.04 | 0.03 | 0.34 | 0.56 | 8.61 |
| 24. Chemicals | 28.2 | 0.5 | 0.9 | 3.8 | 0.25 | 55.16 | 44.84 | | | 1.50 | 2.58 | 4.09 | 2.05 | 1.38 | 15.90 | 11.16 | 69.89 |
| 25. Cement and bricks | 55.0 | 1.4 | 1.3 | 7.4 | 0.42 | 68.98 | 31.02 | | | 1.50 | 24.15 | 4.09 | 2.05 | 0.03 | 0.21 | | |
| 26. Petroleum refining | 19.4 | 0.6 | 1.5 | 2.9 | 0.36 | 71.95 | 28.05 | | | 1.50 | 28.96 | 4.09 | 2.05 | | | 9.71 | 50.11 |
| 27. Other manufacturing | 25.4 | 2.6 | 5.0 | 2.6 | 1.75 | 67.99 | 32.01 | | | 1.50 | 4.39 | 4.09 | 2.05 | 16.61 | 33.17 | 54.00 | 71.03 |

| va | | | | | | | | | | | | | | |
|---|---|---|---|---|---|---|---|---|---|---|---|---|---|---|
| *Other industry* | 6.6 | 6.6 | | 7.2 | | | | | | | | 0.0 | 0.0 | 0.0 |
| 28. Energy | 60.8 | 3.4 | 2.8 | 4.0 | 1.69 | 80.00 | 20.00 | ¯.50 | 5.02 | 2.08 | 1.04 | | | 0.0 |
| 29. Construction | 41.6 | 3.2 | 3.8 | 0.4 | 5.48 | 50.00 | 50.00 | 1.50 | 0.16 | 2.08 | 1.04 | | | |
| *Services* | | 53.5 | 41.5 | | 72.4 | | | | | | | 17.5 | 17.5 | 5.2 |
| 30. Commerce | 84.0 | 15.3 | 9.1 | 0.4 | 26.52 | 20.00 | 80.00 | 1.50 | 0.00 | 2.08 | 1.04 | 0.07 | 0.07 | 0.21 | 0.35 |
| 31. Transport | 53.9 | 11.8 | 10.9 | 1.5 | 11.73 | 20.00 | 80.00 | 1.50 | 0.27 | 2.08 | 1.04 | | 17.38 | 17.38 | 15.88 |
| 32. Housing | 81.8 | 4.9 | 3.0 | | | | | 1.50 | 0.03 | 2.08 | 1.04 | | | |
| 33. Private services | 53.5 | 12.9 | 12.0 | 1.5 | 12.79 | 20.00 | 80.00 | 1.50 | 0.00 | 2.08 | 1.04 | 0.01 | 0.01 | 5.03 | 5.98 |
| 34. Public services | 66.2 | 8.6 | 6.5 | | 21.35 | 20.00 | 80.00 | 1.50 | 0.00 | 2.08 | 1.04 | | | |
| **Total** | 49.8 | 100.0 | 100 | | 100.0 | 100.00 | | | 0.00 | 2.08 | 1.04 | 100.0 | 10.0 | 100.0 | 14.45 |

*Source:* Dorosh, Niazi, and Nazli (2004).

*Note:* va-value added; x-output.

a. total labor ÷ total capital

b. *sig_va* = substitution parameter in CES production

c. *eta* = export demand elasticity

d. *sig_m* = substitution parameter in CES composite good

e. export ÷ output

f. imports ÷ composite good

**Table 7.2. Model Household Categories, Pakistan**

| 2001–02 social accounting matrix | 2001–02 household integrated economic survey |
|---|---|
| Large-farm households (Punjab, Sindh, other Pakistan) | Landowners with more than 50 acres |
| Medium-farm households (Punjab, Sindh, other Pakistan) | Landowners with more than 12.5, but less than 50 acres |
| Small-farm households (Punjab, Sindh, other Pakistan) | Landowners with less than 12.5 acres |
| Small-farm renters, landless (Punjab, Sindh, other Pakistan) | No landholdings, but rent land for farm activities |
| Rural agricultural workers, landless (Punjab, Sindh, other Pakistan) | No landholdings, agricultural workers |
| Rural nonfarm nonpoor | Rural nonpoor, nonfarmers, nonagricultural workers |
| Rural nonfarm poor | Rural poor, nonfarmers, nonagricultural workers |
| Urban nonpoor | Urban nonpoor |
| Urban poor | Urban poor |

*Sources:* Dorosh, Niazi, and Nazli (2004); Federal Bureau of Statistics (2003).

*Note:* The SAM covers three major provinces: Punjab, Sindh, and other Pakistan, which consists of Azad Kashmir, Balochistan, North-West Frontier Province, Northern Areas (Gilgit-Baltistan), Federally Administered, and Federally Administered Tribal Areas.

The structure of consumption varies among household groups. A composite sector—livestock, cattle, and dairy—shows the highest share in the consumption basket, varying from 14 percent among large- and medium-farm households in other Pakistan to 25 percent among agricultural worker households in Punjab. The other major items in the consumption basket are private services (about 14 percent), transport (about 13 percent), milled wheat (from 4 percent among the urban nonpoor to 12 percent among agricultural workers in other Pakistan), textiles (from 5 percent among large- and medium-farm households in other Pakistan to 7 percent among agricultural worker households in Punjab and the urban poor), other manufacturing (from 1 percent among agricultural worker households in Sindh to 10 percent among large- and medium-farm households in other Pakistan), sugar (from 3 percent among urban nonpoor households to 10 percent among agricultural worker households in other Pakistan), and fruits and vegetables (from 4 percent among large- and medium-farm households in Punjab to 7 percent among agricultural worker households in other Pakistan). Commodities with high foreign trade content are impacted significantly by changes in trade policies and world prices. This has varying effects across household groups because of differences in the household consumption bundles.

The sectoral indirect tax structure is presented in table 7.1. The highest tax rate, 45 percent, applies to other food, the share of which in the consumption of households is only about 1 percent. Indirect taxes are also relatively high on cement, bricks, and petroleum refining, which generally account for less than 1 percent of direct household consumption, but affect housing and transportation costs. The tax rate on cotton lint and yarn is 12 percent, while it is zero on textiles. However, because cotton lint and yarn are major inputs into textile production, an increase in the tax on the former raises the cost of production of textiles. This affects consumers because the share of textiles in the consumption basket is about 5 percent.

Sugar shows the highest tariff rate, 59 percent (table 7.3). Another commodity showing high tariffs, averaging 55 percent, is livestock, cattle, and diary, which account for a large share in the consumption basket of households. Other agricultural commodities showing high tariffs and substantial consumption shares are milled wheat and vegetable oil. A few primary agricultural and light food processing sectors show low or even negative import tariffs. In contrast, tariffs are uniformly relatively high across the manufacturing sectors.

Overall, the foreign trade sector in Pakistan is not large relative to the domestic sector (table 7.1). Of the total domestic output, only 10 percent goes to the export market. Only 15 percent of the total goods and services available in the domestic market are imported. However, there are large differences across sectors. Within agriculture, the sectors with the highest share of production exported are milled IRRI rice, 47 percent; forestry, 31 percent; and fishing, 24 percent. The shares exported are small in the rest of the agricultural sectors. Within the nonagricultural sectors, other food, at 52 percent, has the highest share of production exported; leather is at 43 percent; textiles, 40 percent; and cotton lint and yarn, 27 percent. The textile sector dominates in exports. In the SAM, textiles account for 32 percent of total exports, cotton lint and yarn for 9 percent, and other food for 12 percent.

Because of the large volume of crude oil imports, the mining sector has the highest share of domestic consumption that is imported, at 81 percent. The share of other manufacturing is 71 percent; of chemicals, 70 percent; and of petroleum, 50 percent. Other manufacturing accounts for 54 percent of overall imports; chemicals, 11 percent; and mining and petroleum refining, each about 9 percent. Except for forestry (25 percent) and vegetable oil (20 percent), the shares of domestic consumption that are imported in the agricultural sectors are well under 10 percent.

Table 7.1 includes the values of key elasticity parameters in the model: the import substitution elasticity ($sig\_m$) in the constant elasticity of substitution composite good function and the production substitution elasticity ($sig\_va$) in the constant elasticity of substitution value added production function.[6] The values of the export demand elasticity ($eta$) are the Armington parameters of the global model.

The sources of household income in the model are labor income, capital income, income from land, and other income (table 7.4). Other income is

**Table 7.3. Parameters and Exogenous Demand and Price Shocks Caused by Rest-of-the-World Liberalization, Pakistan**

| Pakistan CGE model | | Linkage model | Trade distortions | | Full trade liberalization, excluding Pakistan | | Agricultural trade liberalization, excluding Pakistan | |
|---|---|---|---|---|---|---|---|---|
| Sector no. | Sector description | Sector description | Tariff, % | Export tax, % | World import price change, % | Export demand shifter[b] | World import price, % change | Export demand shifter[b] |
| *Agriculture* | | | | | | | | |
| *Primary agriculture* | | | | | | | | |
| 1. | Wheat, irrigated | Wheat | -4.9 | 0.0 | 2.41 | 1.0 | 3.12 | 1.00 |
| 2. | Wheat, nonirrigated | Wheat | -4.9 | 0.0 | 2.41 | 1.0 | 3.12 | 1.00 |
| 3. | Paddy, IRRI | Paddy rice | 0.0 | 4.0 | 0.00 | 1.2 | 0.00 | 1.23 |
| 4. | Paddy, basmati | Paddy rice | 0.0 | 4.0 | 0.00 | 1.2 | 0.00 | 1.23 |
| 5. | Cotton | Plant-based fibers | 4.9 | 0.0 | 4.44 | 1.1 | 6.68 | 1.14 |
| 6. | Sugarcane | Sugarcane and beets | 4.3 | 0.0 | 0.00 | 1.0 | 0.00 | 1.00 |
| 7. | Other major crops | Other crops | 15.3 | 0.0 | -1.91 | 1.0 | 0.00 | 1.01 |
| 8. | Fruits and vegetables | Vegetables and fruits | 16.5 | 0.0 | -2.93 | 1.0 | -2.62 | 0.97 |
| 9. | Livestock, cattle, and dairy[a] | Cattle, sheep, and so on | 55.4 | 0.0 | 4.41 | 1.0 | 5.17 | 1.00 |
| 10. | Poultry | Other livestock | 10.8 | 0.0 | -8.00 | 1.0 | -6.77 | 0.99 |
| 11. | Forestry | Other primary products | 14.3 | 18.1 | -0.14 | 1.1 | 0.79 | 1.01 |
| *Lightly processed food* | | | | | | | | |
| 12. | Fishing industry | Other primary products | 14.3 | 18.1 | -0.14 | 1.1 | 0.79 | 1.01 |
| 14. | Vegetable oil | Vegetable oils and fats | 23.7 | 0.0 | 1.78 | 0.9 | 0.40 | 0.93 |
| 15. | Wheat, milled | Other food, beverages and tobacco | 24.9 | 0.0 | 0.00 | 1.0 | -1.68 | 0.97 |
| 16. | Rice, milled IRRI | Processed rice | 0.0 | 4.0 | 8.21 | 1.1 | 10.18 | 1.08 |
| 17. | Rice, milled basmati | Processed rice | 0.0 | 4.0 | 8.21 | 1.1 | 10.18 | 1.08 |
| 18. | Sugar | Refined sugar | 59.0 | 0.0 | 1.62 | 1.0 | 3.44 | 1.00 |

*Nonagriculture*

*Mining and manufacturing*

| | | | | | | | |
|---|---|---|---|---|---|---|---|
| 13. Mining | Other primary products | 14.3 | 18.1 | −0.14 | 1.1 | 0.79 | 1.01 |
| 19. Other food | Other food, beverages and tobacco | 24.9 | 0.0 | 0.00 | 1.0 | −1.68 | 0.97 |
| 20. Cotton lint and yarn | Textile and wearing apparel | 19.9 | 1.1 | −0.68 | 1.0 | 0.48 | 1.00 |
| 21. Textiles | Textile and wearing apparel | 19.9 | 1.1 | −0.68 | 1.0 | 0.48 | 1.00 |
| 22. Leather | Textile and wearing apparel | 19.9 | 1.1 | −0.68 | 1.0 | 0.48 | 1.00 |
| 23. Wood products | Other manufacturing | 16.6 | 5.4 | −0.38 | 1.0 | 0.38 | 1.00 |
| 24. Chemicals | Other manufacturing | 16.6 | 5.4 | −0.38 | 1.0 | 0.38 | 1.00 |
| 25. Cement and bricks | Other manufacturing | 16.6 | 5.4 | −0.38 | 1.0 | 0.38 | 1.00 |
| 26. Petroleum refining | Other manufacturing | 16.6 | 5.4 | −0.38 | 1.0 | 0.38 | 1.00 |
| 27. Other manufacturing | Other manufacturing | 16.6 | 5.4 | −0.38 | 1.0 | 0.38 | 1.00 |

*Other industry*

| | | | | | | | |
|---|---|---|---|---|---|---|---|
| 28. Energy | Services | 0.0 | 0.0 | −0.22 | 1.0 | 0.19 | 1.00 |
| 29. Construction | Services | 0.0 | 0.0 | −0.22 | 1.0 | 0.19 | 1.00 |

*Services*

| | | | | | | | |
|---|---|---|---|---|---|---|---|
| 30. Commerce | Services | 0.0 | 0.0 | −0.22 | 1.0 | 0.19 | 1.00 |
| 31. Transport | Services | 0.0 | 0.0 | −0.22 | 1.0 | 0.19 | 1.00 |
| 32. Housing | Services | 0.0 | 0.0 | −0.22 | 1.0 | 0.19 | 1.00 |
| 33. Private services | Services | 0.0 | 0.0 | −0.22 | 1.0 | 0.19 | 1.00 |
| 34. Public services | Services | 0.0 | 0.0 | −0.22 | 1.0 | 0.19 | 1.00 |

*Source:* Linkage model simulations by van der Mensbrugghe, Valenzuela, and Anderson (see the appendix).

a. This is the trade weighted average of cattle, sheep, other livestock, and dairy in the Linkage model.

b. In equation 2, this is $a = (1 + 0.01 * p)(1 + 0.01 * q)^{(1/ESUBM)}$; where $p$ is export price change, $q$ export volume change; and ESBUM Arimington elasticity, all from the Linkage model.

# Table 7.4. Household Income Sources and Income Taxes, Pakistan, 2001–02

| Households | 2001–02 income Total mil Rs | Per capita, PRs 1,000s | 2001–02 population 1,000s | % distribution | Labor Farm | Unskilled | Skilled | Capital | Land | Other | Direct tax, % |
|---|---|---|---|---|---|---|---|---|---|---|---|
| **Large-farm households** | | | | | | | | | | | |
| –Sindh | 19,079 | 112.9 | 169 | 0.12 | 13.2 | 0.3 | — | 31.4 | 49.8 | 5.3 | — |
| –Punjab | 64,116 | 173.7 | 369 | 0.25 | 8.6 | 0.5 | — | 43.3 | 42.2 | 5.4 | — |
| –Other Pakistan[a] | 10,755 | 152.9 | 70 | 0.05 | 9.8 | 0.2 | — | 52.4 | 32.3 | 5.4 | — |
| **Medium-farm households** | | | | | | | | | | | |
| –Sindh | 44,625 | 30.4 | 1,466 | 1.00 | 14.5 | 3.1 | — | 39.6 | 37.4 | 5.3 | — |
| –Punjab | 145,995 | 48.4 | 3,014 | 2.07 | 10.8 | 4.3 | — | 52.3 | 27.2 | 5.4 | — |
| –Other Pakistan | 35,572 | 34.2 | 1,040 | 0.71 | 14.9 | 2.9 | — | 38.2 | 38.4 | 5.5 | — |
| **Small-farm households** | | | | | | | | | | | |
| –Sindh | 57,648 | 14.9 | 3,873 | 2.65 | 6.8 | 9.0 | — | 57.9 | 20.4 | 5.8 | — |
| –Punjab | 318,888 | 18.1 | 17,605 | 12.06 | 7.9 | 14.2 | — | 51.8 | 20.3 | 5.8 | — |
| –Other Pakistan | 124,985 | 11.9 | 10,493 | 7.19 | 6.0 | 11.6 | — | 63.6 | 12.5 | 6.2 | — |
| **Small-farm renters, landless** | | | | | | | | | | | |
| –Sindh | 43,672 | 7.7 | 5,682 | 3.89 | 11.6 | 18.7 | — | 48.5 | 15.6 | 5.7 | — |
| –Punjab | 45,963 | 10.7 | 4,307 | 2.95 | 9.0 | 20.5 | — | 48.7 | 16.1 | 5.8 | — |
| –Other Pakistan | 14,970 | 8.2 | 1,818 | 1.25 | 10.1 | 14.5 | — | 55.0 | 14.7 | 5.7 | — |
| **Rural agricultural workers, landless** | | | | | | | | | | | |
| –Sindh | 20,782 | 6.4 | 3,241 | 2.22 | — | 51.0 | — | 42.8 | — | 6.2 | — |
| –Punjab | 68,172 | 12.0 | 5,693 | 3.90 | — | 49.3 | — | 45.2 | — | 5.5 | — |
| –Other Pakistan | 9,513 | 14.6 | 653 | 0.45 | — | 18.7 | — | 76.0 | — | 5.4 | — |
| **Rural nonfarm households** | | | | | | | | | | | |
| –nonpoor | 400,771 | 19.8 | 20,233 | 13.86 | — | 43.0 | — | 49.9 | — | 7.2 | — |
| –poor | 134,398 | 5.5 | 24,525 | 16.80 | — | 29.7 | — | 63.4 | — | 6.9 | — |
| **Urban households** | | | | | | | | | | | |
| –nonpoor | 1,744,119 | 58.5 | 29,829 | 20.44 | — | 11.9 | 33.3 | 10.6 | — | 44.2 | 8.4 |
| –poor | 181,413 | 15.3 | 11,880 | 8.14 | — | 76.2 | — | 18.0 | — | 5.8 | — |

*Sources:* Dorosh, Niazi, and Nazli (2004).

a. Other Pakistan—Azad Kashmir, Balochistan, North-West Frontier Province, Northern Areas (Gilgit-Baltistan), Federally Administered, and Federally Administered composed of foreign remittances, which is assumed in the SAM to be distributed proportionately among all households, and dividend income, which is earned only by urban nonpoor households. The sources of income vary across household groups. Farm households are dependent on income from land, farm labor, and capital. Other rural households depend on income from unskilled labor and capital. About three-fourths of the income of urban poor households comes from unskilled labor. Urban nonpoor households derive 44 percent of their incomes from other income (composed largely of dividend income) and 33 percent from skilled labor income. According to the SAM, it is only the urban nonpoor household group that pays income taxes, amounting to 8.4 percent of their incomes.

## Poverty Indicators

The overall poverty rate based on the official national poverty line declined in Pakistan from about 30 percent in the late 1980s to 26 percent in 1990–91. During these years, both urban and rural poverty decreased. However, in 1993–94, the incidence of rural poverty and the incidence of urban poverty started to move in different directions: urban poverty continued to decline, while rural poverty began to rise, thereby widening the poverty gap between urban and rural areas (figure 7.1). The gap reached a peak in 2001–02, which was largely caused by the crippling drought that severely affected agricultural output that year, together with relatively low international agricultural commodity prices. Almost 70 percent of the people live in rural areas, and, because the majority of these people (40 percent of all households nationally) depend on agriculture for income, the incidence of rural poverty increased to 39 percent that year, while urban poverty was stable at 23 percent.

There is some disagreement about the accuracy of recent estimates of poverty. For 2004–05, the estimates of the Planning Commission of Pakistan show the overall incidence of poverty declining from the peak of 34 percent in 2001–02 to 24 percent in 2004–05 (Dorosh and Salam 2009). The World Bank (2007) estimates a smaller decline, to 29 percent. Despite the disparity between these estimates (arising primarily because of the inflation factor used in computing the relevant poverty lines), the estimates show the incidence of poverty declining in urban and rural areas in the most recent years, but highlight the large gap between the rural and urban poverty rates. The depth of poverty indicated by the Foster, Greer, and Thorbecke (1984) poverty gap and the squared poverty gap also suggest that the problem of poverty is more severe in rural areas and that this was especially true during the 2001–02 drought (table 7.5).

**Figure 7.1. Poverty Incidence, Pakistan, 1986–87 to 2004–05**

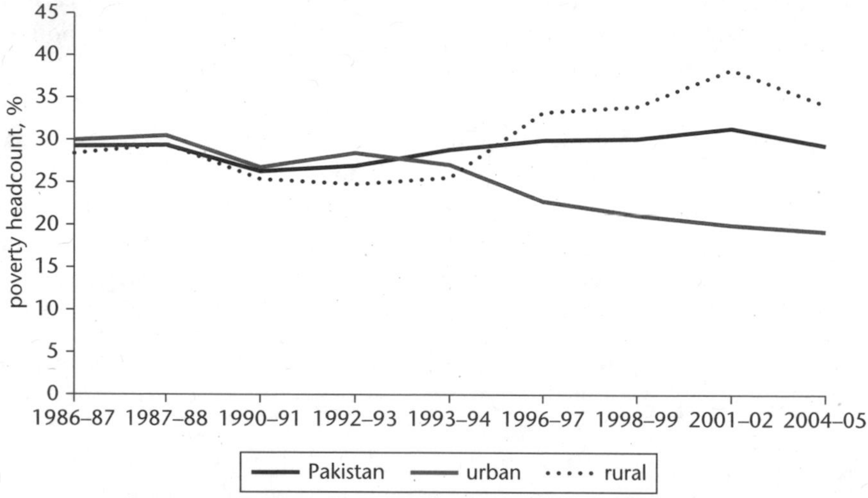

*Sources:* Ministry of Finance (2003); World Bank (2007) for the 2004–05 estimates.

*Note:* Poverty is defined as the share of the population living below the national poverty line. Official data for 1993–94 indicate that the level of overall poverty was above the incidence of poverty in urban and rural areas; see Ministry of Finance (2003).

**Table 7.5. Poverty Estimates, Pakistan, 1998–99, 2001–02, and 2004–05**

| Poverty index | 1998–99 | 2001–02 | 2004–05 |
|---|---|---|---|
| *Poverty incidence* | | | |
| Pakistan | 30.0 | 31.2 | 29.2 |
| Urban | 21.0 | 19.9 | 19.1 |
| Rural | 33.8 | 38.2 | 34.0 |
| *Poverty gap* | | | |
| Pakistan | 6.3 | 6.5 | 6.1 |
| Urban | 4.3 | 3.9 | 3.9 |
| Rural | 7.1 | 8.0 | 7.2 |
| *Squared poverty gap, poverty severity* | | | |
| Pakistan | 2.0 | 2.0 | 2.0 |
| Urban | 1.3 | 1.2 | 1.2 |
| Rural | 2.2 | 2.5 | 2.3 |

*Sources:* Ministry of Finance (2003); World Bank (2007) for the 2004–05 estimates.

*Note:* The table reflects the poverty concepts of Foster, Greer, and Thorbecke (1984).

## Simulations

The first part of this section describes our six policy experiments, while the second part discusses the results. The experiments use direct tax replacement to hold the government fiscal balance fixed. The idea is to replace distorting trade taxes with less-distorting income taxes. The fiscal burden falls on urban nonpoor households because, according to the SAM, other household groups do not pay income taxes (table 7.4). We have also conducted an alternative indirect tax replacement experiment to check the sensitivity of the results to the specification, given that financing a trade reform is a nontrivial issue from the government's point of view (Ahmed, Abbas, and Ahmed 2009). In our analysis, we separate the effects on the economy of reducing distortions in the rest of the world and in domestic markets in Pakistan, and we evaluate the effects of both on income inequality and poverty.

### Design of the policy experiments

Table 7.3 shows the sectoral correspondence between the Pakistan model and the global model. It also shows the sectoral tariff rates and export taxes, which, where possible, are based on the set of estimates on nominal rates of assistance for Pakistan by Dorosh and Salam (2009). We use these trade distortions in all our policy experiments. The table presents the changes in border import prices found through the global model under full trade liberalization and agricultural liberalization by the rest of the world, and it lists sectoral export demand shifters calculated on the basis of equation (7.2). We have used these data as inputs in the six policy experiments we have conducted, as follows:

- *S1A*, full world trade liberalization in all tradable goods sectors by all countries, excluding Pakistan: This experiment uses the results of the global model under full trade liberalization in table 7.3. It retains all existing trade distortions in Pakistan.
- *S1B*, agricultural price and trade liberalization by all countries, excluding Pakistan: This scenario uses the results of the global model. As with S1A, all existing distortions in Pakistan are retained.
- *S2A*, full goods trade liberalization carried out unilaterally in Pakistan: All Pakistan trade distortions are set to zero. There are no changes in the sectoral border export and import prices or in the export demand shifters because there is no rest-of-the-world trade liberalization.
- *S2B*, agricultural trade liberalization carried out unilaterally in Pakistan: All Pakistan distortions in primary agriculture and in lightly processed food are set to zero. Similar to S2A, there are no changes in the sectoral border export and

import prices and in the export demand shifters because there is no rest-of-the-world trade liberalization.

- *S3A*, full world trade liberalization of all tradable goods, including in Pakistan: This combines S1A and S2A.
- *S3B*, agricultural world trade liberalization, including in Pakistan: This combines S1B and S2B.

In analyzing the results under each of the scenarios, we indicate, first, the effects on poverty for the whole of Pakistan, for rural and urban areas, and for major household groups. The results on poverty include changes in the incidence of poverty and in the depth of poverty measured by the poverty gap and the squared poverty gap. These poverty effects are traced and analyzed through the various determining channels: macro, sectoral, commodity, and factor prices, as well as household incomes. In estimating the poverty effects, we apply the results on household incomes and consumer prices for each of the 19 household groups in the CGE model simulations to the household classifications in the Household Integration Economic Survey. Each of the CGE simulations generates a new vector of household income and consumer price for each of the groups, which we use to compute new sets of poverty indexes to compare with the baseline indexes.

### Simulation results

In this subsection, we present the modeling results of our six policy experiments. We continue the discussion with additional results that show the sensitivity of the core results to changes in the treatment of tax adjustments in the model.

### S1A: Trade liberalization by the rest of the world without Pakistan

Full trade liberalization abroad, while retaining all existing trade distortions in Pakistan, causes the overall poverty incidence index to decline by 1.3 percent from its base value, from 31.2 to 30.8 (table 7.6). Households at the bottom of the income ladder benefit the most, as indicated by the greater reduction in the poverty gap (1.6 percent) and the squared poverty gap (1.9 percent). Among rural households, the poorest households—those in the rural nonfarmer group—benefit the most. Thus, rural-urban income inequality is lowered in this scenario also.

What are the forces that drive these reductions in poverty and income inequality? The S1A simulation leads to a real exchange rate appreciation of 1.24 percent (table 7.7).[7] The terms of trade (the ratio of domestic export to import prices) improve by 1.38 percent in agriculture and by 1.56 percent in nonagriculture. This is because of the lower world import prices of some of the agricultural products, as well as most of the nonfarm goods (table 7.3).

# Table 7.6. The Poverty Effects of Prospective Liberalizations, Pakistan

| Indicator | | Index in 2001–02 | 2001–02 population distribution, % | % change from 2001–02 index | | | | | |
|---|---|---|---|---|---|---|---|---|---|
| | | | | S1A | S1B | S2A | S2B | S3A | S3B |
| All Pakistan | –P0 | 31.23 | | –1.3 | –0.1 | –5.2 | –1.6 | –6.4 | –1.8 |
| | –P1 | 6.46 | | –1.6 | –0.1 | –10.0 | –2.3 | –11.5 | –2.5 |
| | –P2 | 1.97 | | –1.9 | –0.1 | –12.1 | –2.8 | –13.8 | –3.0 |
| Gini coefficient | | 0.34 | | –0.03 | –0.02 | –3.3 | –0.1 | –3.3 | –0.2 |
| All urban | –P0 | 19.86 | 29.7 | –1.5 | –0.1 | 2.3 | –2.4 | 0.4 | –2.7 |
| | –P1 | 3.91 | | –1.5 | –0.1 | –13.3 | –3.6 | –14.8 | –3.7 |
| | –P2 | 1.16 | | –1.7 | –0.1 | –16.9 | –4.2 | –18.3 | –4.3 |
| Gini coefficient | | 0.40 | | –0.03 | –0.01 | –2.0 | –0.1 | –2.0 | –0.1 |
| All rural | –P0 | 38.16 | 70.3 | –1.2 | –0.1 | –7.6 | –1.4 | –8.6 | –1.5 |
| | –P1 | 8.02 | | –1.6 | –0.1 | –9.0 | –2.0 | –10.5 | –2.1 |
| | –P2 | 2.47 | | –2.0 | –0.1 | –10.8 | –2.4 | –12.5 | –2.6 |
| Gini coefficient | | 0.26 | | –0.0 | –0.02 | 0.2 | –0.1 | 0.2 | –0.1 |
| Large- and medium-farm households | –P0 | 22.82 | 4.0 | 0.1 | 0.0 | –7.9 | 3.4 | –7.9 | 3.4 |
| | –P1 | 4.06 | | –0.7 | 0.4 | –9.9 | 4.9 | –10.0 | 5.3 |
| | –P2 | 1.13 | | –0.7 | 0.5 | –10.5 | 5.2 | –10.6 | 5.8 |
| Small-farm households and agricultural workers | –P0 | 37.40 | 30.6 | –1.4 | 0.1 | –8.3 | –0.9 | –8.7 | –0.9 |
| | –P1 | 7.47 | | –1.3 | 0.0 | –9.3 | –1.3 | –10.3 | –1.3 |
| | –P2 | 2.20 | | –1.5 | 0.0 | –11.2 | –1.7 | –12.4 | –1.6 |
| Rural nonfarm households | –P0 | 39.89 | 35.7 | –1.1 | –0.2 | –7.2 | –1.9 | –8.5 | –2.1 |
| | –P1 | 8.71 | | –1.9 | –0.2 | –8.9 | –2.6 | –10.6 | –2.8 |
| | –P2 | 2.76 | | –2.2 | –0.2 | –10.6 | –3.1 | –12.6 | –3.4 |

Source: National CGE model simulations by the authors.

Note: P0 = poverty headcount. P1 = poverty gap. P2 = poverty severity.

**Table 7.7. Aggregate Simulation Results of Prospective Agricultural and Nonagricultural Liberalization, Pakistan**

(% change from the base)

| Variables | S1A | | S1B | | S2A | | S2B | | S3A | | S3B | |
|---|---|---|---|---|---|---|---|---|---|---|---|---|
| | Ag | Nonag | Ag | Nonag | Ag | Nonag | Ag | Nonag | Ag | Nonag | Ag | Nonag |
| *Real GDP* | 0.15 | | 0.04 | | 0.81 | | 0.26 | | 0.95 | | 0.29 | |
| *Real and relative prices* | | | | | | | | | | | | |
| Real exchange rate | −1.24 | | −0.13 | | 6.09 | | 1.87 | | 4.79 | | 1.73 | |
| Domestic terms of trade[a] | 1.38 | 1.56 | 0.98 | 0.13 | 12.61 | 9.37 | 17.30 | −0.84 | 14.19 | 11.06 | 18.52 | −0.71 |
| *Prices* | | | | | | | | | | | | |
| Export price in local currency | −0.26 | −0.82 | 0.33 | −0.13 | −1.92 | 0.09 | −0.63 | 1.70 | −2.16 | −0.66 | −0.30 | 1.59 |
| Import price in local currency | −1.70 | −2.35 | −0.73 | −0.24 | −12.26 | −8.34 | −14.49 | 2.57 | −13.74 | −10.41 | −15.13 | 2.33 |
| Domestic price | −0.29 | −0.55 | −0.07 | −0.08 | −2.47 | −1.23 | −1.53 | 1.11 | −2.74 | −1.69 | −1.56 | 1.06 |
| Output price | −0.29 | −0.58 | −0.06 | −0.08 | −2.45 | −1.07 | −1.50 | 1.18 | −2.73 | −1.57 | −1.52 | 1.12 |
| Value added price | 0.16 | −0.12 | 0.03 | −0.06 | −3.14 | 1.32 | −2.88 | 1.01 | −2.98 | 1.24 | −2.79 | 0.97 |
| Consumer price index | −0.51 | | −0.11 | | −2.81 | | −0.27 | | −3.24 | | −0.34 | |
| *Volume* | | | | | | | | | | | | |
| Imports | 2.41 | 0.96 | 0.89 | 0.12 | 22.15 | 4.45 | 29.64 | −0.48 | 24.75 | 5.46 | 30.42 | −0.36 |
| Exports | 0.73 | −0.16 | 1.79 | 0.11 | 4.78 | 13.24 | 6.20 | 3.07 | 5.28 | 13.07 | 8.00 | 3.17 |
| Domestic demand | 0.09 | −0.07 | −0.01 | −0.02 | −0.87 | −1.12 | −1.05 | 0.03 | −0.76 | −1.19 | −1.06 | 0.01 |
| Composite good | 0.18 | 0.12 | 0.02 | 0.01 | 0.09 | −0.08 | 0.20 | −0.07 | 0.30 | 0.05 | 0.22 | −0.06 |
| Output | 0.11 | −0.08 | 0.05 | −0.01 | −0.69 | 0.39 | −0.82 | 0.39 | −0.57 | 0.50 | −0.77 | 0.38 |
| Value added | 0.07 | −0.03 | 0.03 | −0.01 | −0.51 | 0.19 | −0.39 | 0.13 | −0.43 | 0.16 | −0.35 | 0.12 |

*Factor prices*

| | | | | | |
|---|---|---|---|---|---|
| Farm wages | −0.95 | −0.27 | −0.58 | −2.16 | −1.67 | −2.44 |
| Wages of unskilled labor | −0.14 | −0.05 | 1.49 | 0.47 | 1.38 | 0.45 |
| Wages of skilled labor | −0.04 | 0.00 | 2.06 | 0.73 | 2.04 | 0.74 |
| Return to land | −1.00 | −0.32 | −1.90 | −2.52 | −3.06 | −2.85 |
| Return to capital | 1.00 | 0.27 | −5.02 | −3.30 | −3.92 | −3.41 |
| | −0.14 | −0.09 | 1.00 | 1.41 | 0.93 | 1.34 |

*Factor prices less inflation*

| | | | | | |
|---|---|---|---|---|---|
| Farm wages | −0.44 | −0.16 | 2.23 | −1.38 | 1.56 | −2.10 |
| Wages of unskilled labor | 0.37 | 0.05 | 4.30 | 0.74 | 4.61 | 0.79 |
| Wages of skilled labor | 0.47 | 0.11 | 4.87 | 1.00 | 5.28 | 1.09 |
| Return to land | −0.49 | −0.21 | 0.91 | −2.25 | 0.18 | −2.51 |
| Return to capital | 1.51 | 0.37 | −2.21 | −3.53 | −0.69 | −3.07 |
| | 0.37 | 0.02 | 3.87 | 1.68 | 4.17 | 1.68 |

*Source:* National CGE model simulations by the authors.

*Note:* Ag = agriculture. Nonag = nonagriculture.

[a] Change in the ratio of domestic export and import prices.

229

The import prices of agricultural goods drop by 1.7 percent (table 7.7), despite the increases in the import prices of livestock, wheat, vegetable oil, and sugar (table 7.3). This is caused by a number of factors, including the appreciation of the currency; the decline in the border import prices of fruits and vegetables and other major crops (table 7.3), all of which have relatively large import components (table 7.1); and the slight reduction in the border import prices of forestry products, which show high import intensity. The domestic prices of farm products decline by 0.3 percent, which is lower than the drop in import prices. This results in more imports of agricultural goods (a rise of 2.4 percent) and a marginal increase in the domestic demand for agriculture (a rise of 0.1 percent). Because the demand for imported and domestic agricultural products increases, the domestic consumption of farm products increases (by 0.2 percent).

Table 7.3 shows that the border import prices of nonagricultural goods decline. This, together with the appreciation of the exchange rate, reduces the import prices of nonagricultural goods by 2.4 percent (table 7.7). The domestic prices of nonagricultural products also decline, by 0.6 percent, which is lower than the decline in the import prices. Thus, the imports of nonfarm products increase, by 1.0 percent. At the sectoral level, there is a relatively large rise in imports of cotton lint and yarn, textiles, and leather because of the relatively greater decline in the border prices of these products. More imports of nonfarm goods reduce marginally the domestic demand, but, despite this, overall domestic nonagricultural consumption increases by 0.1 percent.

The export prices of farm products decline by 0.3 percent. Because the border prices of these products rise, the decline is caused by appreciation in the exchange rate. There is a slightly greater decrease in the domestic prices of agricultural products. Thus, exports of agriculture improve by 0.73 percent, and the overall output of agriculture increases by 0.11 percent.

The effects on value added, value added prices, and factor prices in agriculture are explained by the changes in sectoral export prices, factor intensities, and import and export intensities. The overall output price of agriculture declines by 0.29, while the value added price increases by 0.16 percent. The difference in the sign is generated by a relatively higher increase in the value added price of milled rice (2 percent) and vegetable oil (1.7 percent).[8] The increase by 1.18 percent in the border export price of milled rice has larger effects on the value added price of milled rice because rice has a high export-intensity ratio (table 7.1). Although the border import price of milled rice increases more (10.18 percent), this has no effects because there are zero imports. The increase by 1.78 percent in the import border price of vegetable oil increases the value added price of vegetable oil because vegetable oil has a high import-intensity ratio.

Farm wages and the returns to land decline by about 1.0 percent. This is caused by the decline in the output and value added prices in primary agriculture, which employs farmers and uses land. The average rate of return to capital in agriculture improves by 1 percent. This is caused by the increase in the value added price of milled rice and vegetable oil. These sectors are relatively capital intensive, showing capital-labor ratios of 3.7 for rice and 6.7 for vegetable oil (table 7.1). Because wage rates increase less than value added prices, returns to capital rise. The returns to capital in these sectors increase by more than 2 percent for milled rice and 1.9 percent for vegetable oil. The change in the returns to capital in livestock and poultry is also positive, but smaller. The change in the returns to capital in the other primary agricultural commodities is negative.

The decline in the value added prices in primary agriculture and in nonagri culture lowers the wages of unskilled labor by 0.14 percent. However, because of the increase in the value added prices of milled rice and vegetable oil, the wages of skilled workers decrease by only 0.04 percent. The average returns to the capital used in nonagriculture decline by 0.14 percent.

We have also included the results on factor prices net of the inflation effects. The overall consumer price index in this experiment decreases by 0.5 percent. Net of the inflation effects, there is a negative result for farm wages and the returns to land, but the other factors show positive net price effects.

All these effects lead to changes in household incomes (table 7.8). The changes in the nominal incomes of households are negative across groups except rural nonfarmers and rural agricultural workers, the latter because of their heavy reliance on agricultural capital incomes (mostly informal capital), as shown in table 7.4, and the increase in the average returns to capital in agriculture (1 percent; see table 7.7). However, the consumer prices for each of the groups decline more rapidly than the drop in nominal incomes because of the greater reduction in import prices. Thus, all household groups realize improvements in real incomes. The largest increases in real incomes occur among rural nonfarmers (0.63 and 0.53 for the nonpoor and poor, respectively; see table 7.8) and agricultural workers in other Pakistan (0.58 percent). This explains the significant reduction in the depth of poverty in rural areas, particularly among rural nonfarmers.

In the scenario, full trade liberalization by the rest of the world thus reduces both poverty and income inequality. It reduces import prices, especially on commodities that have relatively large shares in the consumption basket of consumers. This translates into declining consumer prices. It also enhances agricultural production relative to nonagricultural production because of improvements in the world price of farm commodities. The poorest nonfarm households in rural areas benefit the most from the improvement in the real wages of unskilled labor and in the returns to capital and from the reduction in consumer prices.

**Table 7.8. Household Welfare and Price Effects of the Liberalization in All Goods Trade by the Rest of the World, Pakistan**

| Households | 2001–02 population distribution, % | S1A | | | S1B | | | Change in nominal income, % |
| | | Change in nominal income, % | Change in consumer price, % | EV/ income, % | Change in nominal income, % | Change in consumer price, % | EV/ income, % | |
|---|---|---|---|---|---|---|---|---|
| Large-farm households | | | | | | | | |
| –Sindh | 0.14 | −0.49 | −0.51 | 0.02 | −0.24 | −0.08 | −0.16 | −0.53 |
| –Punjab | 0.17 | −0.35 | −0.58 | 0.23 | −0.20 | −0.09 | −0.11 | −0.48 |
| –Other Pakistan | 0.01 | −0.24 | −0.67 | 0.43 | −0.17 | −0.13 | −0.04 | −0.39 |
| Medium-farm households | | | | | | | | |
| –Sindh | 0.99 | −0.46 | −0.51 | 0.05 | −0.20 | −0.08 | −0.11 | −0.61 |
| –Punjab | 1.89 | −0.30 | −0.58 | 0.28 | −0.15 | −0.09 | −0.06 | −0.50 |
| –Other Pakistan | 0.75 | −0.47 | −0.67 | 0.20 | −0.20 | −0.13 | −0.07 | −0.62 |
| Small-farm households | | | | | | | | |
| –Sindh | 2.79 | −0.19 | −0.44 | 0.25 | −0.12 | −0.06 | −0.06 | −0.33 |
| –Punjab | 12.87 | −0.22 | −0.45 | 0.23 | −0.13 | −0.09 | −0.04 | −0.20 |
| –Other Pakistan | 5.67 | −0.10 | −0.46 | 0.36 | −0.09 | −0.11 | 0.01 | −0.19 |
| Small-farm renters, landless | | | | | | | | |
| –Sindh | 0.16 | −0.22 | −0.38 | 0.16 | −0.12 | −0.07 | −0.06 | −0.03 |
| –Punjab | 1.50 | −0.20 | −0.47 | 0.27 | −0.12 | −0.10 | −0.02 | 0.00 |
| –Other Pakistan | 0.58 | −0.18 | −0.52 | 0.35 | −0.11 | −0.12 | 0.01 | −0.13 |
| Rural agricultural workers, landless | | | | | | | | |
| –Sindh | 4.12 | −0.01 | −0.38 | 0.37 | −0.06 | −0.09 | 0.03 | 0.87 |
| –Punjab | 2.02 | 0.00 | −0.40 | 0.39 | −0.06 | −0.09 | 0.03 | 0.82 |
| –Other Pakistan | 0.86 | 0.10 | −0.48 | 0.58 | −0.04 | −0.13 | 0.09 | 0.07 |
| Rural nonfarm households | | | | | | | | |
| –nonpoor | 17.60 | 0.11 | −0.52 | 0.63 | −0.06 | −0.11 | 0.04 | 0.94 |
| –poor | 18.14 | 0.06 | −0.46 | 0.53 | −0.05 | −0.10 | 0.06 | 0.35 |
| Urban households | | | | | | | | |
| –nonpoor | 22.50 | −0.22 | −0.53 | 0.31 | −0.11 | −0.12 | 0.01 | −7.21 |
| –poor | 7.23 | −0.09 | −0.46 | 0.37 | −0.08 | −0.11 | 0.03 | 1.49 |

*Source:* National CGE model simulations by the authors.

*Note:* EV = equivalent variation.

## S1B: Agricultural liberalization by the rest of the world

This second experiment incorporates the results of the global model for agricultural liberalization by the rest of the world, while retaining all existing trade distortions in Pakistan. Compared with scenario S1A, the border import prices of some commodities increase more in this scenario. For example, there is a greater increase in the border import prices of wheat, livestock, cotton, milled rice, and sugar (table 7.3). Furthermore, the border import prices of nonagricultural products increase in this scenario, while they decline in scenario S1A (table 7.7). Also, for commodities that show declining border import prices, the drop is relatively greater

| ?A | | S2B | | | S3A | | | S3B | | |
|---|---|---|---|---|---|---|---|---|---|---|
| ange in nsumer ce, % | EV/ income, % | Change in nominal income, % | Change in consumer price, % | EV/ income, % | Change in nominal income, % | Change in consumer price, % | EV/ income, % | Change in nominal income, % | Change in consumer price, % | EV/ income, % |
| 2.60 | 2.08 | −1.63 | −0.28 | −1.34 | −1.09 | −3.03 | 1.96 | −1.84 | −0.32 | −1.51 |
| .82 | 2.35 | −1.34 | −0.16 | −1.17 | −0.86 | −3.31 | 2.47 | −1.51 | −0.22 | −1.29 |
| .94 | 2.57 | −1.11 | −0.03 | 1.08 | −0.64 | −3.52 | 2.90 | −1.25 | −0.12 | −1.12 |
| 2.60 | 2.00 | −1.21 | −0.28 | −0.93 | −1.11 | −3.03 | 1.94 | −1.39 | −0.32 | −1.06 |
| .82 | 2.33 | −0.87 | −0.16 | −0.71 | 0.81 | −3.31 | 2.52 | −0.99 | −0.22 | −0.77 |
| .94 | 2.33 | −1.25 | −0.03 | −1.22 | −1.14 | −3.52 | 2.40 | −1.43 | −0.12 | −1.30 |
| .40 | 2.08 | −0.60 | −0.40 | −0.19 | −0.51 | −2.78 | 2.28 | 0.00 | 0.43 | −0.33 |
| 47 | 7.19 | 0.60 | 0.53 | 0.00 | −0.41 | −2.84 | 2.44 | −0.68 | −0.57 | −0.10 |
| .37 | 2.19 | −0.37 | −0.53 | 0.16 | −0.26 | −2.77 | 2.52 | −0.42 | −0.60 | 0.18 |
| .16 | 2.14 | −0.53 | −0.56 | 0.03 | −0.24 | −2.48 | 2.25 | −0.62 | −0.59 | −0.03 |
| .41 | 2.42 | −0.48 | −0.52 | 0.05 | −0.19 | −2.82 | 2.64 | −0.57 | 0.59 | 0.03 |
| 41 | 2.29 | −0.50 | −0.44 | −0.05 | −0.29 | −2.87 | 2.59 | −0.58 | −0.53 | −0.04 |
| 08 | 2.96 | 0.26 | −0.68 | 0.95 | 0.91 | −2.41 | 3.33 | 0.24 | −0.73 | 0.98 |
| 19 | 3.02 | 0.25 | −0.71 | 0.97 | 0.87 | 2.52 | 3.40 | 0.23 | −0.76 | 1.00 |
| 20 | 2.28 | 0.10 | 0.60 | 0.71 | 0.24 | −2.62 | 2.87 | 0.11 | −0.70 | 0.82 |
| 68 | 3.63 | 0.10 | −0.30 | 0.41 | 1.12 | −3.12 | 4.25 | 0.09 | −0.37 | 0.47 |
| 23 | 2.58 | 0.16 | −0.57 | 0.73 | 0.47 | −2.63 | 3.11 | 0.16 | −0.64 | 0.80 |
| 13 | −4.06 | −0.25 | −0.11 | −0.13 | −7.27 | −3.57 | −3.69 | −0.32 | −0.19 | −0.12 |
| 44 | 3.94 | 0.38 | −0.51 | 0.90 | 1.44 | −2.83 | 4.28 | 0.34 | −0.58 | 0.93 |

in this scenario compared with scenario S1A. Thus, the increase in the terms of trade for both agriculture and nonagriculture is lower in this experiment compared with scenario S1A. Also, the increase in the terms of trade is significantly lower in nonagriculture than in agriculture in this scenario relative to scenario S1A.

Table 7.6 shows that, while Pakistan's overall poverty incidence index declines marginally, poverty is not reduced across the board. Poverty in urban areas declines, but not all rural households experience a drop in poverty. Rural non-farmers show the highest poverty reduction, but, among farmers and agricultural workers, there is a slight increase in poverty.

What are the factors that drive these poverty results? The import prices of agriculture decline by 0.7 percent (table 7.7). This is caused by the real exchange rate appreciation of 0.13 percent and the reduction in the border prices of milled wheat, as well as fruits and vegetables, which are import intensive. There are a number of primary agricultural commodities that show relatively greater increases in import prices, but these commodities are not imported. The domestic prices of agricultural goods decrease, but by less than the decline in the import prices of these goods. Thus, the imports of agricultural goods increase by 0.9 percent.

In nonagriculture, the smaller decline in domestic prices relative to import prices leads to a marginal increase in imports by 0.12 percent. This raises slightly the domestic consumption of nonagricultural products.

The increase in the export prices in agriculture by 0.33 percent and the decline in the domestic prices in agriculture by 0.07 percent result in a rise in exports by 1.8 percent. This increases the overall output of agriculture slightly, despite the decline in the domestic demand because of more imports. However, the increase in the exports of nonagricultural goods is not quite sufficient to offset the decline in domestic demand; so, the overall output of nonagriculture declines by 0.01 percent.

The difference in the results between the prices of value added and the output in agriculture is caused by variations in the results across industries within the agricultural sector. The greater increase in the border price of milled rice leads to a higher value added price, which offsets the decline in value added prices in the rest of agriculture. The decline in farm wages by 0.27 percent and the decline in the returns to land by 0.32 percent are caused by the decrease in the value added prices in primary agriculture. There is an increase in the returns to capital in agriculture by 0.27 percent mainly because of the improvement in the value added price of milled rice, a sector which has a high capital-labor ratio. The decline in wages in unskilled labor is smaller than the decline in farm wages because of the increase in the value added price of milled rice, which neutralizes much of the effect of the falling value added prices in the rest of agriculture and in some nonagricultural sectors. Because milled rice requires more skilled labor than unskilled labor (table 7.1), the increase in the value added price of milled rice also offsets the negative effects arising in the rest of the economy; thus, the wages of skilled labor do not change.

Net of the inflation effects, the changes in factor prices involve declining farm wages and declining returns to land, but otherwise rising factor prices. The nominal income effects are negative among all household groups (table 7.8), but they are smaller than the effects generated in scenario S1A. Consumer prices decline, but the decline is not sufficient to offset the drop in the nominal incomes of farmers. However, rural nonfarmers and urban households enjoy marginal improvements in real incomes.

In sum, agricultural liberalization by the rest of the world would generate a marginal change in the terms of trade that favors agriculture compared with the results of scenario S1A. Furthermore, although overall import prices decline, the drop is much smaller in the present case than in scenario S1A. This translates into a smaller decline in consumer prices across household groups that is not sufficient to offset the drop in nominal incomes in some groups. These groups—farmers and agricultural workers—experience a slight increase in poverty. Moreover, given the small share of agriculture in the overall trade of Pakistan (less than 10 percent; see table 7.1), a liberalization only in agriculture has much less impact on the Pakistan economy than a liberalization in all goods trade. Thus, the poverty impact is significantly less in the present case than in scenario S1A.

## S2A: The unilateral liberalization of all goods trade by Pakistan

Our third experiment sets all sectoral import tariffs and export taxes in Pakistan to zero and assumes that there are no changes in policies abroad. Table 7.6 shows that this generates a significant drop in poverty, by 5.2 percent overall. There is also a significant reduction in the depth of poverty: the poverty gap drops by 10 percent, and the squared poverty gap drops by 12 percent. However, the incidence of poverty in urban areas increases by 2.3 percent. The detailed results show that the urban nonpoor suffer a decline in incomes because of the additional tax burden. This is the outcome of the tax replacement method, whereby we replace trade-distorting taxes in Pakistan with a less-distorting income tax that falls disproportionately on urban nonpoor households.[9] The rest of the household groups enjoy higher incomes and therefore lower poverty. Overall, income inequality is also reduced.

Most of the effects arise from the elimination of tariffs, although there are also effects because of the dismantling of the export taxes in a number of sectors (table 7.3). The elimination of tariffs leads to a substantial reduction in import prices. The greatest reduction is in sugar and in livestock, cattle, and dairy because these sectors are exposed to the highest tariff rates. The import prices of vegetable oil, milled wheat, other food, cotton lint and yarn, and textiles also decline notably (table 7.9). Overall, the import prices in agriculture decline by 12 percent, while, in nonagriculture, the import prices decline by 8.3 percent (table 7.7).

Domestic prices also decline. However, the decline in domestic prices in most sectors is less than the decline in import prices. Thus, imports in these sectors surge. The imports of sugar increase by 215 percent; livestock, cattle, and dairy, by 99 percent; milled wheat, by 40 percent; other food, by 38 percent; cotton lint and yarn, by 38 percent; textiles, by 33 percent; and leather, by 28 percent (table 7.9). Other sectors show notable increases as well. Overall, imports in agriculture rise by 22 percent compared with only 4 percent in nonagriculture.

**Table 7.9. The Sectoral Effects of the Unilateral Liberalization of All Goods Trade, Pakistan**

| Sectors | Output | | Domestic demand | | Composite good | | Exports | | Imports | | Value added | | Return to capital |
|---|---|---|---|---|---|---|---|---|---|---|---|---|---|
| | x | px | d | pd | q | pq | e | pe | m | pm | va | pva | |
| Agriculture | | | | | | | | | | | | | |
| *Primary agriculture* | | | | | | | | | | | | | |
| 1. Wheat, irrigated | 2.2 | −2.2 | 0.6 | −2.2 | −0.4 | −1.9 | 58.0 | −2.2 | −30.9 | 11.2 | 2.2 | −0.9 | 2.0 |
| 2. Wheat, nonirrigated | −0.6 | −2.5 | −0.6 | −2.5 | −0.6 | −2.5 | 0.0 | 0.0 | 0.0 | 0.0 | −0.6 | −1.3 | −2.1 |
| 3. Paddy, IRRI | 0.7 | −2.5 | 0.7 | −2.5 | 0.7 | −2.5 | 0.0 | 0.0 | 0.0 | 0.0 | 0.7 | −1.5 | −0.5 |
| 4. Paddy, basmati | 0.9 | −2.6 | 0.9 | −2.6 | 0.9 | −2.6 | 0.0 | 0.0 | 0.0 | 0.0 | 0.9 | −1.7 | −0.5 |
| 5. Raw cotton | 4.3 | −2.6 | 4.3 | −2.6 | 4.3 | −2.6 | 0.0 | 0.0 | 0.0 | 0.0 | 4.3 | −0.8 | 5.0 |
| 6. Sugarcane | −1.3 | −2.7 | −1.3 | −2.7 | −1.3 | −2.7 | 0.0 | 0.0 | 0.0 | 0.0 | −1.3 | −1.8 | −3.5 |
| 7. Other major crops | −0.2 | −1.6 | −1.0 | −1.6 | −0.4 | −1.9 | 32.6 | −1.6 | 13.9 | −8.3 | −0.2 | −1.3 | −1.5 |
| 8. Fruits and vegetables | −0.8 | −1.5 | −2.0 | −1.5 | −0.4 | −2.3 | 32.2 | −1.5 | 15.2 | −9.3 | −0.8 | −1.7 | −2.7 |
| 9. Livestock, cattle, and dairy | −0.5 | −3.3 | −0.6 | −3.3 | 0.1 | −3.6 | 41.8 | −3.3 | 99.0 | −32.0 | −0.5 | −5.0 | −5.7 |
| 10. Poultry | −0.6 | −3.6 | −0.7 | −3.6 | −0.7 | −3.6 | 43.9 | −3.6 | 0.0 | 0.0 | −0.6 | −5.7 | −6.5 |
| 11. Forestry | −21.2 | −1.9 | −3.3 | −1.9 | −0.3 | −3.2 | −41.7 | −1.9 | 9.9 | −7.5 | −21.2 | −1.6 | 0.0 |
| 12. Fishing industry | −4.9 | −9.2 | 0.6 | −9.2 | 0.6 | −9.2 | −18.5 | −9.2 | −3.4 | −7.5 | −4.9 | −13.7 | −19.3 |
| *Lightly processed food* | | | | | | | | | | | | | |
| 14. Vegetable oil | −6.8 | −3.8 | −6.8 | −3.8 | 0.1 | −7.2 | 44.8 | −3.8 | 17.7 | −14.5 | −6.8 | −34.9 | −37.9 |
| 15. Wheat, milled | −0.6 | −1.2 | −1.1 | −1.2 | 0.2 | −1.7 | 34.8 | −1.2 | 39.6 | −15.4 | −0.6 | 0.1 | −0.3 |
| 16. Rice, milled IRRI | 1.5 | 0.7 | −0.1 | 0.7 | −0.1 | 0.7 | 3.3 | 0.7 | 0.0 | 0.0 | 1.5 | 5.5 | 6.5 |
| 17. Rice, milled basmati | 1.3 | 0.3 | −0.3 | 0.3 | −0.3 | 0.3 | 5.2 | 0.3 | 0.0 | 0.0 | 1.3 | 5.0 | 5.9 |
| 18. Sugar | −1.4 | −1.5 | −1.4 | −1.5 | 0.0 | −2.0 | 51.5 | −1.5 | 215.2 | −33.5 | −1.4 | −1.2 | −2.1 |

*Nonagriculture*

*Mining and manufacturing*

| | | | | | | | | | | | | | |
|---|---|---|---|---|---|---|---|---|---|---|---|---|---|
| 13. Mining | −4.0 | −8.6 | 1.1 | −8.6 | −1.3 | −7.5 | −21.0 | −8.6 | −1.9 | −7.3 | −4.0 | −10.4 | −15.1 |
| 19. Other food | 2.6 | 2.9 | −6.0 | 2.9 | −1.1 | 0.2 | 11.3 | 2.9 | 38.1 | −15.4 | 2.6 | 10.3 | 12.2 |
| 20. Cotton lint and yarn | 5.0 | 1.7 | 2.5 | 1.7 | 3.7 | 1.1 | 12.0 | 1.7 | 37.5 | −11.8 | 5.0 | 13.8 | 17.6 |
| 21. Textiles | 4.1 | 1.6 | −0.9 | 1.6 | 0.8 | 0.8 | 12.3 | 1.6 | 32.8 | −11.8 | 4.1 | 9.6 | 12.6 |
| 22. Leather | 8.9 | −0.5 | −0.2 | −0.5 | 1.1 | −1.2 | 22.7 | −0.5 | 27.8 | −11.8 | 8.9 | 20.0 | 27.0 |
| 23. Wood products | −1.8 | −1.7 | −1.8 | −1.7 | −0.5 | −2.3 | 7.2 | −1.7 | 15.9 | −9.3 | −1.8 | −0.3 | −1.5 |
| 24. Chemicals | −2.5 | −4.6 | −6.7 | −4.6 | 0.6 | −8.0 | 21.2 | −4.6 | 3.6 | −9.3 | −2.5 | −4.6 | −6.2 |
| 25. Cement and bricks | −1.4 | −4.7 | −1.4 | −4.7 | −1.4 | −4.7 | 21.7 | −4.7 | 0.0 | 0.0 | −1.4 | −4.8 | −5.7 |
| 26. Petroleum refining | −3.8 | −4.8 | −3.8 | −4.8 | 1.1 | −7.1 | 0.0 | 0.0 | 6.3 | −9.3 | −3.8 | −5.5 | −7.9 |
| 27. Other manufacturing | −0.8 | −3.5 | −7.9 | −3.5 | 1.0 | −7.7 | 15.5 | −3.5 | 4.7 | −9.3 | −0.8 | 0.5 | 0.0 |

*Other industry*

| | | | | | | | | | | | | | |
|---|---|---|---|---|---|---|---|---|---|---|---|---|---|
| 28. Energy | 0.3 | −0.5 | 0.3 | −0.5 | 0.3 | −0.5 | 0.0 | 0.0 | 0.0 | 0.0 | 0.3 | 2.7 | 2.8 |
| 29. Construction | −1.7 | −2.9 | −1.7 | −2.9 | −1.7 | −2.9 | 0.0 | 0.0 | 0.0 | 0.0 | −1.7 | 1.3 | 0.1 |

*Services*

| | | | | | | | | | | | | | |
|---|---|---|---|---|---|---|---|---|---|---|---|---|---|
| 30. Commerce | −0.4 | 0.5 | −0.4 | 0.5 | −0.4 | 0.5 | 11.1 | 0.5 | −5.5 | 5.7 | −0.4 | 1.5 | 1.2 |
| 31. Transport | 1.7 | −1.3 | −0.5 | −1.3 | −0.6 | −1.3 | 15.2 | −1.3 | 0.0 | 0.0 | 1.7 | 3.4 | 4.6 |
| 32. Housing | 0.0 | −11.7 | 0.0 | −11.7 | 0.0 | −11.7 | 0.1 | 0.0 | 0.0 | 0.0 | 0.0 | −13.6 | −13.6 |
| 33. Private services | −0.4 | −0.7 | −0.4 | −0.7 | −0.8 | −0.3 | 13.3 | −0.7 | −6.7 | 5.7 | −0.4 | 1.2 | 0.9 |
| 34. Public services | −0.7 | 0.5 | −0.7 | 0.5 | −0.7 | 0.5 | 0.1 | 0.0 | 0.0 | 0.0 | −0.7 | 2.1 | 0.0 |

*Source:* National CGE model simulations by the authors.

*Note:* x = output. px = output price. pd = domestic price. d = domestic demand. q = composite good. pq = composite price. e = exports. pe = export price. m = imports. pm = import price. va = value added. pva = value added price.

Because world prices are fixed, the decline in prices in Pakistan because of the trade reform increases the country's competitiveness.[10] There is a real depreciation of 6.1 percent in the exchange rate. The results, shown in table 7.9, indicate that, except for forestry and fishing, the exports of agriculture—primary agriculture and lightly processed food—improve. Overall, agricultural exports expand by 4.8 percent. However, this increase does not offset the displacement effects of the surge in imports by 22 percent. Thus, the overall output of agriculture declines by 0.7 percent. The biggest reductions are in forestry (21 percent), vegetable oil (7 percent), and fishing (5 percent). However, there is an improvement in raw cotton production because of the increase in the output of cotton lint and yarn, as well as textiles (see elsewhere below).

In nonagriculture, almost all sectors realize positive growth in exports. Overall, exports in nonagriculture increase by 13 percent. The increase in manufacturing exports is also substantial, especially in major export items such as cotton lint and yarn, textiles, other food, and other manufacturing. There is also a notable increase in the exports of services such as commerce, transport, and private services.

For other food, the increase in imports displaces domestic demand by 6 percent. However, this is offset by the increase in exports; thus, the output of other food improves by 2.6 percent, while the output price improves by 2.9 percent. The impact on textiles may be analyzed in relation to the effects on the cotton lint and yarn sector and the raw cotton sector. The increase in textile imports displaces domestic demand by 0.9 percent. However, this is offset by the increase in textile exports; thus, textile output improves by 4.1 percent, while the output price improves by 1.6 percent. Because the cotton lint and yarn sector supplies materials to the textile sector, the improvement in the output of textiles because of the greater exports leads to an improvement in the domestic demand for cotton lint and yarn by 2.5 percent. The increase in both the exports and the domestic demand for cotton lint and yarn leads to 5.0 percent more output and a rise in the output price by 1.7 percent, which, in turn, leads to 4.3 percent more output of raw cotton.

The negative change in the value added prices in agriculture leads to lower prices for factors that are used heavily in agriculture. The wages of farmers decrease by 0.6 percent; the returns to land fall by 1.9 percent; and the average returns to agricultural capital fall by 5 percent.

The average output price in nonagriculture decreases by 1.1 percent, but the value added price improves by 1.3 percent. The increase arises from the notable improvement in the value added prices of leather (20 percent), cotton lint and yarn (14 percent), other food (10 percent), textiles (10 percent), and transport (3 percent) (see table 7.9). Thus, the prices of the factors used in nonagriculture improve. The wages of unskilled workers increase by 1.5 percent and of skilled labor by 2.1 percent, while the average returns to nonagricultural capital rise by

1 percent. Furthermore, there is a significant decline in the consumer price index. Thus, net of the inflation effects, factor prices improve except for the average returns to the capital used in agriculture.

The nominal incomes of farmers drop (table 7.8). This occurs largely because of the declines in the wages of farmers, in the returns to land, and in the average returns to capital in agriculture. Because of the higher wages of workers, the nominal incomes of nonfarmers improve except for the nominal incomes of urban nonpoor households. The incomes of the urban nonpoor decline because of the income tax replacement imposed on this group. However, the decline in consumer prices is significant for all groups. This offsets the decline in nominal incomes except in the case of the urban nonpoor.

In sum, all households, except urban nonpoor households, realize an increase in real incomes, which leads to a significant decline in poverty. The urban poor experience the largest increase in incomes and the largest drop in the depth of poverty. Income inequality is reduced.

### S2B: Unilateral agricultural liberalization by Pakistan

Our fourth experiment sets only agricultural price distortions in Pakistan at zero, while retaining all nonagricultural trade taxes and assuming no changes in the global model.[11] Overall, the poverty effects are significantly lower in this experiment compared with the S2A scenario. Furthermore, there are differences in the effects across households. Urban households experience a decline in poverty, and, although overall poverty in rural areas declines, large- and medium-farm households face increasing poverty.

The results at the macro, sectoral, factor, and commodity price levels explain these poverty effects. At the sectoral level, the import prices of agriculture drop by 14 percent (table 7.7). The largest declines are in sugar (36 percent); livestock, cattle, and dairy (34 percent); milled wheat (18 percent); and vegetable oil (18 percent).[12] There is also a reduction in domestic prices, but this is significantly smaller than the drop in import prices. Thus, the imports of agricultural goods surge by 30 percent.

This agricultural liberalization results in a real exchange rate depreciation. Because tariffs and subsidies in nonagriculture are retained, the average import prices in nonagriculture increase by only 2.6 percent, while the domestic prices in nonagriculture increase by 1.11 percent. Thus, the imports of nonagricultural products decline by 0.5 percent. On the other hand, the exports of nonagricultural products improve by 3.1 percent. At the sectoral level, the increase is caused by the strong export effect on leather, wood products, cotton lint and yarn, and commerce. Because world prices are fixed and the domestic and output prices of nonagriculture increase, the increase in nonagricultural exports is caused by the depreciation in the exchange rate. The increase in nonagricultural exports, together with the marginal increase in the domestic demand for nonagricultural products, leads to an improvement in nonagricultural output by 0.4 percent.

The prices of the factors used in agriculture decline. The wages of farmers decrease by 2.2 percent; the returns to land, by 2.5 percent; and the average returns to capital, by 3.8 percent. However, the prices of factors used heavily in nonagriculture improve. We observe a similar pattern in factor prices after we net out the marginal decline of 0.27 percent in the consumer price index.

The nominal incomes of farmers decline, while the nominal incomes of non-farmers improve. The marginal decline in the consumer price index does not offset the decrease in the nominal incomes of farmers, especially large- and medium-farm households. Thus, the real income of these farm households is lower. However, non-farmers enjoy higher real incomes, except for the urban nonpoor, among whom real incomes fall slightly as a result of the tax burden they bear. Nonetheless, the additional tax burden is not sufficiently large to push the urban nonpoor below the poverty line (unlike the case of scenario S2A); so, poverty declines in urban areas. Although the overall poverty in rural areas declines, large- and medium-farm households face increasing poverty because of declining real incomes.

### S3A: Full trade liberalization by Pakistan and the rest of the world

Our fifth experiment combines the trade liberalization in the rest of the world with that in Pakistan in all sectors. The effects of the unilateral trade liberalization in Pakistan are larger than the effects of the rest-of-the-world trade liberalization. The combined impact on both exports and imports is strongly positive. There is also a large decline in the consumer price index. Factor prices in agriculture decline, but they improve in nonagriculture. However, net of the inflation effects, the only decline in factor returns occurs in the average returns to the capital used in agriculture. The nominal incomes of farmers decline, while the nominal incomes among nonfarmers improve. The large reduction in the consumer price index contributes to an increase in the real incomes of all households except urban nonpoor households.

This scenario generates the largest reduction in poverty. Another point worth highlighting is that, while the incidence of poverty among the urban nonpoor increases, the increase is much smaller in this experiment than in scenario S2A.

### S3B: Agricultural liberalization by Pakistan and the rest of the world

Our sixth experiment combines the agricultural liberalization of the rest of the world with that in Pakistan. It turns out that the effects of the reform in Pakistan dominate those of the agricultural liberalization in the rest of the world. There is also an upward response in imports and exports, but in agriculture only. The surge in agricultural imports displaces local production. This results in lower prices for the factors used in agriculture. Factor prices in nonagriculture increase because the sector remains protected. Therefore, farmers have lower incomes, while nonfarmers benefit.

### Sensitivity analysis: Indirect versus direct tax replacement

The results discussed above are derived using a replacement income tax. Because the SAM we have used to calibrate the model has an income tax on urban non-poor households only (table 7.4), the direct tax replacement puts all the burden of financing the trade reform on this group. As an alternative, we consider, in this subsection, the assessment of indirect taxes to offset the losses in government tar-iff revenue that are generated by reform. We focus on the poverty effects of these two tax replacement schemes in scenarios S3A (full trade liberalization of all goods in the rest of the world and in Pakistan) and S3B (agricultural liberalization in the rest of the world and in Pakistan).

The effects on real income across households are presented in table 7.10. In scenario S3A, in which all sectors are liberalized, changing the tax replacement from a direct tax to an indirect tax completely alters the results. Under the direct tax replacement, all households enjoy higher real incomes except urban nonpoor households. This tax replacement scheme therefore redistributes income from the urban nonpoor to the rest of the household groups. These latter household groups benefit from the reduction in consumer prices and from the redistribution of income from the urban nonpoor households. However, if an indirect tax replacement is used, consumer prices increase because of the taxes, and the bur-den is shared among all household groups depending upon household consump-tion structures. There is a reduction in household incomes among most of the groups except the three relatively wealthy groups (the large-farm households in other Pakistan, the rural nonpoor, and the urban nonpoor). Under this tax replacement scheme, there is a significant increase in domestic prices because of the higher indirect taxes.

If the trade liberalization is focused on agriculture only under S3B, the income results are not sensitive to the tax replacement scheme used. This is because the net government budget implications of the elimination of the distortions are not as large in agriculture as in nonagriculture. Thus, the impact on domestic prices through higher indirect taxes is not as significant in the case of agricultural liber-alization as in the case of the trade liberalization of all goods. In both tax replace-ment schemes, farmers, particularly large- and medium-farm households, are negatively affected, while nonfarmers are favorably affected. However, in the direct tax replacement scheme, the urban nonpoor are still negatively affected, while they are favorably affected in the indirect tax replacement scheme.

**Table 7.10. Sensitivity Analysis of Household Welfare Effects, Two Tax Replacement Schemes, Pakistan**

| Households | 2001–02 population distribution, % | S3A Direct tax | S3A Indirect tax | S3B Direct tax | S3B Indirect tax |
|---|---|---|---|---|---|
| Large-farm households | | | | | |
| –Sindh | 0.1 | 1.96 | −0.49 | −1.51 | −1.65 |
| –Punjab | 0.2 | 2.47 | −0.08 | −1.29 | −1.42 |
| –Other Pakistan | 0.0 | 2.90 | 0.18 | −1.12 | −1.26 |
| Medium-farm households | | | | | |
| –Sindh | 1.0 | 1.94 | −0.75 | −1.06 | −1.20 |
| –Punjab | 1.9 | 2.52 | −0.31 | −0.77 | −0.92 |
| –Other Pakistan | 0.8 | 2.40 | −0.40 | −1.30 | −1.45 |
| Small-farm households | | | | | |
| –Sindh | 2.8 | 2.28 | −0.70 | −0.25 | −0.40 |
| –Punjab | 12.9 | 2.44 | −0.55 | −0.10 | −0.25 |
| –Other Pakistan | 5.7 | 2.52 | −0.56 | 0.18 | 0.03 |
| Small-farm renters, landless | | | | | |
| –Sindh | 0.2 | 2.25 | −0.92 | −0.03 | −0.18 |
| –Punjab | 1.5 | 2.64 | −0.53 | 0.03 | −0.13 |
| –Other Pakistan | 0.6 | 2.59 | −0.51 | −0.04 | −0.20 |
| Rural agricultural workers, landless | | | | | |
| –Sindh | 4.1 | 3.33 | −0.48 | 0.98 | 0.80 |
| –Punjab | 2.0 | 3.40 | −0.36 | 1.00 | 0.82 |
| –Other Pakistan | 0.9 | 2.87 | −0.47 | 0.82 | 0.66 |
| Rural nonfarm households | | | | | |
| –nonpoor | 17.6 | 4.25 | 0.55 | 0.47 | 0.29 |
| –poor | 18.1 | 3.11 | −0.41 | 0.80 | 0.63 |
| Urban households | | | | | |
| –nonpoor | 22.5 | −3.69 | 0.63 | −0.12 | 0.10 |
| –poor | 7.2 | 4.28 | −0.14 | 0.93 | 0.71 |

*Source:* National CGE model simulations by the authors.

Table 7.11 presents the poverty results based on this sensitivity analysis. Trade liberalization in all goods globally under the indirect tax replacement scheme is poverty increasing in scenario S3A. This is because of the declining real incomes among most groups. This effect arises largely because of the higher consumer prices resulting from the indirect tax replacement scheme. The higher consumer prices wipe out the gains accruing because of the higher border export prices, the lower border import prices, and the lower tariffs.

Agricultural liberalization alone entails a smaller fiscal burden. Therefore, both the direct income tax replacement scheme and the indirect tax replacement scheme

**Table 7.11. Sensitivity Analysis of Poverty Effects, Two Tax Replacement Schemes, Pakistan**

| | | S3A | | S3B | |
|---|---|---|---|---|---|
| Poverty index | 2001–02 index | Direct tax | Indirect tax | Direct tax | Indirect tax |
| All Pakistan | | | | | |
| –P0 | 31.2 | –6.4 | 0.5 | –1.8 | –1.2 |
| –P1 | 6.5 | –11.5 | 1.5 | –2.5 | –1.8 |
| –P2 | 2.0 | –13.8 | 1.8 | –3.0 | –2.2 |
| All urban | | | | | |
| –P0 | 19.9 | 0.4 | 0.0 | –2.7 | –2.3 |
| P1 | 3.9 | –14.8 | 0.6 | –3.7 | –2.9 |
| –P2 | 1.2 | –18.3 | 0.7 | –4.3 | –3.3 |
| All rural | | | | | |
| –P0 | 38.2 | 0.6 | 0.6 | –1.1 | –0.9 |
| –P1 | 8.0 | –10.5 | 1.7 | –2.1 | –1.5 |
| –P2 | 2.5 | –12.5 | 2.1 | –2.6 | –1.9 |
| Large- and medium-farm households | | | | | |
| –P0 | 22.8 | –7.9 | 2.2 | 3.4 | 3.4 |
| –P1 | 4.1 | –10.0 | 2.4 | 5.3 | 6.0 |
| –P2 | 1.1 | –10.6 | 2.8 | 5.8 | 6.6 |
| Small-farm households and agricultural workers | | | | | |
| –P0 | 37.4 | –8.7 | 1.5 | –0.9 | –0.3 |
| –P1 | 7.5 | –10.3 | 2.2 | –1.3 | –0.6 |
| –P2 | 2.2 | –12.4 | 2.6 | –1.6 | –0.9 |
| Rural nonfarm households | | | | | |
| –P0 | 39.9 | –8.5 | 0.0 | –2.1 | –1.5 |
| –P1 | 8.7 | –10.6 | 1.5 | –2.8 | –2.2 |
| –P2 | 2.8 | –12.6 | 1.8 | –3.4 | –2.7 |

*Source:* National CGE model simulations by the authors.

*Note:* P0 = poverty headcount. P1 = poverty gap. P2 = poverty severity.

generate favorable effects on poverty. In the case of the indirect income tax replacement scheme, although it increases consumer prices, it does not wipe out the gains achieved through the higher border export prices, the lower border import prices, and the lower trade taxes on agricultural commodities. Because of the negative effects of the agricultural liberalization on domestic agriculture in Pakistan, farmers will be hurt, especially large- and medium-farm households. However, this is a small segment in the total population and exhibits the lowest incidence of poverty (23 percent in 2001–02 compared with 37 percent among small-farm households and agricultural workers and 40 percent among rural nonfarmers).

## Summary and Policy Implications

In this chapter, we have linked the results of two economic models—the Linkage model of the World Bank and the Pakistan CGE model that we have developed—to analyze and compare the poverty effects of trade liberalization abroad with the corresponding effects of unilateral reform by Pakistan. We have conducted six policy experiments: two rest-of-the-world trade liberalization experiments (full liberalization that covers all goods sectors and agriculture only), two unilateral trade liberalization cases (all goods and agriculture only), and two combined scenarios. The results are evaluated under a direct tax replacement scheme among household incomes; the direct tax is paid only by the urban nonpoor. We also examine an alternative tax replacement scheme, an indirect tax on commodities.

A number of policy insights may be drawn from our simulation results. The impacts on the Pakistan economy and on the extent of poverty in the country from own-country liberalization are significantly larger than the impacts from rest-of-the-world trade liberalization. The effects of agricultural liberalization (both in the rest-of-the-world market and in Pakistan) are considerably smaller than the effects of the liberalization of all goods trade. This is because of the smaller share of agricultural trade in overall exports and imports in Pakistan, in which trade is dominated by nonagricultural products.

The income from trade taxes is a major source of revenue for the government. The trade tax revenue is considerably lower from agricultural commodities than from nonagricultural products. Thus, the elimination of the trade taxes on all tradable commodities creates a large dent in government income and in the fiscal balance. It therefore entails a significant government demand for tax revenue from other sources. The poverty and income effects of full trade liberalization greatly depend upon how the tax replacement is implemented. If an additional tax is imposed on household incomes to generate funds to finance the reduction in trade taxes in all sectors, there is a notable decline of consumer prices and a large income redistribution from urban nonpoor households to the rest of the household groups. There is therefore a considerable decline in the incidence of poverty, in the depth of poverty, and in income inequality. This is because the burden of the additional tax falls entirely on the urban nonpoor, while the rest of the groups benefit from higher real factor prices and larger reductions in consumer prices. However, if the tax replacement is imposed as additional indirect taxes on commodities, consumer prices increase and eliminate the benefits generated from the reduction in trade distortions. In this case, poverty rises.

The trade tax revenue is considerably lower from agricultural commodities than from nonagricultural products. If trade liberalization is focused on agricultural commodities only, the fiscal refinancing requirement is substantially less urgent. The poverty reduction effects, although smaller, are robust to the change in tax policy, that is, poverty is reduced under both tax replacement schemes if only agricultural markets are liberalized.

All these results are derived using a static model. The dynamic impact of trade reform on capital accumulation from the changes in prices has not been accounted for. For example, if the rates of return to capital are high in sectors in which the poor are heavily engaged, this will attract investment, thereby increasing capital accumulation in these sectors and output from these sectors. This would have favorable implications for poverty. (It is also possible that the results would be reversed and would therefore generate negative effects on the poor.) Furthermore, the dynamic effects would have an impact on technological progress, the movement of the labor of farm households into nonfarm employment, factor and total productivity, and the flow of foreign direct investment. These are all empirical issues that are relevant topics for further research.

## Notes

1. Estimates of agricultural assistance in Pakistan, based on Dorosh and Salam (2009), are incorporated in the World Bank's Distortions to Agricultural Incentives Project Database (Anderson and Valenzuela 2008). The estimates cover five decades. The representative values for CGE modeling as of 2004 that are used here are available in Valenzuela and Anderson (2008).

2. The specification of the Pakistan CGE model is based on EXTER (see Decaluwé, Dumont, and Robichaud 2000).

3. Cororaton and Orden (2008) include a dynamic analysis in which sectoral capital adjusts over time.

4. The direct tax replacement on household income is specified as:

$$dyh = yh(1 - dtxrh[1 + ndtxrh]),$$

where $dyh$ is disposable income; $yh$ is income before income taxes; $dtxrh$ is the income tax rate at the base; and $ndtxrh$ is the income tax replacement. The indirect tax replacement on commodities is specified as:

$$pd = pl(1 + itxr)(1 + nitx),$$

where $pd$ is the domestic price; $pl$ is the local price before indirect taxes; $itxr$ is the indirect tax rate at the base; and $nitx$ is the indirect tax replacement.

5. Sectoral informal capital is also in the SAM. The returns to informal capital may be considered primarily as payments to labor outside the formal labor market. However, instead of modeling informal capital separately, we have aggregated it with formal capital. There is no significant underestimation of household incomes because informal capital is still being paid based on the returns to capital. However, this aggregation makes the labor share in agriculture appear relatively low.

6. We have set the sectoral values of the parameter $eta$ in the export demand function equal to the Armington elasticities in the global model. The sectoral values of the parameter $sig\_e$ in the export supply function and the sectoral values of the parameter $sig\_m$ in the import demand function are half the values of $eta$.

7. There is no real exchange rate variable in the model. The real exchange rate is defined as the world price, multiplied by the nominal exchange rate, divided by the local price, where the world price is the trade-weighted world import and export prices and the local price is the sectoral output-weighted local prices.

8. Detailed sectoral results are shown only for scenario S2A (see table 7.9). Detailed comparable sectoral results for the other scenarios are available from the authors on request.

9. In the model, the overall government revenue from tariffs is PRs 154 billion and from export taxes, PRs 15 billion. Total government revenue is PRs 446 billion. The total income of the urban nonpoor is PRs 1.73 trillion.

10. In our model, Pakistan is facing a downward-sloping world demand curve. Because the perfect substitution assumption is imposed between exports and domestic sales in Pakistan, the export supply curve is horizontal. The decrease in output prices raises export supply, which shifts the horizontal export supply curve downward.

11. The total tariff revenue from agricultural imports is PRs 14.2 billion, while farm export tax revenue is PRs 4.3 billion in the baseline.

12. Detailed sectoral results generated under this scenario are available from the authors upon request.

## References

Ahmed, V., A. Abbas, and S. Ahmed. 2009. "Taxation Reforms: A CGE-Microsimulation Analysis for Pakistan." Unpublished working paper, Modeling and Policy Impact Analysis Program, Poverty and Economic Policy Research Network, Université Laval, Quebec.

Anderson, K., and E. Valenzuela. 2008. "Estimates of Global Distortions to Agricultural Incentives, 1955–2007." Data spreadsheet, October, World Bank, Washington, DC. http://go.worldbank.org/YAO39F35E0.

Cororaton, B. C., and D. Orden. 2008. *Pakistan's Cotton and Textile Economy: Intersectoral Linkages and Effects on Rural and Urban Poverty*. IFPRI Research Report 158. Washington, DC: International Food Policy Research Institute.

Decaluwé, B., J.-C. Dumont, and V. Robichaud. 2000. *Basic CGE Models*. Vol. II of *MIMAP Training Session on CGE Modeling*. Micro Impacts of Macroeconomic and Adjustment Policies Program, International Development Research Centre, Canadian Centre for International Studies and Cooperation, and Université Laval, Quebec. http://www.pep-net.org/fileadmin/medias/pdf/volume2.pdf.

Dorosh, P. 2005. "Wheat Markets and Pricing in Pakistan: Political Economy and Policy Options." Wheat Policy Note, South Asia Rural Development Unit, World Bank, Washington, DC.

Dorosh, P., M. K. Niazi, and H. Nazli. 2004. "A Social Accounting Matrix for Pakistan, 2001–02: Methodology and Results." PIDE Working Paper 2006–9, Pakistan Institute of Development Economics, Islamabad. http://econpapers.repec.org/paper/pidwpaper/2006_3a9.htm.

Dorosh, P., and A. Salam. 2009. "Pakistan." In *Distortions to Agricultural Incentives in Asia*, ed. K. Anderson and W. Martin, 379–407. Washington, DC: World Bank.

Federal Bureau of Statistics. 2003. "Household Integrated Economic Survey: Round 4, 2001–02." Federal Bureau of Statistics, Islamabad. http://www.statpak.gov.pk/depts/fbs/statistics/hies0102/hies0102.html.

Foster, J., J. Greer, and E. Thorbecke. 1984. "A Class of Decomposable Poverty Measures." *Econometrica* 52 (3): 761–66.

Horridge, M., and F. Zhai. 2006. "Shocking a Single-Country CGE Model with Export Prices and Quantities from a Global Model." In *Poverty and the WTO: Impacts of the Doha Development Agenda*, ed. T. W. Hertel and L. A. Winters, 94–104. London: Palgrave Macmillan; Washington, DC: World Bank.

Ministry of Finance. 2003. *Economic Survey of Pakistan 2002–03*. Islamabad: Economic Advisers Wing, Finance Division, Government of Pakistan. http://www.accountancy.com.pk/docs/Economic_Survey_2002-03.pdf.

Valenzuela, E., and K. Anderson. 2008. "Alternative Agricultural Price Distortions for CGE Analysis of Developing Countries, 2004 and 1980–84." Research Memorandum 13 (December), Center for Global Trade Analysis, Department of Agricultural Economics, Purdue University, West Lafayette, IN. https://www.gtap.agecon.purdue.edu/resources/res_display.asp?RecordID=2925.

van der Mensbrugghe, D. 2005. "Linkage Technical Reference Document: Version 6.0." December, World Bank, Washington, DC. http://go.worldbank.org/7NP2KK1OH0.

World Bank. 2007. *Pakistan, Promoting Rural Growth and Poverty Reduction*. Report 39303-PK. Washington, DC: Sustainable Development Unit, South Asia Region, World Bank.

# 8

# THE PHILIPPINES

## Caesar B. Cororaton, Erwin Corong, and John Cockburn*

The agricultural sector in the Philippines employed 36 percent of the labor force and accounted for roughly 14 percent of the nation's GDP in 2004, or 26 percent of GDP if the agriculture-based food processing sector is included.

From the 1950s to the 1970s, government policies were biased against agriculture. Until the 1980s, these policies included the import-substitution policy, which created a bias in favor of manufacturing and penalized the returns to agricultural investments and exports. Export taxes and exchange rate overvaluation greatly reduced earnings from agriculture, and government intervention through the creation of government corporations siphoned off much of the gains from trade (Intal and Power 1990, David 2003). Then, the trade reform program in the 1980s led to a shift from taxing to protecting agriculture relative to nonagricultural sectors, and these policies became more pronounced when the country became a member of the World Trade Organization in 1995. As a result, the current system of protection favors agriculture through both applied tariff rates and nominal rates of assistance (NRAs) in agriculture that are substantially higher than the NRAs in manufacturing (Aldaba 2005; David, Intal, and Balisacan 2009). However, two decades of protection have failed to induce competitiveness and productivity growth in agriculture.

This chapter analyzes the poverty and inequality implications of the removal of agricultural and nonagricultural price distortions in the domestic markets of the

*The authors are grateful to Kym Anderson, Thomas Hertel, Will Martin, Ernesto Valenzuela, Dominique van der Mensbrugghe, and workshop participants for helpful comments.

Philippines and in markets abroad. As exogenous shocks, our analysis relies on the results of the rest-of-the-world trade liberalization simulations of the Linkage model of the World Bank, here also called the global model (see the appendix by van der Mensbrugghe, Valenzuela, and Anderson; see also van der Mensbrugghe 2005). We use these exogenous shocks, along with national liberalization shocks, to derive effects based on the computable general equilibrium (CGE) model for the Philippines by Cororaton and Corong (2009). The global model incorporates new estimates of agricultural protection and assistance for various developing countries, including the Philippines, and simulates scenarios involving full world trade liberalization in all sectors and in agriculture alone.[1] The global simulations generate changes in export and import prices at the border in the Philippines, as well as changes in world export demand for the products of the Philippines.[2] We apply these results, together with the new estimates of protection and assistance for the Philippines by David, Intal, and Balisacan (2009), as shocks to the CGE model for the Philippines to analyze the distributional, welfare, and poverty impacts of various trade liberalization scenarios for the country.

We conduct our simulation analysis in stages to assess the differing impacts that international market liberalization and domestic market liberalization may entail. In the first stage, we extract changes in the border export and import prices and changes in the world export demand for the products of the Philippines from the global model, and we apply these in the model for the Philippines without altering the existing trade protection system in the country. In the second stage, we simulate unilateral trade liberalization in the Philippines without incorporating any changes from the global model. Finally, we combine the rest-of-the-world liberalization shocks and the unilateral liberalization shocks to assess the total effects.

We conduct six policy experiments using separate scenarios for trade liberalization in all sectors and trade liberalization in the agricultural sector alone. We define the agricultural sector to include primary agriculture and lightly processed food.[3] In each scenario, we generate results at the macrolevel and sectoral level, as well as vectors of changes in household incomes, consumer prices, and sectoral employment shares. We then use the vectors of changes as inputs in a microsimulation procedure to calculate the impact on poverty and inequality. This calculation draws on data from a national household survey conducted in 2000.

The chapter is organized as follows. The next section sheds light on the degree of price distortions and trade protection and on poverty trends in the Philippines. The subsequent section presents the structure of the CGE model for the Philippines, which is based on the national social accounting matrix as of 2000. We then discuss the policy experiments and the results. The final section provides a summary of our findings and examines some policy implications.

## Trade and Assistance Policies and Poverty Trends

In 1949, the Philippines embarked on a development strategy geared toward industrial import substitution with a lesser emphasis on the agricultural and export sectors. The strategy provided protection to domestic producers of final goods through high tariff rates on nonessential consumer goods and low tariff rates on essential producer inputs. However, the policy was not effective: the growth of manufacturing value added and industrial employment increased minimally. In 1970, the government shifted toward export promotion by offering tax exemptions and fiscal incentives to capital-intensive firms located in export processing zones. This strategy also achieved little: the highly skewed structure of the tariff protection in favor of import-substituting manufactured goods remained. Moreover, the imposition of export taxes, an overvalued exchange rate, and the presence of government corporations that not only regulated domestic prices, but also siphoned off much of the gains from domestic and international trade created a strong bias against agriculture and exports.

The restrictive trade policies adopted between the 1950s and the late 1970s prevented efficient resource allocation and the smooth functioning of markets and penalized the domestic economy in three respects. First, import controls resulted in an overvalued exchange rate that favored import-substituting firms. Second, continued protection increased domestic output prices, which impeded forward links. Third, tariff escalations and import controls weakened backward links because the tariffs on capital and intermediate goods were maintained at low levels relative to the tariffs on finished products (Austria and Medalla 1996). This also promoted rent seeking and distorted the economic incentives for investment in agriculture. The agricultural sector, which served as the country's backbone in providing the necessary foreign exchange needed by the import-dependent manufacturing sector, stagnated. Meanwhile, the industrial sector ventured into import-dependent assembly operations with minimal value added content and little or no forward and backward links.

Realizing the pitfalls of the import-substitution policy and the unsuccessful export-promotion strategy, the government implemented a series of trade reform programs starting in 1981.[4] The Philippines has also been participating more actively in the multilateral trading system since it joined the World Trade Organization in 1995. For example, between 1995 and 1999, the country complied with all its multilateral commitments within the prescribed time frames (WTO 1999). These commitments included tariff bindings at a maximum of 10 percentage points over the 1995 applied rate on roughly 65 percent of all tariff lines, tariff bindings on selected information technology products, and bindings on market access in selected service sectors (Austria 2001). Nonetheless, there continues to be a substantial tariff binding overhang, especially in agriculture.[5]

By around 2000, the country had slowed the pace of trade reform (WTO 2005). Although the average applied most favored nation tariff rate declined from 9.7 to 5.8 percent between 1999 and 2003, it then rose to 7.4 percent in 2004. This reversal of the tariff adjustment process was brought about by presidential discretion and was aimed at helping problematic domestic industries and responding to lobbying from domestic interest groups.

### Estimates of the NRA to agriculture

David, Intal, and Balisacan (2009) have estimated the NRA to key industries in the agricultural sector. The NRA is the percentage difference between the domestic and the border price; it thus measures the direct effect of policy-induced distortions on producer incentives.

The NRA for coconuts (copra or dried coconuts) is negative throughout the years shown in table 8.1, largely because of export taxes, a coconut levy, and a copra export ban. The currency devaluation in the 1970s and the world commodity boom in the middle of that decade did not translate into higher profits for coconut farmers; rather, it translated into higher revenue for the government and lower raw material costs for the coconut oil milling industry. Although these policies began to be eliminated in 1986, coconut farmers remain penalized owing to the continued existence of a government corporation that controls 70–80 percent of coconut oil milling, thereby retaining a monopsonistic command over the domestic price of copra.

The NRA for corn has always been positive and exhibits an increasing trend. There is not much political pressure on corn compared with rice because corn is a subsistence crop among upland farmers in the southern part of the country. Nonetheless, it is also a major animal feed ingredient.

Among agricultural crops, sugar has had the highest NRA since the 1960s. In the 1960s and early 1970s, a major part of domestic production was exported to the high-priced U.S. market through a preferential access quota allocated to Philippine producers and sugar processors (known as the Laurel-Langley Agreement). This agreement ended in 1974, resulting in a dramatic drop in sugar exports from the Philippines to the United States.[6]

The NRA for chicken has been consistently high and well above the NRA for pork. However, the government imposed the same level of in-quota and out-of-quota tariffs for both commodities after the ratification of the World Trade Organization agreement in 1995.

Cattle were not included on the sensitive products list for the Philippines at the World Trade Organization. The NRA for cattle has therefore been low relative to the NRAs for chicken and pork. In the early 1990s, the government attempted to

**Table 8.1. The NRAs to Major Agricultural Commodities, the Philippines, 1960–2004**

*(percent)*

| Commodity | 1960–64 | 1965–69 | 1970–74 | 1975–79 | 1980–84 | 1985–89 | 1990–94 | 1995–99 | 2000–04 |
|---|---|---|---|---|---|---|---|---|---|
| Rice | 6 | −1 | −10 | −18 | −16 | 14 | 21 | 53 | 51 |
| Corn | 19 | 38 | 14 | 24 | 20 | 60 | 63 | 79 | 55 |
| Sugar | 18 | 121 | −12 | 2 | 60 | 13 | 49 | 97 | 79 |
| Domestic | 4 | 78 | −39 | −29 | 14 | 112 | 45 | 99 | 75 |
| Export | 28 | 154 | 16 | 17 | 89 | 161 | 77 | 90 | 130 |
| Coconut | | | | | | | | | |
| Copra | −12 | −20 | −25 | −17 | −27 | −21 | −15 | −8 | −14 |
| Coconut oil | −3 | −18 | −21 | −8 | −17 | −4 | 7 | 1 | 6 |
| Beef | 60 | −16 | −47 | −18 | −2 | −8 | 26 | 15 | −17 |
| Pork | −30 | 14 | 3 | −6 | 36 | 51 | 25 | 21 | −8 |
| Chicken | — | 67 | 29 | 28 | 38 | 43 | 57 | 42 | 52 |
| Other | 10 | 10 | 32 | 32 | 16 | 17 | 10 | 5 | 5 |

*Source:* David, Intal, and Balisacan (2009).

*Note:* — = no data are available.

promote the fattening of cattle and allowed duty-free imports of young cattle, while imposing more restrictive nontariff barriers on beef. Nonetheless, cattle fattening activities did not prosper because the tariffs on beef imports fell.

Before the mid-1980s, the NRAs for agricultural inputs such as fertilizer, agricultural chemicals, and farm machinery were generally higher than the NRAs for agricultural crops, averaging well above 20 percent (David, Intal, and Balisacan 2009). This was largely caused by the government's industrial promotion policies, which raised the domestic prices of the manufactured inputs to agriculture. However, after this period and during the trade liberalization process, there were substantial reductions in agricultural input protection, down to around 10 percent in the late 1990s and to a uniform 3 percent in 2000–04.

### Poverty trends

In rural and urban areas, over 60 percent of the expenditure of poor households goes for food, of which almost half is cereals, primarily rice and corn (table 8.2). Rural dwellers spend proportionately more than their urban counterparts on food. Food consumption among nonpoor households is relatively somewhat less (39 percent), and urban nonpoor households spend the least on food and cereals in relative terms (8 percent).

Figure 8.1 presents the evolution of the poverty headcount index between 1985 and 2000. The national headcount index decreased from almost 50 to roughly 34 percent over the period. However, the decline was concentrated mainly in urban areas, especially in the National Capital Region, where poverty was already low. In contrast, the rural headcount index fell only modestly, from 56 to 49 percent, compared with the fall in urban areas from 44 to 23 percent.

### Table 8.2. Poverty Incidence and Food Expenditure Shares, the Philippines, 1997 and 2000

*(percent)*

| Indicator | Rural | | Urban | |
|---|---|---|---|---|
| | 1997 | 2000 | 1997 | 2000 |
| Poverty incidence, % of population | 50.7 | 48.8 | 21.6 | 18.6 |

| Indicator | Poor | | Nonpoor | | Poor | | Nonpoor | |
|---|---|---|---|---|---|---|---|---|
| | 1997 | 2000 | 1997 | 2000 | 1997 | 2000 | 1997 | 2000 |
| Expenditure shares, % of total | | | | | | | | |
| All food | 63.6 | 63.6 | 47.6 | 47.6 | 61.4 | 60.8 | 38.8 | 38.7 |
| Cereals (mostly rice) | 29.5 | 28.8 | 15.4 | 14.6 | 24.5 | 23.0 | 8.6 | 8.2 |

*Source:* NSO (1997, 2000).

**Figure 8.1. Trends in Poverty Indexes, the Philippines, 1985–2000**

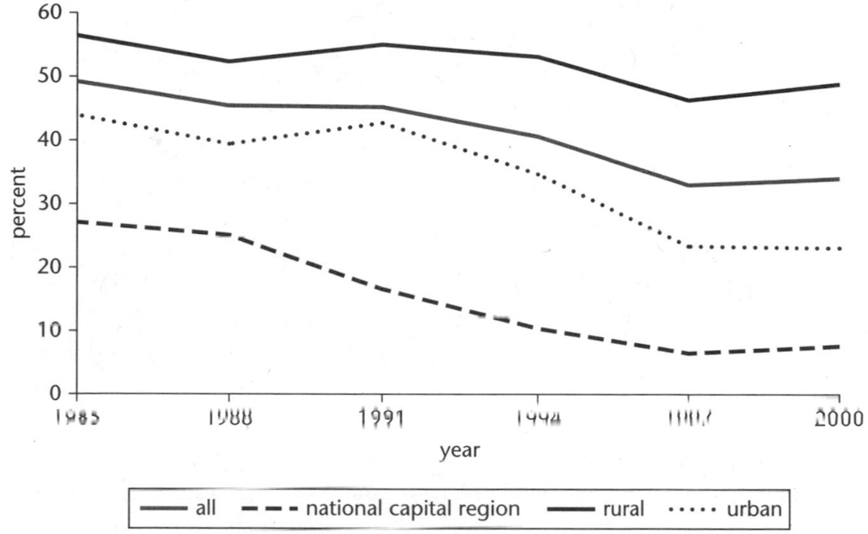

Source: NSO (1985–).

## The CGE Model

The national CGE model we use in our study is calibrated to the social accounting matrix of the Philippines for 2000.[7] There are 41 production sectors and four factors: two labor types (skilled workers with at least a college diploma and unskilled workers), plus capital and land. Institutions include the government, firms, households, and the rest of the world. Household categories are defined according to income deciles. Output ($X$) is a composite of value added ($VA$) and intermediate inputs. Output is sold either to the domestic market ($D$), or to the export market ($E$), or both. The model assumes perfect substitutability between $E$ and $D$. We assume a finite elasticity of export demand. There are two sources of domestic market supply: domestic output and imports ($M$). There is substitution between $D$ and $M$ depending on the changes in the relative prices of $D$ and $M$ and on a constant elasticity of substitution function.

Sectoral output is a Leontief function of intermediate inputs and value added. Value added in agriculture is a constant elasticity of substitution function of skilled labor, unskilled labor, capital, and land. Nonagricultural value added is also a constant elasticity of substitution function of the same factors, except land. Capital and land are each sector specific. Skilled and unskilled labor are mobile across sectors, but limited within skill category, and land use is mobile within the agricultural sector.

Households earn incomes from factors of production, transfers, foreign remittances, and dividends, while paying direct income taxes to the government. Household savings are a fixed proportion of disposable incomes, and household demand is represented by a linear expenditure system.

Government revenue is the sum of the direct taxes on the incomes of households and firms, indirect taxes on domestic and imported goods, and other receipts. The government spends on the consumption of goods and services, transfers, and other payments. In the present version of the model, we assume a fixed government balance. Since shifts in policy will result in changes in government income and expenditure, the government balance is held fixed through a tax replacement variable. For the present analysis, we use an indirect tax replacement on domestic sales, but we also compare the results with the effects of a direct tax replacement on household incomes. In either case, the tax replacement is endogenously determined so as to maintain a fixed government balance.

Foreign savings are held fixed. The nominal exchange rate is the model's numéraire. We introduce a weighted price of investment and derive total investment in real prices; total investment is held fixed by introducing an adjustment factor in the household savings function. Equilibrium is achieved in the model if the supply of and the demand for goods and services are equal and if investment is equal to savings.

Table 8.3 presents the production structure in the social accounting matrix. Generally, the agricultural and service sectors show greater shares of value added (as a percent of output) relative to the industrial sector. In agriculture, coconut and forestry have the largest shares of value added, almost 90 percent, while petroleum refining has the lowest share among the industrial sectors, at 14 percent. The capital-output ratio is generally lower in agriculture than in industry and the service sectors. The largest employer of labor is the service sector. More than 90 percent of the labor input in agricultural production is represented by unskilled labor. The share of skilled labor employed in the industrial sector is substantially greater than the corresponding share in the agricultural sector. The structure of indirect taxes reveals that tobacco and alcohol (23 percent), followed by petroleum (18 percent), are exposed to the highest indirect tax (table 8.3, last column).

Table 8.4 shows that almost 50 percent of total exports are electrical products. Almost 90 percent of the production of electrical products is exported. A major part of this sector is the semiconductor industry. A sizable share of exports are represented by machinery and transport equipment. This industry has a high export-intensity ratio, 73 percent.[8] It is followed in the size of the ratio by other manufacturing, coconut oil, leather, fertilizer, other chemicals,

**Table 8.3. Production Structure, the Philippines, 2000**
*(percent)*

| Sector | Value added/ output, % | % of value added | % of output | % of employment | Capital/ labor, % | % of skilled labor | % of unskilled labor | Land/ output, % | Indirect tax rate |
|---|---|---|---|---|---|---|---|---|---|
| **Agriculture** | | | | | | | | | |
| *Primary agriculture* | | | | | | | | | |
| Palay (rice) | 77.5 | 2.0 | 1.4 | 3.1 | 41 | 6.2 | 93.8 | 7.3 | 3.3 |
| Corn | 78.5 | 0.6 | 0.4 | 1.0 | 25 | 6.2 | 93.8 | 5.3 | 3.5 |
| Coconuts | 88.9 | 0.6 | 0.4 | 0.8 | 59 | 6.2 | 93.8 | 10.3 | 0.9 |
| Fruits and vegetables | 79.7 | 2.2 | 1.5 | 2.4 | 88 | 6.2 | 93.8 | 11.3 | 3.4 |
| Sugar | 69.7 | 0.3 | 0.2 | 0.3 | 83 | 6.2 | 93.8 | 11.2 | 1.8 |
| Other crops | 77.3 | 0.6 | 0.4 | 0.5 | 105 | 6.2 | 93.8 | 13.7 | 1.3 |
| Hogs | 63.7 | 1.4 | 1.1 | 1.6 | 84 | 9.5 | 90.5 | 6.8 | 2.2 |
| Cattle | 71.9 | 0.4 | 0.3 | 0.4 | 111 | 9.5 | 90.5 | 11.0 | 1.2 |
| Chickens | 60.7 | 1.3 | 1.1 | 1.4 | 92 | 9.5 | 90.5 | 8.7 | 2.4 |
| *Lightly processed food* | | | | | | | | | |
| Meat processing | 20.5 | 1.1 | 2.8 | 0.8 | 196 | 25.0 | 75.0 | n.a. | 1.6 |
| Milk and dairy | 31.1 | 0.3 | 0.5 | 0.2 | 210 | 25.0 | 75.0 | n.a. | 1.0 |
| Coconut and edible oil | 28.7 | 0.5 | 0.9 | 0.2 | 574 | 25.0 | 75.0 | n.a. | 0.9 |
| Milled rice and corn | 34.8 | 1.4 | 2.1 | 1.2 | 126 | 25.0 | 75.0 | n.a. | 2.0 |
| Milled sugar | 22.0 | 0.2 | 0.4 | 0.1 | 191 | 25.0 | 75.0 | n.a. | 1.4 |

*(Table continues on the following pages.)*

**Table 8.3. Production Structure, the Philippines, 2000 (*continued*)**
(*percent*)

| Sector | Value added/ output, % | % of value added | % of output | % of employment | Capital/ labor, % | % of skilled labor | % of unskilled labor | Land/ output, % | Indirect tax rate |
|---|---|---|---|---|---|---|---|---|---|
| **Nonagriculture** | | | | | | | | | |
| *Other primary products and mining* | | | | | | | | | |
| Agricultural services | 84.7 | 0.4 | 0.2 | 0.5 | 61 | 6.2 | 93.8 | 10.0 | 2.8 |
| Forestry | 89.4 | 0.2 | 0.1 | 0.1 | 217 | 16.9 | 83.1 | 33.0 | 3.9 |
| Fishing | 77.4 | 2.8 | 1.9 | 2.1 | 216 | 2.4 | 97.6 | 3.8 | 1.7 |
| Mining | 63.0 | 0.6 | 0.5 | 0.4 | 253 | 30.5 | 69.5 | n.a. | 2.2 |
| Crude oil and natural gas | 34.6 | 0.0 | 0.0 | 0.0 | n.a. | n.a. | n.a. | n.a. | 0.0 |
| *Highly processed food and tobacco* | | | | | | | | | |
| Fruit processing | 36.5 | 0.4 | 0.5 | 0.3 | 166 | 25.0 | 75.0 | n.a. | 2.2 |
| Fish processing | 28.5 | 0.3 | 0.6 | 0.2 | 355 | 25.0 | 75.0 | n.a. | 1.3 |
| Other processed food | 30.9 | 1.3 | 2.3 | 1.2 | 162 | 25.0 | 75.0 | n.a. | 1.6 |
| Tobacco and alcohol | 40.4 | 1.0 | 1.4 | 1.0 | 156 | 57.7 | 42.3 | n.a. | 22.9 |
| *Manufacturing* | | | | | | | | | |
| Textiles | 37.3 | 1.0 | 1.4 | 1.0 | 130 | 6.4 | 93.6 | n.a. | 0.7 |
| Garments and footwear | 46.1 | 2.1 | 2.4 | 1.9 | 162 | 4.5 | 95.5 | n.a. | 0.5 |
| Leather and rubber-wear | 42.9 | 0.7 | 0.9 | 0.7 | 143 | 9.8 | 90.2 | n.a. | 0.4 |
| Paper and wood products | 39.3 | 1.7 | 2.3 | 1.5 | 163 | 23.5 | 76.5 | n.a. | 0.7 |
| Fertilizer | 39.7 | 0.1 | 0.2 | 0.1 | 140 | 37.8 | 62.2 | n.a. | 0.5 |

| | | | | | | | | |
|---|---|---|---|---|---|---|---|---|
| Other chemicals | 41.1 | 1.9 | 2.4 | 1.5 | 201 | 37.8 | 62.2 | n.a. | 1.0 |
| *Petroleum* | 14.2 | 0.7 | 2.6 | 0.8 | 114 | 42.4 | 57.6 | n.a. | 17.7 |
| Cement and related products | 41.7 | 0.7 | 0.9 | 0.6 | 165 | 29.8 | 70.2 | n.a. | 1.9 |
| Metal and related products | 36.9 | 1.9 | 2.7 | 1.4 | 210 | 8.4 | 91.6 | n.a. | 1.1 |
| Machinery and transport equipment | 40.0 | 3.6 | 4.8 | 1.8 | 368 | 30.4 | 69.6 | n.a. | 1.7 |
| Electrical and related products | 45.5 | 8.5 | 9.9 | 7.3 | 171 | 39.5 | 60.5 | n.a. | 1.2 |
| Other manufacturing | 48.1 | 1.4 | 1.6 | 1.4 | 135 | 6.7 | 93.3 | n.a. | 1.8 |
| *Other industry* | | | | | | | | |
| Construction | 53.0 | 3.9 | 3.9 | 5.5 | 67 | 14.9 | 85.1 | n.a. | 1.4 |
| Utilities | 68.3 | 3.4 | 2.6 | 1.9 | 324 | 43.7 | 56.3 | n.a. | 3.2 |
| *Services* | | | | | | | | |
| Transportation and communications | 53.6 | 7.0 | 6.9 | 5.3 | 210 | 18.2 | 81.8 | n.a. | 1.2 |
| Wholesale trade | 66.1 | 13.2 | 10.6 | 10.7 | 192 | 25.6 | 74.4 | n.a. | 1.1 |
| Other services | 63.5 | 20.2 | 16.8 | 17.5 | 171 | 31.5 | 68.5 | n.a. | 2.9 |
| Public services | 72.2 | 8.2 | 6.0 | 19.3 | 41 | 60.7 | 39.3 | n.a. | 0.0 |

*Source:* Based on the national model in Cororaton and Corong (2009).

*Note:* n.a. = not applicable.

## Table 8.4. Trade Structure and Elasticity Parameters, the Philippines, 2000

| Sector | Elasticities[a] | | | | Exports, % | | Imports, % | |
|---|---|---|---|---|---|---|---|---|
| | sig_va | sig_m | eta | sig_e | Share | Intensity[b] | Share | Intensity[b] |
| **Agriculture** | | | | | | | | |
| *Primary agriculture* | | | | | | | | |
| Palay (rice) | 0.8 | 2.2 | 4.5 | 2.2 | 0.0 | 0.0 | 0.0 | 0.0 |
| Corn | 0.8 | 2.5 | 4.9 | 2.5 | 0.0 | 0.1 | 0.1 | 8.4 |
| Coconuts | 0.8 | 2.4 | 4.8 | 2.4 | 0.0 | 0.2 | 0.0 | 0.0 |
| Fruits and vegetables | 0.8 | 2.0 | 3.9 | 2.0 | 1.2 | 15.1 | 0.3 | 6.2 |
| Sugar | 0.8 | 3.0 | 5.9 | 3.0 | 0.0 | 0.0 | 0.0 | 0.0 |
| Other crops | 0.8 | 2.0 | 3.9 | 2.0 | 0.1 | 2.8 | 1.2 | 44.2 |
| Hogs | 0.8 | 2.0 | 3.9 | 2.0 | 0.0 | 0.0 | 0.0 | 0.0 |
| Cattle | 0.8 | 2.0 | 3.9 | 2.0 | 0.0 | 0.2 | 0.1 | 9.2 |
| Chickens | 0.8 | 2.0 | 3.9 | 2.0 | 0.0 | 0.0 | 0.0 | 0.4 |
| *Lightly processed food* | | | | | | | | |
| Meat processing | 1.5 | 2.0 | 3.9 | 2.0 | 0.0 | 0.0 | 0.4 | 3.4 |
| Milk and dairy | 1.5 | 2.0 | 3.9 | 2.0 | 0.0 | 1.7 | 1.0 | 33.6 |
| Coconut and edible oil | 1.5 | 2.0 | 3.9 | 2.0 | 1.5 | 32.9 | 0.6 | 19.0 |
| Milled rice and corn | 1.5 | 2.2 | 4.5 | 2.2 | 0.0 | 0.0 | 0.8 | 8.8 |
| Milled sugar | 1.5 | 3.0 | 5.9 | 3.0 | 0.2 | 8.3 | 0.1 | 8.2 |
| **Nonagriculture** | | | | | | | | |
| *Other primary products and mining* | | | | | | | | |
| Agricultural services | 0.8 | 2.2 | 4.3 | 2.2 | 0.0 | 0.0 | 0.0 | 0.1 |
| Forestry | 0.8 | 2.2 | 4.3 | 2.2 | 0.1 | 10.3 | 0.0 | 0.6 |
| Fishing | 0.8 | 2.2 | 4.3 | 2.2 | 0.8 | 7.9 | 0.0 | 0.3 |
| Mining | 0.8 | 2.2 | 4.3 | 2.2 | 0.4 | 15.8 | 1.4 | 45.8 |
| Crude oil and natural gas | 0.8 | 2.2 | 4.3 | 2.2 | 0.0 | 0.0 | 7.5 | 99.6 |
| *Highly processed food and tobacco* | | | | | | | | |
| Fruit processing | 1.5 | 2.0 | 3.9 | 2.0 | 0.7 | 24.1 | 0.3 | 13.9 |
| Fish processing | 1.5 | 2.0 | 3.9 | 2.0 | 0.7 | 22.0 | 0.2 | 7.4 |
| Other processed food | 1.5 | 2.0 | 3.9 | 2.0 | 0.6 | 4.8 | 0.9 | 9.3 |
| Tobacco and alcohol | 1.5 | 2.0 | 3.9 | 2.0 | 0.1 | 1.4 | 0.3 | 5.7 |
| *Manufacturing* | | | | | | | | |
| Textiles | 1.5 | 2.1 | 4.1 | 2.1 | 1.2 | 16.9 | 2.7 | 36.7 |
| Garments and footwear | 1.5 | 2.1 | 4.1 | 2.1 | 0.2 | 1.8 | 0.1 | 1.3 |
| Leather and rubber-wear | 1.5 | 2.0 | 4.1 | 2.0 | 1.3 | 26.6 | 2.3 | 45.6 |
| Paper and wood products | 1.5 | 2.0 | 4.1 | 2.0 | 2.3 | 19.7 | 1.8 | 19.3 |
| Fertilizer | 1.5 | 2.0 | 4.1 | 2.0 | 0.1 | 16.8 | 0.5 | 49.4 |
| Other chemicals | 1.5 | 2.0 | 4.1 | 2.0 | 0.9 | 7.4 | 5.0 | 35.4 |
| Petroleum | 1.5 | 2.0 | 4.1 | 2.0 | 1.6 | 11.8 | 1.8 | 16.6 |

**Table 8.4. Trade Structure and Elasticity Parameters, the Philippines, 2000 (*continued*)**

| Sector | Elasticities[a] | | | | Exports, % | | Imports, % | |
|---|---|---|---|---|---|---|---|---|
| | sig_va | sig_m | eta | sig_e | Share | Intensity[b] | Share | Intensity[b] |
| Cement and related products | 1.5 | 2.0 | 4.1 | 2.0 | 0.4 | 9.5 | 0.5 | 13.8 |
| Metal and related products | 1.5 | 2.0 | 4.1 | 2.0 | 2.5 | 17.4 | 4.2 | 31.7 |
| Machinery and transport equipment | 1.5 | 2.0 | 4.1 | 2.0 | 18.3 | 73.2 | 12.5 | 70.6 |
| Electrical and related products | 1.5 | 2.0 | 4.1 | 2.0 | 45.9 | 89.0 | 35.2 | 88.9 |
| Other manufacturing | 1.5 | 2.0 | 4.1 | 2.0 | 3.7 | 44.3 | 2.0 | 36.1 |
| *Other industry* | | | | | | | | |
| Construction | 1.5 | 1.0 | 2.1 | 1.0 | 0.3 | 1.5 | 0.3 | 1.9 |
| Utilities | 1.5 | 1.0 | 2.1 | 1.0 | 0.0 | 0.0 | 0.0 | 0.0 |
| *Services* | | | | | | | | |
| Transportation and communications | 1.5 | 1.0 | 2.1 | 1.0 | 3.7 | 10.2 | 8.1 | 24.2 |
| Wholesale trade | 1.5 | 1.0 | 2.1 | 1.0 | 2.9 | 5.2 | 0.6 | 1.5 |
| Other services | 1.5 | 1.0 | 2.1 | 1.0 | 8.4 | 9.5 | 6.9 | 10.0 |
| Public services | n.a. | n.a. | n.a. | n.a. | n.a. | n.a. | n.a. | n.a. |

*Source:* Based on the national model in Cororaton and Corong (2009).

*Note:* n.a. = not applicable.

a. *sig_va* = substitution parameter in the constant elasticity of substitution value added function.
  *sig_m* = substitution parameter in the constant elasticity of substitution composite good function.
  *eta* = export demand elasticity.
  *sig_e* = substitution parameter in the constant elasticity of transformation.
b. Exports, divided by output; imports divided by the composite good's consumption.

garments, fruit processing, and fish processing. On the import side, electrical products, as well as machinery and transport equipment, have high import-intensity ratios, accounting for 35 and 12 percent of total domestic sales, respectively. Other sectors in which imports are a major source of domestic supply include other crops, cattle, mining and crude oil, milk and dairy, fruit processing, fish processing, coconut oil, sugar milling, other food, textiles, leather, paper, fertilizer, other chemicals, petroleum, cement, and transportation and communications.

Table 8.4 also shows the values of key elasticity parameters used in the model: the import substitution elasticity (*sig_m*) in the constant elasticity of substitution composite good function, the production substitution elasticity (*sig_va*) in the constant elasticity of substitution value added production function, and the export demand elasticity (*eta*), which is obtained from the Armington parameter of the global model.

The consumption structure of households is presented in table 8.5. Rice is a significant staple among Filipinos, especially among poorer households. It accounts for 14.3 of total expenditure among the first household decile, but the share decreases substantially as households become richer. Fish and meat, fruits and vegetables, and other food are the other significant items in household consumption. Generally, the lower-income groups show substantial expenditure on food and food-related products. For instance, food items account for 42.4 percent of total expenditure among the first decile compared with 13.4 percent among the tenth decile. Richer households spend more on services relative to poorer households. Products of special interest are corn, sugar, chicken, meat processing, milk and dairy, processed fruit, processed fish, milled rice and corn, and milled sugar. The shares of expenditure on these special products decline as households become richer: they account for 25 percent of consumption among the first decile, but only 8.6 percent among the tenth decile.

## Simulations

All policy experiments reported in our study rely on an indirect tax replacement scheme to maintain fixed government balance. We generate results at the macrolevel and the sectoral level, as well as vectors of changes in household incomes, consumer prices, and sectoral employment shares. We then use the vectors of changes as inputs in a microsimulation procedure to calculate the impacts on poverty and inequality based on a household survey in 2000. We also undertake a sensitivity analysis with an alternative direct tax replacement scheme.

### Definition of policy experiments

Table 8.6 shows the sectoral correspondence between the CGE model for the Philippines and the global model, as well as information on the sectoral tariff rates and export subsidies based on new estimates of nominal rates of protection and assistance for the Philippines. The CGE model for the Philippines is initially solved using these new estimates of protection and assistance to create the base with which all subsequent simulations may be compared. In certain policy experiments, we use the global simulation results from the global model as policy shocks for the model for the Philippines, following the method proposed by Horridge and Zhai (2006).

**Table 8.5. Structure of Household Expenditure, by Decile, the Philippines, 2000**
(percent)

| Sector | Decile | | | | | | | | | |
|---|---|---|---|---|---|---|---|---|---|---|
| | 1 | 2 | 3 | 4 | 5 | 6 | 7 | 8 | 9 | 10 |
| **Agriculture** | | | | | | | | | | |
| *Primary agriculture* | | | | | | | | | | |
| Corn | 0.5 | 0.4 | 0.4 | 0.3 | 0.3 | 0.2 | 0.2 | 0.2 | 0.1 | 0.1 |
| Coconuts | 0.3 | 0.3 | 0.3 | 0.3 | 0.2 | 0.2 | 0.2 | 0.2 | 0.2 | 0.1 |
| Fruits and vegetables | 4.1 | 3.8 | 3.6 | 3.4 | 3.1 | 2.8 | 2.5 | 2.2 | 1.9 | 1.3 |
| Sugar | 0.0 | 0.0 | 0.0 | 0.0 | 0.0 | 0.0 | 0.0 | 0.0 | 0.0 | 0.0 |
| Other crops | 0.2 | 0.2 | 0.2 | 0.2 | 0.2 | 0.1 | 0.1 | 0.1 | 0.1 | 0.0 |
| Chickens | 0.8 | 0.9 | 0.9 | 1.0 | 1.1 | 1.1 | 1.1 | 1.1 | 1.0 | 0.7 |
| *Lightly processed food* | | | | | | | | | | |
| Meat processing | 4.2 | 4.6 | 4.9 | 5.6 | 6.2 | 6.8 | 7.1 | 6.8 | 6.3 | 4.2 |
| Milk and dairy | 1.1 | 1.2 | 1.3 | 1.3 | 1.4 | 1.3 | 1.3 | 1.2 | 1.1 | 0.8 |
| Coconut and edible oil | 0.7 | 0.6 | 0.6 | 0.6 | 0.5 | 0.5 | 0.4 | 0.4 | 0.3 | 0.2 |
| Milled rice and corn | 14.3 | 12.9 | 11.7 | 10.0 | 8.4 | 6.9 | 5.7 | 4.5 | 3.4 | 1.8 |
| Milled sugar | 1.2 | 1.1 | 1.0 | 1.0 | 0.9 | 0.8 | 0.7 | 0.6 | 0.5 | 0.3 |
| **Nonagriculture** | | | | | | | | | | |
| *Other primary products and mining* | | | | | | | | | | |
| Forestry | 0.0 | 0.0 | 0.0 | 0.0 | 0.0 | 0.0 | 0.0 | 0.0 | 0.0 | 0.0 |
| Fishing | 6.8 | 6.4 | 6.1 | 5.5 | 4.9 | 4.2 | 3.6 | 3.1 | 2.5 | 1.5 |
| Mining | 0.1 | 0.1 | 0.1 | 0.0 | 0.0 | 0.0 | 0.1 | 0.1 | 0.1 | 0.1 |
| *Highly processed food, and tobacco* | | | | | | | | | | |
| Fruit processing | 1.2 | 1.1 | 1.0 | 0.9 | 0.9 | 0.8 | 0.7 | 0.6 | 0.5 | 0.4 |
| Fish processing | 2.0 | 1.9 | 1.8 | 1.5 | 1.4 | 1.2 | 1.1 | 0.9 | 0.7 | 0.4 |

(Table continues on the following page.)

**Table 8.5. Structure of Household Expenditure, by Decile, the Philippines, 2000 (*continued*)**
(*percent*)

| Sector | Decile | | | | | | | | | |
|---|---|---|---|---|---|---|---|---|---|---|
| | 1 | 2 | 3 | 4 | 5 | 6 | 7 | 8 | 9 | 10 |
| Other processed food | 5.1 | 4.8 | 4.7 | 4.3 | 4.0 | 3.7 | 3.3 | 2.9 | 2.5 | 1.6 |
| Tobacco and alcohol | 4.5 | 4.8 | 4.9 | 4.8 | 4.5 | 4.2 | 3.6 | 3.1 | 2.6 | 1.6 |
| *Mining and manufacturing* | | | | | | | | | | |
| Textiles | 0.8 | 0.9 | 1.0 | 1.0 | 1.0 | 1.0 | 0.9 | 0.9 | 0.9 | 0.8 |
| Garments and footwear | 1.7 | 1.9 | 2.1 | 2.2 | 2.2 | 2.1 | 2.1 | 2.0 | 2.0 | 1.7 |
| Leather and rubber-wear | 0.3 | 0.4 | 0.4 | 0.4 | 0.4 | 0.4 | 0.4 | 0.4 | 0.4 | 0.3 |
| Paper and wood products | 0.8 | 0.7 | 0.7 | 0.7 | 0.6 | 0.6 | 0.6 | 0.6 | 0.7 | 0.9 |
| Fertilizer | 0.0 | 0.0 | 0.0 | 0.0 | 0.0 | 0.0 | 0.0 | 0.0 | 0.0 | 0.0 |
| Other chemicals | 2.7 | 2.4 | 2.2 | 2.1 | 1.9 | 1.8 | 1.8 | 1.9 | 2.2 | 3.1 |
| Petroleum | 1.9 | 1.6 | 1.6 | 1.6 | 1.6 | 1.5 | 1.5 | 1.4 | 1.3 | 0.9 |
| Cement and related products | 0.1 | 0.1 | 0.1 | 0.1 | 0.1 | 0.1 | 0.1 | 0.1 | 0.1 | 0.1 |
| Machinery and transport equipment | 0.1 | 0.3 | 0.3 | 0.5 | 0.7 | 0.9 | 1.0 | 1.1 | 1.1 | 1.3 |
| Electrical and related products | 0.3 | 0.7 | 0.8 | 1.1 | 1.5 | 1.8 | 1.9 | 2.1 | 2.2 | 2.4 |
| Other manufacturing | 0.6 | 0.8 | 0.9 | 0.9 | 1.0 | 1.1 | 1.1 | 1.1 | 1.1 | 1.0 |
| *Other industry* | | | | | | | | | | |
| Utilities | 3.4 | 3.0 | 2.9 | 2.9 | 2.9 | 2.8 | 2.8 | 2.6 | 2.3 | 1.7 |
| *Services* | | | | | | | | | | |
| Transportation and communications | 6.0 | 7.0 | 7.3 | 8.2 | 9.4 | 10.1 | 11.5 | 12.9 | 14.7 | 17.4 |
| Wholesale trade | 17.8 | 17.5 | 17.1 | 16.7 | 16.3 | 15.9 | 15.7 | 15.5 | 15.3 | 14.6 |
| Other services | 16.5 | 17.5 | 18.8 | 20.8 | 22.2 | 24.8 | 26.9 | 29.3 | 32.0 | 38.7 |
| Total | 100.0 | 100.0 | 100.0 | 100.0 | 100.0 | 100.0 | 100.0 | 100.0 | 100.0 | 100.0 |

*Source:* Based on the national model in Cororaton and Corong (2009).

*Note:* There is no household consumption of agricultural services, crude oil and natural gas mining, and several other categories.

**Table 8.6. Exogenous Demand and Price Shocks Caused by Rest-of-the-World Liberalization**
*(percent)*

| Philippine CGE model | Linkage model | Trade distortions | | Full trade liberalization, excluding Philippines[a] | | | Agricultural trade liberalization, excluding Philippines[b] | | |
|---|---|---|---|---|---|---|---|---|---|
| | | Tariff, % | Export subsidy, % (<0 = tax) | Export price, % change | Import price, % change | Export demand shifter,[c] % | Export price, % change | Import price, % change | Export demand shifter,[c] % |
| **Agriculture** | | | | | | | | | |
| *Primary agriculture* | | | | | | | | | |
| Palay (rice) | Paddy rice | 19.6 | 0.0 | 0.0 | 0.0 | 1.0 | 0.0 | 0.0 | 1.0 |
| Corn | Other grains | 29.6 | 0.0 | 0.0 | | 1.0 | 0.0 | 5.7 | 1.0 |
| Coconuts | Oilseeds | 4.8 | −10.0 | 0.0 | −0.8 | 1.0 | 0.0 | −0.5 | 1.0 |
| Fruits and vegetables | Vegetables and fruits | 8.7 | 0.0 | 5.7 | | 1.1 | 3.8 | 1.7 | 1.2 |
| Sugar | Sugarcane and beets | 0.0 | 0.0 | 0.0 | | 1.0 | 0.0 | 0.0 | 1.0 |
| Other crops | Other crops | 3.9 | 0.0 | 5.9 | | 1.0 | 3.9 | 1.4 | 1.0 |
| Hogs | Other livestock | −18.7 | 0.0 | 5.6 | | 1.0 | 3.6 | 0.1 | 1.0 |
| Cattle | Cattle | −18.7 | 0.0 | 5.6 | | 1.0 | 3.6 | 0.1 | 1.0 |
| Chickens | Cattle, sheep, other | 10.0 | 0.0 | 0.0 | | 1.0 | 0.0 | 5.5 | 1.0 |
| *Lightly processed food* | | | | | | | | | |
| Beef and sheep meat | Meat processing | 9.0 | 0.0 | 3.7 | | 0.5 | 2.0 | 4.5 | 0.5 |
| Dairy products | Milk and dairy | 4.1 | 0.0 | 4.9 | | 1.1 | 4.2 | 7.4 | 1.1 |
| Coconut and edible oil | Vegetable oils and fats | 4.4 | 0.0 | 2.6 | | 1.0 | 0.9 | −1.7 | 1.0 |
| Milled rice and corn | Processed rice | 29.0 | 0.0 | 5.3 | | 0.8 | 3.3 | 1.6 | 0.8 |
| Milled sugar | Refined sugar | 73.2 | 0.0 | 3.9 | | 1.5 | 2.0 | 0.8 | 1.6 |

*(Table continues on the following pages.)*

**Table 8.6. Exogenous Demand and Price Shocks Caused by Rest-of-the-World Liberalization** (*continued*)
(*percent*)

| Philippine CGE model | Linkage model | Trade distortions | | Full trade liberalization, excluding Philippines[a] | | | Agricultural trade liberalization, excluding Philippines[b] | | |
|---|---|---|---|---|---|---|---|---|---|
| | | Tariff, % | Export subsidy, % (<0 = tax) | Export price, % change | Import price, % change | Export demand shifter,[c] % | Export price, % change | Import price, % change | Export demand shifter,[c] % |
| *Nonagriculture* | | | | | | | | | |
| *Other primary products and mining* | | | | | | | | | |
| Agricultural services | | 2.7 | −1.0 | 2.8 | 0.6 | 1.1 | 1.0 | 0.9 | 1.0 |
| Forestry | | 2.7 | −1.0 | 2.8 | 0.6 | 1.1 | 1.0 | 0.9 | 1.0 |
| Fishing | Other primary products | 2.7 | −1.0 | 2.8 | 0.6 | 1.1 | 1.0 | 0.9 | 1.0 |
| Mining | | 2.7 | −1.0 | 2.8 | 0.6 | 1.1 | 1.0 | 0.9 | 1.0 |
| Crude oil and natural gas | | 2.7 | −1.0 | 2.8 | 0.6 | 1.1 | 1.0 | 0.9 | 1.0 |
| *Highly processed food and tobacco* | | | | | | | | | |
| Fruit processing | | 6.0 | 0.0 | 3.6 | 1.6 | 1.2 | 2.0 | −0.4 | 1.0 |
| Fish processing | Other food, beverages, | 6.0 | 0.0 | 3.6 | 1.6 | 1.2 | 2.0 | −0.4 | 1.0 |
| Other processed food | and tobacco | 6.0 | 0.0 | 3.6 | 1.6 | 1.2 | 2.0 | −0.4 | 1.0 |
| Tobacco and alcohol | | 6.0 | 0.0 | 3.6 | 1.6 | 1.2 | 2.0 | −0.4 | 1.0 |
| *Manufacturing* | | | | | | | | | |
| Textiles | Textiles and | 8.0 | −1.7 | 2.0 | −0.2 | 1.0 | 1.1 | 0.4 | 1.0 |
| Garments and footwear | wearing apparel | 8.0 | −1.7 | 2.0 | −0.2 | 1.0 | 1.1 | 0.4 | 1.0 |
| Leather and rubber-wear | | 8.0 | −1.7 | 2.0 | −0.2 | 1.0 | 1.1 | 0.4 | 1.0 |
| Paper and wood products | | 3.5 | 0.0 | 2.1 | 1.5 | 1.0 | 0.7 | 0.3 | 1.0 |
| Fertilizer | | 3.5 | 0.0 | 2.1 | 1.5 | 1.0 | 0.7 | 0.3 | 1.0 |
| Other chemicals | | 3.5 | 0.0 | 2.1 | 1.5 | 1.0 | 0.7 | 0.3 | 1.0 |

| | | | | | | | | |
|---|---|---|---|---|---|---|---|---|
| Petroleum | Other manufacturing | 3.5 | 0.0 | 2.1 | 1.5 | 1.0 | 0.7 | 0.3 | 1.0 |
| Cement and related products | | 3.5 | 0.0 | 2.1 | 1.5 | 1.0 | 0.7 | 0.3 | 1.0 |
| Metal and related products | | 3.5 | 0.0 | 2.1 | 1.5 | 1.0 | 0.7 | 0.3 | 1.0 |
| Machinery and transport equipment | | 3.5 | 0.0 | 2.1 | 1.5 | 1.0 | 0.7 | 0.3 | 1.0 |
| Electrical and related products | | 3.5 | 0.0 | 2.1 | 1.5 | 1.0 | 0.7 | 0.3 | 1.0 |
| Other manufacturing | | 3.5 | 0.0 | 2.1 | 1.5 | 1.0 | 0.7 | 0.3 | 1.0 |
| *Other industry* | | | | | | | | | |
| Construction | Services | 0.0 | 0.0 | 2.9 | −0. | 1.0 | 1.1 | 0.2 | 1.0 |
| Utilities | | 0.0 | 0.0 | 2.9 | −0. | 1.0 | 1.1 | 0.2 | 1.0 |
| *Services* | | | | | | | | | |
| Transport and communications | Services | 0.0 | 0.0 | 2.9 | −0. | 1.0 | 1.1 | 0.2 | 1.0 |
| Wholesale trade | | 0.0 | 0.0 | 2.9 | −0. | 1.0 | 1.1 | 0.2 | 1.0 |
| Other services | | 0.0 | 0.0 | 2.9 | −0. | 1.0 | 1.1 | 0.2 | 1.0 |

*Source:* Linkage model simulations by van der Mensbrugghe, Valenzuela, and Anderson (see the appendix).

a. Rest-of-the-world liberalization in all sectors, excluding the Philippines.

b. Rest-of-the-world liberalization in agriculture only, excluding the Philippines.

c. Derived using $(1 + 0.01 * p) (1 + 0.01 * q)^{\wedge}(1/ESUBM)$, where $p$ is the export price change; $q$ is the export volume change; and $ESUBM$ is the Armington import elasticity taken from the global (Linkage) model.

The six policy experiments are as follows:

- *ROW-ALL*, rest-of-the-world trade liberalization in all sectors, excluding the Philippines: This experiment uses the results of the global model under full rest-of-the-world liberalization in table 8.6 and retains all existing trade distortions (tariff rates and export subsidies) in the Philippines.
- *ROW-AGR*, rest-of-the-world trade liberalization in agriculture and lightly processed food only: As with *ROW-ALL*, this experiment uses the results of the global model, but only under rest-of-the-world liberalization in agriculture and lightly processed food, and retains all existing trade distortions in the Philippines.
- *PHIL-ALL*, unilateral trade liberalization in all sectors: All trade distortions in the Philippines are eliminated. No changes in the sectoral border export prices and import prices or in export demand are included in this unilateral liberalization.
- *PHIL-AGR*, unilateral agriculture trade liberalization: All trade distortions in primary agriculture and lightly processed foods in the Philippines are eliminated. Similar to *PHIL-ALL*, there are no changes in the sectoral border export prices and import prices or in export demand in this unilateral liberalization.
- *COMB-ALL*, full trade liberalization in the rest of the world and in the Philippines: This scenario combines *ROW-ALL* and *PHIL-ALL* in a global liberalization.
- *COMB-AGR*, liberalization in agriculture and lightly processed foods in the rest of the world and in the Philippines: This scenario combines *ROW-AGR* and *PHIL-AGR*.

## Results

In this subsection, we present the modeling results of our six policy experiments and then report the impacts on household income and welfare and on poverty and inequality. The subsection concludes with additional results that show the sensitivity of the core results to changes in the treatment of tax adjustments in the model.

### Rest-of-the-world trade liberalization in all sectors (*ROW-ALL*)

The results of the Linkage model in table 8.6 indicate that this first policy experiment leads to higher export prices and greater export demand for the products of the Philippines. Within agriculture, a significant shift in export demand is observed in milled sugar, as well as raw fruits and vegetables (at 1.5 and 1.1 percent, respectively). This is also true in fruit and fish processing (1.2 percent), whereas slightly more modest shifts in export demand are observed in other industrial and service sectors. Meanwhile, full rest-of-the-world liberalization leads to higher world import prices for most Philippine goods.

Table 8.7 shows that export prices overall rise more in the agricultural sectors than in the nonagricultural sectors (by an average of 3.6 versus 2.4 percent in local currency). So, too, do export volumes: they expand 9.8 percent in agriculture compared with a modest 0.3 percent rise in nonagriculture. Local import prices also increase more in agriculture than in nonagriculture (3.0 versus 1.1 percent). Substitution toward imported goods is observed owing to a larger rise in the prices of domestically produced goods relative to the prices of the corresponding imported products. Because of this, agricultural and nonagricultural import volumes increase by 0.9 and 1.1 percent, respectively (table 8.7, second column).

The entire agricultural sector benefits from the improved international market conditions. Agricultural output and value added prices increase by 3.5 and 3.9 percent, respectively. Thus, the returns to agriculture-specific factors, particularly land and agricultural capital (which increase by 5.1 and 4.7 percent, respectively), rise relative to wage rates (3 percent) and to the returns to nonagricultural capital (2.9 percent). Unskilled wages increase slightly more than skilled wages because unskilled workers are used more intensively in the expanding agricultural sector.

In contrast, in the nonagricultural sectors, the fall in domestic sales offsets the export expansion. Thus, the volume of output contracts by 0.1 percent. Essentially, this is traceable to the import–domestic price substitution effects (see elsewhere above), the fall in the world import prices for essential consumer goods such as garments (table 8.6), and the appreciation in the real exchange rate. Despite falling output volumes, nonagricultural output prices still increase by 2.5 percent owing to the higher export prices. Hence, the returns to factors such as nonagricultural capital and skilled workers, which are used intensively in nonagriculture, increase as well.

### Rest-of-the-world trade liberalization in agriculture only (ROW-AGR)

The results of the ROW-AGR scenario are similar, but smaller in magnitude relative to the results of the ROW-ALL scenario. We only focus on the results that are different in this scenario because the mechanisms driving the model results are essentially the same in the ROW-ALL and ROW-AGR scenarios. Agricultural exports increase by 11 percent mainly because of a significant export demand shift in sugar, as well as raw fruits and vegetables (1.6 and 1.2 percent, respectively; see tables 8.6 and 8.7). A distinct feature of this scenario is that domestic agricultural prices increase relatively less than agricultural import prices (1.7 versus 2.7 percent). In the face of more expensive agricultural imports, domestic demand expands, while imports fall (0.1 and 1.2 percent, respectively). Agricultural output

**Table 8.7. Aggregate Simulation Results of Prospective Liberalizations in Agriculture and Nonagriculture, the Philippines**

*(percent change from the baseline)*

| Indicator | ROW-ALL | | ROW-AGR | | PHIL-ALL | | PHIL-AGR | | COMB-ALL | | COMB-AGR | |
|---|---|---|---|---|---|---|---|---|---|---|---|---|
| | Ag | Nonag | Ag | Nonag | Ag | Nonag | Ag | Nonag | Ag | Nonag | Ag | Nonag |
| Real GDP | 0.3 | | 0.1 | | 0.8 | | 0.2 | | 1.1 | | 0.3 | |
| *Prices* | | | | | | | | | | | | |
| Real exchange rate | −1.0 | | −0.4 | | 1.6 | | 0.8 | | 0.6 | | 0.4 | |
| Export price in local currency | 3.6 | 2.4 | 2.0 | 0.8 | −1.8 | −1.0 | −1.3 | −0.3 | 1.8 | 1.4 | 0.7 | 0.4 |
| Import price in local currency | 3.0 | 1.1 | 2.7 | 0.3 | −7.2 | −2.1 | −7.9 | 0.1 | −4.5 | −1.1 | −5.4 | 0.5 |
| Domestic price | 3.5 | 2.6 | 1.7 | 0.9 | −2.3 | −1.7 | −2.2 | −0.7 | 1.2 | 0.8 | −0.5 | 0.2 |
| Output price | 3.5 | 2.5 | 1.7 | 0.9 | −3.1 | −1.6 | −2.3 | −0.6 | 0.4 | 0.9 | −0.6 | 0.3 |
| Value added price | 3.9 | 2.9 | 2.0 | 1.0 | −4.0 | −1.6 | −2.9 | −0.7 | −0.1 | 1.3 | −0.8 | 0.2 |
| Consumer price index | 2.6 | | 1.0 | | −1.3 | | −1.1 | | 1.2 | | −0.1 | |
| *Volume* | | | | | | | | | | | | |
| Imports | 0.9 | 1.1 | −1.2 | 0.3 | 15.1 | 2.1 | 17.0 | 0.7 | 16.2 | 3.2 | 15.8 | 1.0 |
| Exports | 9.8 | 0.3 | 11.0 | −0.1 | 8.5 | 3.5 | 6.2 | 1.1 | 19.5 | 3.8 | 18.2 | 0.9 |
| Domestic demand | 0.2 | −0.2 | 0.1 | −0.1 | −3.1 | −0.6 | −2.8 | 0.2 | −2.9 | −0.8 | −2.6 | 0.0 |

| | | | | | | | | | | | |
|---|---|---|---|---|---|---|---|---|---|---|---|
| Composite good | 0.2 | 0.2 | 0.0 | 0.0 | -0.8 | 0.0 | -0.4 | 0.1 | -0.6 | 0.1 | -0.4 | 0.1 |
| Output | 0.6 | -0.1 | 0.6 | -0.1 | -2.5 | 0.3 | -2.4 | 0.3 | -1.9 | 0.3 | -1.7 | 0.2 |
| Value added | 0.7 | -0.1 | 0.7 | -0.1 | -2.3 | 0.3 | -2.4 | 0.3 | -1.6 | 0.2 | -1.5 | 0.2 |
| *Factor prices* | | | | | | | | | | | | |
| Nominal wages of skilled workers | 2.9 | | 1.0 | | -1.6 | | -0.9 | | 1.3 | | 0.1 | |
| Nominal wages of unskilled workers | 3.1 | | 1.1 | | -2.2 | | -1.2 | | 0.8 | | -0.1 | |
| Nominal returns to land | 5.1 | n.a. | 3.0 | n.a. | -4.7 | n.a. | -3.5 | n.a. | 0.3 | n.a. | -0.5 | n.a. |
| Nominal returns to capital | 4.7 | 2.9 | 2.9 | 0.9 | -5.7 | -1.3 | -4.5 | -0.5 | -1.2 | 1.6 | -1.7 | 0.4 |

*Source:* National CGE model simulations of the authors.

*Note:* Ag = agriculture, which includes primary agriculture and lightly processed food. Nonag = nonagriculture, which includes other primary products, highly processed foods, manufacturing, and services. n.a. = not applicable.

therefore expands because domestic demand in agriculture accounts for a larger share of domestic agricultural output.

The absence of nonagricultural liberalization results in a 0.1 percent decline in nonagricultural exports because most nonagricultural goods show little or no change in world export demand (table 8.6). Nonagricultural imports rise, while domestic demand declines (0.3 versus 0.1 percent) because domestic prices increase relatively more than import prices (0.9 versus 0.3 percent). The contraction in domestic demand, together with the 0.1 percent decline in exports, leads to a 0.1 percent drop in nonagricultural output. Nonetheless, nonagricultural output and value added prices still increase, owing to higher export and domestic prices.

### Full unilateral trade liberalization in the Philippines (*PHIL-ALL*)

This experiment eliminates all sectoral tariff rates and export subsidies in the Philippines and assumes that there are no changes in the global model. *PHIL-ALL* leads to a 7.2 and 2.1 percent decline in the local prices of imported agricultural and nonagricultural products, respectively (table 8.7). Import prices fall more, and import volumes correspondingly increase more in agriculture than in non-agriculture because the initial distortions are greater in agriculture. In the face of cheaper imports relative to domestic prices, the domestic demand declines for local agricultural and nonagricultural producers. Meanwhile, these producers benefit from cost savings on imported inputs, resulting in falls of 2.3 and 1.7 percent in the domestic cost of production in the agricultural and nonagricultural sectors, respectively. The real exchange rate depreciates by 1.6 percent, meaning that products made in the Philippines are relatively cheaper in international markets. Coupled with falling domestic prices in the face of cheaper imports and input cost savings, this encourages producers to reallocate resources toward the export market (table 8.7).

While exports rise in both agriculture and nonagriculture, domestic demand falls relatively more in agriculture. Because domestic demand represents a larger share in agricultural output, agricultural output contracts, while nonagricultural output expands. Output and value added prices in both agriculture and nonagriculture fall, but the fall in the former is higher than the fall in the latter. The result of all these adjustments is a fall in all factor returns. The factors used intensively in agriculture experience a much greater reduction: the returns to agricultural capital and land decline by 5.7 and 4.6 percent, respectively, whereas nonagricultural capital returns fall by only 1.3 percent. The nominal wages for unskilled workers fall relatively more than the wages for skilled workers because unskilled workers are used more intensively in agriculture.

**Unilateral trade liberalization only in agriculture in the Philippines**
(*PHIL-AGR*)
Unilateral liberalization in agriculture and lightly processed food results in substantial expansion in agricultural imports (17 percent) owing to the significant decline in local agricultural import prices (7.9 percent). At the same time, the removal of domestic agricultural distortions also generates cost savings in the export-oriented lightly processed food sector because of this sector's reliance on primary agricultural inputs. Thus, agricultural industries, which, in the context of our study, include lightly processed food, reorient production toward the export market, resulting in a 6.2 percent expansion in exports and a 2.8 percent reduction in domestic sales. The net result is a contraction in agricultural output because domestic sales comprise a larger share of total agricultural output. As a result, agricultural value added and value added prices fall, along with the returns to all agricultural factors. The returns to land drop 3.5 percent, and the returns to agricultural capital decline by 4.5 percent, while the wages of unskilled workers fall by 1.2 percent.

The results in the nonagricultural sectors are the opposite. Import prices increase marginally by 0.1 percent, while domestic prices fall by 0.7 percent, resulting in a 0.2 percent expansion in domestic sales. Domestic prices decrease relatively more than world prices (0.7 versus 0.3 percent), leading to a 1.0 percent export expansion. Together with greater domestic demand, this allows overall nonagricultural output to expand by 0.3 percent.

A comparison of the sectoral results of *PHIL-ALL* and *PHIL-AGR* in table 8.7 confirms the heavier price burden of agricultural protection in the Philippine economy. Indeed, the removal of agricultural distortions accounts for at least two-thirds of the price reduction in exports, imports, domestic production, value added, and the consumer price index.[9] This is also true of factor prices: 40 to 80 percent of the fall in factor returns is traceable to the removal of agricultural protection.

**Rest-of-the-world and Philippine trade liberalization in all sectors**
(*COMB-ALL*)
This experiment combines rest-of-the-world trade liberalization and domestic trade liberalization. The impact of the rest-of-the-world trade liberalization dominates the effects of the unilateral trade liberalization in both agricultural and the nonagricultural sectors. Local import prices decline in the agricultural sector despite the increase in world commodity prices, indicating the substantial level of domestic distortions in the Philippines. The cheaper imports crowd out the corresponding domestic products, leading to a contraction in the domestic sales of domestic producers; this affects the agricultural sector more negatively than the

nonagricultural sector. At the same time, rising world export prices, real exchange rate depreciation, and cost savings on imported inputs allow domestic producers to reorient a large share of their production successfully toward the more profitable export market. Given the greater reliance of the agricultural sector on domestic sales, the net impact is a contraction in agriculture and an expansion in the nonagricultural sectors.

The output prices for both agricultural and the nonagricultural sectors increase (0.4 and 0.9 percent, respectively). Agriculture experiences a smaller increase owing to the substantial level of domestic agricultural distortion in the base. With the exception of the returns to agricultural capital, all factor prices increase. Factor prices increase especially in the nonagricultural sectors, although they increase by less in this scenario than in the *ROW-ALL* scenario. The impacts in output volumes are the opposite: the effects of unilateral liberalization dominate the effects of rest-of-the-world trade liberalization. Thus, overall agricultural output declines, while overall output in the nonagricultural sectors improves ($-1.9$ and 0.3 percent, respectively).

### Rest-of-the-world and Philippine trade liberalization in agriculture only (*COMB-AGR*)

The unilateral agricultural trade liberalization scenario (*PHIL-AGR*) dominates the global agricultural trade liberalization scenario (*ROW-AGR*) within the *COMB-AGR* scenario. In the *COMB-AGR* scenario, output, prices, and volumes in agriculture decline, as do agricultural factor prices. Local import prices in agriculture decline despite rising world commodity prices. This indicates that the level of domestic distortions is substantial in the Philippines. The positive impact of the higher world commodity prices is dominated by the negative impact of the domestic agricultural distortions imposed by the government. Thus, the returns to the factors used intensively in agriculture (land, agricultural capital, and unskilled wages) fall in response to the declining agricultural output prices.

In contrast, local import prices in the nonagricultural sectors increase. This is expected because the country's nonagricultural trade distortions are already low relative to international standards.[10] Thus, the overall output prices of nonagricultural products increase by 0.2 percent, resulting in output expansion and, consequently, higher returns to nonagricultural factors (table 8.7).

### Household income, the consumer price index, and welfare

The changes in nominal household incomes, nominal consumer price indexes (based on household-specific consumer baskets), and real incomes and welfare are presented in table 8.8. In interpreting the changes in household-specific consumer prices, recall from above that primary and processed food account for a

**Table 8.8. Effects of Prospective Liberalizations on Real Household Consumption, by Income Group, the Philippines**

(percent)

| Household | ROW-ALL | | | ROW-AGR | | | PHIL-ALL | | |
|---|---|---|---|---|---|---|---|---|---|
| | Change in nominal income | Change in consumer price | EV | Change in nominal income | Change in consumer price | EV | Change in nominal income | Change in consumer price | EV |
| Decile 1 | 3.3 | 2.9 | 0.4 | 1.3 | 1.2 | 0.1 | −1.9 | −2.2 | 0.3 |
| Decile 2 | 3.3 | 2.9 | 0.4 | 1.3 | 1.1 | 0.1 | −1.9 | −2.0 | 0.2 |
| Decile 3 | 3.3 | 2.8 | 0.4 | 1.3 | 1.1 | 0.1 | −1.9 | −2.0 | 0.1 |
| Decile 4 | 3.2 | 2.8 | 0.4 | 1.2 | 1.1 | 0.1 | −1.8 | −1.8 | 0.0 |
| Decile 5 | 3.2 | 2.8 | 0.4 | 1.2 | 1.1 | 0.1 | −1.8 | −1.7 | −0.1 |
| Decile 6 | 3.1 | 2.7 | 0.4 | 1.2 | 1.1 | 0.1 | −1.7 | −1.6 | −0.2 |
| Decile 7 | 3.0 | 2.6 | 0.4 | 1.1 | 1.1 | 0.1 | −1.7 | −1.4 | −0.2 |
| Decile 8 | 2.9 | 2.6 | 0.4 | 1.1 | 1.0 | 0.1 | −1.6 | −1.3 | −0.3 |
| Decile 9 | 2.8 | 2.5 | 0.3 | 1.1 | 1.0 | 0.0 | −1.5 | −1.2 | −0.3 |
| Decile 10 | 2.9 | 2.4 | 0.5 | 1.1 | 1.0 | 0.1 | −1.4 | −1.0 | −0.4 |
| Overall | 3.0 | 2.6 | 0.4 | 1.1 | 1.0 | 0.1 | −1.6 | −1.3 | −0.3 |

(Table continues on the following page.)

**Table 8.8. Effects of Prospective Liberalizations on Real Household Consumption, by Income Group, the Philippines** (*continued*)

(*percent*)

| Household | ROW-ALL | | | ROW-AGR | | | PHIL-ALL | | |
|---|---|---|---|---|---|---|---|---|---|
| | Change in nominal income | Change in consumer price | EV | Change in nominal income | Change in consumer price | EV | Change in nominal income | Change in consumer price | EV |
| Decile 1 | −1.2 | −2.0 | 0.8 | 1.4 | 0.7 | 0.7 | 0.1 | −0.8 | 0.9 |
| Decile 2 | −1.2 | −1.8 | 0.7 | 1.4 | 0.8 | 0.6 | 0.1 | −0.7 | 0.8 |
| Decile 3 | −1.2 | −1.8 | 0.6 | 1.4 | 0.8 | 0.5 | 0.1 | −0.6 | 0.7 |
| Decile 4 | −1.2 | −1.6 | 0.4 | 1.4 | 0.9 | 0.4 | 0.1 | −0.5 | 0.5 |
| Decile 5 | −1.1 | −1.5 | 0.3 | 1.4 | 1.0 | 0.3 | 0.1 | −0.4 | 0.4 |
| Decile 6 | −1.1 | −1.3 | 0.2 | 1.3 | 1.1 | 0.2 | 0.1 | −0.2 | 0.3 |
| Decile 7 | −1.1 | −1.2 | 0.1 | 1.3 | 1.2 | 0.1 | 0.0 | −0.1 | 0.2 |
| Decile 8 | −1.1 | −1.1 | 0.0 | 1.3 | 1.2 | 0.1 | 0.0 | 0.0 | 0.1 |
| Decile 9 | −1.1 | −1.0 | −0.1 | 1.3 | 1.3 | 0.0 | 0.0 | 0.0 | 0.0 |
| Decile 10 | −1.0 | −0.8 | −0.3 | 1.4 | 1.4 | 0.0 | 0.0 | 0.2 | −0.1 |
| Overall | −1.1 | −1.1 | 0.0 | 1.4 | 1.2 | 0.1 | 0.0 | −0.1 | 0.1 |

*Source:* National CGE model simulations of the authors.

*Note:* EV = equivalent variation in income.

significant share of household expenditure, especially among the lower-income groups, and that the initial tariff rates are higher on primary and processed food items than on other goods (tables 8.4 and 8.5).

*ROW-ALL*, the scenario of global trade liberalization in all sectors, excluding the Philippines, registers the greatest increase in nominal household incomes because rising world prices translate into higher factor returns. For the same reason, consumer prices also increase the most in this scenario. Nonetheless, the greater nominal income growth among all households outweighs the detrimental effects of rising consumer prices, with the result that welfare improves among all household groups. Variations in incomes and consumer prices tend to be greater in the poorest deciles, which are more tightly linked to the agricultural sector and which post generally better welfare results in the scenario. The results under *ROW-AGR* are similar, but less than half as large. The results are qualitatively similar and also display a generally pro-poor effect (table 8.8).

The two domestic liberalization scenarios (*PHIL-ALL* and *PHIL-AGR*) result in falling consumer prices, which are driven by the reduction in local import and export prices following the elimination of trade-related distortions in the Philippines. This price reduction is greater if the domestic agricultural and nonagricultural liberalizations are combined. We see that the removal of domestic agricultural distortions reduces consumer prices by more relative to the corresponding effect of the removal of nonagricultural distortions given the high share of agriculture in household consumption and the higher initial levels of protection and, hence, consumer prices. A comparison of the changes in consumer prices in scenarios *PHIL-ALL* and *PHIL-AGR* show that roughly 1.8 of the 2.2 percent reduction in the consumer price index for the first decile is generated by the elimination of domestic agricultural distortions alone (table 8.8).

One may also observe that nominal incomes fall under the two unilateral liberalization scenarios. However, the consumer price effects dominate such that, despite falling nominal incomes, welfare and real incomes increase more under agricultural trade liberalization. Furthermore, these welfare gains accrue proportionately more to the poorer deciles owing to the greater relative agricultural consumption among these deciles.

These welfare gains are bolstered in rest-of-the-world liberalization and unilateral trade liberalization combined. Nominal incomes rise under the full rest-of-the-world and domestic trade liberalization scenario, but this is somewhat offset by soaring consumer prices. Overall, the combined global and domestic agricultural trade liberalization scenario (*COMB-AGR*) provides the greatest increase in welfare. This is because the nominal income gains from the rest-of-the-world trade liberalization are largely conserved, and to these gains are added the consumer price reductions from the domestic trade liberalization. In this case, the poorest deciles emerge as the winners because of both the domestic agricultural trade liberalization and the pro-agricultural nature of the rest-of-the-world trade liberalization.

### The effects on poverty and inequality

The microsimulation process we use in our study relies on the Family Income and Expenditure Survey of the Philippines in 2000 (NSO 2000).[11] To estimate the likely poverty and inequality impacts of the labor market conditions arising from trade liberalization, we apply certain information from the CGE model as an input into the microsimulation procedure in a sequential manner. In particular, we use the vectors of changes in the total incomes of households; wage income, capital income, and other income; household-specific consumer price indexes (to update the nominal value of the poverty line); and sectoral employment shares.

Through a random process, we incorporate changes in the employment status of households after the simulation. In this way, it is possible to capture household laborers moving in and out of employment (at the microlevel) by taking into account the changes in sectoral employment arising from a policy shift (at the macrolevel). For instance, households that have no labor income because of unemployment may become employed and, consequently, earn labor income. Similarly, employed households may become unemployed and earn no labor income at all after the policy change. Household labor income is affected by changes in wages, as well as by the chance of becoming unemployed after the policy shock. The microsimulation process is repeated 30 times, allowing us to derive confidence intervals on our Foster, Greer, and Thorbecke (1984) indexes and Gini coefficient estimates.[12]

To take advantage of the richness of the microsimulation procedure, we calculate poverty indexes and Gini coefficients based on the demographic characteristics of the household heads, especially gender, skill level, and location (urban or rural). In total, the final Foster, Greer, and Thorbecke indexes are derived for eight categories of household heads. Using demographic characteristics instead of income deciles to evaluate changes in poverty and income distribution is preferable because it allows for a more accurate policy evaluation and identification of the gainers and losers from trade liberalization.

The poverty and inequality results in all experiments are summarized in table 8.9. Inequality marginally worsens in all unilateral liberalization scenarios, but slightly improves in the rest-of-the-world liberalization scenarios. The latter outcome arises because of the increase in nominal incomes among poorer households, while the former outcome results from the greater decrease in the nominal incomes of poorer households relative to richer households (table 8.8).

**Table 8.9. Income Inequality and the Poverty Effects of Prospective Liberalizations, by Location, Gender, and Skills, the Philippines**

(percent change relative to the 2000 index)

| Group | Variable | 2000 index | Indirect tax replacement ROW-ALL | ROW-AGR | PHIL-ALL | PHIL-AGR | COMB-ALL | COMB-AGR | Direct tax replacement COMB-ALL | COMB-AGR |
|---|---|---|---|---|---|---|---|---|---|---|
| All Philippines | Gini | 0.51 | -0.2 | -0.2 | 0.4 | 0.3 | 0.2 | 0.1 | 0.1 | 0.1 |
| | P0 | 33.5 | -0.9 | -0.6 | 1.1 | -0.1 | 0.1 | -0.1 | 0.0 | -0.1 |
| | P1 | 10.3 | -1.9 | -1.2 | 1.6 | -0.1 | -0.4 | -0.9 | -0.4 | -0.7 |
| | P2 | 4.3 | -2.8 | -2.0 | 2.0 | -0.4 | -0.8 | -1.5 | -0.9 | -1.3 |
| All urban | Gini | 0.48 | -0.2 | -0.2 | 0.4 | 0.3 | 0.2 | 0.1 | 0.2 | 0.1 |
| | P0 | 18.6 | -1.6 | -0.9 | 2.0 | 0.8 | 0.1 | -0.2 | 0.1 | 0.0 |
| | P1 | 5.0 | -1.9 | -1.0 | 3.2 | 1.7 | 0.4 | -0.1 | 0.4 | 0.1 |
| | P2 | 2.0 | -2.0 | -1.1 | 4.7 | 2.7 | 0.8 | 0.0 | 0.9 | 0.5 |
| Urban men, skilled | P0 | 3.2 | 0.1 | 0.0 | -1.5 | -1.4 | -0.7 | -0.7 | -1.2 | -1.6 |
| | P1 | 0.7 | -1.4 | -0.2 | -2.0 | -3.4 | -2.2 | -2.6 | -3.4 | -3.4 |
| | P2 | 0.2 | -1.7 | -0.4 | -2.6 | -4.4 | -2.7 | -3.3 | -4.4 | -4.3 |
| Urban men, unskilled | P0 | 23.3 | -1.6 | -0.9 | 2.1 | 0.9 | 0.1 | -0.2 | 0.1 | 0.1 |
| | P1 | 6.4 | -1.8 | -1.0 | 3.2 | 1.7 | 0.5 | -0.1 | 0.5 | 0.2 |
| | P2 | 2.5 | -2.0 | -1.1 | 4.8 | 2.8 | 0.8 | 0.1 | 1.0 | 0.5 |
| Urban women, skilled | P0 | 0.9 | 0.0 | 0.0 | -2.3 | -1.9 | -1.0 | -1.5 | -1.2 | -1.4 |
| | P1 | 0.1 | -2.5 | -0.6 | -0.8 | -3.1 | -2.7 | -3.4 | -2.8 | -3.7 |
| | P2 | 0.0 | -4.1 | -1.0 | -0.2 | -4.4 | -4.1 | -5.2 | -4.4 | -5.5 |
| Urban women, unskilled | P0 | 15.2 | -2.1 | -1.2 | 1.8 | 0.4 | -0.1 | -0.4 | 0.1 | -0.2 |
| | P1 | 3.9 | -2.3 | -1.1 | 3.7 | 2.2 | 0.5 | 0.0 | 0.5 | 0.1 |
| | P2 | 1.6 | -2.4 | -1.3 | 5.1 | 3.4 | 1.0 | 0.1 | 1.0 | 0.6 |

(Table continues on the following page.)

**Table 8.9. Income Inequality and the Poverty Effects of Prospective Liberalizations, by Location, Gender, and Skills, the Philippines (continued)**

*(percent change relative to the 2000 index)*

| Group | Variable | 2000 index | Indirect tax replacement | | | | | | Direct tax replacement | |
|---|---|---|---|---|---|---|---|---|---|---|
| | | | ROW-ALL | ROW-AGR | PHIL-ALL | PHIL-AGR | COMB-ALL | COMB-AGR | COMB-ALL | COMB-AGR |
| All rural | Gini | 0.43 | −0.1 | −0.1 | 0.5 | 0.2 | 0.2 | 0.1 | 0.1 | 0.1 |
| | P0 | 48.7 | −0.9 | −0.6 | 0.6 | 0.0 | −0.1 | −0.3 | −0.2 | −0.3 |
| | P1 | 15.9 | −1.4 | −0.8 | 1.6 | 0.4 | −0.1 | −0.6 | −0.2 | −0.5 |
| | P2 | 6.8 | −1.7 | −0.9 | 2.7 | 1.1 | 0.1 | −0.6 | 0.0 | −0.4 |
| Rural men, skilled | P0 | 12.0 | 0.0 | 0.0 | −1.4 | −2.1 | −1.6 | −3.1 | −1.7 | −2.8 |
| | P1 | 3.5 | −1.0 | −0.2 | −1.4 | −2.3 | −1.8 | −2.2 | −1.7 | −1.9 |
| | P2 | 1.4 | −1.2 | −0.3 | −1.5 | −2.7 | −2.2 | −2.6 | −2.0 | −2.3 |
| Rural men, unskilled | P0 | 52.4 | −0.9 | −0.6 | 0.6 | 0.0 | −0.1 | −0.3 | −0.2 | −0.3 |
| | P1 | 17.2 | −1.3 | −0.7 | 1.6 | 0.5 | −0.1 | −0.6 | −0.2 | −0.5 |
| | P2 | 7.4 | −1.6 | −0.9 | 2.7 | 1.2 | 0.1 | −0.6 | 0.0 | −0.4 |
| Rural women, skilled | P0 | 14.7 | 0.0 | 0.0 | −0.7 | −2.1 | 0.0 | −0.8 | −0.2 | −1.0 |
| | P1 | 4.1 | −1.0 | −0.2 | −1.1 | −4.4 | −1.1 | −2.5 | −1.2 | −2.5 |
| | P2 | 1.4 | −1.6 | −0.3 | −1.6 | −6.3 | −1.7 | −3.7 | −1.9 | −3.8 |
| Rural women, unskilled | P0 | 34.9 | −1.3 | −0.9 | 0.8 | 0.2 | −0.2 | −0.4 | −0.2 | −0.1 |
| | P1 | 10.8 | −1.8 | −1.1 | 2.0 | 0.6 | −0.1 | −0.6 | −0.1 | −0.4 |
| | P2 | 4.4 | −2.3 | −1.3 | 3.7 | 1.6 | 0.3 | −0.4 | 0.2 | −0.1 |

*Source:* National CGE model simulations of the authors.

*Note:* Gini = Gini coefficient. P0 = poverty headcount. P1 = poverty gap. P2 = poverty severity.

Rest-of-the-world liberalization reduces poverty at the national level and favors unskilled households because rising world demand and the rising export prices of products made in the Philippines bring about higher agricultural factor returns (table 8.7). In contrast, unilateral liberalization favors skilled households such that national poverty indexes worsen. This is because the removal of distortions within the Philippines results in resource reallocations toward outward-oriented and externally competitive nonagricultural sectors that employ skilled workers intensively.

Poverty generally falls under the combined global and domestic liberalization scenario, wherein the poverty-reducing impact of rest-of-the-world liberalization dominates the poverty-increasing effect of unilateral liberalization. In contrast, inequality marginally rises because the inequality-increasing effect of unilateral liberalization dominates the inequality-reducing effect of rest-of-the-world liberalization. The combined global and domestic agricultural reform is the most poverty-friendly scenario. Although the national poverty headcount decreases marginally, all household groups, with the slight exception of urban households headed by unskilled workers, share in the benefits of the poverty friendliness of trade liberalization. Indeed, the poorest of the poor, particularly those poor residing in rural areas, emerge as winners because they rely on agricultural production and the wages of unskilled labor.

These results are consistent with those obtained by Cororaton, Cockburn, and Corong (2006). However, the results of these authors suggest a worsening in both the poverty gap and the severity of poverty, while our results show the opposite, especially under the combined rest-of-the-world and Philippine agricultural liberalization. This difference is traceable to the use of more-recent estimates of trade protection on key food items (such as rice, corn, sugar, and processed meat), which, if eliminated from the calculation, result in a significant fall in the consumer prices faced by lower-income groups (table 8.7).

### Sensitivity analysis: Indirect and direct tax replacement schemes

The results discussed above are derived using an indirect tax replacement scheme. Are the results sensitive to the tax replacement scheme used? This subsection compares the above results with the results obtained if a direct tax replacement closure is adopted. We focus on an analysis of the poverty and inequality results of *COMB-ALL* (full rest-of-the-world and domestic trade liberalization) and *COMB-AGR* (rest-of-the-world and domestic agricultural trade liberalization).

The sensitivity analysis is summarized in table 8.9. The directions of the changes in the poverty indexes and inequality are generally the same regardless of the tax replacement scheme. However, the magnitudes are marginally greater under the direct tax scenario owing to a smaller increase in consumer prices because direct taxes are used to compensate for foregone tariff revenues.

## Summary and Policy Implications

Starting in the 1980s, the government shifted from taxing to protecting agriculture relative to the nonagricultural sectors. However, two decades of protection failed to induce competitiveness and productivity growth because agriculture became inward looking and inefficient. This study analyzes the poverty and inequality implications of the removal of the agricultural and nonagricultural price distortions in the domestic markets of the Philippines as of 2004 and compares these effects with the results if policies abroad are liberalized.

Rest-of-the-world liberalization reduces poverty at the national level and favors unskilled households in the Philippines because the higher world export prices and rising export demand for products made in the Philippines allow producers in the Philippines to benefit from favorable international market conditions. Nominal incomes improve significantly, outweighing the impact of higher consumer prices. Rest-of-the-world trade liberalization in all sectors generates almost uniform increases in real incomes across household types, while rest-of-the-world trade liberalization in agriculture brings about progressive changes in real incomes that benefit lower-income groups more.

Unilateral trade liberalization leads to a drop in consumer prices, which is driven by the reduction in local import and export prices following the elimination of trade-related distortions induced by policies within the Philippines. Import prices fall more, and import volumes correspondingly increase more in agriculture relative to nonagriculture because the initial distortions are greater in agriculture. However, unilateral liberalization favors skilled households such that national poverty indexes and inequality worsen. This is because the removal of the distortions leads to resource reallocation in the Philippines toward outward-oriented and externally competitive nonagricultural sectors that employ skilled workers intensively.

The combined global and domestic agricultural reform appears to be the most poverty-friendly scenario for the Philippines. Although the national poverty headcount decreases only marginally, all household groups, with the slight exception of urban households headed by unskilled workers, share in the benefits of the poverty friendliness of the trade liberalization. The poorest of the poor, particularly those poor living in rural areas, emerge as winners because of their reliance on agricultural production and the wages from unskilled labor. Thus, it appears to be in the best interest of the Philippines to take a proactive trade liberalization stance by fully participating with the rest of the world in the effort at trade liberalization through the inclusion of its own domestic liberalization. Our sensitivity analysis confirms that the results are not affected by differing tax replacement assumptions because a similar pattern of effects emerge regardless of whether indirect or direct tax replacement schemes are used.

## Notes

1. Estimates of agricultural protection and assistance in the Philippines, based on David, Intal, and Balisacan (2009), are incorporated in the World Bank's Distortions to Agricultural Incentives Project Database (Anderson and Valenzuela 2008). The estimates cover five decades. The representative values for CGE modeling as of 2004 that are used here are available in Valenzuela and Anderson (2008).

2. These vectors of changes are generated by simulating the global model with no Philippine trade liberalization.

3. This definition is maintained throughout the study. Agriculture is defined as primary agriculture (excluding fishing, forestry, and agricultural services) and lightly processed food, while nonagriculture refers to all other sectors, including highly processed foods, tobacco, and beverages.

4. The trade reform programs were major components of the structural programs prescribed by multilateral organizations in the 1980s, including the International Monetary Fund and the World Bank. The Philippines is currently in the fourth phase of the trade reform programs. See Cororaton, Cockburn, and Corong (2006) for a detailed discussion.

5. Tariff binding overhang refers to the difference between a country's bound tariffs and its applied tariffs. Bound tariffs are tariff rates that, according to agreements with the World Trade Organization, the country will not exceed.

6. Sugar exports accounted for only 10 percent of domestic production during this period.

7. The specification of the CGE model is based on EXTER (see Decaluwé, Dumont, and Robichaud 2000). For a complete discussion and specification of the model, see Cororaton and Corong (2009), who also provide details on the construction of the social accounting matrix.

8. The export (import) intensity ratio is the ratio of a sector's exports (imports) to output (domestic supply).

9. See the ratio of prices in PHIL-AGR relative to PHIL-ALL in table 8.7: exports ($-1.3/-1.8 = 0.7$), imports ($-7.9/-7.2 = 1.1$), domestic prices ($-2.2/-2.3 = 1.0$), output ($-2.3/-3.1 = 0.8$), value added ($-2.9/-4.0 = 0.7$), the consumer price index ($-1.1/-1.3 = 0.8$), skilled wages ($-0.9/-1.6 = 0.4$), unskilled wages ($-1.2/-2.5 = 0.5$), the returns to land ($-3.5/-4.7 = 0.7$), the returns to agricultural capital ($-4.5/-5.7 = 0.8$), and the returns to nonagricultural capital ($-0.5/-1.3 = 0.4$).

10. This is because previous rounds of trade reform in the country focused primarily on reducing nonagricultural distortions.

11. Our microsimulation is a modified version of the original approach proposed by Vos (2005).

12. Vos (2005) observes that 30 iterations are sufficient because repeating the process additionally does not significantly alter the results. The results on confidence intervals are available from the contact author, Caesar Cororaton, upon request.

## References

Aldaba, R. M. 2005. "Policy Reversals, Lobby Groups, and Economic Distortions." PIDS Discussion Paper 2005–04, Philippine Institute for Development Studies, Makati, the Philippines.

Anderson, K., and E. Valenzuela. 2008. "Estimates of Global Distortions to Agricultural Incentives, 1955–2007." Data spreadsheet, October, World Bank, Washington, DC. http://go.worldbank.org/YAO39F35E0.

Austria, M. S. 2001. "Liberalization and Regional Integration: The Philippines' Strategy for Rest of the World Competitiveness." *Philippine Journal of Development* 37 (2): 55–86.

Austria, M. S., and E. M. Medalla. 1996. *A Study on the Trade and Investment Policies of Developing Countries: The Case of the Philippines.* PIDS Discussion Paper 96–03. Makati, the Philippines: Philippine Institute for Development Studies.

Cororaton, C. B., J. Cockburn, and E. Corong. 2006. "Doha Scenarios, Trade Reforms, and Poverty in the Philippines: A CGE Analysis." In *Poverty and the WTO: Impacts of the Doha Development Agenda,* ed. T. W. Hertel and L. A. Winters, 375–402. London: Palgrave Macmillan; Washington, DC: World Bank.

Cororaton, C. B., and E. Corong. 2009. *Philippine Agricultural and Food Policies: Implications for Poverty and Income Distribution*. IFPRI Research Report 161. Washington, DC: International Food Policy Research Institute.

David, C. C. 2003. "Agriculture." In *The Philippine Economy: Development, Policies, and Challenges*, ed. A. M. Balisacan and H. Hill, 175–218. Quezon City, the Philippines: Ateneo de Manila Press.

David, C. C., P. S. Intal Jr., and A. M. Balisacan. 2009. "The Philippines." In *Distortions to Agricultural Incentives in Asia*, ed. K. Anderson and W. Martin, 223–54. Washington, DC: World Bank.

Decaluwé, B., J.-C. Dumont, and V. Robichaud. 2000. *Basic CGE Models*. Vol. II of *MIMAP Training Session on CGE Modeling*. Micro Impacts of Macroeconomic and Adjustment Policies Program, International Development Research Centre, Canadian Centre for International Studies and Cooperation, and Université Laval, Quebec. http://www.pep-net.org/fileadmin/medias/pdf/volume2.pdf.

Foster, J., J. Greer, and E. Thorbecke. 1984. "A Class of Decomposable Poverty Measures." *Econometrica* 52 (3): 761–66.

Horridge, M., and F. Zhai. 2006. "Shocking a Single-Country CGE Model with Export Prices and Quantities from a Global Model." In *Poverty and the WTO: Impacts of the Doha Development Agenda*, ed. T. W. Hertel and L. A. Winters, 94–104. London: Palgrave Macmillan; Washington, DC: World Bank.

Intal, P. S., Jr., and J. H. Power. 1990. *Trade, Exchange Rate, and Agricultural Pricing Policy in the Philippines*. World Bank Comparative Studies. Washington, DC: World Bank.

NSO (National Statistics Office). 1985–. *Family Income and Expenditure Survey, the Philippines*. Manila: NSO. http://www.census.gov.ph/data/publications/pubfies.html.

Valenzuela, E., and K. Anderson. 2008. "Alternative Agricultural Price Distortions for CGE Analysis of Developing Countries, 2004 and 1980–84." Research Memorandum 13 (December), Center for Global Trade Analysis, Department of Agricultural Economics, Purdue University, West Lafayette, IN. https://www.gtap.agecon.purdue.edu/resources/res_display.asp?RecordID=2925.

van der Mensbrugghe, D. 2005. "Linkage Technical Reference Document: Version 6.0." December, World Bank, Washington, DC. http://go.worldbank.org/7NP2KK1OH0.

Vos, R. 2005. "Microsimulation Methodology: Technical Note." Unpublished paper, Department of Economic and Social Affairs, United Nations, New York.

WTO (World Trade Organization). 1999. *Trade Policy Review: The Philippines*. Geneva: WTO.

———. 2005. *Trade Policy Review: The Philippines*. Geneva: WTO.

9

# THAILAND

*Peter Warr**

As Thailand has industrialized, successive Thai governments have become increasingly interested in intervening on behalf of producers in the key declining sector, namely, agriculture.[1] Agricultural producers and processors are the intended beneficiaries of these interventions. However, the fact that Thailand is a major agricultural exporter has limited the scope of protection policies as a means of influencing domestic commodity prices. Over time, the direct taxation of agricultural exports has been gradually eliminated. This has been important in the case of rice, on which the high rates of export taxation prior to the mid-1980s were abolished in 1986. Similarly, rubber exports, taxed prior to 1990, have not been taxed since then. Cassava exports have continued to be taxed to a minor extent through the system of export quotas. Taxes on imports of fertilizer, a major input into agricultural production, have been steadily phased out since the early 1990s. Maize exports have been consistently untaxed, as have chicken exports, a commodity not covered by the present analysis because of the lack of suitable price data. Most of this history is a tale of the elimination of the price distortions that once acted against agricultural export industries.

Four commodities depart from this general trend of the liberalization of agricultural markets. Soybeans were an export item prior to 1992 and have been a net import item since then; the imports have been subject to quota restrictions. The change from a net export item to a net import item coincided with a switch from

---

*The author has benefited greatly from the research assistance of Krisada Bamrungwong and Arief Anshory Yusuf, from helpful discussions with Ernesto Valenzuela, and from the comments of John Cockburn. This chapter relies on a modeling approach that is similar to the approach in the author's chapter on Indonesia in this volume (chapter 6) and is meant to be read in conjunction with that chapter. Methodological points that are common to the two studies are not repeated here. The discussion here focuses on methodological points that are different and on the results of the analysis on Thailand.

negative to positive nominal rates of protection. Since the early 1990s, the domestic soybean industry has received a nominal rate of protection of between 30 and 40 percent. Sugar is an export commodity in Thailand, but the domestic sugar industry is protected by a home price system that taxes domestic consumers and transfers the revenue to producers. Nominal rates of protection have averaged over 60 percent. The political power of the highly capital-intensive sugar milling industry explains this pattern of protection. The case of palm oil is qualitatively similar to the case of sugar, but the rates of protection are somewhat lower. Finally, Thailand's small dairy industry is protected from competition by imported milk powder. It has not been possible to obtain sufficient data to quantify dairy protection for the purposes of our study, but informed sources report that the rate of protection is comparable with the rate for sugar. The prospects for additional trade liberalization in Thailand are not encouraging unless this occurs through bilateral preferential trading arrangements such as the scheme proposed with the United States.[2]

Almost all of Thailand's poor people reside in rural areas, and most are directly involved in agricultural production (Warr 2005). The Thai public is well disposed to finding ways to reduce rural poverty, and Thai governments have responded to this sentiment. Interventions on behalf of rural people have been important, but Thailand is unusual in that, except for the cases discussed above, these interventions have seldom taken the form of initiatives in agricultural commodity markets. The strong export-orientation of Thai agriculture is an important reason for this because assistance through commodity markets would require a large production of export subsidy outlays. Instead, cash transfers to village organizations, subsidized loan schemes not linked to agricultural production, and a generally good system of public infrastructure have been the main instruments of intervention in support of rural areas. Unfortunately, with the exception of the investment in rural infrastructure, these transfers have seldom been directed in any systematic way at raising the productivity of rural people or at assisting them in finding better economic opportunities outside agriculture. The long-term contribution of these transfers to any reduction in rural poverty will probably be small.

We use the JamlongThai general equilibrium model of the Thai economy (Warr 2008b), in conjunction with the Linkage global economic model (van der Mensbrugghe 2005), to analyze the effects on the incidence of poverty in Thailand of agricultural and other policies at home and abroad. JamlongThai is structurally similar in most respects to the Wayang model of the Indonesian economy, described in detail in chapter 6 by Warr, and the simulations we perform using this model are also similar to those described in the Indonesian case study.

The next section describes the JamlongThai general equilibrium model of the Thai economy, the principal analytic tool we use in this study. The subsequent section describes the simulations we perform with this model, in combination with the global Linkage model. The simulations involve both unilateral agricultural and trade policy reform in Thailand and reform by the rest of the world. We do this to assess the relative importance of own-country versus rest-of-the-world policies to Thai households. We present the results with a focus on the implications for poverty incidence within Thailand. The final section concludes.

## A General Equilibrium Model of the Thai Economy: JamlongThai

JamlongThai is a general equilibrium model of the Thai economy based on 65 sectors and 200 households. It has been constructed for the analysis of the effect of trade policy and other policy shocks on poverty incidence in Thailand. Unless otherwise stated, the database of the model refers to the year 2000. JamlongThai shares many structural features with the highly influential ORANI general equilibrium model of the Australian economy (Dixon et al. 1982) and the general equilibrium model of the global economy established through the Global Trade Analysis Project (Hertel 1997), which also belong to the Johansen (1964) category of economy-wide models. The specific structure of JamlongThai draws on a revised version of the ORANI model, called ORANI-G (Horridge 2004), and the PARA and Wayang general equilibrium models of the Thai and Indonesian economies, respectively, described in detail in Warr (2001, 2005). We have adapted this general structure of the model to reflect the specific objectives of our study and important features of the Thai economy.

### Industries

The JamlongThai model contains 65 industries, of which 24 are in agriculture. Each industry produces a single output, and the set of commodities therefore coincides with the set of industries. Exports are not identical with domestically sold commodities. In each industry, the two are produced by a transformation process with a constant elasticity of transformation.[3] The core of the production side of the model is an input-output table of 65 sectors. This table has been aggregated from an input-output table of 180 sectors that has been produced by the National Economic and Social Development Board (NESDB 2004). At the time of our study, the latest input-output table available for Thailand related to the year 2000. We have used this data set for our study.

The cost structure of the Thai economy, with an emphasis on the agricultural sector, is summarized in table 9.1. The agricultural sector relies on almost no skilled (educated) labor, but it is intensive in the use of unskilled labor. Unskilled and skilled labor are fully mobile across all industries.

**Table 9.1. Cost Shares of the Major Factors of Production, Paddy and Other Industries, Thailand, 2000**

*(percent of total costs)*

| Cost components | Paddy | Other agriculture | Nonagriculture | All industries |
|---|---|---|---|---|
| Skilled | 0.0 | 0.0 | 10.5 | 9.9 |
| Unskilled | 24.9 | 15.0 | 4.6 | 5.2 |
| Mobile capital | 2.1 | 5.1 | 29.3 | 28.0 |
| Land | 45.7 | 44.1 | 0.0 | 2.3 |
| Intermediate inputs | 27.3 | 35.8 | 55.7 | 54.6 |
| Total | 100.0 | 100.0 | 100.0 | 100.0 |

*Source:* Database of the JamlongThai model, based on NESDB (2004) and agricultural cost survey data of the Ministry of Agriculture and Cooperatives.

**Table 9.2. Sources of the Factor Incomes of Broad Household Groups, Thailand, 2000**

*(percent)*

| Household category | Skilled | Unskilled | Mobile capital | Land | Total factor income |
|---|---|---|---|---|---|
| 1. Farm, northeast | 15.5 | 28.0 | 42.8 | 13.6 | 100.0 |
| 2. Farm, north | 6.3 | 15.5 | 44.0 | 34.2 | 100.0 |
| 3. Farm, other | 10.1 | 12.9 | 47.5 | 29.6 | 100.0 |
| 4. Farm worker, all regions | 9.6 | 78.3 | 6.0 | 6.1 | 100.0 |
| 5. Entrepreneur, paid employees | 2.2 | 0.7 | 97.0 | 0.1 | 100.0 |
| 6. Entrepreneur, no paid employees | 1.6 | 1.6 | 96.6 | 0.2 | 100.0 |
| 7. Professional | 71.2 | 4.8 | 20.1 | 3.9 | 100.0 |
| 8. Clerical employee | 47.5 | 27.7 | 21.3 | 3.5 | 100.0 |
| 9. Production and construction | 31.6 | 51.8 | 13.5 | 3.1 | 100.0 |
| 10. Economically inactive | 7.8 | 4.6 | 38.2 | 50.1 | 100.0 |

*Source:* Database of the JamlongThai model, based on NSO (2003).

## Households

The JamlongThai model contains 10 major household categories, which are based on the socioeconomic survey classifications used by the National Statistical Office (NSO 2003). Table 9.2 summarizes these 10 household categories, which are classified according to the occupation of the heads of household. Four are farm households: farmer, northeast; farmer, north; farmer, other region; and farm worker, all regions. Six are nonfarm: entrepreneur with paid employees; entrepreneur without paid employees; professional; clerical employee; production, construction, or general laborer; and economically inactive. Each of these categories is divided into

20 groups of equal population size that are sorted by household income per person.[4] There are thus a total of 200 household subcategories.

The incomes of each of these 200 household subcategories depend on the household ownership of factors of production, the returns to these factors, and nonfactor incomes, mainly transfers from others. Since our focus is on income distribution, the sources of the incomes of the various households are of particular interest. These differ significantly among the 10 household categories.

Our household data are extracted from the 2000 household socioeconomic survey of the National Statistical Office (NSO 2003). A social accounting matrix has been constructed for Thailand based on data of the household socioeconomic survey, the input-output tables (NESDB 2004), the national accounts, and trade data, all for 2000. The database for the JamlongThai model draws upon this matrix.

The consumer demand equations for the various household types are based on a Cobb-Douglas demand system, using data on expenditure shares extracted from the 2000 household socioeconomic survey. Within each of the 10 major categories, the 20 subcategories thus differ according to per capita expenditures, budget shares in consumption, and sources of factor and nonfactor incomes.

Table 9.2 summarizes the sources of the factor incomes of the 10 major household categories, and table 9.3 summarizes the share of these categories in the overall population and in the overall incidence of poverty in Thailand based on the official poverty line.

**Table 9.3. Characteristics of the Major Household Categories, Thailand, 2000**
(number and percent)

| Household category | Total population, millions | Share of total population, % | Poverty incidence,[a] % |
|---|---|---|---|
| 1. Farm, northeast | 8,460 | 13.9 | 40.7 |
| 2. Farm, north | 3,287 | 5.4 | 27.3 |
| 3. Farm, other | 4,920 | 8.1 | 14.5 |
| 4. Farm worker, all regions | 4,565 | 7.5 | 29.3 |
| 5. Entrepreneur, paid employees | 1,953 | 3.2 | 0.7 |
| 6. Entrepreneur, no paid employees | 8,354 | 13.7 | 5.9 |
| 7. Professional | 4,866 | 8.0 | 1.6 |
| 8. Clerical employee | 7,934 | 13.0 | 2.5 |
| 9. Production and construction | 8,967 | 14.7 | 7.7 |
| 10. Economically inactive | 7,613 | 12.5 | 11.6 |
| 1–10. Total population | 60,916 | 100.0 | 14.4 |

Source: Author calculations based on NSO (2003).

a. Headcount measure of poverty incidence using the national poverty line.

## Simulations

The effects of agricultural trade policy reform are simulated using the JamlongThai model of the Thai economy, combined with the Linkage model of the world economy (van der Mensbrugghe 2005). The simulations involve both unilateral agricultural and trade policy reform in Thailand and reform by the rest of the world. We do this to assess the relative importance of own-country versus rest-of-the-world policies for Thai households. We also compare the reform of agriculture alone with the reform of all goods markets to gauge the relative contribution of agricultural policies to the measured impacts on households.

We consider three sets of policy reforms below: unilateral reform in Thailand (simulation A); global reform, excluding Thailand (simulation B); and the combination of these two sets of reforms, that is, global reform, including Thailand (simulation C).

The structure of these simulations is identical to the structure described for the simulations on Indonesia by Warr in chapter 6; the reader should therefore refer to chapter 6 for details. By reform, we mean the complete elimination of all tariffs, the tariff equivalents of any nontariff barriers, export taxes and export subsidies, and domestic agricultural policies in so far as they alter the producer or consumer prices of farm products in various countries. Each of our three simulations is conducted twice: one time each in which the reductions to protection in Thailand and in the rest of the world apply to all commodities (labeled simulations A1, B1, and C1) and one time each in which the reductions apply only to agricultural commodities, including lightly processed food (labeled simulations A2, B2, and C2).

The initial rates of industry assistance in Thailand used in the simulations are derived from the database of the Linkage model (see table 9.4). We have reduced these rates to zero in simulations A and C. In simulations B and C, we use the Linkage model simulations conducted by van der Mensbrugghe, Valenzuela, and Anderson (see the appendix) to estimate the changes in the import prices and export demand shifters that result from the liberalization in all countries except Thailand. We then apply these results as shocks in the JamlongThai model. The changes to border prices, derived from the Linkage model, are shown in table 9.5.

### The results of the liberalization of markets for all goods

While our emphasis in this study is on the effects on poverty and income inequality, an understanding of these effects requires that we look first at the macroeconomic effects.

**Table 9.4. Industry Assistance Rates Used in Modeling, Thailand, 2004**

*(percent)*

| Commodity | Tariff | Export subsidy | Output subsidy |
|---|---|---|---|
| Paddy rice | 12.5 | 0.0 | −0.3 |
| Wheat | 26.8 | 0.0 | −0.2 |
| Other grains | 26.5 | 0.0 | −0.2 |
| Vegetables and fruits | 44.6 | 0.0 | −0.1 |
| Oilseeds | 32.9 | 0.0 | −0.1 |
| Sugarcane | 0.0 | 0.0 | −0.1 |
| Plant-based fibers | 5.0 | 0.0 | −0.2 |
| Other crops | 38.0 | 0.0 | −0.1 |
| Cattle, sheep, and so on | 9.6 | 0.0 | −0.1 |
| Other livestock | 13.9 | 0.0 | −0.1 |
| Raw milk | 0.0 | 0.0 | −0.1 |
| Wool | 7.2 | 0.0 | −0.1 |
| Other primary products | 2.4 | −0.9 | −2.4 |
| Beef and sheep meat | 49.3 | 0.0 | −1.2 |
| Other meat products | 40.9 | 0.0 | −1.2 |
| Vegetable oils and fats | 39.2 | 0.0 | −1.2 |
| Dairy products | 18.1 | 0.0 | −1.2 |
| Processed rice | 19.6 | 0.0 | −0.5 |
| Refined sugar | 0.0 | 0.0 | −5.0 |
| Other food, beverages, tobacco | 39.7 | 0.0 | −19.9 |
| Textiles and wearing apparel | 23.5 | −0.6 | −1.1 |
| Other manufacturing | 13.9 | 0.0 | −3.3 |
| Services | 0.0 | 0.0 | −3.7 |

*Source:* Valenzuela and Anderson (2008), based on the estimates compiled by Anderson and Valenzuela (2008).

## Macroeconomic effects

The simulated macroeconomic effects of trade reform in all goods markets are summarized in table 9.6 (simulations A1, B1, and C1). Real GDP rises in Thailand under all three reform scenarios. Aggregate real household consumption also rises. The increases in real GDP and aggregate real household consumption in simulation A1 far exceed the corresponding increases in simulation B1. Unilateral liberalization is more beneficial to Thailand in macroeconomic terms than the liberalization of all other countries combined.

By turning to the effects of these reforms on real factor returns, we may discern clues to the income distributional impacts of the reforms. The real factor returns, deflated by the consumer price index, rise in the case of unskilled labor, skilled

**Table 9.5. Exogenous Border Price Shocks Caused by Rest-of-the-World Liberalization, Thailand**

*(percent deviation from base)*

| Commodity | Export price shocks[a] | | Import price shocks[b] | |
|---|---|---|---|---|
| | Reform of all goods | Agricultural reform only | Reform of all goods | Agricultural reform only |
| Paddy rice | 7.3 | 5.7 | 0.0 | 0.0 |
| Wheat | 0.0 | 0.0 | 3.3 | 4.0 |
| Other grains | 6.4 | 4.8 | 4.9 | 4.5 |
| Oilseeds | 6.0 | 4.7 | −6.0 | −5.6 |
| Sugarcane and beets | 0.0 | 0.0 | 0.0 | 0.0 |
| Plant-based fibers | 6.8 | 5.2 | 6.4 | 7.9 |
| Vegetables and fruits | 7.2 | 5.6 | 1.8 | 1.1 |
| Other crops | 7.3 | 5.8 | 1.7 | 1.6 |
| Cattle, sheep, and so on | 6.2 | 4.6 | 3.6 | 2.8 |
| Other livestock | 5.4 | 3.7 | 0.6 | 1.1 |
| Raw milk | 0.0 | 0.0 | 0.0 | 0.0 |
| Wool | 0.0 | 0.0 | 5.5 | 5.3 |
| Beef and sheep meat | 4.1 | 2.2 | 10.0 | 10.1 |
| Other meat products | 4.5 | 2.7 | 1.6 | 2.5 |
| Vegetable oils and fats | 2.6 | 0.9 | 0.7 | 1.2 |
| Dairy products | 4.4 | 2.6 | 12.2 | 12.5 |
| Processed rice | 6.6 | 4.9 | 1.4 | 0.5 |
| Refined sugar | 4.6 | 2.7 | 0.0 | 0.0 |
| Other food, beverages, tobacco | 3.5 | 1.7 | 0.9 | −1.4 |
| Other primary products | 3.3 | 1.2 | 0.5 | 0.8 |
| Textiles and wearing apparel | 3.2 | 1.4 | −0.4 | 0.5 |
| Other manufacturing | 2.9 | 1.1 | 1.3 | 0.3 |
| Services | 3.3 | 1.2 | −0.2 | 0.2 |
| Agriculture and food | 4.6 | 3.0 | 1.7 | 0.9 |
| Agriculture | 7.0 | 5.5 | 1.1 | 1.6 |
| Processed foods | 4.3 | 2.7 | 2.1 | 0.5 |
| Other manufacturing | 3.0 | 1.2 | 1.1 | 0.3 |
| Nontradables | 3.3 | 1.2 | −0.2 | 0.2 |
| Total | 3.3 | 1.4 | 1.0 | 0.4 |
| Merchandise trade | 3.3 | 1.5 | 1.2 | 0.4 |

*Source:* Linkage model simulations by van der Mensbrugghe, Valenzuela, and Anderson (see the appendix).

a. Simulated as shocks to the inverse export demand equations for Thailand.
b. Simulated as shocks to the exogenous import prices for Thailand.

**Table 9.6. Aggregate Simulation Results of the Prospective
Liberalization of All Commodities, Thailand**

| Indicator | Sim A1: unilateral liberalization | Sim B1: rest-of-the-world liberalization | Sim C1: global liberalization |
|---|---|---|---|
| *Macroeconomic aggregates, % change from base* | | | |
| Real GDP, expenditure side, GDP deflator | 0.27 | 0.04 | 0.30 |
| Real household consumption, CPI deflator | 4.32 | 0.16 | 4.43 |
| Import volume index, duty-paid weights | 4.68 | 0.12 | 4.79 |
| Export volume index | −0.04 | 0.01 | −0.03 |
| GDP price index, expenditure side | 8.24 | 2.11 | 10.49 |
| Consumer price index | 7.69 | 2.64 | 10.45 |
| *Nominal change, baht, millions* | | | |
| GDP | 482,697 | 121,566 | 611,829 |
| Consumption | 397,015 | 90,448 | 493,626 |
| Investment | 7,775 | 19,905 | 28,127 |
| Inventory | 2,516 | 38 | 2,610 |
| Government expenditure | 75,390 | 11,175 | 87,466 |
| *Real returns to factors, % change from base, using CPI deflator* | | | |
| Unskilled labor | 3.3 | −0.5 | 2.8 |
| Skilled labor | 10.0 | −0.8 | 9.1 |
| Agricultural capital | −3.3 | −0.3 | −3.5 |
| Nonagricultural capital | 9.9 | −0.3 | 9.5 |
| Land | −3.8 | −0.5 | −4.2 |
| *Real household expenditure, % change from base, using CPI deflator* | | | |
| 1. Farm, northeast | 2.6 | 0.8 | 3.3 |
| 2. Farm, north | 2.9 | 0.7 | 3.5 |
| 3. Farm, other | 4.4 | 0.6 | 4.9 |
| 4. Farm worker, all regions | 1.1 | 0.5 | 1.6 |
| 5. Entrepreneur, paid employees | 5.7 | 0.1 | 5.8 |
| 6. Entrepreneur, no paid employees | 5.7 | 0.3 | 6.0 |
| 7. Professional | 5.7 | −0.4 | 5.3 |
| 8. Clerical employee | 4.3 | −0.1 | 4.1 |
| 9. Production and construction | 2.7 | 0.1 | 2.7 |
| 10. Economically inactive | 3.8 | 0.4 | 4.1 |

*Source:* Thailand computable general equilibrium model simulations by the author.

*Note:* CPI = consumer price index.

labor, and nonagricultural capital in simulation A1 (unilateral liberalization). The returns to agricultural capital and land decline following liberalization, indicating that the structure of protection favors industries that are intensive in the use of agricultural capital and land. Another way of viewing this result is that the structure of protection in Thailand is such that the real returns to skilled and unskilled labor, as well as nonagricultural capital, are lowered, while the real returns to agricultural capital and land are raised. The removal of the protection has the opposite effect.

Simulation C1 is approximately the sum of simulations A1 and B1. It is dominated by the effects of unilateral liberalization.

In all three reform scenarios, real household expenditures increase among all household categories except household group 7, the households headed by professionals. The negative effect under simulation B1 is small relative to the gains achieved by most other household categories.

### The effects on poverty incidence and inequality

The poverty effects of the reforms are summarized in table 9.7. The measured level of the incidence of poverty depends on the poverty line used in the calculations, and this may also be true of the simulated changes in poverty incidence that result from particular economic shocks. We present the effects on the incidence of poverty using two poverty lines: the national poverty line and the international US$2-a-day poverty line at purchasing power parity.[5]

For our calculations with each of the poverty lines, we use the same calibration method, as follows. First, we assemble the data on the ex ante distribution of household expenditures according to information in the model database.

Second, we use the published level of poverty incidence based on one and then the other of the two poverty lines to find the value of the poverty line, measured in the domestic currency, that generates the particular level of poverty incidence we have found in the data on household expenditures in the model database. We take these published levels of poverty incidence from data of the National Economic and Social Development Board in the case of the national poverty line and from PovcalNet (2008) in the case of the US$2-a-day poverty line. This then becomes the base level of the poverty line we use in our subsequent calculations.

Third, the ex post levels of real expenditure for each household group are simulated within the model so as to reflect the effects of the shocks applied to the model. We perform these calculations of real household expenditures using the individual household consumer price index as the deflator so as to reflect the particular household's consumption bundle.

Fourth, we then compare these ex post real expenditures with the poverty line described above to obtain ex post levels of poverty incidence.

**Table 9.7. The Poverty and Inequality Effects of the Prospective Liberalization of All Commodities, Thailand**

| Group | Ex ante level | Change, ex post – ex ante | | |
|---|---|---|---|---|
| | | Sim A1: unilateral liberalization | Sim B1: rest-of-the-world liberalization | Sim C1: global liberalization |
| *Poverty incidence at the national poverty line, %* | | | | |
| 1. Farm, northeast | 40.7 | −6.2 | −2.9 | −9.1 |
| 2. Farm, north | 27.3 | −2.6 | −1.3 | −4.0 |
| 3. Farm, other | 14.5 | −12.2 | −5.8 | −18.0 |
| 4. Farm worker, all regions | 29.3 | −3.4 | −0.2 | −3.6 |
| 5. Entrepreneur, paid employees | 0.7 | −0.7 | 0.0 | −0.7 |
| 6. Entrepreneur, no paid employees | 3.9 | −11.3 | −5.7 | 17.2 |
| 7. Professional | 1.6 | −2.3 | −1.0 | −3.3 |
| 8. Clerical employee | 2.5 | −3.0 | −1.0 | −4.1 |
| 9. Production and construction | 7.7 | −9.0 | −6.7 | −15.7 |
| 10. Economically inactive | 11.6 | −4.9 | −0.6 | −7.5 |
| Farm households | 30.1 | −3.5 | −0.9 | −4.4 |
| Nonfarm households | 5.9 | −3.3 | −0.6 | 3.9 |
| All households | 14.4 | −3.4 | −0.7 | −4.1 |
| *Poverty incidence at the US$2-a-day poverty line, %* | | | | |
| Farm households | 21.03 | −1.55 | −0.31 | −1.86 |
| Nonfarm households | 15.19 | −1.10 | −1.18 | −2.28 |
| All households | 25.20 | −1.84 | −1.00 | −2.84 |
| *Inequality, Gini coefficient* | | | | |
| Urban households | 0.152 | 0.006 | 0.006 | 0.012 |
| Rural households | 0.334 | 0.004 | 0.005 | 0.009 |
| All households | 0.339 | 0.005 | 0.007 | 0.012 |

*Source:* Thailand computable general equilibrium model simulations by the author.

Finally, the changes in poverty incidence reported in table 9.7 and table 9.9 (see below) are the ex post levels of poverty incidence, minus the ex ante levels corresponding to each of the two poverty lines described above. A positive number thus indicates an increase in the simulated level of poverty incidence as a result of the shocks identified.

In addition to the effects on poverty incidence, we also report simulated effects on inequality in the distribution of household real expenditures. We accomplish this using the Gini coefficient as the measure. The Gini coefficient takes values between zero and 1; higher values reflecting greater inequality. These coefficients are estimated by constructing Lorenz curves from the distributions of ex ante and ex post real expenditures and then calculating the Gini coefficients corresponding to these distributions. These results are also presented in table 9.7.

Unilateral liberalization (simulation A1) delivers reduced poverty to all household categories and to farm and nonfarm households in aggregate. The benefits in terms of poverty reduction in Thailand that derive from global across-the-board liberalization (simulation C1) arise primarily from Thailand's own liberalization. Only one-fifth of the total reduction in the incidence of poverty may be attributed to the effects of liberalization elsewhere (simulation B1). Liberalization in Thailand and in the rest of the world increases inequality within Thailand somewhat. Skilled labor gains proportionately more than unskilled labor. However, in absolute terms, poor households have a strong stake in trade liberalization, especially liberalization within their own country regardless of whether or not other countries participate.

### The results of the liberalization of only agricultural markets

The macroeconomic effects of liberalization that is confined to agricultural products alone are summarized in table 9.8. The simulated effects are quite different from those arising from liberalization in the markets for all goods. Unilateral agricultural liberalization in Thailand raises real household consumption and marginally raises the consumer price index. It reduces the real value of unskilled labor marginally and increases skilled wages significantly. It also reduces the returns to agricultural capital, along with the returns to land. Relative to the rest of the economy, the agricultural industries in Thailand use much smaller shares of skilled labor and much larger shares of unskilled labor. Reduced agricultural protection reduces the size of the agricultural sector and raises the size of the nonagricultural sector. In the process, it raises real skilled wages and lowers real unskilled wages, along with the real returns to agricultural capital and land.

Unilateral agricultural liberalization in Thailand raises the incidence of poverty among farm households (table 9.9) because it reduces the real returns to unskilled labor (slightly)—deflated by the consumer price index—and also the real returns to agricultural capital and land (more significantly). Agricultural liberalization in the rest of the world raises the international prices of Thailand's agricultural exports (table 9.4). This increases the real returns to skilled and unskilled labor and the returns to land in Thailand. Farm-level poverty in Thailand declines, along with poverty among nonfarm households. Measured solely by the incidence of poverty in Thailand, these results suggest that Thailand has a stake in agricultural liberalization, but only if other countries participate as well.

## Table 9.8. Aggregate Simulation Results of the Prospective Liberalization of Only Agricultural Commodities, Thailand

| Indicator | Sim A2: unilateral liberalization | Sim B2: rest-of-the-world liberalization | Sim C2: global liberalization |
|---|---|---|---|
| Macroeconomic aggregates, % change from base | | | |
| Real GDP, expenditure side, GDP deflator | 0.01 | 0.03 | 0.04 |
| Real household consumption, CPI deflator | 0.12 | 0.14 | 0.25 |
| Import volume index, duty-paid weights | 0.12 | 0.10 | 0.21 |
| Export volume index | 0.00 | −0.01 | −0.01 |
| GDP price index, expenditure side | 0.21 | 0.99 | 1.20 |
| Consumer price index | 0.12 | 1.25 | 1.37 |
| Nominal change, baht, millions | | | |
| GDP | 12,633 | 57,660 | 69,886 |
| Consumption | 7,733 | 44,919 | 52,352 |
| Investment | 2,587 | 7,767 | 10,304 |
| Inventory | 80 | 51 | 131 |
| Government expenditure | 2,232 | 4,923 | 7,099 |
| Real returns to factors, % change from base, using CPI deflator | | | |
| Unskilled labor | −0.07 | 0.25 | 0.18 |
| Skilled labor | 0.51 | 0.36 | 0.87 |
| Agricultural capital | −1.34 | 0.20 | −1.14 |
| Nonagricultural capital | 0.47 | 0.08 | 0.52 |
| Land | −1.46 | 0.42 | −1.04 |
| Real household expenditure, % change from base, using CPI deflator | | | |
| 1. Farm, northeast | −0.16 | 0.47 | 0.32 |
| 2. Farm, north | −0.10 | 0.42 | 0.32 |
| 3. Farm, other | 0.07 | 0.37 | 0.44 |
| 4. Farm worker, all regions | −0.11 | 0.33 | 0.23 |
| 5. Entrepreneur, paid employees | 0.20 | 0.14 | 0.33 |
| 6. Entrepreneur, no paid employees | 0.24 | 0.26 | 0.48 |
| 7. Professional | 0.26 | −0.15 | 0.10 |
| 8. Clerical employee | 0.15 | 0.00 | 0.15 |
| 9. Production and construction | 0.03 | 0.10 | 0.12 |
| 10. Economically inactive | 0.05 | 0.26 | 0.30 |

Source: Thailand computable general equilibrium model simulations by the author.

Note: CPI = consumer price index.

**Table 9.9. The Poverty and Inequality Effects of the Prospective Liberalization of Only Agricultural Commodities, Thailand**

| | | Change, ex post − ex ante | | |
|---|---|---|---|---|
| Group | Ex ante level | Sim A2: unilateral liberalization | Sim B2: rest-of-the-world liberalization | Sim C2: global liberalization |
| *Poverty incidence at the national poverty line, %* | | | | |
| 1. Farm, northeast | 40.7 | 0.3 | −0.8 | −0.5 |
| 2. Farm, north | 27.3 | 0.1 | −0.3 | −0.2 |
| 3. Farm, other | 14.5 | −0.1 | −1.1 | −1.1 |
| 4. Farm worker, all regions | 29.3 | 1.0 | −4.7 | −3.7 |
| 5. Entrepreneur, paid employees | 0.7 | −0.4 | −0.7 | −1.1 |
| 6. Entrepreneur, no paid employees | 5.9 | −0.1 | −0.2 | −0.3 |
| 7. Professional | 1.6 | 0.0 | −0.6 | −0.6 |
| 8. Clerical employee | 2.5 | 0.1 | −1.5 | −1.4 |
| 9. Production and construction | 7.7 | 0.2 | −1.0 | −0.8 |
| 10. Economically inactive | 11.6 | 0.1 | −0.5 | −0.4 |
| Farm households | 30.1 | 0.3 | −1.6 | −1.3 |
| Nonfarm households | 5.9 | 0.0 | −0.8 | −0.7 |
| All households | 14.4 | 0.1 | −1.1 | −0.8 |
| *Poverty incidence at the US$2-a-day poverty line, %* | | | | |
| Farm households | 21.03 | 0.09 | −0.31 | −0.24 |
| Nonfarm households | 15.19 | −0.03 | −0.14 | −0.17 |
| All households | 25.20 | 0.04 | −0.24 | −0.28 |
| *Inequality, Gini coefficient* | | | | |
| Urban households | 0.152 | 0.001 | 0.006 | 0.007 |
| Rural households | 0.334 | 0.000 | 0.005 | 0.005 |
| All households | 0.339 | 0.001 | 0.007 | 0.008 |

*Source:* Thailand computable general equilibrium model simulations by the author.

## Conclusions and Comparison with the Study on Indonesia

The comparative static analysis in our study indicates that across-the-board trade liberalization is poverty reducing in Thailand, whether other countries participate in the liberalization or not. This poverty reduction occurs among farm and non-farm households, and the qualitative outcome is not dependent on the particular poverty line used in the analysis. The reduction in farm and nonfarm poverty incidence occurs despite an increase in inequality in Thailand. Liberalization raises real skilled wages relative to real unskilled wages, and this effect increases inequality. Both Thailand's own liberalization and the liberalization of the rest of the world reduce poverty among farm and nonfarm households, but the largest benefits from across-the-board liberalization, measured in terms of the effects on poverty, arise from Thailand's own liberalization.

If the trade liberalization is confined to agricultural products alone, the results are somewhat different. A similar increase in inequality occurs, but unilateral agricultural liberalization in Thailand raises the incidence of poverty among farm households, while reducing it slightly among nonfarm households. This negative effect on rural households arises from the reduction in real unskilled wages. If the rest of the world also liberalizes agricultural trade, the increase in farm-level poverty in Thailand disappears. Thailand's farm poor thus have an interest in agricultural liberalization, but only if the rest of the world also liberalizes.

Our analyses of trade liberalization in Thailand in this chapter and the study by Warr on Indonesia in chapter 6 use similar modeling frameworks, but the structure of agricultural trade and agricultural protection in the two countries is quite different. A direct comparison of the simulated effects of liberalized trade policies is therefore possible and offers insights.

The unilateral liberalization of all commodities reduces the incidence of poverty among farm and nonfarm households in both countries. In both countries, skilled and unskilled real wages rise as a result of this liberalization. However, the magnitude of the rise in unskilled wages is greater in Thailand. This reveals a key difference in the effects of the overall structure of the distortions to incentives in the two countries. In Thailand, industry assistance policies act more strongly against the interests of unskilled workers by favoring industries that are less intensive in the use of this factor. The result is that across-the-board liberalization has a much larger poverty-reducing effect in Thailand than in Indonesia, although it reduces the incidence of poverty among all socioeconomic groups in both countries.

Rest-of-the-world liberalization in all commodities is poverty reducing among all socioeconomic groups in both countries, but the magnitude of this effect is larger in Indonesia. Rest-of-the-world liberalization raises the prices of agricultural products relative to the prices of manufactured goods. Indonesia's poor are more dependent on agricultural production, and the magnitude of the poverty reduction that occurs following rest-of-the-world liberalization is therefore greater in Indonesia.

If liberalization occurs only in agricultural products, the returns to agricultural capital and land decline in both countries. In Indonesia, unskilled wages also decline significantly, whereas, in Thailand, this effect is negligible. This divergence in outcomes reflects a difference in the structure of agricultural assistance in the two countries. Indonesia's agricultural distortions are more biased toward unskilled labor–intensive agricultural industries, of which rice—highly protected in Indonesia, but not in Thailand—is the most important example. Meanwhile, because rice is a staple consumer good among Indonesia's poor, a reduction in agricultural assistance benefits many poor households, rural as well as urban. The outcome of unilateral agricultural liberalization is, in both countries, a reduction in the incidence of urban poverty and an increase in the incidence of rural poverty. The net effect is a small overall reduction in national poverty incidence in Indonesia and a small overall increase in Thailand. Rest-of-the-world liberalization in agricultural products alone is poverty reducing among all socioeconomic groups in both countries.

Overall, the key results common to both countries are as follows:

- The poor have a strong interest in across-the-board liberalization both in their own country and in the rest of the world; this applies to the rural poor and the urban poor.
- The urban poor have an interest in unilateral agricultural liberalization, while the rural poor do not.
- Agricultural liberalization in the rest of the world is poverty reducing among all socioeconomic groups in rural and urban areas.

## Notes

1. Structural change in the Thai economy is reviewed by Warr (2007), and a fuller discussion of Thailand's agricultural trade policies is provided by Warr (2008a) and Warr and Kohpaiboon (2009). The estimates of agricultural assistance for Thailand supplied by Warr and Kohpaiboon (2009) are incorporated in the World Bank's Distortions to Agricultural Incentives Project Database (Anderson and Valenzuela 2008). The estimates cover four or more decades. The representative values for computable general equilibrium modeling as of 2004 that are used here are available in Valenzuela and Anderson (2008).

2. A bilateral trading arrangement with the United States was under negotiation prior to February 2006, but the negotiations are currently suspended. The protection of Thailand's soybean industry would be an important issue in the negotiations.

3. This treatment differs from that used by us in the Indonesian case study in chapter 6, in which the commodities exported and sold domestically are identical, but the quantity of exports in import-competing industries is fixed exogenously.

4. The population sizes of the 10 major categories are not the same, but, *within* each category, the population sizes of the 20 subcategories are the same.

5. Poverty incidence at the US$1-a-day level is extremely low in Thailand. We have been unable to measure it with any hope of accuracy using our methods in this study.

## References

Anderson, K., and E. Valenzuela. 2008. "Estimates of Global Distortions to Agricultural Incentives, 1955–2007." Data spreadsheet, October, World Bank, Washington, DC. http://go.worldbank.org/YAO39F35E0.

Dixon, P. B., B. R. Parmenter, J. Sutton, and D. P. Vincent. 1982. *ORANI: A Multisectoral Model of the Australian Economy*. Amsterdam: North-Holland.

Hertel, T. W., ed. 1997. *Global Trade Analysis: Modeling and Applications*. New York: Cambridge University Press.

Horridge, M. 2004. "ORANI-G: A Generic Single-Country Computable General Equilibrium Model." Centre of Policy Studies, Monash University, Melbourne.

Johansen, L. 1964. *A Multi-sectoral Study of Economic Growth*. Amsterdam: North-Holland.

NESDB (Office of the National Economic and Social Development Board). 2004. *Input-Output Tables of Thailand, 2000*. Bangkok: National Accounts Office, NESDB.

NSO (National Statistical Office). 2003. *Report of the Household Socio-economic Survey, 2000*. Bangkok: Economic Statistics Division, NSO.

PovcalNet. World Bank, Washington, DC. http://go.worldbank.org/NT2A1XUWP0 (accessed May 2008).

Valenzuela, E., and K. Anderson. 2008. "Alternative Agricultural Price Distortions for CGE Analysis of Developing Countries, 2004 and 1980–84." Research Memorandum 13 (December), Center for Global Trade Analysis, Department of Agricultural Economics, Purdue University, West Lafayette, IN. https://www.gtap.agecon.purdue.edu/resources/res_display.asp?RecordID=2925.

van der Mensbrugghe, D. 2005. "Linkage Technical Reference Document: Version 6.0." December, World Bank, Washington, DC. http://go.worldbank.org/JWPFA73LH0.

Warr, P. 2001. "Welfare Effects of an Export Tax: Thailand's Rice Premium." *American Journal of Agricultural Economics* 83 (4): 903–20.

———. 2005. "Food Policy and Poverty in Indonesia: A General Equilibrium Analysis." *Australian Journal of Agricultural and Resource Economics* 49 (4): 429–51.

———. 2007. "Long-Term Economic Performance in Thailand." *ASEAN Economic Bulletin* 24 (1). 1–26.

———. 2008a. "Trade Policy and the Structure of Incentives in Thai Agriculture." *ASEAN Economic Bulletin* 25 (3): 249–70.

———. 2008b. "World Food Prices and Poverty Incidence in a Food Exporting Country: A Multi-household General Equilibrium Analysis for Thailand." *Agricultural Economics* 39 (3): 525–37.

Warr, P., and A. Kohpaiboon. 2009. "Thailand." In *Distortions to Agricultural Incentives in Asia*, ed. K. Anderson and W. Martin, 255–79. Washington, DC: World Bank.

# PART IV

# NATIONAL CGE APPROACHES: AFRICA

# 10

# MOZAMBIQUE

## Channing Arndt and James Thurlow

Mozambique has considerable agricultural potential. Only about 20 percent of its vast tracts of decent quality land and an even smaller share of its water resources are currently being exploited. The country's long coastline contains multiple harbors, which face eastward toward the dynamic markets of Asia. Regional markets also offer promise in the short and long term.

Despite this potential, Mozambique earned the unwanted label of poorest country in the world in the early 1990s. The country's severe poverty and poor economic performance were the result of a number of factors, including the character of Portuguese colonization, a failed socialist experiment, and more than a decade of vicious civil war that lasted until 1992 (Tarp et al. 2002). Since the end of the war, Mozambique has performed much better, and most development indicators have shown substantial improvement (Arndt, Jones, and Tarp 2006). Nonetheless, its low starting point underlines the country's need for substantial growth over an extended period if it is to reach even the average conditions among developing countries.

So, while much improved over the past two decades, the economic situation in Mozambique remains sobering, particularly in rural areas, where 70 percent of the population resides. About half of the rural population is considered absolutely poor, meaning that these households have difficulty acquiring even the most basic necessities such as sufficient food to meet calorie requirements (Arndt and Simler 2004). Rural dwellers, particularly the poor, depend heavily on crop agriculture for their incomes. Technology is generally rudimentary, and agricultural value added remains concentrated in cassava, cereals (particularly maize), and beans. Only a small minority of rural households report using improved seeds, fertilizers, and

**303**

pesticides (Uaiene 2008). Rural households tend to consume most of their production directly; they market only a relatively small share. Overall, approximately three-quarters of the population (rural and urban) depend on agriculture for the majority, often a large majority, of their incomes. Urban households also rely on domestically produced agricultural goods, particularly urban households outside Maputo, the capital city. Given the weight of agriculture in the economic life of most Mozambicans, growth in agriculture is widely regarded as a potentially powerful lever for reducing poverty (Thurlow 2008, Tarp et al. 2002).

Agriculture is also a potential driver of exports and economic growth. Mozambique already exports a range of traditional crops, such as tobacco, sugarcane, and cotton. These crops contribute to upstream processing in the manufacturing sector, which has grown rapidly over the last decade. Moreover, the country's underutilized natural resources have attracted considerable foreign investment interest.[1] However, most options for rapid growth in agriculture depend on foreign demand through exports of primary or processed products.

The critical role of international markets in agricultural growth stems from two facts. First, the import penetration in agriculture is relatively limited: imports represent only about 4 percent of the total demand for agricultural products.[2] While there is room to displace processed food imports, the overall scope for growth via import substitution is narrow. Second, because of geographical factors, even the relatively small volume of existing imports would be difficult to displace. The large majority of agricultural imports are consumed in the south of the country, particularly in Maputo. However, the agricultural potential in the south is limited. The more favorable growing areas are located 1,000 to 2,000 kilometers away in the northern and central regions of the country. Because of the large distances, inadequate infrastructure, the inefficiencies in storage, and, especially, the high cost of capital, exporting surplus from the north and importing the same products in the south is generally more efficient than attempting to transport surpluses across space (north to south) and time (from the postharvest period to the hungry season; for example, see Arndt, Schiller, and Tarp 2001; Cruz 2006). Hence, for agriculture to grow substantially, an export orientation is crucial. This may be achieved through exports of primary agriculture or processed farm products.

The links among international agricultural markets, agricultural growth, and the prospects for overall growth and poverty reduction provide the motivation for our study. Similar to other chapters in this volume, this chapter examines whether distortions to agricultural markets hamper the prospects for reducing poverty and income inequality. Two sources of distortions are considered: the distortions to domestic agricultural markets imposed by the government of Mozambique and the distortions imposed by other countries that influence Mozambique's export prospects and import prices.

The chapter is structured as follows. The next section provides basic information on the structure of the Mozambican economy and summarizes the results of a detailed study of domestic agricultural distortions. The subsequent section presents the modeling framework we use for our analysis. The following section discusses our simulations and results. A final section concludes.

## Economic Structure and Agricultural Distortions in Mozambique

The structure of the Mozambican economy is summarized in table 10.1. Agriculture represents about 26 percent of total GDP and 19 percent of exports. Exports are dominated by fisheries, which generate two thirds of raw agricultural export earnings. The low import penetration in agriculture is reflected in the small share of agriculture in total imports and by the small share of imports in the total domestic demand for agricultural goods. Agriculture has strong links to agriculture related processing in the manufacturing sector. Sugar processing, for instance, relies on domestically sourced sugarcane, as do cotton and tobacco processing and grain milling. Together, these processing sectors represent about 0.6 percent of total GDP and 3 percent of exports. Agriculture's upstream links are therefore an important part of the sector's overall contribution to the economy.

The relatively large share of manufacturing in total exports is driven by aluminum smelting, which accounts for around half of all export earnings and 5 percent of total GDP. As documented by Andersson (2001), aluminum smelting is largely an enclave sector characterized by high capital intensity, specific capital requirements, foreign ownership, limited taxation, expatriate labor, and imported intermediates. All aluminum production is exported, and the links between the aluminum sector and the rest of the economy are weak. If aluminum were removed, agriculture would represent 37 percent of exports and 28 percent of GDP.

The agricultural sector has undergone progressive liberalization and the gradual elimination of government intervention since 1987. In particular, the country shifted from central planning to a market economy. The reform program has substantially reduced government involvement in agriculture. A detailed study of the agricultural distortions in Mozambique finds that, since the period of reform from a centrally planned to a market economy, there has been hardly any substantial government intervention in the sector, and few distortions are observed (Alfieri, Arndt, and Cirera 2009). The government intervention that does exist relies primarily on the use of import tariffs. There are a few exceptions, such as the cotton, cashew, and sugar sectors, in which more complex policies have been implemented. Nonetheless, the overall picture is one of distinctly limited government involvement.

**Table 10.1. The Economic Structure in 2002 and Price Distortions in 2004, Mozambique**
*(percent)*

| Sectors | GDP share | Output subsidy | Imports | | | Exports | | |
|---|---|---|---|---|---|---|---|---|
| | | | Share | Intensity | Tariff | Share | Intensity | Tax rate |
| Total | 100.0 | 0.1 | 100.0 | 24.0 | 9.3 | 100.0 | 11.4 | -0.1 |
| Agriculture | 26.1 | 0.7 | 2.9 | 4.8 | 5.2 | 19.0 | 13.0 | — |
| Maize | 3.5 | -0.1 | 0.3 | 4.4 | 10.0 | 0.2 | 1.0 | — |
| Sorghum | 1.1 | -0.1 | — | — | — | — | — | — |
| Unshelled rice | 0.7 | -0.2 | 0.0 | 0.0 | 25.9 | — | — | — |
| Wheat | — | — | 1.7 | 100.0 | 2.5 | — | — | — |
| Cassava | 7.2 | — | — | — | — | — | — | — |
| Roots and tubers | 0.2 | — | 0.0 | 2.2 | 10.9 | 0.0 | 0.0 | — |
| Beans | 1.0 | — | 0.0 | 2.2 | 10.9 | 0.0 | 0.3 | — |
| Groundnuts | 0.9 | 24.6 | 0.1 | 2.1 | 0.8 | 0.0 | 0.0 | — |
| Cashews | 0.4 | — | 0.0 | 0.2 | 10.9 | 1.6 | 43.6 | — |
| Vegetables | 1.7 | -0.9 | 0.0 | 1.5 | 19.0 | 0.0 | 0.0 | — |
| Fruits | 1.6 | -0.9 | 0.0 | 1.3 | 19.0 | 1.7 | 19.3 | — |
| Leaf tea | 0.0 | — | — | — | — | — | — | — |
| Tobacco | 0.3 | — | 0.3 | 40.4 | 10.9 | 0.8 | 47.7 | — |
| Sugarcane | 0.1 | 8.4 | — | — | — | — | — | — |
| Cotton | 0.3 | -3.1 | — | — | — | — | — | — |
| Other crops | 0.8 | -0.8 | 0.2 | 6.5 | 8.2 | 0.0 | 0.1 | — |
| Livestock | 0.5 | -1.4 | 0.0 | 2.3 | — | 0.0 | 0.4 | — |
| Forestry | 2.8 | -0.7 | 0.1 | 0.6 | 3.0 | 1.6 | 10.7 | — |
| Fisheries | 2.3 | -0.7 | 0.0 | 0.0 | 3.0 | 12.7 | 63.6 | — |

| | | | | | | | |
|---|---|---|---|---|---|---|---|
| Industry | 23.2 | 0.0 | 76.0 | 44.6 | 2.1 | 67.1 | 23.6 | −0.1 |
| Mining | 0.3 | −0.7 | 0.2 | 6.6 | 3.0 | 0.3 | 4.9 | — |
| Manufacturing | 13.7 | 0.0 | 70.3 | 57.9 | 2.4 | 55.5 | 35.7 | −0.1 |
| Meat processing | 1.5 | — | 0.3 | 3.1 | 9 | 0.0 | 0.0 | — |
| Other food products | 1.4 | — | 4.2 | 34.4 | 8.7 | 1.6 | 8.5 | — |
| Grain milling | 1.6 | — | 8.5 | 45.0 | 8.7 | 0.2 | 0.7 | — |
| Sugar processing | 0.1 | — | 0.7 | 49.9 | 9.9 | 0.5 | 15.1 | — |
| Beverages | 0.8 | — | 1.3 | 18.6 | 7 | — | — | — |
| Tobacco processing | 0.1 | — | 0.4 | 36.4 | 7 | — | — | — |
| Cotton processing | 0.4 | −0.2 | 2.5 | 66.2 | 3 | 2.7 | 64.5 | −2.0 |
| Textiles and clothing | 0.6 | −0.2 | 2.0 | 40.3 | 3 | 0.7 | 10.3 | — |
| Wood products | 0.8 | −0.2 | 3.1 | 39.0 | 3 | 0.5 | 4.5 | — |
| Chemicals | 0.4 | — | 20.2 | 86.1 | 2 | 0.4 | 6.4 | — |
| Nonmetals | 0.7 | — | 2.3 | 37.8 | 2 | 0.1 | 0.7 | — |
| Metal products | 5.2 | — | 5.3 | 71.6 | 2 | 48.6 | 94.8 | — |
| Machinery | 0.0 | — | 17.3 | 99.4 | 2 | — | — | — |
| Other manufacturing | 0.0 | — | 2.4 | 96.8 | 2 | 0.2 | 46.7 | — |
| Electricity | 1.9 | — | 5.5 | 81.0 | 3 | 11.3 | 79.9 | — |
| Water | 0.3 | — | — | — | — | — | — | — |
| Construction | 7.1 | — | — | — | — | — | — | — |
| Services | 50.7 | — | 21.1 | 9.2 | — | 13.9 | 3.2 | — |

Sources: Social accounting matrix for Mozambique in 2002 (Thurlow 2008) adjusted to reflect the developing-country distortions compiled by Anderson and Valenzuela (2008) and harmonized with the Global Trade Analysis Project model and the Linkage model in Valenzuela and Anderson (2008).

Note: Import intensity is the share of imports in each sector's total domestic demand. Export intensity is the share of exports in each sector's total domestic output. — = data are not available or the indicator is not applicable.

The social accounting matrix we use for our analysis reflects this situation. The only meaningful distortions in the matrix are import tariffs. These are also shown in Table 10.1. To maintain consistency with other studies in this volume, we impose the tariffs in the Linkage model on the Mozambican computable general equilibrium (CGE) model.[3] Similar to many other least developed countries, Mozambique views tariffs as a tool for both raising revenue and influencing prices and incentives within the economy (Arndt and Tarp 2008). Consistent with the revenue-raising goal, most rates are positive, but relatively low. The exceptions are the rates imposed on processed sugar (nearly 100 percent), rice (26 percent), and many processed food commodities (around 20 percent). More recently, the sugar tariff, which is implemented as a variable levy, has declined to near zero because of increases in the world price of sugar. The tariffs on rice have also declined. For our study, we retain the applied rates from 2004 in our estimates of the impact of the removal of domestic price distortions.

## The Modeling Framework

The CGE model used in our study contains 56 activities and commodities, including 24 agricultural and 7 food processing sectors.[4] We identify five factors of production: three types of labor (unskilled, semiskilled, and skilled), agricultural land, and capital. Factor intensities for each sector are shown in table 10.2. Rural and urban labor markets are segmented, such that rural nonfarm and urban nonagriculture are distinguished. We assume that the factors in the model are fully employed at flexible real wages. The only exceptions are rural and urban unskilled laborers, who are unemployed at fixed nominal wages, and capital in the metals and electricity sectors, which is immobile and earning sector-specific returns.[5] The former captures the underemployment of lower-skilled workers in Mozambique, while the latter reflects a dependence on foreign direct investment. Using these factors, producers in the model maximize their profits under technologies exhibiting constant returns to scale, and the choice among factors is governed by a constant elasticity of substitution function. We then combine factors with fixed-share intermediates using a Leontief specification. Under profit maximization, the factors receive income such that marginal revenue equals marginal cost based on endogenous relative prices.

The possibility of substitution exists between production for domestic and production for foreign markets. The decision of producers is governed by a constant elasticity of transformation function that distinguishes between exported and domestic goods to capture any time or quality differences between the two types of products. Profit maximization drives producers to sell in the markets in which they are able to achieve the highest returns. These returns are based on domestic and export prices (whereby the latter is determined by the world price, multiplied by the exchange rate and adjusted for any taxes). Under the small

**Table 10.2. Factor Intensities of Production, Mozambique, 2002**

| Sector | Labor | | | | Capital | Land | Total |
|---|---|---|---|---|---|---|---|
| | Skilled | Semiskilled | Unskilled | All | | | |
| Total | 10.7 | 13.8 | 39.7 | 64.1 | 6.1 | 29.8 | 100.0 |
| Agriculture | 0.6 | 1.9 | 59.6 | 62.1 | 23.3 | 14.6 | 100.0 |
| Maize | 0.6 | 1.9 | 58.1 | 60.6 | 29.7 | 9.7 | 100.0 |
| Sorghum | 0.6 | 2.0 | 61.6 | 64.2 | 26.6 | 9.2 | 100.0 |
| Unshelled rice | 0.5 | 1.8 | 54.5 | 56.8 | 30.7 | 12.5 | 100.0 |
| Wheat | — | — | — | — | — | — | — |
| Cassava | 0.5 | 1.8 | 56.0 | 58.3 | 30.3 | 11.4 | 100.0 |
| Roots and tubers | 0.4 | 1.3 | 39.6 | 41.3 | 42.1 | 16.6 | 100.0 |
| Beans | 0.4 | 1.4 | 42.7 | 44.6 | 38.7 | 16.8 | 100.0 |
| Groundnuts | 0.6 | 2.2 | 65.1 | 67.9 | 20.4 | 11.7 | 100.0 |
| Cashews | 0.3 | 1.2 | 35.8 | 37.3 | 42.7 | 20.0 | 100.0 |
| Vegetables | 0.6 | 2.0 | 60.2 | 62.8 | 26.8 | 10.5 | 100.0 |
| Fruits | 0.4 | 1.2 | 36.5 | 38.1 | 43.8 | 18.1 | 100.0 |
| Leaf tea | 0.4 | 1.3 | 38.5 | 40.1 | 41.2 | 18.6 | 100.0 |
| Tobacco | 0.6 | 1.9 | 56.2 | 63.6 | 29.7 | 11.6 | 100.0 |
| Sugarcane | 0.1 | 0.2 | 7.1 | 7.4 | 73.3 | 19.3 | 100.0 |
| Cotton | 0.4 | 1.3 | 38.6 | 40.2 | 41.4 | 18.4 | 100.0 |
| Other crops | 0.5 | 1.8 | 56.6 | 59.0 | 29.5 | 11.5 | 100.0 |
| Livestock | 0.8 | 2.5 | 78.0 | 81.3 | 18.7 | — | 100.0 |
| Forestry | 0.6 | 2.0 | 63.2 | 65.8 | 34.2 | — | 100.0 |
| Fisheries | 0.8 | 2.8 | 87.2 | 90.9 | 9.1 | — | 100.0 |

*(Table continues on the following page.)*

**Table 10.2. Factor Intensities of Production, Mozambique, 2002 (*continued*)**

| Sector | Labor | | | | Capital | Land | Total |
|---|---|---|---|---|---|---|---|
| | Skilled | Semiskilled | Unskilled | All | | | |
| Industry | 10.7 | 9.7 | 20.8 | 41.2 | 58.8 | — | 100.0 |
| Mining | 1.4 | 2.8 | 11.6 | 15.7 | 84.3 | — | 100.0 |
| Manufacturing | 10.9 | 8.3 | 17.3 | 36.6 | 63.4 | — | 100.0 |
| Meat processing | 18.4 | 14.1 | 29.3 | 61.7 | 38.3 | — | 100.0 |
| Other food products | 18.4 | 14.1 | 29.3 | 61.7 | 38.3 | — | 100.0 |
| Grain milling | 24.5 | 18.8 | 39.1 | 82.3 | 17.7 | — | 100.0 |
| Sugar processing | 15.8 | 12.1 | 25.2 | 53.2 | 46.8 | — | 100.0 |
| Beverages | 3.3 | 2.5 | 5.3 | 11.1 | 88.9 | — | 100.0 |
| Tobacco processing | 3.3 | 2.5 | 5.3 | 11.1 | 88.9 | — | 100.0 |
| Cotton processing | 23.4 | 17.9 | 37.3 | 78.7 | 21.3 | — | 100.0 |
| Textiles and clothing | 24.0 | 18.3 | 38.1 | 80.4 | 19.6 | — | 100.0 |
| Wood products | 24.4 | 18.7 | 38.8 | 81.8 | 18.2 | — | 100.0 |
| Chemicals | 8.9 | 6.8 | 14.1 | 29.8 | 70.2 | — | 100.0 |
| Nonmetals | 3.0 | 2.3 | 4.8 | 10.0 | 90.0 | — | 100.0 |
| Metal products | 0.2 | 0.1 | 0.3 | 0.6 | 99.4 | — | 100.0 |
| Machinery | 8.4 | 6.4 | 13.3 | 28.1 | 71.9 | — | 100.0 |
| Other manufacturing | 8.2 | 6.3 | 13.0 | 27.4 | 72.6 | — | 100.0 |
| Electricity | 9.0 | 6.9 | 14.3 | 30.2 | 69.8 | — | 100.0 |
| Water | 6.5 | 7.7 | 17.0 | 31.3 | 68.7 | — | 100.0 |
| Construction | 11.4 | 13.5 | 29.9 | 54.8 | 45.2 | — | 100.0 |
| Services | 15.9 | 21.7 | 38.0 | 75.7 | 24.3 | — | 100.0 |

*Source:* CGE model for Mozambique by the authors (see Thurlow 2008).
*Note:* — = data are not available.

country assumption, Mozambique faces perfectly elastic world demand curves at fixed world prices (global liberalization is discussed below). The final ratio of exports to domestic goods is determined by the endogenous interaction of the relative prices for these two commodity types.

Additional substitution possibilities exist between imported and domestic goods under a constant elasticity of substitution Armington specification. In this case, substitution may take place in both final and intermediate usages. The elasticities vary across sectors; the lower elasticities reflect greater differences between domestic and imported goods. Under the small country assumption, Mozambique faces an infinitely elastic world supply at fixed world prices. The final ratio of imports to domestic goods is determined by the cost-minimizing decision making of domestic demanders based on the relative prices of imports and domestic goods (both of which include the relevant taxes).

In global liberalization, the results from the World Bank's model of global trade (the Linkage model, see van der Mensbrugghe 2005) are transmitted to the Mozambique model via changes in the import prices, export prices, and export quantities faced by Mozambique. We simply apply the import price changes to the exogenous import prices in the Mozambique model. We apply export price and quantity changes derived from the Linkage model in the manner developed by Horridge and Zhai (2006). Specifically, export demand functions of the form $Q = (FP/P)^{ES}$ (where $Q$ is the quantity exported; $P$ is the export price; $ES$ is the elasticity of demand for exports; and $FP$ is a shift parameter) have been added to the Mozambique model to mimic the global Linkage model. Horridge and Zhai (2006) show that the export price and quantity changes generated by Linkage may be mimicked in a country model through shocks to the shifter parameter $FP$. Using lowercase to indicate percentage change, one may derive the percentage change in $FP$ applied to the Mozambique model as follows: $fp = p + q/ES$.

The model distinguishes among various institutions, including enterprises, the government, and 10 representative household groups. Households are disaggregated across rural and urban areas and national income quintiles. Households and enterprises receive incomes in payment for the use of their factors of production by producers. Households and enterprises pay direct taxes to the government (based on fixed tax rates), save (based on marginal propensities to save), and make transfers to the rest of the world. Enterprises pay their remaining incomes to households in the form of dividends. Households use their incomes to consume commodities under a linear expenditure system of demand.

Home consumption is important among rural households. It represents about half of the commodity consumption among all but the top quintile of rural households; among the top quintile, the share of home consumption in total commodity consumption is about one-quarter (table 10.3). Home consumption is driven in large

**Table 10.3. Household Income and Expenditure Shares, Mozambique, 2002**
(percent)

| Households | Labor | | | Capital | Land | Other income | Total |
|---|---|---|---|---|---|---|---|
| | Skilled | Semiskilled | Unskilled | | | | |
| All households | 11.7 | 15.0 | 43.4 | 22.4 | 6.7 | 0.8 | 100.0 |
| Rural | 0.8 | 5.2 | 68.6 | 7.7 | 17.5 | 0.2 | 100.0 |
| Quintile 1 | 0.1 | 1.9 | 84.2 | 2.5 | 11.3 | 0.1 | 100.0 |
| Quintile 2 | 0.2 | 2.4 | 74.5 | 3.2 | 19.6 | 0.2 | 100.0 |
| Quintile 3 | 0.4 | 3.7 | 65.8 | 5.2 | 24.6 | 0.1 | 100.0 |
| Quintile 4 | 0.2 | 4.3 | 69.5 | 5.8 | 20.0 | 0.2 | 100.0 |
| Quintile 5 | 2.4 | 10.2 | 59.9 | 16.4 | 10.8 | 0.2 | 100.0 |
| Urban | 18.4 | 21.1 | 27.9 | 31.4 | 0.0 | 1.2 | 100.0 |
| Quintile 1 | 0.1 | 12.4 | 77.9 | 9.5 | 0.0 | 0.1 | 100.0 |
| Quintile 2 | 2.8 | 18.9 | 61.6 | 16.6 | 0.0 | 0.1 | 100.0 |
| Quintile 3 | 1.4 | 15.5 | 69.8 | 13.0 | 0.0 | 0.3 | 100.0 |
| Quintile 4 | 5.1 | 25.0 | 46.2 | 23.3 | 0.0 | 0.3 | 100.0 |
| Quintile 5 | 23.5 | 21.3 | 18.0 | 35.8 | 0.0 | 1.5 | 100.0 |

| Households | Household expenditures | | | | | | |
| | Own goods | | Purchased goods | | Taxes | Savings | Total |
| | Food | Nonfood | Food | Nonfood | | | |
|---|---|---|---|---|---|---|---|
| All households | 8.6 | 6.7 | 19.0 | 62.7 | 1.7 | 1.3 | 100.0 |
| Rural | 22.6 | 17.7 | 12.3 | 46.5 | 0.3 | 0.7 | 100.0 |
| Quintile 1 | 36.3 | 15.6 | 14.0 | 34.0 | 0.0 | 0.1 | 100.0 |
| Quintile 2 | 30.1 | 16.4 | 13.3 | 39.7 | 0.0 | 0.5 | 100.0 |
| Quintile 3 | 28.2 | 18.9 | 12.4 | 39.8 | 0.3 | 0.4 | 100.0 |
| Quintile 4 | 20.3 | 21.5 | 12.7 | 45.2 | 0.1 | 0.3 | 100.0 |
| Quintile 5 | 10.2 | 14.9 | 10.4 | 62.2 | 0.7 | 1.6 | 100.0 |
| Urban | 0.0 | 0.0 | 23.1 | 72.7 | 2.6 | 1.6 | 100.0 |
| Quintile 1 | 0.0 | 0.0 | 56.8 | 42.5 | 0.3 | 0.3 | 100.0 |
| Quintile 2 | 0.0 | 0.0 | 43.1 | 55.5 | 0.6 | 0.9 | 100.0 |
| Quintile 3 | 0.0 | 0.0 | 44.9 | 53.1 | 0.8 | 1.2 | 100.0 |
| Quintile 4 | 0.0 | 0.0 | 30.2 | 66.8 | 1.7 | 1.3 | 100.0 |
| Quintile 5 | 0.0 | 0.0 | 18.1 | 77.1 | 3.0 | 1.8 | 100.0 |

*Source:* CGE model for Mozambique by the authors (see Thurlow 2008).

*Note:* Other income refers to government transfers (for example, pensions) and foreign remittances received. Own goods are goods produced and consumed by a household.

measure by substantial divergences between farmgate and consumer prices because of high transaction costs. These margins are captured in the model, wherein transactions costs potentially differ among domestic, imported, and exported goods. The modeling of home consumption and margins follows Arndt et al. (2000).

The government receives income through imposing activity, sales and direct taxes, and import tariffs and then makes transfers to households, enterprises, and the rest of the world. The government also purchases commodities in the form of government consumption expenditures. The remaining income of government is (dis)saved. All savings by households, enterprises, government, and the rest of the world (foreign savings) are collected in a savings pool from which investment is financed.

The model includes three broad macroeconomic accounts: the government balance, the current account, and the savings and investment account. To bring about balance among the various macroaccounts, we must specify a set of macroclosure rules. These provide a mechanism through which macroeconomic balance may be achieved. Consistent with other analyses in this volume, we assume a savings-driven closure to balance the savings and investment account. Under this closure, the marginal propensities to save of households and enterprises are fixed, while investment adjusts to changes in incomes to ensure that the level of investment and savings are equal. For the current account, we assume that a flexible exchange rate adjusts to maintain a fixed level of foreign savings. Thus, the external balance is held fixed in foreign currency terms. Finally, in the government account, we assume that the fiscal deficit remains unchanged and that government revenues and expenditures are balanced through changes in the direct tax rates on households and enterprises.

The CGE model is calibrated to a 2003 social accounting matrix (Thurlow 2008) that was constructed using information from national accounts, trade and tax data, and household income and expenditure data in the 2002 national household survey (INE 2004). Trade elasticities are taken from the Global Trade Analysis Project (Dimaranan 2006). The model is calibrated so that the initial equilibrium reproduces the values of the base year in the social accounting matrix. The results of the CGE model are passed back down to the household survey on which the model is based and in which the poverty measures are calculated. More specifically, the changes in the real commodity expenditures of each representative household in the CGE model are applied to the expenditures of the corresponding household in the survey. Total expenditures are compared to real expenditure poverty lines, and standard poverty measures are recalculated.

## The Simulations and the Results

In this section, we present the results of four simulations. The first two simulations assess the impact of the removal of distortions in the rest of the world without any changes in the tariffs and subsidies in Mozambique. We do this for all commodities (simulation 1) and then only for agriculture and agriculture-related processing (simulation 2). As with other case studies in this volume, the impacts of global liberalization are taken from the Linkage model (see the appendix by van der Mensbrugghe, Valenzuela, and Anderson). The impacts include changes in world import and export prices, as well as changes in the demand for Mozambican exports (table 10.4). The implications of global liberalization as derived from the Linkage model are imposed as in Horridge and Zhai (2006). These two simulations therefore model the impact on Mozambique if the rest of the world removes agricultural and nonagricultural distortions, while Mozambique does not.

The remaining two simulations (3 and 4) assess the impact if Mozambique removes its distortions. These include import tariffs and, to a much lesser extent, export and output taxes and subsidies. In both of these national simulations, there are no changes in the rest-of-the-world distortions. World prices therefore remain unchanged because we retain the small country assumption for Mozambican exports.

### Simulation 1: The global liberalization of all commodities

The results from the Linkage model indicate that Mozambique's terms of trade improve by 1.3 percent once the distortions on all the commodities in the rest of the world are removed (table 10.5). World demand for Mozambique's main exports increases, which is a strong driver in the results that follow. World import prices decline for Mozambique's main imported goods, such as clothing and other heavier manufactures; together, these account for more than half of total imports. Import prices rise for some commodities, such as processed foods, but these are less significant import commodities and show relatively low import penetration ratios (table 10.1).

Rising export prices encourage producers to increase their production for foreign markets, thereby causing an appreciation of the real exchange rate of 2.8 percent (table 10.5). Import demand, which is already rising because of falling world prices, increases additionally as a result of the appreciation, while the expansion of exports is only partially offset. The appreciation of the exchange rate also reduces the value of foreign inflows (mostly the value of foreign assistance measured in local currency) and, hence, lowers investment demand. However, the real appreciation and cheaper imported goods drive down consumer prices, causing a substantial rise in private consumption. Overall, the increase in exports and consumer spending outweighs any additional import penetration, and there is an increase in total GDP of 0.9 percent.

The increase in GDP is driven by agriculture and agriculture-related processing (table 10.6). Greater agricultural production occurs mainly because of increased fisheries exports, which already dominate exports (table 10.7) and are

**Table 10.4. The Exogenous Demand and Price Shocks Caused by Rest-of-the-World Liberalization, Mozambique**

*(percent change from the baseline)*

| Sector | Simulation 1: All commodities | | | Simulation 2: Agriculture only | | |
|---|---|---|---|---|---|---|
| | | Export | | | Export | |
| | Import price | Price | Quantity | Import price | Price | Quantity |
| Agriculture | | | | | | |
| Maize | 2.6 | 1.1 | 3.4 | 4.1 | 1.4 | 19.7 |
| Sorghum | 2.6 | 1.1 | 3.4 | 4.1 | 1.4 | 19.7 |
| Unshelled rice | 8.5 | — | — | 9.7 | — | — |
| Wheat | -0.9 | — | — | -0.8 | — | — |
| Cassava | -0.7 | 1.1 | 8.7 | 0.3 | 1.4 | 16.0 |
| Roots and tubers | -0.7 | 1.1 | 8.7 | 0.3 | 1.4 | 16.0 |
| Beans | -0.7 | 1.1 | 8.7 | 0.3 | 1.4 | 16.0 |
| Groundnuts | -1.2 | 1.0 | -9.7 | 0.1 | 1.3 | -2.8 |
| Cashews | -1.2 | 1.0 | -9.7 | 0.1 | 1.3 | -2.8 |
| Vegetables | -2.7 | 0.6 | 496.8 | -1.5 | 0.9 | 567.8 |
| Fruits | -2.7 | 0.6 | 496.8 | -1.5 | 0.9 | 567.8 |
| Leaf tea | -0.7 | 1.1 | 8.7 | 0.3 | 1.4 | 16.0 |
| Tobacco | -0.7 | 1.1 | 8.7 | 0.3 | 1.4 | 16.0 |
| Sugarcane | — | — | — | — | — | — |
| Cotton | — | 0.7 | 48.4 | — | 1.2 | 56.4 |
| Other crops | -0.7 | 1.1 | 8.7 | 0.3 | 1.4 | 16.0 |
| Cattle | — | — | — | — | — | — |
| Poultry | -1.7 | — | — | -0.1 | — | — |
| Other livestock | -1.7 | — | — | -0.1 | — | — |
| Forestry | 0.6 | 0.8 | 38.4 | 0.4 | 1.1 | -3.1 |
| Fisheries | 0.6 | 0.8 | 38.4 | 0.4 | 1.1 | -3.1 |

| Industry | | | | | | |
|---|---|---|---|---|---|---|
| Mining | 0.6 | 0.8 | 38.4 | 0.4 | 1.1 | −3.1 |
| Meat processing | −1.3 | — | — | 0.1 | — | — |
| Other food products | 1.9 | 0.4 | −5.8 | −0.3 | 0.7 | −15.7 |
| Grain milling | 1.9 | 0.4 | −5.8 | −0.3 | 0.7 | −15.7 |
| Sugar processing | −1.4 | 0.4 | −21.9 | −0.1 | 0.9 | −11.9 |
| Beverages | 1.9 | 0.4 | −5.8 | −0.3 | 0.7 | −15.7 |
| Tobacco processing | 0.6 | 0.8 | 38.4 | 0.4 | 1.1 | −3.1 |
| Cotton processing | 0.6 | 0.8 | 38.4 | 0.4 | 1.1 | −3.1 |
| Textiles and clothing | −1.3 | 0.3 | 22.4 | 0.6 | 0.8 | −3.2 |
| Wood products | −0.8 | 0.2 | −7.6 | 0.2 | 0.7 | −5.1 |
| Chemicals | −0.8 | 0.2 | −7.6 | 0.2 | 0.7 | −5.1 |
| Nonmetals | −0.8 | 0.2 | −7.6 | 0.2 | 0.7 | −5.1 |
| Metal products | −0.8 | 0.2 | −7.6 | 0.2 | 0.7 | −5.1 |
| Machinery | −0.8 | 0.2 | −7.6 | 0.2 | 0.7 | −5.1 |
| Other manufacturing | −0.8 | 0.2 | −7.6 | 0.2 | 0.7 | −5.1 |
| Electricity | −0.3 | 0.3 | 1.7 | 0.3 | 0.7 | 1.0 |
| Water | −0.3 | 0.3 | 1.7 | 0.3 | 0.7 | 1.0 |
| Construction | −0.3 | 0.3 | 1.7 | 0.3 | 0.7 | 1.0 |
| Services | −0.3 | 0.3 | 1.7 | 0.3 | 0.7 | 1.0 |

Source: Results from the World Bank Linkage model (see the appendix by van der Mensbrugghe, Valenzuela, and Anderson).

Note: — = data are not available or the indicator is not applicable.

**Table 10.5. The Macroeconomic Simulation Results of Prospective Liberalization Abroad and Nationally, Mozambique**

*(percent)*

| | | Change from the base | | | |
| | | Rest-of-the-world liberalization | | Unilateral liberalization | |
| Indicator | Base share | Full | Agriculture | Full | Agriculture |
|---|---|---|---|---|---|
| Real GDP at market prices | 73.5 | 0.9 | −0.1 | 1.2 | 0.7 |
| Consumption | 59.1 | 1.4 | −0.2 | 1.0 | 1.1 |
| Investment | 18.8 | 0.5 | −0.2 | 1.6 | −0.9 |
| Government | 10.4 | 0.0 | 0.0 | 0.0 | 0.0 |
| Exports | 14.1 | 3.8 | 0.1 | 9.8 | 6.4 |
| Agriculture | 19.0 | 19.5 | 0.1 | 28.4 | 19.5 |
| Industry | 67.1 | 0.6 | −0.2 | 2.8 | 1.4 |
| Services | 13.9 | −2.4 | 1.5 | 18.0 | 12.5 |
| Imports | −28.8 | 2.6 | −0.4 | 4.8 | 3.1 |
| Agriculture | 2.9 | 3.5 | −1.2 | −0.7 | −0.1 |
| Industry | 76.0 | 2.6 | −0.3 | 7.2 | 4.9 |
| Services | 21.1 | 2.2 | −0.4 | −3.5 | −3.0 |
| Consumer price index | — | −0.5 | 0.0 | −2.4 | −2.3 |
| Real exchange rate | — | −2.8 | 0.1 | 5.2 | 4.0 |
| World export prices | — | 1.0 | −0.4 | 0.0 | 0.0 |
| World import prices | — | −0.3 | 0.2 | 0.0 | 0.0 |
| Terms of trade | — | 1.3 | −0.6 | 0.0 | 0.0 |

*Source:* Simulations by the authors using the CGE model for Mozambique.

*Note:* The domestic price index is the numéraire in the model. — = data are not available or the indicator is not applicable.

generated by price rises and demand increases for Mozambican fish following global liberalization (table 10.4). There is also an expansion in cotton processing because the rice import and export prices and export demand increase. Some other traditional exports also benefit and contribute to the greater upstream production of processed goods. However, sectoral links work against sugarcane production because sugar processing declines as a result of falling world prices and greater import competition (tables 10.7 and 10.8). Finally, the overall increase in Mozambique's international trade generates additional demand for the domestic trade and transport sectors, which, together, drive most of the rise in service sector GDP under this simulation.

The improved terms of trade and the stimulus to export demand for primary and processed agricultural products resulting from global liberalization boost the demand for unskilled workers (greater employment), as well as the returns to the

**Table 10.6. The Effects of Prospective Liberalization Abroad and Nationally on GDP, by Sector, Mozambique**

(percent)

| Sector | Base share | Rest-of-the-world liberalization Full | Rest-of-the-world liberalization Agriculture | Unilateral liberalization Full | Unilateral liberalization Agriculture |
|---|---|---|---|---|---|
| Real GDP at factor cost | 100.0 | 0.9 | −0.1 | 0.9 | 0.3 |
| Agriculture | 26.1 | 2.6 | −0.1 | 2.9 | 1.9 |
| Maize | 3.5 | 1.0 | 0.0 | −1.4 | −1.6 |
| Sorghum | 1.1 | 2.4 | −0.2 | 2.3 | 1.4 |
| Unshelled rice | 0.7 | 0.9 | −0.4 | −3.3 | 3.3 |
| Wheat | 0.0 | 0.0 | 0.0 | 0.0 | 0.0 |
| Cassava | 7.2 | 0.8 | −0.1 | 0.2 | 0.0 |
| Roots and tubers | 0.2 | 0.3 | 0.2 | −0.9 | 0.5 |
| Beans | 1.0 | 0.8 | −0.1 | 0.2 | 0.2 |
| Groundnuts | 0.9 | 0.9 | 0.0 | 21.9 | 22.0 |
| Cashews | 0.4 | −4.3 | −0.2 | 10.1 | 8.3 |
| Vegetables | 1.7 | 1.0 | −0.2 | −1.0 | −0.9 |
| Fruits | 1.6 | −0.6 | −0.2 | 0.9 | 0.9 |
| Leaf tea | 0.0 | 0.7 | 0.2 | 6.8 | 6.8 |
| Tobacco | 0.3 | −3.3 | 8.9 | 15.4 | 9.9 |
| Sugarcane | 0.1 | 0.8 | −0.4 | −2.3 | −2.2 |
| Cotton | 0.3 | 5.3 | 0.9 | 2.6 | −2.2 |
| Other crops | 0.8 | 0.5 | −0.4 | −3.5 | −3.6 |
| Livestock | 0.5 | 0.3 | −0.3 | −2.9 | −2.5 |
| Forestry | 2.8 | 2.8 | −0.1 | 0.8 | 0.4 |
| Fisheries | 2.3 | 20.2 | −1.0 | 21.5 | 13.8 |
| Industry | 23.2 | 0.1 | −0.1 | −0.7 | −1.3 |
| Mining | 0.3 | 0.1 | 0.0 | 0.1 | 0.1 |
| Manufacturing | 13.7 | 0.0 | −0.1 | −2.0 | −1.8 |
| Meat processing | 1.5 | 1.2 | −0.2 | −1.2 | −0.8 |
| Other food products | 1.4 | 0.8 | −0.8 | −1.9 | −2.1 |
| Grain milling | 1.6 | 1.2 | −0.3 | −3.5 | −3.8 |
| Sugar processing | 0.1 | −6.2 | −1.4 | −40.1 | −40.3 |
| Beverages | 0.8 | 0.5 | −0.2 | −2.3 | −1.8 |
| Tobacco processing | 0.1 | 0.6 | −0.1 | −1.8 | −1.6 |
| Cotton processing | 0.4 | 15.5 | 1.1 | 18.8 | 9.0 |
| Textiles and clothing | 0.6 | −3.0 | 0.6 | −10.5 | −11.1 |
| Wood products | 0.8 | −3.9 | 0.2 | −11.4 | −13.0 |
| Chemicals | 0.4 | −7.1 | 0.4 | −3.8 | 7.3 |
| Nonmetals | 0.7 | −3.6 | 0.2 | −1.7 | 2.6 |

(*Table continues on the following page.*)

**Table 10.6. The Effects of Prospective Liberalization Abroad and Nationally on GDP, by Sector, Mozambique (*continued*)**

(percent)

| Sector | Base share | Rest-of-the-world liberalization | | Unilateral liberalization | |
|---|---|---|---|---|---|
| | | Full | Agriculture | Full | Agriculture |
| Metal products | 5.2 | 0.0 | 0.0 | 0.0 | 0.0 |
| Machinery | 0.0 | −5.8 | 0.5 | −4.8 | 6.4 |
| Other manufacturing | 0.0 | −10.7 | −0.9 | 64.6 | 62.3 |
| Electricity | 1.9 | −0.1 | 0.1 | 0.3 | 0.2 |
| Water | 0.3 | −0.5 | −0.3 | −4.4 | −3.2 |
| Construction | 7.1 | 0.5 | −0.1 | 1.5 | −0.8 |
| Services | 50.7 | 0.3 | 0.0 | 0.6 | 0.3 |

*Source:* Simulations by the authors using the CGE model for Mozambique.

other factors (fully employed workers). Because agricultural production relies on unskilled rural labor and land intensively (the factor intensities are listed in table 10.2), the employment of unskilled rural labor rises by 3.2 percent, while the real returns to land rise by 3.0 percent (table 10.9). The increases in the demand for urban labor and more highly skilled labor are less pronounced, thereby reducing the pressure on factor prices. In addition, skilled workers are often employed by the government, and we assume that recurrent and wage bill expenditures are unaffected by rest-of-the-world liberalization (see the unchanged government spending in table 10.5). Capital returns rise slightly in nominal terms, alongside mild increases in production in the industry and service sectors.

All households in the model benefit from full global liberalization. However, the main beneficiaries are lower-income and rural households (measured by the equivalent variation). This is because these households derive a larger share of their incomes from agricultural production and processing, and these sectors are stimulated by the rest-of-the-world liberalization. In contrast, higher-income urban households receive a larger share of their incomes from capital earnings and skilled labor. The improved household welfare is also reflected in changes in the poverty headcount. The share of the population living below the US$1-a-day poverty line falls by 1.4 percent. The decline in poverty is only slightly larger among rural households, and there is no significant change in the inequality measures. Thus, the removal of global distortions on all commodities increases GDP and household welfare and reduces poverty in Mozambique, but has little impact on national inequality.

**Table 10.7. The Effects of Prospective Liberalization Abroad and Nationally on the Real Value of Exports, Mozambique**

(percent)

| Sector | Base share | Change from the base | | | |
| --- | --- | --- | --- | --- | --- |
| | | Rest-of-the-world liberalization | | Unilateral liberalization | |
| | | Full | Agriculture | Full | Agriculture |
| Total exports | 100.0 | 3.8 | 0.1 | 9.8 | 6.4 |
| Agriculture | 19.0 | 19.5 | 0.1 | 28.4 | 19.5 |
| Maize | 0.2 | 0.2 | 12.2 | 4.8 | 3.6 |
| Sorghum | 0.0 | 0.0 | 0.0 | 0.0 | 0.0 |
| Unshelled rice | 0.0 | 0.0 | 0.0 | 0.0 | 0.0 |
| Wheat | 0.0 | 0.0 | 0.0 | 0.0 | 0.0 |
| Cassava | 0.0 | 0.0 | 0.0 | 0.0 | 0.0 |
| Roots and tubers | 0.0 | 1.4 | 11.4 | 10.0 | 9.7 |
| Beans | 0.0 | −0.4 | 13.8 | 23.8 | 20.6 |
| Groundnuts | 0.0 | 402.7 | 504.8 | 169.3 | 162.5 |
| Cashews | 1.6 | −10.6 | −0.3 | 24.3 | 20.6 |
| Vegetables | 0.0 | −8.0 | −0.2 | 5.0 | 4.2 |
| Fruits | 1.7 | −10.2 | −0.2 | 13.9 | 12.0 |
| Leaf tea | 0.0 | 0.0 | 0.0 | 0.0 | 0.0 |
| Tobacco | 0.8 | −2.1 | 15.6 | 33.0 | 23.8 |
| Sugarcane | 0.0 | 0.0 | 0.0 | 0.0 | 0.0 |
| Cotton | 0.0 | 0.0 | 0.0 | 0.0 | 0.0 |
| Other crops | 0.0 | −2.1 | −0.1 | 2.0 | 0.9 |
| Livestock | 0.0 | −2.4 | 0.0 | 4.2 | 3.0 |
| Forestry | 1.6 | 20.4 | 0.0 | 17.1 | 13.5 |
| Fisheries | 12.7 | 29.5 | −1.3 | 32.6 | 21.2 |
| Industry | 67.1 | 0.6 | −0.2 | 2.8 | 1.4 |
| Mining | 0.3 | 15.9 | 0.2 | 13.7 | 11.6 |
| Manufacturing | 55.5 | 0.6 | −0.4 | 2.8 | 1.5 |
| Meat processing | 0.0 | −6.1 | 0.2 | 19.3 | 17.4 |
| Other food products | 1.6 | −6.2 | −8.0 | 6.4 | 5.2 |
| Grain milling | 0.2 | −6.7 | −8.7 | 7.3 | 5.1 |
| Sugar processing | 0.5 | −18.4 | −5.9 | −27.7 | −29.7 |
| Beverages | 0.0 | 0.0 | 0.0 | 0.0 | 0.0 |
| Tobacco processing | 0.0 | 0.0 | 0.0 | 0.0 | 0.0 |
| Cotton processing | 2.7 | 23.7 | 1.2 | 35.7 | 22.1 |
| Textiles and clothing | 0.7 | 4.7 | 0.3 | 12.2 | 9.2 |
| Wood products | 0.5 | −10.1 | −1.3 | 8.1 | 1.6 |
| Chemicals | 0.4 | −10.6 | −1.2 | 15.3 | 18.1 |
| Nonmetals | 0.1 | −9.9 | −1.4 | 15.7 | 14.4 |

(Table continues on the following page.)

**Table 10.7. The Effects of Prospective Liberalization Abroad and Nationally on the Real Value of Exports, Mozambique (*continued*)**

(percent)

| | | Change from the base | | | |
| | | Rest-of-the-world liberalization | | Unilateral liberalization | |
| Sector | Base share | Full | Agriculture | Full | Agriculture |
|---|---|---|---|---|---|
| Metal products | 48.6 | 0.0 | −0.1 | 0.5 | 0.0 |
| Machinery | 0.0 | 0.0 | 0.0 | 0.0 | 0.0 |
| Other manufacturing | 0.2 | −12.6 | −1.7 | 107.3 | 92.5 |
| Electricity | 11.3 | −0.1 | 0.3 | 2.5 | 0.8 |
| Water | 0.0 | 0.0 | 0.0 | 0.0 | 0.0 |
| Construction | 0.0 | 0.0 | 0.0 | 0.0 | 0.0 |
| Services | 13.9 | −2.4 | 1.5 | 18.0 | 12.5 |

*Source:* Simulations by the authors using the CGE model for Mozambique.

### Simulation 2: The global liberalization of agricultural commodities only

In the global agricultural simulation, we model the impact of the removal by the rest of the world of only agricultural distortions, while the distortions in Mozambique are unchanged. Unlike the full global liberalization simulation, Mozambique now experiences a deterioration in the terms of trade of 0.6 percent. However, the demand rises for certain agricultural exports, while the demand declines for all processed commodities, such as processed tobacco, cotton, and sugar.

The principal macroeconomic effects of global agricultural liberalization are small and typically opposite in sign relative to the results of the full global simulation (compare table 10.5, columns 2 and 3). The changes at the sectoral level are correspondingly small (table 10.4), reflecting the relatively mild price and quantity changes that occur in the global markets for products of importance to Mozambique as a result of the rest-of-the-world agricultural trade liberalization (table 10.4). The impacts on factor rewards, welfare, and poverty are also relatively small (table 10.9).

### Simulation 3: The domestic liberalization of all commodities

In the third simulation, we assess the impact of the removal by Mozambique of all its own distortions, while the distortions of the rest of the world remain unchanged. Mozambique's largest distortions revolve around its import tariffs (table 10.1). There is also a small export subsidy for cotton processing, as well as output taxes on

**Table 10.8.  The Effects of Prospective Liberalization Abroad
and Nationally on the Real Value of Imports,
Mozambique**

(percent)

| Sector | Base share | Rest-of-the-world liberalization Full | Rest-of-the-world liberalization Agriculture | Unilateral liberalization Full | Unilateral liberalization Agriculture |
|---|---|---|---|---|---|
| Total imports | 100.0 | 2.6 | −0.4 | 4.8 | 3.1 |
| Agriculture | 2.9 | 3.5 | −1.2 | −0.7 | −0.1 |
| Maize | 0.3 | 2.1 | −4.4 | 3.4 | 4.1 |
| Sorghum | 0.0 | 0.0 | 0.0 | 0.0 | 0.0 |
| Unshelled rice | 0.0 | −17.1 | −36.6 | 146.1 | 152.5 |
| Wheat | 1.7 | 0.9 | −0.4 | −3.3 | −3.3 |
| Cassava | 0.0 | 0.0 | 0.0 | 0.0 | 0.0 |
| Roots and tubers | 0.0 | 6.8 | −0.7 | 8.1 | 9.9 |
| Beans | 0.0 | 11.2 | −0.9 | 14.4 | 16.3 |
| Groundnuts | 0.1 | 11.1 | 2.2 | −26.9 | −25.4 |
| Cashews | 0.0 | 10.3 | −0.4 | 0.3 | 1.6 |
| Vegetables | 0.0 | 8.0 | −0.5 | 21.3 | 23.4 |
| Fruits | 0.0 | 7.6 | −0.4 | 16.8 | 18.5 |
| Leaf tea | 0.0 | 0.0 | 0.0 | 0.0 | 0.0 |
| Tobacco | 0.3 | 9.2 | −3.6 | 4.0 | 6.6 |
| Sugarcane | 0.0 | 0.0 | 0.0 | 0.0 | 0.0 |
| Cotton | 0.0 | 0.0 | 0.0 | 0.0 | 0.0 |
| Other crops | 0.2 | 7.3 | −0.4 | 1.1 | 2.0 |
| Livestock | 0.0 | 6.2 | −0.3 | −6.7 | −5.4 |
| Forestry | 0.1 | 4.8 | −1.2 | −5.6 | −3.3 |
| Fisheries | 0.0 | −0.2 | −0.5 | −6.6 | −4.2 |
| Industry | 76.0 | 2.6 | −0.3 | 7.2 | 4.9 |
| Mining | 0.2 | 11.0 | −1.2 | 0.3 | 1.3 |
| Manufacturing | 70.3 | 2.6 | −0.3 | 7.8 | 5.8 |
| Meat processing | 0.3 | 16.1 | −1.1 | 59.0 | 64.1 |
| Other food products | 4.2 | 2.4 | 0.2 | 15.1 | 17.1 |
| Grain milling | 8.5 | 2.1 | 0.1 | 14.8 | 16.4 |
| Sugar processing | 0.7 | 8.4 | 0.0 | 137.1 | 142.0 |
| Beverages | 1.3 | 1.5 | 0.0 | 9.0 | 10.9 |
| Tobacco processing | 0.4 | 2.9 | −0.6 | 9.6 | 11.0 |
| Cotton processing | 2.5 | 3.0 | −0.7 | 12.8 | 14.2 |
| Textiles and clothing | 2.0 | 10.1 | −1.6 | 25.7 | 28.0 |
| Wood products | 3.1 | 6.9 | −0.7 | 22.0 | 23.8 |

*(Table continues on the following page.)*

**Table 10.8. The Effects of Prospective Liberalization Abroad and Nationally on the Real Value of Imports, Mozambique (*continued*)**

*(percent)*

| | | Change from the base | | | |
| | | Rest-of-the-world liberalization | | Unilateral liberalization | |
| Sector | Base share | Full | Agriculture | Full | Agriculture |
|---|---|---|---|---|---|
| Chemicals | 20.2 | 2.2 | −0.2 | 1.7 | −1.8 |
| Nonmetals | 2.3 | 6.9 | −0.7 | 6.2 | −6.0 |
| Metal products | 5.3 | 1.4 | −0.6 | 3.9 | −2.0 |
| Machinery | 17.3 | 1.0 | −0.2 | 1.2 | −1.6 |
| Other manufacturing | 2.4 | 2.3 | −0.4 | −1.3 | −4.4 |
| Electricity | 5.5 | 3.0 | −0.5 | 0.7 | −5.3 |
| Water | 0.0 | 0.0 | 0.0 | 0.0 | 0.0 |
| Construction | 0.0 | 0.0 | 0.0 | 0.0 | 0.0 |
| Services | 21.1 | 2.2 | −0.4 | −3.5 | −3.0 |

*Source:* Simulations by the authors using the CGE model for Mozambique.

groundnuts and raw sugarcane. Given the relatively few nontariff distortions, the reduction in import tariffs dominates in the results of this simulation.

The removal of import tariffs leads to a 4.8 percent increase in import demand. Highly protected sectors experience greater import penetration. Imports more than double in the most highly protected industry, sugar processing (table 10.8). However, highly protected commodities represent only a small share of total imports (see elsewhere above). Thus, the import tariffs on manufactures are low, and it is the increased domestic demand for these manufactured goods that drives the overall increase in imports. Furthermore, rapidly rising import demand places pressure on the current account, thereby inducing a 5.2 percent depreciation in the real exchange rate.

The depreciation improves export competitiveness. Recall that the major export, aluminum, is highly capital intensive and tied to existing manufacturing facilities. As a result, aluminum exports effectively do not respond to exchange rate signals, transferring the onus of the export supply response onto primary and processed agriculture, the second-largest exporting sector. Agricultural exports grow by 28 percent. Large increases in exports cause agricultural GDP to rise by 2.9 percent. In contrast, the manufacturing sector experiences a contraction almost across the board, with particularly marked declines in sugar processing; the overall decline is 2 percent. This is, however, insufficient to offset the expansion in agriculture, and real GDP rises by 0.9 percent under full domestic liberalization.

**Table 10.9. The Effects of Prospective Liberalization Abroad and Nationally on Employment, Welfare, and Poverty, Mozambique**

| Indicator | Base value | Rest-of-the-world liberalization | | Unilateral liberalization | |
|---|---|---|---|---|---|
| | | Full | Agriculture | Full | Agriculture |
| Real factor returns[a] | Index | Change from the base, % | | | |
| Rural skilled labor | 1.0 | 4.5 | −0.2 | 6.2 | 4.2 |
| Rural semiskilled labor | 1.0 | 3.2 | −0.2 | 5.2 | 3.0 |
| Rural unskilled | 1.0 | 0.5 | 0.0 | 2.4 | 2.3 |
| Urban skilled labor | 1.0 | 1.5 | −0.1 | 4.5 | 2.2 |
| Urban semiskilled labor | 1.0 | 1.9 | −0.2 | 3.9 | 2.0 |
| Urban unskilled | 1.0 | 0.5 | 0.0 | 2.4 | 2.3 |
| Capital | 1.0 | 0.6 | −0.5 | 5.7 | 3.2 |
| Agricultural land | 1.0 | 3.0 | 0.1 | 5.4 | 3.8 |
| Unskilled employment | Index | | | | |
| Rural | 1.0 | 3.2 | −0.1 | 3.0 | 1.5 |
| Urban | 1.0 | 1.0 | −0.1 | 1.0 | −0.3 |
| Equivalent variation, welfare | n.a. | 1.4 | −0.2 | 0.9 | 1.0 |
| Rural | | | | | |
| Quintile 1 | n.a. | 2.8 | −0.1 | 3.9 | 2.9 |
| Quintile 2 | n.a. | 2.8 | −0.1 | 4.3 | 3.2 |
| Quintile 3 | n.a. | 2.7 | −0.1 | 4.1 | 3.2 |
| Quintile 4 | n.a. | 2.8 | −0.1 | 4.3 | 3.2 |
| Quintile 5 | n.a. | 2.6 | −0.2 | 3.1 | 2.4 |
| Urban | | | | | |
| Quintile 1 | n.a. | 0.9 | −0.2 | 2.0 | 1.4 |
| Quintile 2 | n.a. | 1.0 | −0.2 | 2.5 | 2.0 |
| Quintile 3 | n.a. | 0.9 | −0.2 | 1.8 | 1.5 |
| Quintile 4 | n.a. | 0.8 | −0.3 | 0.9 | 1.1 |
| Quintile 5 | n.a. | 0.3 | −0.3 | −1.9 | −0.9 |
| Poverty headcount ratio | % | Change from the base, percentage points | | | |
| US$1-a-day poverty line | 36.2 | −1.4 | 0.0 | −1.7 | −1.3 |
| Rural | 36.0 | −1.5 | 0.0 | −2.1 | −1.6 |
| Urban | 36.5 | −1.3 | 0.0 | −0.9 | −0.5 |
| Inequality measures | Value | Change from the base, percentage points | | | |
| Gini coefficient | 0.477 | 0.1 | −0.1 | −1.5 | −1.2 |
| Theil entropy | 0.532 | 0.3 | −0.2 | −3.7 | −3.2 |

*Source:* Simulations by the authors using the CGE model for Mozambique.

*Note:* n.a. = not applicable.

a. Real factor returns are adjusted to reflect changes in the consumer price index (hence, the change in unskilled wages that are fixed in nominal terms).

Cheaper imported capital goods reduce the cost of investment, while the depreciating exchange rate raises the domestic value of foreign inflows. This causes an increase in investment demand and explains the 1.5 percent rise in construction value added. Cheaper imports also lower consumer prices. This would typically boost consumer spending. However, to replace lost tariff revenues, the government must raise personal and corporate tax revenues. Thus, even with the increase in GDP, the share of direct taxes in GDP more than doubles, rising from 2.1 to 5.3 percent.

We assume that tax rates adjust proportionally such that most of the additional tax burden falls on enterprises and higher-income urban households. This is realistic. Obtaining direct tax revenue from rural and urban poor households is effectively impossible. The new tax burden causes the welfare outcomes to be negative among urban households in the top quintile (table 10.9), despite the relatively large increases in the real returns to skilled labor and capital. The growth in agricultural exports and output drives a 3.0 percent gain in employment in unskilled rural labor and increases the factor prices for rural skilled labor and land by even larger shares. Welfare improves among rural households and all but the richest quintile among urban households.

Our assumptions about tax incidence greatly influence the distributional impacts of the removal of domestic distortions. If each household in Mozambique experiences the same percentage point increase in tax rates, then the gains are distributed much more evenly across households. However, if tax rates increase proportionally, as we have assumed, then most of the tax burden falls on high-income urban households. The latter assumption represents the only feasible direct tax policy. Sensitivity analysis reveals that other policies, such as increasing activity taxes or sales taxes, also tend to concentrate the tax incidence on urban households because of the significant dependence of rural households on home consumption, which evades taxation. As a result, under all feasible revenue replacement options, rural and lower-income urban households tend to gain more than proportionately from own-country trade liberalization. Moreover, a larger reduction in rural household incomes and poverty relative to urban household incomes and poverty causes national inequality to decline slightly, as reflected in the Gini coefficient.

### Simulation 4: The domestic liberalization of primary and processed agricultural commodities

In our final simulation, we consider the impact of the removal by Mozambique of distortions only in the country's agricultural sector, including agricultural processing and textiles. As in simulation 3, we assume that other countries do not alter their own distortions. In many ways, the results of this simulation are similar to the results of simulation 3, though they are somewhat more limited (table 10.5). Reducing tariffs causes imports to rise, the real exchange rate to depreciate, and exports to expand. Total GDP increases by 0.7 percent, in part because of an expansion in unskilled employment. However, there is a notable difference in the components of GDP compared with simulation 3. The combination of the less pronounced nominal depreciation (with implications for the pool of foreign savings), the increases in taxes on high-income urban households and enterprises, and the price rises in the construction sector imply that real investment actually declines. This allows the consumption aggregate to grow more relative to the result in simulation 3.

Because the largest distortions (the ones generated by import tariffs) occur in agricultural processing (textiles also enjoyed fairly significant protection, at 19 percent), the primary impact of the liberalization is to expand the imports of processed products, which are treated as part of industry in table 10.5. Primary agricultural imports actually decline slightly in the aggregate, despite the reduction in protection. Because agriculture is the major source of exports at the margin, the liberalization of agriculture, processed agriculture, and textiles actually stimulates agricultural production; the strongest production gains are registered in fisheries and groundnuts, which had low initial protection.

Commensurate with the consumption aggregate, aggregate household welfare improves slightly more relative to the results under full liberalization. The distributional outcomes are driven by the expansion in agriculture, which generally favors rural labor and land, and the mechanism used to replace lost tariff revenues, which affects the highest urban household quintile the most. Because the aggregate stimulus to agriculture is less in this simulation compared with the result in the full liberalization of all markets, the consumption gains are more evenly distributed across factors and, hence, across households. This leads to reductions in poverty that are slightly less pronounced than the ones in simulation 3 (table 10.9). There is, however, a similar reduction in national inequality because of the larger income gains and more significant poverty reductions among rural households relative to urban households.

## Conclusions

Agriculture is adversely affected by current global distortions, which are biased against some of Mozambique's key export sectors, such as fisheries. Removing all global distortions would reduce the prices for key imported commodities. It would, however, raise the prices of imported food items, dampening the gains in the terms of trade. Overall, Mozambique's terms of trade would improve. The production responses to a new global environment favor agriculture because of the stimulation of agricultural exports and import-competing food sectors. Agricultural GDP rises once all trade distortions in the rest of the world are eliminated, which reduces poverty in Mozambique. In contrast, the removal of only agricultural price distortions abroad has little effect on Mozambique's agricultural sector. The gains in traditional export crops, such as cotton and tobacco, are offset by heightened import competition in processed foods, which has adverse effects on downstream food-crop farmers. Thus, the net impact is a small decline in agricultural GDP and a small increase in national poverty if only agricultural distortions are removed in the rest of the world.

Mozambique's own distortions are also biased against agriculture. The producers of processed agricultural products enjoy high levels of protection. The removal of these barriers causes a significant expansion in agricultural GDP despite the associated elimination of tariffs on primary products. The primary agricultural sectors lose little from these tariff reductions because of the relatively low initial protection rates and low import penetration. The rise in agricultural GDP is driven by increased agricultural exports, especially fisheries. Full liberalization nonetheless provides a bigger stimulus to the agricultural sector. Poverty reduction is greater in the full liberalization case because of the relatively greater pro-poor distribution of the welfare gains to households. Inequality also declines through the reduction in domestic distortions.

The results of the model suggest that the removal of domestic and global distortions would have positive implications for agriculture and the expansion of the overall economy of Mozambique. It would also contribute to reducing poverty, which is particularly severe in rural areas. Thus, while improvements in agricultural productivity and rural infrastructure remain the most pressing challenges in the effort to stimulate pro-poor agricultural growth in Mozambique, there are also gains to be made from the elimination of the bias against agriculture caused by existing price distortions at home and abroad.

## Notes

1. For a study of the impacts of current biofuel proposals in Mozambique, see Arndt et al. (2008).

2. Fossil fuels represent more than 10 percent of total imports. The general prospects for import substitution are therefore greater for biofuel crops.

3. Estimates of agricultural protection and assistance for Mozambique, based on Alfieri, Arndt, and Cirera (2009), are incorporated in the World Bank's Distortions to Agricultural Incentives Project Database (Anderson and Valenzuela 2008). The estimates cover five decades. The representative values for developing-country agriculture as of 2004 that we use in the global CGE modeling for our study are summarized in Valenzuela and Anderson (2008).

4. We use the International Food Policy Research Institute's static model in this study (see Lofgren, Harris, and Robinson 2002).

5. We assume that capital is sectorally mobile and earning flexible returns, except in the metals and electricity sectors, in which we assume capital to be fixed.

# References

Alfieri, A., C. Arndt, and X. Cirera. 2009. "Mozambique." In *Distortions to Agricultural Incentives in Africa*, ed. K. Anderson and W. A. Masters, 127–46. Washington, DC: World Bank.

Anderson, K., and E. Valenzuela. 2008. "Estimates of Global Distortions to Agricultural Incentives, 1955–2007." Data spreadsheet, October, World Bank, Washington, DC. http://go.worldbank.org/YAO39F35E0.

Andersson, P. A. 2001. "The Impact of the Mega Projects on the Mozambican Economy." Gabinete de Estudos Discussion Paper 18, Ministry of Planning and Finance, Maputo, Mozambique.

Arndt, C., R. Benfica, F. Tarp, J. Thurlow, and R. Uaiene. 2008. "Biofuels, Poverty, and Growth: A Computable General Equilibrium Analysis of Mozambique." Discussion Paper 63E, Ministry of Planning and Development, Maputo, Mozambique.

Arndt, C., H. T. Jensen, S. Robinson, and F. Tarp. 2000. "Agricultural Technology and Marketing Margins in Mozambique." *Journal of Development Studies* 37 (1): 121–37.

Arndt, C., S. Jones, and F. Tarp. 2006. "Aid and Development: The Mozambican Case." Discussion Paper 06–13, Department of Economics, University of Copenhagen, Copenhagen. http://www.econ.ku.dk/Research/Publications/pink/2006/0613.pdf.

Arndt, C., R. Schiller, and F. Tarp. 2001. "Grain Transport and Rural Credit in Mozambique: Solving the Space-Time Problem." *Agricultural Economics* 26 (1): 59–70.

Arndt, C., and F. Tarp. 2001. "Estimating Utility Consistent Poverty Lines." Discussion Paper 6E, Ministry of Planning and Development, Maputo, Mozambique.

Arndt, C., and F. Tarp. 2008. *Taxation in a Low Income Economy*. London: Routledge.

Chiconela, J. 2004. "Estimativas e Perfil da Pobreza em Moçambique." Discussion Paper 7P, Ministry of Planning and Development, Maputo, Mozambique.

Cruz, A. S. 2006. "Maize Trade in Southern Africa: Comparative Advantage on Storage Costs." Discussion Paper 32E, Ministry of Planning and Development, Maputo, Mozambique.

Dimaranan, B. D., ed. 2006. *Global Trade, Assistance, and Protection: The GTAP 6 Data Base*. West Lafayette, IN: Center for Global Trade Analysis, Department of Agricultural Economics, Purdue University. https://www.gtap.agecon.purdue.edu/databases/v6/v6_doco.asp.

Horridge, M., and F. Zhai. 2006. "Shocking a Single-Country CGE Model with Export Prices and Quantities from a Global Model." In *Poverty and the WTO: Impacts of the Doha Development Agenda*, ed. T. W. Hertel and L. A. Winters, 94–104. London: Palgrave Macmillan; Washington, DC: World Bank.

INE (National Statistics Institute). 2004. *Inquérito Nacional aos Agregados Familiares sobre Orçamento Familiar 2002/3* [National Household Budget Survey]. Maputo, Mozambique: INE.

Lofgren, H., R. L. Harris, and S. Robinson. 2002. "A Standard Computable General Equilibrium (CGE) Model in GAMS." Microcomputers in Policy Research 5, International Food Policy Research Institute, Washington, DC.

Tarp, F., C. Arndt, H. T. Jensen, S. Robinson, and R. Heltberg. 2002. *Facing the Development Challenge in Mozambique: An Economy-wide Perspective*. IFPRI Research Report 126. Washington, DC: International Food Policy Research Institute.

Thurlow, J. 2008. *Agricultural Growth Options for Poverty Reduction in Mozambique*. Washington, DC: International Food Policy Research Institute.

Uaiene, R. 2008. "Determinants of Agricultural Technical Efficiency and Technology Adoption in Mozambique." PhD dissertation, Department of Agricultural Economics, Purdue University, West Lafayette, IN.

Valenzuela, E., and K. Anderson. 2008. "Alternative Agricultural Price Distortions for CGE Analysis of Developing Countries, 2004 and 1980–84." Research Memorandum 13 (December), Center for Global Trade Analysis, Department of Agricultural Economics, Purdue University, West Lafayette, IN. https://www.gtap.agecon.purdue.edu/resources/res_display.asp?RecordID=2925.

van der Mensbrugghe, D. 2005. "Linkage Technical Reference Document: Version 6.0." December, World Bank, Washington, DC. http://go.worldbank.org/7NP2KK1OH0.

# 11

# SOUTH AFRICA

*Nicolas Hérault and*
*James Thurlow*

South Africa rapidly reentered global markets after apartheid ended in the early 1990s. The country had previously faced economic sanctions, which created severe foreign exchange shortages and forced the government to restrict imports and encourage exports through a complex system of tariffs and subsidies (Bell 1993). The result was a heavily distorted economy designed to maintain self-sufficiency and macroeconomic stability. Following the change in government, sanctions were lifted, and South Africa became a member of the World Trade Organization. The new government placed trade liberalization at the center of its export-oriented growth strategy (Department of Finance 1996). Import tariffs were reduced; export subsidies were eliminated; and most quantitative restrictions were replaced by tariffs. However, despite these reforms, South Africa's system of protection remains complex; import tariffs still favor a narrow range of sectors (Cassim, Onyango, and van Seventer 2004).

South Africa's economic performance improved during the 1990s, and annual growth had reached 5 percent by 2005. Evidence suggests that the removal of trade distortions contributed positively to growth during this period without reducing aggregate employment (Jonsson and Subramanian 2001, Edwards 2001). Studies also find that trade-induced growth did not contribute to the rise in poverty during the 1990s and may even have helped reduce poverty in more recent years (Hérault 2007, Thurlow 2007). However, the past distortions were biased in favor of lower-skilled workers, especially workers in the protected textiles and clothing sectors (Edwards 2001). The removal of these distortions has thus exacerbated income inequality (Thurlow 2007).

During the 1990s, a rural-urban divide also emerged and grew. The share of the poor population living in rural areas rose from 60 to 70 percent during 1995–2000 (Hoogeveen and Özler 2005).[1] Agriculture is an important sector for rural livelihoods, employing one in four rural workers. If upstream activities are included, the share is larger. However, agriculture grew only half as quickly as nonagriculture during 1990–2005 because the gains from export growth were more than offset by rising import penetration (World Bank 2008; Jooste, Van Schalkwyk, and Groenewald 2003). This poor performance is undoubtedly responsible for some of the rise in rural poverty. Why agricultural growth was slow is unclear, as is the extent to which global or domestic price and trade policies were biased against agriculture and rural development. One study suggests that domestic policies may have hurt agriculture during the late 1990s when the effective rate of protection was negative, implying that tariffs on inputs more than offset output protection (van Seventer 2001). There is also evidence that global distortions were biased against agriculture (Krueger, Schiff, and Valdés 1991). However, a more recent study indicates that the support in agriculture was greater than that in other tradable goods sectors during 1961–2006 (Kirsten, Edwards, and Vink 2009).

In this chapter, we examine the impact on the South African economy of the removal of distortions in global and domestic prices. More specifically, we estimate the size of the remaining bias against agriculture and identify the transmission channels through which trade distortions influence poverty and income inequality. We do this using a top-down computable general equilibrium (CGE) and microsimulation models.

The next section describes South Africa's economic structure and the current distortions. The following two sections outline the methodology and present the results from the model simulations. The final section offers concluding comments.

## Economic Structure and Trade Distortions in South Africa

Table 11.1 describes the South African economy in 2002, when agriculture, a small sector, generated 4 percent of GDP. However, the sector does have strong links to upstream processing, which represent another 5 percent of GDP. Agriculture and processing together contribute 8.5 percent to total export earnings and account for some of the country's more heavily traded commodities; 17 percent of agricultural output is exported. Summer cereals (maize), fruits, cotton, tobacco, and livestock are the main export sectors, accounting for more than 90 percent of total agricultural exports. Agricultural growth during the 1990s was driven by the strong export performance of maize, fruits, and livestock, although this was offset by rising import demand for these commodities caused by larger declines in agricultural tariffs. Import penetration remains low, but it doubled during the 1990s as South Africa opened to global markets (Jooste, Van Schalkwyk, and Groenewald 2003). Import penetration is particularly high in winter cereals (wheat), cotton, and

**Table 11.1. Economic Structure and Price Distortions,
South Africa, 2002**

| Sector | GDP share, % | Imports, % Share | Intensity | Tariff | Exports, % Share | Intensity | Tax rate | Elasticity |
|---|---|---|---|---|---|---|---|---|
| Total | 100.00 | 100.0 | 13.3 | 5.3 | 100.0 | 13.2 | 0.8 | 3.10 |
| Agriculture | 4.33 | 1.8 | 8.1 | 4.8 | 4.3 | 17.3 | 0.1 | 2.03 |
| Summer cereals | 0.54 | 0.2 | 5.0 | 1.0 | 0.3 | 7.9 | 0.0 | 1.30 |
| Winter cereals | 0.21 | 0.4 | 23.3 | 14.6 | 0.0 | 2.4 | 0.0 | 4.45 |
| Oilseeds and legumes | 0.11 | 0.1 | 14.0 | 4.1 | 0.0 | 4.3 | 0.0 | 2.45 |
| Fodder crops | 0.03 | 0.0 | 2.4 | 2.5 | 0.1 | 28.2 | 0.0 | 3.25 |
| Sugarcane | 0.26 | 0.0 | 0.0 | 0.0 | 0.0 | 0.0 | 0.0 | 2.70 |
| Cotton and tobacco | 0.06 | 0.4 | 91.8 | 3.9 | 0.3 | 95.0 | 0.0 | 0.30 |
| Vegetables | 0.77 | 0.0 | 0.3 | 2.8 | 0.1 | 7.0 | 0.0 | 1.85 |
| Fruits | 0.97 | 0.1 | 6.7 | 2.8 | 2.8 | 58.9 | 0.0 | 1.85 |
| Livestock | 1.58 | 0.3 | 2.8 | 0.5 | 0.4 | 4.5 | 0.0 | 1.53 |
| Fishing | 0.01 | 0.1 | 95.8 | 1.7 | 0.1 | 97.3 | 2.0 | 1.25 |
| Forestry | 0.29 | 0.2 | 15.1 | 1.7 | 0.2 | 10.7 | 2.0 | 2.50 |
| Industry | 33.10 | 86.1 | 22.1 | 6.2 | 80.9 | 22.5 | 0.9 | 3.31 |
| Mining | 8.36 | 11.0 | 43.1 | 0.1 | 31.4 | 67.7 | 1.8 | 0.96 |
| Manufacturing | 19.97 | 75.1 | 23.3 | 7.2 | 49.4 | 18.4 | 0.4 | 3.71 |
| Meat | 0.07 | 0.2 | 2.0 | 5.9 | 0.1 | 0.9 | 0.0 | 3.85 |
| Fish | 0.11 | 0.4 | 31.5 | 19.7 | 0.1 | 15.7 | 0.0 | 4.40 |
| Fruits | 0.16 | 0.2 | 12.6 | 14.6 | 1.1 | 44.8 | 0.0 | 3.30 |
| Oils | 0.08 | 1.0 | 39.9 | 24.2 | 0.2 | 12.9 | 0.0 | 3.30 |
| Dairy | 0.22 | 0.2 | 5.5 | 66.9 | 0.1 | 5.0 | 0.0 | 3.65 |
| Grain milling | 0.27 | 0.9 | 15.3 | 4.8 | 0.3 | 6.1 | 0.0 | 2.60 |
| Animal feeds | 0.08 | 0.2 | 7.5 | 19.9 | 0.0 | 1.3 | 0.0 | 2.00 |
| Bakeries | 0.25 | 0.1 | 2.6 | 47.0 | 0.0 | 1.3 | 0.0 | 2.00 |
| Sugar | 0.20 | 0.0 | 0.8 | 48.2 | 0.2 | 12.9 | 0.0 | 2.70 |
| Confectionery | 0.14 | 0.0 | 3.6 | 18.8 | 0.1 | 5.3 | 0.0 | 2.00 |
| Other foods | 0.31 | 0.5 | 16.1 | 22.0 | 0.4 | 13.6 | 0.0 | 2.00 |
| Beverages and tobacco | 1.14 | 0.8 | 6.0 | 6.5 | 1.6 | 15.7 | 0.0 | 1.15 |
| Textiles | 0.36 | 1.8 | 21.2 | 22.7 | 0.4 | 6.9 | 2.0 | 3.74 |
| Clothing and footwear | 0.57 | 2.4 | 17.3 | 43.8 | 0.5 | 6.4 | 1.9 | 3.92 |
| Wood and paper | 1.91 | 2.4 | 10.1 | 7.7 | 1.3 | 6.0 | 1.9 | 4.05 |
| Chemicals | 4.75 | 14.5 | 18.9 | 4.9 | 11.3 | 16.4 | 0.3 | 3.21 |

*(Table continues on the following page.)*

**Table 11.1. Economic Structure and Price Distortions, South Africa, 2002 (*continued*)**

| | GDP share, % | Imports, % Share | Imports, % Intensity | Tariff | Exports, % Share | Exports, % Intensity | Tax rate | Elasticity |
|---|---|---|---|---|---|---|---|---|
| Sector | | | | | | | | |
| Nonmetals | 0.69 | 1.4 | 18.3 | 11.6 | 0.8 | 11.4 | 0.3 | 2.90 |
| Metals | 3.41 | 7.1 | 17.7 | 4.1 | 13.3 | 28.7 | 0.4 | 3.76 |
| Machinery | 1.59 | 22.6 | 52.8 | 2.9 | 6.0 | 27.4 | 0.3 | 4.22 |
| Transport equipment | 1.92 | 16.7 | 37.4 | 9.7 | 8.7 | 24.6 | 0.3 | 3.88 |
| Other manufacturing | 1.75 | 1.8 | 11.9 | 5.5 | 2.9 | 20.9 | 0.3 | 3.75 |
| Other industry | 4.77 | 0.1 | 0.2 | 0.0 | 0.1 | 0.1 | 0.3 | 2.28 |
| Private services | 47.58 | 12.1 | 4.3 | 0.0 | 14.9 | 4.9 | 0.0 | 1.90 |
| Public services | 14.99 | 0.0 | 0.0 | 0.0 | 0.0 | 0.0 | 0.0 | 1.90 |

*Source*: 2002 social accounting matrix for South Africa.

*Note*: Import intensity is the share of imports in total domestic demand. Export intensity is the share of exports in total domestic output. Elasticity is the trade elasticity applied to import demand and export supply functions.

tobacco. International trade is therefore becoming increasingly important for agriculture, and the sector is responsive to changing trade distortions.

Despite its small and declining share in the economy, agriculture remains an important source of employment. In 2003, more than a million people were working in agriculture within the total employment of 11.5 million (Casale, Muller, and Posel 2004). Around 70 percent of agricultural workers are employed as laborers on large commercial farms, where they earn an average of one-third of the national average wage. The 60,000 commercial farms occupy 87 percent of the total agricultural land and produce 95 percent of all marketed output (Vink and Kirsten 2003). The remaining 300,000 agricultural workers are smallholder farmers, who occupy 13 percent of the agricultural land in the more remote regions of the country. These subsistence-oriented farmers earn less than 5 percent of the national average wage (Casale, Muller, and Posel 2004). Thus, not only is there a growing rural-urban divide, but there is also a divide within agriculture. Smallholders derive much of their income from subsistence production and are thus less likely to be affected by changes in price and trade distortions. In contrast, factors affecting commercial farming may have large impacts on national employment and rural incomes.

Mining has historically been the cornerstone of the South African economy, primarily as a source of export earnings. However, the mining sector also has strong upstream links to metals processing, and, together, these sectors represent about 10 percent of total GDP. However, these sectors are more capital intensive and generate a smaller share of total employment. Construction, textiles, and clothing are among South Africa's more labor-intensive sectors. Food processing is another important manufacturing sector, generating 15 percent of total manufacturing GDP and employment. Dairy products, grain milling, and sugar refining are key processing sectors. Nonfood processing is dominated by the capital-intensive metals and chemicals sectors.

Most export taxes and subsidies were eliminated during the 1990s. The government stopped intervening in input and product markets, allowing farmers to respond more effectively to climate variability and changing market opportunities (Van Schalkwyk, Groenewald, and Jooste 2003). Thus, the largest remaining price distortions are import tariffs. The average tariffs in South Africa are, however, relatively low, at 5.3 percent. The tariffs on agricultural commodities are especially low, at 2 or 3 percent, with the exception of a 14.6 percent wheat tariff. Upstream food processing enjoys far greater protection, with average tariffs of 16.8 percent. Especially high tariffs are applied to dairy products and refined sugar. Of the remaining manufacturing sectors, considerable protection is afforded to textiles, clothing, and motor vehicles. These are considered sensitive sectors and have received special dispensation under South Africa's various trade agreements. Thus, despite far-reaching reforms during the 1990s, import tariffs are not uniformly applied across sectors, and efforts at rationalization are often subjected to pressure by trade unions, especially in the metals, textiles, and clothing sectors. Indeed, tariff revenues account for less than 6 percent of total government income, and the tariffs on agriculture and processed food generate less than 15 percent of these earnings. The removal of trade distortions would therefore have direct implications for a few key sectors, but little impact on overall government revenues.

## The Modeling Approach

In our analysis, we draw on the rest-of-the-world results—that is, the results without the participation of South Africa—in the global trade liberalization scenario in the World Bank's Linkage model (see van der Mensbrugghe 2005). This model provides the estimated changes in the world import prices, world export prices, and export quantities facing South Africa (see the appendix by van der Mensbrugghe, Valenzuela, and Anderson). These world price and export quantity changes are imposed exogenously on the South African CGE model, wherein the additional impacts of domestic trade reforms are also modeled. The CGE model estimates the impact of global and domestic reforms on domestic commodity prices and factor employment and returns. These results are then passed down to a microsimulation model, which estimates poverty and inequality effects. This section describes the South African CGE and microsimulation models.

### The CGE model

The national CGE model contains 110 activities and commodities, including 17 agricultural and 12 food processing sectors.[2] The model identifies four factors of production: three types of labor (unskilled, semiskilled, and skilled) and the capital factor.[3] Agricultural land is not distinguished from other forms of capital.[4] Skilled labor and capital are assumed to be fully employed at flexible wages and returns. To reflect South Africa's high levels of unemployment, we assume that the supply of semiskilled and unskilled labor is perfectly elastic at a fixed nominal wage.[5] In the model, labor returns are calibrated to capture sectoral wage differentials, such that agricultural wages are lower than the wages in most nonagricultural sectors. In addition, labor is fully mobile across sectors. Producers in the model maximize profits under constant returns to scale, and the choice among factors is governed by a nonnested constant elasticity of substitution function. Factors are combined by fixed-share intermediates under a Leontief specification.

Based on a constant elasticity of transformation function, possibilities of substitution exist between production for the domestic market and production for foreign markets. Profit maximization drives producers to sell in the markets in which they are able to achieve the highest returns. The returns are based on domestic and export prices; the latter are determined by the world prices, multiplied by the exchange rate, which is adjusted for any border taxes or subsidies. Similar substitution possibilities also exist between imported and domestic goods under a constant elasticity of substitution Armington specification. The final ratio of imports to domestic goods is determined by the cost-minimizing decision making of those responsible for domestic demand based on the relative prices of imports and domestic goods (including relevant taxes). Under the small country assumption, South Africa faces perfectly elastic world demand and supply at fixed world prices. However, this small country assumption is dropped if we are modeling the impacts of global liberalization. In other words, world import prices are exogenous in the South African CGE model, while world export prices and quantities are determined using the approach outlined in Horridge (2004).

The model distinguishes among various types of institutions, including enterprises, the government, and a single representative household group. Households and enterprises receive incomes in payment for the use by producers of household and enterprise factors of production. Households and enterprises pay direct taxes to the government (based on fixed tax rates), save (based on marginal propensities to save), and make transfers to the rest of the world. Enterprises pay their remaining incomes to households in the form of dividends. Households, unlike enterprises, use their incomes to consume commodities under a linear expenditure system of demand. The government receives income from imposing activity, sales and direct taxes, and import tariffs and then makes transfers to households, enterprises, and the rest of the world. The government also purchases commodities in the form of government consumption expenditure, and the remaining income of government is (dis)saved. All savings from households, enterprises, the government, and the rest of the world (foreign savings) are collected in a savings pool from which investment is financed.

To balance the model's macroeconomic accounts, it is necessary to specify a set of closure rules. A savings-driven closure is assumed to balance the savings-investment account. Under this closure, the marginal propensities to save of households and enterprises are fixed, while investment adjusts to changes in incomes to ensure that the level of investment and savings are equal. For the current account, we assume that a flexible exchange rate adjusts to maintain a fixed level of foreign savings. Finally, for the government account, the fiscal deficit is fixed in absolute terms, and government revenues and expenditures are balanced through uniform changes in the direct tax rates on households and enterprises. Table 11.2 shows the current direct tax rates for poor, nonpoor, rural, and urban households as observed in the microsimulation model. The tax rates are highest for urban households in the top income decile. Changes in the tax rates based on the existing tax structure mainly affect higher-income households, while poor households are largely unaffected because their incomes generally fall below the lowest income tax bracket. Accordingly, proportional changes in income tax rates influence income inequality, leaving the poverty effects of trade reforms largely unchanged.

The CGE model is calibrated to a 2002 social accounting matrix. We have taken information on nonagricultural production from the 2002 supply-use tables and national accounts (StatsSA 2004, SARB 2008). We have disaggregated agricultural production across crops and sectors using the 2002 census of commercial agriculture (StatsSA 2002). We have drawn information on labor employment and wages from the 2000 income and expenditure survey and the labor force survey of September 2004 (StatsSA 2000–, 2001). We have taken trade elasticities from the Global Trade Analysis Project (Dimaranan 2006); household income elasticities are those estimated in Case (2000). The initial price distortions, such as import

## Table 11.2. Direct Tax Rates on Households, South Africa, 2000
*(percent)*

| Households | Taxes as a share of gross household income | | |
|---|---|---|---|
| | Rural areas | Urban areas | All areas |
| Poor, US$2-a-day poverty line | 0.0 | 0.0 | 0.0 |
| Nonpoor | 1.6 | 4.2 | 3.2 |
| Richest, top income decile | 11.3 | 18.1 | 17.2 |

*Source*: South Africa microsimulation model of the authors based on StatsSA (2000–, 2001).

*Note*: Direct taxes only concern formal labor income.

tariff rates, are consistent with the global Linkage model; the agricultural distortions in this model are based on Valenzuela and Anderson (2008).

## Microsimulation model

The predicted impacts in the national CGE model are passed down to a microsimulation model for South Africa. Under a top-down specification, the changes in commodity prices, household tax rates, factor returns, and employment levels in the CGE model are imposed on the microsimulation model, which we then use to estimate behavioral responses at the household level for each of the 26,000 households in the income and expenditure survey of 2000 and the labor force survey.[6] There are two parts to the microsimulation model. First, a selection model predicts the employment status of working-age individuals (that is, inactive, unemployed, subsistence agricultural workers, informal workers, or formal workers). The probability that an individual will have a particular status is derived from a linear utility function based on the characteristics of individuals. Second, a regression model predicts formal and informal earnings. The regression and selection models are econometrically estimated for four demographic groups: single women, partnered women, single men, and partnered men.

The structure of household incomes for poor, nonpoor, and rich households in urban and rural areas is shown in table 11.3. Since occupational choices are

**Table 11.3. Household Income Shares, South Africa, 2000**
(percent)

| Indicator | Rural | | | Urban | | |
|---|---|---|---|---|---|---|
| | Poor, US$2-a-day | Nonpoor | Rich, top income decile | Poor, US$2-a-day | Nonpoor | Rich, top income decile |
| Skilled labor | 0.3 | 1.2 | 9.8 | 0.2 | 5.6 | 35.5 |
| Semiskilled labor | 3.1 | 9.9 | 26.6 | 5.7 | 26.4 | 31.4 |
| Unskilled labor | 20.5 | 35.4 | 38.8 | 32.8 | 40.7 | 11.9 |
| Unspecified labor | 3.4 | 1.9 | 1.3 | 3.9 | 2.4 | 2.2 |
| Home production | 4.4 | 3.0 | 0.9 | 0.4 | 0.1 | 0.1 |
| Capital income | 4.3 | 6.9 | 12.3 | 5.0 | 6.7 | 14.4 |
| Government transfers | 34.5 | 23.2 | 5.4 | 33.1 | 11.1 | 2.6 |
| Interhousehold transfers | 29.5 | 18.5 | 4.9 | 19.0 | 7.0 | 2.0 |
| Total | 100.0 | 100.0 | 100.0 | 100.0 | 100.0 | 100.0 |

Source: South Africa microsimulation model of the authors based on StatsSA (2000–, 2001).

endogenous, these income shares are not assumed to be fixed (and may thus be affected by trade reforms). The labor earnings of individuals are added to other income sources and adjusted to reflect new tax rates so as to update household disposable incomes in the survey. This is then deflated by a household-specific consumer price index based on the household-specific budget shares (table 11.4) and on changes in commodity prices from the CGE model. This reestimated level of household expenditures is then compared with various poverty lines to determine changes in poverty.

**Table 11.4. Household Expenditure Shares, South Africa, 2000**
(percent)

| Sector | Rural | | | Urban | | |
| --- | --- | --- | --- | --- | --- | --- |
| | Poor, US$2-a-day | Nonpoor | Rich, top income decile | Poor, US$2-a-day | Nonpoor | Rich, top income decile |
| Total | 100.0 | 100.0 | 100.0 | 100.0 | 100.0 | 100.0 |
| Agriculture | 16.3 | 12.9 | 6.7 | 10.1 | 6.1 | 2.4 |
| Food processing | 44.4 | 39.7 | 26.7 | 41.1 | 32.5 | 15.4 |
| Meat products | 8.8 | 9.6 | 7.2 | 10.0 | 8.9 | 4.3 |
| Fish products | 1.4 | 1.5 | 0.9 | 1.3 | 1.1 | 0.7 |
| Fruits and vegetables | 0.8 | 0.9 | 0.8 | 0.8 | 1.1 | 0.9 |
| Oils and fats | 2.3 | 1.7 | 1.0 | 2.0 | 1.2 | 0.4 |
| Dairy products | 3.1 | 2.9 | 2.0 | 3.3 | 2.9 | 1.7 |
| Grain mill products | 9.4 | 6.2 | 2.9 | 6.0 | 3.3 | 1.0 |
| Animal feeds | 0.0 | 0.0 | 0.0 | 0.0 | 0.1 | 0.2 |
| Bakery products | 5.9 | 5.7 | 3.3 | 6.7 | 4.6 | 1.3 |
| Sugar products | 5.9 | 3.4 | 1.4 | 3.6 | 1.5 | 0.4 |
| Confectionary products | 0.1 | 0.1 | 0.2 | 0.1 | 0.2 | 0.3 |
| Other processed foods | 4.3 | 3.6 | 2.5 | 4.2 | 3.2 | 1.6 |
| Beverages and tobacco | 2.5 | 4.1 | 4.5 | 3.1 | 4.1 | 2.6 |
| Textiles and clothing | 7.3 | 8.1 | 8.1 | 6.0 | 7.5 | 4.4 |
| Other manufacturing | 17.4 | 18.1 | 22.2 | 18.0 | 17.3 | 22.4 |
| Other industry | 2.7 | 3.5 | 4.5 | 8.9 | 7.2 | 5.9 |
| Services | 11.9 | 17.6 | 31.8 | 16.0 | 29.4 | 49.5 |

Source: South Africa microsimulation model of the authors based on StatsSA (2000–, 2001).

The top-down approach we use to link the microsimulation model to the CGE model is described in detail in Hérault (2006). The approach ensures that changes in prices, direct tax rates, earnings from wages and salaries, returns to capital, and employment levels are transmitted from the CGE model to the microsimulation model. Thus, the microsimulation model predicts how the behavior of individuals and household incomes are affected by the economy-wide impacts predicted by the national CGE model.

## The Model Results

We have run four simulations to examine the effects of price distortions on agriculture, poverty, and inequality. We begin by considering the effects of distortions in the rest of the world on the South African economy. The first simulation assesses the impact of the removal of all merchandise trade policy measures and domestic agricultural policies in other countries of the world without any change in South Africa's own distortions. The second simulation considers only the removal of agricultural sector distortions in the rest of the world. The effects at South Africa's borders of these liberalizations are drawn from the World Bank's Linkage model. These include changes in the country's import and export prices, as well as changes in the demand for South African exports (table 11.5). The remaining two simulations examine the effect on South Africa of the removal of only its own price distortions, first for all tradable goods sectors and then only within agriculture. In both of these latter simulations there are no changes in the rest of the world.

### The liberalization of all commodities by the rest of the world

Full liberalization by the rest of the world results in a positive terms of trade shock in South Africa: the weighted world price of exports rise; and the prices of imports fall. The quantity of agricultural and food products demanded by the rest of the world expands for most items, but contracts for horticultural goods, which are the main source of agricultural exports (table 11.1). Demand also expands for other primary products, which is a key export sector because mining accounts for one-third of all export earnings. However, demand contracts for nonfood manufactures (table 11.5, column 3). On the import side, prices fall for nonfood manufactures and for most farm products (table 11.5, column 1). Overall, the terms of trade improve by 1.4 percent, which causes exports to rise more rapidly than imports. This reduces the trade deficit and places pressure on the current account balance, which, by assumption, is fixed

## Table 11.5. Exogenous Demand and Border Price Shocks of Rest-of-the-World Liberalization, South Africa

*(percent change from the baseline)*

| Sector | Sim 1: Rest-of-the-world, all commodities | | | Sim 2: Rest-of-the-world, agriculture only | | |
|---|---|---|---|---|---|---|
| | Import price | Exports | | Import price | Exports | |
| | | Price | Quantity | | Price | Quantity |
| *Primary sector* | | | | | | |
| Rice | 0.00 | 0.00 | 0.0 | 0.00 | 0.00 | 0.0 |
| Wheat | 0.73 | 0.46 | 21.6 | 0.72 | 0.35 | −15.9 |
| Other grains | −5.49 | 0.46 | 48.6 | −5.45 | 0.35 | 59.3 |
| Oilseeds | −2.28 | 0.47 | −25.5 | −2.02 | 0.34 | −13.8 |
| Sugarcane | 0.00 | 0.00 | 0.0 | 0.00 | 0.00 | 0.0 |
| Cotton | −1.21 | 0.44 | 53.2 | −0.11 | 0.33 | 52.9 |
| Fruits and vegetables | 0.90 | 0.17 | 30.6 | 0.42 | 0.34 | −55.7 |
| Other crops | 1.87 | 0.49 | 7.0 | 2.81 | 0.35 | 10.9 |
| Cattle and sheep | −2.21 | 0.50 | 5.7 | −0.44 | 0.33 | 17.1 |
| Other livestock | 0.74 | 0.57 | −10.5 | 1.37 | 0.34 | 1.2 |
| Other primary products | 0.19 | 0.55 | 0.3 | 0.71 | 0.41 | 1.0 |
| *Secondary sector* | | | | | | |
| Beef and sheep meat | 5.06 | 0.51 | 443.5 | 5.82 | 0.38 | 489.9 |
| Other meat products | 3.71 | 0.57 | −11.4 | 4.77 | 0.42 | −1.9 |
| Oils and fats | −1.80 | 0.33 | −1.1 | −2.50 | 0.14 | 0.7 |
| Dairy products | 16.58 | 0.57 | 405.9 | 17.47 | 0.46 | 447.6 |
| Grain milling | 5.03 | 0.59 | −47.2 | 4.57 | 0.47 | −41.5 |
| Sugar refining | 1.15 | 0.49 | 147.2 | 2.09 | 0.39 | 173.5 |
| Other food and beverages | 4.97 | 0.53 | 58.3 | −0.41 | 0.36 | −10.4 |
| Textiles and clothing | −0.94 | 0.32 | −21.2 | 0.50 | 0.43 | −0.1 |
| Other manufacturing | −0.34 | 0.45 | −2.3 | 0.20 | 0.41 | −1.2 |
| Services | −0.14 | 0.55 | −2.7 | 0.27 | 0.43 | −0.6 |

*Source:* Results from the World Bank Linkage model (see the appendix by van der Mensbrugghe, Valenzuela, and Anderson).

in foreign currency. This induces an appreciation of the real exchange rate by 0.8 percent, which stimulates import demand additionally, while partially offsetting export competitiveness. The net effect is that the volume of exports rises by only 0.2 percent, while the volume of imports rises by 2.3 percent. Among primary agricultural goods, exports fall 13 percent and imports rise 5 percent (table 11.6).

**Table 11.6. Macroeconomic Simulation Results of Prospective Liberalization Abroad and Nationally, South Africa**

(percent)

| Indicator | Base share of GDP | Change from the base | | | |
| --- | --- | --- | --- | --- | --- |
| | | Rest-of-the-world reform | | Unilateral reform | |
| | | All goods | Agriculture only | All goods | Agriculture only |
| Real GDP at market prices | 100.0 | 0.3 | 0.1 | 1.0 | 0.1 |
| Consumption | 61.9 | 1.0 | 0.6 | 1.2 | 0.3 |
| Investment | 16.1 | 1.6 | 1.0 | 1.6 | −0.3 |
| Government | 18.4 | 0.0 | 0.0 | 0.0 | 0.0 |
| Consumer price index | n.a. | −0.4 | −0.1 | −1.0 | −0.3 |
| Real exchange rate | n.a. | −0.8 | −0.6 | 1.9 | 0.3 |
| World export prices | n.a. | 1.2 | 1.0 | 0.0 | 0.0 |
| World import prices | n.a. | −0.2 | 0.2 | 0.0 | 0.0 |
| Terms of trade | n.a. | 1.4 | 0.7 | 0.0 | 0.0 |
| Volume of exports | 32.6 | 0.2 | 0.0 | 7.5 | 1.0 |
| Agriculture | 4.3 | −13.2 | −11.0 | 10.7 | 1.8 |
| Mining | 31.4 | 0.3 | 0.2 | −0.4 | −0.1 |
| Manufacturing | 49.4 | 1.7 | 1.1 | 12.3 | 1.5 |
| Other industry | 0.1 | −0.5 | −0.7 | 5.2 | 0.2 |
| Services | 14.9 | −1.2 | −1.2 | 5.5 | 1.0 |
| Volume of imports | −28.9 | 2.3 | 1.6 | 8.4 | 1.1 |
| Agriculture | 1.8 | 5.0 | 2.4 | 6.6 | 8.9 |
| Mining | 11.0 | −1.4 | −1.1 | 3.3 | 0.6 |
| Manufacturing | 75.1 | 2.7 | 1.7 | 11.5 | 1.3 |
| Other industry | 0.1 | 3.7 | 3.4 | −1.3 | −0.5 |
| Services | 12.1 | 3.4 | 2.9 | −2.9 | −0.6 |

Source: Simulation results by the authors using their CGE model for South Africa.

Note: The domestic price index is the numéraire in the model. n.a. = not applicable.

The decline in agricultural export demand causes agricultural GDP to fall by 0.2 percent mainly because of a drop in fruit production (table 11.7). There is also a contraction in the production of oilseeds, but oilseeds represent only a small share of the agricultural sector. Total manufacturing GDP changes only slightly because the increased production of processed foods is offset by the falling production of other manufactured goods, such as textiles, clothing, and machinery, in the face of rising import competition. Dairy and processed sugar production expand substantially, contributing to food processing expansion and generating positive links to

**Table 11.7. The Effects of Prospective Liberalization Abroad and Nationally on GDP, by Sector at Factor Cost, South Africa**

(percent)

| Sector | Base share of GDP | Rest-of-the-world reform | | Unilateral reform | |
|---|---|---|---|---|---|
| | | All goods | Agriculture only | All goods | Agriculture only |
| Total | 100.0 | 0.3 | 0.2 | 0.7 | 0.1 |
| Agriculture | 4.3 | −0.2 | −0.1 | 1.3 | −0.9 |
| Summer cereals | 0.5 | 3.3 | 3.7 | 0.1 | −0.8 |
| Winter cereals | 0.2 | 2.0 | −0.6 | −12.3 | −14.3 |
| Oilseeds and legumes | 0.1 | −1.4 | −1.8 | −4.9 | −6.0 |
| Fodder crops | 0.0 | 10.4 | 12.9 | −11.4 | 1.8 |
| Sugarcane | 0.3 | 8.6 | 8.6 | −0.2 | −0.6 |
| Cotton and tobacco | 0.1 | 40.5 | 40.2 | 25.2 | 6.1 |
| Vegetables | 0.3 | −1.0 | −1.8 | −0.8 | −1.3 |
| Fruits | 1.0 | −14.5 | −15.1 | 8.1 | 0.9 |
| Livestock | 1.6 | 4.2 | 5.3 | −0.8 | −0.6 |
| Fishing | 0.0 | 0.0 | 0.0 | 0.0 | 0.0 |
| Forestry | 0.3 | −1.0 | −0.8 | 2.3 | 1.2 |
| Industry | 33.1 | 0.1 | −0.1 | 0.5 | 0.1 |
| Mining | 8.4 | 0.0 | 0.0 | 0.0 | 0.0 |
| Manufacturing | 20.0 | 0.0 | −0.2 | 0.7 | 0.2 |
| Meat | 0.1 | 6.7 | 7.9 | −0.2 | −0.1 |
| Fish | 0.1 | 0.9 | 2.6 | −13.9 | −16.2 |
| Fruits | 0.2 | −0.8 | −0.8 | 9.2 | −0.5 |
| Oils | 0.1 | −2.2 | −3.2 | −17.8 | −21.1 |
| Dairy | 0.2 | 35.0 | 41.1 | −7.7 | −9.1 |
| Grain milling | 0.3 | 0.7 | 0.4 | 0.4 | −1.0 |
| Animal feeds | 0.1 | 5.0 | 4.7 | −2.5 | −2.7 |
| Bakeries | 0.3 | 1.3 | 0.3 | −0.8 | −1.0 |
| Sugar refining | 0.2 | 19.7 | 22.1 | 0.6 | −0.7 |
| Confectionery | 0.1 | 3.8 | 0.7 | −0.1 | −0.5 |
| Other foods | 0.3 | 8.9 | −1.0 | −2.2 | −3.6 |
| Beverages and tobacco | 1.1 | 8.0 | −1.6 | 1.2 | 0.3 |
| Textiles | 0.4 | −2.8 | −0.5 | −13.4 | 0.6 |
| Clothing and footwear | 0.6 | −1.3 | 0.0 | −13.4 | 0.4 |

(Table continues on the following page.)

**Table 11.7. The Effects of Prospective Liberalization Abroad and Nationally on GDP, by Sector at Factor Cost, South Africa (*continued*)**

*(percent)*

| Sector | Base share of GDP | Change from the base | | | |
| | | Rest-of-the-world reform | | Unilateral reform | |
| | | All goods | Agriculture only | All goods | Agriculture only |
|---|---|---|---|---|---|
| Wood and paper | 1.9 | −0.1 | −0.2 | 0.2 | 0.4 |
| Chemicals | 4.8 | −1.2 | −0.8 | −1.4 | 0.5 |
| Nonmetals | 0.7 | −0.2 | −0.1 | −2.5 | 0.1 |
| Metals | 3.4 | −2.3 | −1.7 | 3.3 | 0.9 |
| Machinery | 1.6 | −2.1 | −1.5 | 4.6 | 0.8 |
| Transport equipment | 1.9 | −2.1 | −1.5 | 7.3 | 1.1 |
| Other manufacturing | 1.8 | −0.9 | −0.7 | 2.4 | 0.6 |
| Other industry | 4.8 | 0.7 | 0.5 | 0.8 | 0.0 |
| Private services | 47.6 | 0.6 | 0.4 | 1.0 | 0.2 |
| Public services | 15.0 | 0.0 | 0.0 | 0.0 | 0.0 |

*Source*: Simulation results by the authors using their CGE model for South Africa.

the dairy and raw sugar sectors. The large service sector expands the most in absolute terms, causing national GDP to increase under full liberalization by the rest of the world. This is because the declining production in the agricultural and non-food processing (manufacturing) sectors reduces the employment of capital and labor, which therefore migrate to the service sector and to construction.

The reduction in the output of farm and textile products reduces the demand for lower-skilled workers, while the expansion in services and other parts of the manufacturing sector raises the demand for capital and skilled workers (table 11.8). The real wages of lower-skilled workers thus decline, and the wages and capital returns of skilled workers increase (table 11.9). However, under our assumption of fixed nominal wages for unskilled and semiskilled workers, the aggregate employment of both types of labor expands by about 1 percent. The increase in the number of jobs among lower-skilled workers more than outweighs the decline in the average real wages of these workers, leading to larger net increases in the factor incomes of these workers relative to either capital or the average real wages of skilled workers. The net result is that, measured by the equivalent variation in income, national economic welfare rises by 1.0 percent (table 11.9, final row).

Falling prices for machinery and construction reduce the cost of investment, which rises as a result. Investment demand is additionally stimulated by the

**Table 11.8. Factor Intensity Structure, South Africa, 2002**

| Sector | Share of factor income in total value-added, % | | | | | Elasticity[a] |
| | Skilled labor | Semiskilled labor | Unskilled labor | Capital | All factors | |
|---|---|---|---|---|---|---|
| Total | 11.9 | 21.7 | 16.5 | 50.0 | 100.0 | 1.44 |
| Agriculture | 3.3 | 1.2 | 19.4 | 76.1 | 100.0 | 1.50 |
| Summer cereals | 2.7 | 1.0 | 16.3 | 80.0 | 100.0 | 1.50 |
| Winter cereals | 3.1 | 1.2 | 18.7 | 77.0 | 100.0 | 1.50 |
| Oilseeds and legumes | 2.9 | 1.0 | 16.8 | 79.3 | 100.0 | 1.50 |
| Fodder crops | 3.0 | 1.1 | 18.5 | 77.4 | 100.0 | 1.50 |
| Sugarcane | 3.4 | 1.3 | 20.0 | 75.4 | 100.0 | 1.50 |
| Cotton and tobacco | 4.6 | 1.7 | 26.7 | 67.0 | 100.0 | 1.50 |
| Vegetables | 4.0 | 1.5 | 23.7 | 70.8 | 100.0 | 1.50 |
| Fruits | 3.9 | 1.5 | 23.5 | 71.1 | 100.0 | 1.50 |
| Livestock | 2.9 | 1.1 | 17.1 | 78.9 | 100.0 | 1.50 |
| Fishing | 3.7 | 1.5 | 22.4 | 72.4 | 100.0 | 1.50 |
| Forestry | 3.2 | 1.2 | 19.2 | 76.4 | 100.0 | 1.50 |
| Industry | 7.8 | 9.4 | 27.6 | 55.3 | 100.0 | 1.31 |
| Mining | 4.1 | 2.9 | 31.5 | 61.5 | 100.0 | 0.75 |
| Manufacturing | 9.1 | 12.4 | 25.2 | 53.2 | 100.0 | 1.50 |
| Meat | 1.2 | 2.5 | 4.2 | 92.2 | 100.0 | 1.50 |
| Fish | 7.1 | 15.1 | 25.8 | 51.9 | 100.0 | 1.50 |
| Fruits | 7.9 | 16.9 | 28.7 | 46.5 | 100.0 | 1.50 |
| Oils | 4.8 | 10.5 | 17.7 | 67.0 | 100.0 | 1.50 |
| Dairy | 8.1 | 17.2 | 29.3 | 45.4 | 100.0 | 1.50 |
| Grain milling | 3.9 | 8.4 | 14.2 | 73.5 | 100.0 | 1.50 |
| Animal feeds | 5.4 | 11.4 | 19.4 | 63.8 | 100.0 | 1.50 |
| Bakeries | 10.5 | 22.5 | 38.2 | 28.8 | 100.0 | 1.50 |
| Sugar | 6.5 | 13.8 | 23.6 | 56.1 | 100.0 | 1.50 |
| Confectionery | 10.2 | 21.8 | 37.0 | 31.1 | 100.0 | 1.50 |
| Other foods | 7.4 | 15.9 | 27.0 | 49.7 | 100.0 | 1.50 |
| Beverages and tobacco | 0.0 | 12.3 | 16.0 | 71.7 | 100.0 | 1.50 |
| Textiles | 1.8 | 6.0 | 54.2 | 38.0 | 100.0 | 1.50 |
| Clothing and footwear | 4.6 | 4.7 | 59.4 | 31.3 | 100.0 | 1.50 |
| Wood and paper | 3.2 | 3.3 | 42.1 | 51.3 | 100.0 | 1.50 |
| Chemicals | 20.4 | 7.7 | 12.7 | 59.2 | 100.0 | 1.50 |

(*Table continues on the following page.*)

**Table 11.8. Factor Intensity Structure, South Africa, 2002 (*continued*)**

| Sector | Skilled labor | Semiskilled labor | Unskilled labor | Capital | All factors | Elasticity[a] |
|---|---|---|---|---|---|---|
| | Share of factor income in total value-added, % | | | | | |
| Nonmetals | 1.4 | 8.2 | 24.6 | 65.8 | 100.0 | 1.50 |
| Metals | 2.2 | 17.0 | 23.7 | 57.1 | 100.0 | 1.50 |
| Machinery | 11.3 | 20.6 | 32.6 | 35.5 | 100.0 | 1.50 |
| Transport equipment | 4.2 | 17.2 | 36.2 | 42.4 | 100.0 | 1.50 |
| Other manufacturing | 9.2 | 6.3 | 12.3 | 72.2 | 100.0 | 1.50 |
| Other industry | 8.7 | 7.8 | 30.4 | 53.1 | 100.0 | 1.50 |
| Private services | 10.2 | 23.1 | 11.0 | 55.7 | 100.0 | 1.50 |
| Public services | 28.5 | 50.5 | 8.7 | 12.3 | 100.0 | 1.50 |

*Source:* 2002 social accounting matrix for South Africa based on StatsSA (2004).

a. Elasticity is the substitution elasticity between factors.

**Table 11.9. The Effects of Prospective Liberalization Abroad and Nationally on Factor Rewards, Employment, and Welfare, South Africa**

| Indicator | Base value | Rest-of-the-world reform All goods | Rest-of-the-world reform Agriculture only | Unilateral reform All goods | Unilateral reform Agriculture only |
|---|---|---|---|---|---|
| | | Change from the base, % | | | |
| Average real factor returns, R 1,000 per year | | | | | |
| Skilled labor | 127 | 0.4 | 0.3 | 1.2 | 0.1 |
| Semiskilled labor | 78 | −0.2 | −0.2 | 0.1 | 0.0 |
| Unskilled labor | 49 | −0.5 | −0.2 | 1.6 | 0.3 |
| Capital | n.a. | 0.6 | 0.4 | 2.3 | 0.2 |
| Employment, 1,000s | | | | | |
| Skilled labor | 969 | 0.0 | 0.0 | 0.0 | 0.0 |
| Semiskilled labor | 2,910 | 1.2 | 0.7 | 2.0 | 0.2 |
| Unskilled labor | 3,519 | 1.0 | 0.6 | 1.6 | 0.0 |
| Capital | n.a. | 0.0 | 0.0 | 0.0 | 0.0 |
| National economic welfare, EV | n.a. | 1.0 | 0.6 | 1.2 | 0.2 |

*Source:* Simulation results by the authors using their CGE model for South Africa.

*Note:* EV = equivalent variation in income. n.a. = not applicable.

increase in private savings resulting from higher factor incomes (mainly capital returns). Falling import prices cause consumer prices to drop and real consumer spending to rise. Overall, the increase in real exports and in consumption and investment spending and the rise in employment among lower-skilled labor lead to a slight increase (0.3 percent) in national GDP, despite the large expansion in imports (table 11.6).

The liberalization of all commodities by the rest of the world causes poverty to fall measured according to all the reported poverty lines (table 11.10). This is mainly because of the expansion in formal employment. This expansion is biased toward lower-skilled workers (see above), which is particularly beneficial for poor households because these households derive almost all their market incomes from low-skilled labor (table 11.3). In addition, poorer households benefit more from lower consumer prices, especially the prices for meat, sugar, and other foods, which form a large share of their expenditures. Food and agricultural products account for more than half the expenditures of poor households, whereas services and the output of nonfood processing in manufacturing account for more than half the expenditures of rich households (table 11.4). At the higher poverty lines, the reduction in poverty tends to be smaller in rural areas than in urban areas.

**Table 11.10. The Effects of Prospective Liberalization Abroad and Nationally on Sectoral Employment, Income Inequality, and Poverty, South Africa**

| Indicator | Base value | Rest-of-the-world reform | | Unilateral reform | |
|---|---|---|---|---|---|
| | | All goods | Agriculture only | All goods | Agriculture only |
| | | *Change from the base, %* | | | |
| Real factor returns, R per year[a] | | | | | |
| Informal sector workers | 12,828 | 2.40 | 1.31 | 6.67 | 0.93 |
| Formal sector workers | 50,488 | −0.20 | −0.23 | 0.83 | 0.41 |
| Employment, 1,000s | | | | | |
| Subsistence agriculture | 736 | −0.10 | −0.07 | −0.16 | 0.01 |
| Informal sector workers | 3,357 | −0.25 | −0.18 | −0.15 | 0.10 |
| Formal sector workers | 7,307 | 0.94 | 0.58 | 1.54 | 0.06 |
| Unemployment, 1,000s | 3,806 | −0.66 | −0.40 | −1.17 | −0.07 |
| Inactive, 1,000s[b] | 28,032 | −0.12 | −0.07 | −0.22 | −0.02 |
| Real per capita income, R per year[c] | 10,874 | 0.91 | 0.61 | 1.13 | 0.42 |

*(Table continues on the following page.)*

**Table 11.10. The Effects of Prospective Liberalization Abroad and Nationally on Sectoral Employment, Income Inequality, and Poverty, South Africa (*continued*)**

| Indicator | Base value | Rest-of-the-world reform | | Unilateral reform | |
|---|---|---|---|---|---|
| | | All goods | Agriculture only | All goods | Agriculture only |
| | % | *Change from the base, percentage points* | | | |
| Poverty headcount ratios | | | | | |
| US$1-a-day poverty, | | | | | |
| R 87 per month | 9.8 | −0.28 | −0.27 | −0.78 | −0.21 |
| Rural | 16.7 | −0.35 | −0.34 | −1.09 | −0.33 |
| Urban | 4.0 | −0.22 | −0.21 | −0.51 | −0.10 |
| US$2-a-day poverty, | | | | | |
| R 177 per month | 29.2 | −0.34 | −0.26 | −1.12 | −0.26 |
| Rural | 46.4 | −0.28 | −0.24 | −1.32 | −0.32 |
| Urban | 14.8 | −0.39 | −0.29 | −0.96 | −0.21 |
| Lower poverty line, | | | | | |
| R 322 per month | 50.1 | −0.39 | −0.23 | −1.05 | −0.25 |
| Rural | 71.5 | −0.18 | −0.12 | −0.72 | −0.22 |
| Urban | 32.2 | −0.56 | −0.32 | −1.33 | −0.28 |
| Upper poverty line, | | | | | |
| R 593 per month | 67.5 | −0.25 | −0.16 | −0.67 | −0.23 |
| Rural | 86.3 | −0.09 | −0.08 | −0.46 | −0.15 |
| Urban | 51.8 | −0.39 | −0.23 | −0.86 | −0.30 |
| Gini coefficient | 0.67 | −0.05 | −0.05 | −0.54 | −0.11 |
| Rural | 0.63 | −0.09 | −0.05 | −0.37 | −0.11 |
| Urban | 0.62 | −0.08 | −0.06 | −0.63 | −0.12 |

*Source:* Simulation results by the authors using their microsimulation model on South Africa.

a. Average real per capita earnings.

b. Includes 652,000 unspecified workers.

c. Average real disposable income per capita.

This is because rural households are more deeply rooted in poverty and because wages are significantly lower among rural workers, so that new jobs generate less income in rural areas than in urban areas.

The rise in average earnings in the informal sector is caused by the trickle-down effect of formal sector development. The migration of informal workers to lower-skilled formal jobs also raises the average skill level and earnings of the remaining informal workers. Conversely, the rise in lower-pay, lower-skilled formal employment places downward pressure on average formal earnings. Overall, however, the effects on inequality are negligible. The small reduction in income taxes and the higher returns to capital and skilled labor contribute to a worsening of income inequality. However, offsetting this effect is the increase in lower-skilled employment and the drop in consumer prices. The net effect is therefore virtually no change in national inequality, as measured by the Gini coefficient (table 11.10, final row).

Thus, in summary, full global liberalization produces slight gains in GDP in South Africa, but hurts the primary agricultural sector. Yet, food processing expands, which offsets some of the decline in the competitiveness of the horticultural sector. Import competition encourages farmers to shift toward more labor-intensive production. The decrease in the real wages of semiskilled and unskilled labor leads to a significant increase in employment among lower-skilled workers. This is the main force driving poverty reduction in this scenario.

### The liberalization only of agricultural commodities by the rest of the world

Even if reform abroad is restricted only to liberalization in agriculture, a positive effect on the terms of trade is still the result in South Africa. Following such liberalization, prices rise for South African exports by somewhat less than the corresponding rise in the previous simulation (table 11.6). This is because the export prices for most product groups except textiles and clothing rise by less following the liberalization in agriculture alone (table 11.5). The outcome is especially important in the production of fruits, which are South Africa's main agricultural export. However, in contrast to the result of the simulation involving the liberalization of all commodities, there is now a small overall increase in import prices (table 11.6). This is because industrial and service sector prices rise instead of falling, which is significant given that heavy manufactures, such as machinery and vehicles, make up almost two-thirds of total imports. The net result in this reform simulation of agriculture alone is a 0.7 percent improvement in the terms of trade of South Africa, which is half the 1.4 percent improvement in the simulation involving the liberalization by the rest of the world of all merchandise trade. The real exchange rate appreciation is also slightly smaller, and the impact on real GDP at market prices is only 0.1 percent instead of 0.3 percent (table 11.6).

The effects on sectoral output differ in this simulation, too (table 11.7). Agricultural GDP decreases by less relative to the simulation involving the liberalization of all commodities, although the production of vegetables and fruits falls slightly more, and wheat production now declines. Livestock production also increases more in this simulation. Industrial GDP now falls slightly, despite rising output in the food processing sector. The drop in manufacturing production adds to the small fall in agricultural GDP, which, as before, causes a migration of workers to the service sector. However, the impact is less pronounced than in the other simulation because of the smaller size of the shock in the terms of trade. Investment demand is bolstered by the increase in private savings resulting from the higher national GDP and the shift to more capital-intensive sectors outside food processing. Finally, while import prices rise in this simulation, the real appreciation is sufficient to offset the rise, and the consumer price index still falls, albeit by less than the case under full merchandise trade reform. Falling prices cause an increase in household real incomes and aggregate consumer spending (table 11.6, rows 1 and 2).

Household incomes also benefit from the increased employment among lower-skilled workers and the higher returns to capital and skilled labor. The changes produced by this more-limited reform are about two-thirds the size of the changes produced by full merchandise trade liberalization, and the increase in national economic welfare is about three-fifths as large (table 11.9). This is a significant result given the relatively small size of the agricultural sector both globally and in South Africa. It reflects the large distortions in agricultural markets in the rest of the world.

The impacts on income inequality and household poverty are similar to the corresponding impacts of the liberalization of all merchandise trade, but slightly smaller in magnitude (table 11.10). The fall in consumer prices plays a more important role in the reduction of poverty in the simulation involving only agriculture, and poor households particularly benefit from the falling food prices.

Thus, in summary, the removal of the agricultural distortions alone in the rest of the world would have a positive impact on GDP, national welfare, inequality, and poverty in South Africa. This impact is roughly two-thirds as large as the impact of full merchandise trade reform, despite the fact that agriculture accounts for less than one-12th of global and South African GDP and trade.

### The unilateral liberalization of all commodity markets

Agricultural import tariffs are generally quite low in South Africa; duty collection rates average 5 percent (table 11.1). Moreover, there are high tariffs on a relatively small range of manufactured goods, including a 15 percent tariff on wheat imports that dominates price distortions in South Africa. Import tariffs are especially high on certain processed foods (dairy and processed sugar), textiles and clothing, and motor vehicles and related parts (for example, tires and engines). In contrast, export taxes are low and uniform across commodities, with the exception of agriculture, which faces no export taxes. Output taxes and subsidies are equally negligible. So, it is the reduction in import tariffs that drives the results in the two unilateral liberalization simulations we now consider in this and the next subsection.

Eliminating all South Africa's border measures and domestic agricultural subsidies causes a substantial increase in import demand (table 11.6). This widens the trade deficit and induces a 1.9 percent depreciation in the real exchange rate, which offsets some of the rise in real imports. Export competitiveness is enhanced by the depreciation, thus encouraging producers to boost their production for foreign markets. Total exports rise by 7.5 percent, while farm and manufactured exports rise by more than 10.0 percent.

The exchange rate depreciation is sufficient to offset the decline in the tariffs on some import-competing industries, causing the related GDP to expand (table 11.7). In contrast, in heavily protected commodities such as wheat, dairy, textiles, and clothing, imports increase and GDP falls. Thus, in line with the initial distribution of tariffs, agricultural imports expand by less than manufactured imports. Export expansion is more evenly distributed across both the agricultural sector and the nonagricultural sector. Cotton, tobacco, and fruits drive the increase in exports within agriculture.

Relative to liberalization by the rest of the world, unilateral liberalization has a larger positive impact on real consumer spending. This is because, following the latter, falling import prices reduce the consumer price index, thereby raising real household incomes. Rising incomes also increase the level of savings and investment in the economy. Investment is additionally supported by the expansion of the metals and machinery sectors and the reduction in the import prices for capital goods, both of which contribute to a reduction in the cost of investment. Ultimately, following unilateral reform, rising consumption, exports, and investment lead to larger increases in total GDP: 1.0 percent compared with less than 0.3 percent after rest-of-the-world reform (table 11.6).

Increased production following unilateral reform also creates more jobs for lower-skilled workers relative to the case of rest-of-the-world reform (table 11.9). Although most of these jobs are lower-pay jobs in agriculture, there is also an increase in higher-paying jobs in the manufacturing sector. New jobs are created in the metals and machinery sectors, both of which pay higher wages than the textiles and clothing sectors, where jobs are lost. Unskilled workers also migrate to service sector jobs, not all of which are in the lower-pay trade sector. Overall, there is a net migration into higher-pay sectors, causing average real wages and total employment to rise among unskilled workers. There is increased demand for skilled workers, although the shift of such workers into higher-pay sectors is less pronounced. For instance, most skilled workers are already employed in the service sector, where wages are typically the highest. So, it is the overall increase in demand rather than intersectoral shifts that drives the increase in wages among these workers. Finally, semiskilled workers are more intensively employed in the textile sectors, and semiskilled workers thus face the largest declines in employment once the protection for these sectors is removed.

Larger increases in factor incomes cause aggregate household welfare to improve by more in this simulation than in the two rest-of-the-world simulations. Poverty reduction is also larger (table 11.10). The increase in unskilled and semi-skilled real wages, combined with the expansion in employment among the related workers, is the main force behind the reduction in poverty. Indeed, low-income households are the most dependent on low-skilled labor. The slight decline in national inequality is caused by the combination of these labor market changes and the substantial rise in income taxes needed to replace lost tariff revenues. In this simulation, aggregate household income taxes rise by more than 10 percent.

Thus, in summary, the unilateral removal of price distortions in South Africa would cause national GDP to expand and would boost agricultural GDP by more than two times the rise in GDP in industry or services. This suggests that the current domestic distortions are strongly biased against the agricultural sector. However, after the reform, much of the benefits to agriculture would accrue to specific export-oriented crops, such as cotton, tobacco, and fruits, while other farm sectors would be adversely affected. Manufacturing employment would also decline, especially in the sensitive textiles and clothing sectors. This decline would be more than offset, however, by new jobs in the heavier industrial and service sectors. Thus, aggregate household welfare would improve; national poverty would decline; and there would be a small decline in inequality.

### The unilateral liberalization of only agricultural commodities

The removal of price distortions only in South Africa's agricultural and food processing sectors produces macroeconomic results similar to, but much smaller than those produced by the unilateral liberalization of all merchandise. Raising import demand and export supply induces a small depreciation in the real exchange rate, which enhances the competitiveness in foreign markets of domestic producers of exports. Falling import prices also lower consumer prices, benefiting private consumption and increasing national GDP, but only by one-ninth as much as in full unilateral liberalization (table 11.6). However, while these effects are similar to those under full domestic liberalization, their size is much smaller. This is not surprising because South Africa's agricultural and food processing sectors are only a small part of national GDP and are not as well protected as the manufacturing sector.

Under the unilateral liberalization of all goods, agriculture benefits from the large depreciation in the exchange rate that is driven by the declining nonagricultural tariffs and rising import penetration of nonagricultural commodities. However, in the unilateral liberalization of agriculture alone, the depreciation is smaller and is driven entirely by the decline in the supports and tariffs in agriculture and food processing. Thus, only agriculture faces an increase in import competition, while the nonagricultural sectors benefit from the resulting depreciation. Accordingly, there is a decline in agricultural GDP in this simulation. This is driven by declining wheat production, which is subject to high initial tariffs. Fruit, cotton, and tobacco, which show substantially increased production under the full unilateral liberalization, now expand more modestly because of the smaller depreciation, while livestock declines because producers shift production toward more export-oriented activities and because the imports of processed meats increase. Food processing suffers the largest drop in production under the liberalization of agriculture alone. For instance, there is now a contraction in the dried fruit and tobacco sectors, which contributes to the decline in agriculture. Production expands in the industrial and service sectors mainly because of greater export demand following the depreciation. The largest increases are in metals, machinery, and motor vehicles. The slowdown in investment, however, causes a slight decline in construction, and the modest expansion of services is driven by trade, which benefits from South Africa's increased openness. Overall, there is a much smaller increase in national GDP under this liberalization scenario because of the smaller size of the shock and the decline in investment demand (table 11.7).

The greater import competition in agricultural commodities and the only modest additional demand created by nonagricultural expansion cause agricultural prices to fall relatively more than nonagricultural prices. This raises the relative returns in nonagriculture, leading workers to migrate from agriculture. The real returns to lower-skilled agricultural labor increase slightly and generate the decline in unskilled employment resulting from the contraction in agricultural production. The increase in nonagricultural production creates additional jobs for semiskilled workers, but these jobs pay wages that are similar to the wages in agriculture, leaving average wages largely unchanged and raising national economic welfare only slightly (table 11.9).

Unilateral liberalization in agriculture alone thus has the smallest impacts on poverty and inequality among our simulations, although the impacts are in the same direction as the impacts of full unilateral liberalization (except in the case of real wages among unskilled labor, which decline slightly). Unlike the other simulations, poverty reduction under unilateral agricultural liberalization is driven mainly by consumer price changes. Although the reduction in the consumer price index is smaller in this simulation than in the full unilateral liberalization, the changes are more beneficial for the poor because there are substantial declines in the prices of food items that account for a large share of the expenditures of poor households. Hence, poverty is reduced and income inequality declines slightly even in this simulation (table 11.10).

Thus, in summary, while the unilateral removal of the distortions in agriculture and food processing has a negative impact on production in this sector, it lowers food prices, and the net effect is a reduction in poverty and inequality in South Africa.

## Conclusions

Our model results indicate that agriculture in South Africa currently benefits from global price distortions, but mainly because of the impact on local fruit producers. Most of the other agricultural sectors are adversely affected by global distortions. This is especially true of traditional export crops, such as tobacco, sugar, and cotton. The global distortions are also biased against the livestock and dairy sectors, which are important components of food processing in South Africa. Thus, despite a decline in agricultural GDP, the removal of global distortions would favor the creation of new formal sector jobs for lower-skilled workers in agriculture and food processing, including some workers who are currently unemployed. There would need to be a period of structural adjustment in the country as manufacturing workers migrate to the service sector. In the long run, these workers would benefit from higher-pay jobs. The removal of global price distortions thus improves national economic welfare, reduces poverty, and lowers income inequality, albeit only slightly.

South Africa's own policies are also biased against agriculture. Tariff protection is greater for nonagricultural commodities than for farm products, such that the removal of the tariffs raises overall agricultural GDP and employment. There is contraction in some farm industries and in textiles and clothing after unilateral reform. The job losses in these sectors are, however, outweighed by job creation elsewhere in agriculture and food processing, such that overall employment rises after the domestic distortions are removed. Household welfare also improves, especially among poorer rural households.

Our findings suggest that current own-country policies are more damaging to welfare, poverty, and inequality in South Africa relative to the effects of distortionary policies in the rest of the world. The rationalization of the country's system of protection so that tariffs are more uniformly applied across sectors would reduce some of the bias against agriculture and the poor. Price distortions may thus explain some of the poor performance in the agricultural sector and in rural development over the last decade. The complete removal of these distortions would increase the benefits of the broader reform process in South Africa. This reform would involve less adjustment in the South African economy if the domestic reforms were accompanied by reform abroad, such as the reforms desired under the World Trade Organization's Doha Development Agenda.

## Notes

1. Measured using the national household income and expenditure survey in 2000 and a US$2-a-day poverty line (Hoogeveen and Özler 2005).

2. We use the International Food Policy Research Institute's static model for this study (Lofgren, Harris, and Robinson 2002).

3. Table 11.8 shows the factor intensities of various aggregate sectors, as well as the factor substitution elasticities used in the sectoral production functions.

4. Agricultural land is not separated out because arable land is underutilized, and land rents are low, at 5 percent of land values (Ortmann and Machethe 2003). Thus, we assume that agricultural production is not so constrained by the lack of the availability of land, but rather by the lack of the availability of other forms of capital (for example, machinery, irrigation infrastructure, and other infrastructure). Furthermore, commercial land rents, like other forms of capital, mainly accrue to high-income households; the poverty effects of agricultural distortions are therefore unaffected by this assumption.

5. South Africa's unemployment rate was 32 percent in 2003 under a strict definition and 43 percent if the nonsearching unemployed are included in the workforce (Casale, Muller, and Posel 2004). While nominal wages are fixed, they may vary in real terms because of changes in consumer prices.

6. See Hérault (2006) for a detailed description of the microsimulation model.

## References

Anderson, K., and E. Valenzuela. 2008. "Estimates of Global Distortions to Agricultural Incentives, 1955–2007." Data spreadsheet, October, World Bank, Washington, DC. http://go.worldbank.org/YAO39F35E0.

Bell, T. 1993. "Should South Africa Further Liberalise Its Foreign Trade?" *State and Market in Post-apartheid South Africa*, ed. M. Lipton and C. Simpkins, 81–128. Johannesburg: Witwatersrand University Press.

Casale, D., C. Muller, and D. Posel. 2004. "Two Million Net New Jobs: A Reconsideration of the Rise in Employment in South Africa, 1995–2003." *South African Journal of Economics* 72 (5): 978–1002.

Case, A. 2000. "Income Distribution and Expenditure Patterns in South Africa." Unpublished paper, Princeton University, Princeton, NJ.

Cassim, R., D. Onyango, and D. E. N. van Seventer. 2004. *The State of Trade Policy in South Africa.* Johannesburg: Trade and Industrial Policy Strategies.

Department of Finance, Republic of South Africa. 1996. "Growth, Employment, and Redistribution: A Macroeconomic Strategy." Government Printer, Pretoria.

Dimaranan, B. D., ed. 2006. *Global Trade, Assistance, and Protection: The GTAP 6 Data Base.* West Lafayette, IN: Center for Global Trade Analysis, Department of Agricultural Economics, Purdue University. https://www.gtap.agecon.purdue.edu/databases/v6/v6_doco.asp.

Edwards, L. 2001. "Globalisation and the Occupational Structure of Employment in South Africa." *South African Journal of Economics* 69 (1): 40–71.

Hérault, N. 2006. "Building and Linking a Microsimulation Model to a CGE Model for South Africa." *South African Journal of Economics* 74 (1): 34–58.

———. 2007. "Trade Liberalisation, Poverty, and Inequality in South Africa: A Computable General Equilibrium-Microsimulation Analysis." *Economic Record* 83 (262): 317–28.

Hoogeveen, J. G., and B. Özler. 2005. "Not Separate, Not Equal: Poverty and Inequality in Post-apartheid South Africa." William Davidson Institute Working Paper 739, William Davidson Institute, Stephen M. Ross Business School, University of Michigan, Ann Arbor, MI.

Horridge, M. 2004. "Shocking a Single Country CGE Model with Export Prices/Quantities from GTAP." Unpublished paper, Centre of Policy Studies, Monash University, Clayton, Victoria, Australia.

Jonsson, G., and A. Subramanian. 2001. "Dynamic Gains from Trade: Evidence from South Africa." *IMF Staff Papers* 48 (1): 197–224.

Jooste, A., H. Van Schalkwyk, and J. Groenewald. 2003. "South African Agriculture and International Trade." In *The Challenge of Change: Agriculture, Land, and the South African Economy*, ed. L. Nieuwoudt and J. Groenewald, 185–210. Durban, South Africa: University of KwaZulu-Natal Press.

Kirsten, J., L. Edwards, and N. Vink. 2009. "South Africa." In *Distortions to Agricultural Incentives in Africa*, ed. K. Anderson and W. A. Masters, 147–74. Washington, DC: World Bank.

Krueger, A. O., M. Schiff, and A. Valdés, eds. 1991. *The Political Economy of Agricultural Pricing Policy.* 3 vols. Baltimore: Johns Hopkins University Press; Washington, DC: World Bank.

Lofgren, H., R. L. Harris, and S. Robinson. 2002. "A Standard Computable General Equilibrium (CGE) Model in GAMS." Microcomputers in Policy Research 5, International Food Policy Research Institute, Washington, DC.

Ortmann, G., and C. Machethe. 2003. "Problems and Opportunities in South African Agriculture." In *The Challenge of Change: Agriculture, Land, and the South African Economy*, ed. L. Nieuwoudt and J. Groenewald, 47–62. Durban, South Africa: University of KwaZulu-Natal Press.

SARB (South African Reserve Bank). 2008. *South African Quarterly Bulletin of Statistics.* Pretoria: SARB.

StatsSA (Statistics South Africa). 2000–. *Labor Force Survey.* Pretoria: Statistics South Africa.

———. 2001. *2000 Household Income and Expenditure Survey.* Pretoria: Statistics South Africa.

———. 2002. *Census of Commercial Agriculture 2002.* Pretoria: Statistics South Africa.

———. 2004. *Final Supply-Use Tables for South Africa, 2002.* Pretoria: Statistics South Africa.

Thurlow, J. 2007. "Trade Liberalization and Pro-Poor Growth in South Africa." *Journal for Studies in Economics and Econometrics* 3 (2): 161–79.

Valenzuela, E., and K. Anderson. 2008. "Alternative Agricultural Price Distortions for CGE Analysis of Developing Countries, 2004 and 1980–84." Research Memorandum 13 (December), Center for Global Trade Analysis, Department of Agricultural Economics, Purdue University, West Lafayette, IN. https://www.gtap.agecon.purdue.edu/resources/res_display.asp?RecordID=2925.

van der Mensbrugghe, D. 2005. "Linkage Technical Reference Document: Version 6.0." December, World Bank, Washington, DC. http://go.worldbank.org/7NP2KK1OH0.

Van Schalkwyk, H., J. Groenewald, and A. Jooste. 2003. "Agricultural Marketing in South Africa." In *The Challenge of Change: Agriculture, Land, and the South African Economy*, ed. L. Nieuwoudt and J. Groenewald, 119–136. Durban, South Africa: University of KwaZulu-Natal Press.

van Seventer, D. E. N. 2001. "Note on the Structure of the South African Tariff Schedule." Paper presented at "Trade and Industrial Policy Strategies Annual Forum," Johannesburg, September 10–12.

Vink, N., and J. Kirsten. 2003. "Agriculture in the National Economy." In *The Challenge of Change: Agriculture, Land, and the South African Economy*, ed. L. Nieuwoudt and J. Groenewald, 3–20. Durban, South Africa: University of KwaZulu-Natal Press.

World Bank. 2008. *World Development Indicators 2008.* Washington, DC: World Bank.

# PART V

# NATIONAL CGE APPROACHES: LATIN AMERICA

# 12

# ARGENTINA

*Martín Cicowiez,*
*Carolina Díaz-Bonilla,*
*and Eugenio Díaz-Bonilla*

Using the most recent estimates of agricultural price distortions, we study in this chapter the economic, poverty, and income inequality impacts of global and domestic agricultural liberalization and total trade liberalization in Argentina, with a special focus on export taxes. Argentina offers an interesting case study because it is the only large agricultural exporter that, at many times in its history, has applied export taxes to several agricultural products. The most recent episode started after the large devaluation of early 2002, when export taxes, which had been abolished during the 1990s, were reinstated; the export taxes have been in place ever since.[1]

Export taxes have been defended by the Argentine government on the grounds that they are needed for poverty reduction, fiscal consolidation, the intersectoral and intrasectoral balance of production, and other reasons. Critics have argued that the taxes reduce growth and even increase poverty (for example, see Nogués et al. 2007, Nogués 2008). We look at these conflicting claims using a general equilibrium approach in an attempt to present a more integrated evaluation of national measures. We also examine the impact on Argentina of the rest of the world's agricultural and trade policies, with a particular focus on the effects on poverty and inequality in Argentina.

More specifically, our analysis combines results from a global economy-wide computable general equilibrium (CGE) model, a national CGE model, and microsimulations. We use the World Bank's global Linkage model (see van der Mensbrugghe 2005) to analyze the impact on the Argentine economy of trade policy interventions in the rest of the world. The model is based on version 7 of the Global Trade Analysis Project Database, which is calibrated to 2004

(Narayanan and Walmsley 2008), while the agricultural distortions in developing countries are taken from the new World Bank database as summarized by Valenzuela and Anderson (2008). The impacts on the terms of trade and export demand faced by Argentina that are generated by rest-of-the-world policies, which are simulated using the global Linkage model (see the appendix by van der Mensbrugghe, Valenzuela, and Anderson), are transmitted as exogenous shocks to a national CGE model of Argentina. The results of the country CGE simulations in regard to changes in employment, factor prices, and the prices of goods and services are linked to a microsimulation model for Argentina, which allows us to analyze the impacts of these various changes on household poverty and inequality according to household survey data. We analyze and compare the effects on Argentina's economy of the removal of rest-of-the-world distortions and Argentina's own import tariffs and export taxes. In addition, our analysis distinguishes between agricultural reforms only and reforms that cover agricultural and nonagricultural trade policies.

The rest of the chapter is organized into four sections. The next section provides background information, including the economic context in which export taxes were implemented by Argentine authorities in response to the economic collapse of 2001–02 and the evolution of poverty and inequality indicators. The subsequent section summarizes the methodology and data for the national CGE and microsimulation models. This is followed by the core section, which discusses the model simulations and results. The final section offers conclusions.

## Background

In 2001–02, Argentina experienced one of the most severe crises in its history. Amid social unrest and street riots that led to more than 30 deaths and hundreds of injuries, the country plunged into a state of institutional disarray. GDP declined 10 percent in 2002, on top of the previous three consecutive years of decline that involved an accumulated GDP loss of another 10 percent. Formal unemployment jumped to more than 25 percent, and almost 60 percent of the population was considered to be living below the national poverty line.

The collapse was the result of a combination of factors. First and foremost were the policy rigidities of the Convertibility Plan, which was established in 1991 during the Menem administration and linked the peso to the U.S. dollar in a (quasi) currency board arrangement at the exchange rate of Arg$1 = US$1. Inflation continued at a high rate for about two years after the exchange rate had been fixed, and the peso became overvalued, affecting the production of tradables. The fixed peg also forced Argentina to follow the appreciation in the U.S. dollar that started in the mid-1990s, thereby additionally punishing production, employment, and the fiscal accounts. Doubts about the sustainability of the peg led to a generalized dollarization of the banking system, which eliminated the possibility of counter-cyclical monetary policy and increased the vulnerability of the domestic financial system to runs against the peso or the banks.

Second, Menem's government had privatized a significant portion of the social security system by the mid-1990s. This generated a substantial transitional fiscal deficit. The deficit added to public indebtedness, which was expected to take several decades to repay.[2]

Third, there was a series of negative exogenous shocks in the late 1990s and early 2000s, including Brazil's devaluation and the decline of agricultural prices. When the government of President De la Rua took office in late 1999, the economy was already decelerating and heading into outright recession after this combination of external shocks.

Fourth, the alliance of parties that constituted the De la Rua government (the first coalition government in many years) broke down under the economic strains of the deepening recession. In the second half of 2000, the vice president resigned, and the party of the vice president left the coalition, weakening the capacity of the government to manage the difficult economic situation.

At the end of 2001, as confidence waned and a run occurred against the peso and against the banking system, the situation became untenable. The administrative constraints imposed by the government on bank withdrawals to stop the run on the banks—because the deposits of the banks were largely in U.S. dollars, the Central Bank, unable to print dollars, could not help the banks much—finally led to widespread riots and the resignation of President De la Rua. A period of turmoil ensued, during which the country had four additional presidents within only a few weeks through early 2002.

By late 2001 and early 2002, it had become clear that there were two separate, but related fiscal and external problems of insolvency: a significant public debt involving a nonfinanceable fiscal deficit and a significant external debt (private and public) involving a nonfinanceable current account deficit. The suspension of debt payments and the subsequent devaluation (abandoning the one-to-one peg to the U.S. dollar) were desperate measures taken by the interim governments in early 2002 to cope with both problems. The exchange rate jumped to almost Arg$4 per US$1 dollar once it had been allowed to float in the first half of 2002. It later declined to about Arg$2.50 per US$1, but, by the end of 2008, the exchange rate was about Arg$3.30 to US$1.

In early 2002, in the middle of a deep recession, aggravated by the banking crises and the devaluation, and needing to shore up fiscal accounts, the government imposed export taxes on agricultural and several other products, including oil and other energy commodities. One of the objectives of these taxes was fiscal; they were imposed during a moment when the collection of more traditional income and value added taxes had dropped significantly because of the recession. Not only had tax receipts declined, but the peso value of the public debt (most of which was denominated in U.S. dollars) had increased significantly during the devaluation. Under the one-to-one exchange rate, Argentina's GDP was valued at almost US$300 billion in the late 1990s, while the public debt was about US$150 billion (a ratio of debt to GDP of 50 percent). After the devaluation, the GDP was valued at less than US$100 billion, but the debt, yet to be renegotiated, remained the same, implying an unsustainable ratio of debt to GDP of more than 150 percent. Through the imposition of export taxes, the negative impacts of the devaluation on public accounts were partially offset.

Export taxes helped increase fiscal receipts by 1.5 to 2.5 percent of GDP (figure 12.1). They were only one component in a more general effort to consolidate fiscal accounts through the more effective collection of all taxes. Figure 12.2 shows that overall tax receipts increased by 8 to 9 percent of GDP beginning in 2002, compared with the 1990s; so, export taxes accounted for less than one-third of the overall boost in taxes. There was also some adjustment in public expenditures, which, during 2002–07, were about 0.8 percentage points of GDP below the average for the previous decade.

A separate and important objective of the government in imposing export taxes in the case of agricultural products, which include important food staples such as wheat, rice, beef, fruits and vegetables, and dairy products, was to moderate the upward impact of the currency devaluation on domestic food prices and, thereby, on real wages and poverty. Early in the development debate in Argentina it was argued that, because Argentina's exports are mainly wage goods (in the terminology

**Figure 12.1. Export Taxes, Argentina, 2001–07**

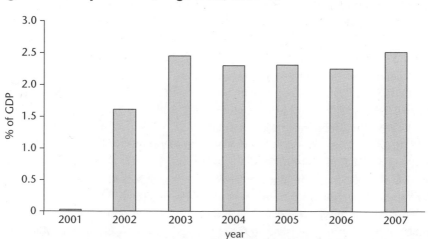

*Source:* Información Económica Database (2008).

**Figure 12.2. Tax Revenue, Argentina, 1991–2007**

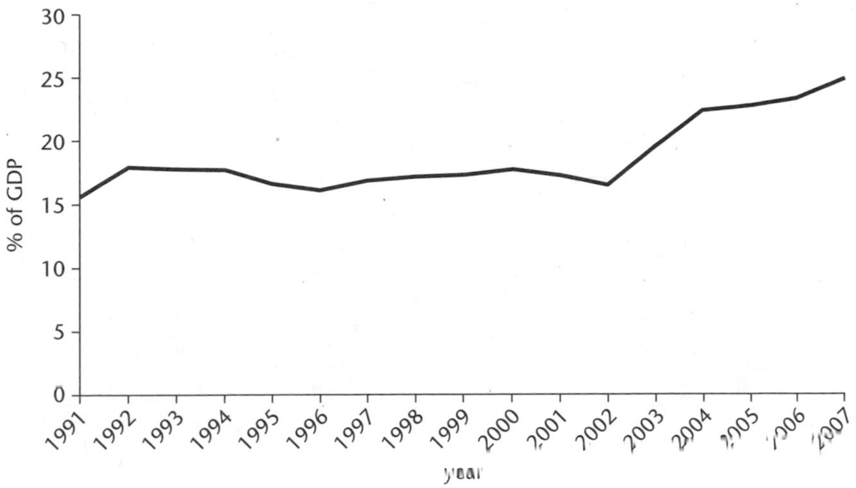

*Source:* Información Económica Database (2008).

of Ricardo), a devaluation would put upward pressure on wages and influence the competitiveness of domestic industry (Díaz-Alejandro 1963, Braun and Joy 1968). By increasing domestic food prices, devaluations would raise the poverty line, which is based on the prices of a basket mainly consisting of food items. For a given income, this would also increase the number of people living below the adjusted poverty line. Because they moderated the increase in domestic food prices, export taxes were seen as a way to reduce this impact of the devaluation.

The government has also maintained a moderate export tax differential (taxing primary products somewhat more than processed items), presumably to compensate domestic producers for the tariff escalation prevalent in the rest of the world.[3]

In addition, export taxes have been imposed on other important export products such as oil and gas, which has kept a lid on the domestic prices of energy, benefiting the productive sectors in proportion to their use of energy inputs. This is important for agricultural production because it has lowered the cost of fuel and fertilizers among farmers.

From 2003 until about the end of 2008, the economy experienced a strong and rapid recovery, growing at about 8.5 percent during the period. To a large extent, the significant growth was based on reductions in the country's macrovulnerability and high volatility, which were the main reasons for the dismal economic performance until recently.[4] The combination of an exchange rate at approximately the real level (deflated by the U.S. consumer price index) of the decades previous to the large overvaluation of the 1990s, fiscal consolidation through increases in taxes and the debt renegotiation, and the accumulation of reserves in the Central Bank has reduced the main causes of macroeconomic vulnerability by sustaining surpluses in the fiscal and current accounts.[5]

The period of economic growth led to improvements in employment, poverty, and income distribution at least through late 2007. The unemployment rate of 7.5 percent in the fourth quarter of 2007 was the lowest since the early 1990s; during the 2001–02 crisis, it had topped 25 percent. The levels of poverty and extreme poverty declined from 58 and 28 percent, respectively, in 2002, to 23 and 8 percent by the end of 2007. Income distribution also improved: the ratio of the top decile to the bottom decile fell from 32 at the beginning of 2004 to 26 in the first quarter of 2007.

What has been the role of agricultural and other trade policies, particularly export taxes, in the positive performance? This is a policy question that may best be addressed using an empirical general equilibrium approach.

It is useful to look, first, at the evolution of agricultural prices and production in Argentina since the imposition of export taxes in 2002. Critics argue that the price-distorting policy reduces farmer incentives and adversely affects growth. The issue of farmer incentives, however, must be analyzed in a broader policy context, along with other measures, particularly the exchange rate.[6] Figure 12.3 shows that domestic producer prices in real terms have been clearly above the 1990s

**Figure 12.3. Agricultural Producer Price Indexes, Argentina, 1992–2006**

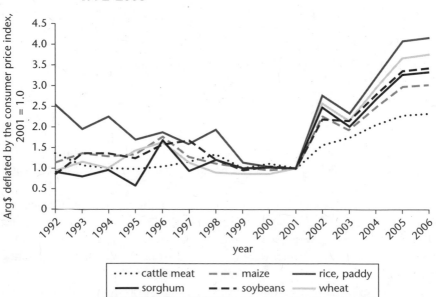

*Sources:* FAOSTAT (2008), Información Económica Database (2008).

values for a variety of farm products, suggesting that the negative impact of export taxes on domestic prices has been more than offset by the devaluation or by a rise in the international prices of farm products.[7] Figure 12.4 shows another indicator of the incentives for agricultural production in Argentina, namely, an index of relative domestic prices for the agricultural sector and the rest of the economy, along with an index of the real exchange rate in Argentina and an index of real international prices (see the definitions in the note to figure 12.4). The significant improvement in the internal terms of trade for agriculture since 2002 has been mainly caused by the adjustment in the real exchange rate, while the changes in world prices show a positive impact only since the second half of 2007.[8]

**Figure 12.4. Indexes of International Agricultural Prices, Relative Domestic Agricultural Prices, and the Real Effective Exchange Rate, Argentina, 1996–2008**

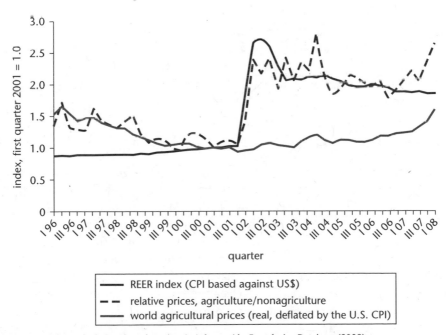

*Source:* Author calculations based on data in Información Económica Database (2008).

*Note:* All variables in the indexes are normalized to 1 for the first quarter of 2001. The index of real prices for world agricultural products is the weighted average of International Monetary Fund indexes for food, beverages, and agricultural raw materials, using International Monetary Fund weights, deflated by the U.S. consumer price index (CPI). The index of relative domestic prices in the agricultural sector is the index of the prices relative to total GDP measured as the ratio of the deflator of agricultural value added in GDP at factor cost to the total GDP deflator at factor cost. The index of the real effective exchange rate (REER) of the Argentine peso against the U.S. dollar is calculated using the average nominal exchange rate (Arg$ per US$) and the consumer price indexes of Argentina and the United States.

In addition to the devaluation, other policies in Argentina have also benefited agriculture, such as the normalization of debt conditions for many producers affected by the 2001–02 macroeconomic collapse, lower energy prices through export taxes on energy products (Argentina is a net exporter of energy), and the expansion of investments in technology and infrastructure. The combination of these policies, plus rising international commodity prices, has contributed to a strong supply-side response from farmers. Thus, Argentina's production of grains and oilseeds in 2003–07 was about 10 percent above the growth trend of the previous 45 years (for details, see Cicowiez, Díaz-Bonilla, and Díaz-Bonilla 2009, appendix 1).

While it is not evident from these recent data that export taxes are harming the agricultural sector, it may be argued that, without export taxes, agricultural growth rates would have been even higher. However, one should bear in mind that lower or no export taxes would have affected fiscal accounts and led to higher interest rates and possibly weaker overall macroeconomic performance. Higher domestic prices may have also led to protests about domestic food prices, compromising the social sustainability of the entire reform program. These possibilities are not explicitly explored in what follows. Rather, we limit ourselves to disentangling the effects of agricultural and trade policies at home and abroad on poverty and income distribution in Argentina, with a special focus on export taxes.

## Methodology and Data

To explore the effects of agricultural and trade policies abroad on poverty and income distribution in Argentina, we use the simulation results from the global Linkage model (see the appendix by van der Mensbrugghe, Valenzuela, and Anderson) as exogenous shocks that are fed into a national CGE model for Argentina, and we use these results, in turn, as inputs in a microsimulation model. We then compare the latter two sets of impacts with the impacts of own-country agricultural and trade policies that we estimate using only the national CGE and microsimulation models. There are no feedback effects from the microlevel to the macrolevel, but the microsimulations are consistent with the aggregates generated by the national CGE model.

At the macrolevel, through the national CGE model, we produce results for a given policy change, including new levels of employment in each economic sector, new wages, and new relative prices. At the household level, we use the microsimulation model to receive the changes in the macrolevel variables and determine new individual wages and employment, a new distribution of household per capita income, and new poverty rates and inequality indicators.

## The CGE model for Argentina

The national CGE model has similarities with the models in Lofgren, Harris, and Robinson (2002) and Lofgren and Díaz-Bonilla (2007). It is based on a 2005 social accounting matrix for Argentina with 24 activities and 26 commodities (table 12.1). This disaggregation matches as closely as possible the disaggregation of the global Linkage model. The national CGE model includes three institutions: a representative household, government, and the rest of the world. There are eight factors, including six labor categories: men and women each divided across unskilled, semiskilled, and skilled workers. We consider land and capital partly sector specific and partly mobile across sectors. Land only moves within the primary agricultural sectors. In the model and database, we consider several

### Table 12.1. Components of the Social Accounting Matrix, Argentina, 2005

| Sectors (26) | | |
|---|---|---|
| **Primary** | **Processed food** | **Other manufactures** |
| 1 Cereals | 10 Meat | 18 Textiles and apparel |
| 2 Vegetables and fruits | 11 Oils and fats | 19 Petroleum refining |
| 3 Oilseeds | 12 Dairy products | 20 Chemical products |
| 4 Other crops | 13 Sugar | 21 Mineral products |
| 5 Sugarcane and beets | 14 Flour, bakery, and pasta | 22 Metal products |
| 6 Livestock, milk, and wool | 15 Feed products | 23 Machinery and equipment |
| 7 Other primary nonagriculture | 16 Other processed food | 24 Vehicles |
| 8 Mining | 17 Beverages and tobacco | 25 Other manufacturing |
| 9 Oil | | 26 Services |
| **Factors (8)** | **Institutions (3)** | **Taxes (9)** |
| 1 Unskilled labor, men | 1 Household | 1 Value added tax |
| 2 Unskilled labor, women | 2 Government | 2 Fuel tax |
| 3 Semiskilled labor, men | 3 Rest of the world | 3 Financial services tax |
| 4 Semiskilled labor, women | | 4 Export tax |
| 5 Skilled labor, men | | 5 Tariffs |
| 6 Skilled labor, women | | 6 Turnover tax |
| 7 Capital, specific and mobile | | 7 Taxes on products |
| 8 Land, mobile only across agriculture | | 8 Income tax |
| | | 9 Factor tax |
| **Savings and investment (1)** | | |
| 1 Savings and investment | | |

Source: Prepared by the authors.

tax instruments, including export taxes, income taxes, and the value added tax. The modeling of the value added tax incorporates rebates for intermediate inputs and investment purchases; so, there is no cascading effect on the prices of the taxes on intermediate goods.

While many CGE models are run under a full-employment specification, our modeling of the labor market allows for endogenous unemployment. This is described through a complementary slackness condition for unemployment and wages. As the economy grows, if the factor market is below full employment, then the unemployment rate is the clearing variable for the market, that is, unemployment decreases for the necessary labor types until a minimum unemployment rate is reached.[9] At full employment (that is, the case wherein the minimum unemployment rate is reached), the economy-wide wage variable adjusts to clear the market.[10]

Because of a modeling characteristic that results from the methodology of the World Bank project, the national model determines export supply behavior, but, regarding demand by the rest of the world, changes are calculated using export demand curves based on parameters and results from the global Linkage model (see Horridge and Zhai 2006). Therefore, we do not adopt the small country hypothesis on the export side. Regarding imports, however, we take the price shocks directly from the global model on the assumption that import supply functions for Argentina are flat (the small country assumption).

The closures for the model are as follows. In the case of the government, we assume that government consumption and savings are fixed in real terms. This means that the level of surplus (or deficit) in the base year is maintained (Argentina had a surplus in 2005); it also means that one or more taxes are the equilibrating variables. Here, we keep all tax rates at the level of the base year except for the direct tax rate, which adjusts to equilibrate fiscal accounts, compensating for the revenue lost through trade liberalization. Therefore, the simulations are fiscally neutral. For the rest of the world, foreign savings—broadly defined to include other nontraded items—are fixed exogenously, while the exchange rate adjusts, that is, the level of trade balance that existed in the base year is maintained in dollar terms, and the exchange rate acts as the equilibrating variable. For the savings-investment balance, investment is driven by savings as in the global Linkage model. Because public savings and foreign savings are fixed, investment arises from changes in household savings behavior; specifically, the marginal propensity to save or consume adjusts.

An understanding of the effects of trade policy reforms is aided by an awareness of the country's trade structure and price distortions in the base year. The trade structure is summarized in table 12.2. Agricultural and agroindustrial products represent about 45 percent of all exports, and petroleum and related products

**Table 12.2. External Trade Structure, Argentina, 2005**
*(percent)*

| Sector | Sectoral share of total goods, exports | Sectoral share of total goods, imports | Share of exports in sectoral production | Share of imports in domestic production |
|---|---|---|---|---|
| *Primary* | | | | |
| Cereals | 5.9 | 0.0 | 55.0 | 0.4 |
| Vegetables and fruits | 2.3 | 0.3 | 29.5 | 4.6 |
| Oilseeds | 4.8 | 0.5 | 30.9 | 3.8 |
| Other crops | 0.8 | 0.4 | 9.9 | 4.8 |
| Sugarcane and beets | n.a. | n.a. | n.a. | n.a. |
| Livestock, milk, and wool | 0.5 | 0.1 | 1.8 | 0.2 |
| Other primary nonagriculture | 0.2 | 0.2 | 8.4 | 9.1 |
| Mining | 3.4 | 2.9 | 29.2 | 23.7 |
| Oil | 1.8 | 0.7 | 15.3 | 3.7 |
| *Processed food* | | | | |
| Meat | 4.1 | 0.2 | 19.0 | 1.0 |
| Oils and fats | 16.3 | 0.1 | 86.8 | 4.0 |
| Dairy products | 1.5 | 0.1 | 13.7 | 0.6 |
| Sugar | 0.3 | n.a. | 19.5 | n.a. |
| Flour, baking, and pasta | 0.7 | 0.1 | 4.1 | 0.7 |
| Feed products | 0.1 | 0.1 | 7.7 | 3.9 |
| Other processed food | 4.6 | 1.2 | 31.6 | 9.5 |
| Beverages and tobacco | 1.2 | 0.2 | 7.7 | 1.0 |
| *Other manufactures* | | | | |
| Textiles and apparel | 3.7 | 4.2 | 18.5 | 18.5 |
| Petroleum refining | 8.7 | 2.6 | 39.4 | 14.6 |
| Chemical products | 9.2 | 19.4 | 26.8 | 40.4 |
| Mineral products | 0.5 | 1.0 | 6.2 | 10.2 |
| Metal products | 7.2 | 7.1 | 21.5 | 19.4 |
| Machinery and equipment | 4.3 | 33.6 | 19.6 | 62.8 |
| Vehicles | 8.1 | 15.9 | 42.4 | 56.0 |
| Other manufacturing | 5.9 | 9.2 | 14.2 | 18.4 |
| Total | 100.0 | 100.0 | 11.8 | 10.8 |

*Source:* Prepared by the authors.

*Note:* n.a. = not applicable.

add another 15 percent. Export and import taxes (or subsidies) are reported in table 12.3 for 2005, the base year for the simulations. To put these data in historical context, Sturzenegger and Salazni (2008) show that the lowering of export taxes in the 1990s was reversed in the next decade such that farm prices for these products during 2000–05 were about one-sixth below international prices;

**Table 12.3. Export Taxes and Import Tariffs, Argentina, 2005**
*(percent)*

| Sector | Import tariffs | Export taxes |
|---|---|---|
| *Primary* | | |
| Cereals | 0.0 | 24.0 |
| Vegetables and fruits | 0.0 | 7.0 |
| Oilseeds | 0.0 | 29.0 |
| Other crops | 0.0 | 6.6 |
| Sugarcane and beets | 0.0 | 0.0 |
| Livestock, milk, and wool | 0.0 | 7.8 |
| Other primary nonagriculture | 1.0 | 0.9 |
| Mining | 1.0 | 0.9 |
| Oil | 1.0 | 30.0 |
| *Processed food* | | |
| Meat | 0.0 | 4.4 |
| Oils and fats | 0.0 | 20.0 |
| Dairy products | 0.0 | 5.0 |
| Sugar | 0.0 | 2.0 |
| Flour, bakery, and pasta | 9.7 | 0.0 |
| Feed products | 6.4 | 0.0 |
| Other processed food | 7.7 | 0.0 |
| Beverages and tobacco | 11.7 | 0.0 |
| *Other manufactures* | | |
| Textiles and apparel | 13.2 | 0.3 |
| Petroleum refining | 0.9 | 0.9 |
| Chemical products | 7.6 | 0.9 |
| Mineral products | 8.1 | 0.9 |
| Metal products | 10.0 | 0.9 |
| Machinery and equipment | 11.1 | 0.9 |
| Vehicles | 13.8 | 0.9 |
| Other manufacturing | 10.4 | 0.9 |

*Sources:* For export taxes: Anderson and Valenzuela (2008); for import tariffs: the social accounting matrix for Argentina in 2005 prepared by the authors.

meanwhile, nominal assistance rates for manufacturing, which were high up until the 1970s, have since come down gradually.

### The microsimulation model

We calculate the results for poverty and inequality at the microlevel by linking the CGE model with a microsimulation model. We use the two in a sequential top-down fashion. Thus, the CGE model communicates with the microsimulation model by generating a vector of prices, wages, and aggregate employment variables, such as labor demand by sector and the unemployment rate. The functioning of the labor market therefore plays an important role; the CGE determines the changes in employment by factor type and sector and the changes in factor and product prices that we then use for the microsimulations.

We use the Permanent Household Survey (Encuesta Permanente de Hogares) (EPH), the main household survey in Argentina, to build the microsimulation model. The EPH is carried out by the National Institute of Statistics and Censuses (INDEC 2006a). It covers all 31 urban areas with more than 100,000 inhabitants. These are home to 71 percent of the urban population in the country. Because urban areas account for 87 percent of the total population in Argentina, the EPH sample represents around 62 percent of the total population. The EPH contains information on individual sociodemographic characteristics, employment status, hours of work, wages, family incomes, types of jobs, education, and migration status. There is no alternative source of household data in Argentina. We have made no attempt to reconcile the household survey data with the national accounts. Instead, the results from the CGE model are transmitted to the microsimulation model as percentage deviations from base values. The productive sectors in the EPH are divided into 10 categories (agriculture; mining; food, beverages, and tobacco; textiles; petrochemicals; metals; machinery; vehicles; other manufactures; and services), and the results from the CGE simulations are adjusted to the sectors of the EPH for the transmission of changes in the relevant variables.

INDEC (2006b) calculates the basic food basket and the total basic consumption basket that determine the extreme poverty line (the "indigence line") and the moderate poverty line (the "poverty line"), respectively. An Engel coefficient captures the relationship between the extreme and moderate poverty lines calculated by the INDEC using the two baskets. Each CGE simulation generates a new level of economy-wide prices for commodities, which lead to changes in the cost of the basic food basket and therefore in the level of the extreme poverty line. The value for the new moderate poverty line is computed by assuming that the Engel coefficient remains constant. These changes in the poverty lines are captured in the last step of the microsimulation methodology (see below) and affect the final estimated moderate poverty and extreme poverty rates.

We introduce the labor market results from the CGE model into the microsimulations to produce a counterfactual labor income for each individual in the household survey. We then recalculate household per capita income and compute the new poverty and income inequality results.

There are two broad approaches to capturing the labor market changes through microsimulations. In one case, the program selects at random (with multiple repetitions) from the corresponding labor groups the individuals who will change sectors and assigns wages to new workers according to parameters for the average groups. This approach is an extension of the earnings inequality methodology developed by Almeida dos Reis and Paes de Barros (1991).

The second general approach is based on econometric techniques. In this approach, one determines the movement of workers across sectors by econometrically estimated probabilities in a sectoral choice model, while one determines the new wages of workers in an econometric model of wage earnings (for example, see Díaz-Bonilla 2005, Díaz-Bonilla et al. 2006). In both approaches, the new wage and employment levels for each individual result in recalculated household per capita incomes that are then used to determine the new poverty and income distribution results.[11]

In this chapter, we use a combination of both approaches. The movement of workers across sectors is estimated through repeated sampling as in the first approach, while the assignment of wages depends on an econometrically estimated equation for the base year. Because the data do not record market wages for an individual who is not working, the human capital theory of Mincer (1962) leads to estimates of wages as a function of human capital variables (for example, experience and education). As in the second approach, a series of wage regressions estimates the sector-specific potential wage for each person according to his or her personal characteristics.

The labor market variables and procedures that link the CGE model with the microsimulations are as follows. $U$ in the tables containing the microsimulations results (see elsewhere below) refers to the impact of changes in the unemployment rate. This effect is simulated by changing the labor status of the active population in the EPH sample based on the results from the CGE model. For instance, if, according to the CGE simulations, unemployment decreases at the same time that employment increases for, say, semiskilled men in sector A, the microsimulation program hires randomly among the unemployed semiskilled men in the EPH sample. Individual incomes for the newly employed are assigned based on the characteristics of the workers (for example, educational level) by using the coefficients of a Mincer equation estimated for these individuals employed in the base year (see above). If the CGE simulations indicate a decrease in employment for a specific labor category and sector, the microsimulation program fires the equivalent share of the workers according to the type of labor and sector, and the counterfactual income for these newly unemployed is zero.

The impact of changes in the sectoral structure of employment is indicated as $S$ in the tables containing the results (see below). This effect is simulated by changing the sectoral composition of employment. For those individuals who move from one sector to another, we simulate a counterfactual labor income based on the characteristics of the individuals and on their new sector of employment by drawing on a Mincer equation estimated for the base year with sectoral dummies.

The impact of changes in relative wages is indicated by $W1$. Wages in a sector are adjusted according to the changes from the CGE simulations, but the aggregate average wage for the economy is held constant. The impact of the change in the aggregate average wage for the economy, $W2$, is simulated by changing all labor incomes in all sectors by the same proportion based on the changes from the CGE simulations. All the above steps are then repeated several times and averaged.

$PL$ is the impact of changes in the poverty line. The official extreme poverty (or indigence) line is recalculated for each scenario based on the changes in the CGE simulations for the prices of the commodities used to compute the extreme poverty line (only food items). The value for the official moderate poverty line is then computed on the assumption that the Engel coefficient stays fixed at base year values.[12]

## Model Simulations and Results

This section describes our main simulations. We then present, first, the overall economic effects of liberalization and, second, the impacts of liberalization on poverty and inequality. Unless otherwise stated (for specific simulations), the closure rules for the government, the rest of the world, and the savings and investment balance are the same across all simulations.

### Simulations

As with the other chapters in this volume, our interest in this case study is in achieving a better understanding of the impact of agricultural and trade policies on poverty and inequality in a specific country. In the base year, no global or domestic liberalization is imposed; rather, the model is calibrated to the actual situation of the country, Argentina, in 2005.

A model scenario involving the global liberalization of all goods markets may provide estimates of bottom-line impacts. On its own, however, such a simulation does not reveal the relative importance of various policies at home and abroad in generating these estimated impacts. Such differentiated analysis requires that the results be disaggregated in various ways. We thus also separately analyze the contribution of agricultural reform alone because, in trade negotiations, this contribution is negotiated separately.

Currently, export taxes are not subject to negotiation in the World Trade Organization (WTO); so, we study a reform in all goods, as well as in agriculture alone, but without reforming export taxes. (We label the related simulations WTO for this reason only, not because they represent the specific negotiating alternatives we discuss.)

We next look separately at rest-of-the-world versus own-country policy reform with and without nonagricultural reform.

Finally, because, in the case of Argentina, the country's agricultural (and mineral and energy) policies are dominated by export taxes, we examine the effects of the unilateral removal by the country of its export tax regime for all goods, as well as for farm products only. We first calculate a base scenario for 2005 and then run the following 10 simulations:

- *Sim 1, GLOB*: This involves the removal of all agricultural subsidies and all import and export taxes on goods trade in the rest of the world and in Argentina.
- *Sim 2, GLOBag*: This is the same as Sim 1 except that only agricultural reform is involved, that is, domestic, import, and export taxes and subsidies are removed only on agricultural products.
- *Sim 3, WTO*: This is the same as Sim 1 except that export taxes are not removed.
- *Sim 4, WTOag*: This is the same as Sim 3 except that only agricultural reform is involved.
- *Sim 5, ROW*: This is the same as Sim 1 except that it covers only the rest of the world, that is, without Argentina. Because it does not include Argentina, export taxes are still imposed in Argentina in this simulation.
- *Sim 6, ROWag*: This is the same as Sim 5 except that it covers agricultural reform alone.
- *Sim 7, ARG*: This is the same as Sim 1 except that it covers Argentina alone.
- *Sim 8, ARGag*: This is the same as Sim 7 except that it covers only agricultural reform.
- *Sim 9, ARG-ex*: This is the same as Sim 7 except that only export taxes are removed in all categories of goods and services.
- *Sim 10, ARGag-ex*: This is the same as Sim 9 except that it covers only agricultural reform.

### Overall economic results

We first look at the impact of the reforms on macroeconomic variables and factor markets. Various indicators are summarized in table 12.4 for the baseline and for our 10 simulations. In particular, it is important to examine the interaction of the changes in the poverty line and in unemployment because these may have opposing impacts on poverty.

The results show a negative effect on the poverty line in all simulations, that is, the poverty line increases relative to the base year because of inflation in consumer prices. Under a scenario of global liberalization that removes all import and export taxes and agricultural subsidies (GLOB and GLOBag), the poverty line increases by more than 6 percent over the base year. The impact on the poverty line is strongest in this simulation because of the combination of increases in the world prices of agricultural goods (from global liberalization) and the elimination of export taxes, which boosts domestic food prices. Although the real exchange rate, which is defined in the model as the price of tradables over nontradables,

**Table 12.4. Aggregate Simulation Results of Prospective Liberalization, Argentina**

| Indicator | Base | GLOB | GLOBag | WTO | WTOag | ROW | ROWag | ARG | ARGag | ARG-ex | ARGag-ex |
|---|---|---|---|---|---|---|---|---|---|---|---|
| GDP factor cost, LCU, billions[a] | 4,395.0 | -0.2 | -0.8 | 1.5 | 0.5 | 0.3 | 0.2 | -0.4 | -0.9 | -1.7 | -0.9 |
| Household consumption, LCU, billions[a] | 3,263.0 | 0.5 | 0.0 | 2.1 | 0.5 | 1.0 | 0.9 | -0.5 | -0.8 | -1.7 | -0.8 |
| Poverty line[a] | n.a. | 6.3 | 6.0 | 2.1 | 1.2 | 1.3 | 1.2 | 4.9 | 4.8 | 4.1 | 4.8 |
| Real exchange rate[a] | 1.0 | -4.6 | -6.3 | 0.5 | -2.9 | -2.0 | -2.9 | -2.7 | -3.5 | -5.3 | -3.5 |
| Terms of trade[a] | n.a. | 0.1 | 1.6 | 1.0 | 2.0 | 2.3 | 2.0 | -2.2 | -0.6 | -1.3 | -0.6 |
| Unemployment rate, %[b] | 12.3 | -0.4 | 0.8 | -2.6 | -0.4 | -0.6 | -0.4 | 0.1 | 1.1 | 2.4 | 1.1 |
| Unskilled labor, women | 29.4 | -0.4 | 0.7 | -2.4 | -0.3 | -0.6 | -0.3 | 0.1 | 0.9 | 1.9 | 0.9 |
| Semiskilled labor, women | 18.8 | 0.1 | 1.0 | -2.4 | -0.2 | -0.4 | -0.2 | 0.4 | 1.1 | 2.4 | 1.1 |
| Skilled labor, women | 5.1 | -0.4 | 1.0 | -2.6 | -0.1 | -0.4 | -0.1 | -0.1 | 1.1 | 2.4 | 1.1 |
| Unskilled labor, men | 14.3 | -0.4 | 0.6 | -3.0 | -0.6 | -0.8 | -0.6 | 0.2 | 1.1 | 2.5 | 1.1 |
| Semiskilled labor, men | 9.4 | 0.0 | 1.0 | -2.8 | -0.4 | -0.5 | -0.4 | 0.4 | 1.3 | 2.8 | 1.3 |
| Skilled labor, men | 4.1 | -1.1 | 0.5 | -1.6 | -0.5 | -0.5 | -0.5 | -0.7 | 0.9 | 2.0 | 0.9 |
| Returns to factors[a] | | | | | | | | | | | |
| Unskilled labor, women | n.a. | 0.0 | 0.0 | 0.0 | 0.0 | 0.0 | 0.0 | 0.0 | 0.0 | 0.0 | 0.0 |
| Semiskilled labor, women | n.a. | 0.0 | 0.0 | 0.0 | 0.0 | 0.0 | 0.0 | 0.0 | 0.0 | 0.0 | 0.0 |
| Skilled labor, women | n.a. | 0.0 | 0.0 | 0.2 | 0.0 | 0.0 | 0.0 | 0.0 | 0.0 | 0.0 | 0.0 |
| Unskilled labor, men | n.a. | 0.0 | 0.0 | 0.0 | 0.0 | 0.0 | 0.0 | 0.0 | 0.0 | 0.0 | 0.0 |
| Semiskilled labor, men | n.a. | 0.0 | 0.0 | 0.0 | 0.0 | 0.0 | 0.0 | 0.0 | 0.0 | 0.0 | 0.0 |
| Skilled labor, men | n.a. | 0.0 | 0.0 | 1.4 | 0.0 | 0.0 | 0.0 | 0.0 | 0.0 | 0.0 | 0.0 |
| Land | n.a. | 62.4 | 59.3 | 20.6 | 12.1 | 12.9 | 12.1 | 46.2 | 44.6 | 37.3 | 44.6 |
| Capital, specific, agriculture | n.a. | 79.1 | 76.3 | 18.4 | 10.7 | 11.2 | 10.7 | 63.8 | 62.2 | 53.9 | 62.2 |
| Capital, specific, nonagriculture | n.a. | 2.6 | -3.1 | 1.6 | -0.7 | -0.6 | -0.7 | 3.5 | -2.4 | 0.9 | -2.4 |
| Capital, mobile | n.a. | 5.4 | 1.4 | 2.7 | 0.1 | 0.2 | 0.1 | 5.1 | 1.2 | 2.4 | 1.2 |

*Source:* CGE model simulations on Argentina by the authors.

*Note:* LCU = local currency unit. n.a. = not applicable.

a. Percent change from the base.

b. Percentage point difference from the base.

declines significantly, this is not sufficient to compensate for the elimination of export taxes, and the domestic prices of food therefore increase. However, the results also show that the impact on the poverty line is smallest in those simulations in which the export taxes in Argentina are not eliminated (WTO, WTOag, ROW, and ROWag).

The GLOB and GLOBag simulations also show negative impacts on GDP, as do the simulations of unilateral liberalization by Argentina (ARG, ARGag, ARG-ex, ARGag-ex). The negative impact on GDP is more significant in the unilateral simulations. This is especially the case if export taxes are eliminated, but not import taxes.[13] In addition, GDP decreases by 1.7 percent in the case of the liberalization of all export taxes in Argentina (ARG-ex) and by 0.9 percent in the case of the liberalization of only agricultural export taxes in Argentina (ARGag-ex). This is partly a result of the assumption that Argentina has some degree of monopoly power in its export markets, but also a consequence of our treatment of unemployment in the model. The simulations without changes in export taxes, but that include the elimination of import taxes and rest-of-the-world liberalization, all appear to increase GDP, particularly the two simulations with more traditional scenarios of national and world liberalization focusing on import taxes alone (WTO and WTOag). In all cases, the liberalization of all goods, rather than the liberalization of only agricultural products, generates a larger GDP increase (or a smaller decrease).

To help us understand the sectoral changes, table 12.5 disaggregates GDP, exports, and imports into agricultural and nonagricultural groups and also presents the value of food consumption by households.[14]

The declines in GDP generated by the elimination of export taxes result from the negative impact on nonagricultural GDP, which outweighs the positive impact on agricultural value added following the change in relative prices. The shift of incentives toward agriculture affects production in other sectors through the usual general equilibrium effect: it extracts capital and labor away from these other sectors once the pool of employable, but unemployed workers has been exhausted. The largest positive impact on agriculture occurs when domestic prices are increased because of higher world prices through liberalization in the rest of the world and because of the elimination of export taxes. Likewise, agricultural exports expand and nonagricultural exports decline except when import tariffs are eliminated for all products (when nonagricultural exports also increase, that is, GLOB, WTO, and ARG). A consequence of this export orientation of agricultural products is that household food consumption declines in all simulations in which export taxes are eliminated (table 12.5, bottom row).

Table 12.4 also shows that unemployment increases in most of the simulations that include the elimination of export taxes, with the exception of the GLOB

**Table 12.5. Sectoral Simulation Results of Prospective Liberalization, Argentina**
(percent change from the base)

| Indicator | Base, LCU, billions | GLOB | GLOBag | WTO | WTOag | ROW | ROWag | ARG | ARGag | ARG-ex | ARGag-ex |
|---|---|---|---|---|---|---|---|---|---|---|---|
| GDP, agriculture | 434 | 16.5 | 16.1 | 5.6 | 6.6 | 6.8 | 6.6 | 10.4 | 10.4 | 8.0 | 10.4 |
| GDP, nonagriculture | 3,961 | −2.0 | −2.7 | 0.6 | −0.5 | −0.4 | −0.5 | −1.6 | −2.1 | −2.8 | −2.1 |
| Exports, agriculture | 470 | 44.0 | 43.8 | 15.3 | 11.4 | 10.9 | 11.4 | 34.4 | 34.6 | 30.4 | 34.6 |
| Imports, agriculture | 15 | 113.5 | 104.2 | 0.2 | −3.0 | −.0 | −3.0 | 115.5 | 116.5 | 113.0 | 116.5 |
| Exports, nonagriculture | 894 | 0.6 | −17.1 | 4.5 | −7.1. | −6.7 | −7.1 | 7.4 | −10.6 | −4.0 | −10.6 |
| Imports, nonagriculture | 1,025 | 19.4 | 6.3 | 12.6 | 2.2 | 2.3 | 2.2 | 17.1 | 3.9 | 7.0 | 3.9 |
| Food consumption, households | 641 | −0.7 | −1.1 | 1.5 | 0.6 | 0.7 | 0.6 | −1.3 | −1.6 | −2.3 | −1.6 |

*Source:* CGE model simulations on Argentina by the authors.

*Note:* LCU = local currency unit.

simulation, which combines complete liberalization in Argentina (that is, the elimination of export and import taxes) with liberalization in the rest of the world for all products (but not if the simulation covers only agricultural products, that is, GLOBag). The worst impact on employment arises from the unilateral elimination of all export taxes in Argentina.

The negative impact on employment of the elimination of export taxes appears more pronounced in the case of unskilled and semiskilled labor and is also more pronounced in the case of women workers rather than men workers. In general, these results are explained by the factor intensities of the sectors that expand and contract after a given policy change (see the discussion below).

Meanwhile, total world liberalization that does not include export taxes (WTO and WTOag) and total rest-of-the-world liberalization that does not eliminate export taxes in Argentina (ROW and ROWag) reduce unemployment; this is so particularly of the simulation WTO. Rest-of-the-world liberalization benefits unskilled labor more and benefits workers who are men more than workers who are women.

To understand the negative results on employment that occur because of the elimination of export taxes, one needs to look at the sectoral composition of export taxes (table 12.3) and the supply-side response. In terms of sectoral composition, the largest export taxes in Argentina are those levied on grains, oilseeds, and oil. The elimination of these taxes increases the supply of products that have three characteristics: first, they are less labor intensive than alternative activities; second, they are inputs into other sectors; and, third, they have an outward orientation of sales that increases significantly after the removal of export taxes. Through various and cumulative channels (discussed below), the consequence of these three characteristics is less employment generally.

Without a full employment specification, the first characteristic (low labor intensity) leads directly to declines in employment. In the case of agriculture in particular, land is shifted from livestock, industrial crops, and other products that tend to be more labor intensive to grains and oilseeds that are less labor intensive. This negative employment effect at the primary level is reinforced because, given that the commodities from these sectors are inputs into other production activities, the increase in prices also affects other activities, in which production and employment then tend to shrink as a result of the higher input prices.[15] Primary products that used to be processed locally are now exported as raw materials, and the domestic industry declines. Oil, in particular, once it has been processed and refined, is an input in most other activities, which are negatively affected by higher oil prices. The outward orientation of the expanding activities also appreciates the real exchange rate (see table 12.4), which generates a form of Dutch Disease among the rest of the tradables.

The positive impact of rest-of-the-world liberalization on GDP and employment is obvious. It creates more markets for Argentina's exports, and, because of the specification of the labor market and the high unemployment that prevailed in the base year, the expansion in aggregate demand leads to more production and employment. In turn, the elimination of import taxes triggers a different mechanism. It leads to more imports that, because of the closure assumption of fixed foreign savings, also require more exports. Therefore, the real exchange rate depreciates, which increases the production of tradables and expands employment. In general, the elimination of import taxes increases imports and moderates the appreciation of the domestic currency in most simulations in which it occurs and, in the WTO simulation for all products, even leads to a small overall depreciation in the real exchange rate (table 12.4).

Note that the terms of trade tend to disfavor Argentina if export taxes are eliminated (table 12.4). This is particularly the case if export taxes are eliminated unilaterally. The specification we follow in this project involves treating countries as though they have a degree of market power (see elsewhere above). The elimination of export taxes therefore depresses the world prices of the products the supply of which expands significantly after such a policy change.[16]

### The results in poverty and income distribution

The main results in poverty are shown in table 12.6, which is based on the national extreme poverty line (the indigence line) and the national moderate poverty line (the poverty line). Table 12.7 presents the results on the Gini coefficient of household per capita income and of labor income. Each of the simulation results shows the observed base year poverty (or inequality) in the first row, followed by the poverty and inequality results under each of the steps discussed elsewhere above in the explanation of our microsimulation model. The second-to-last row shows the cumulative effects of all of the changes ($U$, $S$, $W1$, $W2$, and, in the case of the poverty line, $PL$) on the poverty and inequality results. The last row shows the results as the percent change with respect to the observed base year value.

In terms of poverty, world trade liberalization for all goods (excluding export taxes; simulation WTO) diminishes both moderate and extreme poverty in Argentina. As we have indicated, there are two opposite effects at work, but the end result here is a reduction in poverty. The increase in the poverty line (table 12.4) affects the poor negatively. This increase is also the result of opposing forces: although the elimination of import taxes lowers domestic prices, the rise in world food prices and the devaluation of the domestic currency show effects in the opposite direction. The negative impact of a higher poverty line, however, is more than offset by a strong employment effect. Table 12.4 shows that the WTO trade simulation is the scenario

**Table 12.6. Poverty Effects of Prospective Liberalization, Argentina**
*(percent of the headcount)*

| Effect | Base | GLOB | GLOBag | WTO | WTOag | ROW | ROWag | ARG | ARGag | ARG-ex | ARGag-ex |
|---|---|---|---|---|---|---|---|---|---|---|---|
| *a. Extreme poverty line* | | | | | | | | | | | |
| Observed | 12.7 | 12.7 | 12.7 | 12.7 | 12.7 | 12.7 | 12.7 | 12.7 | 12.7 | 12.7 | 12.7 |
| U | 12.7 | 12.6 | 13.0 | 11.9 | 12.6 | 12.5 | 12.6 | 12.7 | 13.1 | 13.7 | 13.1 |
| U + S | 12.7 | 12.6 | 13.0 | 11.9 | 12.6 | 12.5 | 12.6 | 12.7 | 13.1 | 13.7 | 13.1 |
| U + S + W1 | 12.7 | 12.6 | 13.0 | 11.9 | 12.6 | 12.5 | 12.6 | 12.7 | 13.1 | 13.7 | 13.1 |
| U + S + W1 + W2 | 12.7 | 12.6 | 13.0 | 11.9 | 12.6 | 12.5 | 12.6 | 12.7 | 13.1 | 13.7 | 13.1 |
| U + S + W1 + W2 + PL | 12.7 | 13.7 | 14.2 | 12.2 | 12.8 | 12.7 | 12.8 | 13.6 | 14.0 | 14.4 | 14.0 |
| Change from the base, % | n.a. | 8.5 | 11.8 | −3.4 | 1.1 | 0.6 | 1.1 | 7.5 | 10.9 | 14.0 | 10.9 |
| *b. Moderate poverty line* | | | | | | | | | | | |
| Observed | 34.2 | 34.2 | 34.2 | 34.2 | 34.2 | 34.2 | 34.2 | 34.2 | 34.2 | 34.2 | 34.2 |
| U | 34.2 | 34.1 | 34.7 | 33.0 | 34.1 | 34.0 | 34.1 | 34.3 | 34.8 | 35.6 | 34.8 |
| U + S | 34.2 | 34.1 | 34.8 | 33.1 | 34.1 | 34.0 | 34.1 | 34.3 | 34.8 | 35.6 | 34.8 |
| U + S + W1 | 34.2 | 34.1 | 34.8 | 33.1 | 34.1 | 34.0 | 34.1 | 34.3 | 34.8 | 35.6 | 34.8 |
| U + S + W1 + W2 | 34.2 | 34.1 | 34.8 | 33.1 | 34.1 | 34.0 | 34.1 | 34.3 | 34.8 | 35.6 | 34.8 |
| U + S + W1 + W2 + PL | 34.2 | 36.5 | 37.1 | 33.8 | 34.5 | 34.5 | 34.5 | 36.2 | 36.7 | 37.1 | 36.7 |
| Change from the base, % | n.a. | 6.6 | 8.5 | −1.3 | 0.9 | 0.9 | 0.9 | 5.7 | 7.3 | 8.5 | 7.3 |

*Source:* CGE model simulations on Argentina by the authors.

*Note:* The net impact is the sum of the impacts of changes in five variables. $U$ refers to the impacts arising from changes in the unemployment rate, $S$ to impacts related to changes in the sectoral structure of employment, $W1$ to changes in relative wages, $W2$ to changes in the aggregate average wage in the economy, and $PL$ to changes in the poverty line. n.a. = not applicable.

**Table 12.7. Income Inequality Effects of Prospective Liberalization, Argentina**
*(Gini coefficient)*

| Effect | Base | GLOB | GLOBag | WTO | WTOag | ROW | ROWag | ARG | ARGag | ARG-ex | ARGag-ex |
|---|---|---|---|---|---|---|---|---|---|---|---|
| *a. Household per capita income* | | | | | | | | | | | |
| Observed | 0.499 | 0.499 | 0.499 | 0.499 | 0.499 | 0.499 | 0.499 | 0.499 | 0.499 | 0.499 | 0.499 |
| U | 0.499 | 0.499 | 0.500 | 0.495 | 0.498 | 0.498 | 0.498 | 0.499 | 0.500 | 0.502 | 0.500 |
| U + S | 0.499 | 0.499 | 0.500 | 0.495 | 0.498 | 0.498 | 0.498 | 0.499 | 0.500 | 0.502 | 0.500 |
| U + S + W1 | 0.499 | 0.499 | 0.500 | 0.495 | 0.498 | 0.498 | 0.498 | 0.499 | 0.500 | 0.502 | 0.500 |
| U + S + W1 + W2 | 0.499 | 0.499 | 0.500 | 0.495 | 0.498 | 0.498 | 0.498 | 0.499 | 0.500 | 0.502 | 0.500 |
| Change from the base, % | n.a. | 0.000 | 0.200 | −0.700 | −0.100 | −0.200 | −0.100 | 0.100 | 0.300 | 0.600 | 0.300 |
| *b. Employed labor income* | | | | | | | | | | | |
| Observed | 0.472 | 0.472 | 0.472 | 0.472 | 0.472 | 0.472 | 0.472 | 0.472 | 0.472 | 0.472 | 0.472 |
| U | 0.472 | 0.472 | 0.472 | 0.471 | 0.472 | 0.472 | 0.472 | 0.472 | 0.472 | 0.473 | 0.472 |
| U + S | 0.472 | 0.472 | 0.472 | 0.471 | 0.472 | 0.472 | 0.472 | 0.472 | 0.472 | 0.473 | 0.472 |
| U + S + W1 | 0.472 | 0.472 | 0.472 | 0.471 | 0.472 | 0.472 | 0.472 | 0.472 | 0.472 | 0.473 | 0.472 |
| U + S + W1 + W2 | 0.472 | 0.472 | 0.472 | 0.471 | 0.472 | 0.472 | 0.472 | 0.472 | 0.472 | 0.473 | 0.472 |
| Change from the base, % | n.a. | 0.000 | 0.100 | −0.200 | 0.000 | −0.100 | 0.000 | 0.100 | 0.100 | 0.300 | 0.100 |

*Source:* CGE model simulations on Argentina by the authors.

*Note:* For an explanation of the symbols, see the note to table 12.6.

that generates the largest decline in unemployment (2.6 percentage points). Poverty therefore declines in this trade liberalization simulation. Meanwhile, the same scenario of liberalization, but only in agriculture, does not reduce poverty. In that case, the employment effect is far weaker and is more than offset by the negative impact on poverty of the increase in the poverty line.

Liberalization in the rest of the world (ROW and ROWag) initially reduces poverty slightly through the employment effect, but this is more than offset by the increase in the poverty line because of higher world food prices, resulting in a small increase in poverty overall (which is worse if only agriculture is liberalized, ROWag).[17] This suggests that the positive impact on poverty from the simulation that includes the rest of the world and Argentina (WTO) is driven in good measure by the domestic, not international, liberalization in nonagricultural goods.

If both own liberalization (exports and imports) and liberalization in the rest of the world are considered (GLOB and GLOBag), poverty increases. In the case of the liberalization of all products (GLOB), there is a positive employment effect on poverty (though not if only agricultural products are considered), which is more than offset by the increase in the poverty line.

The main difference in policies in GLOB and GLOBag compared with WTO and ROW is that the export taxes in Argentina are also eliminated. In fact, all simulations that include the elimination of export taxes either on all goods or only for agricultural goods show an increase in the poverty headcount. Particularly negative for the poverty headcount is the unilateral elimination of export taxes by Argentina. The first negative impact arises from the unemployment effect, which, as we have already indicated, results from a combination of a shift from the production of greater value added goods to primary products that are less labor intensive and a form of Dutch Disease in the nonagricultural sectors. A second negative effect, which, in the simulations, is generally stronger than the unemployment effect, results from the increase in the poverty line because of higher food prices (see the line $U + S + W1 + W2 + PL$ in all poverty simulations). In general, the sectoral and wage effects do not make much of a difference in poverty terms.

Table 12.7 shows the results in income distribution. Simulations that include the elimination of export taxes increase income disparities slightly at the household level and also if only the labor incomes of the employed are considered. Meanwhile, liberalization in the rest of the world and in Argentina that does not involve changing export taxes (WTO and WTOag) and liberalization only in the rest of the world (ROW) produce small, but positive effects that reduce inequality. Land receives important increments in factor incomes (not shown here) in all simulations involving the elimination of export taxes, which should increase income inequality (see footnote 13 elsewhere above).

At least within the context of a static framework, the simulation results suggest that export taxes help reduce poverty and inequality, generate additional employment opportunities that the production and export of raw materials would not have provided, and help support a more competitive exchange rate. The simulations also imply that, under the large country assumption, the elimination of export taxes negatively affects the country's terms of trade.[18]

The simulations reported here differ from the results in Nogués et al. (2007) and Nogués (2008), who argue that poverty increases with the use of export taxes. The discrepancies in the results are the consequence of the differences in the methodological frameworks (see the discussion in Cicowiez, Díaz-Bonilla, and Díaz-Bonilla 2009, appendix 2).

## Fiscal and Growth Implications

Two other important issues that the simulations raise are the fiscal and growth effects of the various liberalization scenarios. Regarding fiscal accounts, we run our model with a balanced budget, and the increases in direct tax rates compensate for any change in trade tax revenues. Panel a in table 12.8 shows the revenue from taxes as a share of GDP in the various simulations, with a focus on trade and direct (income) taxes. The simulations involving the elimination only of agricultural export taxes still collect some export tax revenue from other products (about 0.5 percent of GDP, mainly from oil and energy commodities). The increase in direct taxes needed to close the fiscal gap is somewhat more than the direct revenues lost (2.2 percent of GDP) because government consumption is fixed in real terms, which means that the nominal cost of running the government and, therefore, the potential need to collect additional taxes also changes across the simulations. Moreover, because GDP declines, taxes increase somewhat as a share of GDP (and vice-versa in the simulations in which GDP increases).[19]

It has also been suggested that, to counter the poverty effects of export taxes, value added taxes might be reduced to compensate the poor for the higher food prices. In addition, it has been argued that more targeted safety nets, such as conditional cash transfers (such as the Familias Program in Argentina) or food stamps of some sort, might be utilized to counter the negative impacts on poverty of the elimination of export taxes. However, both suggestions would entail even larger losses in fiscal revenue and the negative macroeconomic implications of these losses. Moreover, while these remedies would address the poverty line (*PL*) segment of the impact on poverty, they would not solve the employment issue (*U*). An alternative involving raising the indirect (value added) tax rate (perhaps only on nonfood items so as not to hurt the poor) may also adversely affect employment.

**Table 12.8. Fiscal and Real Investment Effects of Prospective Liberalization, Argentina**

| Indicator | Base | GLOB | GLOBag | WTO | WTOag | ROW | ROWag | ARG | ARGag | ARG-ex | ARGag-ex |
|---|---|---|---|---|---|---|---|---|---|---|---|
| a. Trade and income taxes[a] | | | | | | | | | | | |
| Import tax | 1.5 | 0.0 | 1.5 | 0.0 | 1.5 | 1.5 | 1.5 | 0.0 | 1.5 | 1.6 | 1.5 |
| Export tax | 2.2 | 0.0 | 0.5 | 2.4 | 2.3 | 2.3 | 2.3 | 0.0 | 0.5 | 0.0 | 0.5 |
| Direct (income) tax | 7.5 | 11.2 | 9.2 | 8.4 | 7.3 | 7.2 | 7.3 | 11.3 | 9.3 | 10.1 | 9.3 |
| b. Real investment | | | | | | | | | | | |
| Change from the base, % | 1,114.0[b] | 4.2 | 2.4 | 3.5 | 1.6 | 1.6 | 1.6 | 2.6 | 0.8 | 0.6 | 0.8 |
| As % of GDP at market prices | 20.8 | 21.4 | 21.3 | 21.2 | 21.1 | 21.0 | 21.1 | 21.1 | 21.0 | 21.0 | 21.0 |

*Source:* CGE model simulations on Argentina by the authors.

a. As a percent of GDP. The total tax revenue is kept constant at 29 percent of GDP.

b. In billions of local currency units.

Another important issue is the growth effects of export taxes. It may be argued that, even if the actual effects are the ones reported here in the short term, the elimination of export taxes would generate stronger growth in the medium to longer term that may more than compensate for the immediate negative impact on employment, the poverty line, and inequality. The simulations presented here may offer some indication of the dynamics as time passes via the change in real investment in the various simulations relative to the base year (table 12.8, panel b). The simulations involving the unilateral elimination of export taxes alone (ARG-ex and ARGag-ex) do increase real investment. Although the increase is less than 1 percent, this would accumulate over time and might become significant. In counterargument, one might say that a more-diversified productive structure, in which investments flow to nonagricultural sectors, may have a greater payoff in higher economic growth and less poverty and inequality. These are all legitimate claims worthy of empirical analysis, and they raise the issue of the nature of the development path that would be more pro poor in Argentina: one based mostly on agriculture, or one with a more diversified economic structure.[20] This has long been a matter of policy debate in Argentina, with implications not only for poverty, but also for income distribution given that the country's agrarian structure shows a greater presence of large holdings relative to many other developing countries.

## Final Comments

In this chapter, we have analyzed several simulations of trade liberalization at home and abroad both for all products and only in agriculture, and we have estimated the impacts of these liberalizations on poverty and inequality in Argentina. Global trade liberalization of all products, but not including the elimination of export taxes (the WTO simulation) reduces poverty and inequality. This result is generated by the strong employment effects in this scenario, which are not negated by the increases in the poverty line that also take place. However, if the same liberalization is applied only to agricultural products, poverty and inequality do not improve, but even deteriorate somewhat, mostly because the smaller (but still positive) employment effect is now more than offset by the increase in the poverty line. All other simulations, particularly those involving the elimination of export taxes, affect poverty and inequality more negatively not only because the poverty line increases as food prices rise, but also because the employment effects are small or negative.

Should one then conclude that export taxes, especially on agricultural products, are always good for poverty reduction? Such a conclusion would be premature. First, any statements in this regard must be tempered by the knowledge that the coverage of the EPH household survey is tilted toward urban areas. Although the results from the CGE model, which obviously includes all sectors and populations, show declines in overall employment and increases in the value of the poverty line (all negative effects for the poor), it is not possible to glean from these results what may happen if the rural population not covered by the survey were to be included.

Second, the simulations do not say anything about the impact on the rest of the world of higher agricultural prices or about the impact on poverty outside Argentina that would arise from export taxes.[21]

Third, the model we use in our chapter has other limitations. Thus, it does not include the medium- to long-term dynamic effects on production and technological innovation that may result from policy reforms. Clearly, there remains much scope for additional empirical economic analysis.

## Notes

1. Thus, this policy was unrelated to the sharp increase in world prices in 2007–08, when numerous developing countries that were exporters of agricultural products introduced temporary export controls to reduce domestic food price increases.

2. Recently, the Argentine Congress approved a law that returned the retirement system to a pay-as-you-go scheme, thus eliminating the middle-term transition deficit, but absorbing the longer-term liabilities of the system.

3. Tariff escalation has been discussed at least since the Kennedy Round. The practice in high-income countries of imposing high import taxes on processed goods and lower or no tariffs on primary products (thus granting a higher effective rate of protection to value added in the importing country) reduces significantly the processing capability of developing countries. This places agroindustrial production in developing countries at a disadvantage, tilting the export profile of developing countries toward raw materials (Balassa and Michalopoulos 1986, Díaz-Bonilla and Reca 2000).

4. The country has been in recession about 40 percent of the last half century because of recurrent macroeconomic crises linked to overvalued exchange rates and fiscal and current account deficits that have led to the accumulation of public and external debt.

5. The overall fiscal surplus for the consolidated public sector (central government and provinces) averaged 1.6 percent of GDP during 2003–07 compared with an average annual deficit of 4.2 percent of GDP during 1961–2002. The surplus of the current account of the balance of payments in 2007 was 2.8 percent of GDP, while, during 1976–2002, the country experienced an average annual deficit of 1.7 percent of GDP. The trade surplus for 2007 was more than 4 percent of GDP, against 1.4 percent during 1976–2002. Boosted by high commodity prices in international markets, the value of exports in 2007 increased to about US$56 billion, nearly triple the 1990s average, while the value of imports jumped to around US$43 billion, double the 1990s average. One of the consequences has been that the Central Bank reserves exceeded US$50 billion at the end of the first quarter of 2008, or 16 percent of GDP.

6. After all, domestic producer prices ($PD$) result from the combination of export tax rates ($TX$), the nominal exchange rate ($ER$), world prices ($PW$), and marketing costs and margins ($MCM$), as follows:

$$PD = PW * ER * (1 - TX - MCM).$$

7. These are producer prices in pesos (as reported in FAOSTAT 2008), deflated by the consumer price index in Argentina. It should be noted that current controversies about the changes in the calculation of the Argentine consumer price index do not affect figure 12.3, considering that the data reported in FAOSTAT currently end in 2006.

8. The behavior of relative prices is different now with respect to the period before 2002 when the Convertibility Plan maintained a fixed one-to-one exchange rate between the peso and the U.S. dollar and the internal terms of trade in agriculture basically followed a downward trend in international prices to the lows of 2001. Real international agricultural prices recovered somewhat thereafter and improved significantly in the second half of 2007. By early 2008, they were about 60 percent above the levels in 2001; however, this means only that they were back to the levels of the mid-1990s. There is also a debate now in Argentina over the real level of inflation. The real exchange rate shown in figure 12.4 is based on official statistics. However, even if we use the more extreme estimates of inflation by private analysts, the real exchange rate would still be clearly above the level of 2001 by about 60 percent, instead of around 80 percent using official data.

9. We have run the model using two values for full employment, which is defined by the level of unemployment below which any additional labor demand results in increases in wages rather than in employment. These values are 2.5 percent and 5 percent. The results reported here correspond to the lower value of unemployment (2.5 percent). The direction of our results does not differ much, although the employment multiplier effects are somewhat stronger under the lower value for full employment (2.5 percent) than under the alternative (5 percent) threshold.

10. A reviewer has argued that using employment as the adjustment variable is as extreme as the full employment assumption whereby wages adjust. The key issue, however, is determining which labor closure reflects the economic situation in Argentina more accurately, considering that during the boom years, unemployment was clearly above the frictional level. Also, we must note that the complementary slackness condition allows the labor closure to switch toward wage adjustments once the frictional unemployment rate has been reached. We have also run the model with a full-employment specification, and the results are qualitatively similar, such that poverty is affected by lower salaries (instead of increases in unemployment) and higher food prices. Still, the two labor market closures are not completely symmetrical given that the unemployment closure allows for larger changes in GDP. Finally, the model may also be run with a wage curve, but the simulations, which do not differ much, are not shown here.

11. The microsimulation model in Díaz-Bonilla (2005) and Díaz-Bonilla et al. (2006) has three main components: a sectoral choice model, a model of wage earnings, and a summation of the new wage and employment results for each household (from which the new poverty and income distribution results follow). Rather than on random selection, the sectoral choice component is based on the estimation of a multinomial logit model that determines an individual's probability, given certain characteristics, of working in each of the productive sectors; the multinomial logit model therefore ranks who will move first into a growing sector. The second component of the econometric microsimulation model estimates a wage regression model that determines the labor income received by a new worker. If, instead, the macromodel determines that employment should decrease in a given sector, then those individuals with the lowest probability of working in that sector exit first, and the newly unemployed lose their wages.

12. We have also run the microsimulations with an additional effect resulting from other factor incomes (land and nonhuman capital) that we do not report here. The nonlabor income data from the EPH are weak; they cannot be considered to represent appropriately the distribution of nonlabor incomes and factors across households. In any case, given that the poor do not have much nonlabor income, the introduction of this adjustment does not change the impact on poverty, although it does have an impact on the results on income distribution.

13. In the protection database used in the global model and applied to the Argentina model, the agricultural import tariffs in Argentina are negligible, and the results on the elimination of agricultural import taxes only are therefore also small and are not reported. However, the direction of the results on the elimination of agricultural import taxes alone may be inferred by comparing the simulations in which only export taxes are changed (ARGag-ex) with those in which export taxes and import tariffs are considered jointly (ARGag).

14. As defined in the World Bank project, agricultural activities include agriculture and lightly processed food, but exclude highly processed food, beverages, and tobacco, which are Global Trade

Analysis Project sectors 25 (food products, not elsewhere classified) and 26 (beverages and tobacco products). In our model, they correspond to the following sectors in table 12.1: (1) cereals; (2) vegetables and fruits; (3) oilseeds; (4) other crops; (5) sugarcane and beets; (6) livestock, milk, and wool; (10) meat; (11) oils and fats; (12) dairy products; and (13) sugar.

15. For instance, cereals and oilseeds are inputs in flour mills, oilseed processors, beef and poultry producers and processors, bakeries, and so on, and oil is an input in the refining industry, transportation, and a variety of energy and chemical industries that, in turn, are inputs in other downstream activities.

16. We have also run the simulations with exogenously fixed world prices, that is, with the small country assumption. The effects on unemployment and poverty are comparable in direction and interpretation with the effects presented here. According to a tentative conclusion, which may require additional analysis, the structure of the economy and the development pattern that ensues from the elimination of export taxes—and not necessarily the large country assumption—drive the results in poverty and income distribution discussed here.

17. In any case, given that Argentina does not change agriculture-related policies except for the policies on export taxes in these simulations, the results of WTOag and ROWag are basically the same.

18. We have also run an optimal trade tax simulation based on the notion that, if a country has market power internationally, there must be a positive trade tax rate that maximizes some indicator of welfare for that country. Based on real GDP, the rates in the base year should be increased by about 80 percent, which would mean that, for example, the export tax rate on cereals should rise from 24 to 43 percent, on oilseeds from 29 to 52 percent, and on oil products from 20 to 36 percent. If the objective is to maximize employment, export taxes should be somewhat larger in this case than in the case of GDP maximization. These numbers must be viewed with extreme caution, however, because of the uncertainties about the shape of the demand curves assumed in the World Bank global model. Additional work needs to be completed on the impact of the large country assumption, which may be forcing a more extreme agricultural specialization than is warranted.

19. This result is in contrast to the result estimated by Nogués et al. (2007), who argue that a nontrivial portion of these revenues may be recovered by maintaining the rates of other taxes at the baseline levels. The partial equilibrium analysis of these authors still estimates a net loss in fiscal revenues, but a far smaller one than is suggested by our simulations using a general equilibrium model. Given the high debt-to-GDP ratio and the high public debt payments in Argentina, the negative macroeconomic effects of a drop in tax revenue might be considerable.

20. Gómez Galvarriato and Williamson (2008) and Williamson (2008) provide historical perspectives on the wisdom of countries exploiting the positive terms of trade in primary products and specializing in these products versus maintaining a more diversified production structure.

21. In the case of Argentina, the devaluation and normalization of the real exchange rate within the context of this country's history, although offset in part by export taxes, have delivered a strong production and export response, as we argue (see also Cicowiez, Díaz-Bonilla, and Díaz-Bonilla 2009, appendix 1). All else being equal, the increase in agricultural output that resulted from all the policy reforms followed in Argentina during this decade (notwithstanding the inclusion of new export taxes) should have reduced the upward pressures on agricultural prices in international markets.

# References

Almeida dos Reis, J. G., and R. Paes de Barros. 1991. "Wage Inequality and the Distribution of Education: A Study of the Evolution of Regional Differences in Inequality in Metropolitan Brazil," *Journal of Development Economics* 36 (1): 117–43.

Anderson, K., and E. Valenzuela. 2007. "Do Global Trade Distortions Still Harm Developing Country Farmers?" *Review of World Economics* 143 (1): 108–39.

———. 2008. "Estimates of Global Distortions to Agricultural Incentives, 1955–2007." Data spreadsheet, October, World Bank, Washington, DC. http://go.worldbank.org/YAO39F35E0.

Balassa, B., and C. Michalopoulos. 1986. "Liberalizing Trade between Developed and Developing Countries." *Journal of World Trade Law* 20 (1): 3–28.

Braun, O., and L. Joy. 1968. "A Model of Economic Stagnation: A Case Study of the Argentine Economy." *Economic Journal* 78 (312): 868–87.

Cicowiez, M., C. Díaz-Bonilla, and E. Díaz-Bonilla. 2009. "Impacts of Trade Liberalization on Poverty and Inequality in Argentina." Agricultural Distortions Working Paper 105, World Bank, Washington, DC. http://www.worldbank.org/agdistortions.

Díaz-Alejandro, C. F. 1963. "A Note on the Impact of Devaluation and the Redistributive Effect." *Journal of Political Economy* 71 (6): 577–80.

Díaz-Bonilla, C. 2005. "Poverty and Income Distribution under Different Factor Market Assumptions: A Macro-Micro Model." In "Female Participation, Workers' Sectoral Choice, and Household Poverty: The Effects of Argentina's Structural Reforms during the 1990s," C. Díaz-Bonilla, PhD dissertation, Johns Hopkins University, Baltimore.

Díaz-Bonilla, C., E. Díaz-Bonilla, V. Piñeiro, and S. Robinson. 2006. "The Convertibility Plan, Trade Openness, and Employment in Argentina: A Macro-Micro Simulation of Poverty and Inequality." In *Who Gains from Free Trade? Export-Led Growth, Inequality, and Poverty in Latin America*, ed. R. Vos, E. Ganuza, S. Morley, and S. Robinson, 125–49. New York: Routledge.

Díaz-Bonilla, E., and L. Reca. 2000. "Trade and Agroindustrialization in Developing Countries: Trends and Policy Impacts." *Agricultural Economics* 23 (3), 219–29

FAOSTAT Database. Food and Agriculture Organization of the United Nations. http://faostat .fao.org/default.aspx (accessed September 2008).

Gómez Galvarriato, A., and J. G. Williamson. 2008. "Was It Prices, Productivity, or Policy? The Timing and Pace of Latin American Industrialization after 1870." NBER Working Paper 13990, National Bureau of Economic Research, Cambridge, MA.

Horridge, M., and F. Zhai. 2006. "Shocking a Single-Country CGE Model with Export Prices and Quantities from a Global Model." In *Poverty and the WTO: Impacts of the Doha Development Agenda*, ed. T. W. Hertel and L. A. Winters, 94–104. London: Palgrave Macmillan; Washington, DC: World Bank.

INDEC (Instituto Nacional de Estadística y Censos). 2006a. "Encuesta de Hogares Permanente, Segundo Semestre 2005." Dirección Encuesta Permanente de Hogares, INDEC, Buenos Aires.

———. 2006b. "Incidencia de la Pobreza y de la Indigencia en 28 Aglomerados Urbanos, Resultados Segundo Semestre de 2005." Dirección Encuesta Permanente de Hogares, INDEC, Buenos Aires.

Información Económica Database. Secretariat of Economic Policy, Ministry of Economy and Production, Buenos Aires. http://www.mecon.gov.ar/peconomica/basehome/infoeco.html (accessed September 2008).

Lofgren, H., and C. Díaz-Bonilla. 2007. "MAMS: An Economy-Wide Model for Analysis of MDG Country Strategies." Technical documentation, Development Prospects Group, World Bank, Washington, DC.

Lofgren, H., R. L. Harris, and S. Robinson. 2002. "A Standard Computable General Equilibrium (CGE) Model in GAMS." Microcomputers in Policy Research 5, International Food Policy Research Institute, Washington, DC.

Mincer, J. A. 1962. "On-the-Job Training: Costs, Returns and Some Implications." *Journal of Political Economy* 70 (5): S50–S79.

Narayanan, B. G., and T. L. Walmsley, eds. 2008. *Global Trade, Assistance, and Production: The GTAP 7 Data Base*. West Lafayette, IN: Center for Global Trade Analysis, Department of Agricultural Economics, Purdue University. https://www.gtap.agecon.purdue.edu/databases/v7/v7_doco.asp.

Nogués, J. J. 2008. "The Domestic Impact of Export Restrictions: The Case of Argentina." IPC Position Paper, Agricultural and Rural Development Policy Series, July, International Food and Agricultural Trade Policy Council, Washington, DC. http://www.agritrade.org/ExportRestrictions.html.

Nogués, J. J., A. Porto, C. Ciappa, L. Di Gresia, and A. Onofri. 2007. "Evaluación de Impactos Económicos y Sociales de Políticas Públicas en la Cadena Agroindustrial." Paper presented at the monthly meeting of the Foro de la Cadena Agroindustrial Argentina, with the participation of the Facultad de Ciencias Económicas, Universidad Nacional de La Plata, Buenos Aires, November.

PSD Database (Production, Supply, and Distribution Online). Foreign Agricultural Service, United States Department of Agriculture. http://www.fas.usda.gov/psdonline.

Ravallion, M. 2004. "Pro-Poor Growth: A Primer." Policy Research Working Paper 3242, World Bank, Washington, DC.

Sturzenegger, A. C., and M. Salazni. 2008. "Argentina." In *Distortions to Agricultural Incentives in Latin America*, ed. K. Anderson and A. Valdés, 59–85. Washington, DC: World Bank.

Valenzuela, E., and K. Anderson. 2008. "Alternative Agricultural Price Distortions for CGE Analysis of Developing Countries, 2004 and 1980–84." Research Memorandum 13 (December), Center for Global Trade Analysis, Department of Agricultural Economics, Purdue University, West Lafayette, IN. https://www.gtap.agecon.purdue.edu/resources/res_display.asp?RecordID=2925.

van der Mensbrugghe, D. 2005. "Linkage Technical Reference Document: Version 6.0." December, World Bank, Washington, DC. http://go.worldbank.org/7NP2KK1OH0.

Vos, R., E. Ganuza, S. Morley, and S. Robinson, eds. 2006. *Who Gains from Free Trade? Export-Led Growth, Inequality, and Poverty in Latin America*. New York: Routledge.

Williamson, J. G. 2008. "Globalization and the Great Divergence: Terms of Trade Booms and Volatility in the Poor Periphery 1782–1913." NBER Working Paper 13841, National Bureau of Economic Research, Cambridge, MA.

# 13

# BRAZIL

## Joaquim Bento de Souza Ferreira Filho
## and Mark Horridge*

Brazil exhibits a high degree of income concentration, and this inequality has persisted throughout the dramatic economic and political changes in the country in the past 20 years. The resilience of this problem in income distribution has attracted the attention of researchers inside and outside Brazil. Although increased world trade offers many opportunities for the Brazilian economy to grow, the question addressed in this study is: how much would growth induced by such trade reform benefit the poor?

To answer this question, we provide a quantitative ex ante assessment using a computable general equilibrium (CGE) model of Brazil tailored for income distribution and poverty analysis. The model also has a regional dimension, allowing the comparison of effects across Brazil's 27 states. It builds on earlier studies by the authors, for example, Ferreira Filho and Horridge (2006), that link national CGE and microsimulation (MS) models to analyze the income distribution effects of changes in trade policy. There are two distinctive features of the present analysis. First, the World Bank global Linkage model provides an estimate of the external terms of trade shock that would be caused by rest-of-the-world trade liberalization (see van der Mensbrugghe 2005). Second, we use a full interregional (bottom-up) CGE model of Brazil's 27 states based on the 2001 input-output table.[1] We also bring to bear new farm price distortion estimates for other developing countries to assess the impact of rest-of-the-world trade reform on poverty and inequality in Brazil.[2]

*The authors are grateful to Xiang Tao for research assistance; Harry de Gorter, Alessandro Olper, and Gordon Rausser for discussions and insights on the issues; and Kym Anderson for excellent collaboration and encouragement throughout the project.

The next section offers background on previous, similar analyses, as well as data on poverty and income distribution in Brazil. We then describe our methodology, discuss the relevant literature on the many approaches to the issues, and present the model and the database. A discussion of our results follows. The chapter ends with concluding remarks.

## The Evolution of Poverty and Income Distribution in Brazil

Although Brazil has many poor people, it is not, on average, a poor country. As many as 77 percent of the world's people and 64 percent of nations have average incomes lower than the average in Brazil. However, because of the particularly uneven distribution of income, about 30 percent of Brazilians are poor. The share would be only 8 percent if the incomes were distributed as evenly in Brazil as they are in other countries at similar per capita income, according to Barros, Henriques, and Mendonça (2001). These authors show that, in 1999, about 53 million people, one-third of the Brazilian population, were living in households with incomes below the poverty line (down from 40 percent in 1977), while 14 percent were living in extreme poverty. Whether measured as a share of the population or in terms of a poverty gap, Brazil's poverty stabilized between the second half of the 1980s and 2001 at a lower level than previously. The situation then began to change again, as we see below.

Barros and Mendonça (1997) analyze the impact on poverty of the relationship between economic growth and reductions in inequality in Brazil. They conclude that an improvement in the distribution of income would be more effective for poverty reduction than an economic growth that maintained the current pattern of inequality. According to these authors, because of the high level of income inequality in Brazil, it is possible to reduce poverty in the country dramatically even without economic growth if the level of inequality in Brazil were to become closer to the levels observed in a typical Latin American country.

Brazilian poverty also has an important regional dimension. According to a study by Rocha (1998) on the 1981–95 period, the richer southeast of the country, which accounted for 44 percent of the total population in 1995, had only 33 percent of the poor. The corresponding figures were 15.4 percent for the south (8.2 percent of the poor), and 6.8 percent for the central-west (5.2 percent of the poor). In the poorer regions, in contrast, the share of the population is less than the share of the poor: 4.6 percent (9.3 percent of the poor) in the north and 29 percent (44 percent of the poor) in the northeast, which is the poorest region in the country.

The behavior of wages and the allocation of labor throughout the trade liberalization period in Brazil (1980–99) are analyzed by Green, Dickerson, and Arbache (2001). They point out that wage inequality remained fairly constant in the 1980s and 1990s, with a small peak in the mid-1980s. Trade liberalization had little egalitarian consequence in Brazil during that period, but the authors note the low trade exposure of the Brazilian economy (around 13 percent in 1997), as well as the low 8 percent share of workers who had completed tertiary studies.

The pattern of poverty in Brazil started to change in 2001. Barros et al. (2007a) show that, while there was a 0.9 percent annual increase in national income during 2001–05, the income of the richest fell: the annual increase in income of the top decile (the richest 10 percent) and the top two deciles was −0.3 and −0.1 percent, respectively, while income among the poorest decile grew at 8 percent a year. There was thus a significant decline in the Gini coefficient, 4.6 percent, and a corresponding drop in poverty incidence (4.5 percent). The latter was caused mainly by the decline in inequality and not to the rise in incomes. This is contrary to what has been observed historically in Brazil.

This unusual pattern of poverty reduction has attracted the attention of many experts and uncovered an important aspect of the problem in income distribution. In dealing with this issue, Hoffmann (2006) finds that transfers from the federal government were one of the main determinants of the observed fall in poverty. According to Hoffmann, 31 percent of the drop in the Gini coefficient nationally in 2002–04 (87 percent of the drop in the northeast) and 86 percent of the reduction in poverty were associated with the share of household income accounted for by transfers through the Bolsa Familia Program (family grants), the main federal government income transfer program.[3] Thus, the recent improvements in poverty incidence in Brazil are related to transfer programs and, so, may be regarded as a short-run rather than permanent initiative. This highlights the importance of assessing, as we do in this chapter, the role that might be played by market effects, such as through trade reform, as a source of permanent gains in poverty reduction.

## Methodology and Data

Although CGE models have long been used in poverty analysis, many have relied on a single representative household in examining consumer behavior. However, this limits the scope of the analysis of income distribution and poverty because there are no observations of changes in intragroup income distribution. Recent CGE models take account of several household types, often distinguishing them by income level. For example, Harrison et al. (2003) use a multicountry model drawing on data from the Global Trade Analysis Project and additional data on Brazil in which they recognize 10 urban and 10 rural household types according to income. Because they exhibit varying expenditure shares and differences in incomes and sources of income, the households are affected differently by economic changes. However, income or other differences within a distinct group of households are ignored by Harrison et al.

Other approaches draw on MS techniques. In this case, a CGE model generates aggregate changes that are used to update a large unit record database such as a household survey. This approach allows the model to take into account the full detail in the household data and avoids prejudgments about the aggregation of households into categories. Changes in the distribution of real income are computed by comparing the unit record data before and after updating. Savard (2003) points out that, in this approach, the causality usually runs from the CGE model to the MS model and that there is no feedback between the models. Our methodology addresses this difficulty by constraining certain aggregate results (for example, the aggregate household use of each good) from the MS model to equal, corresponding variables in the CGE model.[4] The main advantages of the two-model approach (CGE and MS) are that it avoids the need to scale the microeconomic data to match the aggregated macrodata; it may accommodate more households in the MS model; and the MS model may incorporate discrete-choice or integer behavior that might be difficult to incorporate in the CGE model alone.

The CGE model we use here, TERM-BR, is a static interregional model of Brazil's economy. It is based on the TERM model of Australia (Horridge, Madden, and Wittwer 2005).[5] It consists of 27 separate CGE models (one for each Brazilian state) that are linked by the markets for goods and factors. For each state, the structure of the CGE model is fairly standard. Each industry and final demander combines Brazilian and imported versions of each commodity to produce a user-specific constant elasticity of substitution composite good. The household consumption of these domestic-imported composites is modeled through the linear expenditure system, while intermediate demand is Leontief (fixed input-output coefficients). The industry demand for primary factors follows a constant elasticity of substitution pattern, while labor is a constant elasticity of substitution function of 10 types of labor. The model distinguishes 41 single-product industries, and the agricultural industry (called agriculture) distributes output between 11 agricultural commodities according to a constant elasticity of transformation constraint. Export volumes are determined by constant-elasticity foreign demand schedules.[6]

The state CGE models are linked by the trade in goods, which is underpinned by large arrays of interstate trade that record, for each commodity, the source state and the destination state, the values of the Brazilian and foreign goods transported, and the associated transport or trade margins.[7] Thus consumers of, say, vegetables in São Paulo substitute between vegetables produced in the 27 states according to the relative prices of the vegetables under a constant elasticity of substitution demand system.[8]

A variety of labor market closures are possible. For the simulations we report here, we assume that the employment of each of the 10 occupational groups is fixed nationally, but that labor migrates to states where real wages grow more (based on a constant elasticity of transformation formulation).

There are 27 states, 42 industries, 52 commodities, and 10 labor types, and the model thus represents around 1.5 million nonlinear equations. We have solved it using Gempack software. The CGE model is calibrated with data from two main sources: the 2001 Brazilian input-output matrix (IBGE 2001a) and shares derived from the Brazilian census of agriculture (IBGE 1996a) and the Brazilian survey of municipal agricultural production (IBGE 2001b).[9]

On the income-generation side of the model, workers are divided into 10 occupation or skill categories according to wages. The wage groups are then assigned to each state industry in the model. Together with revenues from other endowments (capital and land rents), these wages generate household incomes. Each activity relies on a particular mix of the 10 labor categories. Any shift in the activity level alters employment by sector and state. This drives changes in poverty and income distribution. Using data of the consumer expenditure survey (IBGE 1996b), we extend the CGE model to cover 270 different expenditure patterns composed of 10 different income classes in 27 states. In this way, the expenditure side of the MS data set is incorporated entirely within the main CGE model.

There are two main sources of information for the household MS model: the national household sample survey (IBGE 2001a) and the consumer expenditure survey (IBGE 1996b). The household sample survey contains information about households and persons and has produced a total of 331,263 records. As the main output, the survey extracts information on wages by industry and state, as well as other personal characteristics such as years of schooling, gender, age, position in the family, and other socioeconomic details. The consumer expenditure survey covers 11 major metropolitan areas in Brazil, that is, only urban areas. The main information drawn from this survey, which provides the structure of the consumption bundle in 1996 among 16,014 households, revolves around expenditure patterns among 10 separate income groups in the 11 metropolitan areas. We assign one such pattern to each household in the household sample survey according to our income groups in the CGE model. We also map the 11 metropolitan areas in the consumer expenditure survey to the larger set of 27 CGE states.

### The procedure for running the models

The model consists of two main parts: a CGE model and a household MS model (see elsewhere above). We run the models sequentially. We assure consistency between the two models by constraining the MS model to agree with the CGE model. The CGE model is sufficiently detailed, and its categories and data are sufficiently similar to the categories and data of the MS model so that the CGE model closely predicts the MS aggregate behavior that is also included in the CGE model (such as household demand or labor supply). The role of the MS model is to provide extra information about, for example, the variance in income within income groups or the incidence of price and wage changes among groups not identified by the CGE model, such as groups defined by ethnicity, educational level, or family status. To conform with the structure of the global Linkage model, labor supplies are fixed. Furthermore, we assign one of the 270 expenditure patterns identified in the main CGE model to each household in the microdata set. There is thus little scope for the MS model to disagree with the CGE model.

We begin our simulation with a set of trade shocks generated by simulations from the World Bank's Linkage model involving the elimination of distortions to agricultural trade or all merchandise trade outside Brazil. These shocks consist of changes in import prices and in export demand. The changes in export demand are implemented in the Brazil CGE model via vertical shifts in the export demand curves facing Brazil. The results of the applied trade shocks are generated for 52 commodities, 42 industries, 10 households, and 10 labor occupations, all of which vary across the 27 states.

Next, we use the results from the CGE model to update the MS model. Initially, this involves updating data on the wages of and the hours worked by the 263,938 workers in the sample. These changes have geographical and sectoral industry dimensions (27 states, 42 industries). The model then relocates jobs according to changes in labor demand.[10] We accomplish this by changing the weight of each worker in the household sample survey to mimic the change in employment (see the appendix in Ferreira Filho and Horridge 2009 for details). In this approach, job relocation occurs through a process that may have considerable impact on the variance in incomes within the groups, even though it may have little effect on the distribution of wages among the 270 household groups identified in the CGE model.

Although the changes in the labor market are simulated for each adult in the labor force, the changes in expenditures and in poverty are tracked back to the households. A key in the household sample survey links persons to households that contain dependents and one or more adults who are employed in a particular sector and occupation or who are unemployed. In the model, it is possible to recompose changes in household incomes from changes in the wages of individuals. This is an important aspect of the model because it is likely that variations in family incomes are cushioned by this procedure. For example, if one person in a household loses his job, but another in the same household obtains a job, household income may change little or even increase. Because households are the expenditure units in the model, we would expect household spending variations to be smoothed by this income pooling effect. However, the loss of a job will increase poverty more if the displaced worker is the sole earner in the household. National employment in each skill type is fixed, but shifting industry outputs redistribute the jobs among households.

*The base year picture*

Our description of poverty and income inequality in Brazil is extended in this section. The base year for the analysis is 2001. The aggregate indicators of poverty and income inequality for that year are summarized in table 13.1. The rows correspond to household income groups, which are joined according to the consumer expenditure survey definitions in a footnote to the table, such that POF[1] is the lowest income group and POF[10], the highest. The first five income groups, while accounting for 53 percent of the total population of Brazil, receive only 17 percent of total income. Meanwhile, the highest income group accounts for 11 percent of the population and 46 percent of total income. The Gini coefficient associated with income distribution in Brazil in 2001, calculated on an equivalent household basis, is 0.58.[11] This means that income distribution in Brazil is among the most unequal income distributions in the world.

The unemployment rate is also higher among the poor. This is relevant in the modeling. Obtaining a job is probably the main element in lifting people out of poverty, hence, the importance of allowing the poverty model to capture the existence of a switching regime (from unemployment to employment), as well as the information on changes in wages. The unemployment rate is 33 percent among persons above 15 years of age in the lowest income group, but only 4 percent among the richest income group (table 13.1, column 4). The share of white people in the groups also increases considerably as household income rises, while the share of children decreases markedly (table 13.1, columns 5 and 6). Although our analysis does not focus on these aspects, the MS approach allows us to measure the effects of a policy change on groups not distinguished in the main CGE model.

The poverty line we use in our study is set at one-third of the average household income.[12] According to this criterion, 31 percent of Brazilian households were poor in 2001.[13] This share consists of 96, 77, and 54 percent, respectively, of the households in the first three income groups (table 13.1, column 7) or 35 million of the 112 million households in 2001.[14]

Table 13.1 also shows the contribution of each consumer expenditure survey group to two indicators of poverty stressed by Foster, Greer, and Thorbecke (1984). One indicator is the share of households living below the poverty line. In this case, the two lowest income groups account for more than half the 31 percent of households living below the poverty line (column 8). The other indicator is the poverty gap, which is the share by which a group's average household income falls below the poverty line. Among the first (poorest) income group, this share is 73 percent (column 10), which means that there must be large income increases among the poor if the number of poor is to change significantly.

The poverty and inequality picture also has an important geographical dimension in Brazil. Economic activity, particularly manufacturing, is located mainly in the southeast, while agriculture is more dispersed among regions outside the

## Table 13.1. Poverty Indicators, by Poverty Group, Brazil, 2001
*(percent)*

| POF group[a] | Share in total population | Share in total income | Average household income relative to POF[5] | Unemployment rate | Share of whites in population | Share of population under 15 | Share of households below poverty line | Share in all households below poverty line[b] | Poverty gap[c] | Share in poverty gap[c] |
|---|---|---|---|---|---|---|---|---|---|---|
| POF[1] | 10.7 | 0.9 | 0.1 | 32.6 | 35.2 | 46.2 | 96.2 | 11.22 | 73.3 | 8.56 |
| POF[2] | 8.0 | 1.8 | 0.4 | 17.3 | 38.3 | 37.2 | 76.6 | 7.16 | 30.5 | 2.85 |
| POF[3] | 16.0 | 5.2 | 0.6 | 10.4 | 42.0 | 35.1 | 53.6 | 8.77 | 15.0 | 2.45 |
| POF[4] | 7.3 | 3.1 | 0.8 | 8.8 | 45.1 | 32.5 | 28.4 | 2.02 | 5.4 | 0.38 |
| POF[5] | 11.0 | 5.8 | 1.0 | 7.5 | 49.2 | 28.7 | 11.4 | 1.22 | 1.9 | 0.20 |
| POF[6] | 7.9 | 5.1 | 1.2 | 7.4 | 53.4 | 26.4 | 3.9 | 0.29 | 0.5 | 0.04 |
| POF[7] | 12.9 | 11.1 | 1.7 | 6.8 | 60.3 | 24.5 | 0.8 | 0.10 | 0.1 | 0.01 |
| POF[8] | 7.5 | 8.7 | 2.3 | 6.1 | 66.3 | 21.5 | 0.1 | 0.01 | 0.0 | 0.00 |
| POF[9] | 7.7 | 12.7 | 3.1 | 5.9 | 71.2 | 20.5 | 0.0 | 0.00 | 0.0 | 0.00 |
| POF[10] | 10.9 | 45.7 | 7.9 | 4.2 | 81.6 | 17.7 | 0.0 | 0.00 | 0.0 | 0.00 |

*Sources:* IBGE (1996b, 2001a).

a. POF = consumer expenditure survey (see IBGE 1996b). POF[1] is the poorest household group; POF[10] is the richest group. POF[1] ranges from 0 to 2 times the minimum wage, POF[2] from 2+ to 3 times, POF[3] from 3+ to 5 times, POF[4] from 5+ to 6 times, POF[5] from 6+ to 8 times, POF[6] from 8+ to 10 times, POF[7] from 10+ to 15 times, POF[8] from 15+ to 20 times, POF[9] from 20+ to 30 times, and POF[10] more than 30 times the minimum wage. The minimum wage in Brazil in 2001 was US$76 per month.

b. The national average share of households below the poverty line is 30.8 percent, the sum of column 8.

c. The poverty gap is the share by which the average household income of the group falls below the poverty line. The national average is 14.6 percent, which is the sum of column 10.

two big city-states (Rio de Janeiro and São Paulo). The map (figure 13.1) shows the location of the states of Brazil, which are shaded according to share of households living in poverty. The states in the north account for 8 percent of the total population compared with 24 percent in the northeast, 45 percent in the southeast, 16 percent in the south, and 7 percent in the central-west (table 13.2). In the southeast, the state of São Paulo alone accounts for 23 percent of the total population.

Table 13.2, column 5 shows the share of households in each state that are living below the poverty line. The states in the northeast (states 8–16 in the table), plus the states of Pará and Tocantins in the north have the largest shares, indicating that these states are the poorest. However, if state population is taken into account, column 6 shows that the populous states of Bahia, Ceará, Minas Gerais, Pernambuco, and

**Figure 13.1. The Share of the Poor, by State, Brazil, 2001**

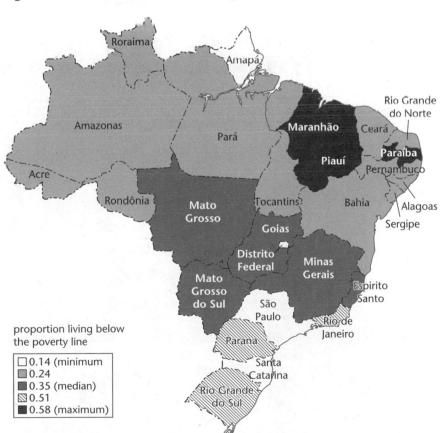

*Source:* Author compilation.

*Note:* The states of Minas Gerais, Parana, Rio de Janeiro, Rio Grande do Sul, Santa Catarina, and São Paulo account for 78 percent of GDP, 58 percent of the total population, and 37 percent of the poor.

**Table 13.2. Poverty and Income Inequality by State, Brazil, 2001**

| State | Region[a] | Share in total population | Share in total agricultural GDP | Share of agriculture in state GDP | Share of poor households in state population | Contribution to national poverty gap[b] | Average poverty gap[b] |
|---|---|---|---|---|---|---|---|
| 1. Rondônia | N | 0.005 | 0.010 | 0.29 | 0.338 | 0.001 | 0.147 |
| 2. Acre | N | 0.002 | 0.004 | 0.30 | 0.356 | 0.000 | 0.176 |
| 3. Amazonas | N | 0.011 | 0.003 | 0.06 | 0.396 | 0.002 | 0.196 |
| 4. Roraima | N | 0.001 | 0.001 | 0.16 | 0.347 | 0.000 | 0.152 |
| 5. Pará | N | 0.023 | 0.031 | 0.25 | 0.425 | 0.005 | 0.194 |
| 6. Amapá | N | 0.003 | 0.002 | 0.13 | 0.151 | 0.000 | 0.069 |
| 7. Tocantins | N | 0.006 | 0.007 | 0.26 | 0.429 | 0.001 | 0.180 |
| 8. Maranhão | NE | 0.029 | 0.014 | 0.23 | 0.579 | 0.008 | 0.288 |
| 9. Piauí | NE | 0.015 | 0.005 | 0.15 | 0.564 | 0.005 | 0.304 |
| 10. Ceará | NE | 0.042 | 0.010 | 0.07 | 0.540 | 0.011 | 0.267 |
| 11. Rio Grande do Norte | NE | 0.016 | 0.006 | 0.07 | 0.471 | 0.004 | 0.218 |
| 12. Paraíba | NE | 0.019 | 0.009 | 0.14 | 0.550 | 0.005 | 0.257 |
| 13. Pernambuco | NE | 0.045 | 0.016 | 0.09 | 0.512 | 0.011 | 0.248 |
| 14. Alagoas | NE | 0.015 | 0.012 | 0.24 | 0.577 | 0.004 | 0.289 |
| 15. Sergipe | NE | 0.010 | 0.002 | 0.05 | 0.503 | 0.002 | 0.239 |
| 16. Bahia | NE | 0.073 | 0.050 | 0.14 | 0.520 | 0.019 | 0.256 |

| | | | | | | | |
|---|---|---|---|---|---|---|---|
| 17. Minas Gerais | SE | 0.108 | 0.141 | 0.18 | 0.301 | 0.014 | 0.133 |
| 18. Espírito Santo | SE | 0.019 | 0.025 | 0.17 | 0.324 | 0.003 | 0.144 |
| 19. Rio de Janeiro | SE | 0.095 | 0.019 | 0.01 | 0.202 | 0.009 | 0.095 |
| 20. São Paulo | SE | 0.229 | 0.219 | 0.06 | 0.166 | 0.019 | 0.083 |
| 21. Paraná | S | 0.059 | 0.112 | 0.19 | 0.237 | 0.006 | 0.100 |
| 22. Santa Catarina | S | 0.034 | 0.076 | 0.18 | 0.136 | 0.002 | 0.055 |
| 23. Rio Grande do Sul | S | 0.067 | 0.084 | 0.12 | 0.179 | 0.005 | 0.073 |
| 24. Mato Grosso do Sul | CW | 0.013 | 0.034 | 0.41 | 0.289 | 0.002 | 0.120 |
| 25. Mato Grosso | CW | 0.015 | 0.053 | 0.46 | 0.251 | 0.002 | 0.106 |
| 26. Goiás | CW | 0.031 | 0.046 | 0.23 | 0.300 | 0.004 | 0.126 |
| 27. Distrito Federal | CW | 0.013 | 0.006 | 0.02 | 0.219 | 0.001 | 0.106 |
| Total | All | 1.000 | 1.000 | 0.10 | 0.308 | 0.145 | 0.145 |

*Source:* IBGE (2001a).

a. N = north, NE = northeast, SE = southeast, S = south, CW = central-west.

b. The poverty gap is the share by which the average household income of the group falls below the poverty line.

São Paulo contribute most to the Foster, Greer, and Thorbecke (1984) poverty gap index.[15] The last column in table 13.2 shows the proportion by which a state's average household income falls below the poverty line (the state poverty gap). The states in the northeast, plus the states of Pará and Tocantins show the largest poverty gaps, while two states in the south, Rio Grande do Sul and Santa Catarina, show the lowest poverty gaps, followed closely by São Paulo.[16]

Table 13.3 contains information on the labor structure of the economy. In this table, the sectoral wage bill is split into the model's 10 occupational groups. The occupational groups are defined in terms of a unit wage ranking. More (less) skilled

**Table 13.3. Share of Occupations in the Activity Labor Bill, by Wage Group, Brazil, 2001**

*(percent)*

| Sector | Occupation, wage group | | | | | | | | | | |
| | 1 | 2 | 3 | 4 | 5 | 6 | 7 | 8 | 9 | 10 | Total |
|---|---|---|---|---|---|---|---|---|---|---|---|
| Agriculture | 40.5 | 30.2 | 5.8 | 6.0 | 5.2 | 3.3 | 3.7 | 1.8 | 1.9 | 1.6 | 100 |
| Mineral extraction | 12.0 | 19.4 | 6.8 | 6.9 | 8.4 | 6.1 | 12.8 | 9.9 | 10.8 | 6.9 | 100 |
| Petroleum and gas extraction, charcoal | 0.0 | 0.0 | 0.0 | 0.9 | 0.9 | 6.1 | 16.1 | 12.1 | 22.8 | 41.1 | 100 |
| Nonmetallic minerals | 7.1 | 18.8 | 7.4 | 8.9 | 11.5 | 11.8 | 14.1 | 7.6 | 7.4 | 5.3 | 100 |
| Iron products | 1.9 | 6.8 | 4.0 | 6.3 | 10.2 | 9.7 | 22.7 | 14.0 | 15.4 | 9.1 | 100 |
| Nonferrous metals | 1.9 | 6.8 | 4.0 | 6.3 | 10.2 | 9.7 | 22.7 | 14.0 | 15.4 | 9.1 | 100 |
| Other metals | 1.9 | 6.8 | 4.0 | 6.3 | 10.2 | 9.7 | 22.7 | 14.0 | 15.4 | 9.1 | 100 |
| Machines, tractors, parts | 0.5 | 4.6 | 1.9 | 4.8 | 6.8 | 9.0 | 19.6 | 17.2 | 16.8 | 18.8 | 100 |
| Electric material | 0.4 | 3.8 | 2.6 | 3.3 | 10.3 | 11.6 | 20.4 | 15.5 | 17.0 | 15.1 | 100 |
| Electronic equipment | 0.4 | 3.8 | 2.6 | 3.3 | 10.3 | 11.6 | 20.4 | 15.5 | 17.0 | 15.1 | 100 |
| Automobiles | 0.3 | 2.5 | 1.0 | 2.4 | 7.7 | 8.6 | 19.6 | 15.7 | 22.4 | 19.8 | 100 |
| Other vehicles, spare parts | 0.3 | 2.5 | 1.0 | 2.4 | 7.7 | 8.6 | 19.6 | 15.7 | 22.4 | 19.8 | 100 |
| Wood and furniture | 8.2 | 11.7 | 6.6 | 8.8 | 12.4 | 11.9 | 16.6 | 9.3 | 9.6 | 5.0 | 100 |
| Paper and graphics | 2.3 | 7.8 | 3.7 | 6.2 | 8.4 | 8.1 | 18.7 | 13.0 | 16.7 | 15.1 | 100 |
| Rubber industry | 0.8 | 4.7 | 3.2 | 4.6 | 14.4 | 5.5 | 24.0 | 13.6 | 16.6 | 12.5 | 100 |
| Chemical elements | 2.1 | 7.8 | 3.0 | 4.2 | 9.1 | 11.8 | 14.2 | 15.6 | 16.4 | 15.8 | 100 |
| Petroleum refining | 0.5 | 1.5 | 2.7 | 0.3 | 9.0 | 5.7 | 13.1 | 7.2 | 10.5 | 49.5 | 100 |
| Various chemicals | 0.0 | 6.8 | 9.6 | 13.4 | 25.3 | 0.0 | 14.5 | 2.8 | 7.9 | 19.7 | 100 |
| Pharmaceutical performance | 1.7 | 5.7 | 3.1 | 6.8 | 4.1 | 7.5 | 13.5 | 11.3 | 18.7 | 27.4 | 100 |
| Plastics | 1.6 | 6.3 | 2.3 | 8.5 | 12.8 | 12.1 | 24.6 | 10.3 | 9.0 | 12.6 | 100 |
| Textiles | 14.7 | 9.0 | 4.9 | 7.2 | 12.5 | 11.0 | 17.6 | 11.3 | 6.2 | 5.5 | 100 |
| Apparel | 3.2 | 17.3 | 7.5 | 15.1 | 16.1 | 9.7 | 15.7 | 5.4 | 4.5 | 5.5 | 100 |
| Shoes and leather products | 4.1 | 16.2 | 6.5 | 13.5 | 18.2 | 13.0 | 14.4 | 5.7 | 4.8 | 3.6 | 100 |

**Table 13.3. Share of Occupations in the Activity Labor Bill, by Wage Group, Brazil, 2001 (*continued*)**

(*percent*)

| Sector | Occupation, wage group 1 | 2 | 3 | 4 | 5 | 6 | 7 | 8 | 9 | 10 | Total |
|---|---|---|---|---|---|---|---|---|---|---|---|
| Industrialized coffee | 8.6 | 14.3 | 6.1 | 9.6 | 13.2 | 11.3 | 15.1 | 8.3 | 7.4 | 6.0 | 100 |
| Vegetable processing | 8.6 | 14.3 | 6.1 | 9.6 | 13.2 | 11.3 | 15.1 | 8.3 | 7.4 | 6.0 | 100 |
| Meats | 8.6 | 14.3 | 6.1 | 9.6 | 13.2 | 11.3 | 15.1 | 8.3 | 7.4 | 6.0 | 100 |
| Dairy products | 8.6 | 14.3 | 6.1 | 9.6 | 13.2 | 11.3 | 15.1 | 8.3 | 7.4 | 6.0 | 100 |
| Sugar | 8.6 | 14.3 | 6.1 | 9.6 | 13.2 | 11.3 | 15.1 | 8.3 | 7.4 | 6.0 | 100 |
| Vegetable oils | 8.6 | 14.3 | 6.1 | 9.6 | 13.2 | 11.3 | 15.1 | 8.3 | 7.4 | 6.0 | 100 |
| Other agriculture | 8.6 | 14.3 | 6.1 | 9.6 | 13.2 | 11.3 | 15.1 | 8.3 | 7.4 | 6.0 | 100 |
| Other industrial products | 16.8 | 13.4 | 6.6 | 6.2 | 11.4 | 7.4 | 13.1 | 7.8 | 10.7 | 6.5 | 100 |
| Public utilities and services | 1.4 | 17.5 | 1.5 | 8.6 | 7.1 | 0.0 | 12.9 | 12.2 | 14.2 | 14.5 | 100 |
| Civil construction | 6.3 | 13.4 | 8.6 | 10.1 | 12.5 | 9.0 | 20.2 | 9.6 | 6.9 | 3.4 | 100 |
| Trade | 10.0 | 14.2 | 6.6 | 8.2 | 10.7 | 8.2 | 15.1 | 8.3 | 10.0 | 8.7 | 100 |
| Transport | 4.6 | 7.0 | 4.4 | 4.7 | 7.5 | 7.1 | 19.0 | 16.1 | 18.1 | 11.6 | 100 |
| Communication services | 1.4 | 4.6 | 2.4 | 5.1 | 7.9 | 9.4 | 18.6 | 13.9 | 17.2 | 19.4 | 100 |
| Financial services | 0.9 | 3.5 | 1.3 | 3.5 | 6.6 | 4.2 | 10.0 | 11.8 | 23.3 | 34.9 | 100 |
| Household services | 16.4 | 20.3 | 7.4 | 8.4 | 9.6 | 6.8 | 12.1 | 6.5 | 7.2 | 5.4 | 100 |
| Enterprise services | 2.9 | 8.1 | 4.3 | 5.7 | 8.1 | 6.4 | 13.0 | 8.6 | 15.7 | 27.2 | 100 |
| Dwellings | 2.0 | 4.3 | 2.7 | 4.8 | 9.9 | 6.3 | 17.1 | 8.8 | 18.4 | 25.7 | 100 |
| Public administration | 1.7 | 13.1 | 3.6 | 7.2 | 7.6 | 6.8 | 13.0 | 12.1 | 19.3 | 15.6 | 100 |
| Nonmerchandise private services | 7.6 | 16.6 | 6.0 | 9.2 | 9.3 | 10.9 | 13.7 | 8.2 | 11.6 | 6.9 | 100 |

*Source:* IBGE (2001a).

workers are those in the highest (lowest) income groups. Agriculture is the activity most dependent on unskilled labor, which absorbs 41 percent of the sector's labor bill, while petroleum and gas extraction, as well as petroleum refining, is the most intensive user of skilled labor. The 10th labor group accounts for more than 40 percent of the wage payments for these activities; financial services follow, at 35 percent. If labor inputs are measured in hours rather than in values, the concentration of low-skill labor in agriculture would be even more pronounced.

Agriculture is also the sector that hires the largest share of unskilled labor in Brazil, around 41 percent of total workers in wage group 1. The trade sector is the second largest employer of this type of labor. The financial and other services sectors hire the largest numbers of higher-wage workers. As a general rule, the wage earnings of higher-wage occupations are concentrated in higher-income households, while the wage earnings of lower-wage occupations are concentrated in lower-income households. Thus, most of the wages earned by workers in wage group 1 accrue to the three poorest household groups, while all the workers in the highest wage group are located in households in the eighth wage group or higher, that is, the household income groups are positively correlated at a high level with the occupational wage earning groups.

## The Model Simulations and Results

In this section, we present the results from a liberalization scenario in which the rest of the world, in addition to Brazil, removes all distortions in merchandise trade. In the case of agriculture and lightly processed agriculture, the reforms involve the removal of all trade taxes (import and export) and subsidies, the removal of all output taxes and subsidies, and the removal of all farm input subsidies.[17] Among other nonagricultural goods, the reforms involve only the removal of all import tariffs and export taxes. We analyze the results with the aid of a decomposition algorithm suggested by Harrison, Horridge, and Pearson (2000) that allows the presentation of the results of the total shocks and the decomposition of the results according to the correspondent partial shocks, that is, liberalization in farm products in the rest of the world (*ROW ag*), liberalization in nonagricultural goods in the rest of the world (*ROW nonag*), liberalization in farm products in Brazil only (*Brazil ag*), and liberalization in nonfarm goods in Brazil only (*Brazil nonag*).

### Model closure

The closure we adopt for the CGE model of Brazil's economy aims to mimic the closure of the World Bank Linkage model that generated the foreign price and export demand shocks. On the supply side, national employment by occupation is fixed.[18] Real wage differentials drive labor migration among states.[19] The model allows industries to substitute between occupations according to relative wages. Similarly, capital is fixed nationally, but is mobile across sectors and states (all rates of return shift as one). The land stock in each state—land is used only in the agricultural and mining sectors—is fixed.[20] However, in the mining sectors (mineral extraction, as well as petroleum and gas extraction), this stock is treated as a natural resources stock and does not affect the price of agricultural land, which is restricted to agriculture. Since agriculture is an activity that produces 11 products, land is allocated to these competing products through relative prices, allowing the crop mix to change.

On the demand side, real government demands are fixed, while investment in each state and sector follows the growth of the corresponding capital stock.[21] A fixed (nominal trade balance–GDP) ratio enforces the national budget balance, which is accommodated by changes in real consumption. The trade balance drives the level of absorption. The national consumer price index is the model's numéraire. A tax replacement mechanism is in force, allowing the direct tax rate to adjust endogenously to maintain total (indirect, plus direct) government tax collection unchanged after the elimination of trade taxes and subsidies. This mechanism is the same as the one used in the Linkage model.

### The CGE model results

The Brazilian economy has limited exposure to external trade. The shares of exports and imports in total GDP were, respectively, 13.8 and 14.7 percent in the 2001 base year (up from 7.0 and 8.9 percent, respectively, in 1996). The significance and structure of Brazilian external trade are summarized in table 13.4. The border price and export demand shocks applied to the national CGE model,

**Table 13.4. The Structure of External Trade, Brazil, 2001**
*(percent)*

| Sector | Sectoral share of total exports | Share of total sectoral output exported | Share of local market supplied by imports | Sectoral share of total imports | Capital-labor ratio |
|---|---|---|---|---|---|
| Coffee | 0 | 0 | 0 | 0 | 0.72 |
| Sugarcane | 0 | 0 | 0 | 0 | 0.72 |
| Paddy rice | 0 | 0 | 2 | 0 | 0.72 |
| Wheat | 0 | 0 | 72 | 1 | 0.72 |
| Soybeans | 3 | 38 | 3 | 0 | 0.72 |
| Cotton | 0 | 0 | 0 | 0 | 0.72 |
| Corn | 1 | 16 | 2 | 0 | 0.72 |
| Livestock | 0 | 0 | 0 | 0 | 0.72 |
| Raw milk | 0 | 0 | 0 | 0 | 0.72 |
| Poultry | 0 | 0 | 1 | 0 | 0.72 |
| Other agricultural products | 2 | 3 | 2 | 1 | 0.72 |
| Mineral extraction | 4 | 56 | 7 | 1 | 0.25 |
| Petroleum and gas extraction, charcoal | 1 | 5 | 24 | 6 | 6.59 |
| Nonmetallic minerals | 1 | 7 | 4 | 1 | 0.71 |
| Iron products | 4 | 16 | 5 | 1 | 7.18 |
| Nonferrous metals | 3 | 19 | 12 | 2 | 3.80 |
| Other metals | 2 | 7 | 8 | 2 | 0.26 |
| Machines, tractors, parts | 3 | 10 | 22 | 8 | 1.93 |
| Electric material | 2 | 14 | 29 | 5 | 0.68 |
| Electronic equipment | 3 | 36 | 56 | 10 | 2.15 |

*(Table continues on the following page.)*

**Table 13.4. The Structure of External Trade, Brazil, 2001 (*continued*)**
(*percent*)

| Sector | Sectoral share of total exports | Share of total sectoral output exported | Share of local market supplied by imports | Sectoral share of total imports | Capital-labor ratio |
|---|---|---|---|---|---|
| Automobiles | 5 | 23 | 14 | 3 | 2.03 |
| Other vehicles, spare parts | 9 | 41 | 25 | 7 | 0.75 |
| Wood and furniture | 3 | 21 | 3 | 0 | 0.53 |
| Paper and graphics | 3 | 11 | 5 | 1 | 1.20 |
| Rubber industry | 1 | 12 | 13 | 1 | 3.31 |
| Chemical elements | 1 | 10 | 18 | 3 | 6.84 |
| Petroleum refining | 5 | 7 | 13 | 10 | 21.68 |
| Various chemicals | 1 | 6 | 17 | 4 | 1.22 |
| Pharmaceutical performance | 1 | 5 | 25 | 4 | 1.65 |
| Plastics | 1 | 6 | 11 | 1 | 0.51 |
| Textiles | 2 | 10 | 10 | 2 | 0.56 |
| Apparel | 0 | 2 | 2 | 0 | 0.39 |
| Shoes and leather products | 4 | 63 | 7 | 0 | 1.31 |
| Industrialized coffee | 2 | 22 | 0 | 0 | 3.77 |
| Vegetable processing | 3 | 14 | 4 | 1 | 0.95 |
| Meats | 4 | 16 | 1 | 0 | 1.36 |
| Dairy products | 0 | 1 | 3 | 0 | 2.17 |
| Sugar | 3 | 37 | 0 | 0 | 3.50 |
| Vegetable oils | 4 | 29 | 2 | 0 | 5.53 |
| Other agriculture | 2 | 8 | 5 | 1 | 0.88 |
| Other industrial products | 1 | 12 | 23 | 2 | 1.89 |
| Public utilities and services | 0 | 0 | 3 | 1 | 1.77 |
| Civil construction | 0 | 0 | 0 | 0 | 4.09 |
| Trade | 1 | 3 | 4 | 1 | 0.16 |
| Transport | 6 | 14 | 10 | 4 | 0.04 |
| Communication services | 0 | 1 | 1 | 0 | 1.90 |
| Financial services | 1 | 1 | 2 | 1 | 0.38 |
| Household services | 3 | 4 | 7 | 5 | 0.10 |
| Enterprise services | 6 | 15 | 18 | 9 | 0.44 |
| Dwellings | 0 | 0 | 0 | 0 | 46.46 |
| Public administration | 1 | 1 | 1 | 2 | 0.00 |
| Nonmerchandise private services | 0 | 0 | 0 | 0 | 0.00 |

*Source:* IBGE (2001c).

shown in table 13.5, have been generated through a previous run of the World Bank global Linkage model (see the appendix by van der Mensbrugghe, Valenzuela, and Anderson). The border price effects in the Brazilian economy have been transmitted to the Brazil CGE model through import price changes and shifts in the demand schedules for Brazilian exports.[22]

**Table 13.5. Exogenous Demand and Border Price Shocks Caused by Prospective Global Trade Liberalization, Brazil**
(percent change)

| Sector | Armington elasticities, Linkage model | Import tariffs | Import CIF prices | Export FOB prices | Vertical shift in the export demand schedule |
|---|---|---|---|---|---|
| Cotton | 6.5 | 0.0 | 0.0 | 9.0 | 10.1 |
| Sugarcane | 5.4 | 0.0 | 0.0 | 0.0 | 0.0 |
| Paddy rice | 10.1 | 0.0 | 4.8 | 0.0 | 0.0 |
| Wheat | 8.9 | −0.3 | −2.8 | 7.1 | 9.3 |
| Soybeans | 4.9 | 0.0 | 1.5 | 8.1 | 2.2 |
| Cotton | 5.0 | 0.0 | 14.4 | 8.7 | 8.2 |
| Corn | 2.6 | 0.0 | 3.3 | 8.4 | 16.2 |
| Livestock | 3.9 | 0.0 | 1.1 | 8.9 | −9.3 |
| Raw milk | 7.3 | 0.0 | 0.0 | 0.0 | 0.0 |
| Poultry | 2.6 | 0.0 | 0.0 | 8.8 | −11.5 |
| Other agricultural products | 3.7 | −2.5 | 2.2 | 8.7 | 4.5 |
| Mineral extraction | 1.8 | −1.7 | −2.6 | 5.6 | −10.2 |
| Petroleum and gas extraction, charcoal | 10.4 | 0.0 | −2.6 | 5.6 | −10.2 |
| Nonmetallic minerals | 5.8 | −5.5 | 0.6 | 5.1 | −0.7 |
| Iron products | 5.9 | −5.2 | 0.6 | 5.1 | −0.7 |
| Nonferrous metals | 8.4 | −4.5 | 0.6 | 5.1 | −0.7 |
| Other metals | 7.5 | −8.4 | 0.6 | 5.1 | −0.7 |
| Machines, tractors, parts | 8.6 | −7.4 | 0.6 | 5.1 | −0.7 |
| Electric material | 8.1 | −7.5 | 0.6 | 5.1 | −0.7 |
| Electronic equipment | 8.8 | −6.4 | 0.6 | 5.1 | −0.7 |
| Automobiles | 5.6 | −7.8 | 0.6 | 5.1 | −0.7 |
| Other vehicles, spare parts | 8.6 | −5.5 | 0.6 | 5.1 | −0.7 |
| Wood and furniture | 6.8 | −7.4 | 0.6 | 5.1 | −0.7 |

(Table continues on the following page.)

**Table 13.5. Exogenous Demand and Border Price Shocks Caused by Prospective Global Trade Liberalization, Brazil (*continued*)**

*(percent change)*

| Sector | Armington elasticities, Linkage model | Import tariffs | Import CIF prices | Export FOB prices | Vertical shift in the export demand schedule |
|---|---|---|---|---|---|
| Paper and graphics | 5.9 | −3.6 | 0.6 | 5.1 | −0.7 |
| Rubber industry | 6.6 | −8.4 | 0.6 | 5.1 | −0.7 |
| Chemical elements | 6.6 | −4.9 | 0.6 | 5.1 | −0.7 |
| Petroleum refining | 4.2 | −3.0 | 0.6 | 5.1 | −0.7 |
| Various chemicals | 6.6 | −5.8 | 0.6 | 5.1 | −0.7 |
| Pharmaceutical performance | 6.6 | −4.5 | 0.6 | 5.1 | −0.7 |
| Plastics | 6.6 | −9.5 | 0.6 | 5.1 | −0.7 |
| Textiles | 7.5 | −11.4 | 0.1 | 5.4 | 1.2 |
| Apparel | 7.4 | −12.4 | 0.1 | 5.4 | 1.2 |
| Shoes and leather products | 8.1 | −6.1 | 0.1 | 5.4 | 1.2 |
| Industrialized coffee | 2.3 | −1.5 | 7.3 | 6.1 | 25.5 |
| Vegetable processing | 4.0 | −2.8 | 5.9 | 6.1 | 25.4 |
| Meats | 8.4 | −1.8 | 3.7 | 7.7 | 25.4 |
| Dairy products | 7.3 | −2.7 | 10.5 | 7.0 | 38.9 |
| Sugar | 5.4 | −0.7 | 0.0 | 6.5 | 25.3 |
| Vegetable oils | 6.6 | −4.5 | −0.8 | 6.8 | −1.3 |
| Other agriculture | 3.8 | −5.1 | 7.3 | 6.1 | 25.5 |
| Other industrial products | 7.5 | −7.2 | 0.6 | 5.1 | −0.7 |
| Public utilities and services | 5.6 | 0.0 | −0.2 | 5.9 | −0.7 |
| Civil construction | 3.8 | 0.0 | −0.2 | 5.9 | −0.7 |
| Trade | 3.8 | −1.8 | −0.2 | 5.9 | −0.7 |
| Transport | 3.8 | 0.0 | −0.2 | 5.9 | −0.7 |
| Communication services | 3.8 | −1.2 | −0.2 | 5.9 | −0.7 |
| Financial services | 3.8 | 0.0 | −0.2 | 5.9 | −0.7 |
| Household services | 3.8 | −0.1 | −0.2 | 5.9 | −0.7 |
| Enterprise services | 3.8 | 0.0 | −0.2 | 5.9 | −0.7 |
| Dwellings | 3.8 | 0.0 | −0.2 | 5.9 | −0.7 |
| Public administration | 3.8 | −1.5 | −0.2 | 5.9 | −0.7 |
| Nonmerchandise private services | 3.8 | 0.0 | −0.2 | 5.9 | −0.7 |

*Source:* Linkage model simulations (see the appendix by van der Mensbrugghe, Valenzuela, and Anderson).

*Note:* CIF = cost, insurance, and freight. FOB = free on board.

An inspection of tables 13.4 and 13.5 gives an idea of the importance of these shocks, combined with a view on the importance of each commodity in Brazil's external trade. The exports are spread across many different commodities, and there is no strong specialization. Primary agricultural products have a small share (mostly soybeans) in total exports. Nonetheless, processed agricultural and agricultural based exports, including wood and furniture, rubber, paper, textiles, and apparel, account for a significant 30 percent share of total exports in the base year, highlighting the importance of agriculture in the broader sense in the economy. The significant products in terms of the shares of domestic production imported are wheat, petroleum, machinery, electric materials, electronic equipment, and chemical products. In terms of shares in total imports, the highest ranking sectors are petroleum products (raw and refined), machinery, electric materials, electronic equipment, and chemical products.

The agricultural sector is modeled as a multiproduction sector; it produces 11 commodities. Thus, the value based ratio of capital to labor in table 13.4 is the same for every agricultural product. The value of land is not included in the value of capital, but, if it were, the value of the ratio of capital to labor in agriculture would rise to 1.11.[23]

Agriculture— primary agriculture and livestock production—is the only sector with a negative production tax in the database: 0.7 percent or −0.007 points in the levels. To eliminate this tax, the scenario includes an increase of 0.007 points in this tax rate. In the lightly processed sectors, there are production subsidies, and the shocks on these sectors are meats (−0.046), dairy products (−0.047), sugar (−0.048), and vegetable oils (−0.046).

The national macroeconomic effects of this global liberalization shock are shown in table 13.6. Because the closure fixes the total supply of all primary factors (land, the 10 categories of labor, and capital), GDP shows only a slight increase of 0.1 percent. The real exchange rate rises as a result of the shocks (a revaluation), with corresponding gains in the external terms of trade. The table also shows the subtotals associated with each partial shock. As one may see, the liberalization of agricultural product markets in the rest of the world generates the largest increase in real GDP and real household consumption in Brazil.

Recall that land is used only by agriculture, while capital and the 10 types of labor are fixed nationally, but mobile across sectors. As a result of the simulation, the average (aggregated) rental return on capital rent increases by 0.7 percent. Because total capital stocks and labor are fixed, expanding industries attract capital and labor from contracting ones, driving up real wages by 1.3 percent, on average. The increase is 21 percent for the lowest wage group, less for medium skills, and negative, at around −3 percent, for higher skills. In those industries

**Table 13.6. The Macroeconomic Impacts of Prospective Trade Liberalizations, Brazil**

*(percent change from the baseline)*

| Indicator | ROW ag | ROW nonag | Brazil ag | Brazil nonag | Global ag + nonag |
|---|---|---|---|---|---|
| Real household consumption | 1.05 | −0.20 | −0.03 | −0.15 | 0.66 |
| Real investment | 0.10 | −0.02 | 0.02 | 0.04 | 0.14 |
| Real government expenditure | 0.00 | 0.00 | 0.00 | 0.00 | 0.00 |
| Export volume | 0.71 | −0.91 | 0.63 | 4.85 | 5.29 |
| Import volume | 5.12 | −1.61 | 0.57 | 3.84 | 7.92 |
| Real GDP | 0.08 | −0.01 | 0.00 | 0.03 | 0.10 |
| Aggregate employment | 0.00 | 0.00 | 0.00 | 0.00 | 0.00 |
| Average real wage | 0.43 | −0.10 | 0.34 | 0.62 | 1.28 |
| Average real return to farmland | 22.43 | 0.94 | 3.72 | 0.86 | 28.00 |
| Average real return to capital | 0.11 | 0.04 | 0.34 | 0.22 | 0.71 |
| Aggregate capital stock | 0.00 | 0.00 | 0.00 | 0.00 | 0.00 |
| GDP price index | 0.23 | −0.10 | 0.06 | −0.06 | 0.13 |
| Consumer price index | 0.00 | 0.00 | 0.00 | 0.00 | 0.00 |
| Export price index | −0.10 | −0.13 | −0.25 | −0.19 | −0.68 |
| Import price index | −4.28 | 0.59 | −0.20 | 0.53 | −3.37 |
| Terms of trade | 4.31 | −0.73 | −0.05 | −0.74 | 2.78 |
| Real exchange rate | 4.66 | −0.71 | 0.27 | −0.61 | 3.62 |
| Nominal GDP | 0.31 | −0.11 | 0.06 | −0.03 | 0.22 |
| Nominal land price | 22.43 | 0.94 | 3.72 | 0.86 | 28.00 |
| Gini coefficient[a] | −1.4 | −0.1 | −0.2 | 0.1 | −1.7 |
| Poverty headcount[b] | −2.3 | −0.1 | −0.5 | −0.4 | −3.5 |

*Source:* CGE model simulations for Brazil by the authors.

a. The baseline value is 0.58.
b. The baseline value is 31 percent.

with falling capital-labor ratios, the marginal productivity of capital increases, and, hence, so do capital returns. The real price of agricultural land also shows a 28 percent rise nationally, reflecting the boost in the demand for land in every state as a consequence of the expansion in production activities relying on this factor, that is, in agriculture. The bulk of this effect is generated by the liberalization of agricultural markets in the rest of the world.

The increase in export volume (5.3 percent) is generated mainly by the liberalization in nonagricultural markets in Brazil. This is because the trade balance is fixed as a share of GDP in the closure. The trade shocks on the import side are generated by the liberalization in imported manufactured goods, on which the bulk of protection is concentrated in Brazil (table 13.5). Because GDP does not change much, the increase in the import volume (7.9 percent) must be matched by an increase in the export volume (5.3 percent), which is facilitated by an exchange rate devaluation (−0.61).

National-level changes in industry output are shown in table 13.7. Agriculture and agricultural related industries expand, and there is a general drop in manufacturing output following the trade liberalization. This suggests that regions specializing in manufacturing would fare worse, which is, indeed, the case. (See table 13.8, in which the states are grouped according to geographical regions.) For each of the 10 labor types, total employment is fixed; so, labor demand is redistributed across regions according to changes in regional industry output. Employment falls in the most populous and most industrialized states, Rio de Janeiro and São Paulo in the southeast, and also in Amazonas and Rio Grande do Norte, where there are free export zones (table 13.8). Thus,

**Table 13.7. The Effects of Prospective Global Trade Liberalization on Sectoral Outputs, Exports, and Imports, Brazil**
(percent change from the baseline)

| Sector | Output | Exports | Imports |
|---|---|---|---|
| Coffee | 12.2 | 0.0 | 0.0 |
| Sugarcane | 18.2 | 0.0 | 0.0 |
| Paddy rice | 12.6 | −82.8 | 116.6 |
| Wheat | 2.2 | 105.7 | 16.5 |
| Soybeans | 3.2 | 0.5 | 5.8 |
| Cotton | −2.3 | 107.8 | −16.5 |
| Corn | 8.2 | 10.0 | 28.3 |
| Livestock | 18.0 | −76.8 | 71.6 |
| Raw milk | 6.3 | 0.0 | 0.0 |
| Poultry | 12.8 | −55.0 | 34.3 |
| Other agricultural products | 3.5 | 6.9 | 4.9 |
| Mineral extraction | −12.1 | −16.5 | −5.9 |
| Petroleum and gas extraction, charcoal | −4.2 | −57.1 | −2.7 |
| Nonmetallic minerals | −2.6 | −15.0 | 15.9 |
| Iron products | −9.4 | −14.3 | 11.6 |
| Nonferrous metals | −11.8 | −16.2 | 7.5 |
| Other metals | −6.9 | −18.4 | 27.0 |
| Machines, tractors, parts | −6.6 | −23.7 | 10.8 |
| Electric material | −5.8 | −14.3 | 9.0 |
| Electronic equipment | −4.8 | −13.1 | 1.6 |

(Table continues on the following page.)

**Table 13.7. The Effects of Prospective Global Trade Liberalization on Sectoral Outputs, Exports, and Imports, Brazil (*continued*)**

*(percent change from the baseline)*

| Sector | Output | Exports | Imports |
|---|---|---|---|
| Automobiles | 0.8 | −5.4 | 2.6 |
| Other vehicles, spare parts | −11.7 | −16.5 | 10.1 |
| Wood and furniture | −5.5 | −23.7 | 17.8 |
| Paper and graphics | −2.8 | −17.1 | 10.4 |
| Rubber industry | −8.6 | −12.9 | 23.6 |
| Chemical elements | −12.0 | −46.4 | 27.1 |
| Petroleum refining | −1.3 | −5.2 | 3.3 |
| Various chemicals | −1.6 | −11.6 | 14.5 |
| Pharmaceutical performance | −0.2 | −15.7 | 3.4 |
| Plastics | −5.0 | −13.3 | 30.3 |
| Textiles | −2.9 | 9.3 | 35.8 |
| Apparel | 0.4 | −8.0 | 21.1 |
| Shoes and leather products | −12.8 | −17.5 | 14.1 |
| Industrialized coffee | 14.3 | 34.3 | 11.1 |
| Vegetable processing | 15.1 | 102.8 | 1.3 |
| Meats | 19.0 | 132.4 | 45.0 |
| Dairy products | 7.9 | 960.3 | −20.9 |
| Sugar | 59.6 | 137.1 | 22.1 |
| Vegetable oils | 4.5 | 7.2 | 4.7 |
| Other agriculture | 8.6 | 104.3 | −0.1 |
| Other industrial products | −7.8 | −23.7 | 13.7 |
| Public utilities and services | −1.1 | −19.8 | 8.2 |
| Civil construction | 0.0 | −13.3 | 6.0 |
| Trade | 1.2 | −15.5 | 8.2 |
| Transport | 0.2 | −7.7 | 3.2 |
| Communication services | 0.2 | −11.1 | 5.1 |
| Financial services | −0.3 | −10.2 | 4.7 |
| Household services | −1.5 | −18.9 | 9.3 |
| Enterprise services | −2.9 | −12.3 | 4.6 |
| Dwellings | −0.2 | 0.0 | 0.0 |
| Public administration | −0.2 | −13.5 | 6.8 |
| Nonmerchandise private services | −0.8 | 0.0 | 0.0 |

*Source:* CGE model simulations for Brazil by the authors.

**Table 13.8. The Effects of Prospective Global Trade Liberalization
on Output, by State, Brazil**
*(percent change from the baseline)*

| State | Region[a] | Real GDP | | | | | Aggregate employment |
|---|---|---|---|---|---|---|---|
| | | ROW ag | ROW nonag | Brazil ag | Brazil nonag | Global ag + nonag | Global ag + nonag |
| 1. Rondônia | N | 2.8 | 0.0 | 0.3 | 0.1 | 3.2 | 1.5 |
| 2. Acre | N | 2.5 | 0.0 | 0.3 | 0.1 | 2.9 | 1.3 |
| 3. Amazonas | N | −0.7 | −0.1 | −0.2 | 0.5 | −0.5 | −0.5 |
| 4. Roraima | N | 1.7 | 0.0 | 0.1 | 0.1 | 1.8 | 0.8 |
| 5. Pará | N | 1.8 | −0.3 | 0.5 | 0.0 | 2.1 | 1.1 |
| 6. Amapá | N | 1.4 | −0.2 | 0.3 | 0.0 | 1.5 | 0.7 |
| 7. Tocantins | N | 3.3 | 0.0 | 0.3 | 0.0 | 3.6 | 2.3 |
| 8. Maranhão | NE | 3.3 | 0.0 | 0.4 | −0.1 | 3.6 | 2.2 |
| 9. Piauí | NE | 2.1 | 0.0 | 0.3 | 0.1 | 2.3 | 1.3 |
| 10. Ceará | NE | −0.1 | 0.3 | 0.1 | 0.0 | 0.2 | 0.0 |
| 11. Rio Grande do Norte | NE | −0.3 | −0.2 | 0.0 | −0.2 | −0.6 | −0.2 |
| 12. Paraíba | NE | 1.2 | 0.1 | 0.3 | 0.0 | 1.6 | 0.7 |
| 13. Pernambuco | NE | 1.0 | 0.0 | 0.2 | −0.1 | 1.1 | 0.5 |
| 14. Alagoas | NE | 4.6 | 0.1 | 1.1 | 0.0 | 5.9 | 2.9 |
| 15. Sergipe | NE | 0.3 | 0.3 | 0.1 | −0.2 | 0.4 | 0.2 |
| 16. Bahia | NE | 0.4 | 0.0 | 0.0 | −0.2 | 0.3 | 0.2 |
| 17. Minas Gerais | SE | 0.5 | −0.1 | 0.1 | 0.0 | 0.5 | 0.2 |
| 18. Espírito Santo | SE | 0.8 | −0.4 | 0.0 | 0.0 | 0.4 | 0.1 |
| 19. Rio de Janeiro | SE | −0.9 | −0.1 | −0.2 | −0.2 | −1.4 | −1.0 |
| 20. São Paulo | SE | −0.6 | 0.0 | −0.1 | 0.1 | −0.5 | −0.5 |
| 21. Paraná | S | 1.5 | 0.0 | 0.2 | 0.1 | 1.8 | 1.0 |
| 22. Santa Catarina | S | 0.6 | −0.3 | 0.1 | 0.1 | 0.5 | 0.7 |
| 23. Rio Grande do Sul | S | −0.3 | 0.3 | −0.1 | 0.1 | 0.1 | 0.1 |
| 24. Mato Grosso do Sul | CW | 4.4 | 0.1 | 0.6 | 0.1 | 5.2 | 3.1 |
| 25. Mato Grosso | CW | 4.2 | 0.1 | 0.4 | 0.1 | 4.8 | 3.0 |
| 26. Goiás | CW | 2.4 | 0.1 | 0.4 | 0.0 | 2.9 | 1.8 |
| 27. Distrito Federal | CW | 0.3 | −0.1 | −0.1 | −0.1 | 0.0 | 0.0 |

*Source:* CGE model simulations for Brazil by the authors.

a. N = north, NE = northeast, SE = southeast, S = south, CW = central-west.

trade liberalization redistributes economic activity toward the poorer regions of Brazil, a result mainly driven by the liberalization in agricultural markets in the rest of the world.

### The results in poverty and income distribution

Because of the differences in the results among states, regions, and industries, there are marked changes in income inequality and poverty as a result of trade liberalization. The changes in the consumer price index specific to income groups are presented in table 13.9. The Gini coefficient of inequality falls by a nonnegligible 1.7 percent as a result of the reallocation effects that change wages and the labor demand structure in expanding and contracting sectors.

**Table 13.9. The Effects of Prospective Global Trade Liberalization on Poverty and Income Inequality, by Household Income Group, Brazil**

(percent change from the baseline)

| Household income group[a] | Average nominal income | Consumer price index | Share of households living below the poverty line | Poverty gap[b] |
|---|---|---|---|---|
| POF[1] | 34.5 | 0.48 | −2.7 | −8.3 |
| POF[2] | 7.7 | 0.42 | −3.1 | −9.4 |
| POF[3] | 4.8 | 0.35 | −5.6 | −9.4 |
| POF[4] | 2.7 | 0.24 | −6.7 | −3.5 |
| POF[5] | 1.6 | 0.22 | −4.5 | 9.6 |
| POF[6] | 0.5 | 0.19 | 7.3 | 53.9 |
| POF[7] | −0.4 | 0.10 | 56.5 | 313.5 |
| POF[8] | −1.2 | 0.03 | 470.4 | 2,032.7 |
| POF[9] | −1.7 | −0.12 | 0.0 | 0.0 |
| POF[10] | −2.4 | −0.36 | 0.0 | 0.0 |
| Original value, base year | n.a. | n.a. | 30.8 | 14.5 |
| % change | n.a. | n.a. | −3.45 | −7.59 |
| Gini coefficient | −1.7 | | | |

Source: CGE model simulations for Brazil by the authors.

Note: n.a. = not applicable.

a. See note a in table 13.1 for definitions of the income groups.
b. The poverty gap is the share by which the average household income of the group falls below the poverty line.

The literature on poverty recognizes the importance that a change in inequality may have in growth. Barros et al. (2007a) have estimated the equivalent growth for Brazil, which they define as the growth rate that would produce a reduction in poverty equal to the reduction caused by a particular fall in inequality. According to their estimates, the 4.6 percent decline in inequality observed in Brazil in 2001–05 was equivalent, from a poverty point of view, to a balanced growth rate of 11 percent with no change in inequality. This leads to the conclusion that a 1 percent decline in inequality is equivalent to an increase in income of 2.4 percent. Thus, one might say, the poor in Brazil would be indifferent whether there was a 1 percent drop in the Gini coefficient or a 2.4 percent balanced increase in per capita income. The simulation result of a 1.7 percent decline in the Gini coefficient would therefore be the equivalent, in terms of poverty reduction, of a 4.1 percent GDP increase above trend between the old and the new static equilibrium.

Although the results on the consumer price index a differ less across house holds than the income results, the trend is the same: living costs go up more for the poor, who spend relatively more of their budgets on food. There is a significant increase in the agricultural prices for some products, such as meats, which is driven mainly by the liberalization in the rest of the world. This contrasts with the expectation of Rocha (1998), who posited that opening the Brazilian economy to external markets—a unilateral liberalization—would help reduce inequality in Brazil by reducing prices in the poorest regions. Our results suggest that the consumer price index would actually go up more among the lowest income groups, but that this would be more than offset by increases in income (table 13.10). The strong positive real income effect on the poorest households is caused mainly by the liberalization in agricultural markets in the rest of the world.

The largest positive changes in household incomes are concentrated in the lowest income households, and the changes decrease monotonically as household income increases. Indeed, as one may see in table 13.9, the reduction in the number of poor households is concentrated in the poorest groups. The high positive numbers among groups 6, 7, and 8 in the consumer expenditure survey represent percent changes in low numbers because, as shown in table 13.1, there are few poor households in these income groups.[24]

The headcount ratio index (table 13.9, third column) captures only the extension of poverty, not the intensity of poverty. The change in the intensity of poverty may be seen in the fourth column, which shows the change in the poverty gap. A reduction in the poverty gap means that there has been a reduction in the severity of poverty within each household income group. The poverty gap is reduced

**Table 13.10. Decomposition of the Effects of Liberalization on Real Incomes, by Household Income Group, Brazil**
(percent change from the baseline)

| Household income group[a] | ROW ag | ROW nonag | Brazil ag | Brazil nonag | Global ag+ nonag |
|---|---|---|---|---|---|
| POF[1] | 27.38 | 2.60 | 3.80 | 2.66 | 34.02 |
| POF[2] | 5.56 | 0.21 | 0.97 | 0.46 | 7.28 |
| POF[3] | 3.14 | 0.21 | 0.66 | 0.47 | 4.45 |
| POF[4] | 1.57 | 0.00 | 0.42 | 0.47 | 2.46 |
| POF[5] | 0.69 | 0.00 | 0.42 | 0.48 | 1.38 |
| POF[6] | −0.25 | −0.10 | 0.20 | 0.48 | 0.31 |
| POF[7] | −0.86 | −0.10 | 0.07 | 0.49 | −0.50 |
| POF[8] | −1.45 | −0.20 | −0.06 | 0.49 | −1.23 |
| POF[9] | −1.74 | −0.21 | −0.04 | 0.51 | −1.58 |
| POF[10] | −2.11 | −0.23 | −0.09 | 0.56 | −2.04 |

Source: CGE model simulations for Brazil by the authors.

a. See note a in table 13.1 for definitions of the income groups.

relatively more than the headcount ratio among the poorest three household income groups, thus reducing income inequality, but not sufficiently to drive a large number of individuals (or households) out of poverty because of the high value of these indictors during the base year.

The breakdown in the changes in poverty by state is reported in table 13.11. Only in the large, industrialized states of Rio de Janeiro and São Paulo and in Amazonas, where there is a free trade processing zone specialized in electronic products, would there be an increase in the number of households living below the poverty line. This result is generated because of the high concentration of manufacturing industries in Rio de Janeiro and São Paulo, mainly automobiles, machinery and tractors, electric materials, electronic equipment, other vehicles and spare parts, and chemicals. The poverty gap increases in Rio de Janeiro, but not in Amazonas or São Paulo. This is because the share of agriculture and lightly processed food in GDP is larger in Amazonas than in Rio de Janiero or São Paulo (see table 13.2, column 3). The higher wages and employment in agriculture reduce the poverty gaps in these states, even though the fall in manufacturing activities causes the number of poor to increase. Rio de Janeiro, meanwhile, is less agricultural so that rising agricultural wages and employment do not compensate for the fall in manufacturing industries.

**Table 13.11. The Effects of Prospective Global Trade Liberalization
on Poverty, by State, Brazil**
(percent change from the baseline)

| State | Share of households living below the poverty line | Poverty gap[a] |
|---|---|---|
| 1. Rondônia | −6.3 | −7.9 |
| 2. Acre | −4.5 | −8.5 |
| 3. Amazonas | 0.1 | −0.9 |
| 4. Roraima | −5.4 | −7.4 |
| 5. Pará | −4.3 | −7.5 |
| 6. Amapá | −0.6 | −2.3 |
| 7. Tocantins | −9.5 | 15.6 |
| 8. Maranhão | −5.4 | −14.2 |
| 9. Piauí | −4.2 | −8.4 |
| 10. Ceará | −2.6 | 6.1 |
| 11. Rio Grande do Norte | 3.3 | −6.1 |
| 12. Paraíba | −4.5 | −9.3 |
| 13. Pernambuco | −4.5 | −9.2 |
| 14. Alagoas | −6.9 | −14.8 |
| 15. Sergipe | −3.6 | −6.9 |
| 16. Bahia | −2.8 | −7.7 |
| 17. Minas Gerais | −5.1 | −9.2 |
| 18. Espírito Santo | −4.5 | −10.7 |
| 19. Rio de Janeiro | 2.9 | 1.9 |
| 20. São Paulo | 1.9 | −0.8 |
| 21. Paraná | −7.1 | −11.1 |
| 22. Santa Catarina | −3.9 | −6.9 |
| 23. Rio Grande do Sul | −6.2 | −10.3 |
| 24. Mato Grosso do Sul | −14.3 | −19.4 |
| 25. Mato Grosso | −10.1 | −21.3 |
| 26. Goiás | −8.6 | −13.9 |
| 27. Distrito Federal | −0.3 | −1.7 |
| Change in the total number of poor households, millions | −0.53 | |
| Change in the total number of the poor, millions | −1.94 | |

Source: CGE model simulations for Brazil by the authors.

a. The percent by which the average household income of the group falls below the poverty line.

## Conclusions

Our simulated global trade liberalization scenario shows positive impacts on poverty in Brazil, a result mainly driven by the liberalization in the agricultural markets of the rest of the world. Although the country is not particularly oriented toward external trade, the strong push in border prices and external demand generated by trade liberalization causes agriculture to expand considerably, with positive effects on poverty. This highlights the importance that agriculture still has among the poorest households in Brazil. Despite the steady decline in agriculture's share in GDP over the years, the sector still employs most of the nation's poorest. The agricultural sector is thus uniquely important to the poorest workers.

This means that, in Brazil's manufacturing states, particularly Rio de Janeiro and São Paulo, but also in Amazonas, though on a much smaller scale, the number of poor households increases. This occurs because the protection of import-competing manufacturing is reduced by own-country liberalization, and agriculture expands (because of the rest-of-the-world reform), while manufacturing contracts. This is important. Like most of the other countries in Latin America, Brazil once pursued import-substitution policies that benefited the manufacturing sector. Our model results show that the trade liberalization scenario would reverse this outcome somewhat, benefiting agriculture at the expense of the industrial sectors.

Another important point arising from our analysis is the fall in inequality, which is even more dramatic than the fall in the number of people living in poverty. This improvement in inequality would be equivalent, in terms of poverty reduction, to a significant boost in GDP per capita. Furthermore, the biggest narrowing in the poverty gap occurs among the poorest household groups, suggesting that the poorest households in Brazil would tend to benefit most from global trade liberalization. In fact, this result holds for every state in Brazil except Rio de Janeiro.

In this chapter, we have avoided a rural versus urban analysis because of the difficulties of this sort of approach in the case of Brazil. However, the composition of our household groups takes into account the occupational diversity in the economy. It also captures the multiactivity phenomenon, that is, many households include workers in both agriculture and manufacturing. This phenomenon has been intensely researched in Brazil.[25] Approaching poverty through the prism of households and tracking the changes in the labor market from individual workers to households are important modeling issues. In the 2001 data of the national household sample survey we use here, the incomes of household heads account for only 65 percent of household incomes. Using head-of-household income as a proxy for household income may therefore poorly predict the effect of policy changes, as convincingly argued by Bourguignon, Robilliard, and Robinson (2003). The more that spending (and welfare) is a household phenomena, the more appropriate is the method we use here.

Giambiagi and Franco (2007) note that one of the strategies used by the federal government to fight poverty, namely, increases in the minimum wage, seems to be close to reaching the limits in terms of effectiveness, especially in the poorest region, the northeast. This region would be among the regions to benefit the most from global trade liberalization. Thus, a global freeing of trade would provide an alternative channel for helping the poor in Brazil.

## Notes

1. This approach follows closely that of Ferreira Filho, Santos, and Lima (2007). Previous studies have used a simpler top-down or interregional model involving regional differentiation in quantity changes, but not price changes, and reliance on the 1996 input-output table.

2. Estimates of agricultural protection and assistance in Brazil, based on Lopes et al. (2008), are incorporated in the World Bank's Distortions to Agricultural Incentives Project Database (Anderson and Valenzuela 2008). These estimates cover five decades. The representative values for developing-country agriculture as of 2004 that are used in the global CGE modeling for our study are summarized in Valenzuela and Anderson (2008).

3. Barros et al (2007b) find an even larger effect. According to these authors, federal government transfers were responsible for about 50 percent of the observed fall in inequality in Brazil in 2001–05.

4. Following Savard (2003), another approach involves iteration, whereby the CGE simulation is rerun with adjustments to make it consistent with the previous results from the MS model. The process may be repeated until the results converge.

5. Versions of TERM have been prepared for Australia, Brazil, China, Finland, Indonesia, and Japan. Related material may be found at http://www.monash.edu.au/policy/term.htm.

6. For the simulations reported here, we set the export demand elasticities to values derived from the Linkage model so as to increase consistency between the results of the global model and the Brazil model.

7. The dimensions of this margins matrix are 52 * 2 * 2 * 27 * 27.

8. For most goods, the interstate elasticity of substitution is fairly high. To ease the computational burden, we assume that all users of good $G$ in state $R$ draw the same share of their demands from state $Z$.

9. The 2001 Brazilian Input-Output Database we use in this study has been generated by Ferreira Filho, Santos, and Lima (2007) based on the Brazilian national accounting system tables because the last official input-output table published by the IBGE, the Brazilian statistical agency, ends in 1996.

10. This quantum method is described in more detail by Ferreira Filho and Horridge (2005; 2009, annex).

11. The concept of the equivalent household measures the subsistence needs of a household by attributing weights to household members: 1 to the head, 0.75 to each other adult, and 0.5 to each child. Because we define poverty on an equivalent basis, a few (large) families in the middle-income groups fall below the poverty line.

12. This poverty line was equivalent to US$48 in 2001.

13. Working with a poverty line that takes nutritional needs into account, Barros, Henriques, and Mendonça (2001) find that 34 percent of households were poor in 1999.

14. The shares of households living below the poverty line in the other income groups are 0.284 percent in the fourth group, 0.14 percent in the fifth, 0.04 percent in the sixth, 0.008 percent in

the seventh, and 0.001 percent in the eighth. There are no households living below the poverty line in the two highest (richest) income groups.

15. The values of the poverty gap and poverty line are constructed based on adult equivalent per capita household income.

16. While Amapá, in the north, shows a poverty gap in line with the gaps in the richer states of the south and southeast, this should be viewed with caution because Amapá has only a small share in the total population and the result may be generated by a sampling bias. The national household sample survey (an urban survey) does not cover the rural areas in the north, in which poverty is usually concentrated.

17. Highly processed agriculture, beverages, and tobacco (sectors 25 and 26 in the database of the Global Trade Analysis Project) are included as part of manufacturing rather than agriculture. In the classification system in the model for Brazil, these sectors correspond to industrialized coffee (CoffeeInd), vegetable processing (VegetProcess), and other agricultural products (OthAg).

18. There is a tension between this labor closure and the Brazilian reality. The microdata show substantial unemployment among less-skilled groups in all states. An alternate scenario, whereby fixed real wages replace national labor constraints, yields results similar to those we report here.

19. For a particular occupation and state, the intersectoral wage variation has been fixed. In the MS, it is assumed that jobs created (or lost) in a state are allotted to (or taken from) the households in that state.

20. The factor market closure causes the model to generate percent changes in the factor prices for the 10 labor groups, capital, and land; the price changes vary across states. In addition, the percent changes in the demand for each of the 12 factors vary by sector and state. Each adult in the national household sample survey microdata is identified by state and labor group; the employed are also identified by sector. Changes in poverty levels in the microdata are driven by wage changes and by the redistribution of jobs among sectors and states (and, hence, among households).

21. Thus, investment-capital ratios are fixed. Because national capital stock is fixed, changes in aggregate investment are also limited, but do arise from intersectoral variations in the initial investment-capital ratios, although the model is static.

22. We have calculated the shifts in the demand schedules for Brazilian exports based on the export price and quantity results (and export demand elasticities) from the World Bank Linkage model. We have used the method of Horridge and Zhai (2006). The Armington elasticities, reported in table 13.5, are borrowed from the Linkage model. The export demand elasticities (not shown in the table) are equal to the Global Trade Analysis Project state-generic elasticity of substitution among imports in the Armington structure.

23. The primary factor shares in agriculture are land (0.19), labor (0.47), and capital (0.34). The labor bill in agriculture has been adjusted to take wage income from self-employment into account.

24. Some middle-income households have many family members. Because of the low per capita income, they fall below the poverty line.

25. See, for example, Del Grossi and Graziano da Silva (1998), Graziano da Silva and Del Grossi (2001), and Nascimento (2004).

# References

Anderson, K., and E. Valenzuela. 2008. "Estimates of Global Distortions to Agricultural Incentives, 1955–2007." Data spreadsheet, October, World Bank, Washington, DC. http://go.worldbank.org/YAO39F35E0.

Barros, R. P. de, M. Carvalho, S. Franco, and R. Mendonça. 2007a. "A Importância da Queda Recente da Desigualdade na Redução da Pobreza." Texto para Discussão 1256, Instituto de Pesquisa Econômica Aplicada, Rio de Janeiro.

———. 2007b. "Determinantes Imediatos da Queda da Desigualdade da Renda Brasileira." Texto para Discussão 1253, Instituto de Pesquisa Econômica Aplicada, Rio de Janeiro.

Barros, R. P. de, R. Henriques, and R. Mendonça. 2001. "A Estabilidade Inaceitável: Desigualdade e Pobreza no Brasil." Texto para Discussão 800, Instituto de Pesquisa Econômica Aplicada, Rio de Janeiro.

Barros, R. P. de, and R. Mendonça. 1997. "O Impacto do Crescimento Econômico e de Reduções no Grau de Desigualdade sobre a Pobreza." Texto para Discussão 528, Instituto de Pesquisa Econômica Aplicada, Rio de Janeiro.

Bourguignon, F., A.-S. Robilliard, and S. Robinson. 2003. "Representative Versus Real Households in the Macro-economic Modeling of Inequality." Working Paper 2003–05, Department et Laboratoire d'Economie Théorique et Apliquée, Centre National de la Recherche Scientifique, Ecole des Hautes Etudes en Sciences Sociales, Paris.

Del Grossi, M. E., and J. Graziano da Silva. 1998. "A pluriatividade na agropecuáriabrasileira em 1995," *Estudos Sociedade e Agricultura* 11: 26–52.

Ferreira Filho, J. B. S., and M. Horridge. 2005. "The Doha Round, Poverty, and Regional Inequality in Brazil." Policy Research Working Paper 3701, World Bank, Washington, DC.

———. 2006. "The Doha Round, Poverty, and Regional Inequality in Brazil," In *Poverty and the WTO: Impacts of the Doha Development Agenda*, ed. T. W. Hertel and L. A. Winters, 183–218. London: Palgrave Macmillan; Washington, DC: World Bank.

———. 2009. "Would Trade Liberalization Help the Poor of Brazil?" Agricultural Distortions Working Paper 106, World Bank, Washington, DC.

Ferreira Filho, J. B. S., C. V. Santos, and S. M. P. Lima. 2007. "Tax Reform, Income Distribution, and Poverty in Brazil: An Applied General Equilibrium Analysis." PEP-MPIA Working Paper 2007–26, Modeling and Policy Impact Analysis Program, Poverty and Economic Policy Research Network, Université Laval, Quebec.

Foster, J., J. Greer, and E. Thorbecke. 1984. "A Class of Decomposable Poverty Measures." *Econometrica* 52 (3): 761–66.

Giambiagi, F., and S. Franco. 2007. "O Esgotamento do Papel do Salário Mínimo Como Mecanismo de Combate à Pobreza Extrema." Texto para Discussão 1290, Instituto de Pesquisa Econômica Aplicada, Rio de Janeiro.

Graziano da Silva, J., and M. E. Del Grossi. 2001. "Rural Non-Farm Employment and Incomes in Brazil: Patterns and Evolution." *World Development* 29 (3): 443–54.

Green, F., A. Dickerson, and J. S. Arbache. 2001. "A Picture of Wage Inequality and the Allocation of Labor through a Period of Trade Liberalization: The Case of Brazil." *World Development* 29 (11): 1923–39.

Harrison, G. W., T. F. Rutherford, D. G. Tarr, and A. Gurgel. 2003. "Regional, Multilateral, and Unilateral Trade Policies of MERCOSUR for Growth and Poverty Reduction in Brazil." Policy Research Working Paper 3051, World Bank, Washington, DC.

Harrison, W. J., M. Horridge, and K. R. Pearson. 2000. "Decomposing Simulation Results with Respect to Exogenous Shocks." *Computational Economics* 15 (3): 227–49.

Hoffmann, R. 2006. "Transferência de Renda e Redução de Desigualdade no Brasil e Cinco Regiões." *Econômica* 8 (1): 55–81.

Horridge, M., J. Madden, and G. Wittwer. 2005. "The Impact of the 2002–2003 Drought on Australia." *Journal of Policy Modelling* 27 (3): 285–308.

Horridge, M., and F. Zhai. 2006. "Shocking a Single-Country CGE Model with Export Prices and Quantities from a Global Model." In *Poverty and the WTO: Impacts of the Doha Development Agenda*, ed. T. W. Hertel and L. A. Winters, 94–104. London: Palgrave Macmillan; Washington, DC: World Bank.

IBGE (Brazilian Institute of Geography and Statistics). 1996a. "Censo Agropecuário do Brasil" [Census of agriculture]. Instituto Brasileiro de Geografia e Estatística, Rio de Janeiro.

———. 1996b. "Pesquisa de Orçamentos Familiares" [Consumer expenditure survey]. Instituto Brasileiro de Geografia e Estatística, Rio de Janeiro.

———. 2001a. "Pesquisa Nacional por Amostra de Domicílios" [National household sample survey]. Instituto Brasileiro de Geografia e Estatística, Rio de Janeiro.

————. 2001b. "Produção Agrícola Municipal" [Municipal agricultural production]. Instituto Brasileiro de Geografia e Estatística, Rio de Janeiro.

————. 2001c. "Contas Nacionais do Brasil" [National accounts]. Instituto Brasileiro de Geografia e Estatística, Rio de Janeiro.

Lopes, M., I. V. Lopes, M. S. de Oliveira, F. C. Barcelos, E. Jara, and P. R. Bogado. 2008. "Brazil." In *Distortions to Agricultural Incentives in Latin America*, ed. K. Anderson and A. Valdés, 87–118. Washington, DC: World Bank.

Nascimento, C. A. do. 2004. "Pluriatividade, pobreza rural e serviço doméstico remunerado." *Revista de Economia e Sociologia Rural* 42 (2): 341–64.

Rocha, S. 1998. "Desigualdade Regional e Pobreza no Brasil: A Evolução, 1985/95." Texto para Discussão 567, Instituto de Pesquisa Econômica Aplicada, Rio de Janeiro.

Savard, L. 2003. "Poverty and Income Distribution in a CGE-Household Sequential Model." International Development Research Centre, Dakar.

Valenzuela, E., and K. Anderson. 2008. "Alternative Agricultural Price Distortions for CGE Analysis of Developing Countries, 2004 and 1980–84." Research Memorandum 13 (December), Center for Global Trade Analysis, Department of Agricultural Economics, Purdue University, West Lafayette, IN. https://www.gtap.agecon.purdue.edu/resources/res_display.asp?RecordID=2925.

van der Mensbrugghe, D. 2005. "Linkage Technical Reference Document: Version 6.0." December, World Bank, Washington, DC. http://go.worldbank.org/7NP2KK1OH0.

# 14

# NICARAGUA

## Marco V. Sánchez and Rob Vos

The Doha Round of multilateral trade negotiations stalled in 2006 owing in no small measure to a lack of agreement on the terms of a substantial reduction in trade-distorting support for agricultural products. The round aims to address the needs of developing countries, but there is controversy regarding the extent to which a reduction in trade barriers and domestic supports for agricultural commodities would, in fact, be beneficial to developing countries, and, in particular, whether it would unequivocally reduce poverty. Nicaragua presents an interesting case in point. It is one of the poorest economies in Latin America and still has a relatively large agricultural sector and significant rural poverty.

At the end of 2005, Nicaragua joined the Dominican Republic–Central America Free Trade Agreement (DR-CAFTA), a regional free trade agreement between the Central American countries, the Dominican Republic, and the United States. Before Nicaragua signed the agreement, there was substantial debate in the country, especially over concerns regarding the repercussions on poverty. Some feared poverty would become more widespread, particularly in rural areas. An ex ante impact assessment of DR-CAFTA showed that the openness in trade resulting from the agreement would yield positive overall welfare gains and poverty reduction effects, but that these, at best, would be small and that traditional agriculture and the rural poor would be among the likely losers (Sánchez and Vos 2006a, 2006b). Most welfare gains accruing to Nicaragua because of DR-CAFTA would arise from an export quota that would provide greater access to textile and clothing markets in the United States, while tariff cuts and expanded agroindustrial export quotas would contribute relatively little. However, the agreement would liberalize trade only with the United States. While the United States is the most important trading partner of Nicaragua, it was unclear if multilateral trade liberalization involving all the trading partners of the country would yield better outcomes in national welfare, poverty, and income inequality.

In this chapter, we provide a quantitative analysis addressing this question in the debate about the DR-CAFTA agreement, now signed. We do so using a computable general equilibrium (CGE) model for Nicaragua, coupled with a microsimulation methodology. The next section supplies background information on trade reform policies and macroeconomic trends in Nicaragua with special reference to the agricultural sector and rural poverty. The subsequent section describes the main features of the CGE model and the microsimulation methodology we use to assess the impact on poverty and inequality. We then lay out the model simulations we consider, which include the liberalization of agricultural trade and the liberalization of all merchandise goods trade by the rest of the world and by Nicaragua. In the following section, we provide a summary analysis of the results. This analysis includes tests for the sensitivity of the results with respect to assumptions regarding the responsiveness of trade to price liberalization, as identified through the relevant trade elasticities. The final section concludes and offers a discussion of possible policy implications.

## Trade Reform, Agricultural Development, and Poverty in Nicaragua

In this section, we describe the role of trade and agriculture in the economy of Nicaragua, the recent liberalization associated with DR-CAFTA, and the remaining national distortions to agricultural incentives. We then add a brief discussion on the nexus between agriculture and poverty in Nicaragua.

### Trade and agriculture

Agriculture is a mainstay of the economy of Nicaragua. Its share in GDP is larger in Nicaragua than in other Central and South American countries. The sector's growth in Nicaragua averaged a little over 4 percent per year between 1994 and 2006, keeping pace with the rest of the economy and thereby maintaining its contribution to real GDP at around 20 percent. The nominal share declined from 32 to 18 percent over the period, however, because factor costs in agriculture increased at a slower rate than the average for the economy as a whole (tables 14.1 and 14.2).

Agricultural activity is concentrated in the production of basic staple grains, which dominate in land use and among export crops. About 80 percent of the cultivated land is rainfed and planted with corn, beans, rice, and sorghum. Export crops such as coffee, sesame, sugar, tobacco, and peanuts occupy the other 20 percent of the arable land. Yet, basic staple grains contributed no more than 30 percent of agricultural GDP in 2006, while export crops contributed 50 percent, and other crops and livestock the remaining 20 percent.

**Table 14.1. Macroeconomic Indicators, Nicaragua, 1990–2005**
*(annual averages)*

| Indicator | 1990–94 | 1995–99 | 2000–05 |
|---|---|---|---|
| Average real wage growth rate, %[a] | −19.2 | 2.3 | 3.1 |
| Annual consumer price inflation, % | 2,096.3 | 11.2 | 7.7 |
| GDP growth rate, % | 0.6 | 5.4 | 3.2 |
| Agriculture | — | 4.6 | 4.0 |
| Industry | — | 6.2 | 3.9 |
| Services | — | 5.5 | 3.5 |
| Employment growth rate, % | 2.1 | 5.6 | 3.7 |
| Exports, plus imports, % of GDP | 66.4 | 66.1 | 76.6 |
| Exports of goods and services, % of GDP | 20.0 | 21.4 | 24.8 |
| Traditional exports[b] | | | |
| % of merchandise exports | 73.9 | 52.7 | 37.? |
| Annual growth rate, % | 1.8 | 10.8 | 0.9 |
| Nontraditional exports | | | |
| % of merchandise exports | 26.1 | 47.3 | 62.8 |
| Annual growth rate, % | 28.6 | 24.6 | 20.1 |
| Nontraditional exports, excluding *maquila*[c] | | | |
| % of merchandise exports | 24.7 | 33.0 | 40.0 |
| Annual growth rate, % | 16.6 | 17.5 | 12.1 |

*Sources:* World Development Indicators Database (2008) for GDP, exports of goods and services, inflation, and trade. All other data are from the Central Bank of Nicaragua.

*Note:* — = no data are available.

a. Data for the first period cover only 1991–94.
b. Traditional exports include coffee, bananas, sugar, bovine meat, cattle, seafood products (shrimp and lobster), sesame seeds, gold, and silver.
c. A *maquila* is a factory that imports raw materials free of tariffs for assembly or manufacturing and then exports the output, usually to the country that has supplied the raw materials.

Nicaragua's agricultural sector reached a high, but volatile rate of growth during the 1990s. Most of this growth was achieved by bringing more land under cultivation rather than through productivity gains, which occurred mostly in large-scale export agriculture (World Bank 2003). Between 1990 and 2000, the share of land under cultivation increased from 51 to 57 percent of the total land area, but the share has not expanded since then.

Agricultural exports account for 50 to 70 percent of Nicaragua's total merchandise export earnings. Coffee exports alone make up 25 to 30 percent of the total value of exports, depending on the price of coffee. Coffee has been a major engine of growth in Nicaragua. It contributed an average 5.3 percent of GDP and generated 32 percent of rural employment during the 1990s. About 30,000 households grow coffee, and another 150,000–200,000 households receive some part of their

**Table 14.2. Structure of Value Added by Sector at Factor Cost, Nicaragua, 1995, 2000, and 2004**

*(percent)*

| Sector | 1995 | 2000 | 2004 |
|---|---|---|---|
| Agriculture | 31.5 | 27.6 | 26.1 |
| Agriculture[a] | 23.4 | 20.9 | 17.8 |
| Light food processing[b] | 8.2 | 6.7 | 8.3 |
| Mining and quarrying | 0.7 | 0.8 | 1.4 |
| Manufacturing | 10.6 | 10.3 | 9.9 |
| Electricity, gas, and water supply | 2.0 | 3.3 | 3.1 |
| Construction | 5.9 | 7.0 | 5.9 |
| Services | 49.2 | 50.9 | 53.7 |
| Total | 100.0 | 100.0 | 100.0 |

*Sources:* Personal communication, Central Bank of Nicaragua.

a. Including livestock, forestry, and fishing.
b. Including processed food and excluding beverages and tobacco.

incomes through full- or part-time labor in coffee production, processing, or marketing. Together, coffee and fish have contributed about 40 percent of total exports since 2000.

Agricultural exports increased by only 20 percent between 1990 and 2006, much less than the increase elsewhere in Latin America. Traditional agricultural exports grew relatively well during the first half of the 1990s, but, since then, most growth has been dominated by nontraditional products, which now comprise almost two-thirds of total merchandise exports (table 14.1). Exports of all types recovered notably in the early 1990s following the end of the trade embargo by the United States and after the period of macroeconomic instability. Nontraditional export growth was stimulated by special export promotion measures, including the creation of an export processing zone. The zone has favored the development of the *maquila*-type production of textiles and wearing apparel, which is highly import dependent and, yet, has created many new jobs.[1] Nearly 40 percent of the nontraditional export growth during 2000–05 was accounted for by the maquila industry. Owing to its high import content, the maquila industry has only weak links with the rest of the economy.[2]

*Trade reform and DR-CAFTA*

Nicaragua joined the Central American Common Market in 1960 with the aim of pursuing deeper regional economic integration. Trade with the rest of the world was liberalized in the early 1990s following a decade of civil strife in Nicaragua and an international boycott. Around 1990, the pacification process was initiated, and financial and commercial relations with the United States and multilateral financial institutions were restored. Unilateral trade liberalization was part of a broader set of market-oriented reforms. Tariffs on imports were reduced, including in agricultural commodities and processed food products. Quantitative restrictions on imports and exports, import surcharges, and all state monopolies trading in food staples were phased out, and customs procedures were simplified. Most export taxes were eliminated in 1993, and the agricultural sector began benefiting from tax exemptions for imports of raw materials and capital goods. Temporary tax-credit certificates, used extensively in the 1990s to promote non-traditional exports, were subsequently eliminated. These reforms increased the degree of trade openness—the total share of exports and imports in GDP—from 66 to 77 percent of GDP between 1990–94 and 2000–05 (table 14.1). The greater trade openness has not boosted agricultural productivity, however. Empirical evidence suggests that the gains in productivity growth have been modest at best and are concentrated in the large-scale farm production of export crops, while productivity growth has been stagnant in smallholder farming (Deininger, Zegarra, and Lavadenz 2003; Bravo-Ortega and Lederman 2004; World Bank 2003).

The importance of the United States as Nicaragua's main trading partner is likely to increase through DR-CAFTA. In 2000–05, Nicaragua's exports to and imports from the United States represented 42 percent of total exports and 29 percent of total imports. Under DR-CAFTA, 92.5 percent of Nicaragua's trade with the United States will be fully liberalized over a period of 20 years, and, for many of the remaining products, the country's access to the markets of the United States will be enhanced through tariff rate quotas and other preferential access quotas. In return, Nicaragua is offering the United States greater access to its domestic markets. The weighted average tariff rate for imports from the United States in 2003, before the signing of DR-CAFTA, was around 6.2 percent; it is projected to fall to 0.2 percent by 2020. The agricultural sectors would initially benefit from greater protection against agricultural imports from the United States. The reduction in the tariffs on agricultural goods will be gradual, especially for sensitive products such as rice, beans, corn, meats, dairy products, and sugarcane. For some of these products, DR-CAFTA includes safeguard measures in the event of massive imports, and some of these products (such as white corn) have been excluded from the tariff reduction program. Even so, the cuts in the tariffs on agricultural imports from the United States would be ample: by 2020, the weighted average tariff rate should have dropped to 2.1 percent (figure 14.1). Domestic agricultural producers in Nicaragua fear that this trade opening will put many of them out of business and induce more rural poverty, especially if farmers in the United States continue to receive subsidies.

**Figure 14.1. Tariff Rates on Agricultural and Total Imports from the United States under DR-CAFTA, Nicaragua, 2003–20**

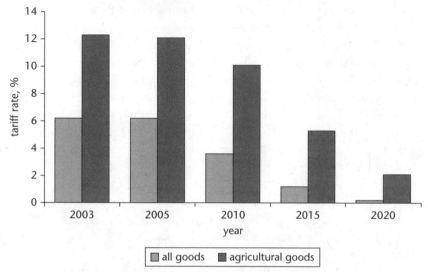

*Source:* Author construction based on data in Sánchez and Vos (2006b).

*Note:* The tariff rates are weighted average nominal rates. DR-CAFTA was implemented immediately after it was ratified on October 10, 2005.

The United States has also agreed to open its markets to Nicaraguan exporters under DR-CAFTA. Reductions in the tariffs on imports from Nicaragua are likely to have a minor impact because the tariffs are already fairly low and even nonexistent in some cases. This is because of unilateral preferences granted by the United States through the Generalized System of Preferences and the Caribbean Basin Initiative and its extensions.[3] Nearly 80 percent of Central America's exports to the United States are already subject to duty-free access owing to unilateral preferential programs of the United States (USTR 2005). It may therefore be expected that exports from Nicaragua to the United States will not increase notably through additional tariff cuts. However, DR-CAFTA makes previously unilateral preferential access permanent. The unilateral preferences of the United States may be revoked at any time for countries that do not have a trade agreement with the United States. Exports from Nicaragua to the United States are expected to increase more notably if tariff rate quotas granted by the United States are fully implemented. Nicaragua has also obtained temporary preferential access quotas, or tariff preference levels, that allow the use of third-country yarn and cloth if equal amounts of U.S. cloth are imported. In the case of Nicaragua, up to the equivalent of 100 million square meters of cloth would be allowed to enter the United States annually free from the restrictions of rules of origin for the first 10 years, a benefit arising from Nicaragua's status as a heavily indebted poor country.

### The distortions to farmer incentives

Domestically produced farm inputs are not subsidized in Nicaragua, but the agricultural sector (including the light processing of food) historically receives some output price support. Agricultural activities are generally untaxed.[4] Furthermore, imported inputs for agricultural production and some agroindustries are exempt from duties. Export taxes, which were nontrivial in the past, have generally been eliminated. Export subsidies are limited and are being phased out to comply with World Trade Organization commitments. Taken together, the average overall nominal rate of assistance (NRA) for farmers in Nicaragua has been close to zero since the early 1990s; import-competing assistance, which increased until 2000, but has since fallen to near zero, has been slightly more than offset by export taxes, which are levied on a production weighted basis (figure 14.2). The slightly negative NRA for tradable agricultural products contrasts with the average NRA for nonfarm tradables, which has been around 10 percent; so, the relative rate of assistance has fluctuated between −5 and −15 percent since the early 1990s (figure 14.3).[5] Since 2004, the direct influence

**Figure 14.2. The NRAs for Exportable, Importable, and All Covered Farm Products, Nicaragua, 1991–2004**

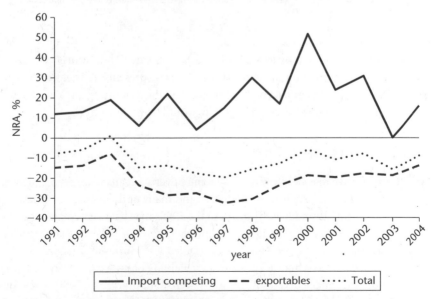

*Source:* Berthelon, Kruger, and Saavedra (2008).

**Figure 14.3. The NRAs for Agricultural and Nonagricultural Tradable Sectors and the RRAs for Farmers, Nicaragua, 1991–2004**

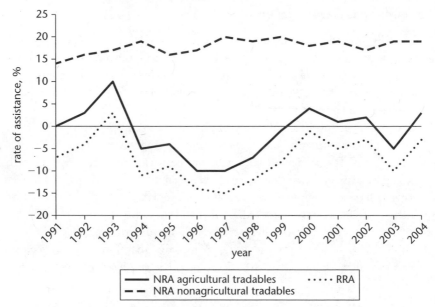

Source: Berthelon, Kruger, and Saavedra (2008).

Note: The relative rate of assistance (RRA) is defined as $100 * [(100 + NRAag^t)/(100 + NRAnonag^t) - 1]$, where $NRAag^t$ and $NRAnonag^t$ are the percentage NRAs for the tradables part of the agricultural and nonagricultural sectors, respectively.

of trade and agricultural policies on farm prices in Nicaragua has thus been rather modest. This is important for the simulation analysis we present below; it leads one to expect that the estimated impact on farm output and the economy generally from the elimination of agricultural taxes and subsidies would be small.

## Agriculture and poverty

Agricultural growth may be effective in reducing poverty because the vast majority of Nicaraguan farmers are small-scale producers, and many of them are poor. The agricultural sector's rapid, broadbased growth in the 1990s may have represented the single most important cause of the significant reduction in poverty that occurred between 1993 and 2001 (World Bank 2003; see table 14.3). However, the sources of this growth—high export commodity prices, the availability of unoccupied land, and the return to normalcy after a decade of civil war—were temporary. None of these factors should be expected to continue as pillars of sustained growth in the years ahead.

**Table 14.3. The Poverty Headcount Ratio and the Gini Coefficient
of Income Inequality, Nicaragua, 1993–2005**

| Indicator | 1993 | 1998 | 2001 | 2005 |
|---|---|---|---|---|
| Poverty headcount ratio at US$1 a day[a] | 44.0 | 42.2 | 43.0 | 39.4 |
| Urban | 26.0 | 24.9 | 27.5 | 22.3 |
| Rural | 69.2 | 62.8 | 64.7 | 60.7 |
| Poverty headcount ratio at US$2 a day[a] | 74.0 | 77.8 | 78.0 | 75.8 |
| Urban | 61.2 | 66.1 | 67.0 | 63.0 |
| Rural | 92.0 | 91.6 | 93.3 | 91.9 |
| Inequality in consumption, Gini coefficient[b] | 0.49 | 0.44 | 0.43 | 0.40 |
| Urban | 0.45 | 0.43 | 0.41 | 0.38 |
| Rural | 0.43 | 0.36 | 0.35 | 0.34 |
| Income inequality, Gini coefficient[c] | 0.58 | 0.58 | 0.58 | — |
| Urban | 0.55 | 0.55 | 0.56 | — |
| Rural | 0.54 | 0.56 | 0.51 | |

*Sources:* Data of the National Institute of Statistics and the Census, except for the Gini coefficient for income inequality, which is from ECLAC (2008).

*Note:* — = no data are available.

a. The share of the population whose per capita consumption is below the respective poverty line.
b. Inequality in the distribution of per capita consumption.
c. Inequality in the distribution of per capita household income.

Indeed, the world prices for Nicaragua's main export crops were subject to declines and substantial volatility in 1998–2001 such that poverty increased in some rural areas, especially in the principal coffee-growing areas of the central region, where the farmers are most vulnerable to price shocks. National-level poverty continued to decline though, mainly because of the reconstruction boom, which followed Hurricane Mitch (late 1998) and came to an end in 2001. After 2001, the buoyant commodity prices in world markets, including coffee and basic grain prices, helped boost agricultural incomes; this led to another period of declining rural poverty. The enhanced living conditions were clearly not underpinned by any substantial improvements in farm productivity, but rather by more favorable world market conditions.

## Modeling the Macro-Micro Impact of Trade Liberalization

We now examine the impact on national economic welfare, inequality, and poverty of price-distorting agricultural and trade policies at home and abroad in 2004, the most recent year for which there is a complete data set of such policy measures for the world. (The data have been compiled by Anderson and

Valenzuela 2008 and made available for modelers by Valenzuela and Anderson 2008.) To provide a quantitative ex ante assessment of the effects of the removal of these policies, we use a CGE model of Nicaragua tailored for the analysis of income distribution and poverty. The model builds on our earlier analyses (for example, Sánchez and Vos 2006a, 2006b) that link a country-specific CGE model and a microsimulation methodology. A distinctive feature of the analysis we present in this chapter is the use we make of the World Bank's global Linkage model to provide the external shocks on the terms of trade caused by rest-of-the-world trade liberalization. We also use, for the first time, the new estimates compiled by Anderson and Valenzuela (2008) on farm price distortions in developing countries, including Nicaragua, to assess the impact of rest-of-the-world trade reform on the country's income inequality and poverty. The World Bank global Linkage model is already well documented (see van der Mensbrugghe 2005). We therefore now describe only the CGE model for Nicaragua.

### Theoretical foundations of the national CGE model

To analyze the impact on Nicaragua of agricultural and total trade liberalization, we use a CGE framework that consists of a static block and a dynamic block. The static part of the model provides within-period equilibrium solutions, starting from the base year, and it shares most of the features of the generic CGE model developed at the International Food Policy Research Institute and documented in Lofgren, Harris, and Robinson (2002).[6] The main changes we have made to the generic model are the inclusion of bilateral trade in import and export functions and in an export demand function, a decomposition of foreign savings into capital flows and foreign direct investment, and a wage function to deal with sector-specific conditions regarding wage indexation and labor market adjustment.[7]

The dynamic part of the model is recursive in the sense that it connects the within-period equilibrium solutions over time through lagged variables and through updates of stock variables (particularly factors of production) and selected parameters that are either fixed or absent in the first within-period solution. We consistently link all within-period equilibrium solutions for the desired number of simulation periods (years) to generate the baseline scenario.[8]

We model trade using a standard Armington constant elasticity of substitution function that defines optimal combinations of domestically produced and imported commodities. The model also includes an export supply function of the standard constant elasticity of transformation format, although exports are effectively driven in the model by world demand (see below). Both the export and the import functions are adapted to account for bilateral agreements with trading partners (see Sánchez and Vos 2009, appendix, equations 21–2 and 25–6). Tariff reductions may be simulated by adjusting the tariff parameter in the equation that determines the domestic prices of imports by commodity and trading partner (see Sánchez and Vos 2009, appendix, equation 1). Likewise, changes in export taxes and subsidies are transmitted through an equation that defines the domestic price of exports by commodity and trading partner. The world import prices involved in determining domestic prices may be manipulated to impose shocks in the terms of trade.

The model also specifies an export demand function by commodity and by trading partner (see above). The function serves to link Nicaragua's CGE model to a global trade model and facilitates simulations of the worldwide liberalization of trade and domestic agricultural prices. The global Linkage model of the World Bank is used to simulate the liberalization of trade and agricultural policies in the world, excluding Nicaragua. These simulation results provide information on the expected changes in world import and export prices and in the demand for Nicaraguan exports; these changes are subsequently imposed on the Nicaraguan CGE model.[9] Unlike typical country models, global trade models generally do not use constant elasticity of transformation functions to define the export supply behavior of individual countries. Instead, they assume downward-sloping export demand schedules derived from the Armington assumption applied to the import behavior of trading partners. To match information from both types of models, we did not remove the constant elasticity of transformation function from the Nicaraguan CGE model, but, instead, gave the high value of 20 to the elasticities of transformation such that the constant elasticity of transformation function no longer has any major influence on export supply behavior and exports become, in effect, driven by demand shifts.[10] By implication, the small country assumption no longer holds.

### The factor market closure rules

In the base year solution, we have assumed that capital is underutilized and fixed and may not be reallocated across sectors. Activity-specific rents assure that fixed activity utilization levels are consistent with profit maximization through a flexible adjustment of activity-specific wage-distortion factors.[11] Firms are allowed to increase their capacity utilization rate in response to an increase in the demand for capital in the subsequent period solutions, however, such that capital is no longer fixed. The capital market begins to clear through a flexible adjustment in the economy-wide rent, while the activity-specific wage-distortion factor remains fixed. Aggregate real investment generated at the end of each period is reallocated for use as capital in the next period. We do this by allowing activities with higher past profitability to gain larger shares of investable funds, as suggested in Dervis, de Melo, and Robinson (1982). The ratio of aggregate real investment at the end of the past period to the aggregate capital stock at the beginning of the past period determines the growth in capital stock in sectors and in the economy. The initial economy-wide and sectoral stocks of capital in any given period (excluding the base year) are defined as the capital stocks of the past period, adjusted by the growth rate of the capital stocks, less the rate of depreciation.

Labor is classified by occupational category (wage and nonwage), skill level (skilled and unskilled), and gender (men and women). We assume that the quantity of the labor demand for each type is endogenous in all period solutions and for all activities except in fishing and mining. We assume that labor supply increases at constant population growth rates for each category. We specify wage adjustment rules as much as possible in accordance with the existing institutional setting of labor markets in Nicaragua. The market clears in all segments (with a few exceptions) through adjustments in the level of employment, implying that there is unemployment in the economy, and activity-specific wages are fixed. Wages are not fully fixed for unskilled or skilled workers in government services and public utility sectors, but are indexed to consumer prices following trade-union bargaining. Another exception is workers in the fishing and mining sectors; in the case of Nicaragua, these workers tend to face difficulties in finding jobs in other sectors. Hence, labor is assumed to be specific to these two sectors, that is, the demand for workers in these sectors is fixed, and the activity-specific wage equilibrates the labor market (through changes in the activity-specific wage-distortion factor).

### The macroeconomic closure rules

The macroclosure rules are the same in the base year and all other period solutions. In the fiscal adjustment process, we assume that government savings are fixed (at the base year level) and that direct tax rates adjust to maintain real government spending and fiscal balance. For the purposes of our analysis, we keep the distributional effects of the changes in direct tax rates neutral across domestic institutions. This government closure rule enables us to calculate the amount of direct taxes that would need to be collected to compensate for any loss of revenue from the taxes on trade (net of any subsidy change) in each trade liberalization simulation. The exchange rate adjusts to maintain a fixed current account balance in nominal terms (that is, foreign savings are fixed). Investment is driven by savings; thus, we use fixed marginal propensities to save so that the private savings of domestic nongovernmental institutions are determined endogenously. Aggregate investment passively adjusts to match aggregate savings.

*Model calibration and the baseline*

We implement the base year calibration of the Nicaraguan CGE model using a social accounting matrix for 2000. We have compiled this matrix in collaboration with government experts in Nicaragua.[12] The key economic activities and commodities relevant for the analysis of trade liberalization, including special entries for the commodities produced in the export processing zone, are all captured in the matrix. Nicaragua's social accounting matrix (and CGE model) has 40 productive sectors and the same number of commodities. In addition, the matrix has external accounts for trade and other current account flows, which are disaggregated by main trading partner.

Because 2000 is the base year of the social accounting matrix, the model is solved recursively up to 2004 to enable us to conduct counterfactual simulations of what would happen if the protection structure were fully dismantled in 2004. Prior to conducting the counterfactual simulations, the matrix was complemented with other data to generate two alternative baseline scenarios for the period from 2000 to 2004. In the first baseline scenario, we have solved the dynamic recursive CGE model using two types of Armington elasticities that we have borrowed from the World Bank global Linkage model. At the top level of the nested function are the elasticities of substitution between domestic goods and aggregate imports. We have used these in the Nicaraguan CGE model to calibrate the Armington function exponent. At the second level are the elasticities of substitution across imports, which, in general, are defined as the top-level elasticities, times two. In the Nicaraguan CGE model, we have used these to calibrate the export demand function exponent. In the second baseline scenario, the Armington elasticities are parameter values that we have estimated using country-specific data and sensitivity analysis.[13] The country-specific Armington elasticities range from 0.46 to 1.42 for the top-level elasticities and from 0.83 to 2.83 for the second-level elasticities, while those in the global Linkage model are between 2.08 and 5.91 and between 4.16 and 11.82, respectively. Hence, trade liberalization policies would likely produce weaker trade effects in Nicaragua if country-specific elasticities were used. Consequently, different assumptions regarding the Armington elasticities may also yield different welfare effects.[14]

The two baseline scenarios differ solely in the Armington elasticities. We have estimated all other model parameters and elasticities based on country-specific data, as explained in more detail in Sánchez and Vos (2006b), where the data sources and the estimation methods are listed and described. In addition, we have taken base year employment and population data from the employment and wages survey produced by the National Institute of Statistics and the Census of Nicaragua for November 2000. Both the population and the labor force grow according to estimations provided to us by the institute for 2001–04.

The two baseline scenarios also account for an exogenous update in several parameters. We have updated trade taxes and subsidies for 2001–04 using data of the Customs Office of the Ministry of Finance of Nicaragua. We have additionally adjusted the agricultural protection structure to make it compatible with the corresponding structure generated for 2004 by Berthelon, Kruger, and Saavedra (2008), which is also the structure used for Nicaragua in the global Linkage model. For this purpose, the global Linkage model was calibrated using version 7 of the Global Trade Analysis Project protection database for 2004 once this had been amended to incorporate new estimates of distortions to agricultural and food markets in developing countries.[15] To complete the recursive calibration of Nicaragua's CGE model, we have also updated world export and import prices to 2004 using trade price deflators provided by the Central Bank of Nicaragua. We have also updated autonomous foreign direct investment (and, implicitly, foreign savings) for 2001–04 using data from the Central Bank of Nicaragua. Lastly, we have exogenously updated total factor productivity to enable the reproduction of actual economic growth during 2001–04.

### Modeling the impact on poverty

Because CGE models typically only specify a limited number of representative households, they provide insufficient detail regarding changes in income distribution and expenditures to allow one to make robust statements regarding poverty outcomes. In consequence, the CGE analysis needs to be supplemented by certain assumptions (such as fixed within-group distributions) or, as we have done for the empirical analysis reported here, by a microsimulation method that applies the labor market outcomes (relative remunerations, employment, changes in skill levels) from the CGE model for different types of workers to a microdata set (based on a household survey) to obtain the required detail about income distribution for the poverty analysis. Bourguignon, Robilliard, and Robinson (2002), Ganuza, Barros, and Vos (2002), and Vos et al. (2006) offer a discussion and application of such methods in conjunction with CGE model analysis. The approach we follow here is that of Ganuza, Barros, and Vos (2002) and Vos et al. (2006), which was designed for application in the context of a static CGE model. This method adjusts the original labor market structure ($\lambda$) as observed in a household survey to simulate the sequential effects of a new labor market structure ($\lambda^*$) with consequent changes in employment, household income, and employment and income distribution. The original labor market structure, that is,

$$\lambda = f(P_j, U_j, S_{jk}, O_{jk}, W1_{jk}, W2, M_{jk}), \tag{14.1}$$

is adjusted using simulated CGE labor market outcomes to obtain the new labor market structure, that is,

$$\lambda^* = f(P_j^*, U_j^*, S_{jk}^*, O_{jk}^*, W1_{jk}^*, W2^*, M_{jk}^*), \tag{14.2}$$

where $P$ and $U$, respectively, are the participation and unemployment rates for labor type $j$; $S$ and $O$ represent the structure of employment by, respectively, sector and occupational category for labor type $j$ in segment $k$; $W1$ is the relative remuneration (that is, relative to the mean) for labor type $j$ in segment $k$; $W2$ is the average consumption wage per worker; and $M$ is the structure of employment by the skill (education) level of workers of type $j$ in segment $k$.

In the microsimulation procedure, we assume that workers move among occupational situations and economic sectors according to a random process in a normal distribution. We generate confidence intervals using a Monte Carlo procedure. A more elaborate exposition of this procedure and the related assumptions is found in Ganuza, Barros, and Vos (2002) and Vos et al. (2006). Meanwhile, for the application of this microsimulation methodology in a dynamic setting, a number of additional assumptions are required because observed survey data are only available for the base year (and a few subsequent years). In essence, we assume that no demographic shifts (such as migration or population aging) take place during the simulation period. This is an obvious limitation of the methodology, but justifiable to the extent that the CGE model does not model or consider such demographic change either. Thus, we essentially use the labor market outcomes in the CGE model scenarios to generate labor market structures for $t$ periods ($\lambda_t$ and $\lambda_t^*$) and apply them to a single microdata set (for a given $t$).[16]

We have implemented the microsimulation methodology using the 2001 round of the Living Standards Measurement Study of the National Institute of Statistics and the Census. The CGE model provides baseline and simulation results for the parameters of the labor market structure for 2000–04.[17] We have imposed the changes in the labor market structure with respect to 2001 on the Living Standards Measurement Study, and this has enabled us to generate poverty and inequality indicators for the baseline and the simulated scenarios. Before implementing this method, we have adjusted per capita household incomes to be able to reproduce the official poverty figures of the National Institute of Statistics and the Census for 2001. We have produced these by comparing per capita consumption rather than per capita income with respect to different total and extreme poverty lines. We have followed two steps. First, we have matched per capita household income with per capita consumption among nonpoor families the per capita incomes of which were lower than their per capita consumption and among poor families the per capita incomes of which were above their per capita consumption. Second, for some families, we have detected that their labor incomes are larger than their total incomes; we have imputed the difference to total family income.

Our adjusted per capita household income is defined as follows:

$$ypc_h = \frac{1}{n_h}\left[\sum_{i=1}^{n_h} yp_{hi} + yq_h\right], \tag{14.3}$$

where $n_h$ is the size of household $h$; $yp_{hi}$ is the labor income of member $i$ of household $h$; and $yq_h$ is the sum of all nonlabor incomes of the household, defined as:

$$yq_h = \sum_{i=1}^{n_h} yqp_{hi} + yqt_h, \tag{14.4}$$

where $yqp_{hi}$ is the individual nonlabor income of member $i$ of household $h$, and $yqt_h$ is other household incomes. In the simulations, $yp_{hi}$ is altered for some individuals $i$ of household $h$ as a result of changes in the labor market parameters.

We have used the endogenous poverty lines produced through the CGE model to generate the poverty results and to generate the poverty effect of trade liberalization through the cost of basic consumption. We have first calibrated the US\$1-a-day and US\$2-a-day poverty lines (at purchasing power parity) using the 2001 round of the Living Standards Measurement Study to replicate the official poverty numbers for 2001 of the National Institute of Statistics and the Census.[18] We have transformed the calibrated real poverty lines for 2001 into monetary poverty lines for all years in the simulation period (that is, 2000–04). For this purpose, we have used the composite (consumption) price for each commodity from the CGE model, which, for all commodities, has been indexed to unity in 2001. For all other years, the composite price of each commodity differs from 1. We have measured the influence of the composite price of each commodity in the computation of the monetary poverty lines for all years of the simulation period through commodity-based weights (that is, using the gamma parameter in the linear expenditure system of the CGE model; see Sánchez and Vos 2009, appendix, equation 34).

## Liberalization Simulations

We are interested in assessing the impact, particularly on the poor in Nicaragua, arising from the removal of all forms of trade protection and farm price support measures in Nicaragua and in the rest of the world. Because most of the policies that were distorting agricultural incentives in Nicaragua were eliminated during the 1990s, we expect additional own-country liberalization to have only a limited impact. The elimination of the much more substantial distortions in the rest of the world, especially in agriculture, may be more important for farmers in Nicaragua because of the impact this would have on the border prices for agricultural products.

To assess the welfare implications of the various levels of trade and domestic price liberalization in Nicaragua that would result from unilateral and rest-of-the-world reforms, we have performed four static simulations and assessed their impacts through comparisons with the two alternative baselines. We have simulated the liberalization of trade through the removal of trade (import and export) taxes and subsidies for all tradable commodities, as well as all agricultural domestic supports.[19] The four simulations are as follows:

- *trdlib1*: the unilateral liberalization of trade in agricultural commodities and the domestic markets for agriculture
- *trdlib2*: the unilateral liberalization of trade in all tradable commodities and the domestic markets for agriculture
- *trdlib3*: the worldwide liberalization of trade in agricultural commodities and the domestic markets for agriculture, that is, simulation *trdlib1*, plus the changes in export and import prices (terms of trade shocks) resulting from the rest-of-the-world elimination of agricultural support measures
- *trdlib4*: the worldwide liberalization of trade in all tradable commodities and the domestic prices for agriculture, that is, simulation *trdlib2*, plus the changes in export and import prices (terms of trade shocks) resulting from the rest-of-the-world liberalization of all trade, including the elimination of agricultural support measures

Because Nicaragua has already liberalized most of its domestic agricultural markets, simulations *trdlib1* and *trdlib2* reflect mainly the impact of the removal of the remaining import tariffs. The worldwide trade liberalization scenarios (*trdlib3* and *trdlib4*) reflect, in addition, the effects on export and import prices in Nicaragua that such reform is expected to generate. We have performed all four simulations as static simulations as of 2004 because the global Linkage model is calibrated with data for 2004. We have calibrated the base run of the model so as to reproduce an agricultural protection structure consistent with that of the global Linkage model.

## The Effects of Agricultural and Trade Liberalization

The changes in the export and import prices of Nicaragua in the global Linkage model after worldwide agricultural and nonagricultural trade liberalization through simulations *trdlib3* and *trdlib4* are shown in table 14.4. The border price changes are shown for the commodity breakdown in the global Linkage model. For our present analysis, we have reweighted these changes to fit the commodity

**Table 14.4. Trade Structure and World Price Shocks Imposed in the Global Trade Liberalization Simulations, Nicaragua, 2004**

*(percent)*

| Sector | Shares in exports | World export price, % change over 2004 trdlib3 | World export price, % change over 2004 trdlib4 | Shares in imports | World import price, % change over 2004 trdlib3 | World import price, % change over 2004 trdlib4 |
|---|---|---|---|---|---|---|
| Paddy rice | 0.00 | 0.00 | 0.00 | 1.39 | 9.66 | 8.52 |
| Wheat | 0.00 | 0.00 | 0.00 | 1.72 | 3.13 | 2.06 |
| Other grains | 0.00 | 0.00 | 0.00 | 0.48 | 17.64 | 16.42 |
| Oilseeds | 2.81 | 7.18 | 6.11 | 0.00 | 0.00 | 0.00 |
| Vegetables and fruits | 2.62 | 0.70 | −0.18 | 0.31 | 4.55 | 2.62 |
| Other crops | 7.91 | 0.92 | −0.12 | 0.26 | 9.15 | 7.17 |
| Sugarcane and beets | 0.00 | 0.00 | 0.00 | 0.00 | 0.00 | 0.00 |
| Plant-based fibers | 0.00 | 0.00 | 0.00 | 0.00 | 0.00 | 0.00 |
| Other primary products | 0.98 | 0.97 | −2.21 | 4.46 | 2.09 | −0.47 |
| Cattle, sheep, and so on | 2.09 | 6.91 | 5.36 | 0.06 | 21.03 | 18.65 |
| Other livestock | 0.07 | −0.11 | −1.62 | 0.43 | 3.72 | 1.70 |
| Raw milk | 0.00 | 0.00 | 0.00 | 0.00 | 0.00 | 0.00 |
| Wool | 0.00 | 0.00 | 0.00 | 0.00 | 0.00 | 0.00 |
| Beef and sheep meat | 6.88 | 6.04 | 4.97 | 0.34 | 3.12 | 2.02 |
| Other meat products | 0.14 | 10.21 | 8.98 | 0.17 | 7.74 | 5.92 |
| Vegetable oils and fats | 0.59 | −1.19 | −1.77 | 2.58 | 1.29 | −0.08 |
| Processed rice | 0.00 | 0.00 | 0.00 | 0.16 | 1.11 | −0.07 |
| Dairy products | 1.86 | 2.39 | 0.99 | 0.30 | 7.72 | 5.82 |
| Refined sugar | 2.24 | 6.44 | 5.21 | 0.00 | 0.00 | 0.00 |
| Other food, beverages, and tobacco | 8.97 | 0.22 | 2.85 | 6.74 | 1.42 | 1.15 |
| Textiles and wearing apparel | 35.59 | 0.75 | 1.94 | 13.87 | 0.63 | 0.21 |
| Other manufactured goods | 13.07 | 0.48 | −2.11 | 56.30 | 1.02 | 0.01 |
| Services | 14.18 | 0.22 | −0.20 | 10.42 | 0.16 | −0.36 |

*Source:* Linkage model simulations of van der Mensbrugghe, Valenzuela, and Anderson (see the appendix).

*Note:* See the text for an explanation of the simulations.

classification of the Nicaragua CGE model.[20] The table shows that export and import prices would increase among most commodity groups. In the reclassified commodity groupings of the Nicaragua model, there would be a decline only in other manufactures in the simulation of the worldwide trade liberalization of all goods (*trdlib4*). For virtually all other industries, the simulated worldwide liberalization would result in higher export and import prices in Nicaragua.

In aggregate, the terms of trade of Nicaragua would improve by a slight 0.3 and 1.2 percent in the global simulations used as inputs for *trdlib3* and *trdlib4*, respectively. Table 14.5 shows that export prices would increase an average of 1.8 and 1.5 percent, respectively, in the two simulations, while import prices would rise by, respectively,

## Table 14.5. The Impact of Prospective Trade Liberalization on the Macroeconomy, Nicaragua, 2004

*(percent deviation from the baseline)*

| Indicator | trdlib1 | trdlib2 | trdlib3 | trdlib4 |
|---|---|---|---|---|
| GDP, factor cost | | | | |
| Simulations with global Linkage model elasticities | 0.3 | 0.5 | 1.2 | 1.5 |
| Simulations with country-specific elasticities | 0.4 | 0.8 | 0.7 | 1.1 |
| Private consumption | | | | |
| Simulations with global Linkage model elasticities | 1.1 | 1.6 | 1.7 | 2.7 |
| Simulations with country-specific elasticities | 0.8 | 1.5 | 0.9 | 2.0 |
| Fixed investment | | | | |
| Simulations with global Linkage model elasticities | 1.1 | 3.4 | 1.4 | 4.7 |
| Simulations with country-specific elasticities | 0.9 | 3.1 | 0.9 | 3.8 |
| Exports | | | | |
| Simulations with global Linkage model elasticities | 6.9 | 10.0 | 11.6 | 14.1 |
| Simulations with country-specific elasticities | 2.1 | 4.0 | 3.8 | 5.0 |
| Imports | | | | |
| Simulations with global Linkage model elasticities | 4.5 | 7.5 | 6.4 | 10.0 |
| Simulations with country-specific elasticities | 1.9 | 4.3 | 2.6 | 5.2 |
| Real exchange rate | | | | |
| Simulations with global Linkage model elasticities | −1.4 | −2.8 | −3.6 | −4.6 |
| Simulations with country-specific elasticities | −1.2 | −3.1 | −3.2 | −4.4 |
| World export price | | | | |
| Simulations with global Linkage model elasticities | 0.0 | 0.0 | 1.8 | 1.5 |
| Simulations with country-specific elasticities | 0.0 | 0.0 | 1.8 | 1.5 |
| World import price | | | | |
| Simulations with global Linkage model elasticities | 0.0 | 0.0 | 1.3 | 0.3 |
| Simulations with country-specific elasticities | 0.0 | 0.0 | 1.3 | 0.3 |
| Terms of trade | | | | |
| Simulations with global Linkage model elasticities | 0.0 | 0.0 | 0.3 | 1.2 |
| Simulations with country-specific elasticities | 0.0 | 0.0 | 0.3 | 1.2 |
| Consumer price index | | | | |
| Simulations with global Linkage model elasticities | −0.8 | −1.5 | −0.9 | −1.7 |
| Simulations with country-specific elasticities | −0.7 | −1.4 | −0.8 | −1.5 |

*Source:* Nicaraguan CGE model simulations by the authors.

*Note:* See the text for an explanation of the simulations. Real government consumption is assumed to be fixed in the model such that this variable is not expected to change with respect to the baseline in the trade liberalization simulations.

1.3 and 0.3 percent. The resource allocation effects depend critically on the impact of the trade liberalization on the real exchange rate and domestic (consumer) prices. The real exchange rate appreciates in all simulations; the more comprehensive the trade liberalization, the more significant the appreciation. The initial relative price shock favors exports more than import demand in all simulations. Consequently, the (nominal) trade deficit narrows. Given the external closure rule that keeps foreign savings fixed, the exchange rate adjusts. The real exchange rate appreciation of 1 to 4 percent causes positive second-round effects on import demand and negative effects on exports, weakening the final impact on the real trade balance. However, only in the simulations using the lower country-specific Armington elasticities for the combined agricultural and nonagricultural price liberalization (*trdlib2* and *trdlib4*) does real import demand grow more than exports.

Domestic consumer prices unambiguously fall with respect to the baseline in all the simulations. As expected, the decline is greater if agricultural and nonagricultural commodities are liberalized together and if the liberalization is global rather than only unilateral. The trade opening would also allow private consumption to grow because of the simulated decline in consumer prices. Private investment expands in all simulations (table 14.5).

Real exchange rate appreciation tends to stimulate economic activity in Nicaragua. This outcome, which is embedded in the empirical structure of the country CGE model, occurs because production costs fall in the highly import-dependent Nicaraguan economy and because of the real wage effects under conditions of unemployment. While such stimulus is at work in our simulations, the relative price shifts resulting from trade liberalization appear equally important. Thus, traditional exports (especially coffee and livestock), some manufacturing sectors, construction, and services expand in almost all simulations, although to varying degrees (table 14.6). Farmers cultivating basic grains lose under all simulations because their protection is fully dismantled. Important manufacturing sectors (sugar processing and other food processing) also suffer from the trade opening in most simulations, though less so if we assume the lower country-specific Armington elasticities. Output in the export processing zone suffers heavily in the simulations involving nonagricultural trade liberalization because producers face rising costs for imported inputs that are exacerbated by the exchange rate appreciation and by the full exposure to global competition in the markets for textiles and garments. Thus, much of the maquila industry would lose its competitive edge without preferential market access and support measures. The relatively small industrial sectors with links to livestock production and fishery (dairy products and processed meats and fish) are among the winners in these liberalization simulations.

In aggregate, the national economic welfare gains are modest, but they are somewhat larger if we assume the higher Armington elasticities in the global Linkage model. In the latter case, compared with the baseline, GDP increases

## Table 14.6. The Impact of Prospective Trade Liberalization on Real Sectoral GDP, Nicaragua

*(percent)*

| Sector | Share in real base year GDP | Deviation from the baseline | | | |
|---|---|---|---|---|---|
| | | trdlib1 | trdlib2 | trdlib3 | trdlib4 |
| *Coffee* | | | | | |
| Simulations with global Linkage model elasticities | 3.2 | 8.6 | 17.8 | 28.0 | 41.4 |
| Simulations with country-specific elasticities | 3.2 | 2.6 | 7.1 | 8.3 | 12.9 |
| *Sugarcane* | | | | | |
| Simulations with global Linkage model elasticities | 0.9 | 0.3 | 1.3 | −1.9 | −0.4 |
| Simulations with country-specific elasticities | 0.9 | 0.0 | 0.1 | −0.7 | −0.5 |
| *Basic grains* | | | | | |
| Simulations with global Linkage model elasticities | 3.9 | −7.4 | −7.7 | −5.6 | −5.9 |
| Simulations with country-specific elasticities | 3.9 | −2.4 | −2.5 | −1.7 | −1.7 |
| *Other agricultural production* | | | | | |
| Simulations with global Linkage model elasticities | 4.0 | 1.0 | 2.6 | 5.6 | 7.2 |
| Simulations with country-specific elasticities | 4.0 | 0.4 | 1.0 | 1.1 | 1.8 |
| *Livestock farming* | | | | | |
| Simulations with global Linkage model elasticities | 6.0 | 2.4 | 6.9 | 1.4 | 6.5 |
| Simulations with country-specific elasticities | 6.0 | 0.6 | 2.6 | −0.2 | 1.8 |
| *Forestry, logging, and related service activities* | | | | | |
| Simulations with global Linkage model elasticities | 1.1 | 0.0 | −0.6 | 0.7 | 0.5 |
| Simulations with country-specific elasticities | 1.1 | 0.2 | 0.4 | 0.4 | 1.0 |
| *Fishing* | | | | | |
| Simulations with global Linkage model elasticities | 1.5 | 2.7 | 7.2 | 1.6 | 6.6 |
| Simulations with country-specific elasticities | 1.5 | 0.7 | 2.7 | 0.0 | 2.0 |
| *Mining and quarrying* | | | | | |
| Simulations with global Linkage model elasticities | 0.8 | −0.7 | −1.4 | −1.6 | −3.0 |
| Simulations with country-specific elasticities | 0.8 | −0.7 | −0.9 | 0.3 | 0.5 |
| *Production, processing, and preservation of meat and fish* | | | | | |
| Simulations with global Linkage model elasticities | 1.8 | 4.8 | 13.6 | 2.7 | 12.1 |
| Simulations with country-specific elasticities | 1.8 | 1.2 | 4.7 | −0.3 | 3.0 |

*(Table continues on the following page.)*

**Table 14.6. The Impact of Prospective Trade Liberalization on Real Sectoral GDP, Nicaragua (*continued*)**

*(percent)*

| Sector | Share in real base year GDP | Deviation from the baseline | | | |
|---|---|---|---|---|---|
| | | trdlib1 | trdlib2 | trdlib3 | trdlib4 |
| *Production, processing, and preservation of sugar* | | | | | |
| Simulations with global Linkage model elasticities | 1.0 | −0.2 | 0.3 | −2.8 | −2.0 |
| Simulations with country-specific elasticities | 1.0 | −0.3 | −0.8 | −1.3 | −1.7 |
| *Manufacture of dairy products* | | | | | |
| Simulations with global Linkage model elasticities | 1.0 | −0.8 | −0.5 | 1.1 | 1.8 |
| Simulations with country-specific elasticities | 1.0 | 0.2 | 0.4 | 0.3 | 0.6 |
| *Manufacture of other food products* | | | | | |
| Simulations with global Linkage model elasticities | 2.2 | −6.3 | −7.0 | −6.6 | −7.6 |
| Simulations with country-specific elasticities | 2.2 | −0.5 | −0.6 | −0.5 | −0.4 |
| *Zona franca, export processing zone* | | | | | |
| Simulations with global Linkage model elasticities | 1.4 | 3.6 | −23.8 | 10.6 | −24.4 |
| Simulations with country-specific elasticities | 1.4 | 0.9 | −10.3 | 2.9 | −11.1 |
| *Other manufacturing* | | | | | |
| Simulations with global Linkage model elasticities | 8.1 | 0.0 | 0.0 | 0.0 | 0.0 |
| Simulations with country-specific elasticities | 8.1 | 0.0 | 0.0 | 0.0 | 0.0 |
| *Electricity, gas, and water supply* | | | | | |
| Simulations with global Linkage model elasticities | 3.1 | 0.1 | −0.4 | 0.2 | −0.3 |
| Simulations with country-specific elasticities | 3.1 | 0.1 | −0.1 | 0.2 | 0.0 |
| *Construction* | | | | | |
| Simulations with global Linkage model elasticities | 7.8 | 0.4 | 1.7 | 0.5 | 2.3 |
| Simulations with country-specific elasticities | 7.8 | 0.4 | 1.5 | 0.3 | 1.8 |
| *Services* | | | | | |
| Simulations with global Linkage model elasticities | 52.3 | 0.0 | −0.3 | 0.6 | 0.4 |
| Simulations with country-specific elasticities | 52.3 | 0.0 | 0.3 | 0.3 | 0.6 |

*Source:* Nicaraguan CGE model simulations by the authors.

*Note:* See the text for an explanation of the simulations. The base year is 2000.

by 0.3 percent after the unilateral liberalization in agricultural trade (*trdlib1*) and by 0.5 percent after the unilateral removal of all price distortions under *trdlib2* (table 14.5). If we use the lower country-specific Armington elasticities, the output gains are slightly higher: 0.4 and 0.8 percent, respectively. The difference is explained by the fact that, at lower Armington elasticities, the domestic consumer response to the cheaper imports of basic grains and some manufactured food products is weaker than in the case of the Armington elasticities in the global Linkage model. The output in basic grains and other manufacturing consequently suffers less (table 14.6). The direction of the change is generally the same under the simulations involving worldwide trade liberalization, but the effects are more significant because the global Linkage model results suggest that the associated Armington elasticities would generate positive effects on the terms of trade of Nicaragua. Compared with the baseline, aggregate GDP would be 1.2 percent higher under *trdlib3* and 1.5 percent higher under *trdlib4* (table 14.5). Greater import competition continues to affect the farmers producing basic grains, as well as some of the food processing, but the impact is less unfavorable compared with the outcomes of unilateral trade and domestic price liberalization (table 14.6). The welfare effects of worldwide trade liberalization are much less significant, yet still positive, if we use the lower country-specific Armington elasticities. This is because the responsiveness of domestic producers to the larger world demand for Nicaraguan exports and higher world market prices is weaker.

### The fiscal cost of trade liberalization

The government closure rule of the model assumes a fixed fiscal deficit. Consequently, to maintain the baseline fiscal balance, domestic tax rates need to adjust for any possible gains or losses in trade tax revenue. In the model, we make direct taxes adjust (neutrally) to accommodate. Total government revenue falls initially in all trade liberalization simulations.[21] As shown in figure 14.4, the fiscal costs are not trivial and would be almost 2 percent of GDP under *trdlib2* and *trdlib4*. In the model simulations, we assume that the government is able to raise sufficient extra direct taxes in this way. A reduction in trade barriers only gradually would render this more feasible, such as in the case of DR-CAFTA, and might also allow time to raise funds through public borrowing if this is needed over the short term.

### The labor market effects

The potential productivity gains from trade openness are treated exogenously in the CGE model for Nicaragua. Hence, the simulated output gains from trade liberalization are realized through the greater use of factors of production, especially labor. Employment and real labor incomes generally follow the output effects. Aggregate employment would increase moderately in the unilateral trade liberalization simulations (*trdlib1* and *trdlib2*) and slightly more under the

**Figure 14.4. The Fiscal Cost of Trade Liberalization, Nicaragua**

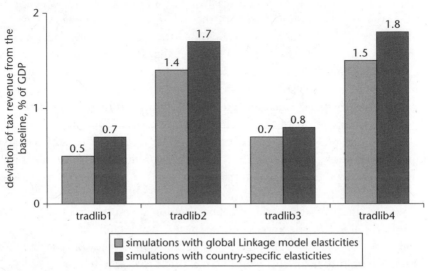

Source: Nicaraguan CGE model simulations by the authors.

assumption of lower trade elasticities. If we use the higher Armington elasticities, around 20,000 jobs are lost on farms producing basic grains, and about 3,000 more jobs are lost in manufacturing in the case of unilateral agricultural liberalization (tables 14.7 and 14.8). Job losses in manufacturing and services are more significant, at around 23,000, if nonagricultural trade is also unilaterally liberalized, especially because of the lower labor demand in the maquila export processing zone. The unemployed workers find new employment opportunities in traditional export farming (coffee and livestock). Although this is not captured by the CGE model, it is unlikely to be a smooth adjustment. In the short run at least, frictional unemployment is likely to emerge given the differences in skill requirements and locations between the lost jobs and the new jobs. Under the assumption of lower country-specific Armington elasticities, the employment effects (both positive and negative) are more substantial (table 14.7, first rows).

Worldwide trade liberalization (*trdlib3* and *trdlib4*) produces more significant employment effects in parallel with the more substantial output effects. In essence, the employment effects would magnify the effects observed under the unilateral trade liberalization simulation, but leave a proportionally larger net employment gain because the job losses in the farming of basic grains are somewhat less under the worldwide scenarios.

Unskilled workers see somewhat greater improvements in their employment opportunities in most simulations, especially unskilled wage laborers in traditional agriculture and particularly if the liberalization is global (tables 14.7 and 14.8).

**Table 14.7. The Impact of Prospective Trade Liberalization on Employment and Real Wages, Nicaragua**

*(percent deviation from the baseline)*

| Indicator | Employment | | | | Real consumption wage per worker | | | |
|---|---|---|---|---|---|---|---|---|
| | trdlib1 | trdlib2 | trdlib3 | trdlib4 | trdlib1 | trdlib2 | trdlib3 | trdlib4 |
| *Total* | | | | | | | | |
| Simulations with global Linkage model elasticities | 0.1 | 0.7 | 1.8 | 2.7 | 1.4 | 2.2 | 0.8 | 1.6 |
| Simulations with country-specific elasticities | 0.4 | 1.2 | 1.1 | 1.9 | 0.9 | 1.8 | 0.8 | 1.7 |
| *Skilled workers[a]* | | | | | | | | |
| Simulations with global Linkage model elasticities | 0.4 | 0.8 | 1.6 | 2.1 | 1.0 | 1.8 | 0.8 | 1.6 |
| Simulations with country-specific elasticities | 0.4 | 1.0 | 0.8 | 1.4 | 0.9 | 1.7 | 0.9 | 1.8 |
| *Unskilled workers[b]* | | | | | | | | |
| Simulations with global Linkage model elasticities | 0.0 | 0.7 | 2.0 | 3.0 | 1.6 | 2.5 | 0.9 | 1.8 |
| Simulations with country-specific elasticities | 0.4 | 1.3 | 1.2 | 2.2 | 1.0 | 1.9 | 0.8 | 1.8 |
| *Wage labor* | | | | | | | | |
| Simulations with global Linkage model elasticities | 0.7 | 0.2 | 2.3 | 1.9 | 0.8 | 1.7 | 0.3 | 1.1 |
| Simulations with country-specific elasticities | 0.6 | 1.0 | 1.3 | 1.7 | 0.7 | 1.5 | 0.6 | 1.5 |
| *Nonwage labor[c]* | | | | | | | | |
| Simulations with global Linkage model elasticities | −0.3 | 1.1 | 1.5 | 3.2 | 1.8 | 2.9 | 1.2 | 2.4 |
| Simulations with country-specific elasticities | 0.3 | 1.4 | 0.9 | 2.1 | 1.1 | 2.1 | 0.9 | 2.0 |

*Source:* Nicaraguan CGE model simulations by the authors.

*Note:* See the text for an explanation of the simulations.

a. Skilled workers have completed nine or more years of formal education and may be employed in wage or nonwage segments of the labor market.

b. Unskilled workers have completed eight or fewer years of formal education and may be employed in wage or nonwage segments of the labor market.

c. Nonwage labor represents self-employed workers.

**Table 14.8. The Impact of Prospective Trade Liberalization on Employment, by Sector, Nicaragua**

(number and percent)

| Sector | Base employment level, 1,000s, 2004[a] | % deviation from the baseline | | | |
|---|---|---|---|---|---|
| | | trdlib1 | trdlib2 | trdlib3 | trdlib4 |
| *Coffee* | | | | | |
| Simulations with global Linkage model elasticities | 139 | 8.2 | 16.9 | 27.3 | 40.0 |
| Simulations with country-specific elasticities | 139 | 2.3 | 6.4 | 7.9 | 12.0 |
| *Sugarcane* | | | | | |
| Simulations with global Linkage model elasticities | 18 | 0.0 | 0.7 | −2.4 | −1.3 |
| Simulations with country-specific elasticities | 18 | −0.2 | −0.4 | −1.0 | −1.2 |
| *Basic grains* | | | | | |
| Simulations with global Linkage model elasticities | 255 | −7.5 | −7.9 | −5.8 | −6.2 |
| Simulations with country-specific elasticities | 255 | −2.5 | −2.7 | −1.8 | −1.9 |
| *Other agricultural production* | | | | | |
| Simulations with global Linkage model elasticities | 195 | 0.6 | 1.9 | 5.0 | 6.2 |
| Simulations with country-specific elasticities | 195 | 0.1 | 0.4 | 0.8 | 1.1 |
| *Livestock farming* | | | | | |
| Simulations with global Linkage model elasticities | 231 | 1.9 | 6.0 | 0.8 | 5.3 |
| Simulations with country-specific elasticities | 231 | 0.3 | 1.9 | −0.6 | 0.9 |
| *Forestry, logging, and related service activities* | | | | | |
| Simulations with global Linkage model elasticities | 47 | −0.4 | −1.3 | 0.2 | −0.5 |
| Simulations with country-specific elasticities | 47 | −0.1 | −0.2 | 0.1 | 0.3 |
| *Fishing* | | | | | |
| Simulations with global Linkage model elasticities | 25 | 4.8 | 13.5 | 2.7 | 12.4 |
| Simulations with country-specific elasticities | 25 | 1.4 | 5.2 | 0.0 | 3.9 |
| *Mining and quarrying* | | | | | |
| Simulations with global Linkage model elasticities | 17 | −2.1 | −4.1 | −4.8 | −8.6 |
| Simulations with country-specific elasticities | 17 | −1.3 | −1.6 | 0.5 | 0.9 |
| *Production, processing, and preservation of meat and fish* | | | | | |
| Simulations with global Linkage model elasticities | 34 | 4.4 | 12.6 | 2.0 | 10.7 |
| Simulations with country-specific elasticities | 34 | 0.8 | 3.9 | −0.8 | 2.0 |

## Table 14.8. The Impact of Prospective Trade Liberalization on Employment, by Sector, Nicaragua (*continued*)

*(number and percent)*

| Sector | Base employment level, 1,000s, 2004[a] | % deviation from the baseline | | | |
|---|---|---|---|---|---|
| | | trdlib1 | trdlib2 | trdlib3 | trdlib4 |
| *Production, processing, and preservation of sugar* | | | | | |
| Simulations with global Linkage model elasticities | 5 | −0.4 | −0.1 | −3.1 | −2.5 |
| Simulations with country-specific elasticities | 5 | −0.5 | −1.2 | −1.5 | −2.1 |
| *Manufacture of dairy products* | | | | | |
| Simulations with global Linkage model elasticities | 24 | −1.3 | −1.5 | 0.4 | 0.4 |
| Simulations with country-specific elasticities | 24 | −0.1 | −0.5 | −0.2 | −0.4 |
| *Manufacture of other food products* | | | | | |
| Simulations with global Linkage model elasticities | 68 | −6.8 | −7.8 | 7.2 | 8.8 |
| Simulations with country-specific elasticities | 68 | −0.9 | −1.4 | −0.9 | −1.4 |
| *Zona franca, export processing zone* | | | | | |
| Simulations with global Linkage model elasticities | 41 | 0.0 | 0.2 | 0.1 | −0.2 |
| Simulations with country-specific elasticities | 41 | 0.0 | 0.1 | 0.0 | −0.1 |
| *Other manufacturing* | | | | | |
| Simulations with global Linkage model elasticities | 88 | −0.5 | −4.2 | −0.1 | −4.2 |
| Simulations with country-specific elasticities | 88 | −0.2 | −1.3 | −0.1 | −1.3 |
| *Electricity, gas, and water supply* | | | | | |
| Simulations with global Linkage model elasticities | 14 | −0.2 | −0.9 | −0.2 | −1.1 |
| Simulations with country-specific elasticities | 14 | −0.1 | −0.5 | −0.1 | −0.6 |
| *Construction* | | | | | |
| Simulations with global Linkage model elasticities | 99 | −0.1 | 0.6 | −0.3 | 0.7 |
| Simulations with country-specific elasticities | 99 | 0.0 | 0.5 | −0.2 | 0.6 |
| *Services* | | | | | |
| Simulations with global Linkage model elasticities | 824 | 0.0 | −0.7 | 0.3 | −0.5 |
| Simulations with country-specific elasticities | 824 | 0.2 | 0.0 | 0.3 | 0.2 |

*Source:* Nicaraguan CGE model simulations by the authors.

*Note:* See the text for an explanation of the simulations.

a. The number employed.

We assume the nominal wage adjustment is rather rigid in Nicaragua, given the prevailing institutional wage-setting mechanisms in most sectors of the economy. For some types of workers in the formal (wage-based) segment of the labor market in the CGE model, wages are partially indexed to year-to-year changes in consumer prices. Labor demand pressures influence the movements in real wages, but only moderately and without clearing labor markets. Real consumption wages are otherwise strongly influenced by changes in consumer prices. As domestic prices fall for consumers relative to the baseline under all the trade liberalization simulations, real wages (labor incomes) increase. This is consistent with the simulated appreciation of the real exchange rate. Real wage increases are similar across types of workers, although the increases are slightly greater among unskilled workers because these workers are in greater demand following the additional trade opening. Consistent with our results above, the real wage effects are more significant under economy-wide liberalization than under agricultural liberalization alone. Growth in the real wage of each worker is somewhat weaker under worldwide trade liberalization compared with the unilateral liberalization because employment grows more markedly under global liberalization.

### The inequality and poverty effects

Although employment growth favors unskilled workers in the trade opening simulations, the estimated effect on inequality in the distribution of labor incomes and per capita household incomes is minimal (table 14.9). The Gini coefficient drops by a slight 0.003 points in the case of the full-blown global liberalization of agricultural and nonagricultural commodities (*trdlib4*) and in a context of high Armington elasticities. This is consistent with the more significant employment effects under *trdlib4*. These inequality-reducing outcomes vanish, however, if we use the lower country-specific Armington elasticities, and, in contrast, inequality drops—again only slightly—under the unilateral trade liberalization simulations. The employment effects are more substantial in the model runs in which we use the higher Armington elasticities, and the job losses in the low-productivity smallholder farming of basic grains and in higher-productivity, more skill-intensive industrial sectors are offset by the growth of jobs in higher-productivity export agriculture. On the whole, though, the compounded effects of shifts in labor demand across skills and sectors produce small distributional effects.

In consequence, the poverty effects are mainly driven by the average wage and employment effects. As table 14.9 shows, the incidence of poverty falls in all simulations and model runs, but typically only by 1 percentage point or less (apart from one exception, under *trdlib2* if we use the lower Armington elasticities). Such a small impact on poverty is to be expected given the modest output and employment effects of trade liberalization. If we assume the lower country-specific elasticities,

| Simulation | Poverty headcount ratio, % | | | | | | Gini coefficient | |
|---|---|---|---|---|---|---|---|---|
| | At US$1 a day | | | At US$2 a day | | | Labor income | Per capita household income |
| | Total | Urban | Rural | Total | Urban | Rural | | |
| *Simulations with global Linkage model elasticities* | | | | | | | | |
| baseline, 2001[a] | 42.9 | 27.5 | 64.4 | 77.9 | 67.7 | 92.3 | 0.569 | 0.536 |
| baseline, 2004 | 41.4 | 26.0 | 63.0 | 72.1 | 59.7 | 89.6 | 0.568 | 0.531 |
| trdlib1, 2004 | 41.3 | 26.3 | 62.3 | 71.8 | 59.6 | 88.9 | 0.568 | 0.530 |
| Deviation from the baseline[b] | −0.1 | 0.3 | −0.7 | −0.4 | −0.1 | −0.7 | 0.000 | −0.001 |
| trdlib2, 2004 | 40.5 | 25.3 | 61.7 | 71.5 | 59.0 | 89.0 | 0.566 | 0.529 |
| Deviation from the baseline[b] | −1.0 | −0.7 | −1.3 | −0.6 | −0.7 | −0.6 | −0.002 | −0.002 |
| trdlib3, 2004 | 41.2 | 25.8 | 62.6 | 71.7 | 59.2 | 89.2 | 0.567 | 0.532 |
| Deviation from the baseline[b] | −0.3 | −0.2 | −0.4 | −0.4 | −0.4 | −0.4 | −0.001 | 0.000 |
| trdlib4, 2004 | 41.0 | 26.3 | 61.7 | 71.6 | 59.2 | 89.0 | 0.565 | 0.529 |
| Deviation from the baseline[b] | −0.4 | 0.2 | −1.3 | −0.5 | −0.4 | −0.6 | −0.003 | −0.003 |
| *Simulations with country-specific elasticities* | | | | | | | | |
| baseline, 2001[a] | 42.9 | 27.5 | 64.4 | 77.9 | 67.7 | 92.3 | 0.569 | 0.536 |
| baseline, 2004 | 42.0 | 27.2 | 62.8 | 72.0 | 59.7 | 89.2 | 0.571 | 0.534 |
| trdlib1, 2004 | 41.1 | 26.0 | 62.3 | 71.3 | 58.5 | 89.2 | 0.567 | 0.531 |
| Deviation from the baseline[b] | −0.8 | −1.1 | −0.5 | −0.7 | −1.2 | −0.1 | −0.003 | −0.003 |
| trdlib2, 2004 | 40.5 | 25.7 | 61.1 | 71.4 | 59.0 | 88.7 | 0.568 | 0.531 |
| Deviation from the baseline[b] | −1.5 | −1.4 | −1.6 | −0.6 | −0.7 | −0.5 | −0.003 | −0.003 |
| trdlib3, 2004 | 41.7 | 27.0 | 62.2 | 72.0 | 59.6 | 89.3 | 0.571 | 0.533 |
| Deviation from the baseline[b] | −0.3 | −0.2 | −0.6 | −0.1 | −0.1 | 0.1 | 0.000 | 0.000 |
| trdlib4, 2004 | 41.1 | 26.7 | 61.2 | 71.1 | 58.4 | 88.9 | 0.571 | 0.534 |
| Deviation from the baseline[b] | −0.9 | −0.5 | −1.5 | −0.9 | −1.3 | −0.3 | 0.001 | 0.000 |

*Source:* Nicaraguan CGE model results and microsimulations by the authors.

*Note:* See the text for an explanation of the simulations.

a. The use of different Armington elasticities does not affect the results for 2001 in the baseline scenario because, in the application of the microsimulations, all changes in the labor market are seen relative to 2001, the year on which the Living Standards Measurement Study that was used was conducted.

b. The differences are expressed as absolute deviations (points or percentage points) from the baseline.

rural poverty reduction is somewhat more substantial among the extreme poor (that is, using the US$1-a-day poverty line). This may be explained by the lower employment and real labor income losses among the poorest in traditional small-holder farming and the income gains among the poorest in other agricultural activities. The poverty reduction in urban areas is somewhat more significant among the moderately poor (people living below the US$2-a-day poverty line) who benefit more from the decline in consumer prices and the related increase in real consumption wages (relative to the baseline).

Along with the output and employment effects discussed above, the poverty reduction tends to be slightly greater if both agricultural and nonagricultural trade are liberalized. Yet, at a drop in the incidence of poverty by 1 percentage point or less, only around 22,000 extreme poor and 17,000 moderately poor are lifted out of poverty. Clearly, an enormous challenge remains in reaching the goal of poverty eradication.[22]

## Conclusions and Policy Implications

Nicaragua's agricultural sector is already close to free of import protection and price interventions; few agricultural and agroindustrial products are still highly protected from import competition. Under DR-CAFTA, much of the country's trade with its major trading partner, the United States, is nearly fully liberalized. In an ex ante impact analysis, Sánchez and Vos (2006a, 2006b) have shown that openness under DR-CAFTA would yield positive overall welfare gains and poverty reduction effects, but that these, at best, would be small and that traditional agriculture and the rural poor are among the likely losers in the process. This analysis demonstrates that only small welfare gains would be obtained through the elimination of taxes on agricultural trade or through enhanced agroindustrial export quotas in trade with the United States; most of the gains for Nicaragua would be obtained if the economy were able to use the full extent of the greater market access granted for textile and clothing exports to the United States.

Our study addresses the question whether the additional liberalization of trade with all trading partners would yield greater welfare outcomes and the question whether full worldwide liberalization of policy barriers to the free flow of agricultural trade would contribute to poverty reduction in Nicaragua. Our analysis confirms that small gains in output and in poverty reduction in Nicaragua may be expected under the various simulations of trade opening we consider. The estimated effects are somewhat greater than those recorded in the 2006a Sánchez and Vos study, but, at best, aggregate output would increase by 1.5 percent, and the reallocation of resources and the labor market adjustments would have only a small impact on income inequality. Modest aggregate employment and real wage growth would contribute to poverty reduction, but by only 1 percentage point from still high levels of extreme and moderate poverty. The extreme rural poor would likely gain somewhat more, however, because much of the employment gains would occur in the rural sector.

It is hardly surprising that we find such modest output gains and poverty reduction, given that import tariffs are already low, most export taxes have been eliminated, and no direct farm-input subsidies exist. Furthermore, the gains in some sectors, especially traditional export agriculture (coffee and livestock) and the meat processing industry, would arise at the expense of incomes and jobs among smallholder farmers. The export taxes that, in 2004, were still being levied on commodities such as vegetables and fruits, cattle and sheep, and meats have since been eliminated; hence, the welfare gains have already materialized. Additional gains in output growth and poverty reduction from more trade liberalization in Nicaragua would likely be even more modest than the gains we report in this chapter.

The fall in government revenue caused by the elimination of import duties and export taxes would be significant, ranging between 0.5 and 1.8 percent of GDP. The broadening of the tax base because of higher aggregate output following trade liberalization is unlikely to offset this loss, not least because it would be politically controversial. An alternative might involve financing the fiscal loss through increased public borrowing or aid inflows, but this, too, would be difficult for the government to accomplish given the country's significant indebtedness and reliance on official development assistance. Thus, a gradual approach to trade reform would be more desirable for fiscal reasons, but also to avoid labor market adjustment problems.

We must make an additional cautionary remark about our simulation results: they are sensitive to the trade elasticity values chosen. The higher trade responsiveness assumed in the global Linkage model of the World Bank tends to magnify output and employment gains (and losses) from trade liberalization relative to the outcome using the relatively lower country-specific elasticities that we have estimated for Nicaragua. Should one consider the estimated elasticities more realistic, then the overall outcomes are even more modest.

Overall, the simulations indicate that agricultural and nonagricultural trade liberalization may be viewed as a mixed blessing for Nicaragua's poor. If history is a guide, such measures, if taken in isolation, may not have a lasting impact on farm output growth or agricultural efficiency; past liberalizations, for instance, have had only a weak impact on the productivity and dynamism of the agricultural sector. The attainment of larger welfare gains would depend on complementary domestic policies directed at strengthening productivity growth and dynamic diversification in the agricultural sector and in other sectors of the economy. Such policies might aim at improving rural infrastructure, enhancing access to credit and to modern farm inputs, building up better marketing and distribution systems, and boosting the investment in human capital in rural areas. Achieving greater welfare gains would also require prudent macroeconomic policies, including keeping the exchange rate competitive and sustaining countercyclical fiscal and monetary stances. The domestic and international liberalization of the markets for agricultural goods and other goods clearly does not represent a quick fix for Nicaragua's structural problems in the development of a dynamic and diversified agricultural sector and the reduction of widespread poverty, particularly in rural areas.

## Notes

1. A maquila is a factory that imports raw materials free of tariffs for assembly or manufacturing and then exports the output, usually to the country that has supplied the raw materials.

2. According to data of the Central Bank of Nicaragua, the import-export ratio of the maquila export processing zone averaged 68 percent per year in 2000–05 and has been above 70 percent since 2004.

3. The trade preferences of the Caribbean Basin Initiative were granted to the countries of the region by the Caribbean Basin Economic Recovery Act, which was enacted by the United States in 1983 and went into effect on January 1, 1984. The benefits of the initiative were expanded in 2000 through the enactment of the Caribbean Basin Trade Partnership Act, which allows duty-free and quota-free treatment for selected items of apparel assembled in qualified initiative countries and applies reduced tariffs to certain other previously excluded products.

4. Agricultural producers only pay arbitrary municipal taxes on sales and services, real state, and registrations and licenses. They also pay a tax under the administration of the Instituto Nacional Tecnológico aimed at the collection of a mandatory 2 percent contribution from payrolls in the formal sector.

5. The relative rate of assistance is defined as $100 * [(100 + NRAag^t)/(100 + NRAnonag^t)-1]$, where $NRAag^t$ and $NRAnonag^t$ are the percentage NRAs for the tradables parts of the agricultural and nonagricultural sectors, respectively.

6. This model belongs to the family of structuralist neoclassical general equilibrium models developed for trade policy analysis. The theoretical foundations are described by Dervis, de Melo, and Robinson (1982) and Robinson (1989).

7. We made the first two extensions because the model was initially used to assess the impact of DR-CAFTA on Nicaragua's economy (Sánchez and Vos 2006a, 2006b).

8. A more-detailed description of the dynamic recursive CGE framework for Nicaragua may be found in Sánchez and Vos (2006a, 2006b), while a summary of the model equations may be found in the appendix by van der Mensbrugghe, Valenzuela, and Anderson.

9. For these purposes, we have followed the procedure that is spelled out in Horridge and Zhai (2006) and that is designed to connect the Global Trade Analysis Project model and a country model.

10. Sánchez and Vos (2006a, 2006b) include the export demand function for various practical purposes in their modeling of the impact of DR-CAFTA in Nicaragua. They use it to impose changes in export quotas by exogenously changing the base year quantity of exports (that is, the shift parameter in the export demand function).

11. The activity-specific wage of each factor is the product of the economy-wide wage of the factor (that is, the average wage by factor type) and an activity-specific wage-distortion factor. The latter measures the extent to which base year activity-specific wages deviate from the economy-wide wage by factor type.

12. Sánchez and Vos (2006b, appendix A3) provide a detailed description of the construction of Nicaragua's social accounting matrix.

13. The Armington elasticities in the global Linkage model are not country specific, but tend to be equal across countries.

14. Indeed, it has been found that, in a context of weak trade responsiveness, the gains from trade may even be reversed. See, among others, Vos (2007) for a review.

15. Unlike previous versions of the Global Trade Analysis Project Database, version 7 merges an input-output table for Nicaragua with world trade flows and protection data. See Narayanan and Walmsley (2008).

16. Sánchez (2004) and Sánchez and Vos (2005, 2006b) present a more detailed discussion of the implementation of the methodology in a dynamic setting, as well as a discussion of the limitations for analysis.

17. The participation rate is a constant in our CGE model and thus does not play a role in the microsimulation analysis. The base year unemployment rate by labor type is a constant in the model, too, but we have changed it inversely (and proportionately) in response to changes in the employment rate by labor type to implement the microsimulations.

18. We have used the international comparable poverty lines as previously defined by the World Bank. At the time we wrote this chapter, the new international poverty line estimates based on new purchasing power parity weights were not yet publicly available. See Chen and Ravallion (2008) for a discussion of the new poverty line estimates and the implications for trends in global poverty. We assume here that the directions of change in the poverty incidence in Nicaragua are not affected by the revised poverty line definition.

19. Nonagricultural commodities include highly processed food products (specifically, beverages and tobacco, which are Global Trade Analysis Project sectors 25 and 26) and all other manufactures and nonfarm primary goods.

20. Because the Nicaragua CGE model disaggregates trade by trading partner, we have adapted the terms of trade shocks additionally using the weighted participation of trading partners in exports and imports during the base year that is indicated in this model.

21. An alternative closure rule for the government would allow savings to fluctuate to balance the fiscal accounts, while direct tax rates would be fixed at base year levels. Under such a closure rule, government savings are found to increase significantly to offset the elimination of revenues from import duties and taxes. In our analysis, however, we assume that there is some sort of fiscal discipline and that the government may increase the tax burden without limit to keep government accounts in balance if trade taxes no longer generate revenue.

22. Our findings here are not dissimilar to the findings obtained on the expected impact of DR-CAFTA, the regional trade agreement with the United States, as analyzed by Sánchez and Vos (2006a, 2006b).

# References

Anderson, K., and E. Valenzuela. 2008. "Estimates of Global Distortions to Agricultural Incentives, 1955–2007." Data spreadsheet, October, World Bank, Washington, DC. http://go.worldbank.org/YAO39F35E0.

Berthelon, M., D. Kruger, and D. Saavedra. 2008. "Nicaragua." In *Distortions to Agricultural Incentives in Latin America*, ed. K. Anderson and A. Valdés, 273–99. Washington, DC: World Bank.

Bourguignon, F., A.-S. Robilliard, and S. Robinson. 2002. "Representative Versus Real Households in the Macro-economic Modeling of Inequality." Unpublished working paper, World Bank and International Food Policy Research Institute, Washington, DC.

Bravo-Ortega, C., and D. Lederman. 2004. "Agricultural Productivity and Its Determinants: Revisiting International Experiences." *Estudios de Economía* 31 (2): 133–63.

Chen, S., and M. Ravallion. 2008. "The Developing World Is Poorer Than We Thought, but No Less Successful in the Fight against Poverty." Policy Research Working Paper 4703, World Bank, Washington, DC.

Deininger, K., E. Zegarra, and I. Lavadenz. 2003. "Determinants and Impacts of Rural Land Market Activity: Evidence from Nicaragua." *World Development* 31 (9): 1385–1404.

Dervis, K., J. de Melo, and S. Robinson. 1982. *General Equilibrium Models for Development Policy*. Cambridge: Cambridge University Press.

ECLAC (United Nations Economic Commission for Latin America and the Caribbean). 2008. *Social Panorama of Latin America 2007*. Report LC/G.2351-P. Santiago, Chile: ECLAC.

Ganuza, E., R. Paes de Barros, and R. Vos. 2002. "Labour Market Adjustment, Poverty and Inequality during Liberalization." In *Economic Liberalization, Distribution and Poverty: Latin America in the 1990s*, ed. R. Vos, L. Taylor, and R. Paes de Barros, 54–88. Cheltenham, United Kingdom: Edward Elgar.

Horridge, M., and F. Zhai. 2006. "Shocking a Single-Country CGE Model with Export Prices and Quantities from a Global Model." In *Poverty and the WTO: Impacts of the Doha Development Agenda*, ed. T. W. Hertel and L. A. Winters, 94–104. London: Palgrave Macmillan; Washington, DC: World Bank.

Lofgren, H., R. L. Harris, and S. Robinson. 2002. "A Standard Computable General Equilibrium (CGE) Model in GAMS." Microcomputers in Policy Research 5, International Food Policy Research Institute, Washington, DC.

Narayanan, B. G., and T. L. Walmsley, eds. 2008. *Global Trade, Assistance, and Production: The GTAP 7 Data Base*. West Lafayette, IN: Center for Global Trade Analysis, Department of Agricultural Economics, Purdue University. https://www.gtap.agecon.purdue.edu/databases/v7/v7_doco.asp.

Robinson, S. 1989. "Multisector Models." In *Handbook of Development Economics*, vol. 2, ed. H. Chenery and T. N. Srinivasan, 885–947. *Handbooks in Economics* 9. Amsterdam: North Holland.

Sánchez, M. V. 2004. *Rising Inequality and Falling Poverty in Costa Rica's Agriculture during Trade Reform: A Macro-Micro General Equilibrium Analysis*. Maastricht, the Netherlands: Shaker.

Sánchez, M. V., and R. Vos. 2005. "Impacto del Tratado de Libre Comercio con Estados Unidos en el Crecimiento, la Pobreza y la Desigualdad en Panamá: Una evaluación ex ante usando un modelo de equilibrio general computable dinámico." Project report, United Nations Development Programme, Panama City.

———. 2006a. "DR-CAFTA: Panacea o fatalidad para el desarrollo económico y social en Nicaragua." Estudios y Perspectivas Series 57, Social Development Unit, Subregional Headquarters, United Nations Economic Commission for Latin America and the Caribbean, Mexico City.

———. 2006b. *Impacto del CAFTA en el crecimiento, la pobreza y la desigualdad en Nicaragua: Una evaluación ex-ante con un modelo de equilibrio general computable dinámico*. Managua: Ministerio de Fomento a la Industria y el Comercio and United Nations Development Programme.

———. 2009. "Liberalizing Trade and Its Impact on Poverty and Inequality in Nicaragua." Agricultural Distortions Working Paper 106, World Bank, Washington, DC.

USTR (Office of the United States Trade Representative). 2005. "CAFTA Facts: The Case for CAFTA; Growth, Opportunity, and Democracy in Our Neighborhood." CAFTA Policy Brief, February, USTR, Washington, DC.

Valenzuela, E., and K. Anderson. 2008. "Alternative Agricultural Price Distortions for CGE Analysis of Developing Countries, 2004 and 1980–84." Research Memorandum 13 (December), Center for Global Trade Analysis, Department of Agricultural Economics, Purdue University, West Lafayette, IN. https://www.gtap.agecon.purdue.edu/resources/res_display.asp?RecordID=2925.

van der Mensbrugghe, D. 2005. "Linkage Technical Reference Document: Version 6.0." December, World Bank, Washington, DC. http://go.worldbank.org/7NP2KK1OH0.

Vos, R. 2007. "What We Do and Don't Know about Trade Liberalization and Poverty Reduction." DESA Working Paper 50, document ST/ESA/2007/DWP/, United Nations Department of Economic and Social Affairs, New York. http://www.un.org/esa/desa/papers/2007/wp50_2007.pdf.

Vos, R., E. Ganuza, S. Morley, and S. Robinson, eds. 2006. *Who Gains from Free Trade? Export-Led Growth, Inequality, and Poverty in Latin America*. New York: Routledge.

World Bank. 2003. *Nicaragua Poverty Assessment: Raising Welfare and Reducing Vulnerability*. Report 26128-NI. Washington, DC: Central America Department, Latin America and the Caribbean Region, World Bank.

World Development Indicators Database. World Bank. http://go.worldbank.org/6HAYAHG8H0 (accessed September 2008).

# BORDER PRICE AND EXPORT DEMAND SHOCKS IN DEVELOPING COUNTRIES FROM REST-OF-THE-WORLD TRADE LIBERALIZATION: THE LINKAGE MODEL

*Dominique van der Mensbrugghe,*
*Ernesto Valenzuela, and Kym Anderson*

A global study by Anderson, Valenzuela, and van der Mensbrugghe—chapter 2 in this volume—uses the World Bank's global Linkage model to examine the economic impacts of agricultural and trade policies on various countries, regions, and the world as a whole as of 2004. It does this by applying shocks to the global Linkage model through the removal of all agricultural price-distorting domestic and border policies both with and without the removal of the price-distorting trade policies affecting all other goods. (The application of the two sets of shocks helps us identify the relative contribution to various indicators that is supplied by agricultural policies and by trade policies directed at other merchandise.)

The sets of shocks are also used in another global study in this volume—chapter 3 by Bussolo, De Hoyos, and Medvedev—to examine, in this case, the implications of price-distorting policies for inequality and poverty in more than 100 countries (by applying the Global Income Distribution Dynamics microsimulation tool, the GIDD Database, of the authors).

The Linkage model is also used by the authors of the 10 national case studies reported in this volume to provide exogenous shocks to the national economy-wide models of these authors on the developing countries in the studies.[1] The effects of the shocks on the national economies are then compared with the effects

**457**

of own-country liberalization by using the same national models, as well as the agricultural protection rates for these countries that are used in the global Linkage model.

In this appendix, we describe the main assumptions that have been adopted to generate the border price and export demand shocks arising from agricultural and trade policy reforms by the rest of the world. We also describe the way these shocks are communicated to the national models.

We use the comparative static version of the World Bank's Linkage model (van der Mensbrugghe 2005, 2006) with a baseline—the base year is 2004—calibrated to prerelease 5 of beta version 7 of the Global Trade Analysis Project (GTAP) data set. The new version of the GTAP global protection database, version 7, has somewhat greater regional coverage than version 6, which was calibrated to a baseline of 2001 (Dimaranan 2006). The sectoral and regional aggregations and concordances are shown in tables A.1 and A.2. We first amend the distortions in version 7 of the GTAP Database (see Narayanan and Walmsley 2008) by replacing the applied tariffs with distortion rates that reproduce the nominal rates of assistance estimated by the authors of the developing-country case studies in the World Bank's research project, Distortions to Agricultural Incentives, as presented for modelers by Valenzuela and Anderson (2008) using the sectors described in the GTAP Database.[2]

## Global Linkage Model Border Shocks to the Single-Country Models

It is important to ensure uniformity in the simulations used in the global and national modeling. Therefore, the results communicated from the Linkage model to the single-country models are rest-of-the-world reforms, that is, they represent global liberalization without liberalization in the country of interest. The shocks imposed are as follows:

- In agricultural and lightly processed food sectors (excluding highly processed food, beverages, and tobacco):
  ○ The removal of all trade (import and export) taxes and subsidies
  ○ The removal of all farm input and output taxes and subsidies
- In other, nonagricultural sectors:
  ○ The removal of all trade (import and export) taxes

**Table A.1. Sectoral Concordance of the Linkage Model and the GTAP Version 7 Database**

| Number | Code | Description |
|--------|------|-------------|
| 1 | pdr | Paddy rice |
| 2 | wht | Wheat |
| 3 | gro | Other grains |
| 4 | osd | Oilseeds |
| 5 | c_b | Sugarcane and beets |
| 6 | pfb | Plant-based fibers |
| 7 | v_f | Vegetables and fruits |
| 8 | ocr | Other crops |
| 9 | ctl | Cattle, sheep, and so on |
| 10 | oap | Other livestock |
| 11 | rmk | Raw milk |
| 12 | wol | Wool |
| 13 | cmt | Beef and sheep meat |
| 14 | omt | Other meat products |
| 15 | vol | Vegetable oils and fats |
| 16 | mil | Dairy products |
| 17 | pcr | Processed rice |
| 18 | sgr | Refined sugar |
| 19 | ofb | Other food, beverages, and tobacco<br>Food products n.e.s. (ofd), beverages and tobacco products (b_t) |
| 20 | prm | Other primary products<br>Forestry (frs), fishing (fsh), coal (coa), oil (oil), gas (gas), minerals n.e.s. (omn) |
| 21 | twp | Textiles and wearing apparel<br>Textiles (tex), wearing apparel (wap), leather products (lea) |
| 22 | omx | Other manufacturing<br>Wood products (lum); paper products, publishing (ppp); petroleum, coal products (p_c); chemical, rubber, plastic products (crp); mineral products n.e.s. (nmm); ferrous metals (i_s); metals n.e.s. (nfm); metal products (fmp); motor vehicles and parts (mvh); transport equipment n.e.s. (otn); electronic equipment (ele); machinery and equipment n.e.s. (ome); manufactures n.e.s. (omf) |
| 23 | srv | Services<br>Electricity (ely); gas manufacture, distribution (gdt); water (wtr); construction (cns); trade (trd); transport n.e.s. (otp); sea transport (wtp); air transport (atp); communications (cmn); financial services n.e.s. (ofi); insurance (isr); business services n.e.s. (obs); recreation and other services (ros); public administration and defense, education, health services (osg); dwellings (dwe) |

*Sources:* van der Mensbrugghe (2005), Narayanan and Walmsley (2008).

*Note:* n.e.s. = not elsewhere specified.

**Table A.2. Regional Concordance of the Linkage Model and the GTAP Version 7 Database**

| Number | Code | Description |
|---|---|---|
| 1 | aus | Australia |
| 2 | nzl | New Zealand |
| 3 | jpn | Japan |
| 4 | kor | Korea, Rep. |
| 5 | twn | Taiwan, China |
| 6 | hyc | Hong Kong, China (hkg); Singapore (sgp) |
| 7 | can | Canada |
| 8 | usa | United States |
| 9 | e15 | EU15 (see next)<br>Austria (aut), Belgium (bel), Denmark (dnk), Finland (fin), France (fra), Germany (deu), Greece (grc), Ireland (irl), Italy (ita), Luxembourg (lux), the Netherlands (nld), Portugal (prt), Spain (esp), Sweden (swe), United Kingdom (gbr) |
| 10 | xer | Rest of Western Europe<br>Cyprus (cyp), Malta (mlt), Switzerland (che), rest of the European Free Trade Association (xef), rest of Europe (xer) |
| 11 | bgr | Bulgaria |
| 12 | cze | Czech Republic |
| 13 | est | Estonia |
| 14 | hun | Hungary |
| 15 | lva | Latvia |
| 16 | ltu | Lithuania |
| 17 | kaz | Kazakhstan |
| 18 | kgz | Kyrgyzstan |
| 19 | pol | Poland |
| 20 | rom | Romania |
| 21 | svk | Slovak Republic |
| 22 | svn | Slovenia |
| 23 | rus | Russian Federation |
| 24 | tur | Turkey |
| 25 | xca | Rest of Europe and Central Asia<br>Albania (alb), Croatia (hrv), Ukraine (ukr), rest of Eastern Europe (xee), Armenia (arm), Azerbaijan (aze), Georgia (geo), rest of former Soviet Union (xsu) |
| 26 | mde | Middle East<br>Iran, Islamic Rep. (irn); rest of Western Asia (xws) |
| 27 | egy | Egypt, Arab Rep. |
| 28 | mar | Morocco |
| 29 | xnf | Rest of North Africa<br>Tunisia (tun), rest of North Africa (xnf) |
| 30 | zaf | South Africa |

**Table A.2. Regional Concordance of the Linkage Model and the GTAP Version 7 Database (*continued*)**

| Number | Code | Description |
|--------|------|-------------|
| 31 | mdg | Madagascar |
| 32 | moz | Mozambique |
| 33 | zmb | Zambia |
| 34 | zwe | Zimbabwe |
| 35 | wcf | Rest of West and Central Africa<br>Rest of West Africa (xwf), Central Africa (xcf), south-central Africa (xac) |
| 36 | uga | Uganda |
| 37 | tza | Tanzania |
| 38 | nga | Nigeria |
| 39 | sen | Senegal |
| 40 | xss | Rest of Sub-Saharan Africa<br>Malawi (mwi), Mauritius (mus), rest of East Africa (xec), Botswana (bwa), rest of Southern African Customs Union (xsc) |
| 41 | chn | China |
| 42 | idn | Indonesia |
| 43 | mys | Malaysia |
| 44 | phl | Philippines |
| 45 | tha | Thailand |
| 46 | vnm | Vietnam |
| 47 | xea | Rest of East Asia<br>Rest of Oceania (xoc), rest of East Asia (xea), Cambodia (khm), rest of Southeast Asia (xse) |
| 48 | bgd | Bangladesh |
| 49 | ind | India |
| 50 | pak | Pakistan |
| 51 | lka | Sri Lanka |
| 52 | xsa | Other South Asia |
| 53 | arg | Argentina |
| 54 | bra | Brazil |
| 55 | chl | Chile |
| 56 | col | Colombia |
| 57 | ecu | Ecuador |
| 58 | mex | Mexico |
| 59 | nic | Nicaragua |
| 60 | xlc | Rest of Latin America and the Caribbean<br>Rest of North America (xna); Bolivia (bol); Paraguay (pry); Peru (per); Uruguay (ury); Venezuela, R.B. de (ven); rest of South America (xsm); rest of Central America (xca); Caribbean (xcb) |

*Sources:* van der Mensbrugghe (2005), Narayanan and Walmsley (2008).

## Macroclosure in the Linkage Model

The macroclosure of the global Linkage model involves the following:

- Fixing the balance of trade
- Fixing regional investment
- Fixing real government spending
- Implementing a tax replacement to offset the lost revenue in trade and production (if present) taxes, net of subsidies that would no longer be paid after the reforms; specifically, a tax on factors of production is implemented to ensure that the share of net tax receipts in net national incomes remains unchanged in the face of the elimination of distortions

## Implementing Global Results in the Single-Country Models

As indicated by Horridge and Zhai (2006), the aim is to allow the single-country models to determine export supply behavior and to use the changes in demand by the rest of the world as presented in the global model. In calculating the export demand curve, one should obtain from the global model the slope—approximately equal to the elasticity of substitution among imports—and the shift ($fp$) of the world demand schedule, where $fp$ is computed as follows:

$$fp = p + q/(\text{Elasticity of substitution among imports}), \qquad (A.1)$$

while $p$ is the percentage change in export prices, and $q$ is the percentage change in export quantities.[3]

On the import side, one takes the import price shocks directly from the global model. In global models such as Linkage, the import supply curves for a small country are flat; in single-country models, the import demand curves are comparatively steep because they typically rely on the import-domestic elasticities suggested by Armington (1969). Hence, vertical shifts in import supply are readily proxied by exogenous price changes.[4]

## The Linkage Model

In a key specification, the Linkage model contains three production technologies for agricultural activities: crops, livestock, and all else.[5] The first technology, crops, attempts to capture the trade-offs between intensive and extensive farming. The second, livestock, captures the trade-offs between extensive grazing and intensive ranch-fed farming by allowing substitution between feedgrains and land. The third is the more traditional capital-labor substitution, albeit with a special, additional nesting for energy use.

Another key model specification is the treatment of land. In the Linkage model, land supply is variable according to region-specific land supply elasticities. A listing of these and other key model elasticities is provided in table A.3. For the purposes of the simulations in this volume, the vintage capital structure elasticities in the Linkage model are imposed in all production functions so that the functions emulate the long-run substitution possibilities.

All runs use the following closure rules:

- Fixed real government expenditures and fiscal balance: To meet ex ante revenue changes (for example, a loss in tariff revenues), the rate of lump sum direct taxation on the single representative household is endogenous. While perhaps unrealistic in some countries in the short run, this specification has the advantage of not adding to existing distortions in the economy.
- Private savings are endogenous and determined by the extended linear expenditure system of demand. Investment is determined as the sum of all available savings: private, public (fixed in real terms), and foreign (fixed in real terms relative to the model numéraire). Because all three forms of savings are more or less invariant (in nominal terms), major changes in the volume of investment are largely driven by changes in the unit cost of investment (for example, a reduction in tariffs on imported capital goods). In the comparative static model, this has only minor impacts that may be attributed to the final composition of demand because investment has no effect on the capital stock in the comparative static version of the model.
- The capital account and, hence, the current account are fixed. The real exchange rate adjusts to clear ex ante changes in the current account. A reduction in import tariffs, for example, leads to an increase in import demand. The demand for additional imports needs to be financed through an increase in exports, most often generated by a fall in the real exchange rate, that is, a depreciation.

Some of the other key features of the model include the following:

- The model numéraire is defined as the export price index of manufactured exports from high-income countries. This is set to 1 in the base year and in subsequent shocks.

## Table A.3. Key Elasticities in the Linkage Model

### a. Production elasticities

| Elasticity | Long-run parameter |
| --- | --- |
| Across inputs, excluding sector-specific and energy inputs | 0.0 |
| Between other inputs and value added, including energy | 0.0 |
| Between labor and the capital and energy bundle | 1.0 |
| Across labor inputs | 0.5 |
| Between capital and energy | 0.8 |
| Between capital and sector-specific factors | 0.0 |
| Across fuel inputs | 2.0 |
| Between chemicals and land-capital inputs | 0.5 |
| Between feed and land | 0.5 |
| Across agricultural chemicals | 0.5 |
| Across livestock feed | 0.5 |

### b. Armington elasticities[a]

| Elasticity | | Value |
| --- | --- | --- |
| pdr | Paddy rice[b] | 4.45 |
| wht | Wheat | 5.85 |
| gro | Other grains | 4.93 |
| v_f | Vegetables and fruits | 3.94 |
| osd | Oilseeds | 4.75 |
| c_b | Sugarcane and beets | 5.91 |
| pfb | Plant-based fibers | 3.94 |
| ocr | Other crops | 3.94 |
| ctl | Cattle, sheep, and so on | 3.94 |
| oap | Other livestock | 3.94 |
| rmk | Raw milk | 3.94 |
| wol | Wool | 3.94 |
| cmt | Beef and sheep meat | 3.94 |
| omt | Other meat products | 3.94 |
| vol | Vegetable oils and fats | 3.94 |
| mil | Dairy products | 3.94 |
| pcr | Processed rice[b] | 4.45 |
| sgr | Refined sugar | 5.91 |
| ofb | Other food, beverages, and tobacco | 3.94 |
| prm | Other primary products | 4.31 |
| twp | Textiles and wearing apparel | 4.11 |
| omx | Other manufacturing | 4.09 |
| srv | Services | 2.08 |

## Table A.3.  Key Elasticities in the Linkage Model (*continued*)

c. Land supply elasticities[c]

| Elasticity[c] | | Value |
|---|---|---|
| aus | Australia | 1.00 |
| nzl | New Zealand | 1.00 |
| jpn | Japan | 0.25 |
| kor | Korea, Rep. | 0.25 |
| twn | Taiwan, China | 0.25 |
| hyc | Hong Kong, China; Singapore | 0.25 |
| can | Canada | 1.00 |
| usa | United States | 1.00 |
| e15 | EU15[d] | 0.25 |
| xer | Rest of Western Europe | 0.25 |
| bgr | Bulgaria | 0.25 |
| cze | Czech Republic | 0.25 |
| est | Estonia | 0.25 |
| hun | Hungary | 0.25 |
| lva | Latvia | 0.25 |
| ltu | Lithuania | 0.25 |
| kaz | Kazakhstan | 1.00 |
| kgz | Kyrgyzstan | 1.00 |
| pol | Poland | 0.25 |
| rom | Romania | 0.25 |
| svk | Slovak Republic | 0.25 |
| svn | Slovenia | 0.25 |
| rus | Russian Federation | 1.00 |
| tur | Turkey | 1.00 |
| xca | Rest of Europe and Central Asia | 0.25 |
| mde | Middle East | 0.25 |
| egy | Egypt, Arab Rep. | 0.25 |
| mar | Morocco | 0.25 |
| xnf | Rest of North Africa | 0.25 |
| zaf | South Africa | 1.00 |
| mdg | Madagascar | 1.00 |
| moz | Mozambique | 1.00 |
| zmb | Zambia | 1.00 |
| zwe | Zimbabwe | 1.00 |
| wcf | Rest of West and Central Africa | 1.00 |
| uga | Uganda | 1.00 |
| tza | Tanzania | 1.00 |
| nga | Nigeria | 1.00 |

(*Table continues on the following page.*)

## Table A.3. Key Elasticities in the Linkage Model (*continued*)

### c. Land supply elasticities[c]

| Elasticity[c] | | Value |
|---|---|---|
| sen | Senegal | 1.00 |
| xss | Rest of Sub-Saharan Africa | 1.00 |
| chn | China | 0.25 |
| idn | Indonesia | 1.00 |
| mys | Malaysia | 1.00 |
| phl | Philippines | 1.00 |
| tha | Thailand | 1.00 |
| vnm | Vietnam | 1.00 |
| xea | Rest of East Asia | 1.00 |
| bgd | Bangladesh | 0.25 |
| ind | India | 0.25 |
| pak | Pakistan | 0.25 |
| lka | Sri Lanka | 0.25 |
| xsa | Other South Asia | 0.25 |
| arg | Argentina | 1.00 |
| bra | Brazil | 1.00 |
| chl | Chile | 1.00 |
| col | Colombia | 1.00 |
| ecu | Ecuador | 1.00 |
| mex | Mexico | 0.25 |
| nic | Nicaragua | 0.25 |
| xlc | Rest of Latin America and the Caribbean | 1.00 |

*Source:* van der Mensbrugghe (2005).

a. The elasticities in this table represent the top-level trade elasticities, that is, the substitution between the aggregate domestic good and aggregate imports. The second-level elasticity, that is, the substitution across imports by region of origin, is double the top-level elasticity using the rule of 2.

b. Because of convergence, the rice trade elasticities for Japan, the Republic of Korea, and Taiwan, China have been set at 1.5, 1.0, and 1.5, respectively, for both levels of the elasticities and for paddy rice and processed rice.

c. Countries and regions are classified as either land abundant (with an elasticity of 1) or land scarce (with an elasticity of 0.25).

d. The 15 members of the European Union prior to 2004; see table A.2.

- Aggregate labor supply is fixed and fully mobile across all sectors. Note that in the version of the model used in the present study, no exogenous assumptions are imposed on the relative rural-urban wage ratio, and wages are assumed to be uniform across sectors. Assuming intersectoral wage differentials (with or without perfect mobility) may lead to different results depending on whether, in aggregate, demand in the high-wage sectors is greater than demand in the low-wage sectors.[6] Skilled labor is a substitute for unskilled labor, and the composite labor bundle may be substituted for capital.
- Aggregate capital supply is fixed and fully mobile across all sectors.[7]
- Agricultural land supply is endogenous, and land is specified as either scarce or abundant. Land is perfectly mobile across agricultural industries.

The price distortion structure in the GTAP Version 7p5 database for 2004 is shown in table A.4, for comparison with the distortion rates drawn from the World Bank project's database for use in the present study in place of the standard GTAP database numbers.

Table A.5 provides the export price, import price, and export demand shocks from rest-of-the-world agricultural and trade policy reform for our selected developing countries. These come from the Linkage model, for use in the other models employed in the present study. In terms of those Linkage model results, we note the following:

- Changes in value added are computed with and without taxes and subsidies on the factors of production. The exception is wage taxes, which are not used in this version of the model. The first definition reflects the cost of value added, inclusive of total taxes and subsidies. The second definition reflects final payments to the owners of the factors of production. In the output provided to the authors, total value added at factor cost (that is, inclusive of taxes and subsidies) is provided.
- Welfare is measured using the Hicksian equivalent variation in income. In the base year, the expenditure function is exactly equal to disposable income and reflects the expenditures on goods, services, and savings. After the shock, the expenditure function reflects the value of the expenditures required to achieve the new level of utility at the base year prices. It is closely approximated by the value of nominal disposable income, deflated by the consumer price index. In some countries, the increase in the income (lump sum) tax may not be fully offset by a decline in consumer prices, even taking into account changes in factor incomes.

Tables A.4 and A.5 provide additional summary material on our data.

**Table A.4. Price Distortion Structure in GTAP Version 7p5 and the Distortion Rates Drawn from the World Bank Project, 2004**

(percent)

| Country, region | GTAP version 7p5 | | | | Amended rates | | | |
|---|---|---|---|---|---|---|---|---|
| | Primary agriculture | Agriculture and lightly processed food | | Other goods | Primary agriculture | Agriculture and lightly processed food | | Other goods |
| | Domestic support | Export subsidy | Import tariff | Import tariff | Domestic support | Export subsidy | Import tariff | Import tariff |
| Australia | 0.0 | 0.0 | 0.7 | 3.3 | 0.0 | 0.0 | 0.5 | 3.3 |
| New Zealand | 0.0 | 0.0 | 2.8 | 3.3 | 0.0 | −0.2 | 0.7 | 3.3 |
| EU15[a] | 1.0 | 10.8 | 7.1 | 0.7 | 1.2 | 12.8 | 6.9 | 0.7 |
| Rest of Western Europe | 2.6 | 8.6 | 52.9 | 2.2 | 2.6 | 13.4 | 53.9 | 2.2 |
| Russian Federation | 1.7 | −0.1 | 7.5 | 7.4 | 1.7 | −0.9 | 18.9 | 7.4 |
| Kazakhstan | −0.9 | 0.0 | 2.9 | 2.7 | −0.9 | 0.0 | 3.4 | 2.7 |
| Kyrgyzstan | −1.0 | −0.1 | 3.1 | 5.0 | −1.0 | −0.1 | 3.8 | 5.0 |
| Turkey | 0.8 | 0.0 | 29.0 | 3.1 | 0.8 | 0.0 | 33.3 | 3.1 |
| Rest of Europe and Central Asia | −1.1 | 0.0 | 9.8 | 5.7 | −1.1 | −0.9 | 9.9 | 5.7 |
| Bulgaria | 0.6 | 0.0 | 17.0 | 11.5 | 0.6 | 0.0 | 14.8 | 11.5 |
| Czech Republic | 0.6 | 10.2 | 3.1 | 0.5 | 0.6 | 0.0 | 3.0 | 0.5 |
| Estonia | 0.0 | 9.7 | 6.2 | 0.9 | 0.0 | 0.0 | 5.0 | 0.9 |
| Hungary | 3.1 | 9.7 | 6.6 | 0.5 | 3.1 | 0.0 | 6.2 | 0.5 |
| Latvia | 13.1 | 9.9 | 3.7 | 0.9 | 13.3 | 0.0 | 3.3 | 0.9 |
| Lithuania | 0.5 | 9.4 | 13.1 | 1.0 | 0.5 | 0.0 | 12.1 | 1.0 |
| Poland | 0.4 | 8.3 | 6.1 | 0.8 | 0.4 | 0.0 | 6.2 | 0.8 |
| Romania | 1.3 | 0.0 | 19.8 | 9.8 | 1.3 | 0.0 | 18.0 | 9.8 |
| Slovak Republic | 0.0 | 10.4 | 5.5 | 0.4 | 0.0 | 0.0 | 5.2 | 0.4 |
| Slovenia | 0.0 | 10.5 | 6.3 | 0.4 | 0.0 | 0.0 | 7.8 | 0.4 |

| | | | | | | | | |
|---|---|---|---|---|---|---|---|---|
| United States | 4.0 | 0.5 | 2.5 | 1.3 | 5.2 | 0.6 | 6.1 | 1.3 |
| Canada | 1.6 | 2.0 | 23.1 | 1.4 | 1.6 | 3.6 | 18.9 | 1.4 |
| Japan | 2.0 | 0.0 | 141.1 | 1.7 | 2.0 | 0.0 | 151.7 | 1.7 |
| Korea, Rep. | 0.0 | 0.0 | 172.7 | 5.9 | 0.0 | 0.0 | 319.4 | 5.9 |
| Taiwan, China | −0.4 | 0.0 | 77.4 | 3.9 | −0.4 | 0.0 | 84.2 | 3.9 |
| Hong Kong, China; Singapore | 0.0 | 0.0 | 0.0 | 0.0 | 0.0 | 0.0 | 0.0 | 0.0 |
| China | 0.0 | 0.0 | 12.6 | 7.1 | 0.0 | 0.2 | 6.5 | 7.1 |
| Indonesia | 0.0 | 0.0 | 6.4 | 4.9 | 0.0 | −1.6 | 7.3 | 4.9 |
| Malaysia | 0.0 | 0.0 | 2.4 | 5.9 | 0.0 | −0.2 | 5.0 | 5.9 |
| Philippines | −4.7 | 0.0 | 20.0 | 3.4 | −4.7 | 0.0 | 7.1 | 3.4 |
| Thailand | −0.2 | 0.0 | 22.1 | 12.9 | −0.2 | 0.0 | 26.2 | 12.9 |
| Vietnam | −3.6 | 0.0 | 15.5 | 18.5 | −3.6 | −0.5 | 21.5 | 18.5 |
| Bangladesh | −1.0 | 0.0 | 16.3 | 22.5 | −1.0 | 0.0 | 9.9 | 22.5 |
| India | 3.9 | 0.0 | 29.8 | 20.9 | 10.1 | 2.5 | 2.9 | 20.8 |
| Pakistan | 0.0 | 0.0 | 10.8 | 18.5 | 0.0 | −0.2 | 19.4 | 18.5 |
| Sri Lanka | 0.6 | 0.2 | 24.3 | 5.8 | 0.6 | −0.3 | 23.8 | 5.8 |
| Rest of South Asia | −0.5 | 0.0 | 5.0 | 15.6 | −0.5 | 0.0 | 6.9 | 15.6 |
| Rest of East Asia | −0.7 | 0.0 | 2.8 | 2.3 | −0.7 | 0.0 | 3.2 | 2.3 |
| Rest of Middle East | −12.4 | 0.0 | 9.0 | 5.7 | −12.4 | 0.0 | 7.5 | 5.7 |
| Egypt, Arab Rep. | 0.0 | 0.0 | 4.0 | 13.5 | 0.0 | 0.0 | 5.0 | 13.5 |
| Morocco | 0.0 | −0.3 | 33.3 | 20.0 | 0.0 | −0.4 | 28.4 | 20.0 |
| Rest of North Africa | −3.9 | 0.5 | 24.9 | 13.1 | −3.9 | 1.3 | 30.7 | 13.1 |
| South Africa | 0.0 | 0.0 | 9.7 | 6.5 | 0.0 | 0.0 | 10.2 | 6.5 |
| Madagascar | 0.0 | 0.0 | 3.9 | 2.7 | 0.0 | −4.4 | 3.4 | 2.7 |
| Mozambique | 0.2 | 0.0 | 12.5 | 10.9 | 0.2 | 0.0 | 14.5 | 10.9 |
| Zambia | −0.8 | 0.0 | 5.6 | 9.0 | −0.8 | 0.0 | 7.0 | 9.0 |
| Zimbabwe | −3.2 | 0.0 | 13.6 | 15.4 | −3.2 | 0.0 | 8.9 | 15.4 |

*(Table continues on the following page.)*

# Table A.4. Price Distortion Structure in GTAP Version 7p5 and the Distortion Rates Drawn from the World Bank Project, 2004 (continued)

(percent)

| Country, region | GTAP version 7p5 | | | | Amended rates | | | |
| --- | --- | --- | --- | --- | --- | --- | --- | --- |
| | Primary agriculture | Agriculture and lightly processed food | | Other goods | Primary agriculture | Agriculture and lightly processed food | | Other goods |
| | Domestic support | Export subsidy | Import tariff | Import tariff | Domestic support | Export subsidy | Import tariff | Import tariff |
| Uganda | 0.0 | 0.0 | 9.5 | 5.5 | 0.0 | −2.6 | 9.2 | 5.5 |
| Tanzania | −0.3 | 0.0 | 11.6 | 13.7 | −0.3 | 0.0 | 11.8 | 13.7 |
| Nigeria | 0.1 | 0.0 | 74.0 | 17.2 | 0.1 | 0.0 | 76.1 | 17.2 |
| Senegal | 0.0 | 0.0 | 8.4 | 8.9 | 0.0 | −1.1 | 6.2 | 8.9 |
| Rest of West and Central Africa | −0.2 | 0.0 | 10.5 | 8.9 | −0.2 | 0.0 | 10.8 | 8.9 |
| Rest of Africa | −0.4 | 0.0 | 10.4 | 14.1 | −0.4 | 0.0 | 10.6 | 14.1 |
| Argentina | −4.9 | 0.0 | 2.9 | 5.7 | 0.0 | −14.8 | 0.0 | 5.8 |
| Brazil | 0.0 | 0.0 | 4.5 | 8.9 | 0.0 | 0.0 | 4.8 | 8.9 |
| Chile | −1.7 | 0.0 | 1.3 | 1.8 | 0.0 | 0.0 | 2.4 | 1.8 |
| Colombia | 0.0 | 0.0 | 12.9 | 9.8 | 0.0 | 0.0 | 21.6 | 9.8 |
| Ecuador | 0.0 | 0.0 | 6.8 | 10.4 | 0.0 | 0.0 | 13.4 | 10.4 |
| Mexico | 1.3 | 0.0 | 8.6 | 3.4 | 1.2 | 0.0 | 6.2 | 3.4 |
| Nicaragua | 0.0 | 0.0 | 8.0 | 3.9 | 0.0 | −2.8 | 9.6 | 3.9 |
| Rest of Latin America and the Caribbean | −1.7 | 0.6 | 9.8 | 9.9 | −1.7 | 0.3 | 9.9 | 9.9 |

Sources: The GTAP version 7p5 rates, which have since been amended, by Narayanan and Walmsley (2008), to create the GTAP Database, version 7; the new rates in the World Bank Agricultural Distortions Global Database compiled by Valenzuela and Anderson (2008).

Note: The price distortion structure is based on the value of production using undistorted prices as weights.

a. The 15 members of the European Union prior to 2004; see table A.2.

**Table A.5. Export Price, Import Price, and Export Demand Shocks to National Models from Rest-of-the-World Agricultural and Trade Policy Reform, Selected Developing Countries**

*(percent deviation from the baseline)*

a. Argentina (global results, excluding Argentina)

| Sector | Export price impact | | Export quantity impact | | Import price impact | |
|---|---|---|---|---|---|---|
| | All goods | Agriculture only | All goods | Agriculture only | All goods | Agriculture only |
| Paddy rice | 4.8 | 5.6 | −98.7 | −98.8 | n.a. | n.a. |
| Wheat | 5.0 | 5.7 | 21.7 | 17.4 | n.a. | n.a. |
| Other grains | 4.7 | 5.5 | 30.8 | 33.6 | 4.8 | 6.5 |
| Oilseeds | 4.8 | 5.6 | 31.1 | 30.1 | 2.8 | 5.0 |
| Sugarcane and beets | n.a. | n.a. | n.a | n.a. | n.a. | n.a. |
| Plant-based fibers | 4.0 | 4.9 | 30.9 | 36.3 | 7.8 | 9.2 |
| Vegetables and fruits | 5.1 | 5.9 | −34.3 | −31.9 | 6.4 | 7.7 |
| Other crops | 5.6 | 6.4 | −24.3 | −22.5 | 3.9 | 4.9 |
| Cattle, sheep, and so on | 5.5 | 6.2 | −36.2 | −33.4 | 1.7 | 2.9 |
| Other livestock | 4.7 | 5.5 | 28.9 | 33.3 | 1.5 | 2.7 |
| Raw milk | n.a. | n.a. | n.a. | n.a. | n.a. | n.a. |
| Wool | 5.4 | 6.2 | −34.1 | −30.2 | 2.7 | 2.6 |
| Beef and sheep meat | 4.5 | 5.3 | 105.2 | 113.8 | 5.7 | 7.4 |
| Other meat products | 4.0 | 4.8 | 148.7 | 154.5 | 5.7 | 6.7 |
| Vegetable oils and fats | 4.2 | 5.0 | −16.2 | −15.9 | 0.4 | 1.6 |
| Dairy products | 3.8 | 4.7 | 426.9 | 439.4 | 7.1 | 9.2 |
| Processed rice | 4.1 | 4.9 | −90.2 | −91.5 | −0.6 | 1.9 |
| Refined sugar | 3.9 | 4.7 | 67.4 | 86.3 | n.a. | n.a. |
| Other food, beverages, and tobacco | 3.3 | 4.1 | 12.3 | −26.5 | 3.5 | 2.1 |

*(Table continues on the following pages.)*

**Table A.5. Export Price, Import Price, and Export Demand Shocks to National Models from Rest-of-the-World Agricultural and Trade Policy Reform, Selected Developing Countries** (*continued*)

*(percent deviation from the baseline)*

a. Argentina (global results, excluding Argentina)

| Sector | Export price impact | | Export quantity impact | | Import price impact | |
|---|---|---|---|---|---|---|
| | All goods | Agriculture only | All goods | Agriculture only | All goods | Agriculture only |
| Other primary products | 3.0 | 3.8 | −21.0 | −19.0 | 2.1 | 2.9 |
| Textiles and wearing apparel | 2.8 | 3.7 | −2.4 | −20.5 | 0.8 | 2.6 |
| Other manufacturing | 2.6 | 3.5 | −25.8 | −18.3 | 0.4 | 1.8 |
| Services | 3.0 | 3.8 | −12.0 | −13.4 | −0.3 | 0.3 |
| Agriculture and food | 4.3 | 5.1 | 21.2 | 17.3 | 4.0 | 4.1 |
| Agriculture | 4.9 | 5.7 | 14.7 | 14.7 | 4.5 | 5.9 |
| Processed foods | 4.0 | 4.8 | 25.2 | 18.9 | 3.7 | 3.1 |
| Other manufacturing | 2.7 | 3.6 | −22.7 | −18.6 | 0.5 | 1.9 |
| Nontradables | 3.0 | 3.8 | −12.0 | −13.4 | −0.3 | 0.3 |
| Total | 3.6 | 4.4 | −0.5 | −0.9 | 0.4 | 1.6 |
| Merchandise trade | 3.7 | 4.5 | 1.1 | 0.9 | 0.6 | 1.9 |

b. Brazil (global results, excluding Brazil)

| Sector | Export price impact | | Export quantity impact | | Import price impact | |
|---|---|---|---|---|---|---|
| | All goods | Agriculture only | All goods | Agriculture only | All goods | Agriculture only |
| Paddy rice | n.a. | n.a. | n.a. | n.a. | 4.8 | 6.4 |
| Wheat | 7.1 | 7.2 | 19.6 | 33.7 | −2.8 | −3.5 |
| Other grains | 8.4 | 8.6 | 19.9 | 21.8 | −3.3 | −3.1 |
| Oilseeds | 8.1 | 8.3 | −23.9 | −21.8 | 1.5 | 3.2 |

| | | | | | | |
|---|---|---|---|---|---|---|
| Sugarcane and beets | n.a. | n.a. | n.a | n.a. | n.a. | n.a. |
| Plant-based fibers | 8.7 | 8.9 | -2.4 | 1.0 | 14.4 | 16.7 |
| Vegetables and fruits | 8.6 | 8.9 | -54.8 | -51.7 | 7.1 | 7.2 |
| Other crops | 9.0 | 9.3 | 6.4 | 14.3 | 0.0 | 0.7 |
| Cattle, sheep, and so on | 8.9 | 9.1 | -51.9 | -47.8 | 1.1 | 2.3 |
| Other livestock | 8.8 | 9.0 | -41.5 | -38.4 | 0.0 | 1.0 |
| Raw milk | n.a. | n.a. | n.a. | n.a. | n.a. | n.a. |
| Wool | 10.8 | 11.1 | -55.5 | -47.7 | n.a. | n.a. |
| Beef and sheep meat | 7.6 | 7.7 | 918.9 | 972.6 | 5.1 | 6.6 |
| Other meat products | 7.8 | 8.0 | 76.2 | 84.7 | -3.4 | -2.7 |
| Vegetable oils and fats | 6.8 | 6.9 | -40.6 | -40.8 | -0.8 | -0.3 |
| Dairy products | 7.0 | 7.1 | 572.8 | 626.0 | 10.5 | 11.1 |
| Processed rice | 6.7 | 6.8 | -27.5 | -28.0 | 4.0 | 5.3 |
| Refined sugar | 6.5 | 6.6 | 140.7 | 164.1 | n.a. | n.a. |
| Other food, beverages, and tobacco | 6.1 | 6.1 | 84.5 | -38.1 | 7.3 | 2.4 |
| Other primary products | 5.6 | 5.7 | -30.5 | -33.5 | -2.6 | 1.4 |
| Textiles and wearing apparel | 5.4 | 5.5 | -27.6 | -30.3 | 0.1 | 1.2 |
| Other manufacturing | 5.1 | 5.2 | -32.4 | -29.5 | 0.6 | 0.7 |
| Services | 5.9 | 5.9 | -21.7 | -20.5 | -0.2 | 0.3 |
| Agriculture and food | 7.5 | 7.7 | 92.8 | 87.0 | 3.4 | 1.9 |
| Agriculture | 8.5 | 8.7 | -12.7 | -8.5 | 0.9 | 1.0 |
| Processed foods | 7.1 | 7.3 | 166.2 | 153.4 | 6.0 | 2.9 |
| Other manufacturing | 5.2 | 5.3 | -31.8 | -30.1 | 0.3 | 0.8 |
| Nontradables | 5.9 | 5.9 | -21.7 | -20.5 | -0.2 | 0.3 |
| Total | 6.1 | 6.3 | 2.2 | 1.9 | 0.3 | 0.7 |
| Merchandise trade | 6.1 | 6.3 | 4.9 | 4.4 | 0.5 | 0.8 |

*(Table continues on the following pages.)*

# Table A.5. Export Price, Import Price, and Export Demand Shocks to National Models from Rest-of-the-World Agricultural and Trade Policy Reform, Selected Developing Countries (continued)

(percent deviation from the baseline)

## c. China (global results, excluding China)

| Sector | Export price impact | | Export quantity impact | | Import price impact | |
|---|---|---|---|---|---|---|
| | All goods | Agriculture only | All goods | Agriculture only | All goods | Agriculture only |
| Paddy rice | 4.2 | 1.8 | 94.9 | 123.6 | n.a. | n.a. |
| Wheat | 3.5 | 1.4 | 15.5 | 45.8 | 2.9 | 3.6 |
| Other grains | 3.9 | 1.6 | 105.1 | 157.7 | 6.5 | 6.5 |
| Oilseeds | 4.0 | 1.7 | 10.3 | 42.9 | -2.8 | -2.3 |
| Sugarcane and beets | n.a. | n.a. | n.a. | n.a. | n.a. | n.a. |
| Plant-based fibers | 3.3 | 1.3 | 30.0 | 51.4 | 10.0 | 11.5 |
| Vegetables and fruits | 4.2 | 1.8 | 185.5 | 232.9 | 1.9 | 1.6 |
| Other crops | 4.5 | 2.0 | -12.7 | 8.4 | 1.3 | 1.5 |
| Cattle, sheep, and so on | 4.4 | 1.9 | -18.6 | -3.1 | 6.5 | 6.6 |
| Other livestock | 3.8 | 1.6 | -20.8 | -0.2 | 0.7 | 1.6 |
| Raw milk | 4.1 | 1.7 | -48.3 | -31.7 | -1.8 | -0.7 |
| Wool | 3.8 | 1.6 | -13.1 | 10.1 | 4.9 | 4.9 |
| Beef and sheep meat | 3.4 | 1.3 | -1.8 | 21.0 | 7.0 | 7.6 |
| Other meat products | 3.5 | 1.3 | 30.7 | 58.1 | 1.9 | 2.8 |
| Vegetable oils and fats | 1.8 | 0.3 | -6.4 | 5.7 | -0.2 | -0.9 |
| Dairy products | 2.9 | 0.8 | 191.2 | 251.6 | 10.9 | 11.4 |
| Processed rice | 3.0 | 0.9 | -148.8 | 192.1 | 4.2 | 3.4 |
| Refined sugar | 3.0 | 0.8 | 410.2 | 560.4 | 1.4 | 2.0 |
| Other food, beverages, and tobacco | 2.9 | 0.8 | 66.4 | -16.0 | 0.0 | -1.0 |

| | Export price impact | | Export quantity impact | | Import price impact | |
|---|---|---|---|---|---|---|
| | All goods | Agriculture only | All goods | Agriculture only | All goods | Agriculture only |
| Other primary products | 2.7 | 0.6 | −7.9 | 2.0 | 0.5 | 1.1 |
| Textiles and wearing apparel | 2.6 | 0.8 | 13.7 | −2.1 | −0.2 | 0.4 |
| Other manufacturing | 2.2 | 0.5 | −3.3 | −1.6 | 0.7 | 0.3 |
| Services | 2.5 | 0.5 | −10.4 | −0.9 | 0.1 | 0.2 |
| Agriculture and food | 3.3 | 1.2 | 66.6 | 33.8 | 1.4 | 1.5 |
| Agriculture | 4.1 | 1.8 | 72.4 | 106.3 | 1.8 | 2.4 |
| Processed foods | 3.0 | 0.9 | 63.5 | −0.4 | 0.9 | 0.3 |
| Other manufacturing | 2.3 | 0.5 | 0.4 | −1.6 | 0.6 | 0.3 |
| Nontradables | 2.5 | 0.5 | −10.5 | −0.9 | 0.1 | 0.2 |
| Total | 2.4 | 0.6 | 2.2 | −0.3 | 0.6 | 0.4 |
| Merchandise trade | 2.4 | 0.6 | 3.2 | −0.3 | 0.7 | 0.4 |

### d. Indonesia (global results, excluding Indonesia)

| Sector | Export price impact | | Export quantity impact | | Import price impact | |
|---|---|---|---|---|---|---|
| | All goods | Agriculture only | All goods | Agriculture only | All goods | Agriculture only |
| Paddy rice | n.a. | n.a. | n.a. | n.a. | 4.3 | 2.7 |
| Wheat | n.a. | n.a. | n.a. | n.a. | 6.8 | 7.1 |
| Other grains | 3.1 | 1.4 | 50.8 | 69.4 | −2.7 | −2.8 |
| Oilseeds | 3.0 | 1.3 | −13.6 | 7.6 | −1.8 | −1.3 |
| Sugarcane and beets | n.a. | n.a. | n.a. | n.a. | n.a. | n.a. |
| Plant-based fibers | 3.1 | 1.4 | 2.8 | 38.2 | 7.6 | 8.7 |
| Vegetables and fruits | 3.1 | 1.4 | 5.4 | 20.9 | 2.6 | 1.9 |
| Other crops | 3.0 | 1.3 | −13.4 | 2.6 | 1.5 | 1.8 |
| Cattle, sheep, and so on | 3.0 | 1.3 | 1.1 | 24.3 | 5.6 | 5.5 |
| Other livestock | 2.7 | 1.1 | −18.3 | −5.2 | −1.9 | −0.6 |

*(Table continues on the following pages.)*

**Table A.5. Export Price, Import Price, and Export Demand Shocks to National Models from Rest-of-the-World Agricultural and Trade Policy Reform, Selected Developing Countries (*continued*)**

*(percent deviation from the baseline)*

d. Indonesia (global results, excluding Indonesia)

| Sector | Export price impact | | Export quantity impact | | Import price impact | |
|---|---|---|---|---|---|---|
| | All goods | Agriculture only | All goods | Agriculture only | All goods | Agriculture only |
| Raw milk | n.a. | n.a. | n.a. | n.a. | n.a. | n.a. |
| Wool | n.a. | n.a. | n.a. | n.a. | 9.8 | 10.0 |
| Beef and sheep meat | 3.0 | 1.4 | −61.2 | −50.8 | 5.6 | 5.7 |
| Other meat products | 2.5 | 0.8 | 185.5 | 265.8 | 3.3 | 3.6 |
| Vegetable oils and fats | 2.5 | 0.9 | 8.9 | 22.5 | 0.4 | 1.1 |
| Dairy products | 2.7 | 1.1 | 419.3 | 514.3 | 8.6 | 8.8 |
| Processed rice | 3.0 | 1.3 | −38.1 | −28.7 | 3.7 | 2.8 |
| Refined sugar | 2.6 | 1.0 | 445.7 | 502.2 | 2.9 | 2.5 |
| Other food, beverages, and tobacco | 2.4 | 0.9 | 106.0 | −12.7 | −0.8 | −0.7 |
| Other primary products | 2.1 | 0.6 | −8.6 | 2.3 | 1.3 | 0.8 |
| Textiles and wearing apparel | 2.1 | 1.0 | 11.4 | −3.9 | −0.3 | 0.4 |
| Other manufacturing | 1.9 | 0.6 | −4.3 | −2.6 | 0.4 | 0.4 |
| Services | 2.1 | 0.6 | −9.0 | −1.4 | −0.2 | 0.2 |
| Agriculture and food | 2.5 | 1.0 | 39.0 | 12.9 | 3.0 | 3.2 |
| Agriculture | 3.0 | 1.3 | −11.2 | 4.4 | 4.1 | 4.5 |
| Processed foods | 2.5 | 0.9 | 51.4 | 15.0 | 1.7 | 1.8 |
| Other manufacturing | 2.0 | 0.6 | −2.4 | −2.0 | 0.4 | 0.4 |
| Nontradables | 2.1 | 0.6 | −9.0 | −1.4 | −0.2 | 0.2 |
| Total | 2.1 | 0.7 | 2.2 | −0.1 | 0.5 | 0.6 |
| Merchandise trade | 2.1 | 0.7 | 3.1 | 0.0 | 0.7 | 0.8 |

## e. Mozambique (global results, excluding Mozambique)

| Sector | Export price impact | | Export quantity impact | | Import price impact | |
|---|---|---|---|---|---|---|
| | All goods | Agriculture only | All goods | Agriculture only | All goods | Agriculture only |
| Paddy rice | n.a. | n.a. | n.a. | n.a. | 8.5 | 9.7 |
| Wheat | n.a. | n.a. | n.a. | n.a. | −0.9 | −0.8 |
| Other grains | 1.1 | 1.4 | 3.4 | 19.7 | 2.6 | 4.1 |
| Oilseeds | 0.6 | 0.9 | 496.3 | 567.8 | −2.7 | −1.5 |
| Sugarcane and beets | n.a. | n.a. | n.a. | n.a. | n.a. | n.a. |
| Plant-based fibers | 0.7 | 1.2 | 48.4 | 56.4 | n.a. | n.a. |
| Vegetables and fruits | 1.0 | 1.3 | −9.7 | −2.8 | −1.2 | 0.1 |
| Other crops | 1.1 | 1.4 | 8.7 | 16.0 | −0.7 | 0.3 |
| Cattle, sheep, and so on | n.a. | n.a. | n.a. | n.a. | n.a. | n.a. |
| Other livestock | n.a. | n.a. | n.a. | n.a. | −1.7 | −0.1 |
| Raw milk | n.a. | n.a. | n.a. | n.a. | n.a. | n.a. |
| Wool | n.a. | n.a. | n.a. | n.a. | n.a. | n.a. |
| Beef and sheep meat | n.a. | n.a. | n.a. | n.a. | −1.3 | 0.1 |
| Other meat products | n.a. | n.a. | n.a. | n.a. | 1.6 | 3.1 |
| Vegetable oils and fats | 0.3 | 0.7 | 13.1 | 10.8 | −0.3 | −0.8 |
| Dairy products | n.a. | n.a. | n.a. | n.a. | −0.9 | 0.4 |
| Processed rice | n.a. | n.a. | n.a. | n.a. | 3.3 | 3.2 |
| Refined sugar | 0.4 | 0.9 | −21.9 | −11.9 | −1.4 | −0.1 |
| Other food, beverages, and tobacco | 0.4 | 0.7 | −5.8 | −15.7 | 1.9 | −0.3 |
| Other primary products | 0.8 | 1.1 | 38.4 | −3.1 | 0.6 | 0.4 |
| Textiles and wearing apparel | 0.3 | 0.8 | 22.3 | −3.2 | −1.3 | 0.6 |
| Other manufacturing | 0.2 | 0.7 | −7.6 | −5.1 | −0.8 | 0.2 |

*(Table continues on the following pages.)*

**478**

## Table A.5. Export Price, Import Price, and Export Demand Shocks to National Models from Rest-of-the-World Agricultural and Trade Policy Reform, Selected Developing Countries (*continued*)

*(percent deviation from the baseline)*

### e. Mozambique (global results, excluding Mozambique)

| Sector | Export price impact | | Export quantity impact | | Import price impact | |
|---|---|---|---|---|---|---|
| | All goods | Agriculture only | All goods | Agriculture only | All goods | Agriculture only |
| Services | 0.3 | 0.7 | 1.7 | 1.0 | −0.3 | 0.3 |
| Agriculture and food | 0.7 | 1.0 | 15.7 | 18.0 | 0.5 | 0.3 |
| Agriculture | 0.9 | 1.3 | 37.7 | 48.9 | −0.5 | 0.0 |
| Processed foods | 0.4 | 0.7 | −6.9 | −13.6 | 1.1 | 0.5 |
| Other manufacturing | 0.2 | 0.7 | −5.2 | −5.0 | −0.8 | 0.3 |
| Nontradables | 0.3 | 0.7 | 1.7 | 1.0 | −0.3 | 0.3 |
| Total | 0.3 | 0.7 | −0.3 | 0.0 | −0.5 | 0.3 |
| Merchandise trade | 0.3 | 0.8 | −1.1 | −0.5 | −0.5 | 0.3 |

### f. Nicaragua (global results, excluding Nicaragua)

| Sector | Export price impact | | Export quantity impact | | Import price impact | |
|---|---|---|---|---|---|---|
| | All goods | Agriculture only | All goods | Agriculture only | All goods | Agriculture only |
| Paddy rice | n.a. | n.a. | n.a. | n.a. | 8.5 | 9.7 |
| Wheat | n.a. | n.a. | n.a. | n.a. | 2.1 | 3.1 |
| Other grains | n.a. | n.a. | n.a. | n.a. | 16.4 | 17.6 |
| Oilseeds | 2.3 | 2.7 | 41.2 | 49.4 | n.a. | n.a. |

| | | | | | | |
|---|---|---|---|---|---|---|
| Sugarcane and beets | n.a. | n.a. | n.a. | n.a. | n.a. | n.a. |
| Plant-based fibers | n.a. | r.a. | n.a. | n.a. | n.a. | n.a. |
| Vegetables and fruits | 2.4 | 2.8 | −18.0 | −15.2 | 2.6 | 4.6 |
| Other crops | 2.5 | 2.9 | −18.2 | −14.2 | 7.2 | 9.1 |
| Cattle, sheep, and so on | 2.8 | 3.3 | 21.7 | 31.3 | 18.7 | 21.0 |
| Other livestock | 3.0 | 3.5 | −30.5 | −24.7 | 1.7 | 3.7 |
| Raw milk | n.a. | n.a. | n.a. | n.a. | n.a. | n.a. |
| Wool | n.a. | n.a. | n.a. | n.a. | n.a. | n.a. |
| Beef and sheep meat | 1.5 | 2.0 | 30.3 | 36.2 | 2.0 | 3.1 |
| Other meat products | 2.3 | 2.8 | 64.1 | 72.7 | 5.9 | 7.7 |
| Vegetable oils and fats | 1.8 | 2.1 | −24.2 | −22.5 | −0.1 | 1.3 |
| Dairy products | 2.2 | 2.5 | −8.7 | −0.6 | 5.8 | 7.7 |
| Processed rice | n.a. | n.a. | n.a. | n.a. | −0.1 | 1.1 |
| Refined sugar | 1.7 | 2.0 | 49.3 | 64.8 | n.a. | n.a. |
| Other food, beverages, and tobacco | 1.8 | 2.1 | 8.5 | −13.3 | 1.1 | 1.4 |
| Other primary products | 1.5 | 1.6 | −27.5 | −4.9 | −0.5 | 2.1 |
| Textiles and wearing apparel | 1.3 | 1.4 | 5.6 | −4.8 | 0.2 | 0.6 |
| Other manufacturing | 1.1 | 1.4 | −23.1 | −7.1 | 0.0 | 1.0 |
| Services | 1.4 | 1.4 | −6.2 | −4.8 | −0.4 | 0.2 |
| Agriculture and food | 2.0 | 2.4 | 9.4 | 8.9 | 2.4 | 3.3 |
| Agriculture | 2.5 | 2.9 | −2.1 | 3.2 | 5.6 | 6.9 |
| Processed foods | 1.7 | 2.1 | 18.1 | 13.1 | 1.0 | 1.7 |
| Other manufacturing | 1.2 | 1.4 | −2.6 | −5.4 | 0.0 | 1.0 |
| Nontradables | 1.4 | 1.4 | −6.2 | −4.8 | −0.4 | 0.2 |
| Total | 1.5 | 1.8 | 1.2 | −0.1 | 0.3 | 1.3 |
| Merchandise trade | 1.6 | 1.8 | 2.5 | 0.6 | 0.4 | 1.4 |

(Table continues on the following pages.)

**Table A.5. Export Price, Import Price, and Export Demand Shocks to National Models from Rest-of-the-World Agricultural and Trade Policy Reform, Selected Developing Countries (continued)**

(percent deviation from the baseline)

g. Pakistan (global results, excluding Pakistan)

| Sector | Export price impact | | Export quantity impact | | Import price impact | |
|---|---|---|---|---|---|---|
| | All goods | Agriculture only | All goods | Agriculture only | All goods | Agriculture only |
| Paddy rice | 1.4 | 1.0 | 117.4 | 138.0 | n.a. | n.a. |
| Wheat | n.a. | n.a. | n.a. | n.a. | 2.4 | 3.1 |
| Other grains | n.a. | n.a. | n.a. | n.a. | 13.6 | 14.6 |
| Oilseeds | 1.6 | 1.2 | 76.7 | 103.1 | 1.5 | 1.9 |
| Sugarcane and beets | n.a. | n.a. | n.a. | n.a. | n.a. | n.a. |
| Plant-based fibers | 1.3 | 1.0 | 57.8 | 59.2 | 4.4 | 6.7 |
| Vegetables and fruits | 1.4 | 1.0 | −20.9 | −13.7 | −2.9 | −2.6 |
| Other crops | 1.5 | 1.1 | −17.7 | −1.6 | −1.9 | 0.0 |
| Cattle, sheep, and so on | 1.4 | 1.0 | −42.1 | −28.1 | n.a. | n.a. |
| Other livestock | 1.4 | 1.0 | −20.5 | −9.1 | −8.0 | −6.8 |
| Raw milk | 1.4 | 1.0 | −36.5 | −27.6 | n.a. | n.a. |
| Wool | n.a. | n.a. | n.a. | n.a. | −10.5 | −8.8 |
| Beef and sheep meat | 1.1 | 0.6 | −39.4 | −31.0 | 2.2 | 3.2 |
| Other meat products | n.a. | n.a. | n.a. | n.a. | 0.2 | 1.4 |
| Vegetable oils and fats | 1.1 | 0.7 | −28.0 | −26.7 | 1.8 | 0.4 |
| Dairy products | 1.2 | 0.7 | 22.0 | 49.6 | 16.8 | 17.8 |
| Processed rice | 1.2 | 0.7 | 25.8 | 34.0 | 8.2 | 10.2 |
| Refined sugar | 1.1 | 0.6 | −26.3 | −5.3 | 1.6 | 3.4 |
| Other food, beverages, and tobacco | 1.1 | 0.6 | 3.6 | −14.0 | 0.0 | −1.7 |
| Other primary products | 1.0 | 0.4 | 20.0 | 1.8 | −0.1 | 0.8 |

| | | | | | |
|---|---|---|---|---|---|
| Textiles and wearing apparel | 1.0 | 0.7 | 3.? | −2.1 | −0.7 | 0.5 |
| Other manufacturing | 0.7 | 0.5 | −2.? | −1.9 | −0.4 | 0.4 |
| Services | 0.9 | 0.5 | −4.? | −0.6 | −0.2 | 0.2 |
| Agriculture and food | 1.2 | 0.8 | 10.8 | 15.0 | 1.6 | 2.0 |
| Agriculture | 1.4 | 1.0 | 15.? | 25.6 | 1.5 | 3.0 |
| Processed foods | 1.1 | 0.7 | 9.? | 11.4 | 1.7 | 0.5 |
| Other manufacturing | 0.9 | 0.7 | 2.? | −2.0 | −0.4 | 0.4 |
| Nontradables | 0.9 | 0.5 | −4.? | −0.6 | −0.2 | 0.2 |
| Total | 1.0 | 0.6 | 2.0 | −0.2 | −0.1 | 0.5 |
| Merchandise trade | 1.0 | 0.7 | 3.? | −0.1 | −0.1 | 0.6 |

## h. The Philippines (global results, excluding the Philippines)

| Sector | Export price impact | | Export quantity impact | | Import price impact | |
|---|---|---|---|---|---|---|
| | All goods | Agriculture only | All goods | Agriculture only | All goods | Agriculture only |
| Paddy rice | n.a. | n.a. | n.a. | n.a. | n.a. | n.a. |
| Wheat | n.a. | n.a. | n.a. | n.a. | 3.0 | 3.9 |
| Other grains | n.a. | n.a. | n.a. | n.a. | 6.1 | 5.7 |
| Oilseeds | n.a. | n.a. | n.a. | n.a. | −0.8 | −0.5 |
| Sugarcane and beets | n.a. | n.a. | n.a. | n.a. | n.a. | n.a. |
| Plant-based fibers | 5.5 | 3.7 | 4.0 | 32.7 | 13.8 | 15.6 |
| Vegetables and fruits | 5.7 | 3.8 | 35.8 | 51.0 | 2.4 | 1.7 |
| Other crops | 5.9 | 3.9 | −30.3 | −10.6 | 1.3 | 1.4 |
| Cattle, sheep, and so on | n.a. | n.a. | n.a. | n.a. | 5.6 | 5.5 |
| Other livestock | 5.6 | 3.6 | −30.0 | −12.2 | −1.0 | 0.1 |
| Raw milk | n.a. | n.a. | n.a. | n.a. | n.a. | n.a. |

(Table continues on the following pages.)

**Table A.5. Export Price, Import Price, and Export Demand Shocks to National Models from Rest-of-the-World Agricultural and Trade Policy Reform, Selected Developing Countries (*continued*)**

*(percent deviation from the baseline)*

**h. The Philippines (global results, excluding the Philippines)**

| Sector | Export price impact | | Export quantity impact | | Import price impact | |
|---|---|---|---|---|---|---|
| | All goods | Agriculture only | All goods | Agriculture only | All goods | Agriculture only |
| Wool | n.a. | n.a. | n.a. | n.a. | n.a. | n.a. |
| Beef and sheep meat | 3.7 | 2.0 | −95.3 | −94.0 | 2.8 | 4.5 |
| Other meat products | 4.7 | 2.7 | 14.0 | 42.0 | −0.2 | 0.3 |
| Vegetable oils and fats | 2.6 | 0.9 | −10.3 | 5.9 | −1.1 | −1.7 |
| Dairy products | 4.9 | 4.2 | 13.0 | 19.6 | 7.0 | 7.4 |
| Processed rice | 5.3 | 3.3 | −65.7 | −59.7 | 4.3 | 1.6 |
| Refined sugar | 3.9 | 2.0 | 885.2 | 1,238.4 | 2.1 | 0.8 |
| Other food, beverages, and tobacco | 3.6 | 2.0 | 73.0 | −20.0 | 1.6 | −0.4 |
| Other primary products | 2.8 | 1.0 | 12.6 | −1.9 | 0.6 | 0.9 |
| Textiles and wearing apparel | 2.0 | 1.1 | 12.4 | −4.0 | −0.2 | 0.4 |
| Other manufacturing | 2.1 | 0.7 | −5.1 | −3.7 | 1.5 | 0.3 |
| Services | 2.9 | 1.1 | −11.9 | −3.6 | −0.1 | 0.2 |
| Agriculture and food | 4.3 | 2.5 | 64.2 | 46.6 | 2.5 | 1.7 |
| Agriculture | 5.7 | 3.8 | 32.6 | 48.1 | 2.6 | 3.0 |
| Processed foods | 3.5 | 1.8 | 82.6 | 45.7 | 2.4 | 1.3 |
| Other manufacturing | 2.1 | 0.7 | −3.8 | −3.7 | 1.3 | 0.3 |
| Nontradables | 2.9 | 1.1 | −11.9 | −3.6 | −0.1 | 0.2 |
| Total | 2.3 | 0.9 | −0.4 | −0.9 | 1.3 | 0.4 |
| Merchandise trade | 2.3 | 0.9 | 0.3 | −0.7 | 1.4 | 0.5 |

i. South Africa (global results, excluding South Africa)

| Sector | Export price impact | | Export quantity impact | | Import price impact | |
|---|---|---|---|---|---|---|
| | All goods | Agriculture only | All goods | Agriculture only | All goods | Agriculture only |
| Paddy rice | n.a. | n.a. | n.a. | n.a. | n.a. | n.a. |
| Wheat | 0.5 | 0.4 | 21.6 | -15.9 | 0.7 | 0.7 |
| Other grains | 0.5 | 0.3 | 48.6 | 59.3 | -5.5 | -5.5 |
| Oilseeds | 0.5 | 0.3 | -25.5 | -13.7 | -2.3 | -2.0 |
| Sugarcane and beets | n.a. | n.a. | n.a. | n.a. | n.a. | n.a. |
| Plant-based fibers | 0.4 | 0.3 | 53.2 | 52.9 | -1.2 | -0.1 |
| Vegetables and fruits | 0.5 | 0.3 | -38.6 | -33.7 | -0.9 | -0.4 |
| Other crops | 0.5 | 0.3 | 7.0 | 10.9 | 1.9 | 2.8 |
| Cattle, sheep, and so on | 0.5 | 0.3 | 5.7 | 17.1 | -2.2 | -0.4 |
| Other livestock | 0.6 | 0.3 | -10.5 | -1.2 | 0.7 | 1.4 |
| Raw milk | 0.5 | 0.3 | -32.0 | -23.8 | n.a. | n.a. |
| Wool | 0.4 | 0.4 | 4.1 | 11.0 | 19.5 | 19.8 |
| Beef and sheep meat | 0.5 | 0.4 | 443.5 | 489.9 | 5.1 | 5.8 |
| Other meat products | 0.6 | 0.4 | -11.4 | -1.9 | 3.7 | 4.8 |
| Vegetable oils and fats | 0.3 | 0.1 | -1.1 | 0.7 | -1.8 | -2.5 |
| Dairy products | 0.6 | 0.5 | 405.9 | 447.6 | 16.6 | 17.5 |
| Processed rice | 0.6 | 0.5 | -47.2 | -41.5 | 5.0 | 4.6 |
| Refined sugar | 0.5 | 0.4 | 147.2 | 173.5 | 1.2 | 2.1 |
| Other food, beverages, and tobacco | 0.5 | 0.4 | 58.3 | -10.4 | 5.0 | -0.4 |
| Other primary products | 0.5 | 0.4 | 0.3 | 1.0 | 0.2 | 0.7 |
| Textiles and wearing apparel | 0.3 | 0.4 | -21.2 | -0.1 | -0.9 | 0.5 |
| Other manufacturing | 0.4 | 0.4 | -2.3 | -1.2 | -0.3 | 0.2 |

(Table continues on the following pages.)

**Table A.5. Export Price, Import Price, and Export Demand Shocks to National Models from Rest-of-the-World Agricultural and Trade Policy Reform, Selected Developing Countries** *(continued)*

*(percent deviation from the baseline)*

i. South Africa (global results, excluding South Africa)

| Sector | Export price impact | | Export quantity impact | | Import price impact | |
|---|---|---|---|---|---|---|
| | All goods | Agriculture only | All goods | Agriculture only | All goods | Agriculture only |
| Services | 0.6 | 0.4 | −2.7 | −0.6 | −0.1 | 0.3 |
| Agriculture and food | 0.5 | 0.4 | 31.3 | 7.7 | 2.2 | 0.6 |
| Agriculture | 0.5 | 0.3 | −23.7 | −18.6 | −0.3 | 0.3 |
| Processed foods | 0.5 | 0.4 | 80.2 | 31.0 | 3.4 | 0.8 |
| Other manufacturing | 0.5 | 0.4 | −2.4 | −0.8 | −0.3 | 0.3 |
| Nontradables | 0.6 | 0.4 | −2.7 | −0.6 | −0.1 | 0.3 |
| Total | 0.5 | 0.4 | 0.8 | 0.1 | −0.2 | 0.3 |
| Merchandise trade | 0.5 | 0.4 | 1.3 | 0.2 | −0.2 | 0.3 |

j. Thailand (global results, excluding Thailand)

| Sector | Export price impact | | Export quantity impact | | Import price impact | |
|---|---|---|---|---|---|---|
| | All goods | Agriculture only | All goods | Agriculture only | All goods | Agriculture only |
| Paddy rice | 7.3 | 5.7 | 82.5 | 118.1 | n.a. | n.a. |
| Wheat | n.a. | n.a. | n.a. | n.a. | 3.3 | 4.0 |
| Other grains | 6.4 | 4.8 | 30.1 | 48.7 | 4.9 | 4.5 |
| Oilseeds | 6.0 | 4.7 | −30.9 | −18.4 | −6.0 | −5.6 |
| Sugarcane and beets | n.a. | n.a. | n.a. | n.a. | n.a. | n.a. |

| | | | | | | |
|---|---|---|---|---|---|---|
| Plant-based fibers | 6.8 | 5.2 | 7.2 | 13.5 | 6.4 | 7.9 |
| Vegetables and fruits | 7.2 | 5.6 | 5.3 | 11.9 | 1.8 | 1.1 |
| Other crops | 7.3 | 5.8 | −33.4 | −21.5 | 1.7 | 1.6 |
| Cattle, sheep, and so on | 6.2 | 4.6 | −17.2 | −3.8 | 3.6 | 2.8 |
| Other livestock | 5.4 | 3.7 | −25.0 | −12.2 | 0.6 | 1.1 |
| Raw milk | n.a. | n.a. | n.a. | n.a. | n.a. | n.a. |
| Wool | n.a. | n.a. | n.a. | n.a. | 5.5 | 5.3 |
| Beef and sheep meat | 4.1 | 2.2 | −91.7 | −89.2 | 10.0 | 10.1 |
| Other meat products | 4.5 | 2.7 | 48.5 | 79.7 | 1.6 | 2.5 |
| Vegetable oils and fats | 2.6 | 0.9 | 5.6 | 20.1 | 0.7 | 1.2 |
| Dairy products | 4.4 | 2.6 | 70.3 | 93.1 | 12.2 | 12.5 |
| Processed rice | 6.6 | 4.9 | 48.5 | 64.4 | 1.4 | 0.5 |
| Refined sugar | 4.6 | 2.7 | 506.3 | 563.6 | n.a. | n.a. |
| Other food, beverages, and tobacco | 3.5 | 1.7 | 47.6 | −17.2 | 0.9 | −1.4 |
| Other primary products | 3.3 | 1.2 | −10.5 | −5.1 | 0.5 | 0.8 |
| Textiles and wearing apparel | 3.2 | 1.4 | −0.5 | −7.6 | −0.4 | 0.5 |
| Other manufacturing | 2.9 | 1.1 | −8.1 | −6.9 | 1.3 | 0.3 |
| Services | 3.3 | 1.2 | −13.0 | −3.7 | −0.2 | 0.2 |
| Agriculture and food | 4.6 | 3.0 | 70.3 | 45.6 | 1.7 | 0.9 |
| Agriculture | 7.0 | 5.5 | 5.5 | 17.4 | 1.1 | 1.6 |
| Processed foods | 4.3 | 2.7 | 80.0 | 49.8 | 2.1 | 0.5 |
| Other manufacturing | 3.0 | 1.2 | −7.4 | −7.0 | 1.1 | 0.3 |
| Nontradables | 3.3 | 1.2 | −13.0 | −3.7 | −0.2 | 0.2 |
| Total | 3.3 | 1.4 | 1.0 | −0.4 | 1.0 | 0.4 |
| Merchandise trade | 3.3 | 1.5 | 3.1 | 0.1 | 1.2 | 0.4 |

Source: World Bank Linkage model simulations by the authors.

Note: n.a. = not applicable.

## Notes

1. The 10 national studies cover Argentina (Cicowiez, Díaz-Bonilla, and Díaz-Bonilla; chapter 12), Brazil (Ferreira Filho and Horridge; chapter 13), China (Zhai and Hertel; chapter 5), Indonesia (Warr; chapter 6), Mozambique (Arndt and Thurlow; chapter 10), Nicaragua (Sánchez and Vos; chapter 14), Pakistan (Cororaton and Orden; chapter 7), the Philippines (Cororaton, Corong, and Cockburn; chapter 8), South Africa (Hérault and Thurlow; chapter 11), and Thailand (Warr; chapter 9).

2. The distortions database of the World Bank research project is documented fully in Anderson and Valenzuela (2008); it is based on the methodology summarized in Anderson et al. (2008a, 2008b).

3. Such a calculation is pertinent for models in which exports and domestic goods are perfect substitutes; see Horridge and Zhai (2006) for details on models that assume imperfect substitution.

4. In this study, the average sectoral trade volumes in the Linkage model are derived using Divisia indexes. These are computed using weights that change over the course of the simulations. In effect, they are an average of before and after shares. In earlier studies, the results from the Linkage model were derived using the Paasche export price index (that is, based on trade volumes after the shocks).

5. There is a special version of the GTAP model known as GTAP-AGR that has an agricultural focus (Keeney and Hertel 2005).

6. A discussion on this and other labor market specification issues is available in van der Mensbrugghe (2007).

7. The fixed factor in the natural resource sectors is aggregated with capital.

## References

Anderson, K., M. Kurzweil, W. Martin, D. Sandri, and E. Valenzuela. 2008a. "Methodology for Measuring Distortions to Agricultural Incentives." In *Distortions to Agricultural Incentives: A Global Perspective, 1955–2007*, ed. K. Anderson, Appendix A. London: Palgrave Macmillan; Washington, DC: World Bank.

———. 2008b. "Measuring Distortions to Agricultural Incentives, Revisited." *World Trade Review* 7 (4): 1–30.

Anderson, K., and E. Valenzuela. 2008. "Estimates of Global Distortions to Agricultural Incentives, 1955–2007." Data spreadsheet, October, World Bank, Washington, DC. http://go.worldbank.org/YAO39F35E0.

Armington, P. S. 1969. "A Theory of Demand for Products Distinguished by Place of Production." *IMF Staff Papers* 16 (1): 159–78.

Dimaranan, B. D., ed. 2006. *Global Trade, Assistance, and Protection: The GTAP 6 Data Base.* West Lafayette, IN: Center for Global Trade Analysis, Department of Agricultural Economics, Purdue University. https://www.gtap.agecon.purdue.edu/databases/v6/v6_doco.asp.

GIDD Database (Global Income Distribution Dynamics Database). World Bank. http://go.worldbank.org/YADEAFEJ30.

Horridge, M., and F. Zhai. 2006. "Shocking a Single-Country CGE Model with Export Prices and Quantities from a Global Model." In *Poverty and the WTO: Impacts of the Doha Development Agenda*, ed. T. W. Hertel and L. A. Winters, 94–104. London: Palgrave Macmillan; Washington, DC: World Bank.

Keeney, R., and T. W. Hertel. 2005. "GTAP-AGR: A Framework for Assessing the Implications of Multilateral Changes in Agricultural Policies." GTAP Technical Paper 24 (August), Center for Global Trade Analysis, Department of Agricultural Economics, Purdue University, West Lafayette, IN. https://www.gtap.agecon.purdue.edu/resources/res_display.asp?RecordID=1869.

Narayanan, B. G., and T. L. Walmsley, eds. 2008. *Global Trade, Assistance, and Production: The GTAP 7 Data Base.* West Lafayette, IN: Center for Global Trade Analysis, Department of Agricultural Economics, Purdue University. https://www.gtap.agecon.purdue.edu/databases/v7/v7_doco.asp.

Valenzuela, E., and K. Anderson. 2008. "Alternative Agricultural Price Distortions for CGE Analysis of Developing Countries, 2004 and 1980–84." Research Memorandum 13 (December), Center for Global Trade Analysis, Department of Agricultural Economics, Purdue University, West Lafayette, IN. https://www.gtap.agecon.purdue.edu/resources/res_display.asp?RecordID=2925.

van der Mensbrugghe, D. 2005. "Linkage Technical Reference Document: Version 6.0." December, World Bank, Washington, DC. http://go.worldbank.org/7NP2KK1OH0.

———. 2006. "Linkage Technical Reference Document: Version 6.1." Draft. World Bank, Washington, DC.

———. 2007. "Modeling the Impact of Trade Liberalization: A Structuralist Perspective?" Paper presented at the 10th Annual Conference on Global Economic Analysis, Purdue University, West Lafayette, IN, June 7–9. https://www.gtap.agecon.purdue.edu/resources/download/3332.pdf.

# INDEX

Figures, notes, and tables are indicated by *f*, *n*, and *t*, respectively.

**A**

Africa. *See* Middle East and North Africa; Sub-Saharan Africa; *specific countries*
agricultural price distortions, poverty, and inequality, xvii–xviii, 3–45
  analytical framework for, 10–14
  defining poverty, 9, 106
  further research required into, 38–40
  global CGE models, empirical results of, 15–25. *See also* Global Income Distribution Dynamics; Global Trade Analysis Project; Linkage model of global economy
  growth-trade-poverty nexus, 39
  levels of global poverty and inequality, 3–5, 4*t*
  liberalization, effects of. *See* liberalization
  measuring inequality, 9
  national CGE models, empirical results of, 25–35. *See also* national CGE models, *and specific countries and regions*
  NRAs in developing versus high-income countries, 6–8, 7*t*
  policy implications of empirical findings, 40–41
  probability of falling into poverty, 39
  reasons for focusing on, 8–10
Ahmed, S. A., 39
AIDADS demand system, 121, 129
Albania
  in GIDD model, 93*f*, 95*f*, 114*f*
  in Linkage model, 460*t*
Almeida dos Reis, J. G., 372
Altertax procedure, 52
analytical framework, 10–14

Anderson, Kym
  acknowledged, 247*n*, 391*n*
  biographical information, xxi
  as chapter author, 3, 49, 457
  cited, 6, 12, 15, 25, 38, 42*n*7, 50, 51, 52, 60, 96, 99, 128, 132, 192, 210, 248, 335, 366, 407, 431–32, 458
  as editor of *Distortions to Agricultural Incentives: A Global Perspective*, xvii
Arab Republic of Egypt. *See* Egypt, Arab Republic of
Arbache, J. S., 392
Argentina, 359–90
  border price and export demand shocks, 471–72*t*
  characteristics of national CGE model, 26*t*
  conclusions regarding, 385–86
  Convertibility Plan, 360
  Dutch Disease, 378, 382
  economic crisis of 2001-02, 360–62
  economic recovery in, 363–66
  export taxes on farm products, 359
    agricultural growth rates and, 366
    agricultural producer price indexes since introduction of, 364–65, 364*f*
    growth effects of, 385
    liberalization effects of removing, 376, 378, 379, 382, 383
    in Linkage model, 83*n*10
    objectives of imposing, 362–63*f*
    poverty and inequality affected by, 35, 37, 379, 382, 383
    in simulations, 373–74
    table of, 369, 370*t*

Argentina (*continued*)
  external trade structure, 368–70, 368*t*
  GDP in, 27, 362, 376, 383
  GIDD model, 100*f*, 102*f*
  index of agricultural prices, 365*f*
  labor market results, 371–73
  liberalization effects, 374–85
    aggregate simulation results, 275*t*, 374–79
    different simulations affecting poverty and
      inequality, 374–76, 379–83, 380–81*t*
    export taxes, removing, 376, 378, 379,
      382, 383
    fiscal and growth effects, 383–85, 384*t*
    GDP, 376, 383
    global liberalization's effects on poverty and
      inequality, 28–30*t*, 31, 32–34*t*, 35, 37
    macroeconomic effects, 374–76
    sectoral changes, 376, 377*t*
    unemployment, 375*t*, 376–79, 382, 383
  Linkage model
    agricultural outputs, imports, and
      exports, 64*t*
    border price and export demand shocks to
      national model from, 471–72*t*
    economic welfare, global and national, 58*t*
    factor prices, 71*t*
    land supply elasticities, 466*t*
    national CGE model, use with, 359–60, 366,
      367, 368
    price distortion structure, 53*t*, 470*t*
    regional concordance, 461*t*
    sectoral value added, 69, 74*t*
  Menem and De la Rua governments, 360–61
  methodology and data, 366–73
  microsimulations, use of, 359–60, 370–73
  national CGE model, 359–60, 367–70
  poverty and inequality
    different simulations affecting, 374–76,
      379–83, 380–81*t*
    global liberalization's effects on, 28–30*t*, 31,
      32–34*t*, 35, 37
    rural versus urban, 28–29*t*, 32–33*t*, 42*n*16
    rural versus urban poverty and inequality in,
      28–29*t*, 32–33*t*, 42*n*16
  safety nets for the poor in, 383
  SAM, 367*t*
  simulations used for, 373–74
  tax replacement schemes, 383
  unemployment in, 12, 14, 364, 368, 375*t*,
    376–79, 382, 383
  VAT proposal, 383
Armenia
  in GIDD model, 93*f*, 95*f*, 112*t*, 114*f*
  in Linkage model, 460*t*
Armington elasticities
  in Chinese CGE model, 153
  in Indonesian Wayang model, 183,
    188–90, 207*n*4

  in Linkage model, 56, 464*t*
  in Mozambique national CGE model, 311
  in Nicaragua model, 432, 433, 435, 442,
    444–46, 450
  in Pakistan national CGE model, 214,
    219, 245*n*6
  in Philippines national CGE model, 260
  in South African national CGE model, 336
Arndt, Channing, xxi, 303
Asia. *See* East Asia and Pacific; Eastern Europe
  and Central Asia; South Asia;
  *specific countries*
Australia
  GIDD model, 95*f*, 100*f*, 102*f*
  Linkage model
    agricultural outputs, imports, and
      exports, 64*t*
    economic welfare, global and national, 59*t*
    factor prices, 69, 72*t*
    land supply elasticities, 465*t*
    price distortion structure, 54*t*, 468*t*
    regional concordance, 460*t*
    sectoral value added, 75*t*
  ORANI general equilibrium model, 182
  TERM CGE model, 394
Austria
  in GIDD model, 95*f*
  in Linkage model, 460*t*
Azerbaijan
  in GIDD model, 93*f*, 95*f*, 112*t*, 114*f*
  in Linkage model, 460*t*

**B**
Balisacan, A. M., 248, 250
Baltic states (Estonia, Latvia, Lithuania)
  GIDD model, 93*f*, 95*f*, 100*f*, 101, 102*f*, 114*f*
  Linkage model
    agricultural outputs, imports, and
      exports, 64*t*
    economic welfare, global and national, 59*t*
    factor prices, 71*t*
    land supply elasticities, 465*t*
    price distortion structure, 54*t*, 468*t*
    regional concordance, 460*t*
    sectoral value added, 74*t*
Bamrungwong, Krisada, 283*n*
Bangladesh
  GIDD model
    empirical results of, 23, 24*t*
    factor prices, 102*f*
    inequality variations in agricultural and
      nonagricultural households, 95*f*
    poverty, effects of global liberalization on,
      110*f*, 111*t*
    real national consumption, effects of global
      liberalization on, 100*f*
    share of population in agriculture and of
      agriculture in total income, 93*f*

Theil Index, income distributional
    changes, 114f
GTAP model, 121
    agricultural versus nonagricultural trade
        reforms, 136–38t, 138
    commodity-specific support, effects of,
        140t, 141t
    contribution of earnings to total poverty
        response, 127t
    elasticities approach to poverty
        headcount, 122t
    percentage change in national poverty
        headcount, 131t
    poverty population, stratum contributions
        to, 124t
    preference erosion resulting from global
        liberalization, 134
    price distortion structure, 469t
    stratum- and earnings-specific elasticities,
        125, 126t
    tax replacement, 131t
Linkage model
    agricultural outputs, imports, and
        exports, 63t
    economic welfare, global and national, 58t
    factor prices, 71t
    land supply elasticities, 466t
    price distortion structure, 53t, 469t
    regional concordance, 461t
    sectoral value added, 74t
Barros, R. P. de, 302, 393, 415, 436, 437
Belarus, in GIDD model, 93f, 95f
Belgium, in Linkage model, 460t
Benin, in GIDD model, 93f, 95f, 111t, 114f
Bolivia
    in GIDD model, 93f, 95f, 111t, 114f
    in Linkage model, 461t
Bolsa Familia Program, Brazil, 393
border price and export demand shocks in
        Linkage model, 457–87
    export price, import price, and export demand
        shocks by country, 467, 471–85t
    global results, implementing, 462
    key specifications, 462–67
    macroeconomic closure rules, 462
    price distortion structure, 468–70t
    regional concordance, 460–61t
    sectoral concordance, 458, 459t
    shocks imposed, 458, 459t
border price and export demand shocks in
        national models
    Argentina, 471–72t
    Brazil, 405–9, 407–8t, 472–73t
    China, 474–75t
    Indonesia, 190–92, 191t, 193t, 475–76t
    Mozambique, 315, 316–17t, 477–78t
    Nicaragua, 439–41, 440t, 478–79t
    Pakistan, 219, 220–21t, 480–81t

Philippines, 263–65t, 481–82t
South Africa, 340, 341t, 483–84t
Thailand, 288, 291t, 484–85t
Botswana, in Linkage model, 461t
Bourguignon, F., 8, 96, 419, 436
Brazil, 391–422
    Bolsa Familia Program, 393
    border price and export demand shocks,
        405–9, 407–8t, 472–73t
    characteristics of national CGE model, 26t
    conclusions regarding, 418–19
    external trade structure, 405–6t, 409
    factor market closure rules, 420n20
    geographic issues
        output, 411–14, 413t
        of poverty and income inequality
            in base year picture, 398–99, 399f,
                400–401f
        liberalization effects on, 416, 417t
GIDD model
    empirical results of, 16, 17t
    factor prices, 102f, 103
    GICs, 108f, 113
    inequality variations in agricultural and
        nonagricultural households, 95f
    poverty, effects of global liberalization on,
        110f, 111t, 113
    real national consumption, effects of global
        liberalization on, 100f, 101
    share of employment in agriculture and
        income levels, relationship between, 92f
    share of population in agriculture and of
        agriculture in total income, 93f
    Theil Index, income distributional
        changes, 114f
GTAP model, 121
    agricultural versus nonagricultural trade
        reforms, 136–38t
    commodity-specific support, effects of,
        140t, 141t
    contribution of earnings to total poverty
        response, 127t
    elasticities approach to poverty headcount,
        122t, 123
    percentage change in national poverty
        headcount, 131t, 132
    poverty population, stratum contributions
        to, 124t
    price distortion structure, 470t
    tax replacement, 131t
labor market
    in base year picture, 402–3t, 402–4
    in national model, 394–95
    unemployment rates, 397
liberalization effects, 405–16
    border price and export demand shocks,
        405–9, 407–8t
    external trade structure, 405–6t, 409

Brazil (*continued*)
  GDP, 409–11, 418
    geographic outputs, 411–14, 413*t*
    global liberalization's effects on poverty and
        inequality, 28–30*t*, 31, 32–34*t*, 36*t*
    macroeconomic effects, 409–10, 410*t*
    national model simulations, poverty and
        inequality effects, 414–16, 414*t*,
        416*t*, 417*t*
    sectoral outputs, 411–12*t*
  Linkage model
    agricultural outputs, imports, and
        exports, 64*t*
    border price and export demand shocks to
        national model from, 472–73*t*
    economic welfare, global and national, 58*t*
    factor prices, 71*t*
    land supply elasticities, 466*t*
    national model, use in, 396, 404–5, 407,
        420*n*22
    price distortion structure, 53*t*, 470*t*
    regional concordance, 461*t*
    sectoral value added, 69, 74*t*
  national model
    base year picture, 397–404, 398*t*, 399*f*,
        400–403*t*
    CGE and microsimulation, use of,
        393–96
    households in, 395
    labor market in, 394–95
    Linkage model, use of, 396, 404–5, 407,
        420*n*22
    macroeconomic closure rules, 404–5
    procedure for running, 395–96
    simulations, 404
    TERM-BR, 394, 419*n*5
  poverty and income inequality
    in base year picture, 397, 398*t*
    geographic aspects of
      in base year picture, 398–99, 399*f*,
        400–401*f*
    liberalization effects on, 416, 417*t*
    global liberalization's effects on, 28–30*t*, 31,
        32–34*t*, 36*t*
    incidence of, 391, 392–93
    national model simulations, 414–16, 414*t*,
        416*t*, 417*t*
    rural versus urban, 28–29*t*, 32–33*t*
    rural versus urban poverty and inequality in,
        28–29*t*, 32–33*t*
    transfer payments (remittances), importance
        of, 127*t*, 128
Bulgaria
  GIDD model, 93*f*, 95*f*, 100*f*, 102*f*, 114*f*
  Linkage model
    economic welfare, global and national, 59*t*
    factor prices, 71*t*
    land supply elasticities, 465*t*

    price distortion structure, 54*t*, 468*t*
    regional concordance, 460*t*
    sectoral value added, 74*t*
Burkina Faso, in GIDD model, 93*f*, 95*f*, 111*t*, 114*f*
Burundi, in GIDD model, 93*f*, 95*f*, 111*t*, 114*f*
Bussolo, Maurizio, xxi, 8, 19, 23, 24, 31, 80, 87,
        96, 457

# C

Cai, J., 22
Cambodia
  in GIDD model, 93*f*, 95*f*, 111*t*, 114*f*
  in Linkage model, 461*t*
Cameroon, in GIDD model, 93*f*, 95*f*, 111*t*, 114*f*
Canada
  GIDD model, 95*f*, 100*f*, 102*f*
  Linkage model
    agricultural outputs, imports, and
        exports, 64*t*
    economic welfare, global and national, 59*t*
    factor prices, 69, 72*t*
    land supply elasticities, 465*t*
    price distortion structure, 54*t*, 469*t*
    regional concordance, 460*t*
    sectoral value added, 75*t*
Caribbean. *See* Latin America and Caribbean;
        *specific countries*
Caribbean Basin Initiative, 428, 454*n*3
cattle. *See* livestock and meat products
Central Asia. *See* Eastern Europe and Central
        Asia; *specific countries*
CGE. *See* computable general equilibrium
        (CGE) modeling
Chen, S., 96, 147, 148
Chile
  GIDD model
    empirical results of, 23, 24*t*
    factor prices, 102*f*
    inequality variations in agricultural and
        nonagricultural households, 95*f*
    poverty, effects of global liberalization on,
        109, 111*t*
    real national consumption, effects of global
        liberalization on, 100*f*
    share of population in agriculture and of
        agriculture in total income, 93*f*
    Theil Index, income distributional
        changes, 114*f*
  global liberalization, effects on incidence of
        poverty and inequality in, 36*t*
  GTAP model, 121
    agricultural versus nonagricultural trade
        reforms, 131*t*
    commodity-specific support, effects of,
        140*t*, 141*t*
    concentration of poverty in agricultural
        households, 121

contribution of earnings to total poverty
   response, 127t
elasticities approach to poverty
   headcount, 122t
percentage change in national poverty
   headcount, 131t
poverty population, stratum contributions
   to, 124t
price distortion structure, 470t
tax replacement, 131t
Linkage model
   agricultural outputs, imports, and
      exports, 64t
   economic welfare, global and national, 58t
   factor prices, 71t
   land supply elasticities, 466t
   price distortion structure, 53t, 470t
   regional concordance, 461t
   sectoral value added, 74t
   transfer payments (remittances), importance
      of, 127t, 120
China, 147–78
   benchmark data, social accounting matrix
      used for, 153–56, 154–55t
   border price and export demand shocks,
      474–75t
   CGE model and data, 149–56
   characteristics of national CGE model, 26t
   Doha Round trade liberalizations, effects of, 149
   factor prices, 161t, 162
   GIDD model
      factor prices, 101, 102f
      inequality variations in agricultural and
         nonagricultural households, 95f
      poverty, effects of global liberalization
         on, 111t
      real national consumption, effects of global
         liberalization on, 100f, 101
      share of employment in agriculture and
         income levels, relationship
         between, 92f
      Theil Index, income distributional
         changes, 114f
   household behavior in, 149–51
   household impact of liberalization, 166–71,
      167–69f
   labor market
      hukou system, 6, 35, 152, 165
      reform/relaxation of hukou system, effects
         of (LABOR), 39, 157t, 159, 161–66,
         161t, 164t, 169f, 170–71, 175–76
   land market rental assumption, 173–75, 174t
   land reform in (LAND), 157t, 159, 161t, 162–66,
      164t, 169f, 170–71, 171t, 175–76
   liberalization effects, 160–75
      global model effects on poverty and
         inequality, 28–30t, 31, 32–34t, 35, 36t, 37
      household impacts, 166–71, 167–69f

land market rental assumption,
   173–75, 174t
macroeconomic effects, 160–63, 161t
national model impacts on poverty and
   inequality, 163–66, 164t
sectoral impacts, 171–73
Linkage model
   agricultural outputs, imports, and
      exports, 63t
   border price and export demand shocks to
      national model from, 474–75t
   economic welfare, global and national, 58t
   empirical results of, 15t, 17, 18t
   factor prices, 70t
   land supply elasticities, 466t
   poverty, effects on, 76–80, 77–79t
   price distortion structure, 53t, 469t
   regional concordance, 461t
   sectoral value added, 69, 73t
NRAs in developing versus high-income
   countries, 7t
policy implications for, 175–76
poverty and inequality
   global model effects on, 28–30t, 31, 32–34t,
      35, 36t, 37
   levels of, 3, 4t, 147
   national model impacts on, 163–66, 164t
   rural versus urban, 28–29t, 32–33t, 147
production, modeling, 152–53
rural versus urban
   current market reforms, impact of, 148
   impact of global liberalization in poverty
      and inequality, 164t, 165
   incidence of poverty and inequality, 28–29t,
      32–33t, 147
   migration from country to city, 151–52,
      160–62, 161t, 163, 173
sectoral impacts of liberalization, 171–73
sectoral structure of benchmark data,
   154–55t, 154–56
simulation design for, 156–59, 157–58t
TERM CGE model, 419n5
trade, modeling, 152–53
WTO accession, 52, 99, 128,
   147–48, 149
Cicowiez, Martin, xxi, 35, 359
Cirera, X., 94
closure. See factor market closure rules;
   macroeconomic closure rules
Cockburn, John, xxi, 3, 247, 279, 283n
Colombia
   GIDD model
      empirical results of, 23, 24t
      factor prices, 102f
      inequality variations in agricultural and
         nonagricultural households, 95f
      poverty, effects of global liberalization on,
         110f, 111t

Colombia (*continued*)
real national consumption, effects of global liberalization on, 100*f*
share of population in agriculture and of agriculture in total income, 93*f*
Theil Index, income distributional changes, 114*f*
global liberalization, effects on incidence of poverty and inequality in, 36*t*
GTAP model, 121
agricultural versus nonagricultural trade reforms, 136–38*t*
commodity-specific support, effects of, 140*t*, 141*t*
concentration of poverty in agricultural households, 121
contribution of earnings to total poverty response, 127*t*
elasticities approach to poverty headcount, 122*t*
percentage change in national poverty headcount, 131*t*, 132
poverty population, stratum contributions to, 124*t*
price distortion structure, 470*t*
self-employed nonagricultural households as share of poor, 124
tax replacement, 131*t*
Linkage model
agricultural outputs, imports, and exports, 64*t*
economic welfare, global and national, 58*t*
factor prices, 71*t*
land supply elasticities, 466*t*
price distortion structure, 53*t*, 470*t*
regional concordance, 461*t*
sectoral value added, 69, 74*t*
transfer payments (remittances), importance of, 127*t*, 128
commodity-specific support in GTAP model, 120–21, 139–40, 140*t*, 141*t*
computable general equilibrium (CGE) modeling
in analytical framework, 11–13
global models. *See* global CGE models
microsimulation modeling, combined with, 8, 13, 19. *See also* microsimulation modeling
national models. *See* national CGE models
Convertibility Plan, Argentina, 360
corn. *See* grains and oilseeds
Corong, Erwin, xxii, 247, 248, 279
Cororaton, Caesar B., xxii, 209, 212, 247, 248, 279
Costa Rica, in GIDD model, 93*f*, 95*f*, 111*t*, 114*f*
Côte d'Ivoire, in GIDD model, 93*f*, 95*f*, 111*t*, 114*f*

cotton. *See* textiles and textile raw materials
Croatia, in Linkage model, 460*t*
Croser, Johanna, 49*n*
Cyprus, in Linkage model, 460*t*
Czech Republic
GIDD model, 95*f*, 100*f*, 102*f*
Linkage model
agricultural outputs, imports, and exports, 64*t*
economic welfare, global and national, 59*t*
factor prices, 71*t*
land supply elasticities, 465*t*
price distortion structure, 54*t*, 468*t*
regional concordance, 460*t*
sectoral value added, 74*t*

**D**
dairy
in Argentina, 367*t*, 369*t*, 370*t*, 388*n*14, 471*t*
border price and export demand shocks, 459*t*, 464*t*, 471–85*t*
in Brazil, 403*t*, 405–8*t*, 411–12*t*, 473*t*
in China, 154*t*, 158*t*, 474*t*
GTAP model, commodity-specific support in, 140*t*
in Indonesia, 191*t*, 193*t*, 476*t*
in Linkage model, 62*t*, 65, 66–67*t*, 68*t*, 69
in Mozambique, 477*t*
in Nicaragua, 440*t*, 479*t*
in Pakistan, 212, 215*t*, 239, 480*t*
in Philippines, 255*t*, 258*t*, 261*t*, 263*t*, 481–82*t*
in South Africa, 250, 342–44, 483*t*
in Thailand, 284, 290*t*, 485*t*
David, C. C., 248, 250
De la Rua government, Argentina, 361
Denmark
in GIDD model, 95*f*
in Linkage model, 460*t*
Dervis, K., 434
Díaz-Bonilla, Carolina, xxii, 35, 359, 367
Díaz-Bonilla, Eugenio, xxii, 35, 359
Dickerson, A., 392
Diffenbaugh, N. S., 39
distortions to agricultural incentives. *See* agricultural price distortions, poverty, and inequality
Distortions to Agricultural Incentives Project Database, 176*n*1, 196, 209, 245*n*1, 281*n*1, 298*n*1, 328*n*3
Divisia indexes, 486*n*4
Doha Development Agenda, 120, 132, 142*n*2, 354
Doha Round
agricultural policy reform as contentious issue in, 8, 49, 87, 423
China, trade liberalization effects on, 149
merchandise trade barriers and subsidies, agricultural price distortions contributing to cost of, 6

poverty reduction potential of, 119
prospective agreement, poverty consequences
of, 11
reasons for participation in, 9
Dominican Republic, in GIDD model, 93*f*, 95*f*,
112*t*, 114*f*
Dominican Republic–Central America Free
Trade Agreement (DR-CAFTA),
423–24, 426–29, 428*f*, 445, 452
Dorosh, P., 209, 212
Dutch Disease, 378, 382

**E**

East Asia and Pacific. *See also specific countries*
GIDD model
empirical results of, 20*t*, 21, 22*t*, 23, 24*t*, 25
factor prices, 101, 102*f*
global liberalization, effects of, 107*t*
population represented in, 89
poverty, effects of global liberalization on,
109, 111*t*
real national consumption, effects of global
liberalization on, 100*f*
share of population in agriculture and of
agriculture in total income, 94
Theil Index, income distributional changes
following global liberalization, 113
global liberalization, effects on incidence of
poverty and inequality in, 37
GTAP model, 121, 469*t*
Linkage model
agricultural outputs, imports, and exports,
63*t*, 65*t*
economic welfare, global and national, 58*t*
empirical results of, 15*t*, 17*t*, 18*t*
factor prices, 70–71*t*
land supply elasticities, 466*t*
poverty, effects on, 77–79*t*
price distortion structure, 53*t*, 469*t*
regional concordance, 461*t*
sectoral value added, 69, 73–74*t*
NRAs in developing versus high-income
countries, 7*t*
poverty and inequality
in GIDD model, 109, 111*t*
levels of, 4*t*
in Linkage model, 77–79*t*
Theil Index, income distributional changes
following global liberalization, 113
Eastern Europe and Central Asia. *See also specific
countries*
developing-country region, treatment as, 52
GIDD model, 89, 94, 100*f*, 102*f*, 112*t*
Linkage model
agricultural outputs, imports, and exports,
64*t*, 65*t*
economic welfare, global and national, 59*t*
empirical results of, 15*t*, 17*t*, 18*t*

factor prices, 71*t*
land supply elasticities, 465*t*
poverty, effects on, 77–79*t*
price distortion structure, 54*t*, 468*t*
regional concordance, 460*t*
sectoral value added, 74–75*t*
Ecuador
banana market in EU, discrimination in, 16, 57
GIDD model
factor prices, 102*f*
inequality variations in agricultural and
nonagricultural households, 95*f*
poverty, effects of global liberalization on,
110*f*, 112*t*, 113
real national consumption, effects of global
liberalization on, 100*f*, 101
share of population in agriculture and of
agriculture in total income, 93*f*
Theil Index, income distributional
changes, 114*f*
Linkage model
agricultural outputs, imports, and
exports, 64*t*
economic welfare, global and national,
57, 58*t*
empirical results of, 16
factor prices, 71*t*
land supply elasticities, 466*t*
price distortion structure, 53*t*, 470*t*
regional concordance, 461*t*
sectoral value added, 69, 74*t*
Egypt, Arab Republic of
GIDD model, 100*f*, 102*f*
Linkage model
agricultural outputs, imports, and
exports, 63*t*
economic welfare, global and national, 58*t*
factor prices, 70*t*
price distortion structure, 53*t*, 469*t*
regional concordance, 460*t*
sectoral value added, 73*t*
El Salvador, in GIDD model, 93*f*, 95*f*, 112*t*, 114*f*
elasticities. *See* Armington elasticities, *and under
specific global and national models*
Estonia. *See* Baltic states
Ethiopia, in GIDD model, 93*f*, 95*f*, 111*t*, 114*f*
European Free Trade Association, 460*t*
European Union/Western Europe. *See also*
Eastern Europe and Central Asia;
*specific countries*
banana market, discrimination in, 16, 57
GIDD model, 92*f*, 95*f*, 99, 100*f*, 102*f*
GTAP model, 128, 468*t*
Linkage model
agricultural outputs, imports, and exports,
60, 64*t*
economic welfare, global and national, 59*t*
factor prices, 69, 72*t*

European Union/Western Europe (*continued*)
    land supply elasticities, 465*t*
    price distortion structure, 54*t*, 468*t*
    regional concordance, 460*t*
    sectoral value added, 75*t*
    preference erosion resulting from global
        liberalization, 134
ex ante simulation analysis used in GIDD, 88
exogenous border price shocks. *See entries at*
        border price and export demand shocks
export demand shocks. *See entries at* border
        price and export demand shocks
exports
    Argentina, export taxes in. *See under*
        Argentina
    Linkage model, prospective effects of global
        liberalization in, 60–68, 62–67*t*
    subsidies. *See* subsidies

**F**
factor market closure rules
    Brazil, 420*n*20
    Nicaragua, 433–34
factor prices
    in China, 161*t*, 162
    in GIDD model, 101–3, 102*f*
    in Linkage model, 68–69, 70–72*t*
FAOSTAT Database, 42*n*9
Ferreira, F. H. G., 96
Ferreira Filho, Joaquim Bento de Souza, xxii, 391
Finland
    in GIDD model, 95*f*
    in Linkage model, 460*t*
    TERM CGE model for, 419*n*5
foreign investment distortions, 82*n*3
Foster, J., 276, 397
France
    in GIDD model, 95*f*
    in Linkage model, 460*t*
Franco, S., 419
fruit. *See* vegetables, fruits, and vegetable oils

**G**
The Gambia, in GIDD model, 93*f*, 95*f*, 111*t*, 114*f*
Ganuza, E., 436, 437
GDP. *See* gross domestic product
Gempack Software, 128, 395
Generalized System of Preferences, 428
Georgia
    in GIDD model, 93*f*, 95*f*, 112*t*, 114*f*
    in Linkage model, 460*t*
Germany, in GIDD model, 95*f*
Ghana, in GIDD model, 93*f*, 95*f*, 111*t*, 114*f*
Giambiagi, F., 419
GICs (growth incidence curves), GIDD model,
    104–5, 104*f*, 107–9, 108*f*, 113, 117*n*20
GIDD. *See* Global Income Distribution
    Dynamics

Gini coefficient of income distribution, as
    measure of inequality, 9, 83*n*12
global CGE models, 14–25. *See also* Global
    Income Distribution Dynamics;
    Global Trade Analysis Project; Linkage
    model of global economy
    in analytical framework, 12–14
    characteristics of national and global models
        compared, 26*t*
Global Income Distribution Dynamics (GIDD),
    8–9, 87–118. *See also under specific*
    *countries*
    agricultural versus nonagricultural
        households
        characteristics of poor in, 91*t*
        global liberalization, global effects of,
            105–6, 105*t*
        income distributions among,
            89–92, 90*f*
        inequality variations, 94, 95*f*
    in analytic framework, 11
    characteristics of national and global models
        compared, 26*t*
    conclusions regarding, 115–16
    empirical findings, 19–23, 20*t*, 21*t*, 22*t*
    ex ante simulation analysis used in, 88
    initial conditions in data set, 89–96, 90*f*, 91*t*,
        92*f*, 93*f*, 95*f*
    labor market effects, accounting for, 98,
        117*n*13
    liberalization effects, 37, 98–115
        macroeconomic general equilibrium
            effects, 99–103, 100*f*, 102*f*
        microsimulation results, 103–15
            GICs, 104–5, 104*f*, 107–9, 108*f*, 113,
                117*n*20
            global poverty and inequality, 105–9,
                105*t*, 107*t*, 108*f*
            regions and countries, poverty and
               inequality effects within, 102*f*, 109–15,
               111–12*t*, 114*f*
            Theil Index, income distributional
              changes, 113–15, 114*f*
    Linkage model, use of, 88, 97, 117*n*13
    methodology of model, 96–98, 97*f*
    microsimulation modeling combined with
        CGE, 88, 96
    poverty and inequality
        agricultural versus nonagricultural
            households, 91*t*, 94, 95*f*
        global, 105–9, 105*t*, 107*t*, 108*f*
        in regions and countries, 102*f*, 109–15,
            111–12*t*, 114*f*
    share of employment in agriculture
        income levels, relationship to, 92*f*
        share of agriculture in total income and,
            92–94, 93*f*
    global inequality, 4*t*, 5

Global Trade Analysis Project (GTAP), 9,
119–43. *See also under*
*specific countries*
adjustments to database, 50, 52, 128–29
agricultural and nonagricultural households
contribution of earnings to total poverty
response, 125–28, 127*t*
elasticities approach, 122–23, 122*t*
poverty population, stratum contributions
to, 124*t*
stratum- and earnings-specific elasticities,
125, 126*t*
stratum classification of, 121–22
in analytic framework, 12
characteristics of national and global models
compared, 26*t*
Chinese benchmark data and, 154
commodity-specific support, effects of,
120–21, 139–40, 140*t*, 141*t*
conclusions regarding, 140–42
countries studied in, 121
empirical findings, 23–25, 24*t*
GTAP-AGR, 82*n*2, 486*n*5
international cross-section approach, 120
liberalization effects, 130–40
agricultural versus nonagricultural trade
reforms, 134–39, 136–38*t*
percentage changes in national poverty
headcounts, 130–32, 131*t*
on poverty and inequality, 37, 38, 131*t*,
133–34
preference erosion, 134
tax replacement, 130, 131*t*, 132–33
Linkage model, use of database for, 51, 52, 56,
458, 467, 468–70*t*
macroeconomic closure rules, 130
methodology of model, 128–30
modifications to model, 129–30
ORANI general equilibrium model for
Australia, 182
poverty and inequality
analytical approach to poverty modeling,
121–28, 122*t*, 124*t*, 126*t*, 127*t*
liberalization effects on, 37, 38, 131*t*,
133–34
utility function and associated consumer
demand system, 121, 129
Golub, A., 121
Gorter, Harry de, 391*n*
grains and oilseeds
in Argentina, 366, 367*t*, 369*t*, 370*t*,
388*n*14–15, 471*t*
border price and export demand shocks in
Linkage model, 459*t*, 464*t*, 471–85*t*
in Brazil, 403*t*, 405*t*, 407*t*, 411*t*, 472–73*t*
in China, 154–55*t*, 158*t*, 474*t*
GTAP model, commodity-specific support in,
139–40, 140*t*, 141*t*

Indonesia
exogenous border price shocks, 193*t*,
475–76*t*
industry assistance rates, 191*t*
protection of sugar and rice industries in,
179–81, 202–5
in Linkage model, 62*t*, 65, 66–67*t*, 68*t*
in Mozambique, 306–7*t*, 308, 309–10*t*,
316–17*t*, 318, 319*t*, 321*t*, 323*t*, 477*t*
in Nicaragua, 424, 440*t*, 446, 478–79*t*
in Pakistan, 211, 212, 215*t*, 218, 220*t*, 232, 234,
236*t*, 239, 480*t*
in Philippines, 250, 251*t*, 255*t*, 258*t*, 260, 261*t*,
263*t*, 481–82*t*
in South Africa, 332, 333*t*, 339*t*, 341*t*, 343*t*,
345*t*, 483*t*
in Thailand, 283, 290*t*, 484–85*t*
Greece
in GIDD model, 95*f*
in Linkage model, 460*t*
Green, L., 392
Greer, J., 276, 397
gross domestic product (GDP)
agricultural GDP and farm household
welfare, relationship between, 8
agricultural share in, 6
in Argentina, 27, 362, 376, 383
Brazil, liberalization effects in, 409–11, 418
Mozambique, liberalization effects in, 315–18,
319–20*t*, 324–26, 327
in Nicaragua. *See under* Nicaragua
South Africa, liberalization effects in, 342,
343–44*t*, 347, 349–54
growth incidence curves (GICs), GIDD model,
104–5, 104*f*, 107–9, 108*f*,
113, 117*n*20
growth-trade-poverty nexus, 39
GTAP. *See* Global Trade Analysis Project
Guatemala, in GIDD model, 93*f*, 95*f*, 112*t*, 114*f*
Guinea, in GIDD model, 93*f*, 95*f*, 111*t*, 114*f*
Guyana, in GIDD model, 93*f*, 94, 95*f*,
112*t*, 114*f*

**H**
Haiti, in GIDD model, 93*f*, 94, 95*f*,
112*t*, 114*f*
Harris, R. L., 367, 432
Harrison, G. W., 393
Harrison, W. J., 130
Heckman, J. J., 153
Henriques, R., 392
Hérault, Nicolas, xxii, 331, 340
Hertel, Thomas W.
acknowledged, 247*n*
biographical information, xxii
as chapter author, 119, 147
cited, 8, 11, 12, 13, 23–25, 27, 39, 120, 121,
122, 129, 148

high-income countries. *See also specific countries*
Linkage model
agricultural outputs, imports, and exports, 64*t*, 65*t*
economic welfare, global and national, 59*t*
factor prices, 72*t*
price distortion structure, 54*t*
sectoral value added, 75*t*
NRAs in developing countries versus, 6–8, 7*t*
Honduras, in GIDD model, 93*f*, 95*f*, 112*t*, 114*f*
Hong Kong, China
in GIDD model, 95*f*, 100*f*, 102*f*
Linkage model
agricultural outputs, imports, and exports, 64*t*
economic welfare, global and national, 59*t*
factor prices, 72*t*
land supply elasticities, 465*t*
negligible influence on, 83*n*8
price distortion structure, 469*t*
regional concordance, 460*t*
sectoral value added, 75*t*
Horridge, Mark
biographical information, xxii
as chapter author, 391
cited, 130, 213, 214, 260, 311, 315, 336, 462
De Hoyos, Rafael, xxiii, 19, 23, 24, 31, 80, 87, 457
Huang, J., 150
*hukou* system, China. *See* subhead "labor market," under China
human capital theory, 372
Hungary
GIDD model
factor prices, 102*f*
inequality variations in agricultural and nonagricultural households, 94, 95*f*
real national consumption, effects of global liberalization on, 100*f*
share of population in agriculture and of agriculture in total income, 93*f*
Theil Index, income distributional changes, 114*f*
Linkage model
agricultural outputs, imports, and exports, 64*t*
economic welfare, global and national, 59*t*
factor prices, 71*t*
land supply elasticities, 465*t*
price distortion structure, 54*t*, 468*t*
regional concordance, 460*t*
sectoral value added, 75*t*

**I**

imports
Linkage model, prospective effects of global liberalization in, 60–68, 62–67*t*
Philippines import-substitution policy, 247, 249
tariffs on. *See* tariffs

income distribution/income inequality. *See* agricultural price distortions, poverty, and inequality, *and under specific countries and regions*
India
domestic policy and trade liberalization in, 39–40
GIDD model
empirical results of, 22*t*
factor prices, 102*f*, 103
GICs, 108*f*, 113
inequality variations in agricultural and nonagricultural households, 95*f*
poverty, effects of global liberalization on, 109, 110*f*, 111*t*, 113
real national consumption, effects of global liberalization on, 100*f*
share of employment in agriculture and income levels, relationship between, 92*f*
share of population in agriculture and of agriculture in total income, 93*f*
Theil Index, income distributional changes, 114*f*
global liberalization, effects on incidence of poverty and inequality in, 36*t*
levels of poverty and inequality in, 3–5, 4*t*
Linkage model
agricultural outputs, imports, and exports, 63*t*
economic welfare, global and national, 58*t*
empirical results of, 15*t*, 17–19, 18*t*
factor prices, 71*t*
land supply elasticities, 466*t*
poverty, effects on, 77–79*t*, 80
price distortion structure, 53*t*, 469*t*
regional concordance, 461*t*
sectoral value added, 74*t*, 76
Indonesia, 179–208
border price and export demand shocks, 190–92, 191*t*, 193*t*, 475–76*t*
characteristics of national CGE model, 26*t*
conclusions regarding, 207
GIDD model
empirical results of, 23, 24*t*, 42*n*11
factor prices, 102*f*
inequality variations in agricultural and nonagricultural households, 95*f*
poverty, effects of global liberalization on, 110*f*, 111*t*
real national consumption, effects of global liberalization on, 100*f*
share of population in agriculture and of agriculture in total income, 93*f*
Theil Index, income distributional changes, 114*f*
GTAP model, 121
agricultural versus nonagricultural trade reforms, 135–38, 136–38*t*

commodity-specific support, effects of,
140*t*, 141*t*
concentration of poverty in agricultural
households, 121
contribution of earnings to total poverty
response, 127*t*
elasticities approach to poverty
headcount, 122*t*
percentage change in national poverty
headcount, 131*t*
poverty population, stratum contributions
to, 124*t*
price distortion structure, 469*t*
tax replacement, 131*t*
liberalization effects, 194–207
agricultural products, liberalization only of,
202 7, 203 6*t*
global liberalization's effects on poverty and
inequality, 28–30*t*, 32–34*t*, 35, 36*t*
incidence of poverty and income inequality,
197 202*t*, 198 99*t*, 201*t*, 202*t*
macroeconomic effects, 194–97, 195*t*
Linkage model
agricultural outputs, imports, and
exports, 63*t*
border price and export demand shocks to
national model from, 475–76*t*
economic welfare, global and national, 58*t*
factor prices, 70*t*
land supply elasticities, 466*t*
price distortion structure, 53*t*, 469*t*
regional concordance, 461*t*
sectoral value added, 73*t*
rice and sugar industries, protection of,
179–81, 202–5
rural versus urban poverty and inequality in,
28–29*t*, 32–33*t*
SAM, 181–82, 185–86, 189
TERM CGE model, 419*n*5
Thai study, comparison with, 296–98
Wayang general equilibrium model,
181–90
assumed rates of industry assistance, 191*t*
border price and export demand shocks,
190–92, 191*t*, 193*t*
commodities, 183
database, 189
elasticities, 190
factors of production, 183–85, 184*t*
households, 185–88, 187*t*
industries, 182–83
macroeconomic closure, 192–94
theoretical/analytical structure, 188
inequality. *See* agricultural price distortions,
poverty, and inequality, *and under
specific countries and regions*
Intal, P. S., 248, 250
intercountry inequality, 5

international cross-section approach in GTAP
model, 120
International Food Policy Research Institute, 432
international inequality, 5
Iran, Islamic Republic of, in Linkage model, 460*t*
Ireland
in GIDD model, 95*f*
in Linkage model, 460*t*
Islamic Republic of Iran, in Linkage model, 460*t*
Israel, in GIDD model, 95*f*
Italy
in GIDD model, 95*f*
in Linkage model, 460*t*
Ivanic, M., 120, 133

**J**
Jamaica, in GIDD model, 93*f*, 95*f*, 112*t*, 114*f*
JamlongThai general equilibrium model. *See
under* Thailand
Janvry, A. de, 22
Japan
GIDD model, 100*f*, 102*f*
Linkage model
agricultural outputs, imports, and
exports, 64*t*
economic welfare, global and national, 59*t*
factor prices, 69, 72*t*
land supply elasticities, 465*t*
price distortion structure, 54*t*, 469*t*
regional concordance, 460*t*
sectoral value added, 75*t*
TERM CGE model for, 419*n*5
Johansen category, 182
Jordan, in GIDD model, 93*f*, 95*f*, 114*f*

**K**
Katz, L. F., 153
Kazakhstan
GIDD model
factor prices, 102*f*
inequality variations in agricultural and
nonagricultural households, 95*f*
poverty, effects of global liberalization on,
112*t*, 113
real national consumption, effects of global
liberalization on, 100*f*
share of population in agriculture and of
agriculture in total income, 93*f*
Theil Index, income distributional
changes, 114*f*
Linkage model
agricultural outputs, imports, and exports, 64*t*
economic welfare, global and national, 59*t*
factor prices, 71*t*
land supply elasticities, 465*t*
price distortion structure, 54*t*, 468*t*
regional concordance, 460*t*
sectoral value added, 75*t*

Keeney, Roman, xxiii, 23–25, 27, 119, 129
Kennedy Round, WTO, 386n3
Kenya, in GIDD model, 93f, 95f, 110f, 111t, 114f
Korea, Republic of
　as developing country, 56
　GIDD model, 95f, 100f, 102f
　Linkage model
　　agricultural outputs, imports, and
　　　exports, 63t
　　economic welfare, global and
　　　national, 58t
　　factor prices, 70t
　　land supply elasticities, 465t
　　price distortion structure, 53t, 469t
　　regional concordance, 460t
　　sectoral value added, 73t
Kurzweil, Marianne, 49n
Kyrgyz Republic, in GIDD model
　factor prices, 102f
　inequality variations in agricultural and
　　nonagricultural households, 95f
　poverty, effects of global liberalization
　　on, 112t
　real national consumption, effects of global
　　liberalization on, 100f
　share of population in agriculture and of
　　agriculture in total income, 93f
　Theil Index, income distributional
　　changes, 114f
Kyrgyzstan, in Linkage model, 460t,
　465t, 468t

**L**

labor market. *See under specific countries*
land market rental assumption, China,
　173–75, 174t
Lao PDR, in GIDD model, 93f, 95f
Latin America and Caribbean. *See also specific
　countries*
　Caribbean Basin Initiative, 428, 454n3
　GIDD model
　　empirical results of, 20t, 22t, 23, 24t, 25
　　factor prices, 101, 102f
　　GICs, 107, 108f
　　global liberalization, effects of, 107t,
　　　109, 115
　　population represented in, 89
　　poverty, effects of global liberalization on,
　　　109, 111t
　　real national consumption, effects of global
　　　liberalization on, 100f
　　share of population in agriculture and of
　　　agriculture in total income, 94
　　Theil Index, income distributional changes
　　　following global liberalization, 113
　global liberalization, effects on incidence of
　　poverty and inequality in, 37
　GTAP model, 121, 470t

Linkage model
　agricultural outputs, imports, and exports,
　　64t, 65t
　economic welfare, global and national, 58t
　empirical results of, 15t, 17t, 18t
　factor prices, 71t
　land supply elasticities, 466t
　poverty, effects on, 77–79t
　price distortion structure, 53t, 470t
　regional concordance, 461t
　sectoral value added, 69, 74t
NRAs in developing versus high-income
　countries, 7t
poverty and inequality
　in GIDD model, 109, 111t
　global liberalization, effects of, 37
　levels of, 4t
　in Linkage model, 77–79t
　Theil Index, income distributional changes
　　following global liberalization, 113
Latvia. *See* Baltic states
Laurel-Langley Agreement, 250
Lay, J., 96
Leite, P. G., 96
Leontief specifications, 188, 253, 308, 336
Lessem, Rebecca, 87n
liberalization
　benefits of, 36–38, 36t
　further research required into effects of, 38–40
　growth-trade-poverty nexus, 39
　national and global CGE models, prospective
　　effects according to. *See under specific
　　models and countries*
　policy implications of, 40–41
　redistributive effects of, 87–88
　reduction of poverty and inequality by,
　　28–30t, 31–35, 32–34t
　services, trade in, 39, 82n3
Lin, Justin Yifu, xviii
Linkage model of global economy, 8–9, 49–85.
　　*See also under specific countries*
　in analytical framework, 12, 13
　border price and export demand shocks. *See
　　border price and export demand
　　shocks in Linkage model*
　caveats regarding, 80–81
　characteristics of national and global models
　　compared, 26t
　conclusions regarding, 81–82
　description of, 55–57
　elasticities, 463, 464–66t
　empirical results, 15–19, 15t, 17t, 18t
　GIDD's use of, 88, 97, 117n13
　GTAP database, use of, 51, 52, 56, 458, 467,
　　468–70t
　key distortions and their effects in 2004,
　　52–55, 53–54t
　key specifications, 462–67

liberalization effects, 37–38, 57–60
    agricultural output, import, and export,
        60–68, 62–67t
    economic welfare, global and national,
        57–60, 58–59t
    poverty, effects on, 76–80, 77–79t
    product and factor prices, effect on, 68–69,
        68t, 70–72t
    regional and sectoral distribution of, 60, 61t
    sectoral value added, 69–76, 73–75t
    simulations used, 37–38, 57–60
    macroeconomic closure rules, 462
Lithuania. *See* Baltic states
Liu, X., 151
livestock and meat products
    in Argentina, 367t, 369t, 370t, 388n14–15, 471t
    border price and export demand shocks in
        Linkage model, 459t, 464t, 471–85t
    in Brazil, 403t, 405–8t, 411–12t, 473t
    in China, 154–55t, 156, 158t, 474t
    in Indonesia, 191t, 193t, 475–76t
    in Linkage model, 62t, 66–67t, 68t
    in Mozambique, 306–7t, 309–10t, 316–17t,
        319t, 321t, 323t, 477t
    in Nicaragua, 440t, 479t
    in Pakistan, 215t, 220t, 232, 236t, 239, 480t
    in Philippines, 250–52, 251t, 255t, 258t, 260,
        261t, 263t, 481–82t
    in South Africa, 332, 333t, 339t, 341t, 343t,
        345t, 483t
    in Thailand, 283, 290t, 485t
Lochner, L., 153
Lofgren, H., 367, 432
Luxembourg
    in GIDD model, 95f
    in Linkage model, 460t

**M**
Macedonia, FYR, in GIDD model, 93f, 95f
MacMaps, 52
macroeconomic closure rules, 14
    Brazilian national model, 404–5
    GTAP model, 130
    Indonesia, Wayang model, 192–94
    Linkage model, 462
    Mozambique national CGE model, 314
    Nicaraguan national model, 434
    South African national model, 337
macroeconomic effects
    Argentine national model, 374–76
    Brazilian national model, 409–10, 410t
    Chinese national model, 160–63, 161t
    GIDD model, 99–103, 100f, 102f
    Indonesia, Wayang model, 194–97, 195t
    Nicaraguan national model, 441–42, 441t
    South African national model, 341, 342t
    in Thai CGE model, 284, 291t, 295t,
        298–92

Madagascar
    GIDD model, 93f, 95f, 100f, 102f, 111t
    Linkage model
        agricultural outputs, imports, and
            exports, 63t
        economic welfare, global and national, 58t
        factor prices, 70t
        land supply elasticities, 465t
        price distortion structure, 53t, 469t
        regional concordance, 461t
        sectoral value added, 73t
maize. *See* grains and oilseeds
Malawi
    GIDD model, empirical results of, 23, 24t
    GTAP model, 121
        agricultural versus nonagricultural trade
            reforms, 136–38t
        commodity-specific support, effects of,
            140t, 141t
        concentration of poverty in agricultural
            households, 121
        contribution of earnings to total poverty
            response, 127t
        elasticities approach to poverty headcount,
            122t
        percentage change in national poverty
            headcount, 131t
        poverty population, stratum contributions
            to, 124t
        tax replacement, 131t
    Linkage model, 461t
Malaysia
    GIDD model, 100f, 102f
    Linkage model
        agricultural outputs, imports, and
            exports, 63t
        economic welfare, global and
            national, 58t
        factor prices, 70t
        land supply elasticities, 466t
        price distortion structure, 53t, 469t
        regional concordance, 461t
        sectoral value added, 73t
Mali, in GIDD model, 93f, 95f, 111t, 114f
Malta, in Linkage model, 460t
*maquila* industry, Nicaragua, 425t, 426, 442, 446,
    454n1–2
Martin, Will, xxiii, 3, 60, 87n, 96, 247n
Mauritania, in GIDD model, 93f, 95f, 111t, 114f
Mauritius, in Linkage model, 461t
McCulloch, N., 94
MDG (Millennium Development Goals), 41, 50
meat. *See* livestock and meat products
Medvedev, Denis, xxiii, 19, 23, 24, 31, 80, 87, 457
Melitz, M., 80
Melo, J. de, 434
Mendonça, R., 392
Menem government, Argentina, 360–61

Mexico
  GIDD model
    empirical results of, 23, 24t
    factor prices, 102f, 103
    inequality variations in agricultural and
      nonagricultural households, 95f
    poverty, effects of global liberalization on,
      109, 110f, 112t
    real national consumption, effects of global
      liberalization on, 100f, 101
    share of population in agriculture and of
      agriculture in total income, 93f
    Theil Index, income distributional
      changes, 114f
  global liberalization, effects on incidence of
    poverty and inequality in, 36t
  GTAP model, 121
    agricultural versus nonagricultural trade
      reforms, 135–38, 136–38t, 139
    commodity-specific support, effects of, 139,
      140t, 141t
    contribution of earnings to total poverty
      response, 127t
    elasticities approach to poverty
      headcount, 122t
    percentage change in national poverty
      headcount, 131t
    poverty population, stratum contributions
      to, 124t
    preference erosion resulting from global
      liberalization, 134
    price distortion structure, 470t
    tax replacement, 131t
  Linkage model
    agricultural outputs, imports, and exports, 64t
    economic welfare, global and national, 58t
    factor prices, 71t
    land supply elasticities, 466t
    price distortion structure, 53t, 470t
    regional concordance, 461t
    sectoral value added, 74t
    transfer payments (remittances), importance
      of, 127t, 128
microsimulation modeling
  in Argentina, 359–60, 370–73
  CGE, combined with, 8, 13, 19
  in GTAP model, 88, 96, 122
  in Nicaragua, 432, 436, 437
  in South Africa, 338–39t, 338–40
Middle East and North Africa. See also specific
    countries
  GIDD model
    factor prices, 101, 102f
    population represented in, 89
    real national consumption, effects of global
      liberalization on, 100f, 101
    share of population in agriculture and of
      agriculture in total income, 94

Linkage model
  agricultural outputs, imports, and exports,
    63t, 65t
  economic welfare, global and national, 58t
  empirical results of, 15t, 17t, 18t
  factor prices, 70t
  land supply elasticities, 465t
  new distortion estimates, lack of, 82n4
  poverty, effects on, 77–79t
  price distortion structure, 53t, 469t
  regional concordance, 460t
  sectoral value added, 69, 73t
migration, rural to urban, in China, 151–52,
    160–62, 161t, 163, 173
Milanovic, B., 5, 57
milk. See dairy
Millennium Development Goals (MDG), 41, 50
Mincer, J. A., 372
Moldova, in GIDD model, 93f, 95f, 112t, 114f
Mongolia, in GIDD model, 95f, 114f
Morocco
  in GIDD model, 93f, 95f, 100f, 102f, 110f
  in Linkage model, 461t, 465t, 469t
Mozambique, 303–29
  agricultural potential of, 303–4
  agricultural price distortions in, 305–8
  border price and export demand shocks, 315,
    316–17t, 477–78t
  characteristics of national CGE model, 26t
  conclusions regarding, 327–28
  economic structure of, 305, 306–7t
  factor intensities of production, 308, 309–10t
  GIDD model, 23, 24t, 100f, 102f
  government income and expenditure, 314
  GTAP model, 121
    agricultural versus nonagricultural trade
      reforms, 136–38t
    commodity-specific support, effects of,
      140t, 141t
    concentration of poverty in agricultural
      households, 121
    contribution of earnings to total poverty
      response, 127t
    elasticities approach to poverty
      headcount, 122t
    percentage change in national poverty
      headcount, 131t
    poverty population, stratum contributions
      to, 124t
    price distortion structure, 469t
    tax replacement, 131t
  household income and expenditure, 311–14,
    312–13t
  liberalization effects, 314–27
    border price and export demand shocks,
      315, 316–17t
    domestic liberalization of agricultural
      products, 326–27

domestic liberalization of all commodities, 322–26, 325t
GDP, 315–18, 319–20t, 324–26, 327
global liberalization's effects on poverty and inequality, 28–30t, 32–34t, 36t
rest-of-the-world agricultural liberalization, 316–18t, 322, 325t
rest-of-the-world liberalization of all commodities, 315–20, 316–25t
simulations used, 314–15
Linkage model
agricultural outputs, imports, and exports, 63t
border price and export demand shocks to national model from, 477–78t
economic welfare, global and national, 58t
factor prices, 70t
land supply elasticities, 465t
national CGE model, use with, 311, 315
price distortion structure, 53t, 469t
regional concordance, 460t
sectoral value added, 69, 73t
macroeconomic closure rules, 314
national CGE modeling framework, 308–14
rural versus urban poverty and inequality in, 28–29t, 32–33t
SAM, 308, 314
simulations, 314–15
tax replacement schemes in, 326
transfer payments (remittances), importance of, 127t, 128
Murphy, K. M., 153

**N**

national CGE models, 25–35. *See also specific countries*
in analytical framework, 11–14
border price and export demand shocks. *See border price and export demand shocks in national models*
characteristics of, 25, 26t
incidence of extreme poverty, 27, 28–30t
incidence of income inequality, 27, 32–34t
reduction of poverty and inequality by global liberalization, 28–30t, 31–35, 32–34t
unweighted averages for poverty results, 28–31, 30t
Nazli, H., 212
Nelgen, Signe, 49n
Nepal, in GIDD model, 93f, 95f, 114f
poverty, effects of global liberalization on, 111t
Netherlands
in GIDD model, 95f
in Linkage model, 460t
New Zealand
GIDD model, 95f, 100f, 101, 102f
Linkage model

agricultural outputs, imports, and exports, 64t
economic welfare, global and national, 59t
factor prices, 69, 72t
land supply elasticities, 465t
price distortion structure, 54t, 468t
regional concordance, 460t
sectoral value added, 75t
Niazi, M. K., 212
Nicaragua, 423–56
agricultural growth affecting poverty and inequality in, 430–31, 431t
agricultural price distortions in, 429–30f
agriculture and agricultural trade in, 424–26, 425–26t
base year calibration of national model, 435–36
border price and export demand shocks, 439–41, 440t, 478–79t
CGE, use of, 432
characteristics of national model, 436t
DR-CAFTA, 423–24, 426–29, 428f, 445, 452
factor market closure rules, 433–34
GDP
agricultural share of, 424, 425t
exports and imports as share of, 427
liberalization effects, 441t, 443–44t, 443–45
GIDD model
factor prices, 102f
inequality variations in agricultural and nonagricultural households, 95f
poverty, effects of global liberalization on, 112t
real national consumption, effects of global liberalization on, 100f
share of population in agriculture and of agriculture in total income, 93f
Theil Index, income distributional changes, 114f
GTAP database, 436, 454n9, 455n15, 455n19, 470t
labor market
liberalization effects, 445–50, 447–49t
structure, 434, 436–38
liberalization effects, 439–52
border price and export demand shocks, 439–41, 440t
fiscal costs, 445, 446f
GDP, 441t, 443–44t, 443–45
on labor market, 445–50, 447–49t
macroeconomic effects, 441–42, 441t
on poverty and inequality
in global liberalization models, 28–30t, 32–34t, 36t
in national model, 450–52, 451t
Linkage model
agricultural outputs, imports, and exports, 64t

Nicaragua (*continued*)
  border price and export demand shocks to
    national model from, 478–79*t*
  economic welfare, global and national, 58*t*
  factor prices, 71*t*
  land supply elasticities, 466*t*
  national model's use of, 432, 433, 439
  price distortion structure, 53*t*, 470*t*
  regional concordance, 461*t*
  sectoral value added, 74*t*
macroeconomic closure rules, 434
macroeconomic indicators in, 424, 425*t*
*maquila* industry, 425*t*, 426, 442, 446,
    454*n*1–2
microsimulation, use of, 432, 436, 437
national model, 26*t*, 431–39
NRAs in, 429–30*f*
policy implications for, 452–54
poverty and inequality
  agricultural growth affecting, 430–31, 431*t*
  under GIDD model, 112*t*
  global liberalization's effects on, 28–30*t*,
    32–34*t*, 36*t*
  modeling methodology, 436–38
  national model's liberalization effects on,
    450–52, 451*t*
  rural versus urban, 28–29*t*, 32–33*t*
  rural versus urban poverty and inequality in,
    28–29*t*, 32–33*t*
  simulations used, 438–39
  tariffs in, 427, 428*f*
  unemployment in, 12, 14
Nigeria
  GIDD model
    factor prices, 102*f*
    inequality variations in agricultural and
      nonagricultural households, 95*f*
    poverty, effects of global liberalization on,
      110*f*, 111*t*
    real national consumption, effects of global
      liberalization on, 100*f*, 101
    share of population in agriculture and of
      agriculture in total income, 93*f*
    Theil Index, income distributional
      changes, 114*f*
  Linkage model
    agricultural outputs, imports, and
      exports, 63*t*
    economic welfare, global and national, 58*t*
    factor prices, 70*t*
    land supply elasticities, 465*t*
    price distortion structure, 53*t*, 470*t*
    regional concordance, 461*t*
    sectoral value added, 73*t*
nominal rates of assistance (NRAs)
  in developing versus high-income countries,
    6–8, 7*t*
  in Nicaragua, 429–30*f*

Philippines, estimates of NRA to agriculture
    in, 250–52, 251*t*
North Africa. *See* Middle East and North Africa;
    *specific countries*
NRAs. *See* nominal rates of assistance
numerical open-economy growth model, 41*n*6

**O**

OECD (Organisation for Economic Co-
    operation and Development), 119,
    128–29, 142*n*7, 157
oils, vegetable. *See* vegetables, fruits, and
    vegetable oils
oilseeds. *See* grains and oilseeds
Olper, Alessandro, 391*n*
ORANI general equilibrium model for
    Australia, 182
Orden, David, xxiii, 209, 212
Organisation for Economic Co-operation and
    Development (OECD), 119, 128–29,
    142*n*7, 157

**P**

Paasche price index, 117*n*14
Pacific Region. *See* East Asia and Pacific, and
    *specific countries*
Paes de Barros, R., 372
Pakistan, 209–46
  agricultural price distortions in, 210–12
  border price and export demand shocks, 219,
    220–21*t*, 480–81*t*
  characteristics of national CGE model, 26*t*
  GIDD model
    factor prices, 102*f*
    inequality variations in agricultural and
      nonagricultural households, 95*f*
    poverty, effects of global liberalization on,
      110*f*, 111*t*
    real national consumption, effects of global
      liberalization on, 100*f*
    share of population in agriculture and of
      agriculture in total income, 93*f*
    Theil Index, income distributional
      changes, 114*f*
  indicators and incidence of poverty, 223,
    224*f*, 224*t*
  liberalization effects, 226–43
    agricultural liberalization
      global, 240–41
      by Pakistan unilaterally, 239–40
      by rest of the world, 232–35
    border price and export demand shocks,
      219, 220–21*t*
    empirical results, 28–30*t*, 31, 32–34*t*, 36*t*
    trade liberalization
      global, 240
      by Pakistan unilaterally, 235–39,
        236–37*t*

by rest of the world, 226–31, 227–29t, 232–33t
Linkage model
agricultural outputs, imports, and exports, 63t
border price and export demand shocks to national model from, 480–81t
economic welfare, global and national, 58t
factor prices, 71t
land supply elasticities, 466t
price distortion structure, 53t, 469t
regional concordance, 461t
sectoral value added, 74t
used in national CGE model, 209, 213–14
national CGE model, 212–23
border price and export demand shocks, 219, 220–21t
consumption structure, 218
household income sources and taxes, 219–23, 222t
households, 211, 210t
Linkage model and, 209, 213–14
SAM, economic structure in, 214, 215–18t
simulations used, 209–10, 225–26
structure of, 212–13
tariffs, 219
policy implications in, 244–45
poverty and inequality
in GIDD model, 110f, 111t
rural versus urban, 28–29t, 32–33t, 42n19
Theil Index, income distributional changes, 114f
rural versus urban poverty and inequality in, 28–29t, 32–33t, 42n19
SAM, 210, 212, 214, 215–18t, 223, 241
tax replacement schemes, 209, 210, 241–43, 242–43t, 245n4
palm oil. *See* vegetables, fruits, and vegetable oils
Panama, in GIDD model, 93f, 95f, 112t, 114f
Paraguay
in GIDD model, 93f, 95f, 112t, 114f
in Linkage model, 461t
Park, A., 151
Pearson, K. R., 130
Pereira da Silva, L. A., 8, 96
Peru
GIDD model
empirical results of, 23, 24t
inequality variations in agricultural and nonagricultural households, 95f
poverty, effects of global liberalization on, 110f, 112t, 113
share of population in agriculture and of agriculture in total income, 93f
Theil Index, income distributional changes, 114f
global liberalization, effects on incidence of poverty and inequality in, 36t

GTAP model, 121
agricultural versus nonagricultural trade reforms, 136–38t
commodity-specific support, effects of, 140t, 141t
contribution of earnings to total poverty response, 127t
elasticities approach to poverty headcount, 122t
percentage change in national poverty headcount, 131t
poverty population, stratum contributions to, 124t
self-employed nonagricultural households as share of poor, 124
tax replacement, 131t
Linkage model, 461t
Philippines, 247–82
agricultural price distortions in, 247, 249–52, 251–52t, 253f
border price and export demand shocks, 263–65t, 481–82t
GIDD model
empirical results of, 23, 24t
factor prices, 102f
inequality variations in agricultural and nonagricultural households, 95f
poverty, effects of global liberalization on, 110f, 111t, 113
real national consumption, effects of global liberalization on, 100f
share of population in agriculture and of agriculture in total income, 93f
Theil Index, income distributional changes, 114f
GTAP model, 121
agricultural versus nonagricultural trade reforms, 136–38t, 138
commodity-specific support, effects of, 140t, 141t
contribution of earnings to total poverty response, 127t
elasticities approach to poverty headcount, 122t
percentage change in national poverty headcount, 131t
poverty population, stratum contributions to, 124t
price distortion structure, 469t
tax replacement, 131t
import-substitution policy, 247, 249
liberalization effects, 266–79
agricultural liberalization
global, 272
by rest of the world, 267–70
unilaterally by Philippines, 271
border price and export demand shocks, 263–65t

Philippines (*continued*)
   consumer price index, 274*t*, 275
   global liberalization's effects on poverty and
      inequality, 28–30*t*, 31, 32–34*t*, 35, 36*t*
   household incomes, 272–75, 273*t*
   national model's effects on poverty and
      inequality, 276–79, 277–78*t*
   trade liberalization
      global, 271–72
      by rest of the world, 266–67, 268–69*t*
      unilaterally by Philippines, 270
      welfare gains, 275–76
   Linkage model
      agricultural outputs, imports, and
         exports, 63*t*
      border price and export demand shocks to
         national model from, 481–82*t*
      economic welfare, global and national, 58*t*
      factor prices, 70*t*
      land supply elasticities, 466*t*
      national CGE model and, 248, 260, 262–65*t*
      price distortion structure, 53*t*, 469*t*
      regional concordance, 461*t*
      sectoral value added, 73*t*
   national CGE model, 253–60
      characteristics of, 26*t*
      consumption structure of households, 260,
         261–62*t*
      Linkage model and, 248, 260, 262–65*t*
      production structure, 254–59, 255–57*t*
      simulations, 260–66
      trade structure and elasticity parameters,
         258–59*t*, 259–60
   NRA to agriculture, estimates of, 250–52, 251*t*
   policy implications, 280
   poverty and inequality
      in GIDD model, 110*f*, 111*t*, 113
      global liberalization's effects on, 28–30*t*, 31,
         32–34*t*, 35, 36*t*
      in GTAP model, 124*t*
      incidence of, 252, 252*t*, 253*f*
      national model's effects on, 276–79,
         277–78*t*
      rural versus urban, 28–29*t*, 32–33*t*
      Theil Index, income distributional
         changes, 114*f*
   rural versus urban poverty and inequality in,
      28–29*t*, 32–33*t*
   SAM, 248, 253
   tariff binding overhang, 249, 281*n*5
   tax replacement schemes, 279
plant-based fibers. *See* textiles and textile raw
      materials
Poland
   GIDD model, 93*f*, 95*f*, 100*f*, 102*f*, 114*f*
   Linkage model
      agricultural outputs, imports, and
         exports, 64*t*

      economic welfare, global and national, 59*t*
      factor prices, 71*t*
      land supply elasticities, 465*t*
      price distortion structure, 54*t*, 468*t*
      regional concordance, 460*t*
      sectoral value added, 75*t*
   policy implications of empirical findings, 40–41
Portugal
   in GIDD model, 95*f*
   in Linkage model, 460*t*
poverty. *See* agricultural price distortions,
      poverty, and inequality, *and under*
      *specific countries and regions*
Powell, A., 121
PPP (purchasing power parity) prices, in GIDD
      data set, 89
preference erosion resulting from global
      liberalization, 134
probability of falling into poverty, 39
product prices, in Linkage model, 68–69, 68*t*
purchasing power parity (PPP) prices, in GIDD
      data set, 89

**R**
Rausser, Gordon, 391*n*
Ravallion, M., 96, 147, 148
regional and sectoral distribution of welfare
      effects, in Linkage model, 60, 61*t*
remittances (transfer payments), 125–28,
      127*t*, 136*t*
replacement of tariff revenue. *See* tax
      replacement schemes
Republic of Korea. *See* Korea, Republic of
Republic of Yemen, in GIDD model, 93*f*, 95*f*,
      114*f*, 1110*f*
República Bolivariana de Venezuela. *See*
      Venezuela, República Bolivariana de
rice. *See* grains and oilseeds
Rimmer, M., 121
Robilliard, A.-S., 419, 436
Robinson, S., 367, 419, 432, 434, 436
Rocha, S., 392, 415
Rodrik, D., 87
Romania
   GIDD model
      factor prices, 102*f*
      inequality variations in agricultural and
         nonagricultural households, 84, 95*f*
      real national consumption, effects of global
         liberalization on, 100*f*
      share of population in agriculture and of
         agriculture in total income, 93*f*
      Theil Index, income distributional changes,
         114*f*
   Linkage model
      agricultural outputs, imports, and
         exports, 64*t*
      economic welfare, global and national, 59*t*

factor prices, 71t
land supply elasticities, 465t
price distortion structure, 54t, 468t
regional concordance, 460t
sectoral value added, 75t
Rozelle, S., 150
rural versus urban. *See also under specific
    countries*
incidence of extreme poverty, 28–29t
levels of inequality, 5, 32–33t
redistributive effects of trade liberalization, 88
Russian Federation
GIDD model
    factor prices, 102f
    inequality variations in agricultural and
        nonagricultural households, 95f
    poverty, effects of global liberalization
        on, 112t
    real national consumption, effects of global
        liberalization on, 100f
    share of employment in agriculture and
        income levels, relationship between, 92f
    share of population in agriculture and of
        agriculture in total income, 93f
    Theil Index, income distributional
        changes, 114f
Linkage model
    agricultural outputs, imports, and
        exports, 64t
    economic welfare, global and
        national, 59t
    factor prices, 71t
    land supply elasticities, 465t
    price distortion structure, 54t, 468t
    regional concordance, 460t
    sectoral value added, 75t
Rutherford, T. F., 41n6

**S**
Sadoulet, E., 22
Salam, A., 209
Salazni, M., 369
SAMs. *See* social accounting matrices
Sánchez, Marco V., xxiii, 423, 432
sectoral and regional distribution of welfare
    effects, in Linkage model, 60, 61t
sectoral concordance of border price and export
    demand shocks in Linkage model,
    458, 459t
sectoral value added, in Linkage model, 69–76,
    73–75t
Senegal
GIDD model
    factor prices, 102f
    inequality variations in agricultural and
        nonagricultural households, 95f
    poverty, effects of global liberalization
        on, 111t

real national consumption, effects of global
    liberalization on, 100f, 101
share of population in agriculture and of
    agriculture in total income, 93f
Theil Index, income distributional
    changes, 114f
Linkage model
    agricultural outputs, imports, and
        exports, 63t
    economic welfare, global and national, 58t
    factor prices, 70t
    land supply elasticities, 466t
    price distortion structure, 53t, 470t
    regional concordance, 461t
    sectoral value added, 73t
services, trade in, 39, 82n3
sheep. *See* livestock and meat products
Shi, X., 152
Sicular, T., 150, 152
Singapore
GIDD model, 95f, 100f, 102f
Linkage model
    agricultural outputs, imports, and
        exports, 64t
    economic welfare, global and national, 59t
    factor prices, 72t
    land supply elasticities, 465t
    negligible influence on, 83n8
    price distortion structure, 469t
    regional concordance, 460t
    sectoral value added, 75t
Slovak Republic
GIDD model, 100f, 102f
Linkage model
    agricultural outputs, imports, and
        exports, 64t
    economic welfare, global and national, 59t
    factor prices, 71t
    land supply elasticities, 465t
    price distortion structure, 54t, 468t
    regional concordance, 460t
    sectoral value added, 75t
Slovenia
GIDD model, 95f, 100f, 102f
Linkage model
    agricultural outputs, imports, and
        exports, 64t
    economic welfare, global and national, 59t
    factor prices, 71t
    land supply elasticities, 465t
    price distortion structure, 54t, 468t
    regional concordance, 460t
    sectoral value added, 75t
social accounting matrices (SAMs), 13
Argentinian CGE model, 367t
China, benchmark data for, 153–56, 154–55t
Indonesian Wayang model, 181–82,
    185–86, 189

social accounting matrices (*continued*)
    Mozambique CGE model, 308, 314
    Nicaraguan model, 435
    Pakistan's CGE model, 210, 212, 214, 215–18$t$,
        223, 241
    Philippines CGE model, 248, 253
    South African CGE model, 337
    Thai CGE model, 287
South Africa, 331–56
    agricultural price distortions in, 335
    apartheid, end of, 331
    border price and export demand shocks, 340,
        341$t$, 483–84$t$
    CGE model, 336–38, 337$t$
    characteristics of national CGE model, 26$t$
    conclusions regarding, 354
    direct tax rates in, 337$t$
    economic structure of, 332–35, 333–34$t$
    factor intensity structure, 344, 345–46$t$
    GIDD model
        factor prices, 102$f$
        inequality variations in agricultural and
            nonagricultural households, 94, 95$f$
        poverty, effects of global liberalization on,
            109, 110$f$, 111$t$
        real national consumption, effects of global
            liberalization on, 100$f$
        share of population in agriculture and of
            agriculture in total income, 93$f$
        Theil Index, income distributional
            changes, 114$f$
    household income and expenditure, 338–39$t$
    liberalization effects, 340–54
        border price and export demand shocks,
            340, 341$t$
        GDP after global liberalization, 342,
            343–44$t$, 347, 349–54
        global liberalization's effects on poverty and
            inequality, 28–30$t$, 31, 32–34$t$, 36$t$
        macroeconomic effects of global
            liberalization, 341, 342$t$
        national model's effects on poverty and
            income inequality, 347–48$t$, 347–49
        rest-of-the-world agricultural
            liberalization, 349–50
        rest-of-the-world liberalization of all
            commodities, 340–49, 341–48$t$
        unilateral liberalization of agricultural
            commodities, 352–54
        unilateral liberalization of all commodities,
            350–52
    Linkage model
        agricultural outputs, imports, and
            exports, 63$t$
        border price and export demand shocks to
            national model from, 483–84$t$
        economic welfare, global and national, 58$t$
        factor prices, 70$t$

land supply elasticities, 465$t$
national CGE model's use of, 335, 338, 340
price distortion structure, 53$t$, 469$t$
regional concordance, 460$t$
sectoral value added, 73$t$
microsimulation model, 338–39$t$, 338–40
national model, 335–40
poverty and inequality
    in GIDD model, 109, 110$f$, 111$t$
    global liberalization's effects on, 28–30$t$, 31,
        32–34$t$, 36$t$
    national model's effects on, 347–48$t$,
        347–49
    rural versus urban, 28–29$t$, 32–33$t$,
        331–32, 334
    Theil Index, income distributional
        changes, 114$f$
rural versus urban poverty and inequality in,
    28–29$t$, 32–33$t$, 331–32, 334
SAM, 337
simulations, 340
unemployment in, 6, 12, 14, 344, 346–47$t$,
    354, 355$n$5
WTO accession, 331
South Asia. *See also specific countries*
    GIDD model
        empirical results of, 20$t$, 22$t$, 23, 24$t$, 25
        factor prices, 102$f$
        GICs, 107, 108$f$
        global liberalization, effects of, 107$t$, 109, 115
        population represented in, 89
        poverty, effects of global liberalization on,
            109, 111$t$
        real national consumption, effects of global
            liberalization on, 100$f$
        share of population in agriculture and of
            agriculture in total income, 94
    global liberalization, effects on incidence of
        poverty and inequality in, 37
    GTAP model, 121, 469$t$
    levels of poverty and inequality in, 4$t$
    Linkage model
        agricultural outputs, imports, and exports,
            63$t$, 65$t$
        economic welfare, global and national,
            57, 58$t$
        empirical results of, 15$t$, 16, 17$t$, 18$t$
        factor prices, 70–71$t$
        land supply elasticities, 466$t$
        poverty, effects on, 77–79$t$, 80
        price distortion structure, 53$t$, 469$t$
        regional concordance, 461$t$
        sectoral value added, 69–76, 73–74$t$
    NRAs in developing versus high-income
        countries, 7$t$
    poverty and inequality
        in GIDD model, 109, 111$t$
        in Linkage model, 77–79$t$, 80

South Korea. *See* Korea, Republic of
Southern Africa Customs Union, 461*t*
soybeans. *See* vegetables, fruits, and
    vegetable oils
Spain
  in GIDD model, 95*f*
  in Linkage model, 460*t*
Sri Lanka
  GIDD model
    factor prices, 102*f*
    inequality variations in agricultural and
      nonagricultural households, 95*f*
    poverty, effects of global liberalization on,
      110*f*, 111*t*
    real national consumption, effects of global
      liberalization on, 100*f*
    share of population in agriculture and of
      agriculture in total income, 93*f*
    Theil Index, income distributional
      changes, 114*f*
  Linkage model
    agricultural outputs, imports, and
      exports, 63*t*
    economic welfare, global and national, 58*t*
    factor prices, 71*t*
    land supply elasticities, 466*t*
    price distortion structure, 53*t*, 469*t*
    regional concordance, 461*t*
    sectoral value added, 74*t*
Sturzenegger, A. C., 369
Sub-Saharan Africa. *See also specific countries*
  GIDD model
    empirical results of, 20*t*, 22*t*, 23, 24*t*, 25
    factor prices, 102*f*
    global liberalization, effects of, 107*t*
    population represented in, 89
    poverty, effects of global liberalization
      on, 111*t*
    real national consumption, effects of global
      liberalization on, 100*f*
    share of population in agriculture and of
      agriculture in total income, 94
  global liberalization, effects on incidence of
    poverty and inequality in, 37
  GTAP model, 121, 469–70*t*
  Linkage model
    agricultural outputs, imports, and exports,
      63*t*, 65*t*
    economic welfare, global and national,
      57, 58*t*
    empirical results of, 15*t*, 16, 17*t*, 18*t*
    factor prices, 70*t*
    land supply elasticities, 465–66*t*
    poverty, effects on, 77–79*t*, 80
    price distortion structure, 53*t*,
      469–70*t*
    regional concordance, 461*t*
    sectoral value added, 69, 73*t*

NRAs in developing versus high-income
  countries, 7*t*
poverty and inequality
  in GIDD model, 111*t*
  global liberalization, effects of, 37
  levels of, 3, 4*t*
  in Linkage model, 77–79*t*, 80
subsidies. *See also* agricultural price distortions,
  poverty, and inequality
  China, benchmark data for, 154–55*t*
  commodity-specific support, effects of,
    120–21, 139–40, 140*t*, 141*t*
  GIDD model simulations based on removal
    of, 99
  Indonesia, simulated shocks in Wayang
    model, 191*t*
  Linkage model, price distortion structure,
    52–55, 53–54*t*
  in South Africa, 335
sugar
  in Argentina, 367*t*, 369*t*, 370*t*, 388*n*14, 471*t*
  border price and export demand shocks in
    Linkage model, 459*t*, 464*t*, 471–85*t*
  in Brazil, 403*t*, 405–8*t*, 405*t*, 407*t*,
    411–12*t*, 473*t*
  in China, 154–55*t*, 158*t*, 474*t*
  GTAP model, commodity-specific support
    in, 140*t*
  in Indonesia, 179–81, 191*t*, 193*t*, 202–5,
    475–76*t*
  in Linkage model, 62*t*, 65, 66–67*t*, 68*t*
  in Mozambique, 306–7*t*, 308, 309–10*t*,
    316–17*t*, 318, 319*t*, 321*t*, 322, 323*t*,
    324, 477*t*
  in Nicaragua, 424, 440*t*, 479*t*
  in Pakistan, 211–12, 215*t*, 219, 220*t*, 232, 236*t*,
    239, 480*t*
  in Philippines, 250, 251*t*, 255*t*, 258*t*, 260, 261*t*,
    263*t*, 266, 481–82*t*
  in South Africa, 333*t*, 339*t*, 341*t*, 342–44, 343*t*,
    345*t*, 350, 483*t*
  in Thailand, 284, 290*t*, 484–85*t*
Sweden
  in GIDD model, 95*f*
  in Linkage model, 460*t*, 465*t*
Switzerland, in GIDD model, 95*f*

**T**
Taber, C., 153
Taiwan, China
  as developing country, 56
  GIDD model, 100*f*, 102*f*
  Linkage model
    agricultural outputs, imports, and
      exports, 63*t*
    economic welfare, global and national, 58*t*
    factor prices, 70*t*
    land supply elasticities, 465*t*

Taiwan (*continued*)
  price distortion structure, 53*t*, 469*t*
  regional concordance, 460*t*
  sectoral value added, 73*t*
Tajikistan, in GIDD model, 93*f*, 95*f*,
    112*t*, 114*f*
Tanzania
  GIDD model
    factor prices, 102*f*
    inequality variations in agricultural and
      nonagricultural households, 95*f*
    poverty, effects of global liberalization
      on, 111*t*
    real national consumption, effects of global
      liberalization on, 100*f*, 101
    share of population in agriculture and of
      agriculture in total income, 93*f*
    Theil Index, income distributional
      changes, 114*f*
  Linkage model
    agricultural outputs, imports, and
      exports, 63*t*
    economic welfare, global and national, 58*t*
    factor prices, 70*t*
    land supply elasticities, 465*t*
    price distortion structure, 53*t*, 470*t*
    regional concordance, 461*t*
    sectoral value added, 73*t*
tariff binding overhang, 249, 281*n*5
tariffs. *See also* agricultural price distortions,
    poverty, and inequality
  aggregate gains following elimination of, 87
  Argentina, table of export taxes and import
    tariffs for, 369, 370*t*
  China, benchmark data for, 154–55*t*
  developing-country cuts in, 119
  GIDD model simulations based on removal
    of, 99
  Indonesia, simulated shocks in Wayang
    model, 191*t*
  Linkage model, price distortion structure,
    52–55, 53–54*t*
  in Nicaragua, 427, 428*f*
  in Pakistan, 219
  in Philippines, 249–50
  in South Africa, 335
  tax replacement. *See* tax replacement schemes
Tarr, D. G., 41*n*6
tax replacement schemes
  Argentina, 383
  GTAP model, 130, 131*t*, 132–33
  Mozambique, 326
  Pakistan, 209, 210, 241–43, 242–43*t*, 245*n*4
  Philippines, 279
TERM CGE model, 394, 419*n*5
textiles and textile raw materials
  in Argentina, 367*t*, 369*t*, 370*t*, 388*n*14–15,
    471–72*t*

border price and export demand shocks in
    Linkage model, 459*t*, 464*t*, 471–85*t*
  in Brazil, 402*t*, 473*t*
  in China, 154–55*t*, 156, 158*t*, 474–75*t*
  GTAP model, commodity-specific support
    in, 140*t*
  in Indonesia, 191*t*, 193*t*, 475–76*t*
  in Linkage model, 62*t*, 66–67*t*, 68*t*
  *maquila* industry, 425*t*, 426, 442, 446,
    454*n*1–2
  in Mozambique, 306–7*t*, 316–17*t*, 318, 319*t*,
    321*t*, 322, 323*t*, 477*t*
  in Nicaragua, 425*t*, 426, 428–29, 440*t*, 442,
    446, 454*n*1, 479*t*
  in Pakistan, 211, 215–16*t*, 218, 219, 220–21*t*,
    232, 236–37*t*, 238, 239, 480–81*t*
  in Philippines, 256*t*, 258*t*, 262*t*, 264*t*, 481–82*t*
  in South Africa, 332, 333*t*, 339*t*, 341*t*, 343*t*,
    345*t*, 350, 351, 483*t*
  in Thailand, 290*t*, 485*t*
Thailand, 283–99
  border price and export demand shocks, 288,
    291*t*, 484–85*t*
  characteristics of national CGE model, 26*t*
  conclusions regarding, 296–98
  GIDD model
    empirical results of, 23, 24*t*, 25
    factor prices, 102*f*
    inequality variations in agricultural and
      nonagricultural households, 95*f*
    poverty, effects of global liberalization on,
      110*f*, 111*t*, 113
    real national consumption, effects of global
      liberalization on, 100*f*
    share of population in agriculture and of
      agriculture in total income, 93*f*
    Theil Index, income distributional
      changes, 114*f*
  GTAP model, 121
    agricultural versus nonagricultural trade
      reforms, 136–38*t*
    commodity-specific support, effects of,
      140*t*, 141*t*
    contribution of earnings to total poverty
      response, 127*t*
    elasticities approach to poverty
      headcount, 122*t*
    percentage change in national poverty
      headcount, 131*t*
    poverty population, stratum contributions
      to, 124*t*
    price distortion structure, 469*t*
    tax replacement, 131*t*, 132
  Indonesian study, comparison with, 296–98
  JamlongThai general equilibrium model,
    285–88
    border price and export demand shocks,
      288, 291*t*

households in, 286–87*t*
industries in, 285, 286*t*
industry assistance rates used in modeling,
    288, 289*t*
Linkage model, used with, 284
simulations, 288
liberalization effects
agricultural liberalization, 294–95,
    295–96*t*, 297
border price and export demand shocks,
    288, 291*t*
global liberalization, 288–94, 291*t*, 293*t*
global models' effects on poverty and
    inequality, 28–30*t*, 31, 32–34*t*, 35, 36*t*
macroeconomic effects, 284, 291*t*, 295*t*,
    298–92
national model's effects on poverty and
    inequality, 292–94, 293*t*, 296*t*
rest-of-the-world liberalization, 290–91*t*,
    292, 293*t*, 294, 297
trade liberalization, 296–97
unilateral liberalization, 290–91*t*, 292, 293*t*,
    294, 297
Linkage model
agricultural outputs, imports, and
    exports, 63*t*
border price and export demand shocks to
    national model from, 484–85*t*
economic welfare, global and national, 58*t*
factor prices, 70*t*
land supply elasticities, 466*t*
national CGE model used with, 284
price distortion structure, 469*t*
regional concordance, 461*t*
sectoral value added, 74*t*
poverty and inequality
in GIDD model, 110*f*, 111*t*, 113
global models' effects on, 28–30*t*, 31,
    32–34*t*, 35, 36*t*
in GTAP model, 122*t*, 124*t*, 131*t*
national model's effects on, 292–94,
    293*t*, 296*t*
rural versus urban, 28–29*t*, 32–33*t*, 284
Theil Index, income distributional
    changes, 114*f*
rural versus urban poverty and inequality in,
    28–29*t*, 32–33*t*, 284
SAM, 287
transfer payments (remittances), importance
    of, 127*t*, 128
Theil Index, income distributional changes
    following global liberalization,
    113–15, 114*f*
Thorbecke, E., 276, 397
Thurlow, James, xxiii, 303, 331
Timmer, Hans, 87*n*
trade in services, 39, 82*n*3
trade liberalization. *See* liberalization

trade taxes. *See* tariffs
transfer payments (remittances), 125–28,
    127*t*, 136*t*
Tunisia, in Linkage model, 460*t*
Turkey
as developing country, 52
GIDD model
    factor prices, 102*f*
    inequality variations in agricultural and
        nonagricultural households, 95*f*
    poverty, effects of global liberalization
        on, 110*f*
    real national consumption, effects of global
        liberalization on, 100*f*
    share of population in agriculture and of
        agriculture in total income, 93*f*
    Theil Index, income distributional
        changes, 114*f*
Linkage model
    agricultural outputs, imports, and
        exports, 59*t*
    economic welfare, global and national, 59*t*
    factor prices, 71*t*
    land supply elasticities, 465*t*
    price distortion structure, 54*t*, 468*t*
    regional concordance, 460*t*
    sectoral value added, 75*t*

**U**
Uganda
GIDD model
    empirical results of, 23, 24*t*
    factor prices, 102*f*
    inequality variations in agricultural and
        nonagricultural households, 95*f*
    poverty, effects of global liberalization
        on, 111*t*
    real national consumption, effects of global
        liberalization on, 100*f*
    share of population in agriculture and of
        agriculture in total income, 93*f*
    Theil Index, income distributional
        changes, 114*f*
global liberalization, effects on incidence of
    poverty and inequality in, 36*t*
GTAP model, 121
    agricultural versus nonagricultural trade
        reforms, 136–38*t*
    commodity-specific support, effects of,
        140*t*, 141*t*
    contribution of earnings to total poverty
        response, 127*t*
    elasticities approach to poverty
        headcount, 122*t*
    percentage change in national poverty
        headcount, 131*t*
    poverty population, stratum contributions
        to, 124*t*

Uganda (*continued*)
   price distortion structure, 470*t*
   tax replacement, 131*t*
   Linkage model
      agricultural outputs, imports, and
         exports, 63*t*
      economic welfare, global and national, 58*t*
      factor prices, 70*t*
      land supply elasticities, 465*t*
      price distortion structure, 53*t*, 470*t*
      regional concordance, 461*t*
      sectoral value added, 73*t*
Ukraine
   in GIDD model, 93*f*, 94, 95*f*, 112*t*, 114*f*
   in Linkage model, 460*t*
unemployment. *See under* specific countries
United Kingdom
   in GIDD model, 95*f*
   in Linkage model, 460*t*
United States
   Caribbean Basin Initiative, 428, 454*n*3
   GIDD model, 92*f*, 95*f*, 100*f*, 102*f*
   Linkage model
      agricultural outputs, imports, and
         exports, 64*t*
      economic welfare, global and national, 59*t*
      factor prices, 69, 72*t*
      land supply elasticities, 465*t*
      price distortion structure, 54*t*, 469*t*
      regional concordance, 460*t*
      sectoral value added, 75*t*
   Mexican agricultural imports purchased
      from, 103
   Nicaragua, trade relations with, 426,
      427–29
   Philippines, sugar exports from, 250
   preference erosion resulting from global
      liberalization, 134
   Thailand, bilateral trade agreement on dairy
      products with, 284
urban versus rural. *See* rural versus urban
Uruguay, in Linkage model, 461*t*
Uruguay Round
   GIDD database and, 99
   GTAP database affected by, 52, 128
Uzbekistan, in GIDD model, 93*f*, 95*f*, 112*t*, 114*f*

**V**
Valenzuela, Ernesto
   acknowledged, 183*n*, 247*n*
   biographical information, xxiii
   as chapter author, 49, 457
   cited, 6, 12, 15, 25, 38, 42*n*7, 50, 51, 52, 96, 98,
      128, 132, 192, 210, 248, 335, 366, 407,
      431–32, 458
value added tax (VAT)
   in Argentina, 383
   as tariff revenue replacement, 131*t*, 133

van der Mensbrugghe, Dominique
   acknowledged, 87*n*, 247*n*
   biographical information, xxiv
   as chapter author, 49, 457
   cited, 6, 15, 25, 38, 42*n*7, 60, 96, 98, 132, 192,
      209, 210, 248, 335, 366, 407
VAT. *See* value added tax
vegetables, fruits, and vegetable oils
   in Argentina, 367*t*, 369*t*, 370*t*, 388*n*14, 471*t*
   border price and export demand shocks in
      Linkage model, 459*t*, 464*t*, 471–85*t*
   in Brazil, 403*t*, 405–8*t*, 411–12*t*, 420*n*17, 473*t*
   in China, 154–55*t*, 156, 158*t*, 474*t*
   in Indonesia, 191*t*, 193*t*, 475–76*t*
   in Linkage model, 62*t*, 66–67*t*, 68*t*
   in Mozambique, 306*t*, 309*t*, 316*t*, 319*t*, 321*t*,
      323*t*, 477*t*
   in Nicaragua, 440*t*, 479*t*
   in Pakistan, 211–12, 215*t*, 218, 220*t*, 236*t*,
      239, 480*t*
   in Philippines, 250, 251*t*, 255*t*, 258*t*, 260, 261*t*,
      263*t*, 266, 481–82*t*
   in South Africa, 332, 333*t*, 339*t*, 341*t*, 343*t*,
      345*t*, 351, 483*t*
   in Thailand, 283–84, 290*t*, 485*t*
Venezuela, República Bolivariana de
   GIDD model
      empirical results of, 23, 24*t*
      inequality variations in agricultural and
         nonagricultural households, 95*f*
      poverty, effects of global liberalization
         on, 112*t*
      share of population in agriculture and of
         agriculture in total income, 93*f*
      Theil Index, income distributional
         changes, 114*f*
   global liberalization, effects on incidence of
      poverty and inequality in, 36*t*
   GTAP model, 121
      agricultural versus nonagricultural trade
         reforms, 136–38*t*
      commodity-specific support, effects of, 139,
         140*t*, 141*t*
      contribution of earnings to total poverty
         response, 127*t*
      elasticities approach to poverty
         headcount, 122*t*
      percentage change in national poverty
         headcount, 131*t*
      poverty population, stratum contributions
         to, 124*t*
      self-employed nonagricultural households
         as share of poor, 124
      tax replacement, 131*t*
   Linkage model, 461*t*
Vietnam
   GIDD model
      empirical results of, 23, 24*t*, 25

factor prices, 102*f*
inequality variations in agricultural and
    nonagricultural households, 95*f*
poverty, effects of global liberalization on,
    110*f*, 111*t*, 113
real national consumption, effects of global
    liberalization on, 100*f*
share of population in agriculture and of
    agriculture in total income, 93*f*
global liberalization, effects on incidence of
    poverty and inequality in, 36*t*
GTAP model, 121
    agricultural versus nonagricultural trade
        reforms, 135–38, 136–38*t*, 139
    commodity-specific support, effects of, 139,
        140*t*, 141*t*
    contribution of earnings to total poverty
        response, 127*t*
    elasticities approach to poverty
        headcount, 122*t*
    percentage change in national poverty
        headcount, 131*t*
    poverty population, stratum contributions
        to, 124*t*
    price distortion structure, 469*t*
    tax replacement, 131*t*, 132
Linkage model
    agricultural outputs, imports, and
        exports, 63*t*
    economic welfare, global and
        national, 58*t*
    factor prices, 71*t*
    land supply elasticities, 466*t*
    price distortion structure, 53*t*, 469*t*
    regional concordance, 461*t*
    sectoral value added, 74*t*
Vos, Rob, xiv, 423, 432, 436, 437

**W**
Wang, Z., 148
Warr, Peter, xiv, 179, 283, 297
Wayang general equilibrium model. *See under*
    Indonesia
welfare
    agricultural GDP and farm household
        welfare, relationship between, 8
    global and national economic welfare,
        in Linkage model, 57–60,
        58–59*t*
    regional and sectoral distribution
        of welfare effects, in Linkage
        model, 60, 61*t*
Western Europe. *See* European Union/Western
    Europe; *specific countries*
wheat. *See* grains and oilseeds
Winters, L. A., 8, 11, 12, 13, 94, 120
wool. *See* textiles and textile raw
    materials

World Bank
    data sets, 8–9, 119. *See also* global CGE
        models
    Distortions to Agricultural Incentives Project
        Database, 176*n*1, 196, 209, 245*n*1,
        281*n*1, 298*n*1, 328*n*3
World Trade Organization (WTO)
    China, accession of, 52, 99, 128,
        147–48, 149
    Doha Round. *See* Doha Round
    export taxes not subject to negotiation in,
        373, 386*n*3
    future rounds of reforms, anticipating results
        of, 51
    Kennedy Round, 386*n*3
    South Africa, accession of, 331
    Uruguay Round. *See* Uruguay Round

**X**
Xiang Tao, 391*n*

**Y**
Yemen, Republic of, in GIDD model, 93*f*, 95*f*,
    114*f*, 1110*f*
Yusuf, Arief Anshory, 283*n*

**Z**
Zambia
    GIDD model, 23, 24*t*, 100*f*, 102*f*
    GTAP model, 121
        agricultural versus nonagricultural trade
            reforms, 136–38*t*, 138
        commodity-specific support, effects of,
            140*t*, 141*t*
        concentration of poverty in agricultural
            households, 121
        contribution of earnings to total poverty
            response, 127*t*
        elasticities approach to poverty headcount,
            122–23, 122*t*
        percentage change in national poverty
            headcount, 131*t*
        poverty population, stratum contributions
            to, 124*t*
        price distortion structure, 469*t*
        tax replacement, 131*t*
    Linkage model
        agricultural outputs, imports, and
            exports, 63*t*
        economic welfare, global and
            national, 58*t*
        factor prices, 70*t*
        land supply elasticities, 465*t*
        price distortion structure,
            53*t*, 469*t*
        regional concordance, 461*t*
        sectoral value added, 69, 73*t*

Zhai, Fan
    biographical information, xiv
    as chapter author, 147
    cited, 148, 213, 214, 260, 311,
        315, 462
Zhang, L., 150
Zhao, Y., 150, 151, 152
Zimbabwe
    GIDD model, 100f, 101, 102f

Linkage model
    agricultural outputs, imports, and
        exports, 63t
    economic welfare, global and national, 58t
    factor prices, 70t
    land supply elasticities, 465t
    price distortion structure, 53t, 469t
    regional concordance, 461t
    sectoral value added, 69, 73t